Selected P
from t
XXII World Congress
of Philosophy

Special Supplement
Journal of Philosophical Research

In cooperation with the

Korean Philosophical Association

and the

Fédération Internationale des Sociétés de Philosophie

Editor in Chief
Myung-Hyun Lee

Editors
Kihyeon Kim and Seon-Wook Kim

Philosophy Documentation Center
Charlottesville, Virginia
2012

The papers in this volume were originally presented at the XXII World Congress of Philosophy in Seoul, Korea (2008). They have been published as a service to the profession, in cooperation with the **Korean Philosophical Association** and the **Fédération Internationale des Sociétés de Philosophie**. All other papers from this congress will also be made available by the **Philosophy Documentation Center**.

The *Journal of Philosophical Research* (ISSN 1053-8364) is a unique scholarly resource that publishes outstanding papers in any branch of philosophy. It has a generous length limit and occasionally publishes supplementary volumes from special events.

Philosophy Documentation Center
P.O. Box 7147 • Charlottesville, Virginia 22906-7147
www.pdcnet.org • order@pdcnet.org

Selected Papers from the XXII World Congress of Philosophy
ISBN-13: 978-1-889680-88-0 • ISBN-10: 1-889680-88-5

Individuals
Print volume: $35
Online access (with *Journal of Philosophical Research*): $35

Institutions
Print volume $45
Online access with *Journal of Philosophical Research*

Single articles from this volume also available online.

For delivery of print copies outside the US please add $8 shipping. Online access includes the *Journal of Philosophical Research* volume 15 (1990) to the present and all supplements. More information at http://secure.pdcnet.org/jpr.

Related Publications:

Ethics and the Life Sciences
2007 (28 contributions, 356 pages)
ISBN-13: 978-1-889680-53-8

Ethical Issues for the Twenty-First Century
2005 (31 contributions, 408 pages)
ISBN-13: 978-1-889680-37-8

Philosophy in America at the Turn of the Century
2003 (7 contributions, 122 pages)
ISBN-13: 978-1-889680-33-0

Journal of Philosophical Research
ISSN 1053-8364, eISSN 2153-7984
http://secure.pdcnet.org/jpr

Selected Papers from the XXII World Congress of Philosophy

TABLE OF CONTENTS

Philosophy in Korea

Lectures

Opening Address

SELECTED PAPERS FROM THE XXII WORLD CONGRESS OF PHILOSOPHY

PREFACE TO *SELECTED PAPERS FROM THE XXII WORLD CONGRESS OF PHILOSOPHY*

MYUNG-HYUN LEE
PROFESSOR EMERITUS, SEOUL NATIONAL UNIVERSITY, SEOUL, KOREA
PRESIDENT, THE KOREAN ORGANIZING COMMITTEE FOR THE XXII WORLD CONGRESS OF PHILOSOPHY

It has now been four years since the XXII World Congress of Philosophy took place in Seoul, 2008. The Congress was held at Seoul National University from July 30th to August 5th, and a total of 2130 scholars from all over the world participated. The Congress program included Plenary Sessions, Symposia, Endowed Lectures, Invited Sessions, Sections for Contributed Papers, Round-Tables, and Society Meetings. In addition, the Korean Organizing Committee for the Congress organized the Korean Philosophical Association Special Sessions and Student Sessions.

The Korean Organizing Committee has made two Proceedings. One is the E-book Proceedings, created in 2010, that contains 1,235 papers in seven different languages presented in 54 Sessions for Contributed Papers. The second is this Paper-book Proceedings that contains the 36 papers presented in Plenary Sessions and Symposia along with the Endowed Lecture papers and the Opening Speech.

With the publication of this volume of the Proceedings, the official role of the Korean Organizing Committee for the XXII World Congress of Philosophy has come to an end. I would like to express our sincere thanks to all the colleagues who helped finish the XXII World Congress of Philosophy in Seoul successfully, and especially to Dr. George Leaman of the Philosophy Documentation Center for his kind support for the publication and distribution of the Proceedings, and to Dr. Seon-Wook Kim for his excellent work for the World Congress both during and long after the main event.

DOI: 10.5840/jpr201237Supplement59

SELECTED PAPERS FROM THE XXII WORLD CONGRESS OF PHILOSOPHY

FOREWORD TO *SELECTED PAPERS FROM THE XXII WORLD CONGRESS OF PHILOSOPHY*

PETER KEMP
PRESIDENT OF THE XXII WORLD CONGRESS OF PHILOSOPHY

This book contains proceedings of the XXII World Congress of Philosophy that was held in Korea at Seoul National University from July 30 until August 5 in 2008 on the theme "Rethinking Philosophy Today." The congress was organized by the International Federation of Philosophical Societies in collaboration with the Korean Philosophical Association. 1,235 papers contributed by participants in fifty-four thematic sections have been published on DVD produced by the Korean Philosophical Association. Here you find nearly all the papers by philosophers invited by the organizer to speak in the plenary sessions, in the symposia, and in the endowed lectures as well as my opening address.

The publication of the proceedings of every world congress is a unique challenge, and this one has been met with a range of technologies. The Philosophy Documentation Center published the proceedings of the 20th World Congress of Philosophy and the Center has digitized all volumes of the 21st World Congress. I am grateful to George Leaman for offering the *Journal of Philosophical Research* for this publication of the proceedings of the 22nd World Congress of Philosophy.

It was the first time in history that the World Congress of Philosophy took place in Asia. The 21st World Congress of Philosophy took place in Istanbul, on the border between Europe and Asia. But this World Congress was held in the heart of Asia, in Korea, between Japan on the one side and China and Russia on the other.

More than ever the papers from this congress testify that philosophy has become a common need and interest for people from all nationalities, and that we must rethink philosophy today in a truly global context.

I thank all those who by their papers and discussions contributed to the success of the World Congress of Philosophy in Seoul. It showed the world what human thinking can be, when it is at its best in facing problems, conflicts, inequalities, and injustices connected with the rise of a transnational civilization.

DOI: 10.5840/jpr201237Supplement35

SELECTED PAPERS FROM THE XXII WORLD CONGRESS OF PHILOSOPHY

INTRODUCTION TO *SELECTED PAPERS FROM THE XXII WORLD CONGRESS OF PHILOSOPHY*

SEON-WOOK KIM
ASSOCIATE PROFESSOR, SOONGSIL UNIVERSITY, SEOUL, KOREA
SECRETARY-GENERAL, KOREAN ORGANIZING COMMITTEE, XXII WORLD CONGRESS OF PHILOSOPHY

The XXII World Congress of Philosophy, known as the Olympic Games of Philosophy, was held in Seoul, Korea, from July 30 to August 5, 2008. It was organized by the Fédération Internationale des Sociétés de Philosophie (FISP) and the Korean Philosophical Association (KPA), and hosted by the Korean Organizing Committee (KOC) of WCP 2008. The venue was Seoul National University.

2,130 scholars from 82 countries and regions registered and stayed at least a day to participate, and among them 1,278 were non-Korean. This number does not include the participants' unregistered families, about 250 student volunteers, philosophy camp participants, and unregistered participants. Thus, the number of all participants is believed to well exceed 3,000.

2,277 papers were received for screening and 1,875 papers were actually presented on site. This number does not include papers presented at Round Tables, Society Meetings, and Invited Sessions. All of the 478 planned sessions were held, including 4 Plenary Sessions, 6 Symposia, 3 Endowed Lectures, 9 Korean Philosophical Association Special Sessions, 11 Invited Sessions, 299 sessions in 54 Sections for Contributed Papers, 73 Round Tables, 54 Sessions for Society Meetings, and 20 Student Sessions. In addition, 5 social meetings, 2 official FISP meetings and several improvised meetings were held during the congress period.[1]

The proceedings for the Congress were divided into two parts; one was created in e-book format and the other in print form. The e-book, published in 2010, contains 1,235 papers from 54 Sections for Contributed Papers. We believe that the e-book is a very democratic format for our purposes. A hard copy of the proceedings would inevitably force us to select only a few papers based on certain criteria due to physical constraints. The electronic format allows us to store every paper in its original language inside a single DVD disc.

Special Supplement, *Journal of Philosophical Research* pp. xi–xii

DOI:

The KOC was originally planning on including the papers selected for this volume in the DVD as well, but upon the suggestion of the FISP it decided to separate the two. Dr. William McBride introduced me to George Leaman, who graciously allowed us to publish this volume of the Proceedings as a Special Supplement of the *Journal of Philosophical Research* by the Philosophy Documentation Center (PDC). This volume with the title *Selected Papers from the XXII World Congress of Philosophy* contains 36 outstanding papers, which were presented at the sessions of Plenary Session and Symposia, and at Endowed Lectures and the Opening Ceremony. The themes of the sessions of Plenary Session and Symposia and their speakers were chosen by the Program Committee of the FISP. This contains all of the papers presented at the above sessions with one exception: Dr. Yanguag Wang's "Ethical Issues and Governance of Stem Cell Research: Chinese Views" is excluded upon his request.

Work on the printed Proceedings began in the fall of 2010 and continued for two years until its completion. I thank Dr. William McBride, Secretary of the FISP during the XXII World Congress and current President of the FISP, who connected us to the publisher and did some copy-editing for this volume, and Dr. Peter Kemp, President of the FISP during the XXII World Congress, who helped us contact the authors we had trouble in reaching. I want to express deep gratitude to Dr. George Leaman and the PDC, who made the e-book Proceedings available to the public by facilitating the distribution of the DVD and digitalizing the individual papers.

I thank Dr. Myung-Hyun Lee for sustaining and directing the KOC as its President until this volume was published. The Korean Philosophy Association made it possible for the KOC to complete its tasks.

I am glad that with the publication of this volume my job as the Secretary-General of the KOC finally comes to an end. I remember the great efforts made by my colleagues and co-workers both in preparing the Congress and finishing various post-Congress tasks, and I give them my deepest thanks.

NOTES

1. For more information of the XXII World Congress of Philosophy, please refer to my short report, "Varia: The XXII World Congress of Philosophy" in *Concordia,* no. 56, 2009.

SELECTED PAPERS FROM
THE XXII WORLD CONGRESS OF PHILOSOPHY

Liberal Democracy and Its Critics: Some Voices from East and West

FRED DALLMAYR
UNIVERSITY OF NOTRE DAME

ABSTRACT: Liberalism and democracy are not identical. In the phrase "liberal democracy" the two terms are conflated—with the result that liberalism tends to trump democracy. My paper challenges this tendency. It first examines critically central features of "minimalist" liberal democracy as formulated by some leading theorists. The discussion then shifts to critical assessments in both the East and the West. Turning first to South Asia, the focus is placed on Gandhi's teachings regarding popular self-rule (swaraj) where the latter does not mean "selfish rule" but rather the ability of people to rule themselves in an ethical manner. Moving to East Asia, I concentrate on Confucianism which emphasizes the basic ethical "relationality" of human life and stands opposed to both radical individualism and collectivism. The paper concludes by invoking the work of John Dewey who famously defined democracy as an ethical community.

Heraclitus notwithstanding, history is not just random flux. Apart from its great or memorable events, every historical period also pays tribute to certain guideposts or guiding ideas—what skeptics call its "idola fori" or idols of the market place. Looking at our contemporary age, it is not difficult to pinpoint a guiding, and probably *the* guiding idea endorsed almost universally by people around the world: that of "liberal democracy." Although originating in Western societies, the idea today is circulating as an orienting loadstar among people in Africa, the Middle East as well as South and East Asia. As can readily be seen, the guidepost is actually a composite phrase combining the two terms "liberal" and "democracy." Yet, despite the possibility of differentiation, the two terms in recent times have been basically conflated or amalgamated—with the result that, in the view of both ordinary people and leading intellectuals, the "democratic" component has become redundant or

DOI: 10.5840/jpr201237Supplement21

been absorbed without a rest in the dominant "liberal" idea. This conflation is particularly evident in, and traceable to, modern economics (with its own idols of the "market"). In large measure, the ongoing process of globalization is fueled by the idea of "neo-liberalism"—a version of the liberal tradition which insists on "down-sizing" political (including democratic) oversight for the sake of promoting individual or corporate "free enterprise."

This preponderance of liberal or neo-liberal agendas is by no means fortuitous. Taking a broad view, the entire trajectory of modern Western history can be seen as a movement of progressive human liberation, above all liberation from clerical and autocratic modes of control. This trajectory was present already in the work of Thomas Hobbes, in his rupture with classical and medieval conceptions of community. The movement was carried forward by John Locke with his accent on the persistence of "natural rights"—especially the right to equal liberty—in the confines of an established commonwealth. The latter emphasis was deepened and fleshed out by later liberal thinkers, like John Stuart Mill and Benjamin Constant—whose arguments in favor of minimal government (laissez-faire) were by then powerfully buttressed by the rise of capitalism and modern market economics. Small wonder that, in view of this long-standing trajectory, individual freedom became at last a catchword or shibboleth. As we know, the Western world calls itself, somewhat boastfully, the "Free World," while America celebrates itself as the "land of the free." As a corollary of this development, democracy as a political regime has come to be equated with an arena of free individual choice—that is, with liberal or libertarian democracy. But how plausible is this outcome? Has freedom in the modern world completely replaced such traditional categories as virtue and the "good life"—with the result that Aristotle's distinction between just and unjust regimes would be leveled into that between free and unfree forms of life?

In the following I want to pursue this line of thought. In a first step, I shall outline the meaning of liberal democracy, as it is defined by some contemporary theorists or philosophers. Subsequently I want to examine efforts to correct this liberal conception, turning first to the South Asian and next to the East Asian context. By way of conclusion I shall review again the relation between liberalism and democracy.

MINIMAL LIBERAL DEMOCRACY

As previously indicated, liberalism has a long history in the course of which it has assumed many different shapes and shadings. During the early period, the time of Hobbes and Locke, liberalism—in the sense of the defense of "natural" individual rights—served precariously as an adjunct or supplement to monarchical and even absolutist regimes. In the post-revolutionary era, liberalism became affiliated with various republican or democratic regimes—but in such a manner that the latter would progressively be trumped by the former (a development in which, as stated, the rise of capitalism played a major role). In the opinion of nineteenth-century liberals, the role of government—including democratic government—was meant to be minimal: seen chiefly as protectors of private property, political regimes were said to govern best when governing least. The dismal experiences of the twentieth century with populist and totalitarian governments have reinforced the liberal preference for political or public minimalism—despite occasional concessions to "welfare" programs during times of economic hardship. As a result of these experiences and developments, the notion of individual freedom has come to be equated preponderantly with "negative liberty" (to use Isaiah Berlin's phrase) or the freedom to be left alone—with only limited allowance made for active or "positive freedom" (mainly on the level of voting rights and lobbying). In his study of John Dewey (who opposed this entire trend), Raymond Boisvert has sketched the stereotype of the minimalist liberal: "an individual with no roots and little connectedness to community; . . . a highly competitive individual fixated on narrow purposes whose practice is marked by expedience rather than conventional ethics."[1]

On a sophisticated level, aspects of democratic minimalism can be found even in the writings of theorists or intellectuals otherwise strongly committed to democratic politics. An example is Robert Dahl's celebrated text *A Preface to Democratic Theory* (first published in 1956). In the very Introduction to his study, Dahl delineates two basic approaches in this field: a "maximizing" theory (relying either on ethical principles or formal axioms) and a purely "descriptive-empirical" and to that extent minimalizing approach. Traditional political theory, he notes, has tended to be "maximizing" by emphasizing "internal checks"—such as conscience and ethical dispositions—to restrain possible excesses of governmental power. Pre-revolutionary writers in particular, he says, insisted upon "moral virtue among citizens as a necessary condition for republican government," a condition which needed to be cultivated through "hortatory religion, sound education, and honest government." This approach, however, has gone out of fashion since the revolutionary period and, in America, since the writings of James Madison. In Dahl's presentation, Madison proceeded to sideline the earlier "maximizing" approach which must have been still "a common assumption of his time." From Madison's perspective, the traditional ethical approach was simply no longer viable given the increasingly competitive and interest-based character of modern politics. Moreover, even if occasionally operative, ethical constraints were no longer reliable given the strength of individual ambitions. Hence, for both Madison and Dahl, modern governments require not traditional but "external [or procedural] checks" to restrain oppressive tendencies. As can readily be seen, however, procedural checks are themselves the result of contractual arrangements and hence dependent on changing individual preferences.[2]

Another example of a democratic theorist leaning in the minimalist direction is Giovanni Sartori, well known for his text *The Theory of Democracy Revisited* (which is a sequel to his earlier *Democratic Theory*, of 1962). Like Dahl's study, Sartori's text distinguishes at the outset between a "prescriptive" or normative conception and a "descriptive" or empirical conception—with the latter version involving greatly reduced demands on democratic politics. In his view, to introduce normative expectations is likely to overburden the democratic regime such as to render it unviable:

"To bring morality into politics is akin to playing with fire—as we have only too well rediscovered since Hegel theorized a 'political ethos' or *Sittlichkeit*." In view of the alleged danger associated with public ethics, Sartori prefers to employ "minimalist" language and to leave phrases like "political morality, social morality, professional ethics" aside. What he finds particularly unhelpful or obnoxious is any association of democracy with public affection or Aristotelian-type friendship—something he derisively calls "demophily." As he insists: "Since real-world democracy consists (this is what renders it real) of a democratic machinery, democracy can do well without demophily." Democratic machinery coincides for him—and many other empirical theorists—with voting behavior, pursuit of individual interests through pressure groups and political parties, and public policy-making on the basic of these interests. Comprising this battery of elements, the democratic machinery basically yields what he calls "demo-power," that is, the power of the people, or predominant segments of the people, to implement and make effective prevailing interests: "Democracy begins with demo-power."[3]

An even more resolutely minimalist approach is propagated by a perspective which, in recent times, has increasingly gained prominence in the social sciences: rational choice theory. This outlook basically transfers neo-classical economic assumptions to social and political life; under the aegis of "neo-liberalism," the perspective is fast emerging as something like a dominant global ideology. As can readily be seen, what is jeopardized or called into question by this model is not only public ethics, but politics, particularly democratic polities, as such. For, even when seen as a minimally shared regime, democracy is bound to be a burden or hindrance for the ambitions of an unrestrained economic agenda. No one has articulated this burden more forcefully than William Riker, a founder of this model, in his book *Liberalism Against Populism* (of 1982). In this text, the term "populism" stands for an interventionaist or perhaps "Jacobin" type of democracy—in a manner which immediately renders democracy suspect (if compared with liberalism). As Riker states at the outset: "The theory of social [or rational] choice is a theory about the way the tastes, preferences, or values of individual persons are amalgamated and summarized into the choice of a collective group or society." Since these preferences are not ethically ranked, the primary focus is on something measurable or quantifiable: in economics monetary profit, in politics "the theory of voting" which is the core of liberal (or libertarian) democracy, barring any interference with voting preferences. Like Dahl, Riker distinguishes between a normative-ethical and an empirical or "analytical" conception of politics—placing rational choice clearly in the second category: the model is "an analytical theory about the way the natural world can [and does] work and what kind of outputs that world can yield."[4]

Again like Dahl, though with modified accents, Riker delineates two different genealogies of modern democracy: a "liberal or Madisonian" type and a "populist or Rousseauistic" type. In the liberal (or libertarian) version, he notes, "the function of voting is to control officials, and *nothing else*"—meaning by "nothing else" the absence of positive political programs promoting something like the common good. As he adds, this Madisonian definition "is *logically* complete, and there is nothing to add. Madison said nothing about the quality of popular decision, whether good or bad." By contrast, "populists"—presumably following Rousseau—desire a more active, participatory role of the people and a polities that creates "a moral and collective body" endowed with "life and will," especially the (in)famous "general will." At this point, Riker endorses whole-heartedly Isaiah Berlin's notion of "negative liberty" and his indictment that "positive liberty, which appears initially innocuous, is the root of tyranny" or oppression. Tellingly, Riker also alludes to some ideological background—not unaffected by the geopolitics of the Cold War. "No government," he asserts, "that has eliminated economic freedom has been able to attain or keep democracy." On the other hand,

> economic liberty is also an end in itself because capitalism is the driving force for the increased efficiency and technological innovation that has produced in two centuries both a vast increase in the wealth of capitalist nations and a doubling of the average life span of their citizens.

Although acknowledging that it may be viewed as "minimalist" by some, Riker concludes that liberal or Madisonian democracy is "the only kind of democracy actually attainable" or feasible in our world.[5]

BEYOND MINIMALISM: VOICES FROM SOUTH ASIA

In large measure, liberal democracy—in the sense of a minimalist, libertarian regime (or non-regime)—tends to occupy centerstage in recent Western social and political thought. As it is important to note, this has not always been the case. During important phases of Western political development, minimalist liberal democracy has been criticized or contested by able thinkers and public intellectuals. One such phase was the American colonial period when the Puritan John Winthrop proposed the formation of an ethical-communitarian republic in Massachusetts Bay. Another, post-revolutionary phase was the era of "Jacksonian democracy" when the ideal of an egalitarian republic was pitted against the laissez-faire ambitions of the emerging manufacturing elite (epitomized by the Bank of America). On a theoretical or philosophical plane, however, the most important development was the rise of "pragmatism" in the late nineteenth century, and especially John Dewey's eloquent defense of "radical" democracy as an antidote to laissez-faire liberalism. In Boisvert's words: for Dewey "democracy as an ideal for community life is not a mere provision for a minimal state which simply leaves citizens alone. Such an individualistic ideal is inimical to the kind of *associated* living which is democratic." To quote Dewey himself: "The clear consciousness of a communal life, in all its implications, constitutes the idea of democracy."[6]

For present purposes, given the contemporary global expansion of liberal (or neo-liberal) democracy, I want to turn my attention to non-Western intellectual contexts. An important context of this kind is South Asia and particularly India, the home of the Mahatma Gandhi. As is well known, Gandhi was not only an astute politician or public leader but also a thinker or intellectual with deep insight into public affairs, including the requisites of democracy. On the latter issue he has pronounced himself repeatedly, but perhaps most forcefully and pithily in his early book of 1909 titled *Hind Swaraj* (or *Indian Home Rule*). In this text, Gandhi takes to task forms of democracy found in Western countries which are often upheld as shining models to the rest of the world. Concentrating his attention particularly on the British model, he delineates a long list of shortcomings or defects, ranging from the venality of parliament, or its subservience to vested interests, to the fluctuating whims of public opinion under the impact of power-hungry politicians or businessmen. Surveying these and a host of related blemishes, Gandhi does not hesitate to trace the malaise to a central underlying cause: the unrestrained pursuit of self-interest and self-indulgence, at the cost of shared ethical commitments to the public good. To be sure, as he acknowledges, modern life—even life in corrupt democracies—has brought greater freedom for many people in different strata of society; this advance, however, is marred and nearly eclipsed by prevailing abuses. In terms of *Hind Swaraj*, the main problem is the sway of self-centered materialism, the fact that people in the modern West "make bodily welfare the [sole] object of life." As the text starkly depicts the situation:

> This civilization takes note neither of morality [*niti*] nor of religion [*dharma*]. . . . [It] seeks to increase bodily comforts, and it fails miserably even in doing so. This civilization is irreligion [*adharma*], and it has taken such a hold on the people in Europe that those who are in its appear to be half mad. . . . They keep up their energy by intoxication.[7]

The remedy proposed in *Hind Swaraj* for this state of affairs is precisely self-rule or "*swaraj*"—which does not mean selfish rule or promotion of self-centered ambitions, but rather the ability to rein in such ambitions for the benefit of the common good, that is, the good of all people. As Gandhi points out, egocentrism or individual self-seeking is contrary not only to ethical and spiritual "rightness" (one sense of *dharma*) but also to the teachings of practically all the great religions of the world—including (next to Hinduism) Christianity, Islam, Judaism, and Zoroastrianism (he might have added Buddhism). What all these religions try to teach us, he writes, is "that we should remain passive [or reticent] about worldly pursuits and active about godly [or ethical] pursuits, that we should set a limit to our worldly ambition, and that our religious [or *dharmic*] ambitions should be illimitable." Despite differences of accent or detail, all religions and ethical-spiritual paths can thus be seen as "different roads converging to the same point." People following these paths are liable to achieve not "civilization in name only," but genuine culture or civilization befitting free and responsible human beings. In Gandhi's terse formulation: "Civilization is that mode of conduct which points out to human beings the path of duty. Performance of ethical duty . . . means to attain mastery over our mind and our passions. In so doing, we come to know ourselves." Even more importantly: in so doing, we come to rule ourselves both as individuals and as people. The clear implication of this view is a new understanding of democracy: in the sense not of the pursuit of individual or collective self-interest but of a transformative popular self-rule (that is, rule of people over themselves) or *swaraj*: "It is *swaraj* when we learn to rule ourselves."[8]

Although composed relatively early in his life (and during an arduous sea voyage from London to South Africa), the basic tenets of *Hind Swaraj* remained firm guideposts during Gandhi's mature years. Although willing to revise minor details, he never disavowed his early text; in fact, he reconfirmed its central argument on repeated occasions in subsequent years. A few examples should suffice to document this continuity. In his "Constructive Program" submitted to the Indian National Congress in 1941, Gandhi strongly reaffirmed his commitment to *swaraj*, explaining the meaning of the term as denoting "complete independence through truth [*satya*] and non-violence [*ahimsa*]" and "without distinction of race, color or creed." A letter written to Jawaharlal Nehru a few years later made explicit reference to the text of 1909, stating: "I have said that I still stand by the system of government envisaged in *Hind Swaraj*." In retrospect, what appeared to Gandhi as the central lesson of his book was the emphasis on ethical self-rule and self-restraint, on a conception of individual and public agency performed within the limits of rightness or truth (*satya*) and non-violent generosity toward others. The most dramatic and direct application of the idea of *swaraj* came in his "Quit India" speech delivered in Bombay in 1942. In that speech, Gandhi—now the leader of a nationwide "*satyagraha*" (civil resistance relying on "truth power")—contrasted his vision of Indian self-rule with the kind of freedom and political rulership found in Britain and the Western world, saying:

> I do not regard England, or for that matter America, as free countries. They are free after their own fashion: free to hold in bondage the colored races of the earth. . . . According to my own interpretation of that freedom, I am constrained to say: they are strangers to that freedom which their [own] poets and teachers have described.[9]

Profiled against dominant Western approaches, Gandhi's idea of *swaraj* discloses a conception of democracy—an ethical conception—sharply at variance with interest-based models of liberal or libertarian democracy. Despite his fondness for Western writers like Ruskin, Thoreau, and Tolstoy, Gandhi was not a radical individualist (in the modern "liberal" sense) ready to separate a vast arena of private freedom from a narrowly circumscribed, perhaps minimalist, public-democratic domain. Faithful to older philosophical traditions (both in India and the West), he preferred to stress a qualitative distinction between modes of human and political conduct—a distinction that cannot readily collapsed into modern private/public or internal/external polarities. Without blandly fusing individual and society or subordinating one to the other, his thought was able to hold the two elements in fruitful, perhaps tensional balance. This aspect is clearly shown in another letter Gandhi wrote to Nehru in 1945. Picking up Nehru's suggestion regarding the importance of human and social development," he fully agreed that it was crucial to "bring about man's highest intellectual, economic, political and moral development," that is, the "flourishing" of all human abilities. The basic issue was how to accomplish this goal. For Gandhi this was impossible without thorough attention to rightness (*dharma*) and without social engagement and responsibility. Echoing Aristotle, and countering the modern Western focus on self-centered individualism carried over from an atomistic "state of nature" into society, he wrote: "Man is not born to live in isolation but is essentially a social animal independent *and* interdependent. No one can or should ride on another's back." A similar view was expressed in an interview of summer 1946 where Gandhi stated that, although the individual does count in important ways, this "does not exclude dependence and willing help from neighbors or from the world. It will be a free and voluntary play of mutual forces."[10]

In speaking of interconnectedness and the "play of mutual forces" Gandhi displays an affinity with the spirit of Jamesian and Deweyan pragmatism. But the parallel can be carried further. Like William James and Dewey, and perhaps even more emphatically, Gandhi was an ethical and spiritual pragmatist, in the great tradition of Indian spirituality. As is well known, the most important source of inspiration for Gandhi throughout his life was the *Bhagavad Gita*, a text which delineates several paths (or *yogas*) guiding toward liberation and blessedness (in the sense of flourishing). Among these paths, Gandhi deliberately chose the path of action or praxis (*karma yoga*) demanding continuous ethical engagement in the affairs of the world. Again like Dewey, he did not assume that human beings are free and equal by nature (or in an original "state of nature"); rather freedom and equality for him were achievements requiring steady practice—a practice involving not only change of outward conditions but primarily self-transformation. In Gandhi's own words, freedom is not an instant boon, but is "attained only by constant heart-churn" or self-giving in service to others. As Ramashray Roy explains, in his thoughtful book *Self and Society*, *karma yoga* for Gandhi was not just a form of activism or worldly busy-ness, but rather a soteriological path or a process of sanctification which sees performance of action as sacred duty: "This sacred duty lies in exerting oneself to the benefit of others, that is, service."[11] Viewed from this angle, achievement of self-rule or *swaraj* involves self-transcendence and a diligent training in the ways of freedom. In a manner akin to Deweyan political thought, pursuit of liberating paths (or *yogas*) demands steady practice and habituation, facilitated by sound education. In a more directly Aristotelian view, such practice revolves around the nurturing of a set of virtues—which Gandhi reformulated under the rubric of ethical and spiritual "vows" (*yamas*).

Comparing Gandhian *swaraj* with dominant forms of modern Western thought, the differences care stark and obvious. What needs to be noted right away is the distance of *swaraj* from prevalent modern conceptions of freedom: those of "negative" and "positive" liberty. In this binary scheme, negative liberty basically designates the freedom to be left alone (that is, liberalism's retreat into private self-satisfaction), whereas positive liberty denotes the unhampered pursuit of collective goals—a pursuit sometimes shading over into social engineering on behalf of ideological panaceas. As can readily be seen, neither of these options shows kinship with Gandhian *swaraj*. Even when highly spiritualized, negative liberty still bears traces of individual self-centeredness, while the positive type—in stressing worldly activism—seems ignorant of self-restraint, releasement and non-attachment to the fruits of action. This distance is clearly pinpointed by Ramashray Roy. As he observers, negative liberty insists on social aloofness, on the retreat into a private realm often coinciding with selfishness or the wanton "satisfaction of desires." On the other hand, while emphasizing social and political engagement, positive liberty sidesteps the task of self-curtailment and self-transcendence by extolling the benefits of collectively chosen goals. For Roy, it was "Ghandi's genius" to have squarely faced this dilemma and have shown an exit from this binary dilemma. The central point of Gandhian *swaraj*, he notes, was the emphasis on self-rule as a transformation process—whereby people are able to rule not so much over others than over themselves.[12]

The arguments regarding freedom or liberty can readily be transferred to the basic meaning of democracy. The difference between Gandhian *swaraj* and the liberal-minimalist conception of democracy has been ably highlighted by the Gandhi-scholar Ronald Terchek, especially in his essay titled "Gandhi and Democratic Theory." Right at the outset Terchek states the crux of the matter: that democracy for Gandhi was not merely "procedural" or minimal but "substantive" in the sense of being grounded in a non-oppressive way of life. He cites Gandhi himself to the effect that, under democracy "the weakest should have the same opportunity as the strongest. And this can never happen except through [political, social, and psychological] non-violence."[13] Basically, for the Mahatma, democracy is a regime not organized or imposed "from the top down" (or from the state down) but one nurtured "from the bottom up." This explains his emphasis on village life and village self-government (through councils or *panchayats*) as well as on economic decentralization and local industries. In Terchek's presentation, Gandhi believed that the means of production (at least of the basic necessaries of life) should remain ultimately in the hands of the people—and not be relinquished or alienated to corporate elites. In contrast to the rampant competition unleashed by the capitalist market, he stressed the need to cultivate cooperative dispositions so that the brute "struggle for survival" would be transmuted into a "struggle for mutual service" or "mutual existence." Such dispositions, in turn, presuppose the fostering of mutual respect and the practice of such civic virtues as inter-personal and inter-group tolerance or recognition. As Terchek observes, paraphrasing Gandhi's own arguments: "Tolerance implies a mutual regard for others; and if it is missing, the [bottom-up] dialogue of the democratic process is diminished, if not destroyed." Gandhi in India, he adds perceptively, "like Dewey in America, saw dialogue as necessary to both individual growth and to the democratic prospect. Indeed, democracy received one of its primary justifications from Dewey because it promoted tolerance and fostered development."[14]

The central point of Terchek's essay is the differentiation of the Gandhian approach from (what he calls) "the dominant model of democracy today" which relies on the unhampered pursuit of self-interest and, politically, on competitive elections where voters choose delegates maximally committed to promoting their interest. From the latter (liberal-minimalist) perspective, interests are individually generated and by no means in a "pre-established harmony." Among a larger group of people, pursuit of self-interest is liable to lead to strife or conflict—whose settlement is secured either through shallow compromise or the intervention of sovereign power. For Gandhi, such settlement is defective under democratic auspices. As Terchek shows, democratic life for him required "both freedom and interdepenence" and the two could only be sustained through ethical dispositions cultivated over time. Moreover, on both the individual and group levels, it was necessary to distinguish genuine needs from private "interests" which are often artificially created by the media (and privilege "greed" over need). Apart from stressing some Deweyan affinities, Terchek also links Gandhi's thought with aspects of the "civic republican" tradition from Cicero to the present. In his words: Civic republicans believed "that freedom could be secured only if people restrained themselves. . . . Accordingly, they attempted to disperse power, institutionalize cooperation, emphasize service, and promote widespread participation" in the political process. Differently phrased, for republicans as well as Gandhi, democracy was predicated on self-rule (in the sense of *swaraj*) and a non-domineering type of public agency—an agency captured by the Gandhian labels of non-violence (*ahimsa*) and "truth-force" (*satyagraha*).[15]

An argument along similar lines has been presented by the Indian political theorist Thomas Pantham, in his article "Beyond Liberal Democracy: Thinking with Mahatma Gandhi." As Pantham points out, Gandhi repeatedly criticized the liberal democratic model—its "objectification and technocratization of the political" (in the state) and its concomitant "alienation of the people's political rights" (by reducing such rights to private interests). The alternative he put forward was that of *swaraj* which, in addition to self-rule, can also be translated as "participatory democracy" where the gulf between "subject and object," between ruler and ruled is erased. For Gandhi, modern liberal thought was based largely on a "one-dimensional conception" of human beings as self-contained and self-seeking creatures whose pursuit of selfish ends could only be tamed by power and non-moral force. It was impossible in his view to escape "the inherent contradictions" of this model "without abandoning the liberal-individualistic conception of humanity and the atomistic, amoral conception of its interests." The escape route he proposed was reliance on "truth-doing" (*satytagraha*) and non-violence (*ahimsa*) as "the most important moral norms"—norms which are "not cloistered virtues" but to be discovered and formed through "the ordinary activities of life" in the social, economic, and political spheres. Once these norms are widely cultivated and taken to heart, a different version of democracy comes into view, one in which freedom and interdependence are closely linked. To quote a statement by Gandhi, written in 1946 and carrying distinct Deweyan (and Aristotelian) echoes:

> I value individual freedom, but you must not forget that man is essentially a social being. He has risen to the present status by learning to adjust his individualism to the requirements of social progress. Unrestricted individualism is the law of the beast of the jungle. We have learnt to strike the mean between individual freedom and social restraint.[16]

BEYOND MINIMALISM: VOICES FROM EAST ASIA

When turning from India to East Asia, similar reservations regarding liberal democracy can readily be found. The critique of radical individualism proceeds there mainly (though not exclusively) on Confucian premises, a philosophy well known for its emphasis on human relationships. Given the essential relatedness of human beings, freedom for Confucians cannot mean either internal retreat or external manipulation and domination. This point is eloquently made by the Chinese-American scholar Tu Weiming. As he observes, Confucianism basically opposes the binary scheme of negative and positive liberty, that is, the construal of freedom in terms of either private self-withdrawal or domineering self-enhancement. "It rejects," he writes, "both an introspective affirmation of the self as an isolable and complacent ego *and* an unrestrained attachment to the external world for the sake of a limitless expansion of one's manipulative power." In lieu of these alternatives, the Confucian "way" or "*tao*"—akin to Gandhian *swaraj*—involves an "unceasing process of self-transformation as a communal act," and thus a linkage of ethics and social engagement whose seasoning effect "can ultimately free us from the constrictions of the privatized ego." As can readily be seen, human freedom from this angle is limited or circumscribed not by the state or external procedures but by the ability of ethical transformation, that is, the ability of people to rule themselves rather than ruling others.[17]

In addition to social engagement and connectedness, Confucianism also fosters the relatedness between human beings and nature as well as the "mutuality between man and Heaven." Ultimately, Tu Weiming notes, the Confucian trajectory points to the human reconciliation with "Heaven, Earth, and the myriad things—with clearly spiritual or religious connotations. In an instructive manner, he also points to the Confucian stress on exemplification, that is, the need not merely to hold fine theories but to exemplify them in daily conduct. Despite his deep modesty, Confucius himself can be seen, and was seen, as an "exemplar" or "exemplary person" (*chün-tzu*) who taught the "way" not through abstract doctrines but through the testimony of responsible daily living. At this point, the affinity with Deweyan philosophy comes clearly into view—a fact which is perhaps not surprising given Dewey's extended visit to China after World War I.[18] As in the case of Gandhian *swaraj*, leading a responsible life in society involves self-restraint and the abandonment of domineering impulses. In Confucius's own words, humaneness or to be properly human (*jen*) means "to conquer oneself (*k'e-chi*) and to return to propriety (*fu-li*)." As Tu Weiming comments, however, the notion of "conquering oneself" should not be misconstrued in the sense of self-erasure in favor of heteronomous forces. The Confucian idea, he writes, does not mean "that one should engage in a bitter struggle" of conquest; rather the concept of *k'e-chi* is "closely linked to the concept of self-cultivation (*hsiu-shen*)" or self-transformation and hence to the task of responsible and responsive social agency.[19]

More difficult to assess is the relation of Confucian thought to modern democracy seen as popular self-rule and self-government. In large measure, the difficulty arises from the fact that, in contrast to the Gandhian legacy, traditional Confucianism is silent on democracy and the political implications of human agency. This silence is often taken as evidence of the utter incompatibility of Confucian teachings and democratic regimes. In the words of the China-scholar Ni Peinim: "The dominant view today still holds that Confucianism and democracy are like water and fire, totally incompatible and antagonistic to each other." According to this view, the former is "authoritarian, repressive, and typically associated with totalitarian policies, uniformity of ideology, social hierarchy, and discrimination against women"—while democracy is "the very opposite."[20] In a similar vein, Wm. Theodore deBary has pointed out that, during much of the twentieth century, Confucianism "was made to stand for all that was backward and benighted in China: it bore all the burden of the past, charged with innumerable sins of the old order." When in 1999—he adds—the "Goddess of Democracy" was publicly displayed in Tiananmen Square, the display was a revolt not only against Communist repression but also against the older Confucian tradition.[21] In this context, traditional Confucian sayings like "The common people are the root or foundation of society" (from the *Shujing*) are widely regarded as pious placebos devoid of concrete political connotations.

At this point, it becomes important to ask what precisely is at issue. Does the claimed incompatibility prevail between Confucianism and democracy *tout court*, or between the former and a certain kind of liberalism or liberal democracy? In the latter case, the meaning of "liberal" and "liberalism" becomes decisive. Do these terms refer to the ethical kind of liberalism which can be traced from Montesquieu and Hegel all the way to Dewey's definition of democracy as an ethical community? Or do we mean the self-seeking, laissez-faire liberalism which ultimately reduces social life to an atomistic state of nature? In the former case—making room for creative adjustments—it seems quite possible to envisage a harmony between Confucianism and modern democracy. In the latter case, harmony or compatibility is clearly excluded—but only because self-centered liberalism is at variance with democracy as such (or only allows for minimalist democracy). The need for a creative adjustment or rethinking of traditional teachings is today acknowledged by many Confucian scholars, especially by such "New Confucians" as Tu Weiming and Liu Shu-hsien. As the latter has aptly stated: "We have to reject the tradition in order to reaffirm the ideal of the tradition."[22] However, such a rethinking of Confucian teachings also requires, as a complementary move, a rethinking of prevalent modern Western ideas—away from the egocentric preferences of democratic minimalism in the direction of a responsible democratic ethos. As it appears to me, such a double rethinking is admirably manifest in the writings of the China scholar Henry Rosemont, Jr.

In several of his texts, Rosemont has eloquently castigated the notion of an egocentric individualism patterned on capitalist economics. As he writes at one point (in a passage with patent Deweyan echoes): "For most of the world's peoples, there are no disembodied minds, nor autonomous individuals; human relationships govern and structure most of our lives, to the point that unless there are at least two human beings, there can be no human beings." As one should note, however, this critique of egocentrism does not induce Rosemont to reject democracy as such. As he states in one of his more well known writings, *The Chinese Mirror*, what he is proposing or suggesting is not a return to autocracy but rather "a somewhat different philosophical view of democracy"—a view more in line with an ethical conception of both liberalism and democracy.[23] The concrete contours of this alternative view are spelled out by Rosemont in another text which intriguingly joins Confucian "relationism" with the pragmatic account on a shared way of life. From this alternative perspective, he states, democracy—including an ethically liberal democracy—might be described as a regime in which every member has the right and duty "to participate in public affairs" and "to take the public welfare of all the other members of society as one's own." As one can see, democracy here is elevated to the height of the vision of a Montesquieu, de Tocqueville, and Dewey. To conclude with another passage from *The Chinese Mirror*, even more distinctly Deweyan in orientation: In a properly constituted democratic community, "the desired would not be equated with the desirable, and democratic participation—being a citizen—would involve engaging in collective dialogue about the appropriate means for achieving agreed-upon ends."[24]

CONCLUDING REMARKS

In the preceding pages, I have delineated critiques of liberal-minimalist democracy, focusing on Gandhian and Confucian teachings. These critical voices could readily be expanded or multiplied. One of the noteworthy developments in Asia in recent decades has been the upsurge of a "new" kind of Buddhism, an outlook which shifts the earlier accent on monastic retreat in the direction of a more worldly engagement and participation. Here again, the twin pitfalls of negative and positive liberty are bypassed (at least in intent). While transgressing the bounds of a purely internal liberation, the turn to engagement carefully steers clear of public manipulation or the pursuit of social blueprints, thus maintaining the central Buddhist focus on "self-emptying" (*sunyata*) and self-transcendence (toward others).[25] Under very different auspices and in a different idiom, tendencies pointing in a similar direction can also be found in strands of contemporary Islamic thought. In this context, the traditional biblical injunction to "pursue justice" above everything else still serves as a powerful incentive to foster an ethically vibrant public life. However, contrary to "fundamentalist" misconstruals, this incentive does not automatically translate into theocracy or clerical despotism. On the contrary, precisely because justice needs to be done in concrete times and places, ordinary people are called upon to act as "vice-regents" or (more prosaically) as co-participants in the formation of ethically just modes of politics. In recent times, the idea of a basic compatibility of Isham and democracy has been defended by a number of able intellectuals, from Muhammad Iqbal to Abdulaziz Sachedina and Abdulkarim Soroush. In Iqbal's pithy phrase: "Islam demands loyalty to God, not to thrones." Paraphrasing and amplifying this idea, the philosopher Soroush has stated: "No blessing is more precious for mankind than the free choice of the way of the prophets. . . . But in the absence of this state of grace, nothing is better for humankind than [democratic] freedom. Because all free societies, whether religious or nonreligious, are properly humane."[26]

As indicated before, the critique of public minimalism is not restricted to non-Western contexts. On the contrary, some of the most eloquent critical voices have been precisely Western and, in fact, American. Just a few years ago, the American political theorist Michael Sandel issued a plea for a renewed "public philosophy" which would re-connect ethics and politics. What stands in the way of such a renewal, in his account, is the predominance of (what he calls) the "voluntarist conception of freedom," that is, the laissez-faire ideology of untrammeled self-seeking, which dispenses with the "difficult task" of cultivating civic dispositions. As an antidote to this ideology, Sandel pleads in favor of a "formative politics" concerned with the formation of ethical civic attitudes and practices; for (he says) "to share in self-rule requires that citizens possess, or come to acquire, certain civic virtues."[27] In issuing this plea, of course, Sandel stands on the shoulders of a series of earlier American thinkers, including the journalist and public intellectual Walter Lippmann. Some seventy years ago, Lippmann had denounced the spreading cult of egocentric will power in economics and politics. As he noted in *The Good Society*, Western modernity had derailed when it moved to equate freedom with individual self-seeking. In opposition to this equation—the "doctrine of laissez-faire, let her rip, and the devil take the hindmost"—Lippmann invoked an older tradition of ethical liberalism congruent with public obligations. Borrowing a leaf from Aristotle as well as American pragmatism, his text observed: "There must be [in democracy] an habitual, confirmed, and well-nigh intuitive dislike of arbitrariness. . . . There must be a strong desire to be just. [And] there must be a growing capacity to be just."[28]

However, the strongest American voice against the derailment into laissez-faire minimalism was John Dewey. As I have stated repeatedly, Dewey was relentless in critiquing a reckless individualism and in upholding social "relationism" and the need for civic bonds. As one should note well, his animus was directed not against liberalism as such, but against a minimalist version incompatible with democratic self-rule. Likewise, his target was not individual liberty (or individual selfhood) per se, but only its imprisonment in the Cartesian fortress of the "ego cogito." In the words of Raymond Boisvert: Whereas old-style individualism connotes "both isolation and self-interestedness," "individuality" in the revised Deweyan sense identifies "the distinctive manner in which someone participates in communal life"; it recognizes "the irreducibility of community and the multiple perspectives associated with it."[29] Such individuality and the multiple perspectives to which it gives rise are not opposed to, but actually constitutive of democratic life. Above all, what needs to be remembered is that, for Dewey, democracy is not a finished state, but an ongoing process of democratizing pointing toward rich untapped horizons. Democracy, he states at one point, is "an end that has not been adequately realized in any country at any time. It is radical because it requires great change in existing social institutions, economic, legal and cultural." To this might be added his observation that, under democratic auspices, "the supreme test of all political institutions and industrial arrangements shall be the contribution they make to the all-round growth [or better: flourishing] of every number of society."[30]

Returning to the theme of self-rule or *swaraj*, it is clear that growth or flourishing cannot mean simply the enlargement of power or managerial control. Rather, to be ethically tenable, democratic self-rule has to involve a practice of self-restraint and self-transformation (even self-emptying) capable of instilling the habit of non-violence (*ahimsa*) and generous openness toward others. As Dewey once remarked, in a very Gandhian spirit: "To take as far as possible every conflict which arises . . . out of the atmosphere and medium of force, of violence as a means of settlement, into that of discussion and of intelligence is to treat those who disagree—even profoundly—with us as those from whom we may learn and, in so far, as friends."[31] This disposition toward non-violence, however, does not come easy. For Dewey, as we know, such a disposition or civic habit is not a ready-made "natural" endowment, but a human potentiality requiring continuous struggle and life-long educational cultivation.

Seen in this light, democracy clearly remains a "promise"—but not an empty pipe-dream nor a mere project of civil engineering. Construed as an ongoing democratization, democracy involves a striving toward human flourishing on both an individual and social level. Transposed into the idiom of Heidegger's philosophy, human *praxis*—in the basic sense of "letting be"—produces no extrinsic objects but an intrinsic good: the achievement or fulfillment of our (promised) humanity.

NOTES

1. Raymond D. Boisvert, *John Dewey: Rethinking Our Time* (Albany, NY: State University of New York Press, 1998), pp. 51–52. Compare also Isaiah Berlin, *Four Essays on Liberty* (London: Oxford University Press, 1977); and for a critique, Charles Taylor, "What's Wrong With Negative Liberty?" in *The Idea of Freedom: Essays in Honor of Isaiah Berlin*, ed. Alan Ryan (Oxford: Oxford University Press, 1979), 175–193.

2. See Robert A. Dahl, *A Preface to Democratic Theory* (Chicago: University of Chicago Press, 1956), pp. 2, 18–19. To Dahl's credit, one has to acknowledge that he stressed not only formal procedural limits but also "inherent social checks and balances." He also refers (pp. 22, 82–83) to an "underlying consensus on policy" existing "prior to politics." But the origin of this consensus is not disclosed.

3. Giovanni Sartori, *The Theory of Democracy Revisited* (Chatham, NJ: Chatham House Publ., 1987), vol. 1, pp. 12–13, 17–18, 241–242; vol. 2, pp. 476–477.

4. William H. Riker, *Liberalism Against Populism: A Confrontation Between the Theory of Democracy and the Theory of Social Choice* (Prospect Heights, IL: Waveland Press, 1982), pp. 1–3.

5. Riker, *Liberalism Against Populism*, pp. 7, 9–12, 246.

6. See Boisvert, *John Dewey*, p. 58. Compare also *John Dewey: The Later Works: 1925–1953*, ed. Jo Ann Boydston (Carbondale and Edwardsville, IL: Southern Illinois University Press, 1981–90), vol. 2, p. 328; and John Winthrop, "A Model of Christian Charity" (1630), in *Individualism and Commitment in America Life*, ed. Robert Bellah et al. (New York: Harper & Row, 1987), pp. 21–27.

7. Mohandas K. Gandhi, *Hind Swaraj and Other Writings*, ed. Anthony J. Parel (Cambridge: Cambridge University Press, 1997), pp. 30–37.

8. Ibid., pp. 42–43, 67, 73.

9. These and similar statements are collected in the "Supplementary Writings" attached by Parel to his edition of *Hind Swaraj*, pp. 149–150, 171, 185. The sources can be found in *The Collected Works of Mahatma Gandhi* (New Delhi: Government of India, 1958–1989), vol. 75, pp. 146–147; vol. 76, pp. 339–401; vol. 81, pp. 319–321. By "their (own) poets and teachers" Gandhi seems to refer to some of his favorite Western authors like Thoreau, Ruskin, and Tolstoy.

10. See "Supplementary Writings" in *Hind Swaraj*, pp. 155, 189. Taken from *The Collected Works of Mahatma Gandhi*, vol. 85, pp. 32–33; and Jawaharlal Nehru, *A Bunch of Old Letters* (London: Asia Publishing House, 1958), p. 512.

11. Ramashray Roy, *Self and Society: A Study in Gandhian Thought* (New Delhi: Sage Publications India, 1984), p. 78. A similar point is made by Bhikhu Parekh in his stellar text *Gandhi* (Oxford: Oxford University Press, 1997), pp. 75–76: "For Gandhi *swaraj* referred to a state of affairs in which individuals were morally in control of themselves and ran their lives in such a way that they needed no external coercion. . . . For Gandhi, *swaraj* thus presupposed self-discipline, self-restraint, a sense of mutual responsibility, the disposition neither to dominate nor be dominated by others, and a sense of *dharma*."

12. Roy, *Self and Society*, pp. 63, 189–190. The possibility of a transformative freedom was actually acknowledged by Isaiah Berlin; but he confined this mode narrowly to mystical or ascetic life-styles—a confinement aptly criticized by Roy (pp. 186–187).

13. Ronald J. Terchek, "Gandhi and Democratic Theory," in *Political Thought in Modern India*, ed. Thomas Pantham and Kenneth L. Deutsch (New Delhi: Sage Publications, 1986), p. 308. The citation is from *Non-Violence in Peace and War*, vol. 1, ed. M. K. Gandhi (Ahmedabad: Navajivan, 1948), p. 269.

14. Terchek, "Gandhi and Democratic Theory," pp. 309, 312. See also Ronald Duncan, *Selected Writings of Mahatma Gandhi* (Boston: Beacon Press, 1951), pp. 78–79.

15. Terchek, "Gandhi and Democratic Theory," pp. 317–319.

16. Thomas Pantham, "Beyond Liberal Democracy: Thinking with Mahatma Gandhi," in Pantham and Deutsch, *Political Thought in Modern India*, pp. 334, 337–339. The citations

are from *Harijan* (March 31, 1946) in Gandhi, *Democracy: Real and Deceptive*, comp. R. K. Prabhu (Ahmedabad: Navajivan, 1961), p. 32; and *Harijan* (May 8, 1937), p. 98.

17. Tu Weiming, *Confucian Thought: Selfhood as Creative Transformation* (Albany, NY: State University of New York Press, 1985), pp. 59, 76–77. Regarding transformative freedom, he adds (p. 78), in a passage critical of modern Western liberalism: "Historically, the emergence of individualism as a motivating force in Western society may have been intertwined with highly particularized political, economic, ethical, and religious traditions. It seems reasonable that one can endorse an insight into the self as a basis for equality and liberty without accepting Locke's idea of private property, Adam Smith's and Hobbes's idea of private interest, John Stuart Mill's idea of privacy, Kierkegaard's idea of loneliness, or the early Sartre's idea of [radical] freedom."

18. Weiming, *Confucian Thought*, p. 175.

19. See Tu Weiming, "The Creative Tension Between *Jen* and *Li*," in his *Humanity and Self-Cultivation: Essays in Confucian Thought* (Berkeley: Asian Humanities Press, 1979), p. 6; also Confucius, *The Analects*, 12:1. Regarding the relation between Confucianism and pragmatism compare David L. Hall and Roger T. Ames, *Thinking Through Confucius* (Albany, NY: State University of New York Press, 1987), p. 15: "If contemporary comparative philosophic activity is any indication, it might be the pragmatic philosophies associated with Pierce, James, Dewey, and Mead, and extended toward process philosophy such as that of A. N. Whitehead, that can serve as the best resource for philosophical concepts and doctrines permitting responsible access to Confucius' thought."

20. Ni Peinim, "Confucianism and Democracy: Water and Fire? Water and Oil? Or Water and Fish? In Defense of Henry Rosemont's View," in *Polishing the Chinese Mirror: Essays in Honor of Henry Rosemont, Jr.*, ed. Marthe Chandler and Ronnie Littlejohn (New York: Global Scholarly Publications, 2008), p. 90.

21. Wm. Theodore de Bary, *The Trouble with Confucianism* (Cambridge, MA: Harvard University Press, 1991), pp. 103–108.

22. Liu Shu-hsien, "From the People-as-the-Root to Democracy" (in Chinese); quoted from Ni Peinim, "Confucianism and Democracy," p. 99.

23. Henry Rosemont, Jr., *A Chinese Mirror: Moral Reflections on Political Economy and Society* (La Salle, IL: Open Court, 1991), p. 93.

24. Rosemont, *A Chinese Mirror*, p. 93; also his "Whose Rights? Which Democracy?" in *Confucianism and Liberalism* (Beijing: Sanlian Shudian, 2001), section 5 (in Chinese). I am following here Ni Peinim's account in his "Confucianism and Democracy," pp. 93–94.

25. See *Engaged Buddhism: Buddhist Liberation Movements in Asia*, ed. Christopher S. Queen and Sallie B. King (Albany, NY: State University of New York Press, 1996). Among the most notable "engaged" Buddhists are Thich Nhat Hanh, Buddhadasa Bhikhu, Sulak Sivaraksa, and the Dalai Lama.

26. *Reason, Freedom, and Democracy in Islam: Essential Writings of Abdolkarim Soroush*, trans. and ed. Mahmud Sadri and Ahmad Sadri (New York: Oxford University Press, 2000), 99, 103. See also Muhammad Iqbal, *The Reconstruction of Religious Thought in Islam* (Lahore: Ashraf, 1971); Abdulaziz A. Sachedina, *The Islamic Roots of Democratic Pluralism* (New York: Oxford University Press, 2001); Khaled Abou El Fadl, *Islam and the Challenge of Democracy* (Princeton: Princeton University Press, 2004); M. A. Muqtedar Khan, ed.,

Islamic Democratic Discourse (Lanham, MD: Lexington Books, 2006); Lahouari Addi, *Islam et démocratie* (Paris: Seuil, 2003); John L. Esposito, *Islam and Democracy* (New York: Oxford University Press, 1996); Timothy D. Sisk, *Islam and Democracy: Religion, Politics, and Power in the Middle East* (Washington, D.C.: United States Institute of Peace Press, 1992); and *Under Siege: Islam and Democracy*, ed. Richard W. Bulliet (New York: Columbia University Press, 1994).

27. Michael J. Sandel, *Public Philosophy: Essays on Morality and Politics* (Cambridge, MA: Harvard University Press, 2005), pp. 9–11, 27, 33.

28. Walter Lippman, *The Good Society* (1936; New York: Grosset and Dunlap, 1943), pp. 194, 237, 346–347. See also my "Introduction" to *In Search of the Good Life: A Pedagogy for Troubled Times* (Lexington, KY: University of Kentucky Press, 2007), pp. 2–8.

29. Boisvert, *John Dewey*, p. 68.

30. Dewey, "Democracy is Radical" (1937), in *John Dewey: The Later Works: 1925–1953*, vol. 11, p. 298; and "Reconstruction in Philosophy" (1920), in *John Dewey: The Middle Works: 1899–1924*, ed. Jo Ann Boydston (Carbondale, IL: Southern Illinois University, 1981), vol. 12, p. 186.

31. Dewey, "Creative Democracy—The Task Before Us" (1939), in *John Dewey: The Later Works, 1925–1953*, vol. 14, p. 228.

Relativisme et polarisation du monde: Une contradiction majeure du capitalisme historique

NKOLO FOÉ
ECOLE NORMALE SUPÉRIEURE (UNIVERSITÉ DE YAOUNDÉ I) CAMEROUN

Abstract: Relativism issues occur in a context characterised by the resurfacing of culturalism and attempts to substitute historical causality based on class struggles with a new causality based on great cycles of civilizations and culture clashes. Symptons include rejection of class struggle, biologisation and culturalisation of social inequalities, and denial of universal values—all linked to the delegitimisation of emancipatory reason, which supposes an ethical approach to social and global issues. In Europe, from the end of the nineteenth century to the beginning of the twentieth, destruction of reason and the neglect of universal values by institutions of capitalism led to the barbaric conquest of non-European societies. In these societies, emancipatory reason and philosophies of freedom have an important role to play in social redemption. The major challenge they face is how to help man free himself from the intolerable universe of constraint (determined by relativism), and bring him to a level of consciousness where freedom of choice is possible. This entails the rehabilitation of universal values and the inscription of the ethics of responsibility at the core of any vision of an alternative modernity.

INTRODUCTION

Les théories de légitimation de la mondialisation recèlent une contradiction majeure: le relativisme. C'est à notre époque que le *bien commun* (Rochet) et l'*excellence universelle* (Mattei) sont attaqués de toutes parts, dans une ambiance d'effervescence dionysiaque et de ferveur barbare. Face au processus «d'ensauvagement de la société et de la vie» (Maffesoli 2002, 40), d' «effervescences anomiques», de mise en scène du «sauvage», du «barbare», il y a urgence à repenser la question décisive de l'«état civil» (Kant 1947), pour souligner à la fois

Special Supplement, *Journal of Philosophical Research* pp. 19–28
DOI: 10.5840/jpr201237Supplement22

la «fonction civilisatrice de la société», l' «avènement d'un Etat de droit» (Delbraccio 2000, 17), la promotion d'un idéal de «société civile universelle» (Kant) et le partage de la responsabilité mondiale.

Pour résumer la destination morale et politique de toute société civilisée, Kant (1947, 33) affirme que «le problème essentiel de l'espèce humaine, celui que la nature contraint l'homme à résoudre, c'est la réalisation d'une Société civile administrant le droit de façon universelle». Cette approche dégage une définition où l'humanité s'absorbe dans l'universalité de l'espèce et pointe en même temps vers la constitution d'un «droit cosmopolitique» et d'une «communauté civile universelle». La virulence barbare oblige à rendre justice à l'universalisme et à relativiser la caricature sur les visées «pacificatrices» du droit cosmopolitique. Car, la «fraternité universelle» est bien plus qu'une «fraternité de voleurs» (Marx 1972). Que, contre le mercantilisme—facteur de discorde entre les hommes—, Kant idéalise le marché mondial, au nom de la civilisation, c'est un fait. Mais le paradoxe aujourd'hui est que, c'est le marché mondial lui-même qui invite la barbarie à ensevelir la civilisation. Avec Rorty, Feyerabend, Lyotard, Maffesoli, etc., il semble que nous soyons loin du «beau jour de l'universalité» tant célébré par Hegel. La raison émancipatrice qui implique l'idée de responsabilité (Samir Amin 2008, 17–18) doit pouvoir relever le défi que lui lancent le relativisme et l'abandon des valeurs universelles.

RELATIVISME ET AUTISME UNIVERSEL

On s'est beaucoup interrogé sur l'audace de ce dernier. En fait, rien ne pouvait plus le freiner, dès lors que la philosophie elle-même avait choisi de capituler face à la furie barbare. Imitant ceux d'hier, les barbares d'aujourd'hui en appellent à une «nouvelle sophistique»: le relativisme cherche à l'étendre «à l'ensemble de la planète pour voir émerger des sociétés démocratiques et libérales» (Biyogo 2005, 123). Rorty lui-même avait posé les bases de l'édifice. Avec lui, la société libérale apparut sous les sombres traits d'une société a-critique et a-philosophique. Si Rorty insista pour que l'ironiste détrônât le philosophe classique démodé, c'est parce qu'il entrevoyait l'avènement d'un nouveau type de citoyen, irrationaliste, privatiste et esthétisant. Mais sous la figure décomposée de ce personnage, on distingue nettement le rictus idiot du consommateur. C'est lui, le pur «résidu intelligible» (Lefebvre), fragmenté, flexible, intuitif et inapte à l'échange social et à la coopération. Il n'y a rien d'étonnant à cela, dès lors que notre époque postmoderne rétablit la «certitude improbable» et la «croyance justifiée». Le relativisme nous interdit de «ridiculiser aucun projet humain, aucune forme délibérée de la vie humaine» (Rorty 1995, 81). Il est donc inutile de chercher à convaincre un interlocuteur ne partageant pas les mêmes points de vue que vous. Pour Deleuze (1991/2005, 31), «il est vain de se demander si Descartes a tort ou raison». Il s'interroge même: «Des présupposés subjectifs et implicites valent-ils mieux que les présupposés objectifs explicites?» (ibid.). C'est en abordant directement la question du débat et de la discussion que l'on mesure la gravité de ces orientations. Le relativisme nous invite à une véritable rébellion contre la culture dialogique héritée de Socrate et de Platon. Deleuze prétend que «la philosophie a horreur des discussions»; qu'elle «a toujours autre chose à faire»; que «le débat lui est insupportable» (p. 33). Nous vivrions en effet une bien curieuse époque, où «tout philosophe s'enfuit quand il entend la phrase: on va discuter un peu» (p. 32). Sans doute, les discussions ne seraient-elles bonnes que pour les tables rondes, car, «le moins qu'on puisse dire est qu'elles ne font pas avancer le travail, puisque les interlocuteurs ne parlent pas de la même chose» (ibid.). Voilà donc l'humanité invitée à l'autisme universel. Rien donc d'étonnant à ce que notre monde libéral et postmoderne soit le monde idéal des schizophrènes et des égoïstes.

EXONÉRATION DU CRIME ET LÉGITIMATION DE L'INJUSTICE

Nous sommes invités à prendre acte du fait que toute «discussion requiert que l'on s'accorde sur la préséance des besoins» (Rorty 1995, 84). Examinons de près cette thèse. Aucun argument, prétend Rorty, ne peut modifier le projet central d'un individu et l'amener à se convertir. Etre «converti» par un «argument» signifierait que l'individu «ne voit plus l'intérêt, la pertinence des arguments qu'il déployait auparavant» (p. 85). La vérité n'existant pas et l'homme lui-même n'étant pas un sujet cognitif, «rien ne peut nous rendre aptes à être convertis par des arguments plutôt que renversés par des forces irrationnelles» (p. 86).

Demandons-nous avec J.-F. Mattéi comment on a pu présenter «comme un progrès, et un progrès absolu, les comportements relativistes présents pour la seule raison, *en fait*, qu'ils ont succédé aux comportements universalistes antérieurs»? (1999, 240). Qui a vraiment pris la mesure du désastre? Comme le précise Mattéi, le relativisme nous invite à accepter par exemple qu'il n'y a pas «de raisons universelles, et objectives, de préférer le système démocratique au système nazi» (ibid.). Par-delà l'indignation, est-il vrai que les sentiments d'horreur qu'inspire Auschwitz sont le simple produit d'un conditionnement historique? Si nous l'accordons à Rorty, alors, l'ethos du fascisme est a priori légitime. N'oublions pas ici que le débat, entré au parlement, sur la légitimité ou l'illégitimité, les bienfaits ou les méfaits de la colonisation et de l'impérialisme, participe des mêmes principes. Par la banalisation du crime et la tactique du harcèlement, le relativisme réussit à conquérir des territoires qui lui étaient jusque-là interdits. Prenons la question des droits de l'homme, jusque-là protégés par la gangue de l'universalité et de l'inconditionnalité. Le relativisme moral les soumet désormais à la conditionnalité. On prétend que ces droits sont inconditionnels, écrit Rorty (p. 120), «qu'ils constituent le cadre fixe des délibérations politiques et morales», ou qu'ils «sont au-delà de toute discussion», étant l' «atout maître qui a préséance sur toute autre considération de nécessité ou d'efficacité sociale»; or, du point de vue pragmatiste, «la notion de droits de l'humanité inaliénables» constitue une banale formule creuse, qui n'est ni plus ni moins bonne que n'importe quelle autre formule. Selon Rorty:

> Quand nous invoquons l'une ou l'autre formule à titre de premier moteur, nous jetons notre as de pique sur la tête; nous admettons que nous sommes à court d'argument. L'analyse philosophique et la critique ne peuvent décemment s'attaquer à la volonté de Dieu ou aux droits de l'humanité, pas plus qu'à 'l'honneur de la famille' ou la 'patrie qui-est-en-danger'.

Il ne sert à rien d'aller au-delà. Ces notions défient l'analyse parce qu'elles ne sont toutes qu'une autre façon de dire: 'C'est ma position: je ne puis rien faire d'autre'» (p. 121). On en est là, aujourd'hui.

La seule autorité de Nietzsche ne suffit pas pour faire des droits de l'homme de «naïves superstitions» ou encore, des «fabrications à l'abri desquels les faibles se protègent des forts» (ibid.). Les opprimés de la terre ne pardonneront jamais tant de frivolités; ils n'accorderont jamais, ni à Rorty ni à Nietzsche, le fait que «la référence aux droits de l'homme n'est qu'une façon commode de résumer certains aspects de *nos* usages, réels ou prétendus» (ibid.). Le relativisme doit faire plus, pour convaincre les victimes que les droits de l'humanité, comme n'importe quelles autres valeurs, constituent le résultat de simples «constructions sociales» (p. 124).

Dans ses vues constructivistes, Feyerabend affirme pour sa part qu'aucune théorie n'est capable de comprendre à elle seule la totalité du «mystère» de la liberté. Mais Bouveresse (1984, 78) lui répond que cela n'implique nullement «que n'importe quelle idéologie exprime un aspect important et irremplaçable de ce 'mystère' qu'il serait dangereux d'ignorer ou de supprimer». Malicieusement, le même penseur (ibid.) souligne que le simple souci de cohérence aurait dû imposer au relativisme de considérer les traditions esclavagistes, racistes ou antisémites comme susceptibles d'apporter, elles aussi, «une contribution substantielle à la liberté et au progrès, même y compris dans leur sens le plus «'tolérant'». Restons donc vigilants.

RESPONSABILITÉ UNIVERSELLE OU TROC DES GÉNOCIDES?

Les objectifs d'un relativisme «tolérant», qui renvoie par exemple dos à dos le rationalisme et le fascisme, les philanthropes et les SS, etc., restent difficiles à saisir, tant qu'on élude la question essentielle de la justice et de la responsabilité. En fait, on exonère le crime, on légitime l'injustice, en prétendant que «tous sont des bêtes», officiers fascistes et philanthropes, nazis et rationalistes. De la même façon, en éludant la question de la constitution d'une hiérarchie stricte des valeurs, on diminue d'autant la responsabilité des hommes les uns vis-à-vis des autres. Or, l'exigence morale et la responsabilité mondiale interdisent la passivité devant l'horreur. La conscience d'une telle responsabilité aurait permis de voir ce qu'il y a d'odieux et de cynique dans cette attitude qui veut que «s'il y a des hommes qui trouvent leur bonheur dans le fait de s'exterminer les uns les autres dans des jeux guerriers dangereux, alors, qu'on leur laisse ce plaisir» (Feyerabend, cité par Bouveresse, 79). En fait, dans son radicalisme, le relativisme recourt à tous les moyens disponibles, même les plus contestables, pour exercer un odieux chantage sur l'universalisme démocratique. Faut-il laisser passer ce chantage? Or, nous savons bien ce que le relativisme cherche à obtenir en contrepartie, mais en fraude: la capitulation sans conditions de la raison, de la morale et de la responsabilité. Avec les idéologies qui l'accompagnent, le capitalisme veut avoir les mains libres pour agir sans entraves et sans responsabilité; dans l'irresponsabilité la plus totale, il veut avoir la liberté de détruire l'être humain et son environnement, de démanteler les économies, de capturer des Etats étrangers, de saccager les nations et d'opprimer les peuples.

Feyerabend met sur la balance la «terreur d'Auschwitz» contre la «terreur blanche» du rationalisme. Feyerabend ne peut croire, ni aux larmes de crocodile des «philanthropes au cœur sensible», ni aux «phrases à propos de la 'terreur d'Auschwitz'», tant que la propagation de leur «humanité dans les écoles, les hôpitaux, les universités, les prisons entraîne une pareille mort des âmes» (ibid., pp. 79–80). Alors, dans le troc des génocides, la reconnaissance du «génocide des âmes», orchestré par la pédagogie rationaliste, constitue-t-elle la monnaie d'échange contre la reconnaissance de la traite des Noirs et de la Shoah?

L'UNIVERS DES CONTRAINTES OU L'HABITUDE DU MALHEUR

Les attitudes de ce type témoignent manifestement d'un manque de jugement. Mais, inlassablement répétées, il finit par s'incruster dans l'esprit des gens l'idée que Socrate, Platon, Jésus, Kant, Marx, etc., «comptent au nombre des plus grands criminels de l'histoire» (p. 79). La chose prêterait à sourire si le destin des millions d'hommes, de femmes et d'enfants n'était en jeu. En fait, depuis Nietzsche et Heidegger, la réaction cherche à *habituer l'humanité au malheur*. Cette étrange attitude est contemporaine de l'époque qui suit immédiatement la défaite du fascisme, époque au cours de laquelle la philosophie occidentale s'appliqua à «dénazifier» Nietzsche. L'habitude du malheur répond à une question que se pose Bouveresse: qui donc espère convaincre Feyerabend lorsqu'il prétend qu'il n'y a pas à choisir entre la bestialité des SS et celle supposée des pédagogues rationalistes et des philanthropes? En fait, l'habitude du malheur émascula complètement les questions cruciales qui rythmèrent la marche de la modernité: justice, libération, droits de l'homme, émancipation des peuples, etc.

C'est donc l'époque structurale elle-même qui interdit toute promesse messianique d'un avenir meilleur. Le drame des peuples captifs, celui des millions d'enfants et de femmes opprimés, peut légitimement nous autoriser à retourner à son envoyeur le fameux «rire philosophique» que Foucault (1966, 353–354) adressait

> à tous ceux qui veulent encore parler de l'homme, de son règne ou de sa libération, à tous ceux qui posent encore des questions sur ce qu'est l'homme en son essence [. . .], à tous ceux qui ne veulent pas penser sans penser aussitôt que c'est l'homme qui pense, à toutes ces formes de réflexion gauche et gauchies.

Mais, nous constatons aujourd'hui que les luttes contre les assujettissements éthiques, obsession de Foucault, laissent intacte la question cruciale de la domination et de l'oppression dans le monde contemporain. Passé dans la banalité quotidienne, le sort des déshérités, celui des populations arrachées à leurs terres ou celui des nations occupées, spoliées, martyrisées, ne serait digne d'aucune grande mobilisation de la philosophie. A travers ses représentants les plus illustres, cette dernière élit des adversaires dignes de son rang. Il s'agit principalement du totalitarisme éthique et du terrorisme de la raison. Mais ces choix philosophiques camouflent des options idéologiques plus profondes, en accord avec l'univers des contraintes lui-même. La mondialisation constitue la preuve que le monde n'est pas sorti de l'époque des nécessités idéalisée par l'idéologie (post)structurale.

Le formalisme, la dépréciation de la raison, l'exaltation de l'impensé, la contestation (post)structurale de l'historique et l'envahissement de l'empirisme et du quantitatif en sociologie, etc., tous ces faits auraient pu alerter que sous des apparences de souplesse—dont procède évidemment le relativisme—, l'époque (post) structurale véhicule en réalité l'un des projets opératoires les plus sévères. Même l'univers postmoderne, idéalisation du capitalisme mondialisé, apparaît comme un monde «administré à son comble» (Meschonnic, 1988, 260).

Depuis Comte, la bourgeoisie n'a jamais véritablement renoncé à l'idée d'une sociocratie, synthèse idéale de la démocratie et de l'aristocratie, la grande obsession du positivisme étant la «reconstruction générale» et non la «révolution». C'est en partisan de l'ordre et de la stabilité que Comte (1966, 31) s'exprime: «Notre situation occidentale» actuelle exclut «le point de vue purement révolutionnaire». L'alternative sociocratique convient d'autant mieux qu'elle permet à la mondialisation de chasser le spectre qui hante le monde moderne: la lutte des classes (dans la nation et le monde). C'est cette alternative qui s'applique à trouver des substituts ethnologiques, culturalistes ou essentialistes à l'idée de contradiction, accusée d'ouvrir la voie à une synthèse universelle. Non seulement l'époque postmoderne est déchirée par la discorde qu'implique l'incompatibilité des cultures, mais aussi elle vit sous l'empire éclaté des ethnosciences. Quel est l'enjeu idéologique de la question?

LA DISCORDE UNIVERSELLE

L'enjeu de la question est l'universalisation de l'esprit de discorde. L'option prise par Feyerabend par exemple est de nature à nourrir le fondamentalisme dans les traditions occidentales et non occidentales, contribuant ainsi à accroître le fossé «culturel» entre le Nord et le Sud. Feyerabend inventa le concept d' «échange libre» entre les traditions pour montrer l'impossibilité d'une entente rationnelle entre les cultures, consécutive à une «discussion critique» des traditions. Or le respect de l'autre (individu, tradition, culture) ne peut procéder que d'un échange argumenté. L'«échange dirigé», me semble-t-il, est la condition même d'un véritable dialogue des cultures et des civilisations. Aujourd'hui encore, les partisans de l' «échange libre» vont et viennent en jurant que l' «échange dirigé» n'accepte qu'une seule tradition et n'admet que les principes conformes à la raison. Comme l'a souligné Bouveresse, Feyerabend se comporte «comme si la tradition rationaliste était pratiquement la seule qui ne soit pas capable de pratiquer l'échange libre, de respecter entièrement ses adversaires et de les traiter autrement que sur le mode de l'exclusion pure» (p. 69).

Mais, pour une fois, ajoutons de l'eau au moulin de Feyerabend. Le capitalisme, pour prendre cet exemple, ne représente pas nécessairement un progrès par rapport aux différents systèmes historiques antérieurs qu'il a détruits ou supplantés. Il suffit de se pencher sur «la masse de connaissances qui ont été perdues du fait de l'expansion mondiale de l'idéologie universaliste» (Wallerstein 1990, 97). Ce constat nous invite à sortir du culturalisme, pour une critique économique et sociale vigoureuse. Cette dernière est seule à même de nous introduire dans les grands problèmes politiques et économiques posés par l'universalisme moderne. Or, une fois la conviction acquise que ce qui se cache sous cet universalisme-là, c'est l'expansion universelle de la forme marchande elle-même, alors, nous pouvons commencer à envisager une sortie de crise, par exemple, en faisant un sort à la question cruciale de la valeur d'usage.

L'erreur du relativisme consiste à croire qu'il suffit de détruire le bien commun et l'excellence universelle, y compris celle que représente l'universalisme démocratique, pour résoudre le problème des inégalités dans le monde. Mais pour l'instant, personne ne propose d'alternative véritablement viable à cette «tradition rationaliste» accusée d'intolérance et d'impérialisme contre les autres traditions. Ce qu'on voit au contraire, c'est, avec Lyotard par exemple, l'irruption d'une énorme phraséologie sur le refus du consensus, le «différend», le «dissensus», le «dissentiment». Que «la prétendue impossibilité de se comprendre qui est supposée séparer des traditions, des cultures, des générations ou des périodes historiques différentes» soit un mythe pur et simple, comme l'a noté Popper (cité par Bouveresse, p. 139), cela n'a pas empêché la postmodernité culturelle et le postcolonialisme en Afrique et en Asie, d'épouser les vues parmi les plus rétrogrades d'un structuralisme et d'un fonctionnalisme qui, on l'oublie trop souvent, donnèrent un fondement idéologique à l'Apartheid en Afrique du Sud. Prenons l'exemple de Malinowski, avec son concept de «contact culturel». En fait, ce concept était compatible avec l'existence d'un système lourd, permanent et dichotomique d' «arrière-pays» auquel chaque partenaire du «contact culturel» se réfère en permanence: le Blanc s'appuyant sur «l'arrière-pays de culture européenne . . . d'où il importe des marchandises et d'où il reçoit des idées, vers lequel, d'une façon ou d'une autre, il retournera»; le Noir se référant quant à lui, à son «arrière-pays, sa culture ancienne qui maintenant fait partie du passé; et dans un autre sens, sa communauté à laquelle il doit revenir après ses courtes prises de contact avec les Blancs» (Malinowski 1970, 40–41).

Sans doute, ces oppositions sont-elles constitutives de l'inconscient capitaliste lui-même. Elles rendent compte d'un schisme traversant l'histoire mondiale et partageant la planète entre un centre développé et dominant d'une part, une périphérie pauvre et assujettie d'autre part. Comme P. Jalée (1973, 154), nous pouvons saisir le monde en termes «d'unité dialectique d'un système capitaliste unique dont la nature contradictoire et opprimante engendre des différences». L'ossification des rapports socio-économiques explique largement certains phénomènes étranges, tels que ceux en rapport avec la psychologie ethnique. Si l'hypothèse capitaliste que j'avance est valable, alors, certaines contradictions notées au sein des théories postmodernes et postcoloniales s'éclairent, par exemple celle qui rend tenue, la marge entre l'essentialisme pur et la «conscience oppositionnelle».

Car, le capitalisme développe un mouvement à double détente. Le mouvement qui correspond au niveau du marché tend à liquéfier les communautés, l'objectif étant de les rendre flexibles. C'est à ce niveau que se structura la vulgate postmoderniste et postcolonialiste sur l'acentrique, l'égalité des cultures, l'éloge de la désorientation éthique, l'affranchissement par rapport aux normes morales contraignantes, les identités multiples, mobiles, le nomadisme, l'hybridité, etc. C'est le marché qui exige la fluidité, la circulation des biens, de la main-d'œuvre, des capitaux, des images. L'universalisme qui correspond à ce stade insinue que le marché est la condition de la liberté et de l'égalité entre les hommes; que le commerce est un facteur de fusion entre les communautés et d'abolition des frontières, que l'échange constitue un ingrédient pour fluidifier les identités. La problématique du métissage et de l'hybridité n'est intelligible que référée aux pratiques universalistes du marché lui-même. Le niveau des grands intérêts capitalistes contredit cette vision idyllique. Elle rétablit donc l'essentialisme et même le racisme. C'est ce niveau des pratiques capitalistes que reflètent l'incommensurabilité et l'incompatibilité des traditions, bien que le «dissensus» et le «différend» puissent également mettre en évidence le comportement du petit bourgeois égoïste, évoluant dans un environnement hostile, où la frontière entre la libre concurrence normale et l'agressivité pure se réduit.

Racisme impérial ou postmoderne, le «choc des civilisations» signifie que pour survivre, l'Empire a besoin de déterminismes culturels; pour être efficace, sa bureaucratie a besoin de marqueurs signifiants. Selon Negri et Hardt (2000, 241), «dans la perspective du racisme impérial . . . il y a des limites à la flexibilité et à la compatibilité des cultures. Les différences entre cultures et traditions sont, en dernière analyse, insurmontables. Il est futile et même dangereux, selon cette théorie, de permettre à des cultures de se mélanger ou d'insister pour qu'elles le fassent: Serbes et Croates, Hutus et Tutsis, Noirs d'Amérique et Coréens d'Amérique doivent être tenus séparés les uns des autres». Il reste à comprendre la signification de cette vision contradictoire au sein d'une même théorie. C'est dans l'Histoire elle-même qu'il faut chercher les sources de la contradiction: le capitalisme moderne refuse de trancher la question du marché libre et celle du mercantilisme. Voilà pourquoi, il favorise les forces du marché tout en manipulant avec désinvolture les vieux démons issus du mercantilisme, le nationalisme en particulier. Mais nous savons le capitalisme incapable de résoudre ce problème crucial, parce que cela impliquerait son autodestruction. Il n'est même pas exclu que cette tension interne constitue le ressort véritable d'un règne qui abandonne aujourd'hui toute référence aux valeurs universelles pour mieux renoncer à l'éthique de la responsabilité.

COMMENT SORTIR LES NATIONS DU SUD DE L'UNIVERS DES NÉCESSITÉS?

L'Empire a mis le paradigme ethnologique au cœur même de son dispositif. Ce paradigme permet de régler des questions gênantes: celles du *temps*, du *progrès* et de l'*histoire*. La *norme*, la *règle* et le *système* sont convoqués, certes pour indiquer, comme on l'a vu, que chaque ensemble (société ou culture) reçoit de lui-même sa cohérence et sa validité propres, mais aussi, pour cimenter idéologiquement la théorie des nécessités. Car, si elle implique le pluralisme et l'égalité des cultures, rien n'empêche l'ethnologie d'être une idéologie des contraintes ou encore des nécessités, en tant que «théorie de l'équilibre entre les différentes forces agissantes dans le monde: système économique et politique, classes, pays industrialisés et pays peu développés» (Lefebvre 1971/1975, 69). L'ethnologie ratifie le *statu quo* au sein de l'Empire et permet de maintenir captives les nations du Sud. Chez Foucault par exemple, la *fonction*, le *conflit* et la *signification* sont contestés parce qu'historiquement, ils sont constitutifs des *philosophies de la liberté*. Là, la *fonction* suppose l'existence d'un sujet actif de l'histoire. Prenant appui sur la raison et la volonté, un tel sujet supporte le *conflit* et les *contradictions* qui travaillent le monde. C'est en les affrontant qu'il donne la pleine mesure de son talent et de sa puissance. Il le fait efficacement parce que le monde qui l'entoure est intelligible et doué de *signification*, contrairement à l'univers opaque de la structure qui renvoie à l'*inconscient* et à l'*impensé*. La pensée de la liberté prend appui sur la connaissance objective des lois de l'histoire, de l'économie et de la société; son ambition est de libérer les opprimés du Système, afin de les insérer dans la communauté des nations en peuples majeurs. Théorie des nécessités, l'ethnologie cherche à maintenir les déshérités dans le Système, en leur conférant une place semblable à celle que Senghor réservait au Noir, au sein de la Civilisation de l'Universel, où dans le grand orchestre de la convergence pan-humaine le chef était l'Europe, l'Afrique occupant la section rythmique. Non seulement elles permettent de sortir de l'impasse du relativisme, mais aussi les philosophies de la liberté constituent une alternative vivante au monde polarisé et administré.

RÉFÉRENCES BIBLIOGRAPHIQUES

Amin, Samir. 2008. *Modernité, religion et démocratie. Critique de l'eurocentrisme, critique des culturalismes*. Lyon: Parangon/Vs.

Biyogo, Grégoire. 2005. *Adieu à Jacques Derrida. Enjeux et perspectives de la déconstruction*. Paris: L'Harmattan.

Bouveresse, Jacques. 1984. *Rationalité et cynisme*. Paris: Minuit.

Comte, Auguste. 1966. *Catéchisme positiviste*. Paris: Garnier-Flammarion.

Delbraccio, Mireille. 2000. «L'idée cosmopolitique et la naissance des sciences de l'homme». In *Du cosmopolitisme*, ed. Mireille Delbraccio and Bernard Pelloile, 9–30. Paris: L'Harmattan.

Deleuze, Gilles. 1991/2005. *Qu'est-ce que la philosophie?* Paris: Minuit.

Feyerabend, Paul. 1979. *Contre la méthode. Esquisse d'une théorie anarchiste de la connaissance*. Paris: Seuil.

Foucault, Michel. 1966. *Les mots et les choses. Une archéologie des sciences humaines*. Paris: Gallimard.

Hardt, Michael et Antonio Negri. 2000. *Empire*. Paris: Exils Editeur.

Jalée, Pierre. 1973. *Le pillage du Tiers monde*. Paris: Maspero.

Kant, Immanuel. 1947. *La philosophie de l'histoire*. Paris: Gonthier.

Lefebvre, Henri. 1971/1975. *L'idéologie structuraliste*. Paris: Anthropos.

Lyotard, Jean-François. 1979. *La condition postmoderne*. Paris: Minuit.

Maffesoli, Michel. 2002. *La part du diable*. Paris: Flammarion.

Malinowski. 1970. *Les dynamiques de l'évolution culturelles Recherches sur les relations raciales en Afrique*. Paris: Payot.

Marx, Karl. 1972. *Critique de l'économie politique*. Paris. Union Générale d'Edition.

Mattéi, Jean-François. 1999. *La barbarie intérieure. Essai sur l'*immonde *moderne*. Paris: PUF.

Meschonnic, Henri. 1988. *Modernité, modernité*. Paris: Verdier.

Rochet, Claude. 2001. *Gouverner par le bien commun. Un précis d'incorrection politique à l'usage des jeunes générations*. Paris: Guibert.

Rorty, Richard. 1995. *L'espoir au lieu du savoir. Introduction au pragmatisme*. Bibliothèque du Collège International de Philosophie/Albin Michel.

Wallerstein, Immanuel. 1990. *Le capitalisme historique*. Paris: La Découverte.

SELECTED PAPERS FROM THE XXII WORLD CONGRESS OF PHILOSOPHY

"Overlapping Consensus" on "Overlapping Consensus"

TONG SHIJUN
EAST CHINA NORMAL UNIVERSITY

Abstract: Many people show great interest in the idea of "overlapping consensus" proposed by John Rawls. On the basis of a careful reading of different understandings of this idea, or the "overlapping consensus" on the idea of "overlapping consensus," we can say that there are three levels of "overlapping consensus." At the first level, people with different positions treat each other in the same reasonable attitude. At the second level, people holding different values support the same norms on the basis of their respective values or by taking each other's perspectives in the moral discourse. At the third level, people who currently hold different "moral sources" of the shared norms are never-the-less ready to be engaged in a common learning process that aims for a "fusion of horizons" in the future. Overlapping consensuses at all these levels should not only be discussed in political philosophy, or discovered in political culture, but also constructed in political practice.

Diversity or pluralism of values has been recognized widely as a major feature of our times both internationally and domestically, including in China, where this phenomenon is regarded as a major reason for the country's efforts to promote the goal of a "harmonious world" abroad and the goal of a "harmonious society" at home.[1] In justifying the goals of "a harmonious world" and "a harmonious society," reference is often made in China to the traditional Chinese idea of "*he er bu tong*," which is often translated in English as "harmony without uniformity." It is close to the proposition of "*qiu tong chun yi*" or "seeking common ground while reserving differences" accepted in the Bandung Conference in 1955, on the one hand, and to the proposition of "unity in diversity" or "united in diversity" accepted as the motto of the European Union, on the other.

All three of these propositions, in my view, contain the idea that we should respect diversity as well as unity, but none of them makes it clear how these two

Special Supplement, *Journal of Philosophical Research* pp. 29–45
DOI: 10.5840/jpr201237Supplement23

sides are to be smoothly connected with each other. This reminds us of the idea of "overlapping consensus," which is used by its major advocator, John Rawls, as well as many others, to deal with the issue of political stability in pluralistic domestic societies and the issue of multiple cultural bases of universal human rights at the global level. In order to see more clearly whether this concept is helpful in answering the problem how diversity and unity can be taken care of at the same time, we are going to have a discussion of the ideas proposed by thinkers in various countries and of different schools of thought in explicating this concept. I want to argue that these different understandings of the idea of "overlapping consensus" can be read as characterizations of different levels of overlapping consensus to be reached in our dealing with pluralism with the aim of "social stability for the right reasons" (in Rawls's words). This also means that some deficiencies found in each of these understandings, especially in the most well-known version or the Rawlsian version of the idea, can be overcome by a mutual complementation between them.

1.

The concept of "overlapping consensus" first appeared in Rawls's *A Theory of Justice* published in 1971 when he said that many disagreements among citizens in their understanding of justice can nevertheless lead to similar political judgments. These similar political judgments, he says, are "overlapping rather than strict consensus."[2] The logical implication of the existence of this kind of consensus is very simple: "different premises can yield the same conclusion."[3]

Since mid-1980s, the idea of overlapping consensus has turned itself from an idea mentioned only in passing in Rawls's earlier book on justice to a major conceptual tool in his later work on political liberalism for dealing with the phenomenon that "the political conception of justice that regulates its basic institutions is endorsed by each of the main religious, philosophical, and moral doctrines likely to endure in that society from one generation to the next."[4] Rawls takes this idea as the first of the three major ideas of his "political liberalism" (the other two being "the idea of the priority of right" and "the idea of public reason").[5]

What is called by Rawls "political liberalism" is different both from the Hobbes's version of liberalism and the Kantian or Mill's version of liberalism. In Hobbes, liberalism is a *modus vivendi*, or a temporary compromise between interests of individuals and groups coordinated and balanced by some well-designed institutions. In Kant or Mill, liberalism is based on certain metaphysical doctrines or "comprehensive" moral doctrines. Neither version, according to Rawls, can solve the problem of social stability under pluralistic conditions: in one case, as soon as the balance of power changes, the existing stability based on it comes to a stop; in another, Kantianism and liberal utilitarianism as comprehensive doctrines respectively with "autonomy" and "individuality" as their key concepts are both held by particular parties, and cannot support the basic institutions of a society in which there are many other comprehensive doctrines as well, secular or not.

The key to this position is "the fact of reasonable pluralism"[6] in Rawls's mind. Here the term "pluralism" refers to the existence of various "comprehensive doctrines," and the term "reasonable" refers first of all to the attitude and mentality of those who, in inter-subjective relations, are ready to be engaged in fair cooperation and to follow public rules in cooperation as long as other equal participants follow them as well. This is different from "rational" in that the latter refers to the careful choice of efficient means for given goals, or the prudent ordering of different goals within a whole life-plan. In order for a society to have a social fact called "reasonable pluralism," citizens in it should be reasonable in this sense. Rawls thinks that the liberal societies in the contemporary West can be characterized in this way; therefore the fact of "reasonable pluralism" can be regarded, in Rawls's view, as the actual basis of, and political cultural support for, his idea of "justice as fairness," among other political conceptions of justice.

In Rawls's position presented above there is an interesting displacement between the role of the philosopher and the role of the citizen: While in Rawls's view the political philosopher should not justify a political conception from a particular philosophical system; the citizen should behave like a philosopher, i.e., he should understand and support the conception of justice from his or her own world-view and value-system in addition to justifying it by means of public reason. Only then, Rawls holds, can there be "stability for the right reasons"[7] under the pluralistic condition. For only then can his idea of "justice as fairness," for example, be met with acceptance by people on the basis of reasons rather than as a result of outside pressure, or one's own ignorance, or acceptance at the shallow level. These "reasons" are different from person to person and the consensus on a certain idea reached by different people for these reasons is the so-called "overlapping consensus."

Since it was advocated, especially since early 1990s, the idea of overlapping consensus has attracted wide attention among political and social theorists. In what follows I will discuss some interpretations or elaborations of the idea that to my view are especially suggestive and helpful in our efforts to explore its full potential in dealing with the issue of political stability in pluralistic domestic societies and the issue of multiple cultural bases of universal human rights at the global level.

2.

The idea of "overlapping consensus" can at the first stage be understood as the situation in which people, though different in their *positions* on a certain relevant issue, are similar in their *attitudes* to each other: they all treat each other in a reasonable way.

The major feature of this understanding of the idea of "overlapping consensus" is to loose the bond between "reasonable" and "consensus" and to stress on the connection between "reasonable" and "disagreement." From C. S. Peirce to J. Habermas, all those who argue for the so-called "consensus theory of truth" have paid special attention to the connection between "reasonableness" and "consensus," regarding "reasonable consensus" or "rational consensus" as the equivalent to, or guarantee for, truth, or in Habermas's words: "The truth of a proposition means the promise to reach a rational consensus on what is said."[8] Habermas does not only apply consensus theory to the problem of truth, but also applies it to the problem of normative rightness, and what makes and redeems the promise to reach a rational consensus is the practical instead of the theoretical discourse. In practical discourses, "just those action norms are valid to which all possibly affected persons could agree as participants in rational discourses."[9]

Although Habermas is clear that real situations of discourse are far from being perfect, and the goal of reaching consensus is far from being certain, he does give us the impression that, of various ideas on the same problem, as long as they differ from each other, at least one is not rational or reasonable. In other words, Habermas seems to admit the possibility of "reasonable consensus" alone and reject the possibility of "reasonable disagreement." But the latter is just a major idea in Rawls's political liberalism. Many disagreements, according to Rawls, are quite possibly not resulted from our prejudices, ignorance, selfishness, and wishful thinking. In normal political life and in the process of practicing our capability of reasoning and judging, the complexities involved in the relation between aims and means, in valuing each person's claims, in applying our theoretical ability and weighing our evidences and so on, there are many difficulties that are hardly avoidable altogether. Rawls calls these difficulties "the burdens of judgment"; as a result of these burdens, even very reasonable people can make different judgments on the same problem: "many of our most important judgments are made under conditions where it is not to be expected that conscientious persons with full powers of reason, even after free discussion, will all arrive at the same conclusion."[10]

Rawls's idea of "reasonable disagreement" is highly regarded by H. Grimen, a Norwegian philosopher, who thinks that Rawls has convincingly shown that "an ideal argumentation situation in Habermas's sense is *subject* to the burdens of judgment,"[11] and we should never expect that disagreements will totally disappear in the long run. A conclusion from this is that "reasonable political actors must learn to live with reasonable disagreements."[12] Because these "reasonable disagreements" resulted from "burdens of judgment" we very often have to be satisfied with "overlapping consensus" rather than "qualified consensus"[13] or what Habermas calls "begruendete Konsensus,"[14] which means consensus on the basis of reasons accepted by all concerned. Grimen's emphasis is not on the indispensability of "overlapping consensus" as a result of the improbability of "qualified consensus," but on the inappropriateness of raising problems on which we cannot possibly expect to reach qualified consensus for public discussion as a result of the reasonableness of "reasonable disagreement." To be more exact, the point Grimen emphasizes is what Rawls calls "the method of avoidance": "In following the method of avoidance, as we may call it, we try, so far as we can, neither to assert nor to deny any religious, philosophical, or moral views, or their associated philosophical accounts of truth and the status of values."[15]

Appropriating the idea of "reasonable disagreement" implied in the idea of "overlapping consensus" is really very important to political unity and social stability under pluralistic conditions, because in many cases we do need to avoid seeking any qualified consensus or any consensus based on shared reasons that is evidently beyond our reach. This understanding of "overlapping consensus," however, has the weakness of being too passive in that it focuses more on "overlapping" than on "consensus," or more on "disagreement" than on "agreement." In the idea of "reasonable disagreement," actually, both "disagreement" and "agreement" play a crucial role: "reasonable disagreement" is "reasonable" because people share the same feature of reasonableness in their attitude to each other, and, as Rawls sometimes also argues, in the doctrines they hold. To say that persons are "reasonable," according to Rawls, is to say that they are ready to "propose principles and standards as fair terms of cooperation and to abide by them willingly, given the assurance that others will likewise do so."[16] To say that a doctrine is reasonable, moreover, is to say that this doctrine meets the theoretical demands for a certain level of consistency and coherence, and meets the practical demands for a certain way of ordering and balancing of various values, and is stable over time and not subject to sudden and unexplained changes.[17]

These two senses of "reasonableness," especially the first one, are, to my view, rooted in our common experiences in the life-world. In some sense it is like what is called *li xing* by Liang Shuming (1893–1988), one of the most important Chinese philosophers in the twentieth century. The Chinese term *li xing* is usually used as the Chinese equivalent of the English words of "reason," "rationality," "reasonablness," and in some cases, "intellect." Liang Shuming made a distinction between "*li xing*" and "*li zhi*," similar to Rawls's distinction between "the reasonable" and "the rational." Both *li xing* and *li zhi* are concerned with speaking, reasoning, and thinking, but *li zhi* is more a matter of calculation of means with regards to ends, while *li xing* is more a matter of co-living and co-experiencing with fellow human beings in a way that takes life as a whole and as the end in itself. "If you observe another person or reflect on yourself," Liang Shuming says, "whenever people are seen to be calm, easy-minded, without anything in their mind, most receptive to others, and most capable of reaching understanding with their partners in speaking with each other, they are people of *li xin*. The so-called *li xing* is nothing but the mental state of being calm and understanding."[18] At this level, that is to say, a monological reflection is sufficient to show what is reasonable, and whether an overlapping consensus at this minimum level has been reached or not.

3.

"Overlapping consensus" can, at the second stage, be understood as the situation in which people disagree in their *values* but agree on *norms*: people holding different values accept and follow a shared set of norms.

The Canadian philosopher Charles Taylor can be regarded as a typical case of the effort to make a conceptual distinction between "norm" and "value" and then applying this distinction to the understanding of the idea of "overlapping consensus." In discussing the problem of what is the unforced consensus on human rights Taylor said: "I suppose it would be something like what Rawls describes in his Political Liberalism as an "overlapping consensus."[19] In all cultures, Taylor says, we can find condemnation of genocide, murder, torture and slavery, and what these condemnations express are the action norms on which there is a universal consensus. Below these shared action norms there are "deep underlying values," which usually "belong to the alternative, mutually incompatible justifications."[20]

Here Taylor relies on the conceptual distinction between norm and value that he himself did not elaborate in detail. In Juergen Habermas's theory of communicative action this distinction plays an important role. The development of this distinction, according to Habermas, is an important achievement both in the process of development of individual moral consciousness and in the process of rationalization of a community's life-world. When he was criticizing Rawls for treating rights as goods in the latter's ideal experiment of "original position," Habermas elaborates the differences between "norm" (to which rights belong) and "values" (to which goods belong) which can be summarized into the following four points:

> norms differ from values, first, in their relation to rule-governed as opposed to purposive action; second, in a binary as opposed to a gradual coding of the respective validity claims; third, in their absolute as opposed to relative bindingness; and, last, in the criteria that systems of norms as opposed to systems of values must satisfy.[21]

These abstract distinctions between norms and values display themselves in the ways of their applications in everyday life: to the same problem "what I should do," a reply on the basis of norms is categorically different from a reply on the basis of values. A norm "commands" me to do something, while a value "advices" me to do something. The former tells us what is good for all, or what is in the equal interest of all, while the latter tells us what is good for me or for us.

Although both accepting the conceptual distinction between norms and values, and agreeing that people with different values can accept and follow the same norms, Habermas and Taylor consider the connection between norms and values differently. While Taylor, like Rawls, thinks that different values can be alternative bases of the same norms, Habermas pays more attention to justifying norms in moral discourse (concerning the question "what is good for all parties concerned") instead of ethical discourse (concerning the question "what is good for me or for us). Habermas admits that in pluralistic societies political consensuses are reached mainly among people holding different "values" (and with different interests) on common "norms" (including "principles" as "higher-level norms"),[22] but he argues that we should make a distinction between "consensus" as a social event and "consensus" as a epistemic achievement, or a distinction between acceptance and acceptability.[23] Individual subjects' agreements on a certain norm on the basis of their respective value systems, can at most converge into an event that is the *acceptance* of the norm; but the persons who claim the *acceptability* of the norm should provide reasons in the process of debating with others and manage to convince them to accept these reasons as valid. Participants in this debate are neither observers of objects, nor members of the same particular cultural community who discuss their shared values, but participants in a "moral discourse" which demands each to have the same "moral point of view," but not the same "ethical way of life." That is to say, participants in moral discourse usually need to reach consensus with people of other cultures and value systems; and in order to do so, they should have the competence to take each other's perspective, or even take an idealized perspective, in order to decide whether a certain norm is in the equal interest of all concerned.

Rawls does not agree with Habermas's criticism of him, but in his reply to Habermas, Rawls seems to be both clearing Habermas's "misunderstanding" of him and moving closer to Habermas's position. The "overlapping consensus" on political conceptions of justice in his sense, he argues, is not the agreement of interests sought by the politicians in everyday politics, but the "*reasonable* overlapping consensus"; and it is reasonable because the political conception is not only given a *pro tanto* justification on the basis of public reason at the first stage, and then given a full justification by members of civil society as individual citizens at the second stage, but also given a public justification by the political society in the form of the overlapping consensus among all the reasonable members of the political society as a result of their embedding the political conception in their several reasonable comprehensive views.[24] Rawls argues that the stability he seeks is thus "stability for the right reasons," and the overlapping consensus that underlies this kind of stability actually demands something that Habermas would call a "moral perspective." In explaining what he calls the "wide and general reflective equilibrium" which is the kernel of this public justification, Rawls makes it clear that "this equilibrium is fully intersubjective: that is, each citizen has taken into account the reasoning and arguments of every other citizen."[25]

Here one point deserves special attention, that is, Habermas argues for making a distinction between "consensus" as a social event and "consensus" as an epistemic achievement, or a distinction between the acceptance of a norm and the acceptability of a norm, not only in order to tell "stability for the right reasons" from stability without right reasons, but also in order to avoid a particularistic or contextualistic understanding of the principles of justice. Rawls emphasizes the role of the political culture in his theory, regarding the political culture of the democratic society in his mind as the realistic basis of political liberalism.

> The political culture of a democratic society," Rawls says, "is always marked by a diversity of opposing and irreconcilable religious, philosophical, and moral doctrines. Some of these are perfectly reasonable, and this diversity among reasonable doctrines political liberalism sees as the inevitable long-run result of the powers of human reason at work within the background of enduring free institutions.[26]

Rawls's concepts such as "reasonable pluralism," "the public use of reason," and the "overlapping consensus" on the conception of justice, etc., both base themselves on this political culture and provide conceptual tools for the latter's self-understanding. Political culture as a "fact," however, is a particular thing; if at the public level the principles of justice are only grounded on the political culture of a particular region or a particular tradition, there is hidden a danger of giving up the demand for universalistic justification for these principles. This particularistic position can lead to two consequences. On the one hand, it would make it difficult to find out elements in the existing political culture as the basis for the immanent critique and immanent transcendence of this culture and the institutions based on it. On the other hand, it would make it difficult to talk about the universality or universal legitimacy of a certain institution outside a particular society and cultural tradition. Habermas does not agree with Richard Rorty, who regards Rawls as a fellow particularist of him with "a thoroughly historicist and antiuniversalistic' attitude."[27] But Habermas insists that, in order to keep a clear distance from this tendency, a conception of justice achieved through a hermeneutical clarification of a contingent tradition should be put up for test in a moral discourse to see whether it is not only accepted, but also acceptable.[28]

When we agree with Habermas in emphasizing the importance of the commonly-made "moral justification" for shared norms vis-à-vis their separately-made value justification or ethical justification, we should add that Habermas may have neglected the fact that it is, after all, very important for the universal political conception and principles of justice to be accepted by people from the bottom of their hearts or on the basis of their deep-rooted values, and the fact that the social stability supported by the acceptance in Rawls's sense is, after all, very different from the social stability kept in other ways, such as a temporary compromise of interests and balance of powers, or even coercion and deception. Given the distinction between norms and values, and the coexistence of the agreement on norms with the disagreement on values, we may well have both types of justification for the shared norms at the same time: the moral justification and the ethical justification (and not just ethical motivation, as a Habermas would say).

4.

"Overlapping consensus" can, at the third stage, be understood as the situation in which different people admit that although they disagree *at present* they are ready to seek agreement *in the future*: people with different views and positions today are engaged in peaceful coexistence and equal communication in order to deepen their mutual understanding and even to seek a "fusion of horizons" tomorrow or the day after tomorrow.

Rawls and Taylor, as mentioned above, both think that it is of great importance for the holders of various values to understand and support the norms they agree with from their respective value systems. Here we should pay more attention to the fact that although agreeing on the importance of the value-based support for norms, they understand this importance from different perspectives. In Rawls, the value-based support for norms or principles provided by comprehensive doctrines is explicated more or less through a hermeneutic circle: on the one hand, comprehensive doctrines will support the political conception of justice as long as they are reasonable; on the other hand, a liberal society is characterized by the "priority of right over the good," and this means that "admissible ideas of the good must respect the limits of, and serve a role within, the political conception of justice."[29] Rawls is basically contented with showing that various reasonable value systems can support the same set of norms or principles, and this kind of support is to him enough for achieving "stability for the right reasons." Therefore Rawls does not try, as Habermas does, to go out of this circle by means of the discourse theory or the universal pragmatics; nor does he, like Taylor, emphasize the inherent significance of the value-based support for shared norms to the dignity of the individual or the community concerned. Taylor thinks that although great differences exist between various theological and metaphysical doctrines, and people often do not behave in ways that they say or think to follow, there is a high degree of consensus on the demands for justice and love, and on their importance. But what is the ground for this consensus? What are the "moral sources" of the norms and standards that we agree on? The moral sources of universal standards, in Taylor's view, are very important, because they concern the problem of how these standards are "experienced."[30] We may well follow these standards simply because we feel obliged to do so or because we would feel guilt or be unsatisfied with ourselves if we do not follow these standards. But, Taylor thinks, "it is quite a different thing to be moved by a strong sense that human beings are eminently *worth* helping or treating with justice, a sense of their dignity or value."[31] In Taylor's view, "there is something morally corrupting, even dangerous, in sustaining the demand simply on the feeling of undischarged obligation, on guilt, or its obverse, self-satisfaction."[32]

It is, however, easy to recognize that universal standards have moral sources, but not so easy to deal with the fact that these moral sources are very often not only different but also in sharp conflicts. Both Rawls's political liberalism and Habermas's discourse theory of democracy are, in the last analysis, proposed to tackle this typically modern and difficult problem. Taylor opposes the efforts, represented by Rawls and Habermas in his view, to avoid the struggle between various moral sources of universal standards by a proceduralistic approach to morality. He also opposes the tendency, seen in critics as well as supporters of modernity, that a certain spiritual value and aspiration is refuted absolutely if it has lead to pain and destruction. It is difficult, Taylor admits, both to keep moral or spiritual sources of various kinds and to avoid their mutual negation and destruction. Towards the end of his book *Sources of the Self* published in 1989, Taylor takes this task to be a serious challenge that must be met, and takes the prospect of meeting this challenge to be a hope that he is both convinced of, but unable to give sufficient reasons for.[33] Taylor did not hide the religious color of this hope at that time, but later he tried to give this hope a philosophical instead of a religious justification, the kernel of which is that various value systems and worldviews can, through dialogues based on mutual respect, strive for mutual understanding, even for a fusion of horizons. Here comes the major point of what I call the overlapping consensus at the third stage.

In the above-mentioned paper published in 1996 on the consensus on human rights, Taylor elaborates the case that human rights can be justified both by humanism or the idea of human agency in the West and by the Buddhist demand for *ahimsa*, and takes it as an evidence that universal standards can receive inter-cultural consensuses. But he immediately points out that this kind of consensus is not a satisfactory end: "Some attempt at deeper understanding must follow or the gains in agreement will remain fragile."[34] Agreement achieved under this condition, for one thing, cannot be a complete one. The relation between the ecological demand for *ahimsa* and the ecological problem, for example, is greatly different from the relation between Western humanism and the ecological problem, and this difference can lead to evident practical consequences. Consensus achieved under the current condition, moreover, is usually not accompanied with sufficient mutual respect, but such respect is indispensable to the need to constantly renew consensuses by dealing with disagreements in our times:

> If the sense is strong on each side that the spiritual basis of the other is ridiculous, false, inferior, unworthy, these attitudes cannot but sap the will to agree of those who hold these views while engendering anger and resentment among those who are thus depreciated.[35]

Therefore Taylor emphasizes the importance of mutual understanding: "The only cure for contempt here is understanding."[36] In some cases, mutual understanding between different values underlying shared norms is a higher level of agreement achieved after the overlapping consensus on the norms, as in the case of the Western humanism and the Buddhist idea of *ahimsa* where they need to move to mutual respect through mutual understanding after they have reached a consensus on human rights. In some cases, however, mutual understanding between different underlying values is the first step towards a possible overlapping consensus between them, because, as the case of the gap between modern Westerners and people of some non-Western societies on the issue of gender equality shows, if between two positions there is no minimum mutual respect it is hard to start to reduce the gap between them from the very beginning.

Mutual understanding between different values or worldviews that have an overlapping consensus on shared norms and principles, to my view, is important not only because the consensus can thus be strengthened, but also because all parties concerned can thus improve and enrich themselves. The overlapping consensus in Rawls's sense is basically static; there seems to be no significant changes within the various worldviews, value systems, or comprehensive doctrines after they have entered into a consensus. Rawls did mention that the political culture of liberal democracy can influence various worldviews and that within this political culture some worldviews will turn more reasonable. But the possibility that different worldviews can have dialogues and that they will change and improve themselves through these dialogues is not seen, or at least not stressed, by Rawls. Taylor demands that "the bare consensus must strive to go on towards a fusion of horizons";[37] with this demand Rawls would not agree, and neither would we agree perhaps, because a full fusion of horizons is not necessarily desirable, even if it were feasible. But some demands implied in the idea of "fusion of horizons" deserve our serious attention: we should, for example, try our best to understand an idea that we do not agree with at first; in order for us to be able to understand this idea, we should try our best to be less indifferent and hostile and more tolerant and respectful to it. Even when others give us a hostile challenge instead of a friendly invitation, we should also try our best to take the task of meeting this challenge as an opportunity to learn something at the same time, and learning in the real sense means not only to enrich ourselves, but also to revise ourselves. "Overlapping consensus" in this sense or at this stage is not only an epistemic achievement, but also a spiritual achievement.

Overlapping consensus in this sense is no longer a mere "social event" referred to by Habermas when he was criticizing Rawls, not even a mere cognitive achievement in Habermas's sense, but also a spiritual growth, or a civilizational progress, which is both inclusive and creative. It is recorded in *The Book of Changes* that Confucius made the famous remark that "in the world there are many different roads (*shu tu*) but the destination is the same (*tong gui*). There are a hundred deliberations (*bai lu*) but the result is one (*yi zhi*)."[38] In terms of the concepts in this remark, the relation between *shu tu* ("many different roads") and *tong gui* ("the same destination"), and that between *bai lu* ("a hundred deliberations") and *yi zhi* ("the one result"), are not the relation between the means and the ends, or the relation between the processes and the aims. In the processes of the collective learning and the civilizational progress in this sense, *tong gui* and *yi zhi* does not mean to replace one for others, nor to bring everything to the same level; neither their contents nor their subjects are predetermined or fixed forever. *Shu tu* and *bai lu*, on the contrary, are not only transcended by but also included in "*tong gui*" and "*yi zhi*"; or rather, "*shu tu*" or "*bai lu*" not only transcend each other, but also transcend themselves, and transcend themselves in close connection with each other.

5.

At the last section of the paper I want to bring up the relation between *theory* and *practice*, which is a focus of attention especially in the Marxist tradition. Reaching overlapping consensus among people and among peoples, to my view, is in the last analysis a historical practice in which we all should participate in a responsible way.

In this connection some ideas of Li Zehou deserve our attention. Li Zehou, one of the most important contemporary Chinese philosophers, speaks highly of Rawls's idea of "overlapping consensus," including one of its major underlying conceptual distinctions: the distinction between "right" and "the good." There are two types of morality, according to Li, one of which is the so-called "societal morality," and the other is the so-called "religious morality." While the societal morality is concerned with the problem of right, the religious morality is concerned with the problem of the good. Rawls's theory of overlapping consensus, Li says, is quite in agreement with this distinction, which means to

> separate the norms of action and rules of life of various societies, regions, countries and cultures in the modern world from the doctrines, beliefs, emotions and ethics promoted by various traditional religions and 'isms', and to cut off the causal connections of these norms and rules both in historical and in theoretical senses. We do not need, for example, to trace the demands for liberty, human rights and democracy in modern societies back to Christianity or Greek culture; we should clearly acknowledge that these are political and legal principles that are commonly followed in modern inter-personal relations.[39]

The last sentence of the passage cited above expresses what Li Zehou thinks to be his own understanding or his own contribution to the understanding of the idea "overlapping consensus." Rawls, according to Li, does not seem to have given a clear explanation to the question how the overlapping consensus at the level of political morality detached from traditional religion, culture and belief is possible or where it comes from. Li's own reply to this problem is based on the classical Marxist thesis that law and morality as superstructure is determined by the basis of economic and material life: the objective universality of the so-called "modern societal morality," Li says, "comes from the convergence or integration of the world in our economic life."[40] As a result of the convergence of our daily material life, including basic necessities of life, medical care, job, transportation, entertainment, information, and so on, changes in our moral and spiritual life are seen by Li Zehou to be inevitable in the direction of the individual's growing self-consciousness, liberation, and independence. "What is demanded by liberalism and modern 'societal morality,'" Li says,

> is only for individuals to abide by minimum obligations in modern life, and to follow minimum public norms and rules, such as keeping contracts, caring for public property, respecting order, following professional ethical rules, fulfilling obligatory military service, and avoiding to harm others, etc. No matter whether it is also a violation of the law, violation of these demands is 'immoral' because it is harmful to the order of our common life and to the rights of other people.[41]

Li Zehou is right in stressing the importance of the problem of the historical or actual basis of the idea of "overlapping consensus." This problem is important because the fact that so many people of such different cultural communities accept and follow the same norms, principles, or standards, needs to be explained and it can be explained at least from two perspectives. On the one hand, these universally accepted norms are functional requirements of the systems in which we lead our life in the modern sense; as long as these systems are functioning, these norms have a binding force that we have to submit ourselves to. On the other hand, as a result of our living in this modern world where these norms are followed as a rule, we tend to internalize them; or, to put it in another way, we have more or less been socialized in a way regulated by these norms. This explains not only why we have to follow these common norms, but also why we usually are quite willing to follow them. To the notoriously "modern" question "why be moral at all?" a moral theorist must give a theoretically justified answer. But for the ordinary people who have undergone normal processes of socialization where what Li Zehou called "societal morality" functions quite well, this has never been a problem in the real sense. Before the problem "why be moral?" (or, for that matter, "why be moral in the way prescribed by "societal morality" in Li's sense?) is raised in theory, it has already been solved in practice or in everyday life. That is implied in Marx's idea that "[a]ll mysteries which misled theory into mysticism find their rational solution in human practice and in the comprehension of this practice."[42] Hence the Marxist idea of the priority of "changing the world" over "interpreting the world."[43]

In the same spirit we should not only look for the actual basis for the willingness to follow shared norms, but also look for the actual basis for the willingness to respect each other's "moral sources" of the shared norms. Moreover, we should not only look for, but also make efforts to build up, if lacking, the actual basis for the willingness to follow shared norms and at the same time respect other people's value-based justifications and motivations for following these norms. "Overlapping consensus" is thus not a mere idea discussed in political philosophy, nor a mere fact discovered in political culture, but also a goal that we should strive for in political practice.

But it is not enough, to my view, to see only the functional necessity of the shared social norms and the psychological mechanism of following these norms. We should not, to be more exact, neglect the dimension of the validity of the norms or reduce the problem of validity of norms to the problem of their facticity. These two problems are highly connected and Li Zehou has done a lot to show this by his interpretation of Kant and his studies of the Chinese intellectual history in the last decades. But the connection between them does not mean the integration of the two. We should not only explain how and why norms of "societal morality" are universally accepted, but also explain why and for what reasons these norms *deserve* to be universally accepted. We should not accept anything as an "ought" simply because it has become an "is" or because of the prediction that it will become an "is." On the one hand, there are always multiple elements and possibi-Zlities in the reality, and we need to make a decision concerning which elements and possibilities are to be kept, developed or realized, and which are to be reduced or even eliminated. On the other hand, we are now in a situation where our technical means of reconstructing our environment and even the Earth as a whole are so powerful that some of the misuses of these means can produce consequences that we and our coming generations will probably have no chance to make up. From this perspective another famous thesis of Marx's can have a new reading: "Men make their own history, but they do not make it just as they please; they do not make it under circumstances chosen by themselves, but under circumstances directly found, given and transmitted from the past,"[44] It is true that we do not make our history as we please, and we always make history under circumstances directly found, given and transmitted from the past. But, if only we have, and I think we do have, a tiny space to choose to do this and not that, we should be clear of the fact that our choice now will immediately become part of "the circumstances directly found, given and transmitted from the past" to our children and our grand children. Given the scale of the technical power we have got now, a small mistake we make now can quite possibly make big difference in the future. In this sense, we have a responsibility to our future generations that is heavier than any preceding generations have had to their succeeding generations. It is irresponsible and dangerous under this condition to emphasize too much the priority of social changes over moral changes and to justify the universal validity of public norms of action simply in terms of the convergence of social and material life.

The reason why the idea of overlapping consensus needs to be taken seriously, actually, is just the fact that the accelerating economic globalization enhanced by information technology and global trade system has a tendency to level out cultural diversities and homogenize culturally different regions of the world. Without a self-reflective regulation of this process the convergence of social and material life would become an "objective ground" not only for the universal validity of the trans-cultural norms of social action, but also for the repressing and replacing cultural and value diversities. We should be serious of the idea of overlapping consensus just in order to resist the "objective tendency" of homogenization and reduction of multiple cultures and values.

The Marxist thesis on the relation between theory and practice, therefore, needs both a serious consideration and an updated understanding when applied in our discussion of the idea of "overlapping consensus." The desirability and possibility of the overlapping consensus in our times is both a theoretical and a practical issue, and these two sides should be considered in tight connection.

Firstly, the "practice" here means the common efforts of the people both in the domestic societies and in the international societies. Admitting that in both types of societies there is a task of establishing "overlapping consensus," we should be clear of the distinction between the two cases: while the boundary of the domestic society is usually the same as the sovereign state, there is not a world government to interact with the international society. More efforts should be made, therefore, to study the limits and features of "plurality" and "consensus" in each case.

Secondly, the "theory" here means the theoretical justification both for the universal validity of norms and for the mutual compatibility between general norms and particular values. Both types of justification are difficult, and the latter is more so. "Overlapping consensus" is an empty word is this kind of compatibility cannot stand.

Last but not least, the "combination" between theory and practice here means not only that those who are specialized in theorizing should care more about the practical basis of their theories and those who are specialized in practicing should care more about theoretical guidance, but also means that both types of people should try to combine the theoretical and practical attitudes in how they are doing as well as in what they are doing. On the one hand, those who are supposed to do theoretical work should be aware of the fact that they are "changing" the world as well by means of "interpreting the world" in a world filled with key words such as "knowledge-based economy," "information age" and "consumption of symbols." From the perspective of the idea of "overlapping consensus," the practical consciousness of those who theorize in this sense reminds us of the importance of avoiding and resisting the activities that would afflict cultural harms upon other communities in the name of freedom of speech seen in some European countries in recent years. On the other hand, those who practices should be aware of the obligation to be engaged in enlightened discourses in order to base our decisions for joint actions on well-informed and well-deliberated judgments. From the perspective of the idea of "overlapping consensus," the theoretical consciousness of the practical workers reminds us of the importance to make more efforts to include various cultural perspectives and value positions in processes of deliberation concerning decision-making and implementing as long as no universal principles and shared norms are violated.

NOTES

This paper was read at the first plenary of the XXII World Congress of Philosophy held in Seoul on July 31, 2008. I want to thank Professor Asger Sørensen for his advices in revising the manuscript. My thanks also go to my young colleagues and students Liu Jin, Ma Ke, Wang Jiangtao and Zhang Lin who read an early version of the manuscript and gave their comments and suggestions.

1. See Hu Jintao, "Hold High the Great Banner of Socialism with Chinese Characteristics and Strive for New Victories in Building a Moderately Prosperous Society in All," report to the Seventeenth National Congress of the Communist Party of China on Oct. 15, 2007, in *Qui Shi* 21 (November 1, 2007).

2. John Rawls, *A Theory of Justice* (Cambridge, MA: The Belknap Press of Harvard University Press, 1971), pp. 387–388.

3. Ibid., p. 387.

4. John Rawls, "The Domain of the Political and Overlapping Consensus," in John Rawls, *Collected Papers*, ed. Samuel Freeman (Cambridge, MA: Harvard University Press, 1999), p. 473.

5. John Rawls, *Political Liberalism* (New York: Columbia University Press, 1996), pp. 173, 212.

6. Ibid., p. 36.

7. John Rawls, "Reply to Habermas," in Rawls, *Political Liberalism*, pp. 388–389.

8. "Die Wahrheit einer Proposition meint das Versprechen, einen vernuenftigen Konsensus ueber das Gesagte zu erzielen." Jürgen Habermas, *Vorstudien und Ergaenzungen zur Theorie des kommunikativen Handelns* (Frankfurt am Main: Suhrkamp, 1995), p. 137. Notice the German original of the English translation "rational consensus" is "vernuenftige Konsensus," where the adjective "vernuenftige" is the same as the one in the German translation of John Rawls (see John Rawls, *Die Idee des politischen Liberalismus: Aufsaetze 1978–1989* [Frankfurt am Main: Suhrkamp, 1992], p. 98) for the English original "reasonable." On this page the English originals "the reasonable" and "the rational" (see John Rawls, *Political Liberalism*, pp. 48–54) are rendered respectively as "das Vernuenftige" and "das Rationale."

9. Jürgen Habermas, *Between Facts and Norms Contributions to a Discourse Theory of Law and Democracy*, trans. William Rehg (Cambridge, MA: The MIT Press, 1996), p. 107.

10. Rawls, *Political Liberalism*, p. 58.

11. Harald Grimen, "Reasonable Disagreement and Epistemic Resignation," in *Philosophy beyond Borders: An Anthology of Norwegian Philosophy*, ed. Ragnar Fjelland and Nils Gilje (Bergen: SVT Press, University of Bergen, 1997), p. 276.

12. Ibid.

13. Ibid., p. 289 n. 3.

14. Jürgen Habermas, *Vorstudien und Ergaenzungen zur Theorie des kommunikativen Handelns* (Frankfurt am Main: Suhrkamp, 1995), s. 135.

15. Harald Grimen, "Reasonable Disagreement," pp. 279–280. See John Rawls, "The Idea of an Overlapping Consensus," in Rawls, *Collected Papers*, p. 434.

16. Rawls, *Political Liberalism*, p. 49.

17. Ibid., p. 59.

18. Liang Shuming, *The Essentials of Chinese Culture*, in *Collected Works of Liang Shuming*, Vol. 3 (Shandong: Shandong People's Publishing House, 1990), p. 123.

19. Charles Taylor, "Conditions of an Unforced Consensus on Human Rights," *East Asian Challenge for Human Rights*, ed. Joanne R. Bauer and Daniel A. Bell (London: Cambridge University Press,1999), p. 124.

20. Ibid., p. 125.

21. Jürgen Habermas, "Reconciliation through the Public Use of Reason," *The Journal of Philosophy* 92, no. 3 (March 1995): 115.

22. Jürgen Habermas, *The Theory of Communicative Action*, Volume 2, trans. Thomas McCarthy (Boston: Beacon Press, 1987, p. 174). The norm that Rawls discusses in his *A Theory of Justice*, especially in his *Political Liberalism*, mainly lies at the level of principles.

23. Habermas, "Reconciliation," p. 122.

24. Rawls, "Reply to Habermas," pp. 386–387.

25. Ibid., p. 385.

26. Rawls, *Political Liberalism*, pp. 3–4.

27. Quoted in Habermas, *Between Facts and Norms*, p. 62.

28. Habermas, "Reconciliation," p. 122.

29. Rawls, *Political Liberalism*, p. 176.

30. Charles Taylor, *Sources of the Self: The Making of the Modernity Identity* (Cambridge, MA: Harvard University Press, 1989), p. 515.

31. Ibid.

32. Ibid., p. 516.

33. Ibid., p. 521.

34. Taylor, "Conditions of an Unforced Consensus on Human Rights," p. 137.

35. Ibid., p. 138.

36. Ibid.

37. Ibid.

38. *A Source Book in Chinese Philosophy*, trans. and comp. Wing-Tsit Chan (Princeton, NJ: Princeton University Press, 1963), p. 268.

39. Li Zehou: *Historical Ontology and Five Essays from 1999* (Beijing: SDX Press), p. 71.

40. Ibid.

41. Ibid., p. 72.

42. Karl Marx: "Theses on Feuerbach," in *The Marx-Engels Reader*, second edition, ed. Robert C. Tucker (New York/London: W.W. Norton & Company, 1978), p. 145.

43. Here I refer to the most famous statement by Karl Marx in his "Theses on Feuerbach": "The philosophers have only *interpreted* the world, in various ways; the point, however, is to *change* it." See Tucker, *The Marx-Engels Reader*, p. 145.

44. Karl Marx: "The Eighteenth Brumaire of Louis Bonaparte," in Tucker, *The Marx-Engels Reader*, second edition, p. 595.

SELECTED PAPERS FROM THE XXII WORLD CONGRESS OF PHILOSOPHY

Réalité, beauté et sens de la vie

TANELLA BONI
UNIVERSITE DE COCODY, ABIDJAN (COTE D'IVOIRE)

Les questions d'ordre métaphysique ne cessent de hanter le monde aujourd'hui. Elles resurgissent là où on les attend le moins. Dans les expressions artistiques, la mort n'est pas une idée mais une réalité contre laquelle nous nous heurtons, sans jamais le faire exprès. La création artistique a, en effet, quelque chose à voir avec la mort, celle de Dieu et la nôtre. Ainsi, la question du sens de la vie se pose en rapport avec la création artistique dans la mesure où nous allons plus loin que nos propres limites d'humain dans la création d'une œuvre, dans la composition d'un poème. Ainsi, créer une œuvre d'art c'est questionner le sens de la vie, «la plus pressante des questions» comme dit Camus.[1]

Parallèlement au champ religieux de plus en plus complexe qui tente de ré-enchanter le monde, l'art est cette appréhension du réel qui, exprimant les correspondances entre le naturel et l'artificiel, s'interroge, au 21ème siècle, sur la part de virtuel dans le réel. Mais l'art ne se demande pas si le réel est imaginaire, il crée de l'imaginaire et de la beauté ou tente de dire quelque chose, de toucher, d'émouvoir là où d'autres discours raisonnent. Cependant, la création artistique n'est-elle pas tout un monde avec ses spécificités d'une discipline à l'autre, d'une culture à l'autre? Peut-être ces univers créés par l'art, ont-ils quelque chose à dire de notre existence? Nous proposent-ils des réponses à nos inquiétudes?

ART ET MÉTAPHYSIQUE

La vie dont nous avons à parler ici est celle réelle et vécue, dans le temps et dans l'espace; cette vie à laquelle nous ne pouvons échapper et à propos de laquelle nous éprouvons un sentiment tragique au moment même où nous prenons conscience de son absurdité. Mais que signifient donc les mots «réelle et vécue»? Et en quoi consiste ce sentiment tragique dont nous parlons? Pour Camus, dès le début du *Mythe de Sisyphe*, ouvrage qui date de 1942, faisant partie de ce qu'il appelle le cycle de l'absurde,[2] «juger que la vie vaut ou ne vaut pas la peine d'être vécue, c'est répondre à la question fondamentale de la philosophie». Si le

Special Supplement, *Journal of Philosophical Research* pp. 47–53
DOI: 10.5840/jpr201237Supplement24

suicide semble être le seul problème philosophique sérieux comme il l'affirme dans cet ouvrage publié pendant la deuxième guerre mondiale, c'est qu'il y a un fossé entre la réalité dans laquelle nous vivons et notre quête de sens. On pourrait espérer qu'il existe une autre vie au-delà de celle-ci. C'est la voie empruntée par les religions pour rendre cette vie habitable. La réalité vécue à laquelle Camus fait allusion c'est la guerre.[3]

D'un continent à l'autre, des événements d'une extrême violence inaugurent un point de non retour dans les mémoires des individus et changent le cours de leur histoire. Ainsi, la deuxième guerre mondiale, le 11 septembre 2001, le génocide au Rwanda en 1994 et quelques autres sont des violences indépassables. La quête de sens qui s'ensuit appartient à la réflexion philosophique mais aussi, paradoxalement, à l'art. Celui-ci laisse des traces, témoignages, paroles infimes, images, musiques de ce qui nous touche, nous ébranle, ravivant notre quête de sens.

On serait donc tenté de dire qu'après vingt-cinq siècles de pensée philosophique en Occident, la banalité de la mort et de l'horreur, par suite de ce que l'humain est capable de faire à son semblable, est quotidienne. Dans l'antiquité grecque, l'art de faire la guerre pouvait être un genre de vie. Il ne s'agissait ni de la banalité de la mort ni du règne de l'horreur. L'esprit de cette époque était tout autre, de même que les valeurs humaines à défendre. Ainsi, Platon en son temps concevait une eschatologie dans laquelle l'âme humaine était d'autant plus heureuse dans l'au-delà qu'elle s'était conduite ici-bas selon le bien, le beau, le vrai, le juste. L'éthique allait de pair avec l'esthétique. Kant redonna, au 18ème siècle, à la faculté de juger son autonomie. Mais aujourd'hui, en regardant certaines œuvres contemporaines, on voit bien comme le goût est une question de culture mais aussi de valeur marchande. L'art se vend et l'artiste a une cote mais donne-t-il pour autant du sens à notre existence? Et il n'est pas sûr qu'il crée de la beauté non plus. Face à certaines créations contemporaines on se sent d'autant plus angoissé que ces œuvres véhiculent l'humeur d'une époque, la nôtre, celle dans laquelle la mort est désacralisée et la violence meurtrière quotidienne, relayée et amplifiée par les médias. Ainsi, l'air du temps fait irruption au cœur des expressions artistiques comme si la réalité, massive et incompréhensible, devenait incontournable, livrant les humains à leurs propres questionnements sur le sens et les limites, sans cesse repoussées, de la vie. Or ces questionnements ne sont-ils pas à proprement parler métaphysiques?

Evoquons encore Camus, l'un des auteurs du 20ème siècle chez qui les expressions artistiques ne sont pas incompatibles avec la métaphysique. Ne dit-il pas qu'écrire un roman c'est aussi penser? Si Platon, dans sa *République,*[4] chasse les poètes de la cité idéale, Camus, dans le *Discours de Suède* prononcé le 10 décembre 1957 à l'occasion de la réception du Prix Nobel, défend l'art et la liberté de l'artiste. «Comment l'art se passerait-il en effet du réel et comment s'y soumettrait-il? L'artiste choisit son objet autant qu'il est choisi par lui.»[5] En effet, l'écrivain et l'artiste ne peuvent plus se permettre de se tenir à l'écart de l'histoire de leur temps. Ils se trouvent être impliqués, «embarqués» dans cette histoire, comme si désormais ils étaient tenus de résister et de survivre malgré les horreurs et les atrocités du monde afin d'être toujours prêts à témoigner. Mais témoigner par l'art est une attitude complexe qui ne signifie pas, d'emblée, faire preuve de «réalisme», en suivant quelques règles ou injonctions venant de l'extérieur. C'est, au contraire, tenir compte de sa propre sensibilité face au monde et prendre ses responsabilités en créant des œuvres toujours singulières.

Mais la demande de sens, métaphysique, ne chemine-t-elle pas avec l'éthique en regard de l'esthétique?

LE MONDE ET LA TERRE HABITÉE

Dans un poème, un tableau, une sculpture, une partition musicale, l'artiste donne-t-il autre chose à voir que son propre monde? Mais qu'est-ce que le «monde»? Les anciens Grecs, concevant «le monde», pensaient sans doute à un «ensemble ordonné», beau de surcroît, se donnant d'abord à voir dans un «ciel» qui pouvait être représenté, conceptualisé sous forme de sphères, figures parfaites, notamment chez Aristote. C'était le temps d'une autre conception du monde physique: clos, fini, parfait. Mais le ciel, lieu composé d'éther élément pur n'était pas le lieu d'habitation des humains et des vivants. Aujourd'hui, longtemps après la révolution copernicienne, la terre tourne autour du soleil, son mouvement n'est pas circulaire. C'est une planète en quête d'équilibre, soumise aux aléas climatiques; elle est plus ou moins obscure selon les régions et selon les saisons. Le soleil ne brille pas pour tous dans le même temps, dans le même monde, ce n'est pas seulement une métaphore mais aussi la manière de désigner ce dont nos regards et nos savoirs prennent connaissance. En ce sens, l'existence d'un monde physique et humain d'inégalités flagrantes, soumis à l'expérience des guerres, des violences et des maux, à la fréquence et à l'intensité des catastrophes naturelles, conduit à la quête de sens dans la mesure où il n'y a pas d'autres espaces pour les humains que la Terre habitée qu'on pourrait appeler aussi «monde» même s'il est loin d'être beau et parfait.

Mais, habitons-nous seuls dans le monde? Chaque culture tente de répondre à cette question et tout artiste créant son propre univers en marge de la réalité massive qui l'entoure apprend, tout en créant, que son monde imaginaire pourrait être habité par d'autres êtres dont l'existence peut ne pas être démontrable par la rationalité instrumentale. Ainsi, le monde de chaque artiste est animé, à son insu ou presque, même s'il n'y croit pas. Le critique pourrait découvrir cette animation en laissant l'œuvre respirer à son propre rythme, en évitant de lui appliquer, comme cela arrive, quelque grille de lecture standard. L'idée de la pièce unique, de la singularité de l'œuvre d'art doit sans doute guider toute lecture.

A l'opposé de l'univers absurde de Camus, dans certaines cultures, parmi lesquelles les cultures africaines, la quête du sens de la vie passe par la conception d'une terre habitée où les humains sont moins seuls à cause de la présence d'autres vivants, corps ou esprits. Ainsi, dans quelques langues de l'Afrique de l'Ouest, «dunya» signifie monde, terre habitée ici-bas par opposition à l'au-delà. Du Sénégal à la Côte d'Ivoire en passant par le Mali, la Guinée, le Burkina Faso, «dunya» se retrouve donc dans ces langues qui, parfois, ont gardé des traces d'une lointaine rencontre avec d'autres cultures encore vivantes sous la forme de l'islam. Mais ce mot n'indique pas que toutes les langues dans lesquelles il se trouve sont marqués par cette religion. Dunya c'est donc le monde terrestre dans lequel certains sont pauvres et d'autres riches. Aucun humain n'y vit seul, d'autres vivants, y compris des plantes, peuplent cette réalité habitée. Voilà pourquoi «cette terre habitée» mérite d'être protégée et conservée comme lieu de passage ici-bas, lieu de repos pour tous ceux qui partent en nous léguant leur souffle. Les esprits des ancêtres, croit-on, habitent là ainsi que les invisibles qui nous accompagnent dans la vie quotidienne et nous facilitent le passage sur la terre en nous protégeant sous le regard d'un Dieu unique. Celui-ci, quelles que soient ses appellations, n'est pas forcément le Dieu des Ecritures. Ce Dieu a de multiples intermédiaires auxquels il est permis de s'adresser en cas de besoin. Il s'agit-là d'un monde mythique qui se transforme, a une histoire et, à supposer qu'il serve de mémoire collective à un travail d'artiste, ce travail se fera sentir sous la forme d'une singularité jamais anonyme.

Malgré l'urbanisation galopante, de nombreuses régions d'Afrique vivent encore sous l'emprise de ce monde «enchanté» par des forces invisibles surnaturelles mais aussi d'autres êtres naturels. En ce sens, la part d'imaginaire et de mythe transformé par la violence historique est à prendre en compte dans la conception de la réalité dans laquelle nous vivons. Car le réel n'est pas seulement ce que nous voyons, sentons ou entendons mais aussi ce que nous imaginons, rêvons, ce auquel nous croyons, ce que nous espérons, en d'autres termes notre monde.

CORRESPONDANCES ET INTERFÉRENCES

Des artistes se sont intéressés à cette conception de la terre habitée, à ses représentations, à l'art qui en est imprégnée. Ainsi, au début du 20ème siècle, les peintres Matisse, Derain et Picasso s'intéressent à la figure féminine et particulièrement à celle venant d'Afrique. Stylisée, elle entre aussi en peinture. Autour des années 1907, au moment où Picasso achève les *Demoiselles d'Avignon* qui inaugure sa période cubiste, l'artiste avait une idée du corps des femmes d'Afrique mais aussi de «l'art nègre». Aujourd'hui, tout artiste africain contemporain habité par une telle conception du milieu de vie est précisément en quête d'une réalité qui lui parle infiniment mais qui, dans le même temps, a été désorganisée, perturbée par ces violences multiples liées à l'histoire. Il recrée donc cette réalité selon sa propre sensibilité.[6] Et la recréation dont il est question ici n'est pas tant celle de la «nature» que celle du «monde» contemporain, capté par un esprit singulier puisqu'elle renvoie à l'univers propre à chaque artiste. Car le travail d'artiste ne consiste-t-il pas à organiser, penser, imaginer, rêver, parler au nom de ces créatures d'encre, de peinture, de bois, de métal, de minéral, ces êtres mixtes nés de la matière façonnée par la main et par l'esprit humain, ou ceux, virtuels ou numériques, qui disent, racontent, questionnent le monde, sont en mouvement, quels que soient les techniques et les matériaux utilisés? Qui a vu les corps splendides sculptés par

Ousmane Sow sait qu'il y a là une interrogation sur ce qu'est un corps d'humain vivant dans telle région d'Afrique et que ce corps incarne l'Afrique qui n'est jamais la même puisqu'elle est celle des contrastes et de la diversité des cultures.

Parlons aussi de la poésie, conçue comme un art total à la fois chant, danse, rythme, comme le montre Senghor dans ses essais.[7] Cet art intègre le poète dans sa communauté. Cependant, il est aussi espace de liberté pour le poète pour qui le langage poétique permet de relier des mots épars, des morceaux de mondes parallèles, dans une langue qui lui appartient en propre et qu'il ne peut exprimer dans aucune autre langue. En ce sens, la poésie n'est pas tant versification ni règles figées que mouvement, rythme, fluidité qui incarnent le temps vécu avec ses ruptures et ses fractures imprévues. C'est la fête des mots qui donnent sens à la vie ordinaire. Ainsi, la poésie, écrite ou orale, va de pair avec la recherche du mot juste—qui n'est pas le mot le plus précis—mais celui qui ouvre des portes dont le poète ignorait l'existence. Le mot juste et celui qui est toujours perdu puisque sa recherche, comme la quête de sens du monde en tant que terre habitée, est la raison d'être de l'art poétique. Au 20ème siècle, les surréalistes semblaient avoir perçu cette manière de poétiser le monde, de l'arracher au poids des divisions et des séparations favorisées par la logique rationnelle et instrumentale autour de laquelle s'ordonne le langage ordinaire. Tout se passe comme s'il fallait rétablir des correspondances rompues et en créer d'autres là où il n'y en avait pas. La poétique étant construction ou reconstruction de la sensibilité, du goût, de l'oreille, de la voyance. Avant les surréalistes, Rimbaud avait déjà, dans la deuxième moitié du 19ème siècle, placé la voyance au cœur des relations et des interférences multiples entre je et l'autre.[8]

Quant au roman, il pourrait être aussi un art de la «donation» de sens en vue d'exorciser la terre habitée des maux et des menaces qui pèsent sur elle par suite des activités humaines aux conséquences imprévisibles mais aussi de ce que chaque humain est capable de faire à son semblable. Chez la plupart des écrivains africains de la fin du 20ème siècle et de ces dix dernières années, la pratique romanesque montre à quel point donner du sens, c'est raconter autrement des histoires sans avoir l'air de raconter puisque le monde extérieur, incompréhensible, ne se raconte pas. Il se donne à entendre dans des mots dont on ne sait jamais d'où ils viennent. Parfois, ils se contentent de porter au jour l'urgence des situations extrêmes vécues sur une parcelle de la terre habitée ou de celle imaginée par le romancier. Ainsi, celui-ci est véritablement «embarqué»—d'après le mot de Camus[9] «dans la galère de son temps».

Les artistes assument donc leur part de responsabilité sur la terre habitée, en créant des récits pour comprendre l'innommable, l'incompréhensible, les paradoxes, les absurdités qui leur échappent. Placés en situation, au pied du mur des bonheurs éphémères ou des horreurs, menaces incalculables qui pèsent sur l'avenir de l'humanité, ils s'en remettent à l'art qui les habite non pas tant pour éviter de se suicider que pour *faire quelque chose* qui ressemble à faire un geste, dire un mot, afin que d'autres, proches ou lointains, cherchent un sens à leur propre existence en comptant sur leurs propres forces. Et, s'ils croient aux éléments et aux êtres de la terre habitée, leur art n'est jamais seul dans l'attente d'un monde meilleur.

Par ailleurs, puisque l'heure n'est plus à l'opposition entre réel et imaginaire et que le virtuel entre en jeu, l'on peut se demander s'il ne s'agit pas là d'un autre lieu à partir duquel le réel peut être pensé. Aujourd'hui semble s'établir un dialogue entre l'art et le virtuel, à la croisée du réel et de l'imaginaire. Les effets spéciaux au cinéma, le dessin animé dont les formes sont de plus en plus variées, les jeux vidéos, toutes ces créations sont symptomatiques de ce que les récits du monde deviennent de plus en plus complexes en tant que passerelles et réseaux entre le réel dans lequel nous vivons et les mondes parallèles que nous sommes capables d'imaginer.

En outre, la notion de monde habitée, l'écoumène, utilisée notamment par les géographes[10] montre à quel point existent des êtres humains, enfants, femmes et hommes aux cultures, religions, histoires et identités multiples vivant aux quatre coins de la planète, aux prises avec les mutations du monde local dans lequel ils veulent habiter, parfois sans y parvenir, vivant au seuil de l'humanitaire, perdant toute humanité aux yeux des autres qui conçoivent beauté et laideur, justice et injustice, qui, tout compte fait, pourraient être des valeurs relatives à moins que l'éthique ne soit la même pour tous.

CONCLUSION

La multiplicité des expériences de vie que nous connaissons ou imaginons grâce aux expressions artistiques nous permettent de revenir à la notion d'universel. Entre le particulier et l'universel se situe le singulier. Et l'œuvre d'art, en tant que telle, est toujours singulière. Elle capte le détail infime, le presque rien qui appartient en propre à telle sensibilité. Que Dieu existe ou non, le pouvoir de créer appartient aussi à l'Homme qui se donne le droit d'inventer de la vie, d'en détruire, de reconstruire d'autres univers qui ont leurs propres lois dans l'interface entre le réel et l'imaginaire. Peut-être la pratique artistique est- elle aujourd'hui cette quête de sens quand l'artiste, quelle que soit la forme d'art qui l'habite, se sent perdu. Comment retrouver son chemin quand celui-ci est invisible ou presque dans la réalité incompréhensible?

Cependant, une autre question reste posée. Si les expressions artistiques nous interpellent aujourd'hui plus que jamais, parlent-elles la langue du beau ou du marché, c'est-à-dire celle de la première réalité économique qui s'impose à l'art en période de mondialisation? Mais, on pourrait aller plus loin. Si Dieu n'est pas mort, l'art est toujours vivant, sans doute en marge de l'espace et du temps pleins de bruits et de fureur caractéristiques de la place médiatique éclairée par les projecteurs des technologies de la communication et des lois du marché. Comme le montre Marc Augé dans un livre récent,[11] la vie politique, artistique ou sportive ne peut plus se concevoir sans le relais des médias qui changent notre relation à l'espace et au temps. L'art ne pourrait donc plus échapper à ce qui apparaît, de plus en plus, comme faisant partie intégrante de sa condition de possibilité?

NOTES

1. Albert Camus, *Le mythe de Sisyphe* (Paris: Gallimard, 1942 [Coll. Folio, essais, 1985]), p. 18.

2. Ce cycle comprend les ouvrages suivants: *Le Mythe de Sisyphe* (1942), *L'étranger* (1942), *Caligula* (1944), *Le Malentendu* (1944).

3. «On ne nie pas la guerre. Il faut en vivre ou en mourir», *Le Malentendu* (Paris: Gallimard, 1947), p. 130.

4. Platon, *République* X, 595a sqq.

5. Camus, *Discours de Suède* (Paris: Gallimard, 1958), p. 52

6. Comme on peut le constater notamment dans les ateliers des peintres et des sculpteurs mais aussi au cours de moments de visibilité comme DAk'Art, la biennale de l'art contemporain africain.

7. Voir L. S. Senghor, *Liberté*, tomes *I*, *III* et *V*, Paris, Seuil; Iba Ndiaye Diadji, *La critique d'art en Afrique. Repères esthétiques pour lire l'art africain* (Paris: l'Harmattan, 2007); Souleymane Bachir Diagne, *Léopold Sédar Senghor. L'art africain comme philosophie* (Paris: Riveneuve éditions, 2007).

8. Au moment où Rimbaud se veut «voyant» apparaît cette formule paradoxale «je est un autre». Voir: Lettre à Georges Izambard du 13 mai 1871: «Je est un autre. Tant pis pour le bois qui se trouve violon, et nargue aux inconscients, qui ergotent sur ce qu'ils ignorent tout à fait»; Lettre à Paul Demeny du 15 mai 1871: «Car Je est un autre. Si le cuivre s'éveille clairon, il n' y a rien de sa faute».

9. Voir Albert Camus, *Discours de Suède*, p. 26, «Tout artiste aujourd'hui est embarqué dans la galère de son temps».

10. Augustin Berque, *Écoumène. Introduction à l'étude des milieux humains* (Paris: Belin, 2000).

11. Marc Augé, *Où est passé l'avenir*? (Paris: Éditions du Panama, 2008).

Politics of Beauty: Aesthetics Today—Its Role and Possibilities

KEN-ICHI SASAKI
NIHON UNIVERSITY

Abstract: This article looks at the past, present, and future of the study of aesthetics. The early modern period, during which aesthetics came into being, was a great historical turning point for civilization. So, too, is our own day. Looked at this way, aesthetics should show a different face than the one we are used to. Aesthetics is generally considered to be the philosophy of art, yet, with art regarded as an autonomous cultural field, aesthetics commonly gives the impression of being isolated from philosophy in general. This article explores a completely different aesthetics. When it was coming into existence, aesthetics was charged with the real and urgent philosophical problem of its time: how to construct a new world.

My subject here is the past, present, and future of our discipline. The early modern period, during which aesthetics came into being, was a great historical turning point for civilization. So, too, is our own day. Looked at this way, aesthetics should show a face rather different from the one we are used to. Aesthetics is generally considered to be the philosophy of art, yet, with art regarded as an autonomous cultural field, aesthetics commonly gives the impression of being isolated from philosophy in general. I wish to talk about a completely different aesthetics. When it was coming into existence, aesthetics was charged with the real and urgent philosophical problem of its time: how to construct a new world.

1. THE CONCEPT OF ART AND THE BIRTH OF AESTHETICS

Baumgarten published the first volume of his *Aesthetics* in 1750. His proposal for a science of sensible cognition, taking art and beauty as its main subject, founded a new branch of philosophy. In this sense, aesthetics is a modern discipline. What is

Special Supplement, *Journal of Philosophical Research* pp. 55–60
DOI: 10.5840/jpr201237Supplement25

called ancient or medieval aesthetics can be said to have come after Baumgarten: previous thinking on beauty and art became worthy of attention only with the establishment of aesthetics. I emphasize the modern origin of aesthetics because its birth occurred against a particular historical background. The first element in this background is the formation of the concept of art, for the notion of art that we are accustomed to was taking shape in Baumgarten's lifetime. Let us look briefly at the history of art.

After the Renaissance, art existed in three forms. One was public or official art, addressing itself to a large audience. Civilization was changing, and political powers needed tangible signs of their existence. Examples would be the Basilica of San Pietro in Vatican City, or the cultural policy of Louis the XIV. In the middle of the seventeenth century, France was politically and culturally an underdeveloped country. The ambitious young king addressed this weakness on both the military and cultural fronts: he wished to be both feared and respected. Versailles was constructed, and Racine, Moliere, and Lully received royal patronage. Generous pensions were even offered to European poets who would produce poems in praise of the king. It was as a buttress to political power that art and artists rose in status. It was such public art that contributed most to the formation of the modern concept of art. We have, however, to acknowledge that this public and large-scale art is rather different from what we now conceive as art.

The second form of post-Renaissance art was the social art intended for the enjoyment of a small number, such as Rococo art. The form of space underwent a radical change: vis-à-vis the palace at Versailles, constituted totally by public space, rococo is a culture of private rooms, especially those of aristocratic ladies. Conversation became an art, and interior decoration as its setting was highly sought after.

But the most important form of art is the third form, that is, reflexive or meditative art. A good example of the evolution from the second to the third forms is provided by Mozart at Paris. Mozart composes his Concerto for Flute and Harp, the masterpiece of Rococo music, in the context of Parisian high society. The sonata for piano in A minor, composed in the same year (1778) is, however, a completely different form of music: one cannot listen to it and pleasantly chat at the same time; it obliges one to concentrate at a deeper level of the mind. The main form of art according to our modern concept is this third one. It is this art that required aesthetics as the philosophy of art, and that philosophy meditated on.

2. SENSIBILITY AND BEAUTY

Baumgarten's aesthetics had as its subjects not only art but also sensibility and beauty, which can be regarded as philosophically more important. Let us begin with sensibility. Baumgarten's idea of aesthetics as the philosophy of sensibility was inspired by Leibniz's epistemology. Among the various modes of cognition classified by Leibniz, it is the category of *clear and confused*—cognitions that are empirically identified but linguistically indeterminable—that corresponds to Baumgartenian aesthetics. Leibniz includes in this category both the perception of sensible qualities such as red and sweet and judgments on poetry and painting, and he applies to them the concept of the "je-ne-sais-quoi." This is the object and the field of aesthetics.

Pascal had stated the importance of sensible cognition a century before Baumgarten. "We know truth, not only by the reason, but also by the heart, and it is in this last way that we know first principles; and reason, which has no part in it, tries in vain to impugn them." What Pascal thought of as the first principle must be God. The existence of God, having fallen under skeptical suspicion, cannot be recovered by reasoning, as was tried by Descartes, but has to be grasped through feeling: where reasoning is futile what is required is existential consent, which is the business of sensibility. This means that sensibility is a matter of values as existential choice and involvement, rather than sensible qualities.

The great turning point of early modern times was literally a crisis. Beauty was an answer to the radical anxiety caused by this crisis. It was Thomas Hobbes who grasped this anxiety. The basis of his political philosophy is human equality in the natural state, from which he deduces the famous thesis: "bellum omnium contra omnes." This notion struck a chord with his contemporaries.

Within this context, Shaftesbury insisted on the role of beauty. Wishing to controvert Hobbes, he presented the beauty of the world as evidence of its rationality, and then by an analogy to such beauty, argued that man is virtuous by nature. His argument contains two steps. In the first step, he justified, from the viewpoint of the total economy of the world, the desire of self-conservation, which Hobbes considered the basic motif of struggle. Emphasizing the rationality of the macro-structure in connection with sexual desire, the conformation of living bodies, and the food chain, he relativizes the good or evil of particular beings, and claims the fundamental goodness of the world. This is the same type of argument as Leibniz's theodicy.

Shaftesbury then points out that the economy of the world is perceived as beauty. The perception of beauty is important because its judgment is not influenced by any personal prejudice or arbitrariness, i.e., it is disinterested. Shaftesbury claims that the same is true with human behavior. This connects with his "moral sense," which testifies to our instinct for virtue. Men do not necessarily struggle with one another to further their selfish desires. Even if the ancient order collapses, human society will continue.

To end this survey of the history of aesthetics, I wish to consider the theory of Creation in Malebranche. His Christian philosophy faced a problem even more puzzling than the existence of evil: why a perfect being, lacking nothing, should create a world at all. Vis-à-vis this difficulty of discovering a motive, Malebranche referred to the work of an architect. His architect, blessed with a modern sense of existence, finds the incentive for his work in his pride in its beauty. It is a gratuitous act. Divine Creation is the same. It is necessary that God loves himself. Because of this essence, God creates the beautiful world, and takes this beauty for his glory. The goodness or value of the world is proven by its beauty, and the artwork is its model.

3. MODERN HOMO-CENTRISM AND AUTONOMOUS AESTHETICS

We have thus sketched the foundations of aesthetics. This early modern aesthetics is, however, very different from the modern aesthetics established in the early nineteenth century. Modern aesthetics is the philosophy of art, with the model of art taken from its solitary and meditative form. In this aesthetics, the position of beauty has essentially changed. For aesthetics as the philosophy of art, beauty becomes increasingly irrelevant as, in line with its homo-centric bias, this aesthetics shifts attention from the work to the author.

The mark of value slides from beauty to depth and originality. Art as high culture became an autonomous activity, and we find its modern history driven by pursuit of novelty, as the expression of the individuality of the artist. Such an autonomous art, insisting on originality, culminates in Duchamp's *Fountain*, which reveals the paradox of art as autonomous institution. The urinal posed a radical question: if the exhibition space or the museum makes the exhibited object an artwork, then why not this one? *Fountain* is now considered the most important artwork of the twentieth century. It criticized the autonomous institution of art, yet was acknowledged as art because of that institution. It illustrates even now the narrow path into which art and the philosophy of art have been led.

The rise of this autonomous art correlates with the decline of nature within aesthetics. The beautiful art of the past was based on the principle of imitation of nature and referred to nature and human history. But art became more and more interested in referring to itself: its focus moved from substance to image. Imagination dreaming the absence was discussed throughout the nineteenth century. The concept of avant-garde (a military metaphor) stemmed from the circle of Saint-Simon, who believed in the leadership of artists in the creation of a new world.

The aesthetics of the nineteenth century, emphasizing image and imagination, embodies modern homo-centrism. We can verify this particularly in the aesthetics of the sublime. The sublime is what exceeds the human pale. In Kant's famous phrase: "Two things fill the mind with ever new and increasing admiration and awe, the oftener and more steadily we reflect on them: the starry heavens above and the moral law within"—the heavens are typically sublime. Theorizing it in the *Critique of Judgment*, Kant however asserts that it is not nature but rather the power of reason comprehending indefinite magnitude or power that is really sublime. This expresses a worldview very different from that of a Shaftesbury. Kant impressed the seal of homo-centrism even onto the aesthetics of the sublime.

The revival of the notion of the sublime around the end of the twentieth century surprised us. We had believed that modern Western civilization had lost any sense of the infinite and that, consequently, the sublime had been lost as an aesthetic category. Adorno obviously follows Kant in his conception of the sublime. He believed that, with the collapse of formal beauty, the only traditional aesthetic category left was the sublime, though the sensible sublime is almost ridiculous. The modern sublime is the self-negating movement imprinted deeply in art, distinguishing it from craft; we can call it sublime because the sublime, as defined by Kant, consists in the mind's resistance to overwhelming power. It is a phenomenon representing the Adornian Enlightenment. But I wonder if we can call "sublime" a sublime that is neither perceived nor felt. Indeed Adorno and his followers might "feel" the sublime in the avant-garde, but only on the basis of a highly cultural-specific association of ideas. The autonomy of art and artistic "beauty" is constituted by such a network of ideas.

I have a reservation. Adorno said that the sensible sublime is now ridiculous. We understand this. It is ridiculous because we perceive in it a gesture of human conceit. How, then, is it possible for the Adornian sublime to escape being ridiculous? The spirit of self-criticism is worthy of respect. But as soon as he calls it "sublime," doesn't he betray its spirit? As a philosopher, Adorno is exceptional in the history of aesthetics, for his insistence on natural beauty. The paradox here is deep-rooted; it is the paradox of modern civilization.

4. ART AS DISCOURSE

The sublime avant-garde is represented by Duchamp's *Fountain*. For a long time, being an artifact was the most fundamental precondition of being an artwork. *Fountain* almost totally lacks this condition, as Duchamp intended. Duchamp, the Dadaist, focused his criticism on the self-evident presupposition of art and art's integration into the system of high culture. This provocative criticism—both accusation and protest—can be reduced to a philosophical question: what is art? Indeed it is a difficult question, since we can find no common point between the Medici Venus and *Fountain*. We might appeal to "family resemblance," but what among acknowledged artworks resembles *Fountain*? Nothing. It is no longer possible to define art by its physiognomy. On this subject, the solution proposed by Prof. Danto is well known. He claimed that art is what the artworld acknowledges, on the basis of its proper history, as art. This definition is apparently empty and evidently tautological: it reflects the structure of a tautological world.

An autonomous world is essentially tautological. This is not only the structure of art, but also of our contemporary, highly information-oriented society itself. It may be what Baudrillard caught with his notion of "simulation." Our society is constituted by a system of signs, having no reference to substances, and not based upon them. Paper money is not convertible any more, and its value is founded solely on credit and expectation. The price of commodities does not represent their value in use, and salaries no longer reflect the value of the productivity of labor. Baudrillard mentions Pop art in connection with simulation, and, indeed, Warhol's *Brillo Boxes* and Lichtenstein's enlarged cartoons are signs of signs. The essence of such art consists in crystallizing the mode of being of contemporary society. It incites philosophical speculation, but, being itself a part of the mechanism of society, such art becomes a kind of fashion and naturally loses any critical power.

Hence the well-known discussion of the end of art. It is important to recognize that the current state of art is the result of its historical development. Moreover, art is now deeply implicated in the phenomena of politics, economics, morality, etc., so that its problems can only be discussed on the total horizon of civilization.

5. THE PHILOSOPHY OF BEAUTY AS CONTEMPORARY AESTHETICS

Humankind now needs philosophy above all. Without doubt globalization has brought about an economic situation based on the law of jungle; what the philosophers of enlightenment would have called barbarism. This wave of change, while producing such excellent results as political liberation, and the sharing of information, has also spread a global disease: the uncritical adoption of econo-centrism. We are being tamed to accept the notion that financial value is the only value; that freedom of economic venture, requiring the autonomous reproduction of the system, is the only freedom. As a result, we cannot effectively cope with the problem of global warming, which is threatening the very ground of our existence, or with the problem of moral decadence. This modern system is our Leviathan. Though our age resembles the early modern period in being a crisis of civilization, the nature of the crisis is very different. At the time of Hobbes, the problem consisted in knowing philosophically the rationality of the world and the ground of morality, and beauty played an important role in that knowing. The monster that is our contemporary social system is, however, immune to the moral good will of individuals. We require a philosophy to analyze the monster, and to discover what form of civilization is really desirable.

Can aesthetics contribute anything to this philosophical task? I believe that beauty and the philosophy of beauty have a real place. What we learn from early modern aesthetics is that when basic values become suspect and or even invalid, aesthetic judgment is the only path towards the establishment of new values. Malebranche looked for the perfection of the world in its beauty, and we find in Genesis a similar notion. Having created the world, God appreciates his creation: "And God saw every thing that he had made, and, behold, it was very good" (I-31). The goodness that is perceived is nothing but beauty.

From the viewpoint of aesthetics, this phrase means two things. In the first place, the fact that the Almighty verified the quality of Creation expresses the aesthetic nature of beauty. Beauty cannot be determined a priori with concepts; it needs always to be verified a posteriori. In other words, beauty is not made but given. Reflecting on that profoundly, we can be cured of arrogance through beauty. As beauty is a grace or gift, and the sole value exceeding human power, we can expect it to play a role in overcoming modern homo-centrism.

In the second place, measuring the goodness of a new world by its beauty can also be an important guide at a turning point in civilization. But consider this: there is beauty in the tracks of missiles flying against a dark sky, and sublimity in the collapse of a glacier. While beauty is the only direct mark of value, it is also involved in an undeniable ambiguity in our contemporary civilization. I am convinced that the most real and important task of aesthetics is to speculate on this ambiguity on the horizon of our global civilization.

SELECTED PAPERS FROM
THE XXII WORLD CONGRESS OF PHILOSOPHY

Les limites de la phénoménalité

JEAN-LUC MARION
UFR DE PHILOSOPHIE

I. LIMITES ET FINITUDE

La philosophie a cette particularité, à la fois un privilège et une tentation constante, de n'avoir par elle-même aucune limite fixe, au contraire de toutes les autres sciences et disciplines. Et de fait, comment en aurait-elle, puisqu'il lui revient en propre de les fixer ou de les reconnaître pour les autres? Car elle se trouve elle-même en charge de l'universel et de l'inconditionné pour le compte des autres, parce qu'il faut bien qu'un discours finisse par assumer, à ses risques et périls et pour le bien de toutes, la tâche sans doute impraticable de la délimitation et de l'architectonique du savoir. Mais, pour cela même, la philosophie, lorsqu'elle doit affronter la tâche de fixer ses propres limites, ne peut que se retrouver seule et démunie.

A chaque époque, d'une manière ou d'une autre, la philosophie doit donc décider de ce qu'elle peut connaître, plus exactement de ce qu'elle peut ambitionner de penser, qu'elle le connaisse ou non; ce qui impose aussi de décider de ce que peut vouloir dire vraiment *connaitre*. Au long de son histoire, la philosophie n'a en effet pas cessé d'en décider suivant des formulations différentes, selon que la limite passe entre l'immuable et le mouvement (pour Platon, Aristote et Plotin), l'éternité et le temporel (pour saint Augustin et jusqu'à saint Thomas d'Aquin), l'infini et le fini (à partir de Jean Duns Scot jusqu'à Leibniz), l'impossible et le possible (à partir de l'*ontologia*, Clauberg, Wolff et Kant jusqu'à Schelling), pour aboutir à l'expérimentable et l'inexpérimentable (avec les positivismes modernes, mais aussi Nietzsche et Husserl, puis toute la phénoménologie), etc. Mais toujours, sous les titres divers de «philosophie première», de «méthode», de «métaphysique», de «critique», de «doctrine de la science», de «système» et «science rigoureuse», la philosophie a tenté de prendre et de maintenir une posture transcendentale. Autrement dit, selon la définition de Kant, elle a prétendu fixer les conditions de possibilité des objets de l'expérience, avant (et afin) de connaître ces objets mêmes: «J'appelle transcendentale toute connaissance qui ne se préoccupe pas tant des objets, que de *notre connaissance* des objets, *en tant que celle-ci doit être possible a priori*».[1]

DOI: 10.5840/jpr201237Supplement26

Mais que voudrait dire la possibilité des objets de l'expérience, si l'on n'entendait ainsi finalement leur compatibilité avec les conditions de l'expérience elle-même, puisque, toujours selon Kant, «. . . les conditions a priori d'une expérience possible en général sont du même coup (*zugleich*) les conditions de possibilité des objets de l'expérience». Pourtant, l'essentiel reste encore au-delà: car que doit-on entendre par les «. . . conditions d'une expérience possible»—pour qui et par rapport à quoi conditionnent-elles l'expérience? La même phrase de Kant poursuit et précise qu'il s'agit des «. . . conditions de la pensée dans son expérience possible»?[2] Mais à nouveau de quelle pensée? D'une pensée telle qu'elle a besoin, pour qu'un objet lui soit donné qu' «il l'affecte d'une certaine manière», à savoir par l'intuition sensible (espace et temps); car elle définit la possibilité de l'expérience «. . . au moins pour nous, les hommes (*uns menschen wenigstens*)».[3] Les conditions des objets de l'expérience ne tombent pas du ciel, ni ne sont gravées dans le marbre de l'éternité: elles se trouvent donc établies par les dimensions et la finitude de notre esprit. Descartes ne prétendait rien d'autre, lorsqu'il posait que les vérités éternelles (logiques et mathématiques) sont aussi créées que notre propre esprit et qu'elles ne lui correspondent si exactement que parce qu'elles partagent la même finitude.—Etablir les limites de la philosophie, donc celles de l'expérience, donc enfin celles des sciences ne fait en droit qu'un avec la reconnaissance et la détermination de la finitude de l'homme. C'est précisément parce que cette finitude conditionne d'avance toute expérience, que nous pouvons en tirer au moins cet avantage négatif, mais littéralement transcendental: prévoir a priori ce qui *ne pourra jamais* devenir un objet de savoir pour nous, parce qu'il outrepasse les limites de ce que nous pouvons recevoir et supporter. Car l'attitude transcendantale ne fixe les conditions de possibilité, qu'en présupposant en deçà d'elle-même une condition ontique à sa propre possibilité épistémologique: la finitude apparaît ainsi comme la possibilité de la fondation des conditions de possibilité en général de l'expérience, donc des objets. Que *fondation* et *condition* fassent ici pléonasme n'a rien d'insignifiant, mais confirme clairement le redoublement de la possibilité transcendentale elle-même par la possibilité de la finitude—ou plutôt par la finitude elle-même comme *la* possibilité.

Il devient dès lors décisif de considérer le statut de la finitude: l'histoire de la philosophie a peut-être consisté en rien d'autre qu'en l'approfondissement et l'universalisation du concept de finitude. A partir de son acception grecque, strictement négative, de simple indétermination (absence de terminaison, de définition), elle devint d'abord le propre de l'homme en tant que créature, face à l'infinité positive de Dieu. Puis, sur la base de cette finitude définitive et délimitante, Descartes a pu établir l'*ego* du *cogito* comme un sol ferme et inébranlable et instaurer un première situation transcendentale. Kant a ensuite pu radicaliser (d'ailleurs dans le prolongement direct de la «création des vérités éternelles» de Descartes) la finitude du *je* transcendental en une finitude de la raison, définitivement marquée par la finitude de l'intuition *sensible*; il assurait le caractère transcendental de toute philosophie, passant de la méthode à la critique, pour penser le phénomène comme simple objet. Heidegger pouvait alors (d'ailleurs prolongeant ainsi fidèlement la phénoménalité finie de Kant) non seulement décrire l'analytique finie du *Dasein*, mais aussi, puisqu'il affermait au *Dasein* la mise à découvert de l'être des étants, parvenir à dégager la finitude *de l'être lui-même*. Dès lors, on ne peut plus esquiver la question, qui demande *jusqu'où* la finitude peut elle-même se radicaliser. Car, de fait, elle se concentre et se radicalise, en sorte qu'elle ne peut pas se définir, ni sans doute se finir: que signifierait une finitude elle-même définie, sinon une contradiction dans les termes? Par définition, la finitude ne peut se finir. En tant que l'agent des limites de la philosophie, elle ne peut que se prolonger d'une indéfinition essentielle.

II. CE QUI SE CONNAÎT COMME OBJET.

Considérons donc la finitude qui nous donne accès aux objets des sciences. Selon l'usage, sans doute simplificateur mais d'autant mieux établi, les sciences se divisent en sciences exacte ou non exactes. Les sciences exactes (dites «dures») obtiennent des énoncés falsifiables, donc aussi vérifiables, soit par l'évidence d'une déduction formelle, soit par production et donc reproduction de processus réglés dans une expérimentation empirique, l'une et l'autre voie aboutissant à d'indiscutables évidences. (Remarquons que la critique, pourtant si courante, du critère de l'évidence n'a guère sens, parce qu'on ne peut jamais critiquer une évidence que par une autre, supposée encore plus *index sui* que la précédente). D'autre part, les sciences autrefois dites "humaines", désormais "sociales", même si elles prétendent parfois au rang supposé plus honorable de "cognitives", et même si elles reposent elles aussi sur des données empiriques souvent surabondantes et éventuellement exactement quantifiées, ne peuvent pourtant pas obtenir les mêmes résultats que des précédentes: elles ne portent en effet pas sur des objets productibles, donc reproductibles à l'identique, en ce sens des objets disponibles à volonté et donc quasi permanents, mais en fin de compte sur des états de choses contingents, des ensembles peu stables, provisoires et toujours en cours d'évaluation. La distinction entre ces deux types de sciences (si d'ailleurs l'on maintient l'univocité du terme, après tout discutable dans ces deux cas fort différents) ne tient pas à l'exactitude des procédures, ni aux méthodes de démonstration, mais plus radicalement à la différence essentielle des temporalités: les sciences «dures» peuvent neutraliser la contingence de leurs objets en les reproduisant à l'identique (en principe et sinon au moins tangentiellement), précisément parce qu'elles parviennent à les produire exhaustivement, tandis que les autres sciences doivent composer avec des objets jamais identiques entre eux, ni d'abord à eux-mêmes: les *data* qui les supportent interviennent non seulement en nombres incommensurables, mais aussi et surtout en des circonstances toujours évoluant et changeantes, en sorte qu'on ne peut assumer l'identité de l'objet que provisoirement. Une temporalité quasi historique reste toujours à l'oeuvre, qui interdit de clôre l'objectivation.

En sorte que l'on y retrouve un reste de la difficulté propre aux sciences de la contingence, telle qu'Aristote l'avait décrite et pour laquelle il avait récusé à la science de la φύσις (précisément *pas* notre physique) le titre de philosophie première:

toujours en changement, l'étant φύσει ne cesse de subir l'affection indéterminante de la ὕλη, qui joue le rôle d'une «cause requise pour que l'accident se comporte autrement que la plupart du temps—ἡ ὕλη ἔσται αἰτία ἡ ενδεχομένη παρά τὸ ὡς ἐπὶ τὸ πολὺ ἄλλως τοῦ συμβεβηκότος».[4] Inégal à soi, sans cesse mutant, l'étant φύσει n'atteint jamais la permanence d'un objet du savoir certain. Cette difficulté a retenu pendant des siècles toute tentative d'interpréter les changements locaux (les mouvements des corps physiques) en termes mathématiques, et a même interdit la quantification de la nature matérielle en général, parce que le privilège des mathématiques—connaître des idéalités stables, productibles et reproductibles—se payait du prix de leur irréalité physique, et que leur application aux étants changeant de la φύσις aurait contredit précisément leur caractère à la fois *physique* et indéterminable, dû à la ὕλη. Il fallut, comme on sait, rien de moins qu'un détour par la théologie chrétienne de la création pour contourner, sinon annuler, cette difficulté principielle, rien de moins qu'un coup de force, assumé comme tel par Kepler et Galilée: attribuer la géométrisation du monde physique à Dieu lui-même, créateur géométrisant: ὁ θέος ἀει γεωμετρεὶ[5] autrement dit, selon Leibniz, «Cum Deus calculat et cogitationem exercet, fit mundus».[6] Soucieux d'une solution plus économique et élégante, Descartes commença d'abord par récuser cette confusion des genres, en refusant que les vérités mathématiques définissent aussi la pensée de Dieu (soit la thèse de la création des vérités éternelles), afin de *permettre* d'autant mieux que ce soit la pensée humaine qui se retrouve autorisée à géométriser la physique et la ὕλη elle-même. Ce qui lui permit de déployer, au lieu de ce coup de force théologique, un coup de force strictement épistémologique: l'assomption que connaître signifie par définition connaître avec certitude, donc suivant le paradigme des mathématiques, au point que, dans quelque domaine de l'étant que l'on tente de connaitre, il faille y procéder comme elles, qui ne supposent dans leurs *objets* rien que l'expérience ait rendu incertain (« . . . objectum ita purum et simplex versantur, ut nihil plane supponant quod experientia reddiderit incertum».[7] Autrement dit, il s'agit toujours, même et surtout dans le domaine du changement physique, de supprimer l'indétermination de la ὕλη, en élaborant un mode de connaissance qui fasse abstraction de la matière elle-même et donc surmonte l'indétermination qu'elle provoque. Mathématiser, ou plus exactement interpréter mathématiquement un étant physique revient ainsi à *dématérialiser* la chose en un objet, qui sera certain en proportion inverse de la matière en lui. Car (contrairement à ce que l'usage répète), il ne s'agit pas, en droit, pour Descartes de promouvoir une mathématisation de la nature, mais son objectivation: désormais, il ne s'agira que de connaître des *objets*, et pour cela d'abord de les *produire*.

Cette opération consiste précisément à constituer des objets, en metttant entre parenthèses la chose, afin d'y éliminer la ὕλη, et de ne retenir de son expérience que les éléments qui satisfont à l'unique condition de la certitude. En termes cartésiens, deux critères décident de ce qu'on doit retenir de la chose pour en constituer l'objet: l'*ordo et mensura*. Par *mensura*, il ne faut pas seulement entendre ce qui se mesure réellement (ce qui s'inscrit déjà et par soi dans les trois dimensions de l'espace euclidien), mais tout ce qui peut se réduire à la mesure par analogie, transposition, imagination, ou toute autre transcription: par exemple le temps, la vitesse qui combine ce temps avec l'espace, l'accélération, qui combine la vitesse une seconde fois avec le temps, la pesanteur, la masse, mais aussi toutes les qualités en tant qu'elles s'étalonnent sur une échelle, etc. Au nombre de ces *dimensiones* (Descartes nomme ainsi ces mesures du non immédiatement spatiales), nous avons aujourd'hui appris à ajouter tous les *paramètres* pensables, y compris et surtout ceux qui mesurent des facteurs *non matériels* (comme dans la psychologie, la sociologie, l'économie et l'écono*métrie*, les sciences commerciales et financières, etc.). Par *ordo*, il ne faut pas entendre l'ordre naturel (ou supposé tel) des choses mêmes, mais la *mise en ordre* des paramètres et des éléments d'un objet, de telle sorte qu'ils s'organisent avec la plus grande évidence possible pour nous et se constituent ainsi suivant la logique de leur *mise en évidence*; il s'agit donc de ce que nous nommons aujourd'hui des *modèles* d'un objet (ou du "concept" d'un produit technologique et commercial). On peut suggèrer que Kant reprendra ce dispositif, en se bornant à le transformer: les paramètres (*mensura*, *dimensiones* de Descartes) renvoient à l'espace (et donc au temps, sens interne) et mettent en oeuvre les catégories de la qualité et, plus encore, celles de la quantité et de la relation; tandis que le modèle (*ordo*) suppose, lui, surtout le temps (et la méthode du schème) pour organiser la constitution des paramètres dans un ensemble; il met donc en oeuvre avant tout les catégories de la modalité—celles précisément qui reportent l'objet à l'esprit qui les constitue. Et, par Kant, faut-il le souligner? la décision prise par Descartes sur les conditions de l'objectivation s'étend à toute la pensée contemporaine: la phénoménologie transcendentale, le positivisme (logique ou non), la métaphysique analytique, etc. Dans tous les cas, le modèle et les paramètres définissent par avance et a priori ce qui, dans l'expérience de la chose en elle-même (en soi), pourra satisfaire à l'exigence de certitude et finira par passer dans l'objet. Car l'objet se distingue fondamentalement de la chose: non seulement il en *réduit* l'expérience à la mesure de ce que la certitude tolère en matière de contingence; mais surtout il *substitue* à la chose ce que les paramètres et l'ordre permettent d'en reconstituer. L'objet ne fournit donc pas une version certaine de la chose, seulement rectifiée «au niveau de la raison»,[8] mais lui substitue une reconstitution, constituée à partir de la réduction de l'expérience imposée par les critères de la certitude. Certitude, qui doit toujours s'entendre comme la certitude *pour notre esprit* et ses pouvoirs de connaître. Suivant en effet la «révolution copernicienne» de Kant, nous ne connaissons certainement d'objet qu'autant que et, littéralement, dans la *mesure* où « . . . comme objet des sens, il se règle sur (*sich richtet nach*) la constitution de *notre* pouvoir d'intuitionner».[9] Plus essentiel à l'objet que la chose, se trouve en lui, ou plus exactement *hors de lui*, le pouvoir de connaître qui le constitue en tant que connaissable—le pouvoir du *Je* transcendental, celui déjà de l'*ego cogito* tel qu'il nous instaure, nous les hommes, « . . . comme maîtres et possesseurs de la nature».[10] Seule l'aliénation de la chose au ministre de la connaissance certaine permet de constituer l'objet. L'objet ne prend la place de la chose, mais par défaut—parce qu'il consent parfaitement à son l'aliénation envers l'*ego* ou au *Je*, tandis que la chose, restant par définition en soi et sur son quant-à-soi, lui résiste. Parler en effet de chose-en-soi revient à n'exprimer qu'un pléonasme: par définition la chose est en soi, tandis que l'objet est par un autre, en fait s'aliène à un autre—le ministre de la certitude. La distinction entre l'objet et la chose, l'aliéné et l'*en-soi* commence lorsque la connaissance impose un autre ordre que l'existence:

> . . . il faut considérer les choses en tant qu'ordonnées à notre connaissance tout autrement que si nous parlons de ces mêmes choses pour autant qu'elles existent vraiment— . . . aliter spectandas esse res singulares *in ordine ad cognitionem nostram*, quam si de iisdem loquamur *prout revera existunt*.[11]

L'objet ne se règle pas sur la vérité de l'existence, mais sur la mise en ordre de l'évidence.

Seule cette transition de la chose à l'objet permet le développement des sciences dites, à juste titre, exactes, parce que seule la substitution de l'objet aliéné à la chose en soi permet de satisfaire à l'exigence de certitude, en éliminant précisément tout ce qui, tel la ὕλη, s'y opposerait de la contingence. Mais cette transition, qui permet historiquement à chaque science exacte de se constituer, il revient à la philosophie de la penser et la justifier, et non pas l'une quelconque de ces sciences exactes, qui d'ailleurs ne s'en soucient guère, occupées qu'elles sont à leurs affaires. En fait, les sciences exactes n'oublient pas que la philosophie pourrait encore garder des prétentions à leur égard, et elles défendent avec vigilance (et parfois avec nervosité) leur autonomie contre tout retour d'un tel impérialisme. Mais c'est la philosophie qui s'oublie elle-même en oubliant que les conditions de possibilité des sciences exactes ne relèvent pas d'une science, même la plus exacte, mais de la philosophie sous sa figure métaphysique—que les sciences le veuillent ou non, et que la philosophie contemporaine puisse encore le penser ou non. La notion d'objet et les règles de l'objectivation proviennent de la philosophie, et que les pratiques scientifiques ne voient parfois plus qu'elles doivent leur rationalité à une instauration (*instauratio magna*) de nature intrinséquement philosophique ne change rien à l'affaire. Et d'ailleurs, elles n'ont pas à le penser, car «les sciences ne pensent pas», mais calculent et objectivisent. (Faut-il rappeler, à rebours d'indignations ignorantes et de commande, que ces mots n'ont rien d'injurieux ou d'irrationnel, mais simplement décrivent et répètent ce que les sciences ont toujours revendiqué, et à bon droit, pour leur *privilège*).

Reste que, quand la philosophie elle-même oublie la décision philosophique qui préside à l'objectivation pratiquée par les sciences exactes, elle commet une double erreur, pour ne pas dire plus.—D'abord elle organise elle-même à sa propre marginalisation, en se faisant le commentateur toujours tardif (l'oiseau de Minerve se lève encore plus tard qu'ailleurs en philosophie des sciences) et souvent superficiel ou anecdotique de la pratique scientifique des sciences exactes elles-mêmes. Inquiète des résultats qu'elle collecte après coup, qu'elle peine à comprendre (d'autant plus que souvent ceux qui les produisent ne les comprennent eux-mêmes guère), qu'elle sait peut-être impossibles à synthétiser, la philosophie se trouve *réduite aux aguets*: elle n'a plus de domaine propre d'interrogation, ni d'investigation, et, dans le domaine qui n'est pas le sien (et ne l'a jamais été), elle perd même à ses propres yeux toute autorité, ne fût-ce qu'une autorité herméneutique. A s'enrôler en supplétif d'une armée qui n'en admet pas, la philosophie se condamne à l'insignifiance d'un commentaire mal assuré de ce qu'il dit et que personne n'a besoin de lire. Les tentatives répétées d'ériger la philosophie en «science rigoureuse», voire seulement en «théorie des sciences», ont toutes régulièrement échoué: il y a sans doute à cela de bonnes raisons—la philosophie permet les sciences exactes, mais à la condition justement de ne pas prétendre en devenir une parmi d'autres (encore moins d'accepter la *diminutio capititis* d'en devenir une).—Mais cette première erreur de la philosophie ne concerne encore qu'elle seule. Il s'en trouve une autre, plus grave parce qu'elle concerne la compréhension et l'organisation des sciences elles-mêmes. En effet, la philosophie, depuis Descartes et peut-être dès Platon (par-dessus l'interdit aristotélicien déniant à la science mathématique le rang de science première) jusqu'à Husserl et Carnap, n'a cessé de prendre appui sur le privilège des mathématiques—la dématérialisation—pour établir son paradigme de toute science certaine. En sorte que, puisqu'elle a elle-même validé la réduction du savoir aux sciences de l'objet, la philosophie doit donc assumer la responsabilité particulière d'en penser le statut et surtout les conséquences. Autrement dit, si le statut de paradigme a été accordé aux sciences les plus objectivantes par la philosophie, si ce paradigme affecte toutes les autres sciences, même non «exactes», et surtout si ce paradigme de limitation du savoir à l'objet aliéné touche aujourd'hui ses limites, la philosophie aurait aussi la charge prioritaire de l'expliquer et de s'en expliquer.

C'est-à-dire de s'interroger sur le mode de finitude qui soutient le projet et le primat de l'objet.

III. CE QUI NE SE CONNAIT PAS COMME OBJET

Les sciences exactes connaissent avec certitude ce que, de l'expérience, elles peuvent constituer en objet selon le type d'*ordo et mensura* (modèle et paramètre) que chacune d'entre elles met en oeuvre avec sa méthode et dans son champ propres. Reste qu'une question ne peut pas ne pas surgir: qu'en est-il de ce qui ne peut se constituer en un objet, de ce qui résiste à son objectivation?

On ne saurait échapper à cette question en la disqualifiant simplement. En particulier, on ne saurait argumenter que nous ne connaissons pas du tout ce que nous ne pouvons constituer en objet par aucune science exacte, donc nous n'avons absolument pas à en tenir compte et qu'ainsi la difficulté ne se pose pas puisqu'elle ne porte à proprement parler (et penser) sur rien. D'abord, la philosophie a longtemps pensé sans se conformer aux exigences de l'objectivité, et l'on ne prétendra pas qu'elle n'a pas pensé du tout. Mais surtout, nous ne laissons pas d'expérimenter, constamment et surabondamment, même ce qui ne laisse pas constituer en objet. Nous l'expérimentons même d'autant mieux que ce non objectivé surgit, comme un résidu irréductible à la dématérialisation, en excès à l'objectivation, en marge de tout objet connu. Car, à la mesure *exacte* où un φύσει ὄν se laisse remplacer par et constituer en objet, surgit, sous une forme de prime abord imprécise et le plus souvent avec l'allure d'une aporie, ce qui ne peut se constituer en objet, le soi de la chose même, le *soi* de la chose en soi. Et il ne s'agit pas là d'apparences provisoires, qu'on devrait tenter encore une fois de réduire à l'objectivité, ni d'objets inconstituables par principe, mais de l'effet de résistance de l'en soi non maîtrisé de la chose. Les exemples ne se trouvent pas loin, puisque les meilleurs proviennent de ce que la métaphysique, sous l'acception de la *metaphysica specialis* a tenté de constituer comme ses trois *objets* privilégiés, sans justement y parvenir sans reste.

Le monde des choses et le monde environnant devraient, pour nous, s'épuiser dans la totalité (même incomplète) des objets que les sciences exactes peuvent constituer, c'est-à-dire des objets que les moyens industriels de la technologie peuvent produire et reproduire. Ce monde d'objets devrait lui-même s'accomplir dans un objet global, sans reste. Or le monde que nous expérimentons en réalité déborde cette objectivation, comme en témoigne exemplairement la menace écologique: le monde des objets ne se substitue pas exactement au monde des choses, mais le déborde ou le contraint par le flux des déchets industriels qu'il produit sans que les choses ne puissent le résorber, l'absorber et le *naturaliser.* L'accumulation des déchets irrécupérables et irrémédiables atteste que l'objectivation comme production ne prend pas en charge ni en vérité les choses du monde, mais les redouble, les dérange et les contredit. A cette accumulation répond, avec une pleine cohérence, une perte—l'épuisement des ressources naturelles fossiles prouve en effet que la contingence demeure irréductible, au point d'imposer une historicité et même une événementialité de l'historicité, qui interdisent l'éternelle croissance d'une production sans fin d'objets techniques. Cette double menace écologique atteste paradoxalement que les choses du monde, ou mieux le monde en soi des choses résiste à son recouvrement par les objets.

La métaphysique a aussi délibérément élaboré un objet divin, un Dieu réduit à son concept, sous les titres successifs et compatibles de *causa sui, ens summe perfectum* et «dieu moral». Cette élaboration, précisément parce qu'elle amenait Dieu à la rationalité univoque du concept, aboutit à une idole, identifiée comme telle par Nietzsche: car la «mort de Dieu» ne déclare aucune guerre contre Dieu, ni ne proclame que nous sommes dispensés de nous en préoccuper; elle *constate* au contraire que l'idole, c'est-à-dire l'objet que la métaphysique a constitué sous ce nom, ne peut pas, en tous les cas ne peut plus porter le poids et la gloire du divin, qui ne cesse pourtant de nous assaillir, désormais sous des figures plus incontrôlées et anonymes. Car la période de la «mort de Dieu» en philosophie (les deux siècles du nihilisme annoncés par Nietzsche)[12] coïncide, sous nos yeux parfois atterrés, avec le retour de flamme incontrôlé de la chose en soi de Dieu, craintivement avouée par la laïcité métaphysique sous le titre de «fait religieux»—l'idole minimale. Pareille résurgence irrépressible du divin atteste que ce que nous ne pensons pas comme un objet et qui est mort comme tel ne cesse de nous imposer son expérience.

Le soi de l'homme enfin s'est trouvé lui-même constitué en un objet par la *metaphysica specialis.* Remarquons pourtant que cette objectivation ne concerne pas seulement, ni même d'abord le *moi* empirique, naturellement disposé au statut d'un objet pour la physique, la physiologie, la psychologie, les sciences cognitives, etc. Elle concerne plus essentiellement ce qui a rendu le concept de *moi* empirique possible: la distinction même entre un *Je* pensant et un *moi* pensé; cette distinction ne va en effet pas de soi et reste inconcevable, si l'on ne voit pas qu'elle résulte directement de l'imposition *à l'homme lui-même* des conditions de l'objectivation. Ce qu'on ne cesse de dénoncer superficiellement (et inefficacement d'ailleurs) sous le titre du dualisme entre esprit et matière relève en fait de la dualité plus essentielle entre une science exigeant la certitude même à propos du soi de la connaissance et ce *soi* lui-même, donc la pensée pensante en acte résiste à son objectivation comme pensée pensée. Cette résistance s'ensuit d'une évidence plus forte que celle de l'objet: que je ne sois pas (sous quelque nom qu'on voudra) le duel de l'objectivant et de l'objectivé, je l'éprouve dans l'épreuve de ma chair (*Leib*, *living body*, etc.); car ma chair me fait non seulement sentir ce qui n'est pas moi, mais aussi sentir que je sens, donc sentir mon sentir originaire lui-même et par lui me fait accèder à mon auto-affection. En un mot, ma chair m'atteste à moi-même comme un *soi*, irréductible à tout objet, y compris le mien propre.

Ainsi la question écologique, le «fait religieux» et la chair de soi mettent en crise rien de moins que les trois objectivations de la *metaphysica specialis*. Mais il y a plus: il ne s'agit pas seulement d'une crise parmi *certains* objets de la connaissance, mais d'une crise *de* la connaissance toute entière en tant que connaissance d'objets; et la résistance à l'objectivation s'étend à toute ce que la *metaphysica generalis* réduit à l'objectivité—à toutes les choses. Ce que l'on a thématisé comme la «fin de la métaphysique» ne consiste pas dans un échec de son entreprise—l'objectivation, la *traduction* des étants en autant d'objets—, mais dans la *réussite* si complète de sa technologie, qu'elle provoque en retour la résistance des choses elles-mêmes à l'objectivation. Le «retour aux choses mêmes» pourrait en effet vouloir dire cette résistance du soi des choses à leur aliénation dans l'objet. Les «arrière-mondes», que dénonce Nietzsche, ne concernent pas seulement les impératifs moraux, mais les valeurs en général, donc d'abord les concepts de la métaphysique et ses catégories (car, en fait d'idoles, il s'agit du sujet, de la causalité et du libre-arbitre dans *Die Götzendämmerung*). Et le *Lebenswelt* du dernier Husserl ne s'oppose au monde de la science qu'en tant qu'il constitué des objets et se reconstitue finalement lui-même comme un objet. Le nihilisme, du moins pris dans son acception sérieuse, se borne à constater que les plus hautes valeurs, donc les plus radicaux des concepts de la *metaphysica*, c'est-à-dire de l'objectivation de l'étant, se dévaluent—autrement dit n'opèrent plus et ne permettent plus la rationalité. Le nihilisme se borne à enregistrer le fait que l'objectivation ne met pas la rationalité en oeuvre, mais en crise.

Nous nous trouvons donc au terme de la situation transcendentale: en conclusion de l'*Analytique transcendentale*, Kant posait comme ultime la distinction des objets entre phénomènes et noumènes: tout se qui se pense se pense dans l'horizon de l'objectivation, mais seuls se connaissent les objets que remplit, soutient et met en scène une intuition sensible; cette distinction s'imposera si parfaitement qu'elle se simplifiera bientôt en une opposition plus sommaire entre les objets, c'est-à-dire les seuls phénomènes dotés d'intuition sensible, et les non-objets, c'est-à-dire les noumènes sans intuition sensible, donc aussi les choses que leur *soi* rend précisément irréductibles à l'expérience, puisqu'on l'entend au sens de ce que l'objectivation en abstrait—l'*ordo et mensura*, le modèle et les paramètres. Il se pourrait donc que, sauf à s'installer dans le nihilisme en entérinant les apories de l'objectivation, il faille envisager une autre distinction fondamentale—non plus celle de tous les objets entre phénomènes et noumènes, mais de tous les phénomènes entre objets et *non-objets*. En d'autres termes, il faudrait élargir la raison au-delà des limites de l'objectivation: élargir au double sens de l'étendre, mais aussi de la libérer. Sans doute, ce faisant, on semble faire fi d'un avertissement solennel de Kant:

> Les principes fondamentaux, par lesquels la raison spéculative s'imagine transgresser ses bornes, n'ont pas pour résultat un élargissement (*Erweiterung*), mais, en y regardant de plus près, inévitablement, un resserrement (*Verengung*) de notre usage de la raison.[13]

Pourtant, pour résister à cette autorité, il s'en trouve d'autres. Car, dans l'un de ses derniers efforts, Husserl envisage bel et bien l'hypothèse que « . . . le domaine du logique est beaucoup plus grand (*viel größer*) que celui dont la logique traditionnelle s'est jusqu'ici occupée». Ce «sens plus vaste et compréhensif», ce «concept compréhensif (*umfassender*) du logique et du logos»,[14] fait écho, toute différence étant entendue, avec la demande de Nietzsche pour une raison élargie: «Tu dis "Je" et tu es fier de ce mot. Mais plus grand est ce que tu ne veux pas croire—ta chair et sa grande raison (*dein Leib und seine grosse Vernunft*), qui ne dit pas "Je", mais qui le fait».[15]

IV. LA PHILOSOPHIE COMME LA «GRANDE RAISON»

L'état de la question conduit donc à contester une décision essentielle prise par Kant. Il pose en effet que, si en métaphysique classique, de Scot à Wolff, le possible (dans son couple avec l'impossible) constitue «der höchste Begriff», en fait, pour la philosophie transcendentale, il faut en ajouter encore un plus grand («noch ein höherer»), celui d'objet.[16] Disposons-nous de bonnes raisons pour dépasser la primauté même de l'objet? Faudrait-il renverser leur rapport et, entendant le possible en un sens radical et non-métaphysique, l'établir à son tour plus haut que l'objet et son effectivité aliénée—conformément à une remarque assez énigmatique de Heidegger: «Höher als die Wirklichkeit, steht die Möglichkeit»?[17] Or, non seulement nous ne manquons pas de raisons pour le tenter, mais nous avons en fait déjà commencé à le faire, et de multiples manières.

L'élargissement de la rationalité provient d'abord de l'*horizon* que nous assignons à la phénoménalité (ou qu'elle s'assigne à elle-même). Or, en fait d'horizon, ce qui apparaît ne résulte pas toujours de sa constitution transcendentale comme un objet: il peut aussi apparaître comme un étant, qui se montre comme tel et à partir de lui-même. Le phénomène signifie alors, suivant du moins Heidegger, « . . . ce qui se montre soi-même en soi-même, le manifeste—das *Sich-an-ihm-selbst-zeigende*, das Offenbare» (*Sein und Zeit*, §7,28,35). Ainsi seulement peuvent se manifester des étants non-objectivables: et d'abord le *Dasein* ou le monde comme *In-der-Welt-sein*, dans un horizon non plus objectivant, mais ontologique—du moins au sens de la répétition de la question de l'être par l'analytique du *Dasein*, à l'encontre précisément de l'interprétation métaphysique de l'*ens* comme un *cogitabile*, un objet pour l'*ego* du *cogito*. Pourtant cet élargissement lui-même suppose que ce qui se montre se montre bien à partir de soi, au lieu de s'aliéner en se soumettant à une constitution venue d'ailleurs, de l'ego. Mais comment un phénomène pourrait-il disposer de soi, s'il ne dispose en lui-même d'aucun *soi*? Comment comprendre le *soi* d'un phénomène, qui ne soit pas déjà un *ego*? A cette question, on ne peut répondre qu'en quittant non seulement l'horizon de l'objet, mais aussi l'horizon de l'être et en passant à celui de la donation: en effet, un phénomène ne peut apparaître en soi (comme une chose), que s'il vient au visible à partir de soi (comme un événement); et il ne vient à partir de *soi*, que si d'abord il se donne. Tout ce qui se montre (au sens strict de se montrer à partir de soi), doit d'abord se donner de *soi*-même. Seul le donné dispose de soi et d'un soi. Heidegger lui-même témoigne de ce dépassement de l'horizon de l'être, lorsqu'il insiste que ni le temps, ni l'être ne *sont* (car seuls sont des étants), et donc qu'il faut en dire «cela donne—*es gibt*», qu'ils adviennent en se donnant (thèse qui ne surgit pas seulement en 1962, dans *Zeit und Sein*, mais dès 1927, en *Sein und Zeit*, §§43–44). En fait, Husserl sans doute avait déjà franchi le pas vers la donation, à sa façon, directement à partir de l'objectivité de l'objet et, pour ainsi dire, sans passer par l'être, lorsqu'il formulait le «principe de tous les principes»: « . . . *tout ce qui se propose à nous originairement dans l'«intuition»* (autant dire dans son effectivité charnelle), *doit se recevoir simplement pour ce qu'il se donne (als es sich gibt)*, mais aussi seulement dans les bornes, *dans lesquelles il se donne ici (nur in den Schranken in denen es sich gibt)*».[18] Les phénomènes, tous sans exception, avant de s'objecter à un *Je*, avant d'être des étants face au néant, adviennent à partir d'eux-mêmes comme se donnant, autant dire comme des événements advenant à partir de leur *soi*. Ainsi en va-t-il précisément de l'événement (collectif et historique, mais aussi individuel), de l'idole, de ma chair et de la face d'autrui, qui apparaissent tous à leur propre initiative, jamais à la mienne et échappent ainsi à l'objectivation; mais qui, non plus, ne sont pas, du moins au sens d'une présence subsistante, ni même d'un étant utilisable, puisque je ne peux pas toujours, en fait presque jamais les voir comme des étants stables, permanents, neutres et publics. Cette détermination des phénomènes comme donnés se pourrait s'avérer si originaire que même les stricts objets pourraient eux aussi se laisser reconduire, en dernière analyse, à des donnés *se* donnant. En effet les modèles et les paramètres, même reproduits à l'identique, ne peuvent s'abstraire totalement de leur inscription irrémédiablement unique, donc contingente et non-reproductible, dans l'espace et le temps: au bout du compte, ils restent toujours encore des événements, assignés chacun à un *ici* et un *maintenant*, dans lesquels ils doivent *se donner*. Ici devient possible une herméneutique: elle tend à retranscrire tous les phénomènes de prime abord considérés comme des objets (ou comme des étants) en phénomènes originairement donnés, parce que *se donnant en soi.* Cette herméneutique des horizons opère le premier élargissement de la phénoménalité.

Une fois identifié l'horizon de la donation, nous pouvons franchir un second pas vers l'élargissement de la phénoménalité. Si tout phénomène se montre, et si, pour se montrer, il faut d'abord qu'il se donne, l'opérateur de la donation reste donc toujours d'abord l'intuition. La description de la *saturation* des phénomènes par leur excès d'intuition opère le second élargissement de la phénoménalité. En effet, rien ne se donne sinon dans et par l'intuition, en sorte que tout phénomène suppose le remplissement, au moins partiel, de son concept (ou de sa signification) par l'intuition donatrice. Car l'intuition ne résulte pas seulement d'une donation («. . . Vorstellung, die vor allem Denken gegeben sein kann»),[19] mais opère cette donation, elle n'est pas tant donnée, que d'abord donatrice: «Sans sensibilité, aucun objet ne serait donné (*kein Gegenstand gegeben wurde*), et sans entendement, aucun ne serait pensé». Ou: «Par la première [réceptivité de la sensibilité, intuition], un objet nous est *donné (ein Gegenstand gegeben wird)*, par la deuxième [spontanéité de l'entendement, concept] il se trouve [. . .] pensé».[20] Ces deux termes permettent, entre autres à Kant et Husserl, de maintenir la définition classique de la vérité comme l'*adequatio*, non plus de la chose avec l'esprit, mais de l'intuition avec le concept. Lorsque, dans des cas d'ailleurs exceptionnels, l'intuition remplit sans reste le concept, on parlera d'évidence, d'expérience subjective pleine de la vérité; dans la plupart des autres cas, on admettra qu'un remplissement seulement partiel du concept par l'intuition suffit à valider la connaissance, selon un régime commun de phénoménalité. Mais tant Kant que Husserl semblent omettre une troisième figure du rapport entre intuition et concept: le cas, après tout lui aussi possible et pensable, où l'intuition déborderait la capacité explicative du concept, au lieu de lui rester égale ou inférieure. Dans ce cas, il ne audrait plus parler d'un phénomène formel, ni d'un phénomène pauvre en intuition (un objet *dématérialisé*, sans ὕλη), ni d'un phénomène commun (partiellement validé par un déficit d'intution), mais d'un phénomène *saturé* d'intuition. Or de tels phénomènes, même si leur phénoménalité se caractérise par un excès exceptionnel (l'intuition s'y *excepte* des limites du concept), n'ont rien que de banal et fréquent dans notre expérience. On en peut distinguer au moins quatre types.—Premièrement, l'événement, qui advient dans l'intuition surabondante de l'histoire, sans qu'aucun concept n'en ait prévu la possibilité et la pensabilité, au point qu'il peut rester, bien après son arrivée effective, inconcevable, impensable et au sens strictement métaphysique du terme, impossible (aussi réclame-t-il l'herméneutique infinie des historiens et des romanciers).—Deuxièmement, l'idole ou l'excès de la qualité sensible, qui déborde ce que les organes de la perception peuvent recevoir et traiter, provoquant l'éblouissement visuel ou sonore, ou de tout autre des cinq sens (la peinture et la musique sont ici concernées au premier chef).—Troisièmement, la chair, ou plus exactement *ma* chair, en tant que j'y fais l'épreuve du sentir se sentant lui-même, c'est-à-dire non plus d'un corps physique (que je sens sans que qu'il ne me sente, et qui donc me reste externe), mais de l'auto-affection (où je me sens me sentir et même me sentir me sentir), qui provoque l'épreuve de soi, l'expérience *du soi*. Ma chair n'admet plus aucun concept, ni n'entre en relation avec rien d'autre qu'elle-même, parce qu'elle s'identifie à et par soi seule (ici se jouent les phénomènes qui l'ont assimilée à la «vie», donc à la mort et à la souffrance, à l'individualité, donc à l'inconscience de soi).—Enfin, le visage d'autrui (ou bien l'icône), tel qu'il se soustrait à la visibilité inerte d'un objet subsistant dans le monde, et même à la présence utilisable d'un étant disponible pour mes finalités, c'est-à-dire tel qu'il devient invisible (n'offrant rien à voir à mon regard intentionnel), mais en revanche me parle, puisqu'il me provoque et convoque par une intentionnalité retournée, qui va désormais de lui vers moi. L'icône ouvre ainsi l'espace de l'éthique, mais sans doute aussi d'autres lieux—tous ceux où je ne dispose pas du concept pour régir le phénomène, mais, dans le meilleur des cas, le reçois comme un impératif.

Cet élargissement ne consiste plus seulement ici en une herméneutique de phénomènes déjà visibles et reçus (les transcrivant de l'objectivité à l'événementialité), mais en l'*invention* des phénomènes saturés, jusqu'alors méconnus en vertu même de leur excès d'évidence. Etrangement, ce qui rend les phénomènes saturés malaisés à admettre ne vient pas d'une difficulté à les expérimenter (car qui n'a pas expérimenté d'événement, sa propre chair, des idoles et le visage parlant d'autrui?), mais au contraire de la surabondance de l'intuition qui y rend inopérant le concept, sa délimitation et sa rationalité finie. Ces phénomènes se dissimulent dans l'éblouissement que provoque leur excès d'intuition. Par éblouissement, on entendra ici non seulement la douleur des yeux qui ne peuvent plus regarder en face la lumière excessive, mais aussi l'épreuve de ne plus pouvoir assigner un concept, ni même une identité à l'intuition donatrice, qui en fait ne donne plus rien qu'elle-même (comme dans un tableau de Turner la lumière dissout le contour des choses et absorbe toutes les formes dans son indistinction submergeante), sans déposer derrière elle, quand elle se retire enfin, aucune figure définie de quoi que ce *soit*. En sorte que le phénomène saturé ne s'offre à aucune expérience directe, parce qu'il ne fournit aucun *objet* d'expérience (ainsi dans le cas de l'icône ou du visage), ni même, souvent, aucun étant présent en permanence (en particulier dans les cas de l'événement ou de ma chair): au mieux, il permet une contre-expérience. Contre-expérience veut dire une expérience, mais indirecte: l'expérience du reflux sur moi de l'intuition, masquant dans ce reflux même l'identité et la forme de ce qui se retire et ne se fait plus connaître que par la résistance qu'il m'impose, à moi et à mon regard intentionnel, désormais privé de tout objet intentionnel, de toute signification visée. Pour autant, la contre-expérience atteste d'autant mieux l'effective présence du phénomène saturé, qu'elle en rend le concept inaccessible: il ne nous est jamais possible de douter du fait d'un phénomène saturé, précisément parce qu'il ne nous est jamais possible de ne pas douter de sa signification. Et ces paradoxes s'exercent avec encore plus de force, lorsque l'on combine les quatre types de phénomènes saturés, pour approcher la phénoménalité des phénomènes de révélation (et ainsi reprendre à nouveaux frais, non plus métaphysiques, mais *phénoménologiques* en un sens nouveau, la question de la manifestation du divin, voire de Dieu).

Au-delà d'une herméneutique et de l'invention de la saturation, on peut encore envisager un troisième élargissement de la phénoménalité: le domaine des *certitudes négatives*. En effet, le motif fondamental de la limitation de la connaissance au champ des objets consiste, on l'a vu, dans le privilège accordé à la certitude. Mais ce privilège n'imposerait aucune limitation au champ de la connaissance, si, plus originairement, il ne s'agissait d'une connaissance finie, la nôtre. Parce que finie, notre connaissance n'atteint la certitude qu'à condition de pouvoir produire des objets, aux lieu et place des choses; or, comme une telle production ne peut se réaliser partout ni dans tous les cas, en particulier pas quand la déréalisation (la dématérialisation) s'avère impraticable (par exemple dans les cas d'excès d'intuition, de phénomènes saturés), le champ de la certitude se trouve lui aussi borné. La finitude de la connaissance, plus exactement la finitude du connaissant, conduit à borner la certitude. Ou plutôt, il ne se trouve de certitude, quelle qu'elle soit, positive ou négative, ample ou bornée, que pour autant que la finitude elle-même la rend possible. Dans cette situation, deux questions peuvent se poser.—On pourrait d'abord demander s'il va de soi que toute connaissance doive ambitionner de devenir une connaissance *certaine*, et si, au contraire, nombre de connaissances non seulement ne peuvent atteindre la certitude, mais ne le *doivent* pas, puisqu'une telle certitude contredirait ce qu'il s'agit de connaitre. Il en va ainsi chaque fois qu'il s'agit de connaître ce qui, en tant que tel, implique une indétermination essentielle. Par exemple la connaissance d'autrui ne devrait, à la fin, jamais prétendre à la certitude, puisqu'autrui implique l'indétermination de sa liberté, faute de quoi il ne pourrait justement plus remplir le rôle, de mon *autre* autrui (et c'est pourquoi on parle, à tort mais constamment, d'une aporie de l'intersubjectivité, alors qu'il s'agit là, au contraire, la voie royale de tout accès à l'autre que moi). Il en va d'ailleurs de même pour la connaissance de soi (l'homme échappe par définition à toute définition et perdrait son humanité si, en la définissant, on l'exposait à se la voir déniée), voire pour la connaissance de Dieu (qui implique par définition l'incompréhensibilité, au point qu'un Dieu compréhensible sombrerait immédiatement au rang d'une évidente idole). De telles connaissances peuvent bien se décrire comme non-certaines, mais non pas se réputer pour autant comme *in*-certaines, parce que l'indétermination joue ici le rôle d'une qualification *positive* de ce qu'il s'agit de connaître, et ne sombre pas en une disqualification de son mode de connaissance. En un mot, la certitude constitue parfois un *obstacle* à la connaissance vraie de certains phénomènes.

En supposant même que l'exigence de certitude ne souffre ni exception, ni contestation, une deuxième question ne s'en poserait pas moins: faut-il toujours, pour connaître avec certitude, énoncer un jugement affirmatif? Ne pourrait-on pas aussi trouver des certitudes dans des connaissances négatives? Il se trouve en effet au moins une excellente raison d'introduire en philosophie le concept de *certitude négative*—le statut transcendental de la connaissance lui-même. Car si la connaissance finie définit du même coup les conditions finies de la possibilité (et donc de l'impossibilité) des objets de la connaissances, il devient non seulement pensable, mais aussi inévitable de déterminer a priori ce qui peut se connaître et ce qui ne le peut pas, et même les questions qui ne peuvent pas et ne pourront a priori jamais recevoir de réponse. Des questions *nécessairement* sans réponse ne doivent (et ne peuvent d'ailleurs) pas toujours être disqualifiées comme des questions mal posées; il arrive au contraire qu'elles se posent très correctement et qu'ainsi même elles fassent apparaître l'impossibilité de principe de la moindre réponse affirmative; réputer toujours dépourvues de sens des questions auxquelles nous ne trouvons aucune réponse témoigne non seulement souvent d'une parfaite mauvaise foi, mais exerce aussi un déni de finitude, qui contredit la revendication apparente de modestie et de scepticisme. Au contraire, si ce n'est pas « . . . par une faute de l'esprit, mais parce que s'y oppose la nature même de la difficulté ou bien la condition d'homme (*non ingenii culpa, sed quia obstat ipsius difficultatis natura, vel humana conditio*)» que l'on sait «*certo*, certainement» ne pouvoir répondre à une question, alors cette connaissance « . . . n'est pas une moindre connaissance, que celle qui découvrirait la nature de la chose en soi (*non minor scientia est, quam illa quae rei ipsius naturam exhibet*)».[21] Toute impossibilité en principe de répondre à une question bien conçue atteste, pour une raison finie, une certitude négative. Et, puisque cette négation même relève de la certitude a priori, elle constitue un élargissement *négatif et réel* des limites de la connaissance. Le relevé et l'analyse des certitudes négatives reste pour l'essentiel à faire, mais on ne peut douter qu'il ne s'en trouve de nombreuses.

Ainsi, précisément en vertu des élargissements indéfinis de la rationalité, la finitude s'attestera elle-même comme indéfinie, ou plus exactement comme positivement infinie. La mise au jour d'une telle *infinie finitude* constitue une tâche prioritaire de la philosophie, si elle veut surmonter le nihilisme en elle.

NOTES

1. *Critique de la Raison Pure*, B 25.
2. *Critique de la Raison Pure*, A 158 / B 197.
3. *Critique de la Raison Pure*, addition de B 33.
4. *Métaphysique E*, 2, 1027 b13–14.
5. Kepler reprend cette formule de Plutarque, qui l'attribue à Platon (*Quaestiones Conviviales* VIII,2) dans le *Mysterium Cosmographicum*, II et dans l'*Harmonice Mundi* V,3 (voir *Gesammelte Werke*, éd. M. Caspar, Munich, 1939sq., respectivement Bd.I, 26 et Bd.VI, 299).
6. Note manuscrite au *Dialogus de connexione inter res et verba et veritatis realitate*, in *Philosophischen Scriften*, éd. Gerhardt, t.7, 199.
7. *Regulae ad directionem ingenii*, II, AT X, 365,16–18;
8. *Discours de la Méthode*, AT VI,14,1.
9. *Critique de la Raison Pure*, B XVII).
10. *Discours de la Méthode*, AT VI, 62,7–8.
11. *Regulae ad directionem ingenii*, II, AT X, 418, 1–2.

12. *Nachgelassene Fragmente*, 11 [411], éd. G.Colli and M.Montinari, *Nietzsche Werke*, Bd. VIII,1, Berlin, 1970, p. 431.

13. *Critique de la Raison Pure*, B XXIV

14. *Expérience et jugement*, §1, [Prague, 1939], éd. L. Landgrebe, Hambourg, 1964, p. 3.

15. *Ainsi parlait Zarathoustra*, I, 4, «De ceux qui méprisent la chair».

16. *Critique de la Raison Pure*, A 290.

17. *Sein und Zeit* §7,38,35.

18. *Ideen zur einen reinen Phänomenologie*, I, §24, Hua.III, 52.

19. *Critique de la Raison Pure*, B132

20. *Critique de la Raison Pure*, A50/B74

21. *Regulae ad directionem ingenii*, VIII, AT X, 393,15–21.

Rethinking Art and Philosophy of Art: Some Preliminary Remarks

GERHARD SEEL
UNIVERSITÄT BERN

Abstract: As an introduction to the plenary session "Metaphysics and Aesthetics" in my article I try to describe the state of philosophy of art today and give an outlook to its future development. In the last century analytical philosophy of art has been occupied with the following four questions: What is the essence of art? What is the ontological status of works of art? What are aesthetic qualities and how do we come to know them? Have aesthetic value judgments objective validity? In the first step I explain why analytical philosophy of art failed to answer these questions and what this failure has to do with the end of art. In the second step I attempt to give a definition of art myself which allows to show that this failure and the end of art were inevitable. Finally I try—as a consequence—to define the general features of the art of the future.

As you know—the main theme of this congress is 'Rethinking Philosophy today.' The organizing committee thought that philosophy needs urgently a reorientation of its tasks, aims, and methods—and rightly so. Because—as I put in one of my papers[1]—on the one hand philosophy is going through a deep crisis of identity today and on the other hand people expect it to become a source of hope and inspiration. Though the whole congress will follow this line of reflection on philosophy it is first and foremost the four plenary sessions and the five symposia that are in charge of achieving this.

Our plenary session today has the special aim of rethinking Metaphysics and Aesthetics. Before I ask our prominent speakers to give their views and proposals on this subject let me try to draw a sketchy picture of the situation we find ourselves in. For, before projecting the way one wants to go it is always judicious to determine precisely the place one has to start from.

Special Supplement, *Journal of Philosophical Research* pp. 77–84
DOI: 10.5840/jpr201237Supplement27

I

During the second half of the last century analytic philosophy of art and aesthetics was occupied mostly with the following questions:

1. What is the essence of art?
2. What is the ontological status of works of art?
3. What are aesthetic qualities and how do we come to know them?
4. Have aesthetic value judgments objective validity?

Now, it seems clear to me that the answers to be given to question (3) and question (4) depend on the answer we give to the first and second questions. Concerning these, philosophy of art suffered two severe reversals, which marked the end of the last century and which are considered by some as true disasters. One occurred in philosophy itself and the other occurred in the arts. The disaster of the philosophers was to have to admit their complete failure in determining the essence of art, the disaster of the artists, or rather of those who make money with art, was the so-called 'end of art' or more precisely the end of the history of art. Both disasters are narrowly linked one to the other and in the same time they contradict each other in a paradoxical way. Let me explain this in a few lines.

1. Since Plato, philosophers have tried to determine the essence of art and the essences of the different kinds of art. But the answers they have traditionally given came under challenge when the arts changed radically, first with the development of abstract art and later with Duchamps's 'fountain' and Andy Wharhole's ready-mades. Under this challenge Nelson Goodman[2] had already diagnosed that the philosophers posed the wrong question. Instead of asking 'what is art?' they should ask 'when is art?' Arthur Danto[3] made a further step declaring that 'everything can be art.' Now, if this is correct, there is no essence of art to be found by philosophers any more, or to put it in a paradoxical way: the essence of art is to lack any essence.[4]

2. At the same time Arthur Danto,[5] following Hans Belting,[6] propounded 'the end of the history of art.' This seems to be the consequence of the fact that art has no essence. For history presupposes that some identifiable entity makes progress toward an end it has in virtue of its essence. So, according to Danto (*After the End of Art*, 136), the history of art was in its first lap the history of the progress in the representation of the real world. This presupposes the conception of art as 'mimesis.' It was in its second lap the progress in the representation of art itself and of its means (ibid., 66). This implies that art is conceived of as a kind of self-reflection. However, as soon as everything can be art and thereby art has lost any essential determination, there is no way any more to make progress in achieving what art is conceived to be. The inevitable consequence is the end of the history of art. It is important to emphasize that the end of the history of art was not brought about by philosophy but by art itself. For it was artists like Duchamps and Warhol who by their works made it clear that everything can be art.

However we have a problem here. If it is the essence of art to have no essence and if thus history of art is impossible, how does it come that we assisted in reality to a history of art that lasted for centuries and is the true object of the endeavour of historians of art? In my view, there is only one way out of this dilemma (Seel, "Wesen der Kunst," 139–141). I found it by reflecting on the role philosophy played in the history of art. Right from the beginning the understanding artists had of what they were doing was largely influenced by what philosophers said about what art had to be. Maybe, at some time artists liked to make imitations of reality, but it was only because some prominent philosophers had defined the essence of art as mimesis that artists, instead of inventing ever new games, engaged in the unique endeavor to bring mimesis to perfection—or in Arthur Danto's words, to produce 'increasingly adequate representations of the world' (*After the End of Art*, 136). This endeavor marked a long period of artistic creation and gave rise to the first type of History of Art. Even when at the end of this period artists began to make art about art, to reflect on the material conditions of making art, it was still the model of philosophy as reflecting on its own conditions and philosophical conceptions of art that were initiating and guiding the new period of the history of art. Finally when at the beginning of the twentieth century one avant-garde chased the other, each convinced to have found the true art, the real motor of this avalanche of radical changes in art was the philosophical idea that there is an essence of art and accordingly that there was only one true art which had to be found if it did not exist already.

The conclusion to be drawn from this is that—until the end of the century—art has proceeded on a misunderstanding of its own nature, caused by past philosophy, and that this misunderstanding made 'history' possible. The history of art was nothing but the attempt to actualize an incorrectly understood 'essence' of art, and the end of art turns out to be the end of this misunderstanding, which has been denounced by art itself and thereby overcome. Thus the end of the history of art coincides with the discovery of the true nature of art. Hence art has come to itself through itself. Philosophy can only take note of that and attempt to explain it.

This is the reason why the end of the history of art is final. Once the misunderstanding that made history possible was discovered and overcome there is no ground for historical development anymore. For the very same reason philosophy does not rule over art anymore and by the same token philosophers have lost their say concerning the future of art. All we can do is wait for the new art. Art is definitely free from the pale of history, the bounds of essence and the rule of philosophy.

II

What does this situation mean for the task of philosophy of art today? Has it become completely superfluous and out of order? Should we renounce saying anything about the essence of art?

I think the first lesson we have learned is that philosophy should renounce dictating to artists what they should do. The enfranchisement of art has to be total and universally recognized. Paradoxically, this is the consequence of a correct determination of the essence of art, philosophy has to acknowledge in the light of the events described above. But how can the reflection on the essence of art come to the conclusion that art has no essence?

Actually, for reasons that I cannot develop here,[7] I am convinced that art is a close cousin, not of searching for truth or striving for moral goodness, but of loving to play. Art, like playing, is an activity we engage in just for the sake of itself and the pleasure we earn from it. This pleasure is in both cases the offspring of the experience of our mastership, good fortune and success in the fulfillment of difficult tasks and endeavors.[8] However these tasks and endeavors are not imposed on the player or the artist from outside, they are her free choice. The freedom of choice is threefold: first of all it concerns the invention of the rules of the play and the agreement upon them, secondly it concerns the participation in the play, and last but not least it concerns the choice of strategies and solutions found out to fulfill the tasks of the play in the most elegant way possible.

For this reason art plays a decisive role in the search for the meaning of life. We do not live in order to work; we work in order to make a living.[9] And the sense of the latter is to allow us to do what we want to do for its own sake. Enjoying art is the activity par excellence we do for its own sake. How boring would our lives be without the pleasures of art and play?

This is in outline my answer to the first question of philosophy of art mentioned above. If I am right in this, the end of art does not make philosophy of art meaningless. On the contrary, my definition opens a way to answer the three other questions as well.

As for the second question, I don't think that all items that normally are considered as works of art have the same ontological status. We have to distinguish at least the following three kinds: (1) Paintings, sculptures, buildings, parks, and so forth; (2) festivals, happenings, concerts, theater performances, readings, shows, and so forth; (3) texts, films, scripts, scores, and so forth. Works of the first kind are individual substances. Aesthetical qualities supervene on the physical properties of these substances according to a given aesthetical context. Works of the second kind are individual events that follow specific aesthetical rules. The third kind of works of art consists of abstract objects, i.e., types the tokens of which are works of the second kind. It is clear that—according to my concept of art—works of the second kind are the core of art, the other play only an auxiliary—though very important—role.

To answer my third and fourth questions I take advantage of the analogy between works of art and games. Games are constituted by a combination of three kinds of rules: (1) semantic rules, (2) rules that allow or forbid certain kinds actions, (3) task-setting rules. The first establish game-relative significations by convention. In soccer, for instance, they fix what kind of action is 'scoring a goal'; what kind of space is a 'soccer field,' what kind of actor is a 'player' etc.

This explains the supervenience of certain types of non-physical properties on types of physical properties. The second and the third kinds of rules allow us to answer the question about the objectivity of aesthetic value judgments. The third kind of rules set certain tasks for the players of the game, for instance to score as much goals as possible and to prevent the adversary from doing the same. The second kind of rules makes this task difficult by, for instance, forbidding touching the ball with the hand. These two kinds of rules are the standards by which an observer can determine whether a player did play well or not. These value judgments are relative to these conventionally fixed rules, but nevertheless objective. Now, if the analogy between arts and games holds,[10] i.e., if a style is nothing but a set of rules of the three kinds, we can easily explain the supervenience of aesthetic properties on physical properties and justify the objectivity of style-relative aesthetic value judgments.[11]

The analogy between games and arts throws also new light on works of art of the first kind. To play a certain game we need a certain kind of playground and a certain kind of tools. The same is true of the second kind of works of art. In order to execute a certain kind of aesthetic activity we need an adequate space and we need adequate tools. Works of art of the first kind are exactly these spaces and tools. For parks and buildings, when they are made for a specific aesthetic function, are the places where we engage in aesthetic activities, and paintings and sculptures are the tools and toys we use in these activities.

III

Let me add a few remarks on the future of art. As I said at the outset, philosophy should renounce dictating what artists should do. This doesn't mean, however, that philosophers have no right to reflect on art and on its future. They even have the duty to do so. So, what appears to be the future of art in the light of what we said about the essence of art and the history of art? I see the following four characteristics of the new art as the inevitable consequence of the end of the history of art—for the most part they have already been diagnosed by Arthur Danto:[12]

A. The age of avant-garde is over.

B. The new art will be 'historic' in a new sense.

C. The new art will be pluralistic.

D. The new art will be esoteric

Let me explain what I mean by these characteristics.

A. The Age of Avant-garde Art Is Over

The first consequence of the end of the history of art is the fact that avant-gardes have lost their role as motors of historical progress. At the end of the nineteenth and during the twentieth century each new self-declared avant-garde articulated and justified the need for overcoming the dominant style and replacing it by a new one. This used to be achieved through the refusal of the rules and canons of the old style and the establishment of new rules and canons for the creative activity of the artists belonging to the avant-garde group. The most spectacular way to make such a revolution was the publication of a 'manifesto,' i.e., a text where the avant-garde articulated its condemnation of the old art and defined its new way of creating art, often declaring that the new art was the only true art. However, the establishment of new rules and canons was not necessarily done by explicit theoretical statements—as in the case of the manifestos—but could also be achieved through the new works of art themselves, which as examples and models implicitly established new rules and canons. During the twentieth century the toppling and replacement of one avant-garde by the next dramatically quickened its pace. At the end one could see the arrival of a new avant-garde nearly every year. This, as I said, has come to an end. Notwithstanding the emergence of radically new styles and the claim of each new group of artist to be the new avant-garde there will be no new avant-garde anymore.

What is the reason for this bold statement? Why should we refuse to these groups the status of an avant-garde? The decisive difference between these groups and a true avant-garde is that the latter—like the determining negation in Hegel's philosophy—presupposes the existence of a preceding style being part of the same history, the same 'narrative' in Arthur Danto's words, in such a way that the negation of it can be understood as a progress. After the end of history no change can be considered as a progress, even not the most radical new inventions. So, even if one style excludes the other and thus is a negation of it, this negation doesn't call for a synthesis. It is not a necessary step in a history that progresses toward an ideal state. This applies to art as well.

B. The New Art Will Be 'Historic' In a New Sense of This Word

The next and the most surprising point is that from now on the term 'art' has no fixed semantics anymore. What the term designs is historically relative though, or rather because, art itself has lost its historicity. In his article "The Work of Art and the Historical Future,"[13] Arthur Danto explains what he means by this: that which can be counted as art at one definite time is no longer art or not yet art at another. In the first place, every artwork has its essence and its worth only in the context of the 'narrative' to which it belongs. However—and this was Arthur Danto's surprising demonstration—artworks, that have their history, can leave it behind them, plunge into a new history and begin a new career.

This means also that history has lost its respectability. The imperatives of historical authenticity, of playing Shakespeare in an imitation of the globe-theatre, of performing Bach's music on historically authentic instruments, are no longer considered as means of finding the historically true meaning of these works of art, but as just one among many ways of playing postmodern games with artworks of the past. These artworks, though belonging in a specific historical context, get the chance of ever new careers. Past history becomes a playground and a quarry for today's art.

C. The New Art Will Be Pluralistic

Here again I follow Arthur Danto's penetrating diagnosis. In a passage from *Beyond the Brillo Box* (229) he declares that the age after the end of art "would be a period then of *deep* Pluralism."

What does Arthur Danto mean by '*deep* pluralism'? He certainly recognizes that art has always displayed a plurality of genres, of styles, and of epochs. However, in the age of history this plurality was organized in a predominantly vertical way. One style followed the other. To be sure the different genres were contemporaneous with one another. Therefore we cannot deny that there was also a kind of horizontal plurality. However, the historians of the visual arts, of literature, and of music are amazed to see how much these genres have in common in each epoch. They speak for instance of baroque painting, baroque architecture, baroque literature, and baroque music. Therefore this plurality is not a deep plurality in Arthur Danto's sense. Deep pluralism means that renaissance, baroque and romantic art exist at the same time. There is no way to organize them in a temporal order of progress, none has precedence over the other, and each has the same right to exist as the other.

D. The New Art Will Be Exoteric

This characteristic is closely linked to what I said about pluralism. For 'pluralism' means plurality of self-sufficient styles. I have defined the term 'style' as a set of rules and canons that a group of artists commonly agree upon.[14] As we have seen before, in the age of history these rules and canons were conceived by every member of the art world as either reactionary and out-of-date or revolutionary and progressive. This divide presupposes a common conception of the overall goal of historic progress. As soon as this is lacking—and it is lacking after the end of history—the difference between reactionary and progressive disappears as well. Therefore, after the end of art, the differences between the styles are no more the proper object of a common evaluation. On the contrary, those who engage in one style will disregard all the others. Furthermore, only those who appreciate a style and follow it will be able to judge the artistic value of the artistic performances and achievements in the frame of it. They will be the only members of the art world who can understand the art of that specific style, the only who will take pleasure in it. Art will be created for these limited groups of 'connoisseurs' and not for humanity as a whole. This means that the art-world itself will split into as many art-worlds, as there are styles.

A comparison with the world of sport and games can again help us to understand this radical change in the art world. We see today a panoply of different sports and games. Each has its own fans and supporters, which normally know the rules, the heroes and the history of their own favorite sport, but know little about the others or ignore them totally. As a consequence, the fans take pleasure only in practicing and watching their favorite sport and find the others rather boring. The same will happen in the art-world. Art will more and more become the concern of insiders and will exclude the rest. In other words, the more art will emancipate itself, the more it will become esoteric.

NOTES

1. Gerhard Seel, "Wozu Philosophie?," in *Studia Philosophica* 66 (2007): 29–45.

2. Nelson Goodman, *Ways of Worldmaking* (Indianapolis: Hackett Pub. Co., 1978), p. 57.

3. Arthur Danto, *After the End of Art* (Princeton, NJ: Princeton University Press, 1997), p. 114.

4. For my arguments, see Gerhard Seel, "Wesen der Kunst—Geschichte der Kunst, Eine unerwartete Begegnung," in *End of Art—Endings in Art*, ed. Gerhard Seel (Basel: Schwabe, 2006), pp. 117–141; and Gerhard Seel, "Kunstwerke als Spielzeuge und Spielplätze," in *Selected Papers of the 15th International Congress of Aesthetics*, Tokyo 2003, ed. Kiyokazu Nishimura, Ken-ichi Iwaki, Tanehisa Otabe, Ken-ichi Sasaki and Eske Tsugami, pp. 383–395.

5. Arthur Danto, "Approaching the End of Art," in Arthur Danto, *The State of the Art* (New York: Prentice Hall Press, 1987); Arthur Danto, "Narratives of the End of Art," in Arthur Danto, *Encounters and Reflections: Art in the Historical Present* (New York: Farrar, Straus & Giroux, 1991).

6. Hans Belting, *Das Ende der Kunstgeschichte?* (München: Deutscher Kunstverlag, 1983), English translation: *The End of the History of Art* (Chicago: University of Chicago Press, 1987); Hans Belting, *Das Ende der Kunstgeschichte: Eine Revision nach zehn Jahren* (München: Beck, 1995).

7. See Gerhard Seel, "Wesen der Kunst—Geschichte der Kunst," pp. 120–134.

8. Compare Gerhard Seel, "Pourquoi l'art nous procure-t-il du plaisir?," in *Revue de théologie et de philosophie* 116 (1984): 275–296.

9. Compare Gerhard Seel, "L'homme a-t-il un droit au travail?," in *Annales 1982–1983 de l'Université de Neuchâtel*: 294–308.

10. For my arguments in favor of this analogy, see Seel, "Kunstwerke als Spielzeuge und Spielplätze," pp. 388–390.

11. Compare Gerhard Seel, "'Cochez votre oeuvre d'art préférée!'—Peut-on déterminer la valeur esthétique d'une œuvre par le suffrage universel?," in *Juger l'art?*, ed. Chr. Genin, Cl. Leroux et A.Lontrade (Paris: Publications de la Sorbonne, 2009), pp. 135–149.

12. See Arthur Danto, *Beyond the Brillo Box: The Visual Arts in Post-historical Perspective* (New York: Farrar Straus Giroux, 1992); and Arthur Danto, *After the End of Art: Contempory Art and the Pale of History* (Princeton, NJ: Princeton University Press, 1997).

13. Arthur Danto, "The Work of Art and the Historical Future," in Gerhard Seel, *End of Art—Endings in Art* (Basel: Schwabe 2006), 93–114.

14. Seel, "Kunstwerke als Spielzeuge und Spielplätze," p. 389; and Seel, "Wesen der Kunst—Geschichte der Kunst," pp. 130–131.

Rethinking Philosophy of Science Today

EVANDRO AGAZZI
UNIVERSIDAD AUTÓNOMA METROPOLITANA MEXICO CITY

Abstract: Modern philosophy of science was, initially, an epistemology of science based on the logical analysis of the language of science. It was superseded by a "sociological epistemology," according to which the acceptance of scientific statements and theories depends on conditionings coming from the social context and powers, and this view has fueled anti-scientific attitudes.

This happened because the sociological turn still expressed an epistemology of science. Science, however, is not only a system of knowledge, but also a complex human activity. Hence, ethical, political, social, religious issues appear legitimate if they concern "doing science."

Therefore, we must "rethink" philosophy of science, accepting in it also an axiology of science that could enable us to retain the cognitive value of science and at the same time to make techno-scientific activity compatible with the satisfaction of a great variety of values that inspire our societies.

PHILOSOPHY OF SCIENCE AS A SPECIALIZED BRANCH OF PHILOSOPHY

In the present paper we shall understand philosophy of science according to its contemporary meaning, that is, not in the general sense of a "philosophical reflection on science," but as the denomination of a specialized branch of philosophy, as a specific philosophical discipline that has acquired also an academic and professional status. Indeed a reflection on science has been present along the whole history of Western philosophy and the very concept of science has undergone a considerable historical evolution (e.g., the most perfect example of science was in antiquity metaphysics, while today it is probably physics). Traditional reflections were not devoted, so to speak, "thematically," to the study of science or of the sciences, but were rather the application to certain sciences of a general discourse,

Special Supplement, *Journal of Philosophical Research* pp. 85–101
DOI: 10.5840/jpr201237Supplement28

usually regarding theory of knowledge, or ontology, because the attention paid to science was only a part of a much broader philosophical conception or "system" in which the interpretation of science found its proper place.

Contemporary philosophy of science, instead, is a philosophical investigaton that is concerned thematically, specifically, and almost exclusively with a single subject matter, science (or some science), and employs intellectual means that are taken from certain sectors of philosophy, but are used as tools for the understanding of science and only to the extent that they are so used. The traditional perspective is somehow reversed: instead of considering a certain "kind of objects" (a certain ontological domain) and trying to see what features should have a science aiming at suitably investigating them, the present way of reasoning consists in analyzing the features of a given science and then trying to infer what kind of ontological reality (if any) could be attributed to the objects if this science. Or, similarly, instead of considering logic as a well established philosophical discipline and trying to see how the arguments used in a given science could be made "logically rigorous," the present tendency is rather that of elaborating, if necessary, a special "logic" tailored to the needs of a given scientific discipline (e.g., quantum logic, non-monotonic logics).

This phenomenon is relatively recent, since one can consider philosophy of science to be born at the beginning of the twentieth century, as a result of two principal factors. The first is the exceptional growth of the natural sciences and mathematics within Western culture during the eighteenth and nineteenth centuries, that had promoted science to a top position in the social and cultural estimation such that it had to attract the interest of philosophy; the second is a serious crisis that affected the exact sciences precisely toward the end of the nineteenth century. It is rather common in the history of philosophy that rethinking or rebirth of certain sectors have been stimulated by the occurrence of a certain crisis, from epistemology to ethics, from political philosophy to metaphysics or aesthetics. In the case of science, we can say that Kant's Critique of Pure Reason had promoted the cognitive model of the physical-mathematical science to the role of paradigm of knowledge as such and, at the same time, had reinforced the "classical" conception of science as a knowledge endowed with absolute certainty, based on the clarity of empirical evidence and intellectual intuition, not less than on the rigor of logical demonstrations. It is precisely this highly ideal model of science that underwent a crisis toward the end of the nineteenth century, a crisis whose comprehension and solution powerfully stimulated the constitution of a specialized sector of philosophical reflection, that is, philosophy of science in its modern sense.

THE CRISIS OF CLASSICAL MATHEMATICS

At the beginning of the nineteenth century, the "working mathematicians" also began to feel in trouble when using, without a sufficient conceptual clarification, such fundamental concepts of analysis as those of infinite, infinitesimal, continuity, function, while in the domain of geometry the old problem of the "Euclidean postulate" was also knowing a significant revival of discussions. In such a way a generalized concern took shape regarding what was later called the "problem of foundations" of mathematics that fuelled during the whole century conspicuous investigations aiming at granting again to mathematical knowledge those self-evident and uncontroversial grounds that could justify the certainty that has been its traditional distinctive mark. Toward the end of the nineteenth century it seemed that set-theory could offer the ultimate ground on which it is possible to logically "construct" the whole building of mathematics, while Frege had come to a similar result following an independent path, that is, by relying on the notion of "class" (not really different from that of "set"), which he considered as purely logical, and claiming in such a way that it was possible to reduce mathematics to logic. But at this point the crisis of the foundations of mathematics exploded, because several antinomies (that is, insoluble contradictions) could be formulated in set-theory and the theory of classes by an unrestricted use of certain apparently "self-evident" principles.

A crisis of the mathematical evidence had also been the outcome of the critical investigations in the domain of geometry. After having abandoned the centuries-old series of frustrating efforts for proving directly the Euclidean postulate from the other unproblematic "evident" postulates of traditional geometry, the new strategy had been adopted to prove it indirectly, by showing that an internal contradiction affected those anti-intuitive geometrical systems obtained by admitting a negation of the Euclidean postulate. But such an internal contradiction could never be discovered and internal consistency was gradually taken as the only criterion of legitimacy for a mathematical theory. This process entailed a deep reconsideration of the axiomatic method, that had been the cornerstone of classical mathematics and of classical science in general, and required that a science be deductively constructed starting from immediately true (or evident) axioms. In the modern perspective, the axioms were reduced to the simple role of "primitive propositions," with no requirement of evidence or truth and, in addition, as "devoid of meaning" and, at most, susceptible of "receiving" a meaning according to different possible interpretations. Once this view is generalized to the conception of every mathematical theory, it follows that no such theory is concerned with the investigation of "its own" domain of objects, and that the requirement of non-contradiction (or "consistency") is the only limitation to the arbitrary construction of axiomatic systems.

All these are well-known historical facts, that show how the "foundational crisis" immediately imposed a series of epistemological and methodological problems, regarding the soundness of what had been considered along the whole history of Western civilization the most perfect example of solid knowledge, endowed with truth, certainty, absolute logical rigor. Therefore, the general conviction was that such a crisis should have a solution, and it is interesting to note that the diagnosis and therapies proposed for overcoming that crisis depended on different ontological conceptions regarding the "kind of existence" of the mathematical objects. For example, the so-called logicists and platonists (such as Frege and Russell) thought that logical and mathematical objects have an actual existence in themselves, and that antinomies only depend on our way of speaking of them; therefore, we must find the remedy in a suitable rigorization of our language (this is the spirit of the Russellian theory of logical types). Intuitionists (such as Brouwer), on the other hand, believed that antinomies were the consequence of having admitted the consideration of actually infinite sets, whereas in mathematics only such entities exist that can be constructed by means of finitely examinable operations. Other scholars believed that the root of the antinomies was the confidence in the content of seemingly "evident" intellectual intuitions, so that a strictly formal axiomatization of all the branches of mathematics (including set theory) should be realized, followed by the proof that no contradiction could be formally derived from such axiomatic systems. The idea that non-contradiction was the necessary and sufficient condition for mathematical existence was at least implicit in this position (called formalism), but the problem was how to prove such a consistency. Hilbert's "programme" was that of showing such a consistency by systematically investigating the proofs realizable in certain axiomatic systems. From a strictly formal point of view they consist in finite manipulations of finite strings of signs according to a finite set of rules, and it seemed reasonable that, through a finite exploration of these possible manipulations, one could obtain the consistency proof at least of the simplest of the mathematically interesting axiomatic systems (that of elementary arithmetic). The famous "Gödel's theorem" of 1931, however, proved the impossibility of such a result and entailed many consequences in various fields.

The short survey outlined here indicates what were the origins of a specialized philosophy of mathematics that flourished along the twentieth century and whose themes regarded the ontology of mathematical objects, the purport of the cognitive methods used in mathematics, the relations between consistency ad existence in mathematics, the meaning of the notion of mathematical truth, the relations between provability and truth, even the difference between human thinking and computer algorithmic functioning. These philosophical discussions have continued, around other topics, also when the impulse coming from the original "foundational schools" became exhausted, and philosophy of mathematics is a well-established sector of philosophy of science in its modern sense.

THE CRISIS OF CLASSICAL PHYSICS

In physics a foundational role similar to that of set-theory in mathematics had been attributed to mechanics, and a theoretical effort was displayed in the nineteenth century by several scientists in order to reduce to mechanics all the branches of physics, in the sense of showing that their fundamental concepts could be defined in terms of mechanical magnitudes, and their empirical laws could be deduced from mechanical laws and principles. The extreme difficulty (and finally the recognized incapability) of proposing correct mechanical interpretations and explanations of the second principle of thermodynamics, on the one hand, and of the electromagnetic field, on the other hand, already toward the end of that century started that "foundational crisis" in physics that was going to know its most dramatic manifestations at the beginning of the twentieth century with the birth of quantum mechanics and relativity theory. Without entering the (rather well-known) details of this crisis, we simply want to point out that the debates among scientists revealed from the start on a clear philosophical (especially epistemological) flavour: physical theories were considered as intellectual constructions intending to be "representations" of the material world but, while in the past they had been easily credited with this capacity, several doubts began to be advanced on this point, and certain authors, such as Mach, for instance, explicitly denied the cognitive purport of scientific theories giving them the simple role of "economically" useful schematizations for the organization of empirical data and for making some predictions. This anti-realist and instrumentalist conception of science was based on a clear philosophical presupposition, that is, radical empiricism that gives to the said crisis its more precise sense of the "crisis of visualizability" of the physical objects, that emerges when these objects appear to be unobservable entities that we try to understand through intuitive models.

Not only sensory intuition, however, was challenged by the advancements of physics. Also that which we could call intellectual intuition (i.e., the clarity not of the images but of the concepts) has been put in trouble by relativity and quantum physics. Let us simply mention the difficulty of coupling continuity and discontinuity in the interpretation of the microworld, the double representation as a particle and as a wave of one and the same microobject, the indeterminacy in the simultaneous attribution of values to conjugate magnitudes at the microlevel, the necessity of considering the mass and the spatial dimensions of a physical body not as its most inalterable intrinsic properties but as variables depending on its velocity, not to speak of the interdependence among two conceptually very distinct "entities" such as space and time and, finally, of the turn from a "deterministic" to a "probabilistic" conception of natural laws with the implicit reconsideration of the principle of causality.

These very well known facts have nourished in the first decades of the twentieth century ample and deep philosophical debates regarding physics in which not only the most prominent scientists of the time have participated, but also several philosophers with a sufficient knowledge of science. Debates that concerned themes of epistemology, ontology, metaphysics, philosophy of nature, methodology of science, and in which the most diverse philosophical positions have appeared. All this is a confirmation that a philosophy of physics has strongly developed out of the crisis of the foundations of physics and has powerfully contributed to the constitution of philosophy of science as a specialized branch of philosophy.

THE PREDOMINANCE OF LOGICAL EMPIRICISM

The subsequent developments of this new branch of philosophy soon acquired a particular direction, due to the fact that philosophy of science became almost monopolized by logical empiricism and the philosophical trends inspired by this movement. The members of the Vienna (and Berlin) Circles had in common the consideration of science as the only genuine form of knowledge and shared with the old positivism a clear antimetaphysical programme reinforced by the adoption of a radical empiricism. In addition they had received the influence of the "linguistic turn" that had characterized a large part of philosophy at the beginning of the century and reduced philosophy to analysis of language. As a consequence of these factors, those scholars conceived philosophy of science as an analysis of the language of science and, in particular, as a logical analysis, logic being understood by them in its most recent sense of mathematical logic with the strictly formalistic interpretation bound to this discipline. Especially the systematic use of such techniques gave to the writings of those people the appearance of a very rigorous and "scientific" exercise and of a kind of philosophical "neutrality" that facilitated the confluence in this stream of many scholars coming from several different countries and cultural traditions. When many of the most prominent representatives of this school went to the United States as a consequence of the nazi racial persecutions, they encountered there a favourable milieu for the expansion of their cultural programme and philosophy of science received that form of an "analytical philosophy of science" that has remained standard for several decades and has been practically considered as the only serious paradigm of this philosophy, to the extent that, after the end of the second world war, this model imposed itself also in Europe, where philosophy of science had found its cradle at the beginning of the century. A not negligible effect of this cultural phenomenon was the following: several important traditions in the philosophy of science that had developed outside the logical-empiricist and analytical line were thrown into the shade, up to the point that in the standard handbooks of philosophy of science (including those written by not English-speaking authors) one does not find the names not only of those great scientists who in the first decades of the twentieth century wrote not trivial things regarding philosophical problems of science, but also names such as those of Duhem, Poincaré, Meyerson, Bachelard, Gonseth, Dingler, Enriques, that is, of authors who explicitly wrote works of philosophy of science not limited to a logical-linguistic analysis of the discourse of science.

This philosophy of science, that we can call "analytical-empiricist" has produced an abundant harvest of publications and also a conspicuous amount of "results," among which the most significant are probably those obtained through a formal-logical analysis of certain metatheoretical properties regarding scientific theories (especially in the domain of mathematics, but also in that of the empirical sciences), such as the reducibility among theories, their mutual relations of consistency, the nature and power of the logical calculi most suitable for their formal treatment, the development of logical calculi for the formalization of the methodologies of empirical confirmation and so on. Less significant, however, seem to be several other results which, though being "correct," appear essentially as a proliferation of cases and subproblems more or less artificially extracted from more important publications, according to a practice common in the domain of the sciences and which corresponds rather well to what Kuhn calls the status of "normal science."

Since we have mentioned Kuhn, we can add that, according to his view (that we share at least partially here) normal science is that which grows up as a development of a given paradigm. In our case we can say that the analytical-empiricist philosophy of science developed under the shelter of the already mentioned paradigm, whose salient features were: the reduction of the sciences to linguistic constructions, radical empiricism as an epistemological presupposition, use of the methods and results of formal logic and philosophy of language as tools for the philosophical analysis. Under this very general umbrella we can encompass several positions characterized by not insignificant differences, such as, for instance, the whole line of the Popperian philosophy of science.

THE CRISIS OF THE ANALYTICAL-EMPIRICIST PHILOSOPHY OF SCIENCE

Kuhn's book The Structure of Scientific Revolutions (1962) is usually considered the work that inaugurated the post-empiricist philosophy of science, and this is to a certain extent true. One cannot overlook, however, that the decline of the preceding paradigm had been produced by internal reasons. The tenet of radical empiricism (i.e., the refusal of a cognitive value of the intellectual intuition) had imposed to the philosophers of science the task of logically "reducing" all theoretical components of the scientific language to an observational basis, but this enterprise (apart from its great technical difficulties) had been blocked by the doctrine of semantic holism defended by Quine, that maintained that all terms in science are "theory-laden" and in this sense theoretical. This thesis is typical of a philosophy of language that, wanting to skip the intellectual nature of meaning, had reduced it to the linguistic context, and was proving detrimental rather than useful for a satisfactory understanding of science. But also the "semantics" elaborated by mathematical logic proved equally inadequate. In fact such a semantics was also inspired by the desire of dispensing with the intellectual "meaning" and, therefore, proposed that the meaning of symbols be obtained by linking them (by means of an interpretation) with certain referents or sets of referents. This is the core of model theory which is a conspicuous part of mathematical logic. Precisely within this theory, however, it appeared that the methods proposed were unable to secure to any empirical theory its "intended model," that is, to justify the fact that it intends to speak about certain specific objects. In conclusion, all the fundamental components of the logical-analytic philosophy of science appeared inadequate for justifying the cognitive purport of science, and this was obviously frustrating for a philosophical school that has considered science as the most genuine and reliable form of knowledge.

But the most serious drawback was still another. The logical and methodological machinery elaborated within that paradigm—that showed serious flaws already regarding the correct understanding of the static structure of science—was absolutely inadequate for understanding the dynamics of science, that is, the transition from a theory to another one, the idea of scientific change and scientific progress, and this especially because the doctrine of the "theory-ladenness" of every scientific concept made impossible to adopt experiments as criteria for discriminating between rival theories. This explains the fortune and the cultural impact of Kuhn's book, that constituted a clear signal of a shifting of interest within philosophy of science from the study of the structure to the study of the dynamics of science, a shifting that, in particular, implied an overcoming of those investigations that, proposing themselves as a "logical reconstruction" of the cognitive structure of science in general, did in fact refer themselves to an extremely idealized and vague model that resembled more or less the presentation of classical physics that we find in schoolbooks. Instead of this vague model, the investigation of the dynamics of science must rely on the study of the concrete history of science, and see what are the real conditions that determine scientific change. In such a way a sociological approach to the understanding of science was emerging and was considered at variance with the logical and analytical approach. As a matter of fact, one could maintain that the two approaches can and should cooperate, once certain tenets of the "received view" are abandoned, but we cannot enter this discourse here.

THE SOCIOLOGICAL TURN

There is certainly no need to summarize here the well known view of science that Kuhn proposes as the outcome of a disenchanted consideration of its history. Scientific knowledge is no longer considered as the (possibly fallible) representation of the status of the physical world, acquired by the scrupulous adhesion from the side of scientists to the fundamental criteria of faithfulness to empirical evidence and logical consistency. Scientists are rather faithful to a paradigm, consisting of a variegated combination of general worldviews, accepted principles, methodological rules, conceptual frameworks, received theories of different sorts. It is within this paradigm that they apply the usual criteria of empirical testing and logical construction in what he calls "normal science," trying to solve the "puzzles" that can emerge from the empirical investigation. When difficulties along this practice appear too frequent and insurmountable, the paradigm enters a status of crisis and can be abandoned if a new paradigm emerges whose initial force may be offered by the capability of solving the most serious insoluble anomalies of the old paradigm, but whose acceptance is a global phenomenon concerning the whole of the scientific community working in a given domain, according to a psycho-sociological process very similar to the ideological or religious conversions, and almost entirely indifferent to empirical and logical constraints. This conception made scientific knowledge entirely dependent on the contingent micro-social context of the scientific communities, almost totally downplaying the criteria for securing a minimal degree of objectivity to such a knowledge. As a consequence, scientific theories became incommensurable and incomparable, and the very notion of scientific progress vanished. Even more, no objective criteria could be defended in order to distinguish science from non-science, to estimate astronomy better than astrology, scientifically based medicine better than witchcraft (as Feyerabend maintained).

It is rather obvious that this turn in philosophy of science has greatly contributed to that disinterest with regard to this discipline that we can ascertain today among working scientists, at variance with the rather generalized interest they had at the time of logical-empiricist philosophy of science which, in spite of its limitations, had the merit of taking science seriously and trying to account for its cognitive endeavours.

Even more radical became these characteristics with the transition from the micro-sociological approach of Kuhn (in which the epistemic conditions of science were made dependent on the scientific community) to a fully fledged sociological view of science that rapidly developed shortly afterwards, according to which science is a "social product" in a literal sense, that is, an activity that is totally conditioned by the dynamics of power that steers society, and produces those contents of knowledge and those applications that are requested by the different powers, independently on any criterion of objective value. This sociologic trend has met with a considerable success in the English-speaking world, where it had been prepared by the academic prestige acquired by sociology of knowledge, but it also had significant resonances in the new-Marxist doctrines (such as those of the Frankfurt school) that maintained the strict dependence of science from the social structure in which it takes place, For all the said reasons this sociological epistemology of science has contributed in a considerable measure to the shaping of that attitude of "anti-science" that was already spreading as a consequence of certain dynamics of a different nature.

FROM SCIENCE TO TECHNOSCIENCE

The sociological turn, both in its Kuhnian initial stage and in its subsequent more radical formulations, can be considered, at least in a certain sense, as the outcome of a "crisis" of the traditional concept of science, a crisis that has ripened slowly and which can be characterized as an overcoming of the purely speculative nature of science in favour of a more integrated speculative-pragmatic view of it. This transition was already more than implicit in the "Galilean revolution" that is usually considered as the most crucial moment of the birth of modern natural science. Galileo's natural science is indeed explicitly grounded on instrumental observation and manipulation of the physical world, and depends in a substantial measure on the technologically accurate realization of instruments. This characteristic has remained fundamental in the whole tradition of modern natural science: scientific knowledge strictly depends on a specific and highly sophisticated doing, and the actual objects of scientific inquiry are those aspects of nature that can be "clipped out" by means of suitable operational procedures. Therefore not only it is true, obvious and well known that modern technology is to a large extent "applied science," but it is also no less true that modern science heavily depends on the advancements of high technology. This interrelation could be seen somehow as a "mutual aid" for a couple of centuries, but it appeared as a real symbiosis when natural science became (as we have already noted) almost entirely a science of the unobservable. As a matter of fact these unobservables were such only with regard to the unaided human sense organs, but a lot of "unobservable" objects could be "observed" in a different (and scientifically more exact) sense thanks to several instrumental apparatuses. For this reason it is correct to qualify contemporary science as technoscience, according to a neologism that has been introduced for different reasons a few decades ago, but that corresponds very well to the specific nature of contemporary science. We shall consider later certain important consequences of this pragmatic dimension of technoscience, and shall pay attention now to another aspect.

A peculiar feature of contemporary science (which was prepared by the developments of nineteenth-century science) consists in the fact that its immediate object is no longer Nature, but the thick layer of mediations science itself has little by little set up through the construction of models and the elaboration of complex theories, with the assistance of ever more refined and "artificial" technologies. If ancient science considered itself inspired by the ideal of observation, and modern science by the ideal of discovery, present-day science is rightly presented as research. It is, in other words, an activity grafted onto what science has already constructed, not as a surely held patrimony, but as an ensemble of constructions that can be revised, criticized, or abandoned. Science feeds on science itself; it corrects itself. In the exchange between one branch and another it discovers instruments, suggestions, and models for advancing, or for radically altering its perspective. New problems arise from the solutions to old ones, and their solutions in turn can come from unexpected sources, provided even by disciplines considered distant. The scientist who is initiated into his research is not "put in contact with Nature," but is placed in a branch which then becomes his field of research. In other words, science no longer feels the pull to go outside of itself to continue to thrive and develop. Even the problems of its "foundation" are increasingly approached and treated from within itself. It is occupied with changes in its own concepts, the definition of their extension, and the creation of new concepts, heedless of the scandals to common sense and the perplexity of philosophers. All this amounts to recognizing that contemporary science has set itself up as an autonomous system, in that it fashions its field of objects by itself. While we have just spoken about natural science, a wholly analogous account could be given with regard to the human sciences.

The above remarks open up easy suggestions in favour of an anti-realist conception of science, but we are not going to discuss this problem here. We want rather to point out that science, especially as far as it is considered as technoscience, appears the product of a specific activity, namely the complex, articulated collective activity of the scientific community. We can continue to call this "product" knowledge, provided that we are not too much interested in specifying "of what" this is knowledge: yes, in the last analysis and indirectly this is, for example, "knowledge of Nature," but Nature in turn appears more and more the many-faceted "referent" of the scientific discourse. Therefore, the cognitive dependence of science on the scientific community is not just a provocative invention of Kuhn (possibly anticipated by other less famous authors) but is a matter of fact that cannot be reduced to the abstractly idealized work of people sticking to a compatibility between empirical evidence and logical consistency. The acceptance of scientific statements and theories within a scientific community depends on a variety of intellectual, cultural, technological factors that justify a considerable part of the Kuhnian "micro-sociological" epistemology of science. Only in part, however, because the fact that technoscience is an "autonomous" system does not entail that it is a "closed" system; in particular, it is open toward some "external world" that it tries to know and to modify (science is not self-referential). This remark allows one not to derive from the Kuhnian view a position of total relativism regarding scientific knowledge. The mention of the "external world," however, cannot be restricted to the consideration of nature, but must also include, in particular, the social context that is "external" to the scientific community, but entertains with this community a dense web of interplays. In such a way we are led to expand the micro-sociological perspective of Kuhn to the macro-sociological perspective of the so-called "social philosophy of science."

FROM THE SOCIAL COMMUNITY TO THE GLOBAL SOCIETY

Kuhn's position can be seen, in a certain sense, as a restriction to the domain of the scientific community of the general perspective of sociology of knowledge, according to which the intellectual categories, the cognitive frameworks and the tools of human knowledge are not something inborn and universal, inscribed in something like the "human nature" or the "human mind," but are featured by the social context of every particular culture. Kuhn maintains that also in the case of science we cannot believe in the existence of a unique and universal model of what is science, but that the very conception of scientific knowledge and of the ways of attaining it are featured in the form of changing paradigms by the historically variable scientific communities. The importance of this step resides in the fact that it eliminated an exception still existing in the original perspective of sociology of knowledge proposed by Mannheim. He had asserted that historical and social environment determines both the content and forms of our knowledge, but had admitted an exception to this epistemological rule and said that mathematics and the natural sciences are exempt from what he calls "existential determination". It is clear that this exception was suggested by the deep conviction that science constitutes a form of objective knowledge and, as such, independent on personal and collective idiosyncrasies, but Kuhn had precisely eroded this conviction. A kind of rebound occurred quickly and consisted in a "dilatation" of the micro-sociological view of Kuhn to the macro-sociological perspective of those authors who maintained that scientific knowledge is a social product not just of a delimited collectivity, but of society in general.

The consequences of maintaining far too great a dependence of science on the social context soon emerged in the debate over epistemologies: radical relativism, antirealism, the disappearance of the notion of truth and even of scientific objectivity, the dissolution of the criteria capable of justifying the preference not only of one scientific theory over another, but also of scientific forms of knowledge over those of pseudo-sciences. These theses, which may seem paradoxical in the openly iconoclastic and provocative writings of a Feyerabend, have received systematic treatment since the 1960s, and make up a solid block of a well known metascientific literature. Of course, there is no reason to give this a negative cast, but certain implications must be taken into account. It is certainly a positive thing in itself to introduce historical and social consciousness into the understanding of science. It is also useful to submit the scientific enterprise to sociological study: the information gained thereby is always interesting and illuminating. It is something completely different, however, to claim to reduce scientific knowledge to nothing but a social product. Herein lies the mistake of a good portion of sociological epistemology, a mistake that can be seen as a consequence of not having distinguished (though without separating) the cognitive dimension of science from other not strictly cognitive ones; in such a way certain negative facts (pertaining mostly to the domain of technology), that have rightly contributed to reshuffle the "received" overoptimistic view of technoscience have produced a generalized negative appreciation of the whole of technoscience, including also its strictly cognitive dimension .

THE CRISIS OF CONFIDENCE IN TECHNOSCIENCE

A wide display of fears, criticisms, and reflections of ethical and social nature have begun to attack technology and, indirectly, science after the end of the second world war. The start was given by the psychological impact produced on public opinion and also on several scientists by the explosion of the first atomic bomb, followed by the fears of a nuclear war that could be the outcome of the arms race opposing the two super-powers, soon expanded into the fears regarding possible disasters accidentally produced by the peaceful use of nuclear energy, and from there to the concerns regarding the contamination of the environment deriving from the acceleration of the industrial development. All these are very well known facts that need no additional explanation. They were accompanied by a deep change in the global evaluation of science. Whereas, in the Western tradition, science had been almost always considered as intrinsically positive and as an essential factor of the progress of humankind, it begun to be considered with suspicion and rather seen as a negative element susceptible of threatening the very survival of humankind.. It is certainly possible to point out that the really occurred damages and the hypothetical dangers derived from certain technological realizations and not from scientific knowledge. However, owing to the already stressed unity of techno-science it is undeniable that it is at most possible to distinguish conceptually science from technology, but not to separate them and, in the common perception, they are easily identified. Therefore, the negative judgment on technology (expressed in general in the name of ethical or social values) has been extended also to science, impairing that which had previously appeared as a fundamental principle of Western culture, that is, the axiological neutrality of science, that was considered the strong point of its objectivity. A rather confusing superposition of such factors of mistrust in the practical usefulness of science, on the one hand, with the mistrust in its cognitive reliability on the other hand, have led to a widespread attitude of hostility against science and technology that makes an appeal to philosophy of science for a necessary clarification. Once more, we are confronted with a crisis, that now is primarily a crisis of confidence in science, but whose solution seems to reside in a new way of conceiving philosophy of science itself.

BEYOND EPISTEMOLOGY OF SCIENCE

We have already explained that science has always meant, within Western culture, the most perfect form of knowledge and that, at a certain historical moment, natural science was considered to have realized the best model of science so that, especially with Kant, the study of the cognitive structure of that model was practically playing the role of a general theory of knowledge, or epistemology. In order to deserve such a privileged status, the "exact sciences" had developed during the nineteenth century that complex quest for rigor and foundation that can be qualified as an "internal" epistemological enterprise but this, as we have seen, ended up with a very serious situation of foundational crisis. Philosophy of science in its modern disciplinary sense was born then in order to come to term with this crisis and, for this reason, was almost entirely concerned with epistemological issues, it was in practice an epistemology of science. The different schools and trends that have been present within philosophy of science were only the expression of different approaches to this epistemological problem, repeating in this case the variety of positions that has been usual along the whole history of general epistemology: the problems were the same, but the philosophical presuppositions and the methodological tools adopted could be very different and produced accordingly different interpretations of the cognitive purport of science. This remains true also in the case of the Kuhnian epistemology of science and even in the case of the social epistemology of science whose most explicit goal was that of pulling down that idealized portrayal of science that pretended it to be the most solid actualization of knowledge. But precisely this was the weakest point of such philosophy of science. Certainly, one cannot minimize the pertinence of many remarks that sociology of knowledge in general and sociology of science in particular have put forth regarding certain conditionings of human knowledge deriving from the social context; neveretheless one cannot deny at the same time that the generalizations and amplifications defended by this school are far from convincing and are not able to impair the substantial objectivity and reliability of scientific knowledge.

The sociological approach, however, while did not produce a sound epistemology of science, has its strong points elsewhere and, perhaps, on issues that it has overlooked. We want to refer to those multifaceted dimensions of science that become patent as soon as we consider science also as a human activity, an activity that has the acquisition of sound knowledge as its primary and specific goal but that, at the same time, is involved in that web of different factors and conditionings that surround every human activity. This, as we have already stressed, is particularly clear if we recognize that contemporary science is actually technoscience and, especially, if we are aware that the great majority (if not the totality) of those problematic situations that have fueled the criticisms of anti-science or inspired the destructive reasoning of a certain social philosophy of science have to do with technoscientific activity and not with scientific knowledge. But if this is the situation, and if we recognize that the present crisis of the public image of science fundamentally depends on this kind of issues, we must conclude that a philosophy of science capable to correspond to its role must cross the limits of an epistemology of science and develop a serious reflection on those dimensions of science that are implicit in its being also a human activity: epistemology of science keeps its legitimacy intact, but it must be incorporated into a philosophical approach that takes much more into account.

The awareness of this fact has not been an easy process and has entailed a real change of paradigm in the way of conceiving philosophy of science, This was especially visible when discussions of ethical, political and social nature regarding science and technology started to become frequent and popular (let us say, at the end of the 1970's). On the one hand, many professional philosophers of science continued to think that this should limit itself to develop those logical-linguistic and methodological analyses that had characterized the empiricist-analytical approach, and considered a lack of "seriousness" the fact of accepting that philosophy of science should give room to such vague considerations and sterile discussions as those of ethical or social nature. At best, they could be the concern of other branches of philosophy. In this attitude, on the other hand, they found themselves in agreement with a certain number of university teachers of ethics, political and social philosophy, who wanted to keep for themselves the treatment of such questions and considered almost as an intrusion in their own domain if a professor of philosophy of science lectured on ethics of science. These were not just manifestations of academic jealousy, but rather the consequence of a crisis of science that pulled a rethinking of philosophy of science. As we have said, this crisis consisted in the emergence of the conception that science is not, essentially, a cognitive enterprise: the inextricable interlacing of science with technology, the thick web of relations of technology with industrial production, the considerable social impacts of this production, and the political and ethical consequences that all this entails represented such a complex situation that necessarily had to reflect itself on science, so that continuing to consider it as a system of "knowledge" appeared at least too partial, if not even misleading. Since making a philosophy of something means essentially to think it, to understand it by means of thought, it easily follows that, to the extent that the complex nature of science in the present world has become patent, also philosophy of science must concentrate its reflection on the nature and consequences of this complexity.

SOME NEW FEATURES OF PHILOSOPHY OF SCIENCE

This means, first, that philosophy of science must become strictly allied with a philosophy of technology, and bring to light those feedback loops that exist between scientific knowledge and technological realizations. It could also not ignore or overlook the impacts and conditionings that "doing science" implies today with regard to the social and political context, and also investigate the ethical, anthropological and cultural issues that emerge from the new situations produced by the increasing of scientific knowledge and of technological development. We could summarize these last issues by saying that an axiology of science is emerging as an important and serious aspect of philosophy of science, and this terminology makes reference in a very general way to the wide spectrum of values that are implied in making science, that is, not simply the typical moral, social and political values, but the rich display of goals and ends that inspire human actions and are considered "worthy" of being pursued. This approach conflicts, at a first sight, with the well known maxim that science must be value-free, but this is not really the case, if one considers the issue more closely. First of all, one must at least recognize that science, even according to its traditional conception, was considered as a search for truth and this was the specific value that ought to characterize scientific activity. In order to pursue this goal, certain criteria have been elaborated by the traditional epistemology of science, such as empirical adequacy and logical rigor but, when it appeared that in several cases they were insufficient for discriminating between rival theories, other criteria were pointed out, such as simplicity, elegance, causal connection, fruitfulness in prediction, and these were also recognized as "values," so that many scholars believed to have already manifested a sufficient open-mindedness toward the presence of values in science by recognizing the role of such values. This alleged open-mindedness, however, was very limited because one could call these epistemic or cognitive values, remaining inside the approach that reduces science to cognition and, in such a way, continuing to subscribe to the real meaning of the thesis that science must be value-free, which means that science must remain unaffected by non-cognitive values of whatever sort. This thesis has also been expressed on various occasions as the affirmation of the neutrality of science, and has a hardly deniable sense, if it is understood as the affirmation that the truth-value or cognitive validity of a scientific statement or theory must be "judged" or evaluated only according to criteria depending on strictly cognitive values. But as soon as we consider scientific activity, and that of technoscience in particular, we must recognize that its ways of being performed, its conditions, motivations, consequences are relevant to many aspects of human life that are oriented by a lot of non-cognitive values, and that it is correct, therefore, to submit the technoscientific doing and its concrete products and consequences to value-judgments of many kinds, from which indications regarding the best way of "doing science" should result. The delicate point is that of assuring the respect of the cognitive autonomy of technoscience and at the same time its capability of satisfying other non-cognitive values. A suitable solution consists in the adoption of a systems-theoretic approach on which, however, we cannot enter here.

In order for all this to remain a task of philosophy of science it is necessary that this admits a broadening of the categories and instruments it makes use of:: for the understanding of that complex reality that is present technoscience it is necessary to make use of all the instruments available in philosophy, not only of those of epistemology, formal logic and philosophy of language, but also, in particular, of those of ethics, social and political philosophy, axiology.

SAFEGUARDING THE COGNITIVE VALUE OF SCIENCE WITHIN A RESPONSIBLE PERFORMANCE OF THE TECHNOSCIENTIFIC ENTERPRISE

The proposals outlined above could meet with a certain diffidence by several people who might see in them a concession made to the sociological trends of the "new philosophy of science" whose effect (if not even the explicit proposal) has been that of discrediting the traditional image of science as objective knowledge, of absorbing science as well into the stream of the present widespread cultural relativism, of portraying the endeavor of science to look for truth (though a partial and fallible truth) as a kind of hypocrisy aiming at masking the actual situation of scientific research as a servant of the interests of the economic and political powers. These negative effects are undeniable but, as we have already noted, depend to a great extent on the fact that these new tendencies have had the pretension of moving on the stage of epistemology, that is, with the intention of breaking the myth of the objectivity of scientific knowledge. But this was, as we have tried to explain, a deplorable equivocation, deplorable because it spoiled precisely the most significant gain implicit in those new approaches, namely the awareness that science is a complex reality that does not reduce itself to the only cognitive dimension. For, while on the one hand it can be considered as a great system of knowledge, it constitutes on the other hand an intricate system of activities that, as such, interacts with all the material, institutional, ideological, ethical, social, religious factors that move and influence the life of society. Instead of taking advantage of this awareness for enriching the understanding of science, too many authors have believed that they were of a direct epistemological character, that they conflicted with the cognitive pretensions of science and were able, in the end, to refute them.

On the contrary we need to recover the sense of the complexity of science that, when it is considered as knowledge, constitutes one of the highest products of human civilization and can be the object of several philosophical investigations. The task of a philosophy of science adequate to this new situation of crisis is precisely that of maintaining and justifying the consideration of science as an objective and rigorous knowledge (though fallible and limited as far as its purport and its research instruments are concerned), capable of making us know more and more aspects of the various realities that surround us; and this without offering us that absolute certainty that is out of reach of humans in every domain, but providing us with certainties that stand "beyond any reasonable doubt." In order to realize this task the traditional analyses of a logical-linguistic kind are still useful, provided that they are not vitiated by prejudices of radical empiricism and remain open to recognize the cognitive capabilities also of the intellect; provided that they are not afraid to use the concept of truth and to admit the ontological purport of knowledge. This correct conception of science as knowledge must then be able to become compatible with all the legitimate considerations that emerge from the ascertainment of the conditions and conditionings that come to the scientific activity from the largely understood social context, and this because the value "knowledge" typically pursued by science is not the only one, and perhaps not even the supreme, that inspires human activity. Therefore, the problem is that of satisfying in the best possible measure the different values at play, without obliging science to renounce its specific end of providing us with objective, rigorous and partially "true" knowledge. And this is compatible with the fact of requiring that science cooperates to the promotion of many "non-cognitive" values that steer the march of civilization ; moreover, technoscience should try to offer means for the most efficacious realizations of such values. In this consists that responsibility of science that can no longer be considered a subject matter alien to philosophy of science and to be left to ethicists, but that requires the convergence of a many-sided reflection in which, in particular, philosophy of science make use of categories and principles found in ethics and political philosophy, but tailored to those situations that only through a scientific investigation can be adequately known.

Against Laws in the Special Sciences

JAEGWON KIM
BROWN UNIVERSITY

Abstract: The traditional view of science holds that science is essentially nomothetic—that is, the defining characteristic of science is that it seeks to discover and formulate laws for the phenomena in its domain, and that laws are required for explanation and prediction. This paper advances the thesis that there are no laws in the special sciences, sciences other than fundamental physics, and that this does not impugn their status as sciences. Toward this end, two arguments are presented. The first begins with Donald Davidson's argument against psychophysical laws and develops a more perspicacious general argument against special science laws. The second is a generalized and more explicitly motivated argument based on J. J. C. Smart's claim that biology, unlike physics, has no laws.

So, then, *why is there anything except physics?* . . . Well, I admit that I don't know why. I don't even know how to *think about* why. I expect to figure out why there is anything except physics the day before I figure out why there is anything at all . . .[1]

—*Jerry Fodor*

There is physics. The rest is engineering.[2]

—*J. J. C. Smart*

In science there is only physics. All the rest is stamp collecting.[3]

—*Sir Ernest Rutherford*

Special Supplement, *Journal of Philosophical Research* pp. 103–122
DOI: 10.5840/jpr201237Supplement29

PHYSICALISM AND THE SPECIAL SCIENCES

The central claim of physicalism is the thesis that the physical domain is all-encompassing. All things in spacetime—all bits of matter and their aggregates, however complex—belong in this domain and behave in accordance with the fundamental laws of physics. This entails the further thesis that this domain is comprehensive and causally closed—closed in the following sense: if a physical event has a cause, then it has a *physical* cause. The closure principle can also be stated in terms of explanation: if a physical event has an explanation, it has a *physical* explanation.[4] That is to say, the physical world is self-sufficient from a casual and explanatory point of view. We also expect basic laws of physics to be reasonably simple and few in number, and formulated in terms of a manageable number of fundamental properties, magnitudes, and forces.

Arguably physicalism is the most influential metaphysical worldview in contemporary science and philosophy—at least, analytic philosophy. Few of us today, however, would be apt to think that physics is the only science. There are also the "special sciences," like biology, geology, astronomy, psychology, cognitive science, and the rest. Most of us believe that these disciplines are no less "scientific" than physics, even though their scope and aspirations may be more limited and modest. We expect these sciences to aim at discovering lawful regularities and causal connections in their domains and often succeed in this effort, thereby generating principled explanations and predictions and helping us control events of interest to us. For most of us, the special sciences, like biology, geology, and psychology, enjoy greater salience and accessibility, and command a wider interest, than basic physics which, at its deeper levels, can be baffling and intimidating if not outright mysterious. It is fair to say that sciences like biology, psychology, and economics have a more direct and visible impact on our lives, from our daily copings with objects and people around us to the control of our physical and biological environments and the management of a nation's finances and economy.

A need to understand how the special sciences are related to physics and, in particular, how laws, explanations, and causal claims of the special sciences stand vis-à-vis those of physics arises from two sources. First, as noted, the domain of physics is thought to be all-encompassing; it includes all objects and events in the spacetime world. In contrast, each special science is "special" just because its domain is a specially demarcated subregion of the physical domain. This means that all entities and phenomena in the domain of any special science also belong in the wider domain of physics and come under the jurisdiction of physical law. Further, as earlier noted, there is a strong sense in which physics is, or widely thought to be, causally closed, in that it does not tolerate injections of nonphysical causal influences into its domain; nor does it allow the possibility of physical phenomena receiving explanations in terms of nonphysical causal forces. This prompts us to wonder how the laws and explanations of a special science are related to those of physics. If the phenomena investigated by the special sciences are part of the universal physical domain, how can there be special-science laws and explanations *in addition to* physical laws and explanations? That is, how are special sciences possible? And even if they are possible, do we *need* them? Why shouldn't developed physics meet all our needs? Or, to repeat Fodor, why is there anything except physics?

Moreover, unless we take a radically irrealist or instrumentalist stance toward the special sciences, we must grant that the special sciences, like physics, are about this one world that we inhabit. All our sciences aim at telling us something about what goes on in the same world—a true story about some aspects of this one reality—and we think that at least sometimes they succeed. So it is perfectly natural for us to want to know how the stories told by these sciences hang together, among themselves and with the story that physics tells us. We want to be able to piece together these stories, stories about genes and photosynthesis, about cognition and behavior, about consciousness and the emotions, about the birth and death of the solar system, about inflations and employment rates, and the rest, into one coherent picture that makes sense to us. Something like this presumably was the goal of the philosophers, like the early positivists, who promoted the idea of "unified science"—that all the sciences form a "unity" in some clear and substantive sense. As everyone knows, few philosophers now subscribe to such an ambitiously monolithic view—either that science is unified in its language or subject matter, or that some identical methodology regulates all the sciences. The idea of a unified science has been out of fashion well over half a century. But do disunity and disorder prevail everywhere as many have claimed?[5] (If they do, should they be allowed to?) What is a realistic picture of the relationship that the special sciences bear to basic physics?

In this paper, I hope to make a start on exploring these issues. But it will be only a start because I am going to focus on a single issue here, the question whether there are laws, or "strict" laws, in the special sciences. I will present two arguments each with the conclusion that, unlike in basic physics, there are no such laws in the special sciences. Obviously this issue is directly relevant to the question in what ways the special sciences differ from, and are related to, basic physics. It is also relevant to questions about the nature of explanations offered by the special sciences and the status of causal claims made in these sciences. These further issues are important and deserve serious attention. But my present concern is with the question of special-science laws. More specifically, I will present three arguments, each with substantial presumptive plausibility, to the effect that there are now laws in the special sciences. The first of these begins with an examination of Donald Davidson's famous, and famously opaque, argument for the claim that psychology is "anomalous"—that is, psychology has no laws. However, the argument I will present goes considerably beyond Davidson. The second argument will take as its starting point J. J. C. Smart's important claim that biology, unlike physics, is not in the business of discovering and formulating its own laws, and that biology is akin to engineering in that it borrows, and makes use of, laws from physics and chemistry.

DAVIDSON AGAINST "STRICT" LAWS IN PSYCHOLOGY

In a series of influential papers published in the 1970s, Donald Davidson advanced the claim, which many found surprising and not credible at the time, that there can be no "strict" laws about psychological phenomena. This is the thesis he called "the Anomalism of the Mental."[6] According to him, there are neither *psychophysical* laws, laws connecting psychological with physical phenomena, nor *purely psychological* laws, laws connecting psychological phenomena with other psychological phenomena. By "psychological" phenomena, he means intentional/representational events and states, like beliefs, desires, and intentions (and we may include their analogues in cognitive science and psychology), and he explicitly excluded from his consideration sensations and other sensory/qualitative states and events. Davidson held that psychology is not, and cannot be made into, a science, and that it is more like philosophy (perhaps hermeneutics?) than a science. He apparently thinks that the discovery of laws and the use of laws to formulate explanations and predictions is a definitive characteristic of science. Since, according to his mental anomalism, no laws are to be found about psychological phenomena, psychology does not qualify as a science. Second, the reason why there are no laws in the mental domain is important. On Davidson's view, it is of the essence of intentional psychological states like belief and desire that they are regulated by normative principles of rationality and coherence, and this precludes a causal-predictive investigation and nomological systematization of these phenomena.[7]

A considerable portion of Davidson's "Mental Events" is devoted to his arguments for psychophysical anomalism, the thesis that there are no laws connecting mental and physical phenomena. He then moves on to wrap things up by showing that there are no purely psychological laws either, laws connecting psychological phenomena with other psychological phenomena. This final phase of Davidson's arguments is contained in the following short and cryptic paragraph:

> It is not plausible that mental concepts alone can provide [a comprehensive and closed framework like that of physics], simply because the mental does not, by our first principle, constitute a closed system. Too much happens to affect the mental that is not itself a systematic part of the mental. But if we combine this observation with the conclusion that no psychophysical statement is, or can be built into, a strict law, we have the Principle of the Anomalism of the Mental: there are no strict laws at all on the basis of which we can predict and explain mental phenomena.[8]

What is a "strict" law? There is some interpretive uncertainty about exactly what Davidson meant by strict laws. One condition on which most are agreed is that, unlike "mere" or "rough" generalizations or "ceteris paribus" laws, strict laws allow absolutely no exceptions.[9] There is the further idea that strict laws occur only as part of "comprehensive" and "closed" theories over a domain, but it is not an idea that is easily made precise in this context, and in any case it isn't clear whether this is to be taken only as a fact about strict laws or it is constitutive of the very idea of strictness. Fortunately, we need not settle this issue, for the only property of strict laws we will be using is their exceptionlessness; for our purposes, then, strict laws are laws that hold without exceptions and tolerate none. In any case, our interest in the quoted paragraph above stems largely from its potential generalizability beyond the psychological domain—that is, we are interested in the question whether an argument along similar lines can be constructed for the conclusion that the special sciences in general are "anomalous." Such an argument would show that there are no "strict" explanatory/predictive laws in biology, geology, and other special sciences any more than in psychology. If an argument to this effect can be constructed, as I believe it can be, that would be a matter of great interest. But what is Davidson's argument?

Return to the quoted paragraph above: Davidson, at this point in "Mental Events," is assuming that he has already established *psychophysical* anomalism, the thesis that there are no strict laws connecting psychological and physical phenomena. To derive the full anomalism of the mental, the claim that there are no laws at all about psychological phenomena, what he needs is *psychological* anomalism, the proposition that there are no purely psychological laws, laws connecting psychological phenomena with other psychological phenomena. His reasoning in the paragraph appears to go like this:

(1) The mental domain is not causally closed—that is, some mental events are caused by nonmental events.

(2) Therefore, there are no purely psychological laws (psychological anomalism).

(3) There are no psychophysical laws (psychophysical anomalism).

(4) Hence, there are no laws about psychological phenomena.

For present purposes, we consider (3) as given; that is, we assume that Davidson has adequately established psychophysical anomalism. Given (2) and (3), the anomalist conclusion (4) immediately follows. The only significant question for us, therefore, concerns the transition from (1) to (2)—how from the failure of causal closure of the psychological domain, Davidson is able to derive the nonexistence of psychological laws.

More than a few philosophers have pondered this question, trying to develop a line of reasoning that would show how the derivation might work, or reveal what Davidson might have had in mind. To my knowledge, none have succeeded. One intractable obstacle is Davidson's appeal to his "first principle" as the source of the failure of causal closure for the mental domain. This principle is the following:

> *Principle of causal interaction.* "At least some mental events interact causally with physical events."[10]

The chief exegetical difficulty lies in the fact that this statement is completely symmetric as between the mental and the physical. The statement that "at least some mental events interact causally with physical events" is trivially equivalent to the statement that "at least some physical events interact causally with mental events." So if this principle entails, or warrants, the claim that causal closure fails for the psychological domain, it becomes unclear, in fact wholly mysterious, why it does not also entail a parallel conclusion, namely that causal closure fails for the physical domain as well. But it is one of Davidson's bedrock beliefs that the physical domain differs from the mental domain—in fact, from all other domains—precisely in that it alone is governed by strict laws, that it alone is a "comprehensive and closed system" of the kind that allows strict laws. It would seem that if we could derive the nonexistence of psychological laws from his "first principle," as Davidson is apparently suggesting, we should also be able to derive the nonexistence of strict physical laws from the very same premise! So clearly something is amiss with Davidson's argument, or our reading of it.

I have come to believe that Davidson's invocation of his "first principle" was a crucially misleading factor, a stumbling block for his readers. Notice that the events that the principle speaks of are most naturally taken as Davidsonian *token events*, that is, concrete dated occurrences, not kinds or properties of events (or events construed as property instantiations).[11] So when Davidson says some mental events causally interact with physical events, what this means is:

> *Token causal symmetry*. Some token events falling under mental event kinds cause, and are caused by, some token events that fall under physical event kinds.

As earlier noted, the first principle understood this way is symmetric for mental and physical events. Possible causal asymmetries between the physical and the mental become visible when—and, I believe, only when—we consider *event types* or *kinds*. For example, consider the following possible mental-physical causal asymmetry, something that isn't implausible and seems consistent with Davidson's views in this area:

> *Type causal asymmetry*. Whenever a mental event, *m*, causes a physical event, *m* is also a physical event, that is, *m* falls under some physical event kind P, whereas it is *not* the case that when a physical event, *p*, causes a mental event, *p* must also be a mental event by falling under some mental event kind M. In the latter case, *p* may be a "purely" physical event, an event that falls under no nonphysical kinds.

This asymmetry is entirely consistent with the symmetry of Davidson's Principle of Causal Interaction. But reading causal asymmetry into Davidson this way is something un-Davidsonian because the basic idea here is that when a mental event does any causal work (passive as well as active), it does so *in virtue of falling under a physical kind*—that is, the causal efficacy it has is due to the fact that it is an event of a certain physical kind. Of course, when a physical event is implicated in a causal relation, it is only the fact that it is an event of a certain physical kind that is causally relevant. Remember that on Davidson's event ontology, an event is mental or physical according as it falls under a mental kind or under a physical kind. The "or" here is nonexclusive: an event can fall under both a physical kind and a mental kind, and therefore it can be both a physical event and a mental event. The mental/physical asymmetry that I am suggesting, therefore, depends on an assumption that Davidson, at least "officially," rejects, namely the thesis that properties of events, or kinds under which events fall, are causally relevant, and that it is in virtue of falling under the event kinds under which they fall that events have the causal efficacy that they have, and enter into the causal relations into which they enter. Davidson has rejected this kind of talk as confused and misguided, insisting that causation is an extensional two-place relation over token events, and that talk of properties "in virtue of which" events cause, or are caused by, other events is incoherent.[12]

In any case, what these reflections show is that causal closure must be formulated in terms of event kinds and types, or properties, not solely in terms of Davidsonian token events. Standardly, physical causal closure is stated something like this:

(C) If a physical event has a cause (occurring) at *t*, it has a physical cause at *t*.

This will not work as intended if "event," or "physical event," is understood within a Davidsonian framework of token events. Something like (C) works only because of the tacit assumption that a physical event is the instancing of a physical property. If an object *x*'s instantiating, or having, a physical property P has a cause—that is, if an event causes this object to have P—then there must be a physical event, namely an event consisting in an object's instantiating some physical property P*, that causes *x* to instantiate P. Perhaps it is more perspicuous to put this in terms of explanation: If there is a causal explanation of why an object has physical property P, there must be a causal explanation of this fact in terms of some object's having a certain physical property P*.

I propose then that we consider the following two causal closure theses formulated in terms of properties/kinds:

Physical causal closure. If *x*'s having a physical property P has a cause that occurs at *t*, there is a physical event, an object *y*'s having a physical property P* at *t*, such that this event, in virtue of being an instancing of P*, causes *x* to instantiate P.

Mental causal closure. If *x*'s having a mental property M has a cause at *t*, there is a mental event, an object *y*'s having a mental property M* at *t*, such that this event, in virtue of being an instancing of M*, causes *x* to instantiate M.

I believe these two principles could be stated for the Davidsonian ontology of token events; however, these restatements would likely be more complex and cumbersome, more so than the already convoluted formulations given here.

In any case, physical causal closure as stated is arguably true; if you believe, as with almost all physicalists, in the comprehensiveness and closedness of physics, our closure principle seems to capture this idea quite nicely—in the way a bare statement like (C) taken to be about token events does not. In contrast, mental causal closure as stated seems plainly false: as Davidson says, "too much happens to affect the mental that is not a systematic part of the mental." Cases in which mental properties are caused to instantiate not by instantiation of other mental properties but by instantiations of nonmental, physical properties are familiar and numerous, as when retinal stimulation causes visual experience, tissue damage causes pain, and all the rest.

The mental/physical asymmetry represented by physical causal closure and the failure of mental causal closure is a good start. But it is not enough to yield the asymmetry we seek, which is the impossibility of *any* strict laws in the mental domain in spite of the presumed existence of such laws on the physical side. The reason is simple: psychological anomalism asserts that there are *no* strict psychological laws at all whereas the failure of mental causal closure only means that there are *some* mental events—*one*, at least—whose causation is not covered by a strict psychological law. Here is where the failure of mental causal closure gives us an idea: What if causal closure failed for *every* putative case of mental causation—that is, everywhere in the mental realm? If that should happen, that must be because no strict mental law could cover any mental event in a causal relation. I suggest then that we consider the following proposition:

> *Massive failure of causal closure for the mental.* Let M and M* be mental event kinds and consider a putative causal relation from an M-event to an M*-event. Then there *always* is a physical event kind P such that if a P-event were to occur along with the M-event, that would prevent the M*-event from occurring. That is to say, every mental-to-mental causal relation is liable to disruption by the occurrence of some physical event.

This, I believe, is not an implausible thesis. We can see that if mind-body supervenience holds, the claim is likely true. For M* to occur, one of its physical supervenience bases must occur. It seems that after the putative cause M occurs we can, perhaps in all cases, intervene and make sure that none of the physical bases of M* occur. (We can always have the brain destroyed—if it must come to that!) Davidson has said that "too much" that is nonmental happens to causally affect the occurrence of mental events; the thesis of massive failure upgrades "too much" to "always" (but weakens "happens" to "could happen"). Every instance of mental-to-mental causation is vulnerable to disruption by the occurrence of a nonmental event.

Given the massive closure failure for the mental, we can quickly show that there are no strict laws in the mental domain. Suppose M → M* is a strict psychological law. This law suffices to ground a causal relation between an M-event and an M*-event.[13] Since the M → M* law is strict, it admits of no exceptions and this means that there can be no physical interfering event to disrupt the M-to-M* causation. This contradicts the thesis of massive failure of causal closure for the mental. It follows that M → M* is not a strict psychological law, and that there are no strict laws on the mental side.[14]

To wrap it up: a strengthened form of the failure of mental causal closure gives us psychological anomalism. To complete the argument for the full anomalism of the mental, we need only to observe that this thesis is a conjunction of psychological anomalism and psychophysical anomalism. For the present purposes, as you may recall, we have conceded the latter to Davidson. Even without this concession, what has been shown is not insignificant: there are no strict laws connecting psychological kinds with other psychological kinds.

THE FRAGILITY OF HIGHER-LEVEL CAUSATION

I believe the reasoning is plausibly generalized to other special sciences. If there are no strict psychological laws and psychological causal relations are in principle vulnerable to disruption, the same must hold for the higher special sciences that psychology underlies, such as sociology and economics. So let us consider biology, a lower-level science in relation to psychology: Can there be strict biological laws and undisruptable biological causation? Not likely: nonbiological physical events (exposure to high levels of radiation, the unavailability of necessary nutrients, ecological changes, natural disasters, and so on) can always intervene to break up biological causal processes. Biological entities are complex aggregates of physical elements subject to physical laws, and something can always, and often do, go wrong with the physical underpinnings of biological processes to interrupt their "normal" progress. Normal developmental processes at the biological level can be affected by all sorts of lower-level nonbiological occurrences. The progress of a pathological condition can be interrupted, or be steered in another direction, by intervention at the physicochemical level, such as administration of drugs or surgical procedures.

It is plausible, then, that a generalized analogue of the massive closure failure for the mental domain holds:

> *General failure of special-science causal closure.* For any putative causal relation from an S_1-event to an S_2-event, involving special-science kinds S_1 and S_2, there always is a lower-level condition C such that if C were to occur along with the S_1-event, that would disrupt the causal process and prevent the S_2-event from occurring.[15]

From this, by the argument sketched above for the mental domain, it follows:

> *The nonexistence of strict special-science laws.* For any special-science kinds S_1 and S_2, there is no strict law of the form $S_1 \rightarrow S_2$.

From this perspective, Davidson's psychophysical anomalism, the thesis that there are no strict laws about mental phenomena, is only a special case. A more general thesis is that there are no laws in any of the special sciences. Strict laws can be found only in fundamental physics. The basic argument for this claim is the same as the argument for mental anomalism: causal/nomological relations at higher levels are always susceptible to disruption from below—that is, to interference from events occurring at a lower level.[16] The physical level being the bottom level, physical causal relations at the fundamental level suffer no similar vulnerability, and this allows for the possibility of strict physical laws.[17]

Davidson is not alone in advancing the thesis that there are no strict laws in some special-science domain. Philip Kitcher, for example, has argued against the reducibility of classical genetics to the lower-level sciences (in particular, molecular biology) in part on the ground that there are no "laws" in classical genetics. On the Nagelian model of bridge-law reduction,[18] assumed by Kitcher, the reduction of one theory to another is accomplished by deriving the laws of the former from those of the latter (with "bridge laws" as auxiliary premises). But if there are no laws of genetics, there is nothing to reduce. Why are there no laws in genetics? According to Kitcher, if there are laws in classical Mendelian genetics, they must be about the transmission of genes. But he can't find any such laws:

> when we read the major papers of the great classical geneticists or when we read the textbooks in which their work is summarized, we find it hard to pick out *any* laws about genes. These documents are full of informative statements. Together, they tell us an enormous amount about the chromosomal arrangements of particular genes in particular organisms, about the effect on the phenotype of various mutations, about frequencies of recombination, and so forth.[19]

But Kitcher doesn't see any laws among these otherwise informative statements. Take, for example, Mendel's "second law," roughly to the effect that the probabilities of a gamete receiving any of the possible genetic combinations are equal. Kitcher points out that this "law" does not hold in general. Once we understand that genes are chromosomal segments, we see that alleles that are on the same chromosome will tend to be transmitted together. Kitcher goes on to argue, plausibly, that various possible restrictions or emendations to Mendel's second law will not make it completely precise and exceptionless.[20]

Let us accept Kitcher's claim that genetic laws are not found in the scientific literature of genetics. But is there a principled argument that would show that, given the nature of genetics, or genetic properties, there *could* not be laws about gene transmission. Perhaps we find no laws of genetics in the scientific literature, but how do we deal with the simple retort that if we would only wait long enough, or allocate generous enough research funds, someone might come up with genetic laws, strict laws about genetic phenomena. When we look through Kitcher's discussion with this issue in mind, we can discern a pattern of considerations that fits well with the quasi-Davidsonian argument just presented. As you will recall, the argument was that for any putative special-science law, there are "lower-level disruptors"—that is, conditions at lower levels such that were they to occur, the law would not hold. Return to the reason Kitcher offers for the failure of Mendel's second law: once we see what lower-level phenomena are involved in genetic transmissions, we realize that Mendel's law cannot hold in general. Or see what Kitcher says in explaining why it will not do to restrict Mendel's second law to genes on nonhomologous chromosomes. He writes: "Unfortunately, this will not quite do. There can be interference with normal cytological processes so that segregation of nonhomologous chromosomes need not be independent."[21] Again, the idea is that lower-level interference can, and often will, disrupt higher-level regularities. All we need to add is that this is something that cannot be avoided, that it will bedevil all higher-level special-science properties everywhere and all the time. It is an instance of what we called the general failure of special-science causal closure: Higher-level regularities and causal relations are fragile—they are liable to breakdowns due to interference from below.

SMART ON BIOLOGY AS ENGINEERING

About two decades before Kitcher argued that there are no laws in genetics, J. J. C. Smart advanced, in his *Philosophy and Scientific Realism* (1963), the claim that there are no laws in biology or psychology, and, by implication, none in any other special science. Physics, according to him, is the only science whose business it is to discover and formulate laws. He wrote:

> Not only do I deny the existence of emergent laws and properties, but I even deny that in biology and psychology there are laws in the strict sense at all. There are, of course, empirical generalizations. There are not any biological laws for the very same reason that there are not any laws of engineering. Writers who have tried to axiomatise biological and psychological theories seem to me to be barking up the same gum tree as would a man who tried to produce the first, second, and third laws of electronics, or of bridge building. We are not puzzled that there are no laws of electronics or of bridge building, though we recognise that the electronic engineer or bridge designer must use laws, namely laws of physics . . . I shall try to show that the important analogy is not between biology and the physical sciences but between biology and the technologies, such as electronics.[22]

I believe this is an insightful perspective—not only about biology but about other sciences such as geology and astronomy. What does Smart mean by "laws in the strict sense"? He writes:

> Physics and chemistry have their *laws*. For example, there are the laws of motion in classical mechanics, the laws of electrodynamics, and the equations of quantum mechanics. . . . These laws are universal in that it is supposed that they apply everywhere in space and time, and they can be expressed in perfectly general terms without making use of proper names or of tacit reference to proper names. Such laws I call "laws in the strict sense."[23]

Smart's "laws in the strict sense," therefore, seem akin to, if not identical with, Davidson's "strict laws." For both, strict laws are wholly exceptionless and completely general, applying everywhere in the spacetime world, and, according to Davidson, they are only found in theories that give a comprehensive and closed coverage of their domains. Both Smart and Davidson claim that there are strict laws only in basic physics.[24]

Smart conceives of the relation between physics and biology in analogy with that between physics and electronic engineering:

> From a logical point of view biology is related to physics and chemistry in the way in which radio-engineering is related to the theory of electromagnetism, etc. . . . Just as the radio-engineer uses physics to explain why a

> circuit with a certain wiring diagram behaves as it does, so the biologist uses physics and chemistry to explain why organisms or parts of organisms (e.g., cell nuclei), with a certain natural-history description, behave as they do.[25]

But why does Smart think that there can't be laws in biology—laws about genes, mutation, photosynthesis, and numerous other biological entities and processes? Prima facie, the existence of biological laws seems consistent with the fact, which we may concede to Smart, that "the biologist uses physics and chemistry to explain" biological phenomena. This could be true not because there are no biological laws but because biological laws are reducible to, or derivable from, laws of physics and chemistry. So we need to ask: what is it about biological entities and processes that make laws about them unavailable? What are the pertinent differences between them and the entities dealt with in physics that explain the nomological differences between them? Smart says that "there are no real laws of biology for the very same reason that there are no special 'laws of engineering'." For Smart, then, biological organisms are like radio receivers, internal combustion engines, and suspension bridges. In designing and building them, and in understanding their behavior (their malfunctions as well as their proper, designed-in behavior), we use laws of physics and chemistry. In engineering there may be useful rough and ready empirical generalizations and rules of thumb; but there seem no laws, or strict laws, about designing or manufacturing radios or internal combustion engines. The analogy with engineering seems apt and thought-provoking, but it does not answer the question why there are no laws in biology—or, for that matter, the question why there no laws of engineering. That is, what do biology and engineering have in common that is responsible for, and explains, there being no laws in either?

It is not easy to give a clear interpretation or reconstruction of Smart's thoughts on this question (it is to his credit that he does raise the question, however). After a meandering discussion, he settles for the claim that the structures of interest to biology, for example, cells, genes, organs, etc., are vastly more *complex* than those studied in physics. In his final paragraph on this topic, Smart writes:

> However, though there is not a sharp division in nature between the objects of the physical sciences and those of the biological sciences, there is, of course, a non-sharp division, which is one of complexity of structure. The methodological division does reflect this non-sharp division in reality.[26]

Smart appears to be saying that on account of the ("non-sharp") differences in the complexity of their respective subject matters, we make a methodological decision, to put physics in the business of coming up with laws and give biology the lesser role of applying the laws discovered by physics. It is clear that this decision makes sense only if structural complexity has a decisive negative impact on the existence of laws.

Such a simple connection between complexity and laws, however, is implausible, for, as we will soon see, structural complexity alone cannot preclude laws. What is of greater relevance is a point that Smart himself refers to when he calls biological entities "complicated and *idiosyncratic* structures" (emphasis added).[27] He continues on to say "No one expects even all motor cars of a certain make and year to behave exactly alike," and points out that a living cell is vastly more complex than an automobile. Here, what does the work is not the complexity of cells but rather what must be a contingent by-product of their complexity, namely their idiosyncrasy—that is, *individual variability* among cells. No two cells are exactly alike—not even those serving identical biological functions in the same organism; hence no two cells behave exactly the same way; hence, we cannot expect to find exceptionless, strict laws about them—or any significant subclasses of them. On this line of reasoning, complexity itself does not have a fundamental role. Cells could be as complex as you please, but if they—or those in some theoretically significant subclass of cells—had an identical microstructure, to the last molecule or basic particle, there would be no prima facie reason, on Smart's general view, why there could not be strict, exceptionless laws about them. They would behave identically in identical situations—just as electrons do. This means that what really accounts for the absence of laws in biology is not structural complexity of biological entities per se but rather its contingent by-product, as I said, namely the individual variability (or, following Smart, "idiosyncrasy") among the entities grouped together under a single biological kind.[28]

I believe these considerations can be generalized to other special sciences along the following lines: the entities of any special science are complex aggregate structures of the entities dealt with in physics, and there inevitably will be structural/compositional differences among entities falling under a single kind in any special-science taxonomic system. This is important because we expect the behavior, or behavioral dispositions, of a complex aggregate system to depend on, and be determined by, its structural/compositional detail. In general, entities that are similar in their microstructure behave in similar ways when placed in similar situations; in fact, the greater the structural similarity the greater the behavioral similarity. The converse of this principle also holds: structurally dissimilar systems are apt to exhibit dissimilar behavior, and, as a general rule, the greater the dissimilarity, the greater the behavioral dissimilarity. Consider all actual and possible samples that fall under a biological kind. We can expect the kind to be idiosyncratic in the sense that these samples show a substantial range of individual variability in their microstructural composition, and given the dependence we just noted of the behavior of wholes on their microstructure, it is highly unlikely that there will be strict laws that apply to this biological kind. It does not strictly follow that there are, or can be, no strict, exceptionless correlations between biological kinds or properties. Let B_1 and B_2 be two biological kinds/properties: it is conceivable that in spite of the high degree of idiosyncrasy of both B_1 and B_2, the range of individual variation allowed by B_1 is matched by that allowed by B_2, generating a precise, strict correlation between them. This is logically possible but highly unlikely. It is true of course that whether or not a generalization holds over all instances of a kind depends on the predicate, or property, projected over them, and that when the projected predicate is extremely general (e.g., "has a mass," "is made of cells," etc.), we can easily secure truth (e.g., "Every heart has a mass," "Kidneys are made up of cells"). But we can safely say that these are not the kind of laws, whether strict or not, we look for in biology.

With these caveats in mind, we can say that the considerations based on the idiosyncrasy of special-science kinds and properties shows, or at least makes it highly likely, that we will not find strict, exceptionless, laws in the special sciences. Moreover, the same considerations also explain why we can expect broad empirical generations of interest and usefulness (you might call them "nonstrict" laws or "ceteris paribus" laws) in the special sciences. This is because in spite of the idiosyncrasy, there are also broad points of compositional similarity and resemblance among samples falling under a given kind.

These considerations invoke two substantive metaphysical premises. One is the thesis, already mentioned, to the effect that the behavior of an aggregate structure of physical entities (elementary particles, quarks, atoms, molecules, or what have you) is determined by, or supervenes on, their basic structural/compositional details. This must be so because the intrinsic properties, and hence the causal potentials, of complex systems supervene on their microstructure. But the premise that plays a more direct role in our argument is the converse of this supervenience principle, namely that structurally dissimilar systems will tend to behave in dissimilar ways under identical conditions. A deep discussion of the grounds for accepting these principles, or of their precise formulations, is beyond the scope of this paper. But it seems to me that principles like these are operative, for example, in our thinking about quality control in industrial manufacturing: In order to maximize a uniform level of performance and functionality across samples of a product, we try to maximize uniformity over the parts to be assembled into the product—that is, to minimize differences (or "idiosyncrasies") among them—and to ensure the uniformity of the mode of assembly as much as possible.

Automobiles rolling off an assembly line are not exactly identical with one another and don't behave in exactly identical ways; the "lemons" would be among the extreme cases—and if there are lemons there must also be "anti-lemons," those samples markedly superior to their cohorts. So there are no exceptionless laws about, say, all samples of the 2006 Honda Accord LX sedan, and it would be silly to look for them. However, they are similar enough to yield many useful empirical generalizations, or rules of thumb, about how they behave and function. That's what makes it possible to write service manuals and owners' handbooks. The same goes for biology: although there are no biological laws, conspecifics are structurally similar enough so that there are informative and useful empirical generalizations (about their longevity, size and weight, developmental phases, susceptibility to diseases, responsiveness to medical interventions, and so on). Smart seems to implicitly endorse the claim that these generalizations are not explanatory; that they are like useful rules of thumb about auto repair and maintenance, and not capable of generating genuine scientific understanding of why organisms function and behave as they do. Smart's position on biology encourages the view that genuine explanatory understanding in biology comes only from applying physicochemical laws to explain why, given its physical structure, an organism functions and behaves as it does. Given the idiosyncrasy of biological kinds, such explanations will not be generalizable even across different samples falling under one biological kind. That is, biological explanations are likely to show as much idiosyncrasy as biological entities do.

These reflections suggest a possible account of why there are, or can be, strict laws in physics. Let us make this assumption: the entities studied in microphysics, like electrons and photons, are metaphysical simples with no internal structure, or, if they are complex, those falling under a basic kind in fundamental physics have an identical structure. On this assumption, the entities belonging to a basic physical kind have exactly the same set of intrinsic properties and hence exactly identical causal potentials (one electron is exactly like the next one, in all intrinsic properties). In consequence, they behave the same way under the same conditions. This is why the basic physical taxonomy makes exceptionless physical laws possible. I am not suggesting that this is the only way in which strict laws can be seen to be possible in basic physics—in particular, I am not saying that this sort of structural consideration applies to all basic laws of physics; nor do I know whether the assumption with which we began the present paragraph is strictly true or will be accepted by the working physicists. So I am leaving this as a speculative conjecture.[29]

IMPLICATIONS: A NEW ARGUMENT FOR DAVIDSON'S ANOMALISM OF THE MENTAL?

The Smart-derived argument of the preceding section suggests a new, and simpler, argument for psychological anomalism. Psychological systems, like human beings and other higher organisms,[30] are complex physical systems, and organisms belonging to the same species can, and do, exhibit a fairly large degree of idiosyncrasy from the point of view of underlying physical/biological structure, though of course as members of the same species they are bound to show a good amount of similarities as well. Moreover, token psychological states, or events, that fall under a single kind, in the scientific or vernacular psychological taxonomy, are certain to show a significant range of individual variability at the underlying biological/physicochemical level, even within the same species—in fact, even for the same organism at different times. As in the case of biology, we should expect that the greater the structural differences are at the biological/physical level, the greater the psychological/behavioral differences will be. Conversely, the greater structural similarity, the greater the psychological similarity. It follows then, first, that strict, exceptionless laws connecting psychological kinds to psychological kinds will likely be unavailable, and, second, that, in spite of that, we can expect to find useful empirical generalizations, or ceteris paribus laws.

It seems that the same line of consideration could also help establish psychophysical anomalism—the claim that there are no strict laws connecting psychological with physical phenomena. Briefly, given the range of individual variability among the token physical/biological states underlying psychological states falling under a psychological kind, it is highly unlikely that the "same" psychological states, that is, states belonging to some single psychological kind, will be followed by, or correlate with, identical physical effects. Human animals, as conspecifics, are biologically/physically quite alike but not exactly so. As a result, they will not behave exactly the same way in psychological contexts any more than they do in purely physical contexts. So there will be no strict laws connecting psychological events with physical events. (There is one exception: *exactly identical* physical conditions in psychological systems will lead to identical psychological behavior.[31] But such laws will be of little practical or scientific interest.) As in the case of laws connecting psychological phenomena with other psychological phenomena, there are enough structural similarities among psychological systems and their properties to yield rough but stable and useful empirical generalizations, and this is part of what makes the psychological and cognitive sciences possible.

If these considerations are not entirely off the mark, it means that we have a new argument for Davidson's Anomalism of the Mental, the claim that there are no strict laws about psychological phenomena. As everyone who has worked through "Mental Events" will agree, Davidson's arguments are complex and difficult to understand as they involve a web of subtle claims and considerations concerning rationality, normativity, holism, radical interpretation, and the like. In contrast, our Smart-derived arguments stay clear of such deep considerations, resting instead on what seem to me to be relatively simple and transparent metaphysical theses about structure and behavior. If this is right, the anomalousness of the mental need have nothing specifically to do with the special character of minds; it is merely one instance of a general and pervasive natural phenomenon, namely the structural idiosyncrasy of psychological systems, including human persons.

Beyond the realm of the sciences, the metaphysical considerations motivating the arguments of this section also explain why there are no strict, exceptionless laws about macro-objects and their observable macro-properties—about rocks, rivers and mountains, rains and sleets, trees and shrubs, tables and chairs, light bulbs, and the rest. These are the familiar sundry things that make up the world in which we pass our lives. Again, our considerations explain why, even though there are no strict laws, there often are useful generalizations about them that are reliable for most purposes and capable of grounding counterfactuals in appropriate cases. Needless to say, without access to such generalizations, it would hardly be possible for us to cope with our constantly changing surroundings and navigate our way through the natural world. These rough and ready generalizations, not the strict laws (if there are any), serve as the indispensable guide for us in our daily dealings with the world.

CONCLUDING REMARKS

There are various pending issues not addressed here which I believe deserve further exploration. One such issue concerns the question how the three arguments presented here are related to each other. Although I have made some comments relevant to this question, there is more to think about and undoubtedly more to say. I am inclined to think that the second, Smart-inspired, argument is the fundamental one, and that the first argument depends on the considerations that motivate and ground it. Second, and more importantly, there is the question what implications our reflections on the laws, or the absence thereof, in the special sciences have on the nature of explanation and causation in these sciences. Does the absence of "strict" laws in the special sciences, assuming this to be the case, mean that special-science explanations are in some ways flawed and imperfect, in comparison with explanations in fundamental physics? What of the causal claims we encounter in the special sciences? In the absence of strict laws how should we understand such claims? What grounds causal relations between special-science phenomena? The problem of mental causation—the problem of accounting for the possibility of causation involving psychological phenomena—has been extensively debated for well over two decades. The problem of special-science causation and explanation will likely turn out to be only a generalized version of the same problem. If so, what we have learned from the mental causation debate may carry important lessons for the general problem. On the other hand, it could be a smart philosophical strategy to tackle the general issues concerning the special sciences first, for the light it may shed on the more special case concerning psychological phenomena. Either way we seem to have a rich set of philosophical problems in this area that should engage us for some time to come.[32]

NOTES

1. Jerry Fodor, "Special Sciences: Still Autonomous After All These Years," *Philosophical Perspectives* 11 (1997): 149–163; the quote is from p. 161 (italics original). In 2004 Barry Loewer gave a colloquium at Brown under the title "Why Is There Anything Except Physics?" and this talk has stimulated me to think about the issues discussed in this paper.

2. J. J. C. Smart, *Philosophy and Scientific Realism* (London: Routledge & Kegan Paul, 1963). This is not a direct verbatim quotation. Smart's view will be discussed in detail later.

3. This is one version of the famous remark attributed to the noted physicist in the early twentieth century.

4. This is the way the closure principle is often formulated but as stated it is slightly defective. It allows the following causal sequence ". . . p_1 causes m causes p_2 . . .", where p_1 and p_2 are physical events and m is a nonphysical event. Note: by transitivity, p_1 causes p_2, and p_2, therefore, has a physical cause. This defect can be easily remedied.

5. See, e.g., John Dupré, *The Disorder of Things* (Cambridge, MA: Harvard University Press, 1993); *The Disunity of Science*, ed. Peter Galison and David J. Stump (Stanford, CA: Stanford University Press, 1996).

6. The most important paper in which this is argued is "Mental Events," reprinted in Davidson, *Essays on Actions and Events* (New York and Oxford: Oxford University Press, 1980). First published in 1970.

7. See "Mental Events." For Davidson's later take on these issues, see "Could There Be a Science of Rationality?" in his *Problems of Rationality* (Oxford: Clarendon Press, 2004), first published in 1995.

8. Davidson, "Mental Events," p. 224.

9. According to the usual understanding, statistical laws can be strict; if there are basic physical laws that are statistical, they do not allow "exceptions"—any more than nonstatistical, deterministic laws do.

10. Davidson, "Mental Events," p. 208.

11. See my "Events as Property Exemplifications," reprinted in *Supervenience and Mind* (Cambridge: Cambridge University Press, 1993). Originally published in 1976.

12. Davidson has not been entirely consistent on this point. See his "Thinking Causes" (in *Mental Causation*, ed. John Heil and Alfred Mele [Oxford: Clarendon Press, 1993]) in which he begins by strongly affirming this point and then goes on to give his own account of the "causal relevance" of mental properties in terms of supervenience.

13. Davidson requires that causal relations be subsumed by strict laws; see "Mental Events."

14. It should be clear that the foregoing considerations (including Davidson's own) apply to what may be called "transition laws," laws that connect psychological events diachronically. They do not affect the possible existence of synchronic, "constitutive," laws involving psychological properties, a possibility that Ron Endicott pointed out to me. However, it will be seen that the second argument below, against special-science laws, affects laws of that sort as well.

15. Wouldn't this mean that there is the following strict law: "If S_1 occurs and C occurs, then S_2 does not occur"? Not necessarily. Even when C occurs, if C* also occurs, it may counteract C and S_1 may still lead to S_2; and so on. Notice also that the consequent of the law is to the effect that a certain psychological phenomenon—to pick an arbitrary special science—does *not* occur. The nonoccurrence of a psychological phenomenon is not itself a psychological phenomenon. For this reason, it would be problematic to consider a law of this form a "psychological" law.

16. To make the argument fully parallel to Davidson's argument, we will need to establish auxiliary premises that correspond to Davidson's psychophysical anomalism—that is, the claim that there are no bio-physical laws, that there are no geological-physical laws, etc.(as Abe Roth has mentioned to me). I believe a general argument to this effect could be constructed on the basis of the same considerations invoked here. There is also the possibility of constructing the needed arguments on the basis of the second and third arguments against special-science laws to follow. For an argument based on considerations of multiple realization to show the nonexistence of laws in the social sciences, see John T. Roberts, "There are no Laws of the Social Sciences," in *Contemporary Debates in Philosophy of Science*,

ed. Christopher Hitchcock (Oxford: Blackwell, 2004). Also of interest is Lee McIntyre, "Davidson and Social Scientific Laws," *Synthese* 120 (1999): 375–394.

17. What if there is no bottom level, there being a lower level for each microphysical level? Would that show that there are no strict laws anywhere? The answer is not clear; whether or not the considerations put forward in the paper (in particular, the idea of "interference from below") will generally apply to microphysical levels seems like an empirical physical question, and I have no idea whether there is received wisdom regarding this question. On the possibility of there being no bottom level, see Ned Block, "Do Causal Powers Drain Away?," *Philosophy and Phenomenological Research* 67 (2003): 133–150; Jonathan Schaffer, "Is There a Fundamental Level?," *Noûs* 37 (2003): 498–517.

18. Ernest Nagel, *The Structure of Science* (New York: Harcourt, Brace and World, 1961). I have elsewhere argued that this is not an adequate model of reduction; see, e.g., *Philosophy of Mind*, 2nd edition (Boulder, CO: Westview Press, 2006), chapter 10; or "Making Sense of Emergence," *Philosophical Studies* 95 (1999): 3–36.

19. Philip Kitcher, "1953 and All That: A Tale of Two Sciences," *Philosophical Review* 93 (1984): 335–373. The quote is from pp. 340–341.

20. Kitcher also argues against possible "bridge" laws connecting biological predicates (e.g., "is a gene") with molecular physical predicates. His argument here appears to be an instance of the classic multiple realization argument.

21. Kitcher, "1953 and All That: A Tale of Two Sciences," p. 342.

22. J. J. C. Smart, *Philosophy and Scientific Realism* (London: Routledge & Kegan Paul, 1963), p. 52.

23. *Philosophy and Scientific Realism*, p. 53.

24. Or, in Davidson's terminology, "developed physics." See Davidson, "Thinking Causes."

25. Smart, *Philosophy and Scientific Realism*, p. 57.

26. Ibid., p. 61.

27. Ibid., p. 55.

28. Actually, the divergence between entities grouped under a biological kind arguably goes much deeper and wider. Biological kinds, like mental kinds, are standardly considered to be "multiply realizable"; think of how diversely, say, the heart or the visual system, is realized in various biological species. The structural differences between two human hearts are very slight indeed when compared with differences between a human heart and a reptilian heart. Issues involving multiple realizability will be taken up in our "third" argument below.

29. As the reader will have noticed, this explanation of why strict laws are possible in physics differs from the explanation I earlier suggested in connection with the "interference from below" argument. I believe there may be interesting connections between the two explanations; however, they have to be set aside for another occasion.

30. If you like, you could include sophisticated computing machines, or robots, as well.

31. If physical identity is understood in terms of identity in *intrinsic* physical properties, that would make this statement highly dubious, at least for many philosophers, in view of

the externalist considerations regarding content-carrying states, such as belief, desire, and intention.

32. For helpful comments, I am indebted to Ronald Endicott, Marc Lange, Jeff Poland, and Barbara von Eckhardt.

L'IDÉE DE RENAISSANCE

BERTRAND SAINT-SERNIN
EMERITUS, PARIS-SORBONNE

ABSTRACT: The term "Renaissance" usually applies to a period in European history during which the Greco-Latin culture was rediscovered and modern science started. We show that "the Idea of Renaissance" indicates a universal process: a community (a nation, for example), identifying needs that it does not know how to satisfy by itself, and recognising that another community already satisfies them, tries first to acclimate the external process, and then becomes a creative entity. Several interpretations of this process have already been given: we study three of them: the law of the three states by Auguste Comte, the notion of "a single revolution" in Kant's *Critic of Pure Reason* and *Critic of Judgement*, and the notion of "scientific revolution" by A. A. Cournot. Thus conceived, Renaissance means a challenge in which all cultures are equally involved: discovering, even elsewhere, the means of satisfy needs which are related to scientific knowledge and know-how; trying to assimilate them; and making them productive and indigenous by becoming creative.

AVANT-PROPOS

Il y a juste un siècle, le Congrès international de Philosophie se tenait en Allemagne, à Heidelberg. Le 28 octobre 1908, peu après le Congrès, lors d'une réunion de la Société française de Philosophie, Henri Bergson fit la réflexion suivante sur les Congrès internationaux de philosophie:

> Si, dans les congrès de physiologistes, de chimistes, de physiciens et de mathématiciens, on approfondit des problèmes généraux ou spéciaux de physiologie, de chimie, de physique et de mathématiques, il me semble que, dans un congrès de philosophes, il faut faire d'abord de la philosophie, la philosophie étant entendue comme une recherche qui, par un côté, est étroitement liée sans doute à la science positive, mais qui en est indépendante par d'autres et possède sa méthode propre.

Special Supplement, *Journal of Philosophical Research* pp. 123–131
DOI: 10.5840/jpr201237Supplement30

C'est en respectant la proximité avec les sciences mais sans croire que la philosophie soit «indépendante des sciences» que je me propose de contribuer au thème choisi pour le Congrès international 2008: «Repenser la philosophie», en traitant de l'idée de «renaissance».

En effet, l'interdépendance croissante entre les nations, les effets des découvertes scientifiques et des inventions technologiques sur la vie quotidienne des hommes et sur la puissance des États, le caractère de plus en plus collectif de la recherche posent des problèmes inédits en philosophie des sciences, comme en politique. Nous nous posons ici la question: comment faire en sorte que, progressivement, toutes les nations entrent dans le réseau scientifique et technologique mondial qui se construit sous nos yeux?

INTRODUCTION

La Renaissance, d'où sortit la science moderne au cours du XVIIe siècle, a-t-elle été un événement unique, impossible à reproduire? Ou bien l'idée de renaissance désigne-t-elle un processus général qui peut se répéter? Dans le 1er cas, étudier la Renaissance telle qu'elle s'est produite en Europe est l'affaire des historiens; dans le 2ème cas, l'idée de renaissance mérite l'attention non seulement des scientifiques et des politiques, mais aussi des philosophes, puisque, si nous savons en décrypter le sens, elle nous fera mieux comprendre comment les nations peuvent se moderniser et accroître leur puissance en entrant dans le réseau scientifique et technologique mondial.

Disposons-nous d'éléments pour choisir entre ces deux hypothèses? La réponse est: oui. La thèse que nous soutenons est la suivante: le terme de "renaissance" ne désigne pas seulement un événement historique dont l'Europe fut le théâtre aux XVe et XVIe siècles; il désigne aussi un ensemble d'attitudes, de démarches et de décisions fondées en raison et susceptibles de se reproduire en d'autres temps et en d'autres lieux.

I. LA RENAISSANCE EUROPÉENNE

1° La Renaissance européenne en tant qu'événement

De quoi est fait l'enchaînement de circonstances d'où naît au début du XVIIe siècle la science moderne?

i) La première Renaissance

À partir des années 1420 et jusqu'à la prise de Constantinople par les Turcs en 1453, des érudits de Byzance firent passer en Italie les manuscrits grecs et latins qu'ils voulaient sauver. De leur côté, les gens cultivés de Florence et, progressivement, de l'ensemble de l'Europe s'attachèrent à redécouvrir l'héritage gréco-latin, dans les sciences, mais aussi en art, en droit, dans les techniques, etc. Ce fut la première Renaissance, celle de la reprise de l'héritage antique et de son assimilation.

ii) La seconde Renaissance

Puis, au sein de la "République des Lettres" (Marc Fumaroli) qui se formait, souvent à l'extérieur des institutions existantes, on s'aperçut qu'il était possible d'aller plus loin que les Anciens, et de découvrir de nouvelles voies dans les sciences, les techniques, la création artistique, le domaine religieux. Ce fut la seconde Renaissance, celle du XVIe siècle.

C'est sur ce terreau que naquit au début du XVIIe siècle la science moderne.

iii) La lenteur du processus de la Renaissance

Si l'on prend comme référence le cas de l'Europe, on constate que la "Renaissance" s'étend sur deux siècles et demi, depuis le transport en Italie des manuscrits scientifiques et philosophiques de l'Antiquité (dans les années 1420–1450) jusqu'à la naissance de la science moderne (1596–1612) et à l'établissement d'une physique universelle (1687).

iv) Les théories sont retravaillées en permanence

À peine conçue, la "première synthèse de la physique"—comme la nomme Whitehead, qui en situe le centre de gravité en 1642 (année de la mort de Galilée et de la naissance de Newton)—donne lieu à des remaniements internes si considérables que, de 1687 à 1787, des *Principia* de Newton à la *Mécanique analytique* de Lagrange, la conceptualisation et le mode d'exposition de la physique changent profondément.

v) Rareté et inégale répartition des lieux d'excellence

Dans la Grèce antique et depuis les débuts de la science moderne jusqu'à aujourd'hui, les foyers de découverte scientifique ont été peu nombreux et très inégalement répartis. Comme la puissance des empires et la sécurité des États ne requéraient pas un dynamisme scientifique propre, cette répartition hétérogène des hauts lieux de connaissance ne préoccupait ni les autorités politiques ni les particuliers. Ce n'est plus le cas aujourd'hui car l'accès aux biens élémentaires (eau potable, électricité, soins médicaux, instruction, sécurité, etc.) dépend de plus en plus de l'insertion des sociétés dans les échanges scientifiques et technologiques.

Bilan: L'élément déclencheur de la Renaissance européenne fut donc la réappropriation de l'héritage gréco-latin par l'Italie et le reste de l'Europe, à partir des années 1420, quand l'Empire byzantin se défait. Les savants craignent que l'héritage intellectuel et spirituel de l'Antiquité disparaisse; ils veulent en assurer la diffusion et la réplication (rôle des copistes, puis des imprimeurs); et prennent conscience que, sur la base de celui-ci, on peut aller plus loin et faire autre chose.

2° Les traits universels de la renaissance européenne

Quand on scrute cet ensemble historique complexe, on y discerne certains traits universels.

i) La Renaissance est le fruit du rationalisme chrétien

La Renaissance européenne est un "miracle chrétien", au sens où Renan parle du "miracle grec". Non seulement parce que les savants qui fondent la science moderne sont croyants; mais surtout parce qu'ils pensent que la raison humaine peut découvrir les opérations de la nature, c'est-à-dire, pour eux, les modalités de la création de l'univers. C'est possible, à leurs yeux, parce que Dieu a créé l'homme «à son image et à sa ressemblance» (*Genèse* 2).

ii) La science est la «sécularisation» du rationalisme chrétien

Cette conviction d'origine religieuse se sécularise (en s'appliquant à la nature) et s'explicite en un programme ouvert de recherches scientifiques. Un grand témoin, à la fois métaphysicien et géomètre, Malebranche (1638–1715), membre de l'Académie des Sciences de Paris, l'atteste à la fin du XVIIe siècle, quand la science moderne a déjà pris racine: parlant de l'idée de l'étendue, idée que «les géomètres et les bons physiciens» contemplent, il déclare: «elle est si féconde en vérités, que tous les esprits ensemble ne l'épuiseront jamais». De son côté, Leibniz, dans les *Essais de théodicée*, publiés en 1710, six ans avant sa mort, va dans le même sens, en se situant, non plus du point de vue de la raison humaine, mais du point de vue de la sagesse de Dieu. Il fait preuve, nous dit Maurice Blondel, d'un «réalisme supérieur».

iii) L'universalité de la raison

Les grands humanistes européens du XVIe et du XVIIe siècles sont convaincus de l'universalité de la raison. À leurs yeux, l'égalité entre les hommes—et, par exemple, entre la civilisation chrétienne de l'Europe et les civilisations d'Extrême-Orient—ne se limite pas à la vie ici-bas. Les hommes sont égaux par la raison; mais ils sont aussi égaux devant l'espérance du salut.

iv) Une nouvelle conception de la liberté

Le rationalisme classique, solidaire de la science moderne, est imprégné d'une idée de la liberté qui s'inspire de la Bible et de la philosophie grecque. Cette conception comporte les traits suivants: (a) Alors que, dans la pensée antique, seul le sage parvient à la liberté, dans la pensée chrétienne, la liberté est un attribut de l'homme en tant qu'homme. Cette idée, une fois laïcisée, a favorisé la notion de démocratie. Bien plus, un dialogue avec Dieu est possible (Abraham); (b) les individus ne constituent pas des entités séparées: ils sont interconnectés si bien que l'Humanité tout entière forme un «corps»; (c) les premiers siècles du christianisme ayant été marqués par des persécutions, les nouveaux convertis savent que «témoigner» peut conduire à la mort. Or tout le monde n'a pas la vocation du martyre: d'où l'idée que, ce que nous ne sommes pas capables de faire en action, nous pouvons au moins l'approcher par l'affection et que, si l'excellence nous fait défaut, nous pouvons en pallier le manque en restant liés aux plus exemplaires: «*si non excellentia connexione*», dit saint Augustin (*Sermo* 280). En d'autres termes, les hommes accèdent à la liberté et à la raison par des efforts conjugués et par la conscience que tous les hommes forment une même communauté; (d) enfin, dès l'origine, on trouve l'amorce de ce que nous appelons aujourd'hui la «laïcité», à savoir l'idée que les hommes, pour s'organiser et faire leur histoire, doivent compter sur leurs ressources propres, et non sur une «loi divine» qu'ils auraient à appliquer.

Bien entendu, ces idéaux ont souvent été perdus de vue et bafoués: il n'en reste pas moins qu'ils ont imprégné l'Europe et, par-là, dans une large mesure, le reste du monde.

> *Bilan*: De ces observations, il ressort que la Renaissance, en tant qu'événement historique singulier, comporte des traits qui se prêtent à une universalisation: (a) croyance que tous les hommes ont part à la liberté et à la raison; (b) assurance que l'esprit humain est armé pour connaître l'univers; (c) conviction que, quoique l'humanité soit fragmentée en "sociétés closes" (Bergson) méfiantes et portées à se faire la guerre, elle a pour vocation de jeter les bases d'une "société ouverte", s'organisant pour régler ses différends par la négociation plutôt que par la violence; (d) certitude que la démocratie et la libre discussion des idées favorisent la recherche (John Herschel, 1830).

II. LA «RENAISSANCE» COMME MODÈLE D'ACQUISITION DE LA CONNAISSANCE

L'idée de renaissance véhicule le message suivant: l'humanité forme une seule communauté. Cependant, à certains moments de leur histoire, les sociétés découvrent dans d'autres cultures des idées, des savoir-faire, des idéaux dont elles ont besoin pour leur propre développement. Pour les acquérir, elles doivent intérioriser un modèle extérieur. Si l'opération réussit, la société qui a assimilé un héritage étranger découvre qu'elle possède en elle-même la capacité d'enrichir cet héritage et de devenir à son tour créatrice.

La renaissance est un processus en trois temps: (a) prise de conscience d'un besoin qu'une autre culture a su satisfaire; (b) assimilation intelligente du modèle extérieur; (c) originalité créatrice.

Pour essayer de comprendre ce processus, nous nous référons à trois modèles du devenir historique dans les sciences: 1° la «loi des 3 états» d'Auguste Comte; 2° la théorie kantienne de l'imitation créatrice; 3° la théorie des "révolutions scientifiques" de Cournot (comparée à celle de Thomas Kuhn).

1° Renaissance et loi des trois états

Selon Auguste Comte, toute société et tout individu passent par trois formes d'intelligence et de sensibilité. La célèbre loi des trois états nous aide à comprendre à quelles conditions une société devient originale et créatrice.

i) L'état théologique

Dans l'état «théologique», la renaissance est l'action de renouer avec une histoire sacrée, avec la sagesse ancienne dont la tradition est porteuse, avec la *science* qu'elle inclut.

Prenons comme exemple la conception selon laquelle l'Afrique a été autrefois détentrice d'une sagesse, voire d'une science qui a fécondé l'Égypte puis la Grèce. Le raisonnement est le suivant: Hérodote et Platon nous disent que c'est de la sagesse de l'Égypte que la Grèce s'est nourrie. Or la civilisation égyptienne vient des sources du Nil, où se trouvaient jadis de puissants royaumes africains. Ceux-ci lui ont donc servi de nourrice. On reconstitue ainsi une filiation sacrée, selon ce qu'Auguste Comte appelle l'état théologique de la pensée: à l'origine les hommes bénéficiaient d'une instruction divine, ils pouvaient ainsi accéder au «laboratoire divin de la nature», selon l'expression de Goethe. Cette sagesse sacrée contenait, sous une forme voilée, la «science» moderne. Savoir, c'est se ressouvenir d'une science enfouie, science plus profonde que nos miettes actuelles. Être sage, c'est retrouver le passé et lui être fidèle; et non essayer d'inventer une science nouvelle.

ii) L'état métaphysique

C'est celui dans lequel l'esprit prend confiance en lui-même: il ne situe plus dans un passé mythique l'état où les hommes partageaient le savoir des dieux; car il estime que l'esprit est porteur d'un pouvoir analogue à celui des dieux. Prenons un exemple moderne: au début du XIXe siècle, la *Naturphilosophie* romantique et l'Idéalisme allemand manifestent une confiance absolue dans les pouvoirs de l'esprit: l'esprit porte en lui-même, pensent-ils, le monogramme de la nature, car Esprit (*Geist*) et Nature (*Natur*) sont faits de la même étoffe. Mais Schelling et Hegel échouent dans le domaine de la physique et de la chimie, parce qu'ils attribuent à tort les mêmes lois à l'Esprit et à la Nature.

iii) L'état positif

Le rêve de pénétrer les causes ultimes des choses disparaît. On accepte l'idée que la nature, c'est l'Autre. Auguste Comte nous dit: Cessons de croire que la nature est à l'image de notre psychisme: ce n'est pas par introspection que nous accédons à ses lois, mais par l'observation et, plus encore, par l'expérimentation. Auguste Comte rejoint Francis Bacon.

Bilan. La loi des 3 états a le mérite de clarifier les conditions qui sont nécessaires pour que l'esprit soit créatif dans le domaine des sciences de la nature. Quand ces conditions nous satisfont, l'esprit peut être dit «positif».

Il aurait très bien pu se faire, en effet, que la nature nous restât opaque: il aurait suffi pour cela que les mathématiques ne nous aident aucunement à formuler des lois, tout simplement parce que rien de stable n'aurait existé dans la nature.

Auguste Comte nous fait comprendre que l'idée de renaissance ne devient féconde au point de vue scientifique qu'à partir du moment où l'esprit reconnaît la nature comme une étrangère dont il faut essayer de percer les lois. L'âge positif est l'âge du rationalisme, c'est-à-dire un état dans lequel l'homme fait confiance à l'ordre des choses.

2° Renaissance et imitation créatrice *(Kant)*

Il existe une 2ème conception de l'enchaînement des événements dans un processus de «renaissance», c'est celle que Kant expose dans la *Critique de la faculté de juger*: dans les sciences—et dans les sciences seulement—, nous pouvons refaire les démarches des découvreurs et, en les imitant, les dépasser. Cela implique deux conditions: i) que le temps ne soit pas cyclique, mais linéaire et progressif; ii) que l'imitation conduise à l'invention.

Kant observe: la reprise d'un modèle antérieur de connaissance ne peut être une action libre et créatrice que dans les sciences. Pourquoi dans les sciences? Et pourquoi *seulement* dans les sciences?

La réponse de Kant à ces deux questions est simple: (1) la recherche de la vérité, dans les sciences, est facilitée par le fait que les grands découvreurs laissent des traces de leurs démarches, si bien qu'on peut mettre ses pas dans les leurs; (2) là où il n'y a pas science, mais art ou technique, l'imitation perd sa transparence parce que les créateurs eux-mêmes ne savent pas comment ils ont produit leurs œuvres (Kant cite l'exemple d'Homère et de Wieland).

Il y a donc dans la science quelque chose d'unique: (1) ses démarches sont assez explicites pour être refaites par d'autres (d'où le fait que les *Éléments* d'Euclide ont servi de manuel de géométrie et d'arithmétique pendant deux millénaires); (2) on constate que ceux qui «imitent» deviennent à leur tour des maîtres qui innovent.

Tel est le modèle kantien du processus de «renaissance»: mettre ses pas dans ceux des découvreurs; les imiter; et aller plus loin qu'eux.

3° Renaissance et révolutions scientifiques

Dans la conception kantienne de la «renaissance», une fois que l'esprit est mis sur la voie de la science, il n'y a plus besoin d'autres «révolutions scientifiques».

Or, au XIXe siècle, il devient évident que la science elle-même a une histoire et que, au cours de ce développement, des changements d'état (de structure, de conjectures, de modes d'observation et d'expérimentation) se produisent. D'où l'idée que ce que nous appelons une «renaissance» est en fait une «révolution scientifique».

i) La théorie des «révolutions scientifiques» de Cournot

Le premier philosophe a avoir proposé une théorie des «révolutions scientifiques», c'est Antoine Augustin Cournot (1801–1877) dans ses *Considérations sur la marche des idées et des événements dans les temps modernes* (1873). L'idée de «révolution scientifique» substitue à l'idée kantienne d'un changement d'état unique et définitif—l'accession de l'entendement à la science—la vue selon laquelle les sciences au cours de leur histoire revêtent une suite d'états différents et que ces changements d'état constituent, dans certains cas, des «révolutions scientifiques».

Une «révolution scientifique», c'est la découverte d'une clef plus puissante que la clef jusque-là disponible pour décrire (et, si possible, expliquer) comment fonctionne la nature. Selon Cournot, la substitution du modèle astronomique de Copernic à celui de Ptolémée ne fut pas une complète «révolution»: en effet, les deux représentations du système solaire sont géométriques; et elles ne fournissent aucune explication du mouvement des corps célestes. La vraie «révolution scientifique», par rapport à l'astronomie de Ptolémée et même de Copernic, est celle qu'opèrent Kepler, Galilée, Descartes et, surtout, Newton. Ce dernier fournit en effet une explication du mouvement des planètes autour du soleil. C'est la fondation de la *dynamique* qui constitue la révolution. Cournot parle d'un *siècle* révolutionnaire.

Cournot aperçoit bien que la clef de la mécanique ne permet pas de pénétrer dans le domaine des liaisons chimiques; la chimie de synthèse, à partir de 1828, va reproduire des substances existantes et en introduire de nouvelles dans la nature..

Il remarque aussi que, dans les années 1860, l'histoire naturelle n'a pas atteint un état scientifique: il loue Darwin, mais il estime que l'usage qu'il fait des probabilités n'est pas adéquat. Il pense donc qu'il y a une révolution probabiliste à venir en physique et dans les sciences de la vie. Il n'est pas relativiste car, selon lui, l'invention d'une clef nouvelle ne disqualifie pas la précédente: elle en conserve les résultats empiriques attestés. Un tel rationalisme est un réalisme.

Cournot est réaliste. Il ne croit pas que la nature recèle des secrets à jamais soustraits à l'observation et à l'analyse. Il estime que l'esprit humain est capable, devant deux constructions logiques, de dire si l'une est une représentation fidèle des processus naturels et l'autre non. Il ne voit pas de raison pour que l'esprit de l'homme soit incapable de découvrir les enchaînements causals des processus naturels: pas entièrement ni partout, bien sûr, mais en tout cas par endroits.

ii) Renaissances et révolutions scientifiques

L'introduction, en philosophie des sciences, de l'idée de «révolution» modifie l'idée de «renaissance»: si, en effet, l'histoire des sciences est ponctuée par l'émergence de théories nouvelles, qui sont comme des clefs de plus en plus puissantes pour expliquer les processus naturels et unifier les lois de la nature, il doit aussi y avoir une pluralité de «renaissances», qui sont comme la reprise d'héritages en vue de les assimiler et de les faire fructifier. La notion de «renaissance» désigne un processus général qui a eu lieu en Europe et qui se produit ailleurs. Il s'agit d'un changement d'état par lequel un ensemble de connaissances retrouve ou conquiert le statut de «science», c'est-à-dire une solidité théorique et empirique.

III. REPENSER L'IDÉE DE RENAISSANCE

i) Le pari du réalisme

Pour que l'idée de renaissance n'en reste pas à l'état théologique ou métaphysique, il faut qu'elle ne soit pas conçue comme le retour mythique à un âge ancien, mais comme un effort systématique et volontaire pour mettre au jour les processus naturels.

C'est un pari philosophique, celui du réalisme. Il exprime la conviction que la nature n'est pas impénétrable à l'esprit fini des hommes. L'esprit humain peut juger si une construction théorique représente fidèlement ou non des opérations de la nature. Il s'agit là d'une conjecture forte, qui n'est pas généralisable à l'ensemble de la nature. Elle n'est testable, en effet, que localement, dans une discipline déterminée.

ii) le pari du travail collectif

Les «renaissances», au XXIe siècle, auront une forme différente de la Renaissance européenne, car la rationalité scientifique et technologique repose davantage aujourd'hui sur l'interaction collective des hommes que sur le seul génie des individus.

Les «renaissances» exigeront, en particulier, des institutions qui favorisent, à l'échelle du monde, ce que, il y a déjà plus d'un siècle, le sociologue Émile Durkheim appelait la «communion des intelligences».

Peut-on préciser en quoi consistera cette «communion des intelligences»? Et quelles sont les institutions qui la favoriseraient? C'est là l'une des questions que recouvre le thème de notre Congrès: «Repenser la philosophie».

iii) Le pari d'une philosophie qui soit une cosmologie ou, comme dit Whitehead, «An Essay in Cosmology»

Puisque nous avons pour tâche de «repenser la philosophie», nous devons essayer de préciser quelles sont les choix qui se présentent à nous. On peut essayer de les présenter sous la forme d'un arbre de décision.

La philosophie peut-elle être indépendante du savoir positif (des sciences) ou non?

Pour ma part, je réponds: Non. Dans cette perspective, on refuse de fonder la philosophie sur la seule connaissance ordinaire: la perception, l'introspection, l'observation du monde social et naturel environnant. C'est le refus de la phénoménologie, fondé sur l'idée que la perception ne nous livre pas les traits les plus profonds du monde réel.

On choisit alors d'asseoir la réflexion philosophique sur les mathématiques, les sciences de la nature (physique, biologie, physiologie, sciences cognitives, etc.) et les sciences sociales. Du même coup, le «réel» n'est plus seulement le monde environnant (*Umwelt*), ni non plus uniquement la Terre, mais l'univers.

Si le réel, c'est l'univers et si nous en sommes des productions, il est clair que nous ne pouvons pas découvrir le sens de notre destinée individuelle et du sort collectif de l'Humanité en négligeant les processus qui nous lient à la nature et, plus généralement, à l'univers.

C'est clair pour ce qui concerne le réchauffement climatique; mais c'est également évident quand on considère les actions que la biologie et la médecine nous permettent de faire.

Repenser la philosophie, c'est donc repenser les liens substantiels (Le «*Vinculum substantiale*» de Leibniz) qui nous attachent à l'univers.

SELECTED PAPERS FROM
THE XXII WORLD CONGRESS OF PHILOSOPHY

«Repenser la philosophie»: une tâche et un problème herméneutique

JEAN GREISCH
ROMANO-GUARDINI LEHRSTUHL, HUMBOLDT-UNIVERSITÄT ZU BERLIN

Abstract: Si «penser» est d'abord un acte, «repenser» l'est aussi. On ne peut «repenser» que ce qui fut déjà pensé une fois. Ce que «repenser» veut dire, nous ne le comprenons que si nous nous demandons au préalable ce que «penser» veut dire. Pour Heidegger, cela revient à se demander ce qui *nous appelle* à penser, pour Kant, c'est se demander comment on peut *s'orienter dans la pensée*, pour Nietzsche, ce qui nous *pousse* à penser, à quoi j'ajouterai la question, moins connue et plus déconcertante, d'Eugen Rosenstock-Huessy dans son essai sur la «pensée dative»: «*Cui cogitatur?*», «À qui nos pensées sont-elles *destinées*?»

À quoi nos pensées sont-elles *dédiées*?, *à qui* sont-elles *destinées*?: c'est la tension féconde entre ces deux questions qui nous met sur la voie d'une réflexion sur le sens que le verbe «repenser» peut revêtir dans la bouche d'un philosophe. À la différence de ceux qui s'imaginent que «repenser» veut dire simplement distribuer un peu différemment les cartes du savoir, les vrais «repenseurs» ne cessent de se demander à quel jeu ils jouent quand il s'efforcent de penser philosophiquement et ils cherchent à avoir une conscience plus nette des enjeux de ces jeux de la pensée.

1
Als er Siebzig war und war gebrechlich
Drängte es den Lehrer doch nach Ruh
Denn die Güte war im Lande wieder einmal schwächlich
Und die Bosheit nahm an Kräften wieder einmal zu.
Und er gürtete die Schuh.

2
Und er packte ein, was er so brauchte:
Wenig. Doch es wurde dies und das.

Special Supplement, *Journal of Philosophical Research* pp. 133–150
DOI: 10.5840/jpr201237Supplement31

So die Pfeife, die er abends immer rauchte
Und das Büchlein, das er immer las.
Weißbrot nach dem Augenmaß.

3
Freute sich des Tals noch einmal und vergaß es
Als er ins Gebirg den Weg einschlug.
Und sein Ochse freute sich des frischen Grases
Kauend, während er den Alten trug.
Denn dem ging es schnell genug.

4
Doch am vierten Tag im Felsgesteine
Hat ein Zöllner ihm den Weg verwehrt:
«Kostbarkeiten zu verzollen?»—«Keine.»
Und der Knabe, der den Ochsen führte, sprach: «Er hat gelehrt.»
Und so war auch das erklärt.

5
Doch der Mann in einer heitren Regung
Fragte noch: «Hat er was rausgekriegt?»
Sprach der Knabe: «Daß das weiche Wasser in Bewegung
Mit der Zeit den mächitgen Stein besiegt.
Du verstehst, das Harte unterliegt.»

6
Daß er nicht das letzte Tageslicht verlöre
Trieb der Knabe nun den Ochsen an
Und die drei verschwanden schon um eine schwarze Föhre
Da kam plötzlich Fahrt in unsern Mann
Und er schrie: «He, du! Halt an!

7
Was ist das mit diesem Wasser, Alter?»
Hielt der Alte: «Intressiert es dich?»
Sprach der Mann: «Ich bin nur Zollverwalter
Doch wer wen besiegt, das intressiert auch mich.
Wenn du's weißt, dann sprich!

8
Schreib mir's auf! Diktier es diesem Kinde!
So was nimmt man doch nicht mit sich fort.
Da gibt's doch Papier bei uns und Tinte
Und ein Nachtmahl gibt es auch: ich wohne dort.
Nun, ist das ein Wort?»

9
Über seine Schulter sah der Alte
Auf den Mann: Flickjoppe. Keine Schuh.
Und die Stirne eine einzige Falte.
Ach, kein Sieger trat da auf ihn zu.
Und er murmelte: «Auch du?»

10
Eine höfliche Bitte abzuschlagen
War der Alte, wie es schien, zu alt.
Denn er sagte laut: «Die etwas fragen
Die verdienen Antwort.» Sprach der Knabe: «Es wird auch schon kalt.»
«Gut, ein kleiner Aufenthalt.»

11
Und von seinem Ochsen stieg der Weise
Sieben Tage schrieben sie zu zweit
Und der Zöllner brachte Essen (und er fluchte nur noch leise
Mit den Schmugglern in der ganzen Zeit).
Und dann war's soweit.

12
Und dem Zöllner händigte der Knabe
Eines Morgens einundachtzig Sprüche ein.
Und mit Dank für eine kleine Reisegabe
Bogen sie um jene Föhre ins Gestein.
Sagt jetzt: kann man höflicher sein?

13
Aber rühmen wir nicht nur den Weisen
Dessen Name auf dem Buche prangt!
Denn man muß dem Weisen seine Weisheit erst entreißen.
Darum sei der Zöllner auch bedankt:
Er hat sie ihm abverlangt.

—Bertolt Brecht, *Legende von der Entstehung des Buches TAOTEKING auf dem Weg des Laotse in die Emigration*

C'est en tant que «citoyens du monde» et non en tant que simples «artistes de la raison» que nous sommes réunis ici à Séoul pour le vingt-deuxième Congrès mondial de philosophie. À la différence de Kant, qui demandait aux philosophes conscients de leur vocation cosmopolitique d'affronter les célèbres quatre questions fondamentales qui récapitulent les grands intérêts de la raison: «Que puis-je savoir?, Que dois-je faire?, Que m'est-il permis d'espérer?», Qu'est-ce que l'homme?», les organisateurs de ce Congrès mondial de philosophie nous confient, semble-t-il, la redoutable tâche de «repenser la philosophie».

«Repenser la philosophie»: qu'est-ce à dire au juste?

Tôt ou tard—sûrement pas trop tôt, mais pas non plus trop tard, à l'heure crépusculaire où le: «Vanité des vanités, tout n'est que vanité»—risque d'engloutir nos certitudes les mieux assurées, tout philosophe devrait écrire son propre Protreptique, c'est-à-dire sa réponse à la question: «Qu'est-ce que la philosophie?». Ce serait probablement la manière la plus efficace, en tout cas la plus «honnête», de «repenser la philosophie».

Un simple examen de la structure lexicale de cette formule nous montre qu'elle se compose d'un verbe («repenser»), d'un article défini («la») et d'un substantif («philosophie»). Ce qui apparaît comme une tâche est en même temps un immense problème. Mais la vocation du philosophe n'est-elle pas justement d'identifier des problèmes et d'inventer les concepts qui permettent de les résoudre?

La difficulté s'accroît encore, si nous rapportons la formule: «repenser la philosophie» au quadrilatère notionnel: «Histoire (de la philosophie), Traditions, Dialogue, Critique» qui figure au programme de notre session plénière d'aujourd'hui. Il importe de désamorcer le soupçon qu'il ne s'agit que d'un simple fourre-tout qui s'accommode aux contenus les plus divers, ou d'une auberge espagnole où chacun vient consommer les aliments et les boissons qu'il a apportées lui-même. Il nous faudra au contraire montrer en quel sens ces quatre termes peuvent entrer en résonance avec la formule directrice «repenser la philosophie», l'éclairant à chaque fois sous un angle nouveau.

C'est à cette double tâche que je m'attellerai ici, en mobilisant pour cela les ressources d'une philosophie «herméneutique», appellation dont la signification s'éclairera «chemin faisant».

I. «LA» «PHILOSOPHIE» A-T-ELLE BESOIN D'ÊTRE «REPENSÉE»?

1. Penser et repenser

Si «penser» est d'abord un acte, «repenser» l'est aussi. On ne peut «repenser» que ce qui fut déjà pensé une fois. Ce que «repenser» veut dire, nous ne le comprenons que si nous nous demandons au préalable ce que «penser» veut dire. Pour Heidegger, cela revient à se demander ce qui *nous appelle* à penser, pour Kant, c'est se demander comment on peut *s'orienter dans la pensée*, pour Nietzsche, ce qui nous *pousse* à penser, à quoi j'ajouterai la question moins connue et plus déconcertante d'Eugen Rosenstock-Huessy dans son essai sur la «pensée dative»: «*Cui cogitatur?*», «À qui nos pensées sont-elles *destinées*?»

À quoi nos pensées sont-elles *dédiées*?, *à qui* sont-elles *destinées*?: la tension féconde entre ces deux questions nous met sur la voie d'une réflexion sur le sens que le verbe «repenser» peut revêtir dans la bouche d'un philosophe.

1. Je dirai d'abord que ce verbe doit être pris ici dans la même extension que celle du verbe «penser» dans un passage célèbre de la *Deuxième Méditation métaphysique* de Descartes: «Mais qu'est-ce donc ce que je suis? Une chose qui pense. Qu'est-ce

qu'une chose qui pense? C'est-à-dire une chose qui doute, qui conçoit, qui affirme, qui nie, qui veut, qui ne veut pas, qui imagine aussi, et qui sent».

Ce qui me fascine dans ce bref passage, c'est que nous y surprenons le penseur Descartes en «flagrant délit» de «repenser» sa première définition du *cogito*. Pour des raisons que Descartes ne précise pas, mais qu'il appartient aux interprètes de deviner et d'expliciter, il ne se contente pas de faire du *cogito* une «chose qui pense». Cette définition pourrait cautionner une conception strictement intellectualiste de l'acte de penser, celle qu'on associe régulièrement avec un «cartésianisme» dont Descartes fut sûrement exempt. Descartes n'est pas un «cartésien», si nous prenons au sérieux la manière dont il relance la compréhension de la pensée, en nous rappelant que «penser», c'est douter, concevoir (produire des concepts, comprendre), affirmer, nier, vouloir, ne pas vouloir, imaginer et même sentir! Rien ne nous interdit d'allonger la liste en y incluant les verbes «désirer» ou même «aimer», comme le faisait le duc de Luynes dans sa traduction française des *Méditations*.

Si «penser» veut dire tout cela, «repenser» également: on «repense» en doutant (y compris en doutant de la légitimité du doute hyperbolique, comme le fait Wittgenstein dans *De la certitude*), en s'efforçant de mieux comprendre et en inventant de nouveaux concepts, en réaffirmant, en «reniant», en voulant (par exemple en consentant à l'involontaire absolu sous la triple figure du caractère, de l'inconscient et de la vie[1]), en refusant (par exemple: en se révoltant), en mobilisant de façon créatrice les ressources de l'imagination, au lieu de n'y voir qu'une source de confusion et d'illusion, et même en «ressentant», d'abord en éprouvant que nous sommes des vivants, puis en faisant un usage «heuristique» de nos affects (la *docta spes* de Bloch; «l'heuristique de la peur» de Hans Jonas), etc.

2. L'idée de «repenser» la philosophie se complexifie encore, si nous prêtons attention aux multiples sens du préfixe: «*re-*»

a) Au niveau le plus élémentaire, il s'agit d'une «répétition». Personne n'aime être taxé de simple «répétiteur», tant il est vrai qu'une répétition «mot à mot», ou une simple paraphrase, représente une menace mortelle pour l'acte vif du penser, dont on ne sait jamais où il nous mènera. Mais suffit-il, pour conjurer ce danger, de vouloir à tout prix du neuf, de l'inédit, du jamais encore pensé? Je n'en suis pas sûr! Kierkegaard et Heidegger nous rappellent que «répéter», (*Wiederholen*), entendu comme reprise et ressaisie peut être une opération créatrice et non l'éternel retour du même.

b) A un second niveau, le préfixe a le même sens que dans le verbe «réfléchir», cher à la tradition française de la philosophie réflexive, dont Jean Nabert fut le dernier témoin. Ce que je retiens de lui pour mes réflexions présentes, c'est sa thèse d'après laquelle la conscience elle-même est indissociable de l'acte de repenser qui ne se focalise pas sur des objets qu'il s'agirait de mieux connaître, mais sur le désir de comprendre dont Nabert dit qu'il est «une reprise exercée sur la subjectivité et l'objectivité à la fois».[2] La question rhétorique: «Pourquoi la philosophie n'accepterait-elle pas que les plus hautes vérités de la philosophie fussent strictement solidaires du mouvement du se comprendre qu'est la philosophie elle-même, et que par ce procès toujours en acte, elles n'eussent aucune demeure?»,[3] nous atteint de plein fouet, si nous acceptons, comme nous y invite explicitement Nabert, de ne pas dissocier le «repenser» et le «se comprendre». J'appliquerai au «repenser» ce que Nabert considère comme «le plus vif du problème» du «se comprendre»: «Entre une objectivité scientifique ou métaphysique qui le passe, qui lui est indifférente, et une croyance subjective ou une foi, le se comprendre doit se frayer un chemin, être plutôt un chemin, conduisant à des affirmations d'une nature singulière: elles n'ont de raison d'être et de valeur que par le se comprendre qui les a mis à jour».[4]

c) En ce point de ma méditation, je suis saisi d'un scrupule «herméneutique»: qu'arrive-t-il au verbe «repenser» si nous le soumettons au test de la traductibilité? Les représentants des différentes langues et traditions représentées dans ce Congrès mondial nous diront comment ce verbe est rendu dans leur propre langue et avec quelles connotations. À l'intérieur des limites étroites des quelques langues européennes qui me sont familières, la langue allemande me semble constituer un cas particulièrement intéressant, dans la mesure où on n'y trouve pas d'équivalent strict du verbe «repenser» des langues romanes ou du *rethinking* anglo-saxon. Au lieu et place d'un introuvable *Wiederdenken*, nous y trouvons une gamme très riche de verbes: *Bedenken*, *Überdenken*, *Nachdenken*, auxquels on pourrait ajouter, dans une optique heideggérienne: *Andenken* et *Zudenken*. Chacun de ces verbes et chacun de ces préfixes contribue à enrichir notre compréhension du verbe «repenser».

2. Repenser le philosopher: du bon usage de «la fonction ϕ»

«La philosophie»: cet article défini a de quoi décourager les plus audacieux, s'il désigne la somme encyclopédique des idées ou du savoir philosophique accumulé depuis des millénaires et consigné dans les bibliothèques universitaires. Rares sont les philosophes contemporains qui croient encore à la possibilité de rédiger une «encyclopédie des sciences philosophiques», à l'instar de celle de Hegel qui se faisait fort de promouvoir un nouveau traitement (*neue Bearbeitung*) de la philosophie, d'après une méthode parfaitement ajustée aux contenus et au but de toute recherche philosophique: «la connaissance scientifique de la vérité».

Dans la préface à la deuxième édition de son *Encycoplédie des sciences philosophiques*, Hegel précisait qu'il s'agit du «chemin le plus difficile», mais qui est en même temps le seul qui ait un intérêt et une valeur pour l'esprit, une fois que celui-ci s'est engagé sur le chemin de la pensée. À condition de garder intacte la volonté et l'audace du vrai, l'esprit découvre que «la méthode seule est capable de maîtriser la pensée et de la guider vers la chose même pour l'y maintenir».

Pour Hegel, un tel cheminement ne peut s'accomplir que comme victoire sur le prétendu «savoir immédiat», quelle qu'en soit la forme. Si, comme le soutient Hegel, la philosophie est la «considération pensante des objets»,[5] elle est par essence un «repenser» (*Nachdenken*), c'est-à-dire une «pensée *réfléchissante* qui a pour *contenu* des *pensées* en tant que pensées qu'elle amène à la conscience».

Parce qu'il est un *Nachdenker*, le philosophe ne saurait revendiquer de régner, tel un monarque absolu ou un despote, sur l'empire de la pensée. Il n'est, pourrait-on dire, qu'un «repenseur», dont la tâche propre est de ressaisir «dans l'élément du Concept» les pensées qui existent déjà sous forme de représentations. Le Concept (*der Begriff*) au sens de Hegel est le travail et le processus dynamique de compréhension conduit jusqu'au bout. L'ouvrier du Concept qu'est le philosophe se heurte nécessairement à l'impatience «de ceux qui voudraient conserver sous le mode de la représentation ce qui est présent dans la conscience en tant que pensée et en tant que Concept».[6]

Il est vrai que, de nos jours, le Concept n'a pas toujours bonne presse. On le soupçonne volontiers, et parfois de manière expéditive, de servir de caution à l'idée de totalité, elle-même suspecte de n'être qu'une simple transposition, dans le champ du pensable philosophique, du «totalitarisme» politique.

C'est en critiquant l'idée de totalité, censée avoir régné sur la philosophie occidentale «d'Ionie à Iéna» que Franz Rosenzweig et Emmanuel Levinas, qui méritent incontestablement le titre de «repenseurs», ont promu une «pensée nouvelle» qui surmonte la Totalité au nom de l'Infini (ou de la «Révélation» dans le cas de Rosenzweig). Ils donnent ainsi une expression philosophique à l'intuition de certains kabbalistes, pour lesquels la lettre *lamed* (la première lettre du mot hébreu désignant l'étude, et la dernière lettre de la Thora) est composée d'un *kaf*, connotant une plénitude «compréhensive», lui-même surmonté d'un *vav*, qui lui imprime un mouvement ascendant. Tout se passe comme si la «Totalité» devrait être «convertie» en «Infini» jusque dans le graphisme de la lettre.

Si nous rechignons à nous engager sur les chemins périlleux d'une mystique des lettres, nous devons nous contenter de donner un sens plus «fonctionnel» que substantiel à l'expression «la philosophie». Ce qu'il s'agit de penser et de repenser dans ce cas, c'est ce que j'appelle «la fonction *méta*» et ce que, dans le contexte de notre Congrès, on pourrait désigner comme «la fonction ϕ», entendons par là l'idée que nous nous faisons du penser en sa spécificité «philosophique».

La manière dont Karl Jaspers décrit les fonctions fondamentales de la philosophie dans sa monumentale trilogie: *Philosophie* nous fournit un excellent exemple d'une relecture «fonctionnaliste» des idées transcendantales de Kant: *S'orienter dans le monde* (*Weltorientierung*), éclaircir l'existence (*Existenzerhellung*), déchiffrer les chiffres de la transcendance: telles sont, repensées par Jaspers, les fonctions fondamentales que la philosophie doit honorer.

Non moins suggestive est la manière dont Emmanuel Levinas, dans la dernière partie d'*Autrement qu'être et au-delà de l'essence*, repense «la fonction ϕ», en donnant une signification nouvelle au vocable «philosophie». Il y voit «la mesure apportée à l'infini de l'être-pour-l'autre de la proximité et comme la sagesse de l'amour», en précisant que la sagesse que vise la philosophie, sans la posséder encore, n'est «sagesse» que si elle se met «au service de l'amour».[7]

Face à des redéfinitions aussi audacieuses, certains philosophes souligneront sobrement que «la fonction ϕ» ne consiste en rien d'autre qu'à analyser l'usage que nous faisons de nos concepts, ce qui revient, d'après Wittgenstein, à condenser les gros nuages de la spéculation métaphysique en quelques gouttelettes de faits linguistiques. Wittgenstein avait-il conscience du fait que, sous des cieux moins cléments que ceux d'Oxford et de Cambridge, les phénomènes de condensation trop brutaux peuvent déclencher des tornades?

Wittgenstein est certainement l'un des grands repenseurs de la philosophie. Dans l'une de ses *Remarques mêlées*, il attire notre attention sur la distinction entre la capacité de jouer à certains jeux, dont on maîtrise les règles, c'est-à-dire, s'agissant des «jeux de langage», la «grammaire», et la question plus radicale de savoir à quel jeu il faut jouer présentement:

> Un peu de la même façon que les anciens physiciens, dit-on, se sont soudainement aperçus qu'ils savaient trop peu de mathématiques, pour dominer la physique, on peut dire que les jeunes gens d'aujourd'hui se trouvent soudain dans une situation où le bon sens ordinaire ne suffit plus pour venir à bout des étranges exigences de la vie. Tout est devenu si compliqué que, pour s'y retrouver, il faut un esprit exceptionnel. Il ne suffit en effet plus de savoir bien jouer le jeu; au contraire, toujours à nouveau surgit la question: est-ce bien à ce jeu-là qu'il faut jouer à présent, et quel est le jeu approprié?[8]

C'est parce que cette question ne cessait de hanter Wittgenstein, qu'il fut l'un des «repenseurs» les plus influents et les plus féconds de la philosophie du dernier siècle.

À la différence de ceux qui s'imaginent que «repenser» veut dire simplement distribuer un peu différemment les cartes du savoir, les vrais «repenseurs» ne cessent de se demander à quel jeu ils jouent quand il s'efforcent de penser philosophiquement et ils cherchent à avoir une conscience plus nette des enjeux de ces jeux de la pensée.

C'est bien sûr aussi ce que Heidegger a tenté de faire: s'arracher au «jeu» du penser métaphysique, identifié à «l'onto-théo-logie», en inventant, en écho au jeu originel de la pensée présocratique (Parménide, Héraclite et Anaximandre), un «autre commencement de la pensée, réglé par le jeu destinal de l'*Ereignis* et en pensant un Dieu tout autre, qu'il appelle le «Dieu ultime» (*der letzte Gott*), sans qu'on sache exactement comment ce Dieu «eschatologique» vient dans une pensée qui se veut essentiellement «méditante» (*Besinnung*).

II. HISTOIRE, TRADITION, DIALOGUE, CRITIQUE: UN FOURRE-TOUT NOTIONNEL OU UN *GEVIERT* HERMÉNEUTIQUE BIEN PORTANT?

Après ces réflexions générales que m'a inspirées le titre de notre congrès, je voudrais maintenant tenter de préciser son sens en référence au quadrilatère notionnel: *histoire (de la philosophie), dialogue, traditions, critique*. On peut les grouper par couples polaires, car là où il y a de l'histoire, il y a aussi des traditions, et là où il y a du dialogue, il y a aussi et nécessairement de la critique.

Pour éviter l'impression que nous avons affaire à un fourre-tout susceptible de rassembler les contenus les plus hétéroclites, il faut nous demander en quoi chacun de ces quatre termes éclaire un aspect particulier des différentes tentatives de «repenser la philosophie».

1. L'histoire: le pari sur la fécondité herméneutique de la distance temporelle

La manière la plus efficace de repenser la philosophie n'est-elle pas de tourner le dos à l'histoire? C'est ce que semble postuler Wittgenstein, quand il écrit, dans l'Avant-propos du *Tractatus logico-philosophicus*: «il m'est indifférent que ce que j'ai pensé, un autre l'ait déjà pensé avant moi». Dans la première phrase du même Avant-propos, Wittgenstein se demande si son livre «ne sera peut-être compris que par qui aura déjà pensé lui-même les pensées qui s'y trouvent exprimées—ou du moins des pensées semblables».[9]

Le dédain souverain de «l'histoire des idées» que Wittgenstein manifeste tout au long de ses écrits a sa grandeur et il était même salutaire à une époque où l'historicisme prétendait tout expliquer par l'histoire. Mais on peut aussi se demander si, loin d'être un obstacle pour le *Selbstdenker*, c'est-à-dire le penseur autonome, l'histoire n'est pas précisément ce qui rend possible et ce qui exige le travail du «repenser».

Si nous accordons crédit à la thèse gadamérienne de la fécondité herméneutique de la distance temporelle, le temps cesse d'être le vilain gouffre qui finit par engloutir les vérités les mieux établies; il se transforme en rampe de lancement, d'où de nouvelles pensées et des vérités nouvelles peuvent prendre leur essor. Abordée dans cette optique, l'histoire de la philosophie ne nous montre pas seulement l'importance des tentatives de repenser la philosophie qui jalonnent son histoire presque dès ses débuts jusqu'à aujourd'hui, mais aussi la multiplicité et la complexité des formes que peut revêtir ce repenser. La «fuite dans les *logoi*» de Socrate, la théorie aristotélicienne des quatre causes, l'invention cartésienne du *cogito*, les thèses de Marx sur Feuerbach (en particulier la onzième), l'introduction à l'*Encyclopédie* de Hegel, la *Krisis* de Husserl: voilà quelques exemples particulièrement remarquables de tentatives de «repenser» la philosophie en se rapportant à son histoire.

Nonobstant leur diversité, elles ont en commun une question qu'en référence à la deuxième *Considération intempestive* de Nietzsche, je formulerai comme suit: «Quels sont les avantages et les désavantages de l'histoire de la philosophie pour la vie de la pensée?»

Emboîtant le pas d'Eugen Fink,[10] je suggère d'appliquer le célèbre ternaire nietzschéen: *histoire monumentale*, *histoire antiquaire*, *histoire critique*, à notre rapport à l'histoire de la philosophie.

L'histoire monumentale nous assure que ce qui fut véritablement grand un jour le restera à jamais. Les grands monuments de la pensée qui ont pour nom: Platon, Aristote, Thomas d'Aquin, Descartes, Spinoza, Kant, Hegel, etc., ne sont pas et ne sauraient devenir des «monuments aux morts», autour desquels on se réunit périodiquement pour une cérémonie commémorative plus ou moins factice. Ils sont encore et pour toujours des interlocuteurs et des challengers pour nous, car une pensée n'est grande que si elle nous donne toujours à penser.

Comme toute activité culturelle, la philosophie se stratifie, elle aussi, en une multitude de traditions et d'écoles de pensée qui ont besoin de l'humble travail des éditeurs, commentateurs et interprètes pour pouvoir se perpétuer. Que saurions-nous de la «métaphysique» d'Aristote, sans le travail éditorial d'un certain Andronicos de Rhodes, le dixième directeur du Lycée? L'*histoire antiquaire*, comprise au sens de Nietzsche, sert elle aussi la vie, même si souvent, elle la dessert. Les «scholiastes» que nous sommes, que nous le veuillions ou non, quand nous enseignons «la philosophie», tenus par un programme scolaire qui ne recoupe pas nécessairement nos propres affinités et prédilections intellectuelles, ne sont pas aussi méprisables qu'on le croit. Eux aussi servent, à leur manière, la vie de la pensée, ne fut-ce que parce qu'un «répétiteur» insignifiant peut avoir pour élève un génie.

Quant à l'*histoire critique*, elle est l'affaire des grands révolutionnaires, qui ont souvent des comptes à régler avec le passé (le leur et celui des autres). Ils s'arrogent le droit de porter un jugement, souvent injuste, sur le passé. «Repenser» veut d'abord dire pour eux rejeter et condamner. La onzième thèse sur Feuerbach de Marx nous en fournit un parfait exemple: «Jusqu'à présent, les philosophes se sont contentés d'interpréter différemment le monde; à présent, il faut le transformer». Gravée en lettres dorées, cette fière devise accueille toujours les étudiants qui franchissent le hall d'entrée de l'université Alexander von Humboldt à Berlin. L'avenir seul nous dira comment les nouvelles générations qui franchissent actuellement les portes de cette université l'auront «repensée».

Si, parmi les multiples tentatives de repenser l'histoire de la philosophie, je devais indiquer celle qui correspond le mieux à ma propre vision «herméneutique» de la *Wirkungsgeschichte* («l'histoire de l'efficience»), je choisirais sans hésiter le célèbre Appendice 28 de la *Krisis* de Husserl. Dans ce texte quasi-testamentaire, écrit en été 1935, Husserl constate avec une amertume proche du désespoir, que le grand rêve qui avait nourri toute sa vie de philosophe: repenser la philosophie de manière à l'établir, une fois pour toutes, comme «science sérieuse, rigoureuse, et même apodictiquement rigoureuse», «est fini»,[11] parce qu'il ne se trouve plus personne pour le partager.

Faute de trouver des interlocuteurs chez les vivants, dont plus personne n'élève encore de «prétention à une vérité inconditionnée, liant tous les hommes et faisant méditation entre eux tous»,[12] Husserl se tourne vers l'histoire, en un geste qui illustre parfaitement l'attitude «monumentale» telle que la définit Nietzsche: «Il n'y a aucun doute: nous devons nous enfoncer dans des considérations historiques, si nous devons nous comprendre nous-mêmes en tant que philosophes, et comprendre ce qui doit sortir de nous comme philosophie».[13] C'est pour se «retrouver» et se comprendre dans une situation de crise et de détresse que «l'auto-penseur philosophe», le *Selbstdenker*, se tourne vers l'histoire de la philosophie qui cesse alors d'être un simple «grenier à dissertations».[14]

Le travail de «relecture» auquel il se livre n'est pas une simple répétition; c'est un travail de redécouverte et de réinvention créatrice comparable à la création poétique. C'est en ce sens que Husserl parle d'un «poème de l'histoire de la philosophie» que chacun d'entre nous doit élaborer s'il veut «repenser la philosophie, et, en la repensant, non seulement mieux se comprendre lui-même, mais ouvrir la philosophie à l'avenir:

Ce qui est historique reste pris dans ce "savoir" obscur comme dans les concepts verbaux des formules, c'est, dans son sens propre, l'héritage spirituel de celui qui philosophe, et il est évident aussi qu'il comprend les autres, en connexion avec lesquels, dans l'amitié et dans l'inimitié critiques, il philosophe. Et philosophant ainsi il est également en connexion avec soi-même, avec sa façon antérieure de comprendre la philosophie et d'en faire, et il sait que dans ce processus la tradition historique, telle qu'il l'a comprise et utilisée, n'a jamais cessé d'intervenir et de le motiver spirituellement. L'image qu'il se fait de l'histoire, en partie forgée par lui-même, en partie reçue, son "poème de l'histoire de la philosophie" n'est pas resté et ne reste pas fixe, il le sait; et pourtant: chaque "poème" lui sert, et peut lui servir, à se comprendre lui-même et son projet, et celui-ci en rapport avec celui des autres et avec leur "poème", et finalement à comprendre le projet commun à tous, qui constitue "la" philosophie en tant que *télos* unitaire avec les tentatives systématiques de remplissement de sens pour nous tous, c'est-à-dire en même temps en connexion avec les philosophes du passé (pour autant que nous puissions en donner diverses "versions poétiques" qui aient du sens pour nous).[15]

2. «Dialoguer»: avec qui et avec quoi?

En parlant d'«amitié et d'inimitié critiques», Husserl nous fournit le mot de passe pour l'intelligence du deuxième terme de notre quadrilatère: «dialogue». «Dialogue» est probablement l'un des termes les plus essentiels, mais aussi les plus galvaudés de la langue philosophique. Qui ne jure pas, les mains sur le cœur, qu'il est un homme ou une femme «de dialogue»? Mais comment mettons-nous ce dialogue en pratique quand nous avons affaire à ceux qui ne pensent pas comme nous? En cette matière, plus qu'en d'autres, «repenser la philosophie» signifie sortir des ornières des évidences trompeuses.

On trouve un excellent exemple d'une telle tentative dans l'introduction à *Qu'est-ce que la philosophie?* de Gilles Deleuze et Félix Guattari. En définissant la philosophie comme «l'art de former, d'inventer, de fabriquer des concepts»,[16] les auteurs de ce *Protreptique* d'un genre nouveau réagissent contre l'idée que la philosophie soit essentiellement «contemplation», «réflexion» ou «communication». Par le fait même, ils nous invitent à nous demander quel genre d'amitié (de *philia*) est présupposé dans la définition même du terme grec de *philosophia*. De qui ou de quoi le «philo-sophe» est-il l'ami? Quel rapport y a-t-il entre l'amitié et la possibilité même de penser?, se demande également Blanchot dans *L'amitié* et dans *L'entretien infini*. Même si cette question n'est pas sans rapport avec celle d'Aristote: «l'homme heureux a-t-il, ou non, besoin d'amis?»,[17] elle radicalise et approfondit la distinction aristotélicienne des trois sortes d'amitiés qui sont autant d'objets-motifs:[18] l'amitié selon le «bon», selon «l'utile» et selon «l'agréable». Penser et repenser peut avoir du «bon», cela peut être «utile» et, souhaitons-le, même «agréable», selon les cas. Ces prédicats ne prennent toute leur valeur que si penser ou repenser nous est devenu nécessaire.

Dès les réflexions liminaires de *Qu'est-ce que la philosophie?*, livre écrit à quatre mains, ce qui en fait aussi l'expression écrite d'une grande amitié, la question: «Que veut dire ami, quand il devient personnage conceptuel, ou condition pour l'exercice de la pensée?»[19] nous alerte sur la multiplicité des figures de l'amitié présentes dans les dialogues de Platon: l'amant, le prétendant, le rival, l'autre, etc., qui sont autant de «déterminations transcendantales»[20] de l'acte même de penser.

L'amitié, entendue en ce sens, sera «créatrice», ou elle ne mérite pas son nom. C'est ce que souligne Deleuze, quand il écrit: «Le philosophe est l'ami du concept, il est puissance de concept».[21] Tout le reste, la «contemplation», la «réflexion», la «communication»—lui sera donné de surcroît. C'est peut-être cela la leçon immémoriale des dialogues de Platon, qui sont des laboratoires de concepts et non des «forums de discussion».

Dans nos sociétés surmédiatisées, où «çà discute beaucoup», souvent à tort et à travers, et bien des fois pour noyer les problèmes plutôt que pour les identifier et les traiter, la thèse de Deleuze, d'après laquelle «la philosophie a horreur des discussions»[22] mérite d'être accueillie comme antidote ou avertissement salutaire:

> Que quelqu'un ait tel avis, et pense ceci plutôt que cela, qu'est-ce que cela peut faire à la philosophie, tant que les problèmes en jeu ne sont pas dits? Et quand ils sont dits, il ne s'agit plus de discuter, mais de créer d'indiscutables concepts pour le problème qu'on s'est assigné. La communication vient toujours trop tôt ou trop tard, et la conversation toujours en trop, par rapport à créer.[23]

3. Repenser les «traditions»

Aussitôt qu'on prononce le terme de «traditions», bien des philosophes se sentent en état de siège et organisent leur défense, comme s'ils avaient affaire à un ennemi mortel. Pour justifier leur levée de boucliers, ils invoquent l'un des plus anciens adages de la philosophie occidentale. C'est le fragment 86 d'Héraclite, rapporté avec approbation par Marc Aurèle:[24] «Il ne faut pas agir et parler comme les enfants de nos parents», c'est-à-dire comme nous l'avons appris par la tradition.

La manière dont Marcel Conche commente ce fragment fait d'Héraclite un précurseur direct de Kant. Tout se passe comme si le philosophe Ephésien avait réussi à condenser en un seul aphorisme le message essentiel de Kant dans son célèbre essai: «Qu'est-ce que les Lumières?». «Celui qui parle et agit en "enfant de ses parents" (en "fils de son père")», commente Conche,

> reste toute sa vie comme sous l'autorité de ses parents et en état d'enfance. Les hommes, pour autant qu'ils reproduisent les croyances et le monde particulier et clos dont ils ont hérité, sont toute leur vie sous la coupe de leurs parents. Ils ne sont que des enfants d'apparence adulte. Si l'âge adulte est l'âge de raison, la seule voie pour y parvenir est la philosophie.[25]

Mais est-ce tout ce qu'il y a à dire en cette matière? Que certaines «traditions» cautionnent l'interdiction de penser, qui est aussi une interdiction de la liberté et une mise sous tutelle de la raison, est un fait historique irrécusable. «Repenser la philosophie», c'est aussi repenser les grands combats pour la reconnaissance qui ont permis à la philosophie de conquérir un droit de cité dans les sociétés humaines. Rien ne nous garantit que, pour l'essentiel, ces combats soient derrière nous.

Mais la philosophie peut-elle se contenter de définir son rapport aux «traditions» de façon purement négative, comme désir de s'émanciper d'une tutelle devenue insupportable? Ce dont nous avons hérité, est-ce nécessairement un «monde particulier et clos» comme semble le postuler Conche? Je n'en suis pas sûr.

En cette matière aussi, il peut être utile de repenser le concept même de tradition, en y distinguant, comme l'a fait Paul Ricœur,[26] plusieurs noyaux de sens qui renvoient chacun à un problème spécifique.

a) Le premier foyer de sens est constitué par le terme de *traditionnalité*. Il désigne un certain «style d'enchaînement de la succession historique», qui ne cesse de conjuguer «l'efficience du passé, que nous souffrons, et la réception du passé, que nous opérons».[27] «La traditionnalité» comprise en ce sens, nous renvoie au phénomène (et au problème) de la *transmission*, qui est constitutif de notre condition historique.

Que le terme de «parricide» surgisse spontanément sous la plume de Conche, quand il commente le fragment 86 d'Héraclite, n'est pas un hasard. Chez bien des philosophes, il est proclamé comme une nécessité et revendiqué avec une légitime fierté: «J'ai été capable de tuer le père, donc je suis quelqu'un!». Mais peut-être devrions-nous également nous intéresser aux relations, souvent tumultueuses, des grands «parricides» de l'histoire de la philosophie à leur propre postérité. Quelles relations entretiennent-ils avec ceux qui veulent être reconnus comme leurs disciples, mais aussi avec ceux qui donnent des signes inquiétants qu'ils pourraient bien être les parricides de la prochaine génération? Parlant des relations conflictuelles de Freud à la «horde sauvage» de ses disciples, et de Husserl à ses propres élèves «hérétiques», en particulier avec l'hérésiarque en chef qu'était à ses yeux Heidegger, Hans Blumenberg formule le paradoxe suivant: «L'acte fondateur ne *devait* pas être répété, mais il ne *pouvait* pas non plus être assumé».[28]

Indépendamment même de l'image dramatique du parricide, toute tentative de «repenser la philosophie» exige une réflexion approfondie sur la manière dont elle se transmet «de génération en génération», et, plus généralement, sur le phénomène de la transmission comme tel. C'est à cette tâche que s'est récemment appliquée Catherine Chalier dans son dernier ouvrage, dont je me permets de citer les dernières lignes:

> Le "soi" ne peut transmettre que ce qui a éclairé—et qui éclaire—ses jours. Le reste, tout ce qu'il sait, ses compétences et ses exigences, le contenu précis de ses paroles—lorsqu'il raconte, explique, démontre, écoute, désire ou témoigne—n'est pas dévalorisé pour autant. Les actes de transmission ont bien un contenu de sens et de connaissances, ils ne peuvent être laissés à la discrétion des sentiments et des émotions. Mais ce contenu n'a de chance de parvenir au "soi" d'autrui—avec, bien sûr, la charge pour lui de

le recevoir et de le faire vivre de façon nouvelle et singulière, au risque de sa liberté—qu'à condition d'avoir été transmis par ceux et celles qui, un instant du moins, ont été "signé" pour lui.[29]

b) Une fois qu'on admet que «la distance temporelle qui nous sépare du passé n'est pas un intervalle mort, mais une *transmission génératrice de sens*» et qu'avant «d'être un dépôt inerte, la tradition est une opération qui ne se comprend que dialectiquement dans l'échange entre le passé interprété et le présent interprétant»,[30] le champ est libre pour porter un regard neuf sur le *plurale tantum des traditions*.

Des traditions, il y en a partout, à l'extérieur comme à l'intérieur de la philosophie, car partout, «nous ne sommes jamais en position absolue d'innovateurs, mais toujours d'abord en situation relative d'héritiers».[31] Nous ne sommes jamais de purs penseurs, mais toujours aussi des repenseurs, des acteurs qui sont en même temps des récepteurs, des interrogateurs interrogés par les traditions qui nous précèdent et dont certaines au moins nous portent et nous nourrissent.

Cette dialectique de l'interrogateur interrogé (ou de "l'arroseur arrosé") ne vaut pas seulement pour les textes issus des différentes traditions philosophiques, mais aussi pour le rapport entre la philosophie et les sources extra-philosophiques de la pensée. Nous pouvons lui appliquer l'adage de Paul Ricœur: Pour commencer de soi, la philosophie doit peut-être avoir des présupposés qu'elle remet en question et résorbe critiquement dans son propre point de départ. Qui n'a pas d'abord des *sources* n'a pas ensuite d'*autonomie*».[32] Les travaux de Martha Nussbaum et de Pierre Aubenque sur le rapport entre la sagesse tragique et la sagesse éthique nous offrent une excellente illustration de la fécondité de ce postulat.

c) C'est ensuite seulement qu'on peut s'intéresser au passage périlleux des traditions, comprise comme «propositions de sens» à *la tradition*, érigée en source unique de vérité. De ce point de vue, il n'y a pas de doute que le «traditionalisme» sous toutes ses formes, qui refuse d'être interrogée et soumis à un examen critique, est l'ennemi mortel de la philosophie.

4. Du bon et du mauvais usage de la «critique»

C'est face à cet ennemi que, dès l'origine de la philosophie, les philosophes ont mobilisé le potentiel critique de la raison réflexive et argumentative. Mais ici aussi, «repenser la philosophie» implique la nécessité de s'entendre sur le bon et les mauvais usages de ce vocable, qui, depuis Platon, fait partie du lexique fondamental de la philosophie.

L'histoire du concept nous confirme que la «critique» est affaire de discernement, par exemple le discernement dont le médecin doit faire preuve dans des situations «critiques», quand il lui faut décider de l'opportunité (*kairos*) d'une intervention chirurgicale, ou le philologue, qui est aussi un critique littéraire, dans la manipulation des sources. Autant dire que la «critique» bien comprise est rarement une machine de guerre et moins encore une guillotine. Le bon «critique» ne se comporte pas comme s'il faisait partie d'un peloton d'exécution!

De l'histoire longue et mouvementée du concept de «critique», je retiens simplement trois indications qui me semblent mériter d'être «repensées».

a) De nos jours, où l'on associe régulièrement le terme de «critique» avec les termes de «méthode» et de «connaissance», il peut être bon de méditer à nouveaux frais la thèse d'Aristote, d'après lequel la «critique» est une caractéristique fondamentale des trois vertus dianoétiques qui viennent compléter la force directive de la *phronèsis*: l'intelligence (*synesis*), terme qu'on peut aussi bien traduire par «faculté de comprendre» ou *Verständnis* en allemand, le jugement perspicace (*gnômè*) ou *Einsicht* et, enfin la «droite raison» ou *équité* (*syngnômè*), traduite en allemand par *Nachsicht*.

Comprise en ce sens inhabituel, la «fonction critique» nous est confiée en tant que nous sommes citoyens du monde, appelés à jouer notre rôle dans ce que Kant appelle «le grand jeu de la vie». Précisément parce que notre monde est bien plus complexe que la cité d'Athènes à l'époque d'Aristote, nous devons résister au chantage des «experts» autoproclamés qui nous serinent sur tous les tons que nous ne sommes pas compétents pour exercer un jugement qualifié.

Aux critiques impitoyables qui se complaisent dans la férocité, on peut prescrire comme antidote de méditer longuement la phrase suivante d'Aristote: «c'est en étant capable de juger des choses (*tô kritikos einai*) rentrant dans le domaine de l'homme prudent qu'on est intelligent, bienveillant et favorablement disposé pour les autres, les actions équitables étant communes à tous les gens de bien dans leurs rapports avec autrui».[33]

b) «Repenser la philosophie» signifie aussi, et peut-être même en premier chef, tirer au clair notre rapport au criticisme de Kant, c'est-à-dire à l'idée d'une raison capable de se fonder elle-même en traçant de l'intérieur ses propres limites. Par le fait même, elle est censée trancher, une fois pour toutes, la question de la possibilité et de l'impossibilité de toute métaphysique, en identifiant les sources, en déterminant l'extension et en mesurant les limites de celle-ci, seule manière de mettre fin à l'oscillation indéfinie du dogmatisme et du scepticisme.

S'agissant de l'idée même de «raison critique», le changement le plus révélateur est le remplacement de l'image d'un champ de bataille où se livrent des combats d'autant plus futiles que les combattants ne savent ni contre qui, ni contre quoi ils bataillent avec tant de férocité, par celle d'un «tribunal de la raison», capable d'arbitrer les litiges et d'instaurer ainsi une «paix perpétuelle», même dans le champ de la philosophie.

Le moins qu'on puisse dire est que l'image que nous donne la philosophie d'aujourd'hui est loin d'un tel rêve. Mais si nous repensons la philosophie dans l'optique des *Paradigmes pour une métaphorologie* de Hans Blumenberg,[34] nous pourrions dire que le «champ de bataille» et le «tribunal de la raison» sont bel et bien des «métaphores absolues» qui nous aident à mieux comprendre le sens philosophique de la critique. Ce n'est qu'à la lumière de la métaphore absolue, c'est-à-dire irréductible, du «tribunal de la raison» qu'on peut comprendre le sens kantien de la critique, que Heidegger glose ainsi:

La critique est l'auto-compréhension (*Selbsterkenntnis*) de la raison placée devant elle-même et reposant sur elle-même. La critique est ainsi l'accomplissement de la rationalité la plus interne de la raison. La critique achève l'élucidation (*Aufklärung*) de la raison.[35]

c) Il est vrai que certains de nos contemporains, se réclamant précisément de Heidegger et de Nietzsche, sont tentés de remplacer la métaphore du «tribunal de la raison» par une nouvelle «métaphore absolue»: celle de la «déconstruction» (*Abbau*) que Heidegger utilise dans le §6 de *Sein und Zeit*, où il traite des tâches d'une «destruction de l'histoire de l'ontologie». Il s'agit d'un travail de «désobstruction» ou d'assouplissement (*Auflockerung*) qui nous fait revenir aux «choses mêmes» et aux expériences originelles qui sous-tendent nos constructions théoriques.

Que la «déconstruction», telle qu'elle est définie ici, soit aussi une manière «critique» de repenser notre rapport à l'histoire de la philosophie se passe de commentaire. Les «déconstructeurs» trop pressés, qui s'imaginent disposer d'une machine de guerre encore plus performante que toutes celles du passé, risquent de perdre de vue le fait qu'il s'agit d'un «retour positif au sens d'une appropriation productive».[36] Contrairement à «l'histoire *critique*», telle que l'entend Nietzsche, la «déconstruction» n'est pas une manière de se débarrasser (*Abschüttelung*) d'un passé encombrant ou gênant. Les déconstructeurs qui s'ébrouent comme un chien sorti de l'eau, pour présenter à leurs contemporains un poil bien luisant, m'inspirent une méfiance invincible, parce qu'ils ne voient pas que «la destruction ne se rapporte pas de façon négatrice au passé», mais que «sa critique touche "l'aujourd'hui"».[37] Nous pouvons leur appliquer l'adage de Karl Barth: «*Kritischer müssten mir die Kritiker sein*», c'est-à-dire: pour être crédibles, les critiques déconstructeurs devraient d'abord faire preuve de davantage de critique envers eux-mêmes.

*
* *

En exergue de ces réflexions, j'ai placé un poème de Bertold Brecht, faisant écho à la légende qui rapporte la genèse du *Taoteking*. Avec beaucoup d'humour, le poète relate l'ultime voyage du vieux sage Lao-Tseu, accompagné d'un disciple, qui s'est fait arrêter à la frontière tibétaine par un douanier qui exige qu'il mette ses pensées par écrit. S'étant acquitté de la tâche, Lao-Tseu poursuit sa route vers une destination inconnue. Dans la dernière strophe du poème, Brecht nous invite à remercier le douanier d'avoir obligé le penseur de consigner ses pensées dans un livre.

Heureusement pour moi, aucun douanier coréen ne m'a demandé quelles idées j'avais à déclarer quand j'ai atterri à l'aéroport international de Séoul. L'eusse-t-il fait, je lui aurais confié, avec une impertinence semblable à celle du disciple du vieux sage, deux paroles de philosophes sur lesquelles j'achèverai ces réflexions.

a) La première est de Martin Heidegger. Elle nous rappelle que nous ne repensons pas la philosophie pour nous amuser, ou pour faire preuve d'une originalité douteuse, mais parce que notre temps nous confronte à des défis nouveaux: «*Das bedenklichste in unserer bedenklichen Zeit ist, daß wir noch nicht denken*». («Le plus inquiétant dans ce temps inquiétant qui est le nôtre, est que nous ne pensons pas encore»[38]).

b) La seconde est de Ludwig Wittgenstein. Elle nous rappelle que le temps de la réflexion et de la compréhension nécessaire pour repenser la philosophie exige une patience et une lenteur comparable à celle du vieux sage cheminant sur son bœuf: «La salutation entre philosophes devrait être: "Prends ton temps!"».

NOTES

1. Paul Ricœur, *Philosophie de la volonté I. Le volontaire et l'involontaire* (Paris: Aubier, 1988), pp. 417–456.

2. Jean Nabert, «La conscience peut-elle se comprendre?,» in *Le désir de Dieu* (Paris: Ed. du Cerf, 1966), p. 416.

3. Ibid., p. 417.

4. Ibid.

5. Enc §2.

6. Enc §43.

7. Emmanuel Levinas, *Autrement qu'être ou au-delà de l'essence* (La Haye: Nijhoff, 1974), pp. 205, 207.

8. Ludwig Wittgenstein, *Remarques mêlées* (Paris: Flammarion, 2001), p. 38 (trad. mod.).

9. Ludwig Wittgenstein, *Tractatus logico-philosophicus*, trad. Gilles-Gaston Granger (Paris: Gallimard, 2001), p. 31.

10. Eugen Fink, *Grundfragen der antiken Philosophie* (Würzburg: Königshausen/Neumann, 1985), pp. 1–18.

11. Edmund Husserl, *Die Krisis der europäischen Wissenschaften und die transzendentale Phänomenologie*, *Hua* VI (La Haye: Nijhoff, 1954); trad. G. Granel, *La crise des sciences européennes et la phénoménologie transcendantale* (Paris: Gallimard, 1976), p. 563.

12. Ibid., p. 564.

13. Ibid., p. 565.

14. Ibid., p. 566.

15. Ibid., p. 568.

16. Gilles Deleuze et Félix Guattari, *Qu'est-ce que la philosophie?* (Paris: Ed. Minuit, 1991), p. 8.

17. Aristote, *Ethique à Nicomaque*, IX, 9.

18. Paul Ricœur, *Soi-même comme un autre* (Paris: Ed. du Seuil, 1990), p. 568.

19. Deleuze et Guattari, *Qu'est-ce que la philosophie?*, p. 9.

20. Ibid., p. 10.

21. Ibid.

22. Ibid., p. 33.

23. Ibid., p. 32.

24. Marc Aurèle, *Pensées pour soi-même*, IV, 46.

25. Marcel Conche, *Héraclite, Fragments* (Paris, PUF, 1987), p. 75.

26. Paul Ricœur, *Temps et Récit III* (Paris: Ed. du Seuil, 1994), p. 318–332.

27. Ibid., p. 318.

28. Hans Blumenberg, *Zu den Sachen selbst und zurück* (Frankfurt: Suhrkamp, 2002), p. 27.

29. Catherine Chalier, *Transmettre de génération en génération* (Paris: Buchet Chastel, 2008), p. 270.

30. Paul Ricœur, *Temps et Récit III*, p. 320.

31. Ibid.

32. Paul Ricoeur, *Lectures* 3. *Aux frontières de la philosophie* (Paris: Ed. du Seuil, 1994), p. 154.

33. Aristote, *Ethique à Nicomaque*, trad. Tricot, VI, 12, 1143 a 29–30.

34. Hans Blumenberg, *Paradigmen zu einer Metaphorologie* (Bonn: H. Bouvier, 1960); trad. D. Gammelin, *Paradigmes pour une métaphorologie* (Paris: Ed. Vrin, 2006).

35. Martin Heidegger, *Die Frage nach dem Ding* (Tübingen: Niemeyer, 1975), p. 96 (trad. pers.)

36. Martin Heidegger, *Sein und Zeit*, Gesamtausgabe vol. 2 (Frankfurt: Klosterman), p. 21; trad. E. Martineau, p. 39.

37. Ibid., p. 22 ; trad. fr., p. 39.

38. Martin Heidegger, *Was heißt Denken?* (Tübingen: Niemeyer, 1971), p. 3.

A New Age in the History of Philosophy: The World Dialogue between Philosophical Traditions

ENRIQUE DUSSEL
UAM-IZ., MÉXICO

Abstract: This paper argues the following points: (1) It is necessary to affirm that humanity has always sought to address certain "core universal problems" that are present in all cultures. (2) The rational responses to these "core problems" first appear as mythical narratives. (3) The formulation of categorical philosophical discourses is a subsequent development in human rationality, which does not however negate all mythical narratives. (4) Modern European philosophy confused its economic, political, and cultural domination, and the resulting crises in other philosophical traditions, with a Eurocentric universality claim, which must be questioned. (5) There are universal aspects in which all regional philosophies coincide, and which respond to the "core problems" at an abstract level. (6) All of this impels entry into a new age of inter-philosophical dialogue, respectful of differences and open to learning from other traditions. (7) A new philosophical project must be developed that is capable of going beyond Eurocentric philosophical modernity, by shaping a global trans-modern pluriverse.

In this paper I will explore a theme that I believe should occupy us for a significant portion of the twenty-first century: *our recognition and acceptance of the meaning, value, and history of all regional philosophical traditions on the planet (European, North American, Chinese, Indian, Arab, African, Latin American, etc.).*

This will be the first time in the history of philosophy that these diverse traditions will be open to an authentic and symmetrical dialogue—a dialogue that will enable us to understand many aspects unknown to us, aspects that may be better developed in some traditions than in others. This dialogue will play a key role in unlocking the contents of the daily life of humanity in other cultures, thanks to the

Special Supplement, *Journal of Philosophical Research* pp. 151–166
DOI: 10.5840/jpr201237Supplement32

enormous machinery of mass media that makes it possible for us to receive news instantaneously of cultures about which we lack first hand knowledge, and will also imply an ethical positioning grounded in the equal recognition of all philosophical communities with equal rights of argumentation. This will make it possible for us to transcend the Eurocentrism of Modernity, so prevalent today, which impedes creativity and often obscures the great discoveries achieved by other traditions.

1. UNIVERSAL CORE PROBLEMS

When I refer to "universal core problems," I mean those fundamental questions (of an ontological character) that *homo sapiens* posed upon attaining a certain level of maturity. Once their level of cerebral development allowed for consciousness, self-consciousness, linguistic, ethical and social development (that is, responsibility for their own acts), human beings confronted the *totality of the real* in order to manage things in such a way as to achieve the reproduction and development of human life in community. Human *admitation* in the face of the possible causes of natural phenomena was further compounded by the unpredictability of their own impulses and behaviors, leading to questions regarding "core problems" such as: What are *real things* in their totality and how do they behave? Such questions encompass phenomena ranging from the astronomical to the simple falling of a stone or the artificial production of fire. They also encompass the mystery of their own human subjectivity, the *ego*, interiority, spontaneity, as well as the nature of freedom and the creation of the *social and ethical world*. In the end, they arrive at the question of how we interpret the *ultimate foundation* of everything that is real, and the universe itself? Which in turn leads to the classic ontological question: "Why *being* and not *nothingness*?" These basic "core problems" have inevitably been faced by all human communities since the remotest period of the Paleolithic age; they are among the many possible variations of the *universal* "whys," and are present in every culture and tradition.

The content and the way of responding to these "core problems" unleashes, impels, and disperses diverse trajectories of *rational* narratives, if by *rationality* we understand simply that reasons have been provided in support of assertions, and that these assertions are intended to interpret or explain phenomena that have "appeared" at the initial level of each of these "core problems."

2. THE RATIONAL DEVELOPMENT OF MYTHICAL NARRATIVES

Throughout all of its stages and dimensions of development, humanity has always and inevitably given linguistic expression to *rational* responses (understood here to mean those that are proffered with some kind of underlying foundation, regardless of its specific character, at least until it is refuted) to core problems such as those described above. This has occurred as the result of a process involving the "production of myths" (or *mytho-poiésis*).

The production of myths was the first rational form of interpretation or explanation of reality (of the world, subjectivity, the ethical practical horizon, and the ultimate reference of reality that is described symbolically). From this perspective myths are symbolic narratives that are not irrational and that do not refer exclusively to singular phenomena. They are symbolic enunciations, and therefore have a "double meaning" that can only be fully elucidated through a hermeneutical process *that uncovers the layers of reasoning* behind them. It is in this sense that they are rational, and that they must be grasped in terms of the extent to which their content has a *universal* significance, given their reference to circumstances that are susceptible to repetition, and constructed upon the basis of *concepts* (cerebral categorizations or cerebral maps that involve millions of neurons and imply the convergence in meaning of multiple and singular empirical phenomena that human beings must confront).

Numerous myths are organized according to their relationship to the *core problems* that I have just highlighted, and have been preserved in the collective memory of communities throughout the world. This was first done through oral tradition, and in written form since 3000 B.C., when they begin to be collected, remembered, and interpreted by communities of sages who had a sense of admiration in the face of reality, in the spirit of Aristotle's affirmation:[1] "but he who finds no explanation (in what he sees, and turns instead to admiration) . . . thereby recognizes his ignorance. This is why he who *loves myth* (*philómythos*) is akin to he *who loves wisdom* (*philósophos*)." This is how mythical "traditions" emerge to provide peoples throughout the world with *rational* explanations related to the questions that have always been most pressing for humanity, and which I have defined here as "core problems." These include peoples as poor and as "simple" in their material culture as the Tupinamba indigenous people of Brazil, who according to Claude Levi-Strauss's studies, carried out the responsibilities inherent in their daily lives in ways embedded in the complex web of meaning provided by their vast number of myths.

According to Paul Ricoeur, each culture has an "ethical and mythical core,"[2] or "vision of the world" (*Weltanschauung*) that provides a framework of interpretation and ethical guidance for the most significant moments in human existence. On the other hand, certain cultures (such as those of China, India, Mesopotamia, Egypt, the Aztec or Mexican, the Arabs, the Hellenic world, Rome, Russia, etc.,) as a result of their political, economic, and military hegemony, were able to consolidate geopolitical dominance. These processes endowed them a degree of universality that included the imposition of their mythical structures over those of subaltern cultures. Such patterns of cultural domination are evident throughout multiple periods of historical development.

As a result of these cultural clashes, certain myths will endure in subsequent stages (even in the age of categorical philosophical discourses and of the science of Modernity itself, up to the present). Myths will never completely disappear as long as some of them continue to *make sense*, as Ernst Bloch argues persuasively in his work *The Principle of Hope.*[3]

3. THE NEW RATIONAL DEVELOPMENT OF DISCOURSES WITH PHILOSOPHICAL CATEGORIES

We have become accustomed, in the context of explanations of the transition from *mythos* to *lógos*, to understand this process as a leap from the *irrational* to the *rational*, from the concretely empirical to the universal, and from the realm of the senses to the realm of concepts. This is false. Each of the narratives at issues has a certain degree of rationality, but their specific character varies. There is a *progression* in terms of degrees of univocal precision, semantic clarity, simplicity, and in the conclusive force with which their foundations have been laid. But there are also *losses* in multiplicity of meaning when symbols displaced, but which can be hermeneutically rediscovered in diverse moments and places (as is characteristic of mythical rational narratives). For example the Promethean or Adamic[4] myths continue to have ethical meaning today.

Thus univocal rational discourse as expressed in *philosophical* categories that are capable of defining conceptual content without recourse to symbols (as in a myth) gains in *precision* but loses in terms of its *resonance* of meaning. All of this nonetheless implies an important civilizational advance, which opens up the possibility of abstraction in modes of analysis. Here, the separation of the semantic content of the object or phenomenon being observed—the description and precise explanation of empirical reality—enables the observer's *management* to be more efficient in the reproduction and development of human life in community.

In this context, *wisdom* can order the diverse responses to the *core problems* that have been enumerated, and becomes the content of a differentiated social "role" focused upon the clarification, exposition, and development of said wisdom. From the perspective of the sociology of philosophy, communities of philosophers form groups differentiated from those of priests, artists, political actors, etc. The members of these communities of sages take on a ritualized form constituting "schools of life" with a strictly disciplinary character (from the Aztecs *calmécac* to the Athenian *academy* or the sages communities of the city of Memphis in the Egypt of the Third Milennium B.C.), and came to be known as the so-called "lovers of wisdom" (*philo-sophoi*) among the Greeks. But from a historical perspective the "lovers of myths" were also, strictly speaking, "lovers of wisdom," and this is why those who will later be described as *philosophers* should be described more aptly as *philo-logists*, if *lógos* is understood to mean a rational discourse that employs philosophical categories and no longer has recourse to mythical symbolic narrative, or only exceptionally and as an example of how philoso-phical hermeneutics holds sway.

This process of leaving behind the purest form of mythical rational expression and stripping away its symbolic content gradually emerged in all of the great urban cultures of the Neolithic. This process gives certain *terms* or *words* a univocal, definable meaning with conceptual content that is the fruit of *methodical* analytical elaboration and is capable of moving from the whole to the parts as it fixes its specific meaning. Key examples of narratives employing *philosophical categories* began to emerge in India (subsequent to the *Upanishads*), in China (from the *Book of Changes* or *I Ching*), in Persia, Mesopotamia, Egypt (in texts such as those described as the "philosophy of Memphis"), in the Eastern Mediterranean between the Phoenicians and the Greeks, in Mesoamerica (the Maya and Aztecs or Mexican), in the Andean region the *amautas* among the Aymaras and the Quechuas, who gave life to Incan civilization, etc. Among the Aztecs, *Quetzal-coatl* was the symbolic expression of a dual ancestral deity ("Quetzal" referring to the green and red feathers of a beautiful tropical bird as a symbol for divinity, and "coatl" referring to a twin or brother, the "duality"). This is what the *tlamatinime* ("those who know things," and whom Bernardino de Sahagún called "philoso-phers"[5]) described as *Ometeotl* (from the roots in the Náhuatl language *omé*, which means two, and *teotl*, which refers to divinity), leaving the symbol aside. This denomination highlighted the "dual origin" of the universe (instead of the unitary origin characteristic of *to én*, or *the One* in Plato or Plotinus, for example). This indicates the beginning of the transition from symbolic rationality to the rationality of *philosophical conceptual categorization* among the Aztecs, as reflected in the historical figure of the poet and philosopher-king Nezahúalcoyotl (1402–1472).

Some authors such as Raúl Fornet-Betancourt in Latin America[6] concede that philosophy was practiced in *Amerindia* (before the European invasion in 1492) or in pre-colonial Africa, without much elaboration of what he understands to be philosophy. Paulin Hountondji's[7] sharp critique of the concept of *ethnophilosophy*, derived from Placide Tempel's book *Bantu Philosophy*,[8] highlights the need to better define what we mean by philosophy in such contexts, in order among other things to distinguish it from myth.

Nonetheless when we carefully read the first sentences of the *Tao Te-king* (or *Dao de jing*) by the legendary Lao-tze: "The Tao that can be spoken of is not the constant Tao; the name that can be named is not the constant name; the nameless is the beginning of Heaven and Earth,"[9] we find ourselves confronted with a text that employs *philosophical categories* distant from those of a purely mythical narrative. It is also impossible today to ignore the argumentative density and rationality characteristic of the philosophy of K'ung Fu-Tsu (Confucius) (551–479 B.C.),[10] and the levels of philosophical development evident in Mo-Tzu (479–380 B.C),[11] whose continuous, even excessive patterns of argumentation criticized the social and moral implications of Confucianism, affirming a universalism with grave political implications, and which was skeptical of rituals and unduly elaborate organizations or "schools." His contributions are one of the pillars of Chinese *philosophy* that predated the great Confucian synthesis of Meng Tzu (Mencius) (390–305 B.C.).[12] This *philosophy* spans some 2,500 years, with classics each century, and even during the period of European Modernity thinkers such as Wang Yang-ming (1472–1529), who founds the neo-Confucian tradition that extends all the way up to the present, influencing Mao Tse-tung and playing a role in the emergence of contemporary capitalism in China and Singapore equivalent to that of Calvinism in Europe. There was also Huang Tsung-hsi (1610–1695) a great renovator of political philosophy.

In the same way the philosophies of the Indian subcontinent are organized in terms of the philosophical expression[13] of the *core problems.* We read in *Chandogya Upanisad*:

> In the beginning, my dear, this world was just Being (*sat*), one only, without a second. Some people, no doubt, say: In the beginning, verily, this world was just Nonbeing (*asat*), one only, without a second; from that Nonbeing Being was produced. But how, indeed, my dear, could it be so? said he. How could Being be produced from Nonbeing? On the contrary, my dear, in the beginning this world was Being alone.[14]

Is it not a philosophical discourse?

In Hinduism the concept of *Brahman* refers to the totality of the universe (as does that of *Pacha* in Quechua among the Incas of Peru); *atman* refers to subjectivity, *karma* to human action, and *moksha* to the relationship between *atman* and *Brahman*. It is with these "core" concepts as points of departure that a discourse undertaken by means of philosophical categories begins to be constructed in the fifth century B.C. It is then with Sankara (788–820 A.C.) that the philosophy of the subcontinent achieves a classical level, which it has continued to develop up to the present.

Buddhist philosophy, meanwhile, beginning with Siddhartha Gautama (563–483 B.C.), rejects the concepts of *Brahman* and *atman*, given its assumption that the totality of the universe is an eternal process unfolding in an interconnected manner (*patitya samatpada*). This even more clearly negates the mythical traditions (such as those of the *Vedas*), contributing instead to the construction of a strictly rational narrative, which is not, as in all philosophies, utterly exempt from mythological moments, such as *ensomátosis*, referring to the successive "re-incorporations of souls."

Meanwhile, Jainism, whose first exponent was Vardhamana Mahvira (599–527 B.C.), ontologically defends the *Tattvartha Sutra* ("no violence, no possession, no determination") from the perspective of a universal vitalism, which has great relevance to the ecological crisis we face today.

All of this clearly implies that philosophy was not born solely or originally in Greece, nor can it be taken as the prototype of philosophical discourse. This error arises from taking Greek philosophy as the definition of philosophy itself, rather than taking a clear *criteria of demarcation* between mythical and philosophical categorical discourse. This confuses the part with the whole: a specific case does not capture the universal sweep of the definition needed. This does not deny Greek philosophy its historical place among these philosophies, or its continuity with the philosophies of the Roman Empire, which in turn opened a cultural horizon towards the so-called Latin-Germanic European Middle Ages. These will culminate in the European philosophy that laid the foundations for the Modernity produced by the European invasion of the American continent, and the emergence of colonialism and capitalism. The Industrial Revolution at the end of the eighteenth century (only two centuries ago) will make Europe the central dominating civilization in the world-system, up to the beginning of the twenty-first century. This domination has obscured and distorted our understanding of history (due to the combined effects of what I have described as hellenocentrism and Eurocentrism), and impeded the global perspective necessary to grasp an authentic history of philosophy.

As a Latin American I am convinced that the future development of world philosophy will be jeopardized if we do not clarify these issues by means of a contemporary dialogue between non-Western philosophical traditions and those of Europe and North America.

In this context, E. Husserl's reflection set forth below, and repeated in general by M. Heidegger and throughout Europe and North America, seems so naïve:

> Thus philosophy . . . is *ratio* in the constant movement of self-elucidation, begun with the first breakthrough of philosophy into mankind. . . . The image of the dawn characterizes Greek philosophy in its beginning stage, the first elucidation through the first cognitive conception of *what is* as universe (*des Seienden als Universum*).[15]

In Latin America, David Sobrevilla essentially supports the same approach:

> I believe that there is a general consensus that the philosophical activity of humanity first emerged in Greece and not in the East. In this regard Hegel and Heidegger appear to be correct, instead of Jaspers, who argues for the existence of three great philosophical traditions: those of China, India, and Greece.[16]

The philosophy of the East would be philosophy understood *in a broad sense*, and that of Greece according to much *narrower* criteria. There is a confusion between the origins of *European* philosophy, which may in part lie in Greece, and the origins of *world* philosophy, which has diverse origins, almost as many as there are fundamental traditions of philosophy. In addition it is assumed that this process was linear, following a sequence "from Greek philosophy to Medieval Latin philosophy and from there to their Modern European expressions." But the true historical trajectory was much more complex. Greek philosophy was cultivated subsequently and principally by Byzantine civilization, and Arab philosophy in turn was the inheritor of Byzantine philosophy, and in particular its Aristotelian tradition. This required the creation of an Arabic philosophical language in the strictest sense.[17]

Latin Aristotelian philosophy in Paris in thirteenth century, for example, has its origin in Greek texts and their Arabic commentaries (translated in Toledo, in Spain, by Arab specialists), and these Greek texts were utilized and commentated by the "Arab Western philosophers" (in the of Cordoba, in Spain), continuing the "Eastern" tradition with origins in Cairo, Bagdad, or Samarkand. This produced a Greek legacy profoundly reconstructed from a Semitic perspective (such as that of Arab civilization), and then passed on to Latins and Germanics in Europe. It is 'Ibn Roshd (Averroes) who marks the origin of the European philosophical renaissance in the thirteenth century.

All of the world's great cultures have created philosophies as well, with varying styles and characteristics of development, but all have produced (some only initially and others with great depth and precision) *conceptual structural categories* that must be recognized as philosophical.

Philosophical discourse does not destroy myth, although it does negate those who lose the capacity to resist the empirical argumentation inherent in such discourse. For example the myths of Tlacaelel among the Aztecs, which justified human sacrifice and provided good reasons for it,[18] completely collapsed once their impossibility was demonstrated, as well as their lack of practical feasibility.

In fact, mythical elements may contaminate even the discourses of great philosophers. For example, Immanuel Kant argues in favor of the "immortality of the soul" in the "pure practical reason dialectics" of his *Critique of Practical Reason*, as a way of resolving the question of the "supreme Good" (since the soul would receive after death the happiness it had earned in its earthly life). But these concepts of the "soul" and of "immortality" demonstrate the persistence of mythical elements of Indian origin in the Greek thought—elements that came to permeate all of the Roman, Medieval Christian, and Modern European world. The supposedly philosophical proofs provided are in these cases tautological and not rationally demonstrative upon the basis of empirical facts. This illustrates the unrecognized (and in this case inappropriate) presence of mythical elements in the *best* philosophies. We might also describe them as examples of unintentional underlying ideologies.

On the other hand, the "Adamic myth" of the Hebrew Semitic tradition, which shows that human freedom is the origin of "evil," and not a deity, as in the Mesopotamian myth of Gilgamesh, is a mythical narrative that can still be interpreted anew in the present, and which resists the rationality of the age of *logos*.[19] The same can be said of the epic narrative of the slaves led by Moses who freed themselves from Egypt—narratives recovered by Ernst Bloch in his previously cited work.

4. THE HEGEMONY OF MODERN EUROPEAN PHILOSOPHY AND ITS UNIVERSALITY CLAIM

Beginning in 1492 Europe conquers the Atlantic, which becomes the new geopolitical center of hegemony in the world, replacing the Mediterranean and extending its sweep all the way to the "Arab sea" (Indian Ocean) and the "China Sea" (the Pacific). This becomes the basis of new colonial empires (almost exclusively centered on the American continent between the fifteenth and seventeenth centuries), which in turn make it possible for a capitalist civilization to develop. It is in this context that Medieval Latin-Germanic philosophy becomes the core of *Modern European philosophy*, in a manner inextricably intertwined with its political and economic hegemonical claim. I believe that the specific philosophical origin of this process is Bartolomé de Las Casas's philosophical critique of the new colonial domination in the Caribbean region in 1514, long before that of Descartes's *Discourse on Method*, written in Amsterdam in 1637. European philosophy was until then singular and *regional* in character, but could now reposition itself in terms of a claim to take on the trappings of *philosophy itself.* It is valid to characterize the domination of European philosophy as *hegemonic* because it imposed its sway on the philosophical communities that had been colonized or reduced to its periphery. It is this hegemony that makes it possible for *modern European philosophy* to develop in a unique manner, unlike any other in the world during the same historical period. My emphasis here, then, is on exploring possible explanations for this development and its universality claim.

Modern colonial expansion through the opening of the Atlantic by Portugal to the West of Africa, and then towards the Indian Ocean (which leapt over the "wall" surrounding the Ottoman Empire), and by Spain towards the Caribbean and the American continent, laid siege to the Islamic world from the end of the 1500s, paralyzing its civilizational and thus, too, its philosophical development. Classic Arab philosophy was not able to survive the crisis in the Caliphate of Baghdad and declined definitively thereafter. The presence of the Mongol Empire similarly destroyed the possibility of new developments in Buddhist and Vedanta philosophies during the sixteenth century. China, meanwhile, began to feel the weight of having failed to complete the Industrial Revolution at the end of the eighteenth century, just as Great Britain[20] began to experience it fully; by the end of the same century China had already ceased to produce new hegemonic philosophy.

In Latin America the process of the Spanish conquest destroyed all of the most outstanding intellectual and cultural resources of the great Amerindian cultures; subsequently the Spanish and Portuguese colonies of the Baroque period were never able to surpass the achievements of the Scholastics of the sixteenth-century Renaissance.

The dominating centrality of Northern Europe as a military, economic, political, and cultural power laid the foundation for the development of its philosophy from the end of the Middle Ages, from the fifteenth century of Nicolás de Cusa (1401–1464) and the Italian Renaissance, with its origins in the presence and influence of the Byzantines expelled by the Ottomans of Constantinople in 1453. This made it possible for its own philosophy to develop and, in the face of the crisis of the other great regional philosophies, elevate its philosophical *particularity* to a *universality claim*.

Modern European philosophy was therefore positioned in such a way as to appear to be a *universal philosophy*—both in its own eyes and in those of the intellectual communities of the colonial world that lay prostrate at its feet, and philosophically paralyzed. It was situated geographically, economically, and culturally in the *center*, able to manipulate the *knowledge and information* wrested from all of the peripheral cultures within its grasp. These cultures were connected to the center along a link running between the Colonial South and the European metropolitan North, but disconnected from each other, without any South-South relations or alliances possible as yet. These relation will evolve during the Age of European Modernity, cultivating an increasing disdain for their own identities and contributions, which includes forgetting their traditions and confusing the high levels of development produced by the Industrial Revolution in Europe with the supposedly *universal truths in its discourse*—both its content and its methods. This is what makes it possible for Hegel to write:

> Universal history goes from East to West. Europe is absolutely the end of universal history."[21] "The Mediterranean Sea is the axis of universal history.[22]

Similarly, certain European mythic narratives will be confused with the supposedly *universal content* of purely European philosophical rationality. Hegel is also the one who wrote that "the Germanic Spirit is the Spirit of the New World [Modernity], whose end is the realization of the Absolute Truth."[23] He fails to note, however, that said "Spirit" is regional (European Christian and not Taoist, Vedanta, Buddhist or Arab), nor is it global, nor does its *content* reflect the problems characteristic of other cultures. For these reasons, it does not constitute a universal philosophical discourse, but instead reflects the characteristics of a mythic narrative. What does it mean in terms of a strictly universal philosophical rationality to speak of the "Spirit of Christianity"? Why not then speak of the "Spirit of Taoism" or of Buddhism or Confucianism? That "Spirit" is completely valid as a component of a mythic narrative with meaning for those who live within the horizons of a regional culture (such as Europe), but not to attribute to it a rational philosophical content with an empirically based universal validity, as modern European philosophy still claims for itself.

Philosophical Eurocentrism is, then, in essence this universality claim of a particular philosophy, many aspects of which may still be absorbed by other traditions. We can assume that all cultures have ethnocentrist tendencies, but it is modern European culture was the first whose ethnocentrism became globalized, with its original regional horizon extended to coincide with that of the emergent world-system itself, as proposed by Immanuel Wallerstein.[24] But this universality claim falls of its own weight when philosophers of other philosophical and cultural traditions become conscious of their own philosophical history and its grounded implications.

5. PHILOSOPHICAL UNIVERSALITY AND CULTURAL PARTICULARITY

None of what I have argued thus far negates that it is possible for philosophical discourse to take into account the fundamental "core problems" and attempt to develop responses with universal validity, as contributions that can be discussed by other cultures, since they would involve problems that are ultimately human and thus universal in character. K.-O. Apel's[25] effort to define the universal conditions of validity necessary for a "argumentative discourse" makes it plain that there must be symmetrical possibilities for each of the participants to engage in the process; otherwise, the conclusions of the discussion will not be valid because participants have not participated under equal conditions. This is an ethical-epistemological formal principle (without any content based in any particular material value judgment of any culture), that can be assessed critically by other cultures. Similarly, the fact that there are historical-material and economic conditions grounded in the affirmation and development of human life, which are universally necessary for human existence (since we are subjects in living bodies as suggested by Karl

Marx), appears to be valid for all cultures. The formal abstract universality of certain statements or principles, which can be shaped differently at the material level of each culture, does not negate that they can be "bridges" which can make it possible for there to be dialogue and debate between different philosophical traditions. This meta-philosophy is a product of all humanity, even if it emerges initially in the context of a specific culture, or in some specific tradition or historical period, which might have been able to make greater progress on this issue than others, but from which all the other traditions could learn from within the bounds of their own historical assumptions.

For example, in the tenth century A.D. in Baghdad, mathematics advanced significantly, immediately contributing to a leap in the development of Arab-Aristotelian philosophy and proving useful to other traditions as well. An *absolutely* post-conventional philosophy is impossible (implying no relationship to any concrete culture), but all philosophies, located inevitably in some specific cultural context, are nonetheless capable of engaging in dialogue with others through the prism of shared "core problems" and categorical discourses of a philosophical character, which are universal to the extent that they are human.

6. THE NEW AGE OF DIALOGUE BETWEEN PHILOSOPHICAL TRADITIONS

It has been asserted for too long that this universal function is fulfilled by modern European philosophy. This insistence has obscured many great discoveries made by other philosophical traditions. This is why the great task that lies before us at the beginning of the twenty-first century is the initiation of an inter-philosophical dialogue.

We must start with a dialogue between North and South, because we will be reminded of the continuing presence of colonialism and its legacies, still with us after five hundred years. This is a multi-dimensional phenomenon that includes economic and political structures and expressions, as well as cultural and philosophical ones. The philosophical communities of the post-colonial world (with their distinct problems and responses) are still not generally accepted, recognized, nor engaged by their counterparts in metropolitan hegemonic communities.

Second (and no less important) is the need to undertake and deepen permanent South-South dialogue, in order to define the agenda of the most urgent philosophical problems in Africa, Asia, Latin America, Eastern Europe, etc., and discuss them together philosophically. The rules for such a dialogue must be patiently developed.

We must lay the pedagogical foundations by educating future generations in multiple philosophical traditions. For example, in the first semester or course in the history of philosophy at the undergraduate level, we should begin with the study of "The First Great Philosophers of Humanity"—the thinkers who developed the original categories of philosophical thinking in Egypt (Africa), Mesopotamia (including the great prophets of Israel), in Greece, India, China, Meso-America, the Incas, etc. In the second semester we should continue with study of "The Great Ontologies," including Taoism, Confucianism, Hinduism, Buddhism, the Greeks (such as Plato, Aristotle, and up to Plotinus), the Romans, etc. A third course should explore later stages of philosophical development in China (beginning with the founding of the Han empire), later examples of Buddhist and Indian philosophy, Byzantine Christian philosophy, and Arab philosophy up to the contemporary period. And so on. *This is how a new generation can begin to think philosophically from within a global mindset.* The same approach should be reflected in the courses specializing in ethics, politics, ontology, anthropology, and even logic (shouldn't we have some notion of Buddhist logic as well?)

Furthermore, we must ask ourselves if other philosophical traditions (beyond those of Europe and North America) have wrestled with questions ignored by our own traditions, even though those traditions might have explored them in different ways, with varying emphases. The differences might provide new perspectives on the particular conditions of the geopolitical environment where they were engaged. There must be dialogue between *East* (an ambiguous concept deconstructed by Edward Saïd) and *West* (equally ambiguous)[26] because Africa, Latin America, and other regions are excluded.

We also need a complete reformulation of the history of philosophy in order to be prepared for such a dialogue. *World Philosophy*, the pioneering work by the sociologist Randall Collins,[27] points to key aspects that must taken into account. His comparative analysis crosses the geography (space) and history (time) of the great Chinese, Indian, Arab, European, North American, and African philosophers, which he categorizes in generations and in terms of their relative importance, although glaring omissions include his failures to devote a single line to five hundred years of Latin American philosophy, and to the nascent philosophies of the urban cultures prior to the conquest. Despite these weaknesses, he provides rich information for further interpretation and gives the philosopher pause, since the author is a sociologist who provides a great deal of material for philosophical thinking.

7. INTER-PHILOSOPHICAL DIALOGUE TOWARDS A TRANS-MODERN PLURIVERSE

After a long crisis resulting from the impact of modern European culture and philosophy, the philosophies of other regions are beginning to recover a sense of their own histories buried beneath the hurricane of Modernity. Take the example of a contemporary Arab philosopher, Mahomed Abed Yabri, at the University of Fez in Morocco, a prestigious university city renowned for over a thousand years, which in the thirteenth century had 300,000 inhabitants and where Moses Maimonides, among others, went to study and teach. In A. Yabri's two works, *The Critique of Arab Reason*[28] and *The Arab Philosophical Legacy: Alfarabi, Avicena, Avempace, Averroes, Abenjaldun*,[29] he begins with an *evaluative assessment* of the philosophy of his Arab cultural tradition. Along the way, a) he rejects the tradition of interpretation prevalent in this historical period (that of the *salafís* or *fundamentalists*), a reaction against Modernity that lacks a creative reconstruction of the philosophical past; b) he rejects of "Marxist *safism*," which forgets its own tradition; and c) he rejects with equal force the liberal Eurocentric tradition that does not accept the existence of a contemporary "Arab philosophy." Instead the author employs his linguistic skills in Arabic as a native speaker and undertakes original research in the philosophical traditions of the great thinkers of the "Eastern" schools (of Egypt, Baghdad, and towards the East, under the influence of Avicenna) and of the "Western" schools (of the Caliphate of Cordoba, including the Berber regions of Fez) that pivot around the contributions of 'Ibn Roshd.

At a second stage in his exploration, A. Yabri undertakes a critique of his own philosophical tradition by employing the resources of Arab philosophy itself, but also drawing from some of the achievements of modern hermeneutics (which he studied in Paris). This combination makes it possible for him to discover new historical elements in his own tradition, for instance, that the Arab "Eastern" tradition had to contend with Persian Gnostic thinking as a principal rival. Thus the *mu'ltazilíes* created the first Arab philosophy: by opposing Persia and at the same time drawing upon Greco-Byzantine philosophy in order to justify the legitimacy of the Caliphate. Subsequently Al-farabi and 'Ibn Sina (Avicenna), employing neo-Platonic categories, will produce a philosophical-mystical tradition of illumination. While Andalusian-Maghrebi "Western" philosophy, inspired by the scientific empiricism and strictly Aristotelian thought (with the characteristic slogan: "abandon the argument based on authority and go back to the sources" as urged by the Almohade 'Ibn Túmert) will produce the great Arab philosopher 'Ibn Roshd, a true philosophical Enlightenment (*Aufklärung*), unlike that which will be imposed as the origin of Latin-Germanic philosophy, the foundation of modern European philosophy. 'Ibn Roshd perfectly defines what inter-philosophical dialogue should consist of:

> Undoubtedly we should build upon and take from the contributions resulting from the research of all who have preceded us (the Greeks, the Christians), as sources of assistance in our process of rational study. . . . Given that this is so, and since the ancient philosophers already studied with great diligence the rules of reasoning (logic, method), it will be appropriate for us to dedicate our labors to the study of the works of these ancient philosophers, and if everything we find in them is reasonable, we can accept it, *and if not, those things that are not reasonable can serve as a warning and a basis for precaution.*[30]

At a third stage, that of new creation based upon one's own tradition and nourished by dialogue with other cultures, we should not allow ourselves to be blinded by the apparent splendor of a modern European philosophy that has laid the groundwork for exploring its own problems, but *not* for exploring the problems particular to the Arab world:

> How can Arab philosophy assimilate the experience of liberalism before the Arab world has experienced that stage, or without having done so?[31]

One more theme must be addressed at this final stage. The dialogue that can enrich each philosophical tradition must be carried out by critical and creative philosophers in each tradition, and not by those who simply repeat the philosophical theses that are the traditional echoes of consensus. An essential element of such a critical stance is for philosophers to assume the responsibility for addressing the ethical and political problems associated with the poverty, domination, and exclusion of large sectors of the population, especially in the Global South (in Africa, Asia, and Latin America). A critical philosophical dialogue presupposes critical philosophers, in the sense of the "critical theory" of the Frankfurt School, which we in Latin America refer to as the Philosophy of Liberation.

European Modernity has impacted cultures throughout the world through colonialism (except for China, Japan, and a few others, who were spared direct European rule). It exploited their resources, extracted information from their cultures, and discarded that which it could not absorb. When I speak of *trans-modernity*, I am referring to a global project that seeks to transcend European or North American Modernity. It is a project that is not post-modern, since post-Modernity is a still-incomplete critique of Modernity by European and North America. Instead, *Trans-modernity* is a task that is, in my case, expressed philosophically, whose point of departure is that which has been *discarded*, *devalued*, and judged *use-less* among global cultures, including colonized or peripheral philosophies. This project involves the development of the potential of those cultures and philosophies that have been ignored, upon the basis of their own resources, in constructive dialogue with European and North American Modernity. It is in this way that Arab philosophy, for example, could incorporate the hermeneutics of European philosophy, develop and apply them in order to develop new interpretations of the *Korán* that would make possible a new, much-needed Arab political philosophy, or Arab feminism. It will be the fruit of the Arab philosophical tradition, updated through inter-philosophical dialogue (not only with Europe, but equally with Latin America, India, China, etc.), oriented towards a *pluriversal future global philosophy*. This project is necessarily *trans-modern*, and thus also trans-capitalist.

For a long time, perhaps for centuries, the many diverse philosophical traditions will each continue to follow their own paths, but nonetheless a global project of a *trans-modern pluriverse* (other than universal, and not post-modern), appears on the horizon. Here, "other philosophies" are possible, because "another world is possible"—as is proclaimed by the Zapatista Liberation Movement in Chiapas, Mexico.

NOTES

1. *Metaphysics*. I, 2; 982 b 17–18.

2. "Civilization universelle et cultures nacional," in *Histoire et Verité* (Paris: Seuil, 1964), pp. 274–288.

3. Ernst Bloch, *Das Prinzip Hoffnung* (Frankfurt: Suhrkamp, 1959), vols. 1–3.

4. See Paul Ricoeur, *La symbolique du mal* (Paris: Aubier, 1963).

5. See my book *The Invention of the Americas* (New York: Continuum, 1995), §7.1. "The Tlamatini."

6. R. Fornet-Betancourt, *Crítica intercultural de la Filosofía Latinoamericana actual* (Madrid: Trotta, 2004).

7. P. Hountondji, *Sur la philosophie africaine. Critique de l'ethnophilosophie* (Paris: Maspero, 1977).

8. P. Tempel, *La philosophie Bantue* (Paris: Présence Africaine, 1949). See Miguel León-Portilla, *Filosofía Nahuatl* (México: UNAM, 1979).

9. *Sources of Chinese Tradition from Earliest Times to 1600*, comp. Wm. Theodore DeBary and Irene Bloom (New York: Columbia University Press, 1999), vol. 1, p. 79.

10. See *Confucius Analects*, trans. Edward Slingerland (Indianapolis: Hackett Publishing Company, 2003).

11. See DeBary and Bloom, *Sources of Chinese Tradition*, vol. 1, pp. 66ff.

12. Ibid., pp. 114ff. See Randall Collins, *The Sociology of Philosophies. A Global Theory of Intellectual Change* (Cambridge, MA: The Belknap Press of Harvard University Press, 2000), pp. 137ff. and 272ff.

13. See *Sources of Indian Tradition From the Beginning to 1800*, ed. Ainslee Thomas Embree (New York: Columbia University Press), vol. 1. Also Collins, *The Sociology of Philosophies*, pp. 177ff. On Japan, ibid., pp. 322ff.

14. 6. 12–14 (Embree, *Sources of Indian Tradition*, vol. 1, p. 37).

15. *Philosophy as Mankind's Self-Reflection; the Self-Realization of Reason*, in *The Crisis of European Sciencies* (Evanston, IL: Northwestern University Press, 1970), pp. 338–339. See §73 of *Die Krisis der europäischen Wissenschaften* (Haag: Nijhoff, 1962), Husserliana VI, p. 273. It is the same text of *The Crisis of European Sciences*, §8, pp. 21ff. (German original, pp. 18ff.). For example, the so call "Pythagoras theorem" was formulated by the Assyrian 1000 B.C. (see G. Semerano, *La favola dell'indoeuropeo* [Milano: Bruno Mondadori, 2005]).

16. D. Sobrevilla, *Repensando la tradición de Nuestra América* (Lima: Banco Central de Reserva del Perú, 1999), p. 74.

17. See for example the *Lexique de la Langue Philosophique D'Ibn Sina (Avicenne)*, ed. A.-M. Goichon (Paris: Desclée de Brouwer, 1938). The 792 different terms analyzed by the editor in 496 large format pages, provide us with an idea of the "precise terminology" of Arab *falasafa* (philosophy). The final entry is: "792. *Yaqini:* certain, known with certitude, relative to a certain knowledge . . .", and thereafter follow 15 lines of explanation with the Arabic expressions, in Arabic script, at the right hand margin.

18. See the subject on Bartolomé de las Casas and the human sacrifices in my book *Política de la Liberación. Una historia mundial y crítica* (Madrid: Trotta, 2007), pp. 203ff.

19. See Ricoeur, *La symbolique du mal*.

20. K. Pommeranz, *The Great Divergence. China, Europe and the Making of the Modern World Economy* (Princeton, NJ: Princeton University Press, 2000).

21. Hegel, *Die Vernunft in der Geschichte, Zweiter Entwurf* (1830), C, c; in *Sämtliche Werke*, ed. J. Hoffmeister (Hamburg: F. Meiner, 1955), p. 243. English version *Lectures on the Philosophy of World History, Introduction: Reason in History* (Cambridge: Cambridge University Press, 1975), p. 197.

22. Hegel, *Die Vernunft*, p. 210; English, p. 171.

23. Hegel, *Vorlesung über die Philosophie der Geschichte*, in *Werke* (Frankfurt: Suhrkamp, 1970), vol. 12, p. 413; *The Philosophy of History* (New York: Colonial Press, 1900), p. 341.

24. I. Wallerstein, *The Modern World-System* (New York: Academic Press, 1980–1989), vols. 1–3.

25. K.-O. Apel, *Die Transformation der Philosophie* (Frankfurt: Surhkamp, 1973), vols. 1–2.

26. And what does the West consist of? Is it only Western Europe, and in that case where does Russia fit, which was certainly a part of the culture of the ancient *Eastern* Byzantine Empire? Is its origin in Greece? But this too is problematic because for Greece the rest of Europe was as barbarous as other regions were to the North of Macedonia.

27. See Collins, *The Sociology of Philosophies*.

28. A. Yabri, *The Critique of Arab Reason* [*Crítica de la razón árabe*] (Barcelona: Icaria-Antrazyt, 2001).

29. A. Yabri, *The Arab Philosophical Legacy: Alfarabi, Avicena, Avempace, Averroes, Abenjaldun* (Madrid: Trotta, 2001).

30. Yabri, *Crítica de la razón árabe*, pp. 157–158.

31. Ibid., p. 159.

Transversality and the Philosophical Politics of Multiculturalism in the Age of Globalization

HWA YOL JUNG
EMERITUS, MORAVIAN COLLEGE

In Memory of My Wife Petee

Abstract: This paper advances the concept of transversality by drawing philosophical insights from Maurice Merleau-Ponty, Calvin O. Schrag, and the Martinicuan francophone Edouard Glissant. By so doing, it attempts to deconstruct the notion of universality in modern Western philosophy. It begins with a critique of the notion of Eurocentric universality which is founded on the fallacious premise that what is particular in the West is made universal, whereas whereas what is particular in the non-West remains particular forever. Eurocentric Universality has no place in the globalization of the multicultural world. It simply ignores the reality of interlacing of multiple life-worlds. The concept of transversality, whose icon is the Maitreyan Middle Way, is proposed to replace universality. It not only reduced ethnocentric particularism but also fosters a hybridity that in fact dissolves the binary opposition between particularism and universalism. In short, transversality is conceived of as a radically new paradigm in philosophical conceptualization or world philosophy.

Gateless is the Great *Dao*,
There are thousands of ways to it.
If you pass through this barrier,
You may walk freely in the universe.
—*Mumon ("Gateless" or "No Gate" in two sinograms)*

Special Supplement, *Journal of Philosophical Research* pp. 167–190
DOI: 10.5840/jpr201237Supplement33

True theory does not totalize, it multiplies.
—*Gilles Deleuze*

Transversal logos replaces the universal logos as the lynchpin for the philosophy of the new millennium.
—*Calvin O. Schrag*

If we keep on speaking the same language together, we're going to reproduce the same history.
—*Luce Irigaray*

I. PROLOGUE: THE IDEA OF GLOBALIZATION

Globalization is a new venture in the civilizational history of humankind everywhere. It is a movement toward the creation of a new world (*mondialisation*). As everything including globalization is a matter of communication, the late Canadian communication theorist Marshall McLuhan fashioned the idea of the shrinking world as "a global village" in an age of electronic media that superseded the Gutenberg era of printing technology. Now his faithful followers "digitalized" the global village—the phenomenon of which may be called "McLuhan 2.0." In terms of media or communication technology, he—who had fancied writing his *magnum opus*, *The Gutenberg Galaxy* (1962), in the medium of sinography—had an unerring sense of the flow and rhythm of history since the Homeric oral culture of ancient Greece. His disputed slogan, "the medium is the message," scales Western history as much as communication theory.

As we are living in the midst of the world which is constituted by a plurality of socio-cultural life-worlds, the neologism *glocalization* signifies the interdependence of the global and the local or the rootedness of the global in the local: the global without the local is empty and the local without the global is myopic. The end of globalization is neither to hold on to anachronistic national/cultural identities nor to establish futuristic "one world" with "one government" if it is ever possible at all. Rather, it fosters a non-polar middle path between the global and the local which shuns abstract universalism on the one hand and ethnocentric particularism on the other.[1]

In the world of multiculturalism, we are not one but many. Interestingly, according to Michael Hardt and Antonio Negri, "we" are neither "people" nor "masses" but a "multitude."[2] The idea of "people" for them reduces many to a single or unitary entity while "masses" is driven to uniformity or conformity. Both "people" and "masses" fail to take into account plurality *cum* difference or diversity. To conserve diversity in the idea of "we," "multitude" is preferred in this essay to describe the contemporary socio-cultural reality which is nothing but a multitudinous web of relationships as well as a multiplicity of experiential realities. "Multitude" for its name sake is a particularly befitting response to both the phenomenon of multiculturalism and the advent of globalization or, better, glocalization.

II. WESTERN MODERNITY AND THE LEGACY OF EUROCENTRISM

Enlightenment thought is the intellectual soul of Western modernity. Its legacy continues and, as its inheritors insist, its project is far from being finished. Some speak of modernity as an unfinished project, a second modernity, even the modernization of modernity, or the second coming of Enlightenment itself. They have an unwavering faith in it as the absolute "end of history." Enlightenment's untamed optimism alleges to promote and crown humanity's progress based on the cultivation of pure and applied reason.

Kant is the paragon of Enlightenment thought, and as such he spelled out its rationale in the clearest and simplest terms: the autonomy of reason was meant to rescue and emancipate humanity from the dark cave of self-incurred immaturity. In so doing, he institutionalized the major agenda of European modernity whose rationality has never been seriously challenged until the auspicious advent of postmodernism found in the voluminous corpus of work in Nietzsche, Heidegger, Lyotard, Foucault, Levinas, Derrida, Vattimo, Deleuze, Irigaray, and others. While privileging and valorizing the autonomy and authority of reason for allegedly human progress and emancipation, European modernity unfortunately left in the cold the (reason's) other, whether it be body, woman, nature, or Orient. Body, woman, nature, and Orient are not randomly isolated but four interconnected (t) issues: most interestingly, it is no accident that the feminine gender is assigned to body, nature, and Orient, while their (binary) opposites—mind, culture, and Occident—are masculine or "malestream" categories.[3] It is worth noting that the heart of postmodernist contention lies in the refutation of these binary oppositions in the thinking or, better, unthinking of Western modernity.

There is nothing trite about emphasizing the fact that all understanding, all thinking, is comparative. Comparison is the source and resource of discovering the limits of the self's discourse in light of the foreign other who is always more or less exotic. For the sake of advancing comparative literature, the American literary theorist Jonathan Culler wisely prods his colleagues to abandon its traditional Eurocentrism and turn "global" or go planetary.[4] The global ex/change of ideas and values would advance a "world republic" of literature (*la république mondiale des lettres*)[5] in the innovative spirit of Goethe's "world literature" (*Weltliteratur*) beyond national boundaries. Since everything is literature (that is, reading, writing, and translating), it is binding on all academic disciplines including philosophy.

Ethnocentrism, great or small, has filtered through some of the finest philosophical minds in the modern intellectual history of the West from Montesquieu to Rousseau, Hegel and Marx to Karl Wittfogel.[6] There are always, of course, exceptions: Voltaire, Leibniz, Humboldt, and Herder who, as a judicious comparativist, refused to identify truth and felicity with just being European or Western. From the very outset, it should be said that the heatedly debated question of rationality in the production of intercultural texts is not so much the question of epistemological absolutism and relativism as of how lateral or transversal truth may indeed be formulated without being entrapped in ethnocentrism.

The institution of the European mindset called Eurocentrism is that hegemonic disposition or propensity of modern Europe (West) which legislates or legitimizes itself as the privileged or anointed guardian of the cultural, scientific/technological, political, economic, and even moral *capital* of the entire globe. By constructing a great dividing wall between the East and the West, in other words, Eurocentrism willfully engages in "a kind of intellectual apartheid regime in which the superior West is quarantined off from the inferior East."[7] "Modernization" is nothing but the all-encompassing catchword given to the totalizing and hegemonizing process of this Eurocentric phenomenon. By positioning itself as the teleological temple of the world, Eurocentrism becomes a tribal idolatry. As the astute interpreter and critic of Western modernity and Eurocentrism, Zygmunt Bauman relates:

> From at least the seventeenth century and well into the twentieth, the writing elite of Western Europe and its footholds on other continents considered its own way of life as a radical break in universal history. Virtually unchallenged faith in the superiority of its own mode over all alternative forms of life—contemporaneous or past—allowed it to take itself as the reference point for the interpretation of the *telos* of history. This was a novelty in the experience of objective time; for most of the history of Christian Europe, time-reckoning was organized around a fixed point in the slowly receding past. Now, . . . Europe set the reference point of objective time in motion, attaching it firmly to its own thrust towards colonizing the future in the same way as it had colonized the surrounding space.[8]

Indeed, this Eurocentric idea of colonizing the future gives a new meaning to the conception of modernity as an unfinished project or as the end of history.

The ugly and ghastly Eurocentric racism of two of the guiding, "enlightened" philosophers of Western modernity certainly tarnishes them as world philosophers: David Hume and Immanuel Kant. They were unquestionably white supremacists. Hume wrote:

> I am apt to suspect the negroes, and in general all the other species of men . . . to be naturally inferior to the whites. There never was a civilized nation of any other complexion than white, nor even any individual eminent either in action or speculation. . . . Not to mention our [British] colonies, there are NEGROE slaves dispersed all over EUROPE, of which none ever discovered any symptoms of ingenuity; tho' low people, without education, will start up amongst us [Whites], and distinguish themselves in every profession. In JAMAICA indeed they talk of one negroe as a man of parts and learning; but 'tis likely he is admired for very slender accomplishments, like a parrot, who speaks a few [English] words plainly.[9]

Kant, who was hailed as the political harbinger of the League of Nations, is reputedly the philosophical paragon of "enlightened" Western modernity. He championed human dignity, obligatory moral integrity, and universal knowledge. Unfortunately, however, he echoed or, better, parroted Hume's racism in *Observations on the Feeling of the Beautiful and Sublime* (1763). In addition to ridiculing the "grotesqueries" of the Indians and Chinese, Kant observed in a singularly unenlightened and prejudiced way:

> The Negroes of Africa have by nature no feeling that rises above the trifling. Mr. Hume challenges anyone to cite a single example in which a Negro has shown talents, and asserts that among the hundreds of thousands of blacks who are transported elsewhere from their countries, although many of them have even been set free, still not a single one was ever found who presented anything great in art or science or any other praiseworthy quality, even though among the whites some continually rise aloft from the lowest rabble, and through superior gifts earn respect in the world. So fundamental is the difference between these two races of man, and it appears to be as great in regard to mental capacities as in color. The religion of fetishes so widespread among them is perhaps a sort of idolatry that sinks as deeply into the trifling as appears to be possible to human nature. A bird feather, a cow's horn, a conch shell, or any other common object, as soon as it becomes consecrated by a few words, is an object of veneration and of invocation in swearing oaths. The blacks are very vain but in the Negro's way, and so talkative that they must be driven apart from each other with thrashings.[10]

The noted nineteenth-century African-American thinker Frederick Douglas had white supremacists such as Hume and Kant in mind when he contended that the complexion of the skin has no bearing on the working of the mind.

III. THE *DAO* OF TRANSVERSALITY

Philosophy often begins anew by inventing concepts to come to grips with the world always already in transition. In today's multicultural and globalizing world, we are in dire need of inventing new concepts to explore changing realities. I would venture to say that transversality is one of those new concepts that replaces the outmoded Eurocentric idea of universality in Western modernity. It is, in a manner of speaking, a phoenix rising from the ashes of universality wedded to Eurocentrism. By decentering or deprovincializing Eurocentrism, it intends to go beyond and transfigure the Eurocentric mega-narratives of universality. It is truly an *interruption* in the etymological sense of the term. Thus it may be conceived of as "*trans(uni)versality*." As a paradigm shift in our thinking, it may be likened to the lateral movement of digging a new hole, instead of digging the same hole deeper and deeper with no exit in sight.[11] Transversality goes beyond the hierarchized binary oppositions, for example, between mind (the rational) and body (the sensorial), man and woman, humanity and nature, East and West, and North and South. It leaves behind the essentialized notion that what is particular in the West is universalized or universalizable, whereas what is particular in the East remains forever particular.

To draw insights from Leszek Kolakowski, what the "priestly" is to Eurocentric universality, the "jesterly" is to transversality. He is incontrovertible when he observes that throughout the ages there is an incurable antagonism between "a philosophy that perpetuates the absolute" and "a philosophy that questions accepted absolutes."[12] That is, there is the antagonism between the "priestly" and the "jesterly," which are the two most general forms of intellectual culture at any given period of time in history. "Priests" are authoritative and ceremonious guardians of the absolute, while "jesters" are those vigilants who distrust the absolute as a stabilized system and intend to unpack it. The "jesterly" play of difference aims at the creation of an alternative or "reversible world" order. As a form of transgression and subversion, it intends to transform a "real" world into a "possible" world.

Inspired directly and indirectly by the insights of Continental philosophers (e.g., Merleau-Ponty, Sartre, Lyotard, Deleuze, and Guattari), the American existential phenomenologist Calvin O. Schrag develops, and spells out, the intricacies of transversality as diacritical engagement and enrichment *across* differences and embraces the conception of truth as the way of communicability.[13] As a derivative concept of geometry, transversality denotes the crossing (Xing) of two diagonal lines in any given parallelogram. Schrag exacts *l'esprit de finesse* by way of a geometric configuration: in addition to the two "diagonals" crossing or intersecting each other at the epicenter of any rectangle, the hermeneutical "circle" and the rhetorical "triangle" also figure in an attempt to resolve the deadlock between Western modernity and postmodernity. Transversality is for Schrag capable of transgression, intervention, re-creation, and new invention. It is in search of "convergence without coincidence," "commonality without identity," and "cooperation without uniformity." What started out to be a refiguration of rationality as a diagonal passageway between the modernist overdetermination and the postmodernist underdetermination of reason has become a radically new project that would be capable of navigating the stormy channel between—in his words—"the Scylla of a hegemonic unification"/"a vacuous universalism," on the one hand, and "the Charybdis of a chaotic pluralism"/"an anarchic historicism," on the other (ibid., "Transversality," 75). One comes to understand transversality by splitting the difference between the two extremes. Most recently Schrag declared that "the transversal logos replaces the universal logos as the lynchpin for the philosophy of the new millennium,"[14] which is already here. In other words, transversality deconstructs Eurocentrism, the mission of which is to proselytize the universality of the rational. It first dismantles or unpacks the status quo and then goes beyond what is given, received, or established by constructing a new formation or constellation of concepts. It attempts to challenge the assumed transparency of truth as universal and overcome the limits of universality as the Eurocentric canon of truth in Western modernity. It means to decenter Europe as the site of universal truth whose "identitarian" and "unitarian" motivation fails to take into account a plurality of cultures or a world of multiculturalism.

What should be noted here is that in transversality differences are negotiated and compromised rather than effaced, absorbed, or assimilated into sameness or unitariness. In transversal engagement what is lacking in one is compensated for or supplemented by the other. Here we should take heed of the pluralist Johann Gottfried Herder, a pupil of Kant, who contended that colonialism "effaces" cultural differences. As Anthony Pagden points out, Western colonialism is for Herder "an evil because it reduces, or threatens to reduce . . . the number of cultural variants that exist in the world. That is an evil because plurality is part of the way the world is constituted."[15] Herder challenges the mainstream Western conception of universal reason in interesting bodily metaphors:

> After dozens of attempts, I find myself unable to comprehend how reason can be presented so universally as the single summit and purpose of all human culture, all happiness, all good. *Is the whole body just one big eye?* Would it not suffer if every part, the hand and the foot, had to serve as the eye and the brain? Reason, too carelessly, too uselessly diffused, may well weaken desire, instincts and vital activity—in fact has already done so.[16]

Insofar as transversality is the negotiated or compromised "middle voice," it touches the soul and heart of Buddhism. I would not hesitate to suggest that the famous wooden statue of Buddha at a Zen temple in Kyoto, Japan, which is now housed in the Kyoto National Museum, embodies the mantra of transversality. The Buddha's face—the "soul of the body" (Wittgenstein's expression) that speaks the world in transformation—marks a new dawn of awakening (*satori*) or signals the beginning of a new regime of ontology, culture, ethics, and politics. From the crack in the *middle* of the old face of Buddha's statue, there emerges an interstitial, liminal face that signifies a new transfiguration and transvaluation of the existing world. The icon of the emerging face symbolizes the arrival of Maitreya (the "future Awakened One," Bodhisattva) or *Middle Way*—the third enabling term of transversality that is destined to navigate the difficult waters of intercultural border-crossings. We are warned not to take it as a middle point between two polarities. Rather, it breaks through bipolarity (e.g., mind and body, and East and West). What is important here is the fact that transversality is the paradigmatic rendition of overcoming any bipolarity. The bipolar solids melt into the air of transversality, as it were.[17]

The French sinologist and philosopher François Jullien calls the effort of decentering Eurocentrism or Western modernity—with Kant in mind—"a new 'Copernican reversal.'"[18] He contends that in "shaking up" Western modernity, China becomes a "philosophical tool." That is to say, he uses Chinese thought to interrogate the limits of Western philosophy and to liberate it from its own "mental cage." Most radically, he wishes to replace the very concept of "truth" itself with that of "intelligibility," because "truth" is bound up with the history of Western philosophy. Jullien puts Foucault to the test in order to vindicate the Eurocentric "legislation" of truth for all global humanity. In his 1978 visit to Japan, the vintage Foucault remarked that knowledge and power are interwoven as one fabric; European imperialism and the era of Western philosophy come to an end. Foucault is not alone in conjecturing that philosophy of the future must be born "outside Europe" or in the "meetings and impacts" between Europe and non-Europe.[19]

Long before either Michel Foucault or French sinologist François Jullien, Maurice Merleau-Ponty spoke of the "lateral universal" and the lateral continuity of all humanity both "primitive" and "civilized" across history. He is unmistakably a consummate transversalist *avant la lettre*. The lateral universal is for him a new paradigm for world-making as well as for world philosophy. For Merleau-Ponty, all history is not only contemporaneous and written in the present tense but also an open notebook in which a new future can be inscribed. It is unfortunate, I think, that his deconstructive effort for comparative philosophy and his sensitivity to the global scope of philosophy have escaped the attention of comparativists and specialists alike. This inattention is likely due to the same tendencies that inform our Eurocentric propensity and orientation in philosophy, including phenomenology.[20]

Merleau-Ponty's deconstructive effort in philosophy, in comparative philosophy, is evidenced in his critique of Hegel's Eurocentrism. In the conceit of Eurocentrism, the modernist Hegel judged the "Oriental philosophy" of China in a cavalier fashion. His grand narratives of *Lectures on the History of Philosophy* show at times an inexcusable philosophical truancy. He totally dismissed the importance of Chinese philosophy in world philosophy as "elementary" (infantile), the Chinese *yin-yang* trigrams and hexagrams as "superficial," and the Chinese composition of elements (fire, water, wood, metal, and earth) as "all in confusion." Then he caps his commentary on Confucius: "We have conversations between Confucius and his followrs in which there is nothing definite further than a commonplace moral put in the form of good, sound doctrine, which may be found as well expressed and better, in every place and amongst every people. Cicero gives us *De Officiis*, a book of moral teaching more comprehensive and better than *all the books of Confucius* [emphasis added]. He [Confucius] is hence only a man who has a certain amount of practical and worldly wisdom—one with whom there is no speculative philosophy."[21] It is transparent that Hegel's judgment is too rash in which Europe is his reference culture. The concept of universal truth is West-generated, that is, born out of "Western narcissism"[22] and "ethnocentric ignorance."[23] Hegel's myopic view of universal truth may be likened to the East-Asian proverbial frog who lived in a deep well, looked up to the sky one day, and squealed with delight: "that's the universe!" For Merleau-Ponty the West invented an idea of truth itself, and there is no one philosophy that contains all philosophies. Rather, philosophy's center is everywhere and its circumference nowhere. Thus truth is concentric/polycentric, that is, transversal.

Merleau-Ponty charges that Hegel arbitrarily drew "a geographical frontier between philosophy and non-philosophy," that is, between the West and the East.[24] For Merleau-Ponty, all philosophies are anthropological types and none has any privilege of, or monopoly on, truth. European philosophy is as much "ethnophilosophical" as Chinese philosophy. However, Hegel's Eurocentric philosophy assumes that what is ethnophilosophical in the West is universalized, whereas what is ethnophilosophical in China (and India) remains ethnophilosophical.[25] Chinese philosophy is dismembered from the exclusive club of philosophy itself. Besides philosophy's own constant vigilance on what it is doing, Merleau-Ponty's phenomenological orientation demands its attention to the ethnography of socio-cultural life-worlds,[26] without which philosophy is a vacuous if not fatal abstraction.

The way of ethnography's "thick" description practiced by Marcel Mauss and Claude Lévi-Strauss, who also taught at the Collège de France, provides Merleau-Ponty with the idea of the lateral continuity of humanity between the "primitive" and the "civilized," that is, with the incessant ethnographic testing of the self by the other and the other by the self, which has a "diacritical value" for humanity's coexistence and its planetary solidarity. Ethnography redeems Western narcissism precisely because it is the human science of understanding the "foreign other." Merleau-Ponty contends that while for Hegel philosophical truth as absolute and universal knowledge is notarized and certified by the Occidental seal of approval alone,[27] the Oriental past must also have an honored place in the famed hall of philosophies to celebrate its hitherto "secret, muted contribution to philosophy." He writes resolutely: "Indian and Chinese philosophies have tried not so much to dominate existence as to be the echo or the sounding board of our relationship to being. Western philosophy can learn from them to rediscover the relationships to being and an initial option which gave it birth, and to estimate the possibilities we have shut ourselves off from in becoming 'Westerners' and perhaps reopen them" (*Signs*, 139). "If Western thought is what it claims to be," he challenges further, "it must prove it by understanding all 'life-worlds'" as multiple geo-sociocultural realities.[28]

Thus Merleau-Ponty suggests that, in contrast to the "overarching universal" of objective sciences, or we might add, Western metaphysics, the "lateral universal" is acquired through ethnographical experience as the way of "learning to see what is ours as alien and what was alien as our own" (*Signs*, 120). His lateral universal is a passport, as it were, that allows us to cross borders between diverse cultures, enter the zone of intersections and discover cross-cultural connections and convergences. While the European geophilosophical politics of identity claims its validity as universal truth, the lateral universal takes into account "local knowledge" prior to planetary knowledge (dubbed by some as "glocalization") and allows the hermeneutical autonomy of the other who may very well be right. Indeed, Merleau-Ponty's lateral universal is contextualized as an open-ended and promiscuous web of temporal and spatial (that is, chronotopic) interlacings.

Merleau-Ponty further contends that the conceited path of Hegel that excludes Chinese thought from universal knowledge and draws a geographical frontier between philosophy and non-philosophy also excludes a good part of the Western past itself. Philosophy as a perpetual beginning is open to examine its own idea of truth again and again, because truth is "a treasure scattered about in human life prior to all philosophy and not divided among doctrines."[29] In this view, Western philosophy itself is destined to reexamine not only its own idea of truth, but also related matters and institutions such as science, economy, politics, and technology. Merleau-Ponty writes with unsurpassable poignancy:

> From this angle, civilizations lacking our philosophical or economic equipment take on an instructive value. It is not a matter of going in search of truth or salvation in what falls short of science or philosophical awareness, or of dragging *chunks of mythology* as such into our philosophy, but of acquiring—in the presence of these *variants of humanity* that we are so far from—a sense of the *theoretical and practical problems* our institutions are faced with, and of rediscovering the existential field that they are born in and that their long success has led us to forget. The Orient's "childishness" has something to teach us, if it were nothing more than the *narrowness* [and rigidity, I might add] *of our adult ideas*. The relationships between Orient and Occident, like that between child and adult, *is not that of ignorance to knowledge or non-philosophy to philosophy*; it is much more subtle, making room on the part of the Orient for all anticipations and "prematurations." *Simply rallying and subordinating "non-philosophy" to true philosophy will not create the unity of the human spirit. It already exists in each culture's lateral relationships to the others, in the echoes one awakes in the other.*[30]

In Hegel's thought, in sum, there can be no genuine dialogue between the "philosophy" of the Occident and the "non-philosophy" of the Orient.

Italo Calvino defines the very notion of multiplicity as an "inability to find an ending": multiplicity multiplies itself.[31] The same cannot be said of Hegel's dialectic, which dictates the Eurocentric march of history. The ultimate synthesis of his dialectic of history is in fact the *identity* of identity (affirmation) and difference (negation). In mapping connections, Deleuze contends that his philosophy of multiplicity based on the "repetitive" logic of difference is "non-dialectizable."[32] In support of Max Weber's conception of sociality as a reconcilable or transversal multiplicity of perspectives (*Vielseitigkeit*), Merleau-Ponty argues that the dialectic is inherently "unstable" and that the only "good dialectic" is "hyperdialectic," i.e., "dialectic without synthesis." Hyperdialectic, he intimates, is "a thought that . . . is capable of reaching truth because it envisages *without restriction the plurality of the relationships and what has been called ambiguity*."[33]

It is the Russian literary theorist Mikhail Bakhtin's dialogical principle or dialogism, as opposed to Hegel's (and Marx's) dialectic, that deserves our close attention, as it uncovers the postmodern *dispositif* of multiplicity as having no ending. Hegel's succession of sublations "finalizes" itself in the *identity* of identity and difference. Bakhtin's dialogical principle, based on Dostoevsky's poetics, is "unfinalizable," that is, it has no ending. Not only is there neither first nor last word but also every past meaning has its homecoming festival. Speaking of Dostoevsky, Bakhtin writes forcefully:

> [A]t the center of Dostoevsky's artistic worlds must lie dialogue, and dialogue not as a means but as an end itself. *Dialogue here is not the threshold to action, it is the action itself.* It is not a means for revealing, for bringing to the surface the already ready-made character of a person; no, in dialogue a person not only shows himself outwardly, but he becomes for the first time that which he is—and, we repeat, not only for others but for himself as well.

> *To be means to communicate dialogically. When dialogue ends, everything ends. Thus dialogue, by its very essence, cannot and must not come to an end.* At the level of his religious-utopian worldview, Dostoevsky carries dialogue into eternity, conceiving of it as eternal co-rejoicing, co-admiration, con-cord. At the level of the novel, it is presented as the *unfinalizability of dialogue*.[34]

In the final analysis, Bakhtin's dialogical principle is predicated upn the eternity of time and the infinity of space, i.e., it is both eternal "chronopolitics" and infinite "geopolitics" that are historically intertemporal and culturally interspatial.

The (Eurocentric) universalist has failed to take into account seriously the question of diversity in the world of multiculturalism. He is still entangled in the cobweb of absolute universal truth and cultural relativism. As difference marks diversity and all relationships, Heidegger's *Differenz* as *Unter/schied* edifies our discussion here because it plays and feeds on the double meaning of the words that connects, preserves, and promotes *both* difference *and* the relational at the same time.[35] In *Differenz* as *Unterschied*, the other is neither assimilated/incorporated nor erased/segregated: the integrity of the other is well preserved. Here we would be remiss if, in light of Merleau-Ponty's above-mentioned "lateral universal" including a critique of Hegel's Eurocentrism, we failed to recognize the seminal contribution of the Caribbean francophone Edouard Glissant to the making of a transversal world.[36] Educated in philosophy and ethnography in France, he is a philosopher, a poet, and a novelist whose "poetics of relation" shaped Caribbean (*antillais*) discourse on "diversality" and creoleness (*créolité*).

Glissant has an uncanny convergence in the name of transversality with Merleau-Ponty in his critique of Hegel the Eurocentric universalist and absolute rationalist when he articulates without equivocation that transversal relation means to replace "the old concept of the universal." "Thinking about One," Glissant puts it concisely, "is not thinking about All" (*La pensée de l'Un ne soit pas la pensée du Tout*).[37] Speaking of Hegel's conception of history, Glissant retorts:

> History is a highly functional fantasy of the West, originating at precisely the time when it alone "made" the history of the world. If Hegel relegated African peoples to the ahistorical, Amerindian peoples to the prehistorical, in order to reserve history for European people exclusively, it appears that it is not because these African or American peoples "have entered History" that we can conclude today that such a hierarchical conception of "the march of History" is no longer relevant.[38]

Glissant unpacks Hegel's history by dissolving it as irrelevant or passé in the postcolonial world of diverse cultures that rejects "the linear, hierarchical vision of a single History."[39]

It is worth exploring further Glissant's transversal philosophy because it is, I submit, an ontology of global relation *à venir*. Transversality embodies the heart of his poetics of relation as cross-cultural encounters. It is the way of *crossing* and going *beyond* (i.e., creolized) ethnic, lingual, and cultural boundaries. The word *errance* means for him "to be at home in several languages and cultures while not cutting off the umbilical cord to one's own native land."[40] For Glissant, therefore, transversality, hybridity, and creoleness may be used interchangeably: transversality is nothing but "*a project to relate*" (italics added). The Caribbean archipelago as a constellation of small islands is a supreme symbol of interconnectedness and interdependence. As he puts it, the relational poetics of diversity seeks "a transversal relation, without any universalist transcendence." Creoleness, too, is the way of discovering Caribbean "subterranean convergence" *from within*. As it is indigenous to the Caribbean archipelago, it is the *métissage* (Glissant's translation of the term is "cross-breeding") of Western and non-Western ethnicity, language, and culture. As *métissage* is "the site of multiple converging paths," the converging histories of the Caribbean multitude liberate them from the all-encompassing vision of a single history. Caribbeanness is the root of a cross-cultural relationship which mutates culturally, ethnically, and linguistically. In brief, it frees the Caribbean multitude from uniformity. The British postcolonial theorist Robert J. C. Young, who regards Eurocentrism as a "white mythology," makes an interesting and unusually astute observation that "postcolonialism is neither western nor non-western, but a dialectical product of interaction between the two, articulating new counterpoints of insurgency from the long-running power struggles that pre-date and post-date colonialism."[41]

The so-called "recognition" or "acknowledgment" of difference, which is not one but many, is not the final but only the first step in the making of hybridity. In *In Praise of Creoleness/Éloge de la Créolité*—a Caribbean manifesto that is purposely written bilingually—"diversality" in opposition to universality is defined as "the conscious harmonization of preserved diversities."[42] When harmonization is understood musically, it enriches the totality and even coloration of "diversality" when two or more tones are put together (i.e., orchestrated); there emerges harmonization (or symphony) in which each individual tone is not lost but preserved, whereas when two colors are mixed together, there is no "harmony" but another color. In the name of "a polyphonic harmony," "diversality" frowns upon "the obsessional concern with the Universal." The above-mentioned Caribbean or "creolized" manifesto begins with the sentence: "Neither Europeans, nor Africans, nor Asians, we proclaim ourselves Creoles" ("*Ni Europeens, ni Africains, ni Asiatiques, nous nous proclamons Créoles*").[43] The Creole (as hybrid) is neither unitarian nor separatist but is likened to a hybrid "butterfly" who frees himself/herself by breaking off from an "ethnocentrist cocoon." Glissant himself describes the principium of creoleness as the end of "diversality," which can hardly be paraphrased:

> Diversity, which is neither chaos nor sterility, means the human spirit's striving for a cross-cultural relationship, without universalist transcendence. Diversity needs the presence of peoples, no longer as objects to be swallowed up, but with the intention of creating a new relationship. Sameness requires fixed Being. Diversity establishes Becoming. Just as Sameness began with expansionist plunder in the West, Diversity came to light through the political and armed resistance of peoples. As Sameness rises *within* the fascination

with the individual, Diversity is spread *through* the dynamism of communities. As the Other is a source of temptation of Sameness, Wholeness is the demand of Diversity. You cannot become Trinidadians or Quebecois, if you are not; but it is from now on true that if Trinidad and Quebec did not exist as accepted components of Diversity, something would be missing from the body of world culture—that today we would feel that loss. In other words, if it was necessary for Sameness to be revealed in the solitude of individual Being, it is now imperative that Diversity should "pass" through whole communities and peoples. Sameness is sublimated difference; Diversity is accepted difference.[44]

IV. EPILOGUE

What does transversality hold for the future? It begins with global dialogue[45] and ends in hybridity or creolization as an "exonomy."[46] The aim of this essay is to explore how transversality plays out as a thought experiment in the globalizing world of multiculturalism as "an asymmetric infinity" whose Many is irreducible to One. The Holy Grail of universality as a an ethnocentric project gives way to transversality: universality may be spelled "trans(uni)versality." This thought experiment of transversality requires a willingness to risk the safety and comfort of philosophical self-sufficiency and self-referentiality. Our journey is to discover the unknown continent of a new reality as well as a new way of philosophizing.[47] In a globalizing world, meanings, ideas, and values do indeed travel and immigrate everywhere in all directions[48]—from West to East, from North to South, and above all diagonally—the phenomenon of which would reduce if not eradicate "ethnocentric ignorance." Merleau-Ponty would call this thought experiment "a thought traveling in a circle" (*VI*, 35).

However, there can be no genuine cross-cultural dialogue in the logic of Eurocentrism—or, for that matter, of any ethnocentrism, e.g., Sinocentrism, Indocentrism, or Afrocentrism—where the "host" culture is conceived of as superior (master) and the "guest" culture as inferior (slave). In Hegel's model of the master-slave struggle between the colonizer and the colonized, there is only the irreconcilable opposition of domination and subordination, which inevitably ends in—to use Hegel's own language of the ultimatum—the death of one against the other. In other words, the aim of a cross-cultural dialogue is to transgress, i.e., to turn the world upside down or inside out or go beyond the question of Hegel's recognition, whose logic inevitably leads to the death of the other or the abolition of difference. His Eurocentrism as well as Hume's and Kant's racism is wholly or partly, I suspect, due to "ethnocentric ignorance," whose banality engenders a colonial or imperialistic mentality. To overcome it, we need first and foremost a phenomenological anthropology of cultural differences.

Transversality is one of philosophy's most inventive modes today. The world of transversality is not a zero-zum game, because everyone wins except ethnocentrists. Transversality, in short, reduces "ethnocentric ignorance." It calls for a radical regime change in philosophizing beyond both "Orientalism" and "Occidentalism."[49] The construction of transversality may be called a "global imaginary" after the fashion of the Canadian political philosopher Charles Taylor.[50] To adopt and modify his conception of "social imaginary," a global imaginary is something broader than an intellectual scheme. Rather, it is life-worldly, that is, it is the way people think and imagine about their social existence in relating themselves to others with global connectedness in mind that is engaging and normative. Thusly viewed, transversality has a global or planetary outlook. It is indeed a newly emerging face in the interstitial, liminal middle of an old face: it is toward future awakening. As the way of the middle or in-betweenness, it neither approves nor promotes irreconcilable binary oppositions of any kind, including what are now known as civilizational clashes. Nor can there be the effacement or defacement of differences. As with the ancient Chinese logic of *yin* and *yang*, which characterizes the way the world works, what is lacking or deficient in one is complemented or supplemented by the other. In short, it makes binary oppositions obsolete.[51] In a transversal world which freely allows border crossings, it is populated with the peoples and events of hyphenation and hybridization.[52]

Recently the Singaporean intellectual/statesman Kishore Mahbubani, who is now Dean of the Lee Kuang Yew School of Public Policy, asked a testy question: "Can Asians think?"[53] What he really meant to ask is this: Can Asians think independently of Western influence or "Westoxification."[54] His question has now become obsolete if not wrong-headed in the world of hyphenations and hybridizations, that is, of confluences.

By the Manichaean "essentialization" of European universalism (philosophy), on the one hand, and non-European particularism (non-philosophy or ethnophilosophy), on the other, Eurocentrism builds a great divide between Europe and non-Europe, which makes no global dialogue conceivable or possible. To reiterate: for global dialogue, there can be neither "Orientalism" nor "Occidentalism." Indeed, there is a geographical if not cultural contiguity between Asia and Europe: Europe is a "cape" of the Asian continent (Paul Valéry's word) or "a little peninsula of Asia" (Nietzsche's expression). The Foucauldian Edward W. Said warned us of the danger of "essentializing" a culture that occasions and spawns "culture wars" and hinders cross-cultural dialogues and conversations. As he puts it, it is the mode of Orientalizing the Orient, Occidentalizing the Occident, Africanizing Africa, Americanizing America, etc.[55] "Essentialization" is the site of civilizational "clashes" and "culture wars." In his new Preface to the 2003 printing of his seminal work *Orientalism* (1978), Said forthrightly asserted:

> Rather than the manufactured clash of civilizations, we need to concentrate on the slow working together of cultures that overlap, borrow from each other, and live together. . . . But for [this] kind of wider perception we need time and patience and skeptical enquiry supported by faith in communities of interpretation that are difficult to sustain in a world demanding instant action and reaction.[56]

Our future world is held in the palm of cultural pluralism marked by hyphenations and hybridizations. Out of a transversal ex-change of the ideas and values of global humanity, the world is poised for transformation. The intersecting middle or crossroads (Xroads) is the way that Merleau-Ponty, Heidegger, and Foucault envisioned the rise of a new paradigm of planetary thinking. Cultural pluralism is rooted in difference, not identity or sameness, which effaces or defaces differences.

The "X factor" in transversal or X-cultural studies goes beyond or, better, dissolves the dichotomous, epistemological and axiological question of relativism and universalism. As relationism is radically distinguished from relativism, transversality is a new face in the miscegenating middle, as it were, for the age of multiculturalism and globalization, which is not one but many. There can be no one philosophy that monopolizes truth: truth is concentric or transversal. In the world of hyphenation and hybridization, no culture can claim its independence, self-referentiality, and self-sufficiency. As the old Chinese saying goes, everything is related to everything else in the cosmos and thus nothing exists in isolation. We are indeed condemned to be *interdependent* with one another not only among humans but also among all things. This web of interdependence privileges humanity for its responsibility to take care of all earthlings without exception.

Transversality is conceived of as a global imaginary that is the pillar of correlating, negotiating, and compromising differences in the postmodern world of multiculturalism. It is a journey of difference without arrival, which may be likened to the saying of a Zen *koan*: "when you get to the top of the mountain, keep climbing." Transversality demands global dialogue that facilitates the intercourse of ideas and values from East and West and from North to South. Indeed, it targets those intersections where two or more lines of thought and action meet. What is deficient in one is hopefully augmented and supplemented by the other(s).

Globalization, too, is the process that facilitates the ex/change of ideas and values at the crossroads (Xroads) of all sides. Ultimately, the future cultivation of global humanity between heaven and earth will become more tri-continental (Asian, African, and Latin American) and less European or Euro-American. Globalization is nothing but the (middle) way of cross-pollinating and cross-fertilizing cultural meanings, ideas, and values in multiplicity. It enhances our chances for cosmopolitanism. The new phoenix of postmodern cosmopolitanism, whose language is interspersed with such prefixes as *inter*, *con*, and *trans*, has risen from the ashes of sovereign nation-states that the modernist Hegel deified as the political *telos* of his dialectic.

As we are living in the midst of the world that is constituted by a plurality of socio-cultural life-worlds, the neologism *glocalization* signifies the interdependence of the global and the local or the rootedness of the global in the local: the global without the local is empty and the local without the global is myopic. The end of glocalization is neither to hold on to anachronistic national/cultural identities nor to establish futuristic "one world" with "one government," if it is ever possible at all. Rather, it fosters a non-polar middle path between the global and the local that shuns abstract universalism, on the one hand, and ethnocentric particularism, on the other.

The essentialization of culture that reifies or vilifies the other is not conducive to cosmopolitanism espoused by the Cynic Diogenes, Marx, Giuseppe Garibaldi, and Virginia Woolf, who called themselves citizens of the world. The civility of cosmopolitanism *à venir* means to feel at home—in the Freudian sense of being *heimliche*—in the world. As an active principle, civility goes beyond the mere toleration of difference. In the language of the postcolonial theorist Paul Gilroy, it is "the desire to dwell convivially with difference."[57] Merleau-Ponty spells out the true spirit of civility when he speaks of the chiasmus or reversibility of "ourselves as strangers" and "strangers as ourselves." In the postmodern age of cosmopolitanism, the virtue of civility advances our communication and interaction with "foreign others" without holding their "foreignness" against them. The cultural polyglot Julia Kristeva echoes and amplifies Merleau-Ponty.[58] Her "utopic" idea or "distant ideal" is "transidentificatory" cosmopolitanism in opposition to "identificatory" nationalism that essentializes and valorizes the modern nation-state as an inviolable and sovereign entity and impenetrable shield. She means to "proselytize"—in the etymological sense of propagating "foreign" or "strange" ideas. As it is a transversal affair, cosmopolitanism is the way of making us at ease with the world that is unmistakably polyphonic. Without it, the buzzword *globalization* or *glocalization* would be an empty slogan or a disguised form of conquest.[59] In tune with global humanity, there is global Korea, global China, global Japan, global USA, and global Europe. Reflecting on the condition of global lifeworlds, philosophy too is poised for radical transformation. What is traditionally called "comparative philosophy" is no longer just a neglected branch of philosophy, but it radically transforms the very conception of philosophy itself.

After all is said and done, the transversalist is a "fox" rather than a "hedgehog." I am alluding here to Isaiah Berlin's often-quoted line from the fragments of the Greek poet Archilochus which reads: "The fox knows many things, but the hedgehog knows one big thing."[60] Thus the transversalist is an interdependent thinker who has both deftness and agility to interweave many things, whereas the universalist has one big magnetizing thought. The history of philosophy both Eastern and Western has been overshadowed by "hedgehogs." In the world of multiculturalism and globalization, the balance should be shifted to the voice of "foxes." In other words, the monistic voice of the universalist gives way to the pluralistic voice of the transversalist. The newly emerging face of the Maitreyan Middle Way mediates and facilitates cultural, disciplinary, speciesistic, and sensorial border-crossings. It is concerned with those "in-between" matters that are intercultural, interdisciplinary, interspeciesistic, interlinguistic, and intersensorial (i.e., intertextual) border-crossings.[61] It cannot be otherwise. It is high time to put an end to the metaphor of philosophy as the "owl of Minerva" that takes its flight at dusk. Philosophy should be metaphorized as the Muse who can play *mousike* (that is, recite, sing, dance, and dramatize) for, and orchestra, the global harmonics of interhuman and interspecific relationships at the dawn of a new day.

NOTES

This essay was prepared for delivery in the Fourth Plenary Session, "Rethinking History of Philosophy and Comparative Philosophy: Traditions, Critique and Dialogue," at the XXII World Congress of Philosophy in Seoul, South Korea, July 30–August 5, 2008. The author is grateful for *Research in Phenomenology* and its editor John Sallis to have given me permission to reprint with some modification this article which was published in its volume 39 (2009): 416–437.

1. Cf. Cornel West, "The New Cultural Politics of Difference," in *Out There*, ed. Russell Ferguson, Martha Gever, Trinh T. Minh-ha, and Cornel West (New York: The New Museum of Contemporary Art, 1990), pp. 19–36; Nishida Kitaro, *Fundamental Problems of Philosophy*, trans. David A. Dilworth (Tokyo: Sophia University, 1970), p. 254; and Paul Ricoeur, *History and Truth*, trans. Charles A. Kelbley (Evanston, IL: Northwestern University Press, 1965), pp. 271–284.

2. Michael Hardt and Antonio Negri, *Multitude* (New York: Penguin Press, 2004), p. xv.

3. See Hwa Yol Jung, "Enlightenment and the Question of the Other: A Postmodern Audition," *Human Studies* 25 (2002): 297–306.

4. Jonathan Culler, "Comparative Literature, At Last!" in *Comparative Literature in the Age of Multiculturalism*, ed. Charles Bernheimer (Baltimore: Johns Hopkins University Press, 1995), pp. 117–121.

5. See Pascale Casanova, *The World Republic of Letters*, trans. M. B. DeBevoise (Cambridge, MA: Harvard University Press, 2004); and "Literature as a World," *New Left Review* 31 (2005): 71–90.

6. See Hwa Yol Jung, "Phenomenology, the Question of Rationality and the Basic Grammar of Intercultural Texts," *Analecta Husserliana*, vol. 46, ed. A.-T. Tymieniecka (Dordrecht: Kluwer, 1995), pp. 169–178.

7. John M. Hobson, *The Eastern Origins of Western Civilisation* (New York: Cambridge University Press, 2004), p. 283.

8. Zygmunt Bauman, *Legislators and Interpreters* (Cambridge: Polity Press, 1987), p. 110.

9. *Essays Moral, Political, and Literary*, ed. T. H. Green and T. H. Grose, 2 vols. (London: Longmans, Green, 1875), I: 252.

10. *Observations on the Feeling of the Beautiful and Sublime*, trans. John T. Goldthwait (Berkeley: University of California Press, 1960), pp. 110–111.

11. See Edward de Bono, *New Think* (New York: Basic Books, 1968).

12. *Toward a Marxist Humanism*, trans. Jane Zielonko Peel (New York: Grove Press, 1968), pp. 9–37.

13. See Calvin O. Schrag, *Philosophical Papers: Betwixt and Between* (Albany: State University of New York Press, 1994); and *Convergence Amidst Difference* (Albany: State University of New York Press, 2004). Cf. also Hwa Yol Jung, "The *Tao* of Transversality as a Global Approach to Truth: A Metacommentary on Calvin O. Schrag," *Man and World* 28 (1995): 11–31; "Transversality and Geophilosophy in the Age of Globalization," in *Calvin O. Schrag and the Task of Philosophy After Postmodernity*, ed. Martin Beck Matuštík and William L. McBride (Evanston, IL: Northwestern University Press, 2002), pp. 74–90; "Transversality and Comparative Political Theory: A Tribute to Fred Dallmayr's Work," in *Letting Be: Fred*

Dallmayr's Cosmopolitical Vision, ed. Stephen F. Schneck (Notre Dame, IN: University of Notre Dame Press, 2006), pp. 230–250; and "Transversality and Comparative Culture," *Ex/Change: Newsletter of Centre for Cross-Cultural Studies* 16 (2006): 11–17.

14. Schrag, *Convergence Amidst Difference*, p. 76.

15. "The Effacement of Difference: Colonialism and the Origins of Nationalism in Diderot and Herder," in *After Colonialism*, ed. Gyan Prakash (Princeton, NJ: Princeton University Press, 1995), p. 414.

16. *J. G. Herder on Social and Political Culture*, trans. and ed. F. M. Barnard (Cambridge: Cambridge University Press, 1969), p. 199 (emphasis added).

17. In phenomenology, meaning is derived from intentionality, which is the meeting of consciousness (ego-*cogito*) and its object (*cogitatum*). Thus meaning is in the middle between consciousness and its object. The American pragmatic semiotician Charles Morris extensively discussed "Maitreyism," in *Paths of Life* (New York: George Braziller, 1956), pp. 151–179. Cf. particularly the works of Lou Marinoff, *The Middle Way* (New York: Sterling, 2007), and Mary Douglas, *Thinking in Circles* (New Haven, CT: Yale University Press, 2007). It is interesting to note that David Farrell Krell sketches *das Geviert* envisioned by Heidegger in the diagram of a rectangle which connects sky, earth, gods, and mortals with two diagonal lines having Being at its epicenter: the cross (X or chi) of Being is not a crossing *out* (*Durchstreichung*) but a crossing *through* (*Durchkreuzen*). See "Analysis," in Martin Heidegger, *Nietzsche*, vol. 4: *Nihilism*, trans. Frank A. Capuzzi (New York: Harper and Row, 1982), p. 289.

Recently I stumbled on the very important and interesting "garden theory" or *Gartenkunst* in Germany in the mid-eighteenth century and the mid-nineteenth century. Instead of detailing it, I wish to note here only its importance for the concept of transversality. The core concept of garden theory is "*Mittelweg*" (middle way). The *Mittelweg* or *Mitte* was intended to be the way of resolving *binary oppositions* such as art and nature, freedom and determinism, rationality and sensibility, and the city and the country. It includes the "'between' condition as a form of unification that incorporates elements of both [extremes whatever they may be]" (see Michael G. Lee, *The German "Mittelweg": Garden Theory and Philosophy in the Time of Kant* ([New York: Routledge, 2006], p. 61). There is an important difference between garden theory's *Mittelweg* and transversality. That is to say, the former focuses on the idea of "mediation," whereas the latter is intended to create a new paradigm.

18. See "Did Philosophers Have to Become Fixated on Truth?," trans. Janet Lloyd, *Critical Inquiry* 28 (2002): 803–824; and "China as Philosophical Tool," *Diogenes* 50 (November 2003): 15–21.

19. See "Michel Foucault and Zen: A Stay in a Zen Temple (1978)," trans. Richard Townsend, in *Religion and Culture*, ed. Jeremy R. Carrette (New York: Routledge, 1999), pp. 110–114. Before he became interested in Japanese aesthetic culture and the Iranian revolution, Foucault wrote with an inerasable sense of a great divide between the East and the West: "In the universality of the Western ratio, there is this divide that is the East; the East thought of as the origin, dreamt of as the dizzy point that is the place of birth, of nostalgia and promises of return, the East which offers itself to the *colonizing reason of the West* but is indefinitely inaccessible, for it remains always as a boundary, the night of beginning in which the West was formed but where it drew a dividing line, *the East is for the West everything which the West is not*, yet it is here that it has to seek whatever might be its originating truth. It is necessary to do a history of this great divide" (Janet Afary and Kevin B. Anderson, *Foucault*

and the Iranian Revolution [Chicago: University of Chicago Press, 2005], 18). The physicist Werner Heisenberg, who is also acquainted with Daoism, too noted that "[i]t is probably true quite generally that in the history of human thinking the most fruitful developments frequently take place at those points where two different lines of thought meet" (quoted in Fritjof Capra, *The Tao of Physics*, 25th anniversary ed. [Boston: Shambhala, 2000], p. 4). Capra was apparently inspired by Heisenberg to "network" or interface modern physics and Eastern mysticism. Capra also encouraged others to discover "networkings."

20. Alisdaire MacIntyre is impeccable when he observed that "a genuine dialogue [between East and West] is for the most part lacking. It is we in the West who are impoverished by our failure to sustain our part in this dialogue" (quoted in Anindita Niyogi Balslev, *Cultural Otherness: Correspondence with Richard Rorty*, 2nd ed. [Atlanta: Scholars Press, 1991], p. 80). Although the late Richard Rorty felt uncomfortable with "a tendency in contemporary political discussion to treat 'the West' as a name for the source of every imaginable oppression" (ibid., p. 101), he agreed with MacIntyre that "Eastern writers and thinkers have done much more work than Western ones to find out what goes on the other side of the world" and that "[i]t is we in the West who are impoverished by our failure to sustain our part in this dialogue" (ibid., p. 89).

In his recent book *Europe, or the Infinite Task: A Study of a Philosophical Concept* (Stanford, CA: Stanford University Press, 2009), Rodolphe Gasché provides a detailed discussion of the idea of Europe or Europa in Husserl, Heidegger, Patočka, and Derrida. However, he overlooks Merleau-Ponty completely, while mentioning Levinas several times in discussing Derrida. The importance of Levinas, I think, is his ethical philosophy of dialogue and responsibility based on the primacy of the other. Dialogism, Levinasian or Bakhtinian, celebrates the primacy of alterity that radically transforms our way of philosophizing ontology, ethics, culture, politics, and economics. Nonetheless, Gasché entertains the idea of multiple universalities. A multiplicity of singular universalities, European and/or non-European, may be called "multiversity" or what Merleau-Ponty calls "lateral universals." What comes after multiversity is the question Gasché does not raise. On the other hand, transversality goes beyond the idea of universality, both singular and multiple, in the direction of hybridity or creoleness in the globalization of the multicultural world. To use the formula of the incomparable Goethe, what the self is to the other, Europe is to non-Europe. Europe is implicated in non-Europe and vice versa. The transversal way of thinking based on Heidegger's (*Differenz* as) *Unterschied*, which fuses "difference" and the "relational" at once, is a radical way of conceptualizing and transforming the very nature of philosophizing itself.

21. Hegel's *Lectures on the History of Philosophy*, trans. E. S. Haldane, vol. 1 (London: Kegal Paul, Trench, Trübner, 1892), p. 121. In reading Amartya Sen's recent work, I find an interesting and striking parallel between Hegel's comments on Chinese philosophy and James Mill's views of India, both of which have influenced the generations of specialists on the subjects: both Hegel and Mill pontificated their views without ever visiting the countries of their subjects and without reading and understanding their languages (*Identity and Violence: The Illusion of Destiny* [New York: W. W. Norton, 2006], pp. 86–87). Bertrand Russell was the first Western philosopher in the twentieth century, I think, who was self-conscious of writing a book on "history of Western philosophy" (see *History of Western Philosophy* [New York: Simon and Schuster, 1945]). He also stressed the fact that philosophy cannot be separated from its social and political context. Robert Bernasconi puts Hegel on trial at the court of the Ashanti or Africa (see "Hegel at the Court of the Ashanti," in *Hegel After*

Derrida, ed. Stuart Barnett [New York: Routledge, 1998], pp. 41–63). To be post-Hegelian is also to be post-colonial as well as post-modern (see Stuart Barnett, "Introduction: Hegel Before Derrida," in *Hegel After Derrida*, pp. 1–37). In her recent book *Hegel, Haiti, and Universal History* (Pittsburgh: University of Pittsburgh Press, 2009), Susan Buck-Morss critically discusses Hegel's Eurocentric cultural racism, while she holds onto his idea of universality or "universal history," which is meant, she argues, to be non-Eurocentric. However, her future projection of "universal history," whether it be Eurocentric or non-Eurocentric, does not justify the globalizing world of multiculturalism or what Glissant calls "diversality." His anti-Hegelian and transversal argument rejects the overarching linear vision of a single history. To reiterate Glissant: thinking about "One" is not thinking about "All."

22. Roland Barthes, *Empire of Signs*, trans. Richard Howard (New York: Hill and Wang, 1982), p. 4.

23. *The World Republic of Letters*, trans. M. B. DeBevoise (Cambridge: Harvard University Press, 2004), 353. See also Pascale Casanova, "Literature as a World," *New Left Review* 31 (Jan.–Feb. 2005): 71–90.

24. M. Merleau-Ponty, "Everywhere and Nowhere," in *Signs*, trans. Richard C. McCleary (Evanston, IL: Northwestern University Press, 1964), pp. 133–140. Cited as *Signs*.

25. Natalie Melas points out that "the unquestioned universality of 'us' (whites) versus the irreparable particularism of 'them' (those 'marked' by color or ethnicity or more ambiguously, gender) is *an extraordinarily stubborn structure of thought and feeling*" ("Re-Imagining the Universal," in *Unpacking Europe*, ed. Salah Hassan and Iftikhar Dadi [Rotterdam: NAi Publishers and Museum Boijamans van Beuningen, 2001], pp. 134–151). For her detailed argument, see her work *All the Difference in the World: Postcoloniality and the Ends of Comparison* (Stanford: Stanford University Press, 2007).

26. John Wild envisions four different kinds of phenomena in the life-world (*Lebenswelt*), "each of which requires a distinct model of scientific investigation: man himself, the realm of nature, other men and the realm of human culture, and, finally, the transcendent" ("Interrogations of John Wild" conducted by Henry B. Veatch, in *Philosophical Interrogations*, ed. Sydney and Beatrice Rome [New York: Holt, Rinehart and Winston, 1964], pp. 119–178). Since phenomenology of the life-world is a global exploration, it is worth noting that Wild once remarked at an East-West philosophical conference that all the major forms of Western philosophical thought are to be found in a vast variety of Eastern schools (see "Certain Basic Concepts of Western Realism and Their Relation to Oriental Thought," in *Essays in East-West Philosophy*, ed. Charles A. Moore [Honolulu: University of Hawaii Press, 1951], p. 258); quoted in Hwa Yol Jung, "Wang Yang-ming and Existential Phenomenology," *International Philosophical Quarterly* 5 (1965): 612.

27. Speaking of Hegel's rationalism, which is "inveterately wedded to the conceptual decomposition of life," the pluralist William James contends that "Hegel was dominated by the notion of a truth that should prove incontrovertible, binding on every one, and certain which should be *the* truth, one, indivisible, eternal, objective, and necessary, to which all our particular thinking must lead as to its consummation. This is the dogmatic ideal, the postulate, uncriticised, undoubted, and unchallenged, of all rationalizers in philosophy. '*I have never doubted*,' a recent Oxford writer says, that truth is universal and single and timeless, a single content or significance, one and whole and complete. Advance in thinking, in the Hegelian universe, has, in short, to proceed by the apodictic words *must be* rather

than by those inferior hypothetic words *may be*, which are all that empiricists can use" (*A Pluralistic Universe* [New York: Longmans, Green, 1909], pp. 100–101).

28. Merleau-Ponty, "Everywhere and Nowhere," in *Signs*, p. 139.

29. Ibid., p. 133.

30. Ibid., p. 139.

31. Italo Calvino, *Six Memos for the Next Millennium* (Cambridge: Harvard University Press, 1988), p. 110.

32. See John Rajchman, *The Deleuze Connections* (Cambridge: Harvard University Press, 2000), p. 50.

33. M. Merleau-Ponty, *The Visible and the Invisible*, ed. Claude Lefort, trans. Alphonso Lingis (Evanston, IL: Northwestern University Press, 1968), pp. 89–95 (italics added). Hereafter *VI*.

34. *Problems of Dostoevsky's Poetics*, ed. and trans. Caryl Emerson (Minneapolis: University of Minnesota Press, 1984), p. 363 (italics added). Cf. Hans-Georg Gadamer concludes his *magnum opus*: "It would be a poor hermeneuticist who thought he could have, or had to have, the last word" (*Truth and Method*, trans. Joel Weinsheimer and Donald G. Marshall, 2nd rev. ed. [New York: Crossroad, 1991], p. 579).

35. See *Identity and Difference*, trans. Joan Stambaugh (New York: Harper and Row, 1969).

36. See *Caribbean Discourse: Selected Essays*, trans. J. Michael Dash (Charlottesville: University Press of Virginia, 1989); and *Poetics of Relation*, trans. Betsy Wing (Ann Arbor: University of Michigan Press, 1997). See also Hwa Yol Jung, "Edouard Glissant's Aesthetics of Relation as Diversality and Creolization," in *Postcolonialism and Political Theory*, ed. Nalini Terese Persram (Lanham, MD: Lexington Books, 2007), pp. 193–225.

37. Glissant, *Poetics of Relation*, p. 33. In her critique of the French politics of the veil or headscarf (*hijab* in Arabic and *foulard* in French) in school, Joan Willach Scott judiciously writes that "oneness" or "unanimity" produces "exclusions that are contrary to democratic ideals of inclusiveness," whereas the concept of "wholeness" recognizes "the existence of disagreement and differences within a 'multitude of citizens' and thus opens the way for the kind of political engagement that negotiates rather than excludes" (*The Politics of the Veil* [Princeton: Princeton University Press, 2007], p. 192).

38. Glissant, *Caribbean Discourse*, p. 49.

39. Here Glissant echoes Merleau-Ponty on Hegel in his Inaugural Lecture at the Collège de France in 1953. Merleau-Ponty emphasized that "[t]he universal history of Hegel is the dream of history. As in our dreams, all that is thought is real, and all that is real is thought. There is nothing at all for men to do who are not already taken up in the system" (see *In Praise of Philosophy*, trans. John Wild and James M. Edie [Evanston, IL: Northwestern University Press, 1963], p. 49). To use this identity logic of the real and the rational (thought), the non-West is excluded from Hegel's system of history. Furthermore, the *contingency* of human events is the pre-condition of history. Otherwise, according to Merleau-Ponty, "[h]istory has no meaning, if this meaning is understood as that of a river which, under the influence of all-powerful causes, flows towards an ocean in which it disappears. Every appeal to universal history cuts off the meaning of the specific event, renders effective history insignificant, and is a *nihilism in disguise*" (italics added). Merleau-Ponty, too, is a radical

empiricist who pays attention to particulars before abstract universals. Nothing is prefixed or predetermined in history under the guise of "Universal History" (ibid., pp. 52–53).

40. See Ivan Ivask, "Edouard Glissant: The New Discourse of the Caribbean," *World Literature Today* 63 (1989): 557–558.

41. Robert J. C. Young, *Postcolonialism* (Oxford: Blackwell, 2001), p. 68. Paul Gilroy's reputed thesis of "the black Atlantic," too, favors "double consciousness" or hybridity that sums up the transcultural intermix of African and European things. Hybridity here is a converging middle path of "multiple, interconnecting axes of affiliation and differentiation." Gilroy's "black Atlantic" is also constructed as "a counterculture of modernity" (Gilroy, *The Black Atlantic* [Cambridge: Harvard University Press, 1993]).

42. Jean Bernabé, Patrick Chamoiseau, and Raphaël Confiant, *In Praise of Creoleness/Éloge de la Créolité* (Paris: Gallimard and Baltimore: Johns Hopkins University Press, 1989). This is the manifesto that is preceded by the francophone Swiss Charles Ferdinand Ramuz's 1914 manifesto of creoleness called *Raison d'être*, which is appropriately called by Casanova "Swiss creoleness" (*The World Republic of Letters*, p. 296).

43. Bernabé, Chamoiseau, and Confiant, *In Praise of Creoleness/Éloge de la Créolité*, p. 13.

44. Glissant, *Caribbean Discourse*, p. 98.

45. Speaking of "global dialogue," Enrique Dussel asks the following interesting and important question: "Should not the constitution of this first *global dialogue* (West/East, North/South) between continental philosophical communities be one of the initial and central tasks of the twenty-first century?" ("Philosophy in Latin America in the Twentieth Century: Problems and Currents," in *Latin American Philosophy*, ed. Eduardo Mendieta [Bloomington: Indiana University Press, 2003], p. 34). Emmanuel Levinas goes one step further: dialogue and ethics are inseparable. "When I speak of first philosophy, I am referring to a philosophy of dialogue that cannot not be an ethics" (*Alterity and Transcendence*, trans. Michael B. Smith [New York: Columbia University Press, 1999], 97). Indirectly, therefore, Levinas's view of ethics, unprecedented in the history of Western philosophy, restores the dignity of Sinism, which was regarded by Hegel, for example, as lack of abstract "speculation." It would be interesting to explore the transversal connection between Confucius and Levinas.

46. In reference to Merleau-Ponty's seminal work *Phenomenology of Perception*, trans. Colin Smith (London: Routledge and Kegan Paul, 1962), Francisco Varela, Evan Thompson and Eleanor Rosch offer an exemplary observation: they speak of the openness of a space between the self and the world as "a middle way, an *entre-deux*" (*The Embodied Mind* [Cambridge: MIT Press, 1993], p. 3). Jean-Luc Nancy's neologism *exonomy* is proposed to move out of "the binary familiarity of the self and the other" (*Philosophical Chronicles*, trans. Franson Manjali [New York: Fordham University Press, 2008], p. 10). It signifies "neither the same nor the other" (ibid.). Exonomy may and can be tied to Nancy's idea of human existence as "Being-in-Common" or of the commonality of common beings (i.e., "communalism"). See "Of Being-in-Common," trans. James Creech, in *Community as Loose Ends*, ed. Miami Theory Collective (Minneapolis: University of Minnesota Press, 1991), pp. 1–12. Moreover, it would be worthwhile to relate Nancy's exonomy or the space of in-betweenness to the East-Asian conception of the human (*ingan* in Korean and *ningen* in Japanese). See particularly Watsuji Tetsuro, *Rinrigaku*, trans. Yamamoto Seisaku and Robert E. Carter (Albany: State University of New York Press, 1996); and Hwa Yol Jung, "Interbeing and Geophilosophy in

the Cultural Topography of Watsuji Tetsuro's Thought," in *Why Japan Matters!* ed. Joseph F. Kess and Helen Lansdowne, vol. 2 (Victoria, BC: Centre for Asia-Pacific Initiatives, University of Victoria, 2005), pp. 691–702. Nancy's exonomy moves into the Eastern "in-betweenness" or Interbeing out of the Western bipolarity of the self and the other.

47. Martin Jay, *Songs of Experience* (Berkeley: University of California Press, 2005), p. 405.

48. While reading Desmond Morris, I came across the fascinating traveling gesture of fig (*fica*)—a slang term in Italian for the female genitalia—which when we were youngsters we learned to use as a gesture of sexual insult during the Japanese occupation of Korea. In fact, the fig gesture originally traveled from Europe to Japan with the Portuguese or the first Europeans in the mid-sixteenth century. Morris comments that the Portuguese must have traded gestures as well as goods on their expeditious visits to Japan. To his amazement he discovered the fig gesture signifying protection while visiting a geisha house in Kyoto for the purpose of academic research, not of *asobi*. What is most interesting here is the fact that not only do ideas, oral and written, travel or transverse, but gestures also migrate (*The Human Animal* [New York: Crown, 1994], pp. 26–27).

49. In his concluding remarks of a comprehensive study of the teaching and research of philosophy in Korea, Yersu Kim writes in the kindred spirit of transversality when he invokes a "philosophical synthesis" which "will not be Eastern or Western, Korean or American, Korean or Chinese, but one 'whose centre is everywhere and its circumference nowhere'" ("Republic of Korea," in *Teaching and Research in Philosophy: Asia and the Pacific* [Paris: UNESCO, 1986], pp. 126–167). Here Kim is quoting Richard Rorty. See Rorty, "Genteel Syntheses, Professional Analyses, Transcendentalist Culture," in *Two Centuries of Philosophy: American Philosophy Since the Revolution*, ed. Peter Caws (Totowa, NJ: Roman and Littlefield, 1980), 239.

50. Charles Taylor, *Modern Social Imaginaries* (Durham: Duke University Press, 2004).

51. Over four decades ago, Chang Tung-sun ably showed and argued that Chinese logic, which is dictated by the social nature of the Chinese language itself, is a logic not of identity but of correlation that both assumes and allows pluralism ("A Chinese Philosopher's Theory of Knowledge," in *Our Language and Our World*, ed. S. I. Hayakawa [New York: Harper and Brothers, 1959], pp. 299–324). In this connection, it is most important to note the cultural psychologist Richard E. Nisbett's empirical and collaborative study of the correlational thinking of East Asian peoples. See *The Geography of Thought* (New York: Free Press, 2003). Since the mid-1980s, I have been using the expression "relational ontology" for the correlational thinking and doing in East Asia.

52. See Homi K. Bhabba, "Afterword: A Personal Response," in *Rethinking Literary History*, ed. Linda Hutcheon and Mario J. Valdés (New York: Oxford University Press, 2002), pp. 194–204. See also his classic and influential work *The Location of Culture* (New York: Routledge, 1996). The American journalist T. R. Reid comments that "East is East and West is West, but anybody who still thinks the twain shall never meet has never been to Baskin-Robbins or Burger King on the far side of the Pacific." Then he mentions the "*nouvelle cousine*" of Asian hybrid or "fusion" delicacies: "the squid pizza, the curry doughnut, the bean-paste Danish, the rice burger, the kimchee burger, the tempura hot dog, the green tea milkshake, the sashimi submarine, and ever-popular BST (that's bacon, seaweed, and tomato) sandwich" (*Confucius Lives Next Door* [New York: Random House, 1999], p. 30).

If you like burgers but not kimchee, Danishes but not bean-paste, milkshakes but not green tea, or bacon and tomatoes but not seaweed, then you may be a purist or essentialist but not a transversalist.

53. Kishore Mahbubani, *Can Asians Think?* (Singapore: Times Books International, 1998).

54. Anthony Pagden, *Worlds at War: The 2,500-Year Struggle Between East and West* (New York: Random House, 2008), p. 521.

55. Edward W. Said, *Culture and Imperialism* (New York: Alfred A. Knopf, 1993), p. 311.

56. Said, preface to *Orientalism* (London: Penguin, 2003); quoted in Hobson, *The Eastern Origins of Western Civilization*, p. 322.

57. Paul Gilroy, *Postcolonial Melancholia* (New York: Columbia University Press, 2005), p. 5.

58. See *Strangers to Ourselves*, trans. Leon S. Roudiez (New York: Columbia University Press, 1991); and *Nations without Nationalism*, trans. Leon S. Roudiez (New York: Columbia University Press, 1993).

59. In *Democracy and the Foreigner* (Princeton: Princeton University Press, 2001), pp. 98–106, Bonnie Honig argues for "a democratic cosmopolitanism" by balancing the local with the international that puts a stop to the hostility between "us" and "them."

60. Isaiah Berlin, *The Hedgehog and the Fox* (New York: Simon and Schuster, 1986), p. 1.

61. Jacques Derrida mentions in passing transversality as an interdisciplinary ("interscientific") approach (*Eyes of the University: Right to Philosophy* 2, trans. Jan Plug and Others [Stanford: Stanford University Press, 2004], p. 241). Martha C. Nussbaum discusses the importance for her program of a new liberal education of cosmopolitanism, non-Western or intercultural studies, and women's studies. See *Cultivating Humanity* (Cambridge, MA: Harvard University Press, 1997). It is instructive for us to read what Barthes says with regard to the nature of interdisciplinarity: "*Interdisciplinary* studies, of which we hear so much, do not merely confront already constituted disciplines (none of which, as a matter of fact, consents to *leave off*). In order to do interdisciplinary work, it is not enough to take a 'subject' (a theme) and to arrange two or three sciences around it. Interdisciplinary study consists in *creating a new object* [emphasis added], which belongs to no one. The Text is, I believe, one such object" (*The Rustle of Language*, trans. Richard Howard [New York: Hill and Wang, 1986], p. 72). So is the hybrid product ("Intertext") of what might be called transversal or intercontinental philosophy, which is the crossing of two or more continental philosophies.

Towards Cosmopolitanism in East and West

TOMONOBU IMAMICHI
TOMONOBU IMAMICHI INSTITUTE FOR ECO-ETHICS

ABSTRACT: The numbers of unfortunate deaths in the twentieth century were the highest compared with any previous century. Such an increase obviates any excuses The idea of technological possibility itself is one of the most basic causes of the destruction of nature in our new human milieu today, the technological conjuncture. But we human beings are also a part of nature. Therefore, without a new ethics understood as eco-ethica nature itself cannot fulfill the necessary conditions for the survival of human beings. For the first time owing to the technological conjuncture human beings bear full responsibility for all human beings tomorrow, for the future of humanity. Nature is no longer just a means to be exploited for the development of human civilization but also a model for how human civilization is to survive. The two great humanistic traditions, Western and Eastern, have developed the same content at the same level. People in the two worlds are really preparing a new cosmopolitanism.

According to my observation, seven untimely human extinctions were salient in the twentieth century. I would like to enumerate these unfortunate deaths according to the degree of the misery that accompanied them:

1) Death from starvation, especially the deaths of children in the developing countries;
2) The victims of traffic accidents, especially innocent people;
3) The war dead, especially civilians;
4) People who died because of pollution, and especially of bad air and poisonous water to which one is most often exposed unconsciously;
5) Victims of political agitations, ideologies, and religious fanaticisms;
6) Suicides, especially those occasioned by alienation; and
7) The victims of murder.

Special Supplement, *Journal of Philosophical Research* pp. 191–196
DOI: 10.5840/jpr201237Supplement34

The numbers of these victims in the twentieth century were the highest compared with any previous century. Some persons might object by pointing out that the world population in the twentieth century reached 5.6 billion people, and hence the numbers of untimely deaths were simply proportionally higher. But the fact of such a remarkably sharp increase of such deaths in the twentieth century defies any excuses. We need to look closely at all this untoward misery and to investigate the definitive causes which have never been brought to the level of philosophical dialogue.

1. THE TECHNOLOGICAL CONJUNCTURE

The idea that technological possibility itself is the principal merit and incentive for human beings is one of the most basic causes of the destruction of nature in our new human milieu today, in what we may call "the technological conjuncture." But we must always be aware of the fact that we human beings are also a part of nature. Without a new ethics understood as an *eco-ethica* nature itself cannot sustain the necessary conditions for the survival of human beings. Such a general catastrophe would mean the destruction not just of all human beings themselves but also of all the brilliance of human culture over many thousands of years. So, the importance of continuing to fashion a new ethics as an eco-ethics, which is what the cardinal expression "the technological conjuncture" suggests, should not be forgotten.

Today we must think in an entirely different way because just now at this moment the technological conjuncture exhibits a dramatic "inversion." The situation of the world has totally changed. This total change is in no ways a reversal but a revolutionary inversion involving the total transformation of human capacities and capabilities.

What has happened, and how has it happened?

The essential form of the situation I am calling the technological conjuncture has become its opposite. While maintaining its function for the new milieu human acts and actions, our vast technological conjuncture has now atrophied and finally become the operative instrument of mostly individual persons.

We might think of the most modern portable telephone by way of illustration. Its rapid development, and especially its multi-functionality perhaps since 2005, has been technologically one of the most wonderful realizations so far in the twenty-first century. If we think that our actual situation may properly be called modernity, then the future which we are facing may be called post-modernity. In my estimation the portable telephone is really the post-modern phenomenon *par excellence.* I would like to call it "post-modern" in this narrow sense in order to avoid any conceptual confusion with the post-modern in the broader sense that was mainly related to the case of architecture in the middle of the twentieth century.

The task of philosophy in the twenty-first century is to analyze this radical inversion of the technological conjuncture as the central phenomenon of post-modernity. Every phenomenon must be viewed from the perspective of an absolute inversion of its form, a kind of absolute negation of the technological conjuncture that has occurred after its recent diminishment.

2. THE "INVERSION" OF THE VECTORIAL DIRECTION OF SCIENCE AND PHILOSOPHY

We must discuss that total *inversion* between "aitiology" or the science of causes (*aitia*) and "archeology" or the science of first principles (the *archê*). Since Aristotle philosophy has had an "archeological" tendency; that is, being has always been reduced to the *archê* (principle in Greek). Doing philosophy mainly came to dealing with the tendencies or directions of the past. By contrast doing science mainly came to dealing with the relations between cause (aitia in Greek) and effect. Science pointed out some causes in order to identify certain effects which had not yet been discovered. This "aitiological" way of thinking was mainly directed to the future—history's direction to the past was not necessary.

What is at stake now, however, is the radical inversion in our human milieu, in the present technological conjuncture. This is what is now most important for human beings. In a word, for the first time thanks to the inversion of the technological conjuncture human beings today bear full responsibility for all human beings tomorrow, indeed for the future of humanity.

3. PHILOSOPHY OF LAW AND ETHICS

In the twentieth century the most developed phenomena of human existence were human rights. For then very many efforts on behalf on human rights were made in very many countries. Human rights, however, is mainly a problem of law. What then do philosophers make of law?

We must try to think deeply once again about a philosophy of law understood as "right" in the terms of Hegel's philosophy of right as he formulated it in his 1820 *Elements of the Philosophy of Right* (*Grundlinien der Philosophie des Rechts*).Thus, I would like to begin our reflections here in this Plenary Session on Rethinking the History of Philosophy and Comparative Philosophy: Traditions, Critique and Dialogue with a summary of Hegel's views.

The reason why I propose that we begin with a reflection on Hegel's *Elements of the Philosophy of Right* is simply because what he writes in that book reflects the deeply thought and widely held common idea of the concept of law as right in the eighteenth century. "When philosophy paints the image of life with its grey in grey," Hegel famously wrote, "then the image of life is an image of life grown old and painted with grey in grey. It cannot be rejuvenated but only understood. The owl of Minerva spreads its wings only with the falling of the dusk."[1]

Hegel believed that his philosophical reflection on law as right (*das Recht*) had to be the final integrated form of the system of law established in the various modern states up until his time. According to Hegel "morality" and "ethics" (*die Sittlichkeit*) are clearly different. Morality is the mental dimension in which the abstract person strains individually and seriously to attain the virtues. Morality is necessary for personal perfection. But according to Hegel individual perfection, namely in the ideal realization of the personal virtues (the perfection of morality), is significant only with respect to individual moral consciousness within the limited personal perspective and so has nothing to do with social justice (*die Gerechtigkeit der Gesellschaft*).

In fact, one person's moral conviction has often changed an unreasonable and savage social custom into a reasonable and civilized custom that is socially just. That is to say, a reasonable morality could change an unreasonable social institution into an acceptable and socially just institution. Perhaps we could say that we can now better understand Hegel's famous adage, "*Was vernünftig ist, das ist wirklich und was wirklich ist, das ist vernünftig*," namely, "What is reasonable is real and what is real is reasonable."

Ethics as *Sittlichkeit* in Hegel's terminology is therefore the social justice that compels the members of a society to be socially just. The famous two lines that are not so simple to understand now become clear thanks to the example of comparing individual morality and social ethics as *Sittlichkeit* in Hegel's terminology. Taking social ethics as *Sittlichkeit* is, according to Hegel, the same as taking the right as law of the State. Therefore the legislative organ of any State is very important because it is the place where the actual details of social ethics as *Sittlichkeit* are decided. To my regret, in Japan the members of the Japanese legislature, the Diet, have not yet understood this idea.

4. COMPARATIVE STUDY IN AESTHETICS

In the West, in the aesthetic realm the classical idea of the arts is no doubt *mimesis*, or the mimetic representation of the object. By contrast, the term " expression" used with respect to subjective pathos is relatively recent. That is, at the end of eighteenth century the Latin word "*expressio*" was an agricultural term designating how grapes were to be pressed in order to squeeze their juice to make wine. At length in the second half of eighteenth century Diderot and Kant worked out the aesthetic nuances of the word in question.

In the Orient, however, the classical idea of the arts was not mimetic representation but the expression of the internal unification of the spirit of the artist with cosmic dynamics, in brief the expression of subjective emotion. And mimetic representation was the modern idea of arts, established at length in the beginning of the eighteenth century.

5. COMPARATIVE STUDY IN ETHICS

In the ethical realm there are two basic concepts, namely, the person as substance and responsibility as an inter-subjective relation. In Western classical ethics the individual existence of the person is regarded as already incorporating elements of Christian religious belief and hence is regarded as having a uniquely important subjective core. But the relevant relational virtue for the individual person with respect to the other, namely the relation of responsibility, was not articulated until the end of the eighteenth century.

By contrast, in Chinese classical ethics one of the most important virtues was responsibility. The subjective concept of the person was not found in the classical books, but an analogous word was coined in the seventeenth century in the book of Wong Yong Ming. The word in question is *ryanchi* (良知) which signifies personal "*Gewissen*" or "*conscience morale*" which is very near to the Western concept of person.

In the history of logic there are some relevant contrasts which comparative study has brought to light. I would like to mention only one example. Confucius stressed the importance of "definition" in his movement with Shang Ming (正名 correcting the term) as Socrates had also stressed in his notion of the correct definition the correct limit of the word. But definition for Confucius is nothing more than words at the moment of departure, for definitions allow no one to enjoy any longer the nostalgic beauty found in various places.

Confucius started with the hypothetical content of correct definitions in his instructive dialogues with his disciples in the interest of resolving the meaning of certain events. Socrates on the other hand wished to clarify problems with the help of dialogues that gradually moved the problems towards resolution with the help of principal definitions of their key ideas. Between these two great rivers of dialogue, the Western dialogue could identify the realms of natural science because of their scientific aspiration to grasp basic ideas. The Confucian dialogue on the other hand with its limited role for definition could not identify any of the sciences and hence remained confined to symbolic thinking only.

Briefly speaking, the two great classical cultures, namely, the Greco-Roman and Christian humanistic tradition on the one hand and the Chinese Confucian and Taoistic humanistic tradition on the other, in roughly the eighteenth century seem to have become conscious of each other as dialogical partners at the same level and tried to overcome their respective deficiencies by opening themselves to their respective resources.

At the present time, at least in the developing countries in East Asia, we can feel the reminiscence of the traditional attitude, i.e., the modest harmonious attitude with respect to nature. Perhaps modern technology must change itself to post-modern technology in which nature is no longer just a means to be exploited for the development of human civilization but also model for how human civilization is to survive.

6. COSMOPOLITANISM

We have noted in cultural phenomena simultaneous developments in the same direction concerning ideas and virtues. We have confirmed that the two great humanistic traditions, Western and Eastern, have developed the same content at the same level. These humanistic traditions, both in the East and in the West, have each overcome their limits in the interests of moving towards a unified understanding of humanism. Concerning the humanistic tradition, the Western tradition and the Eastern tradition have become one. It means that people in the two worlds are really preparing a new cosmopolitanism. Although the system of the modern national State in the sense of Hegel is still dominant, in the cultural dimension the world in post-modernity is developing a truly cosmopolitan dimension, one where philosophical dialogue at the world level is gradually becoming a reality.

NOTE

1. T. M. Knox, *Hegel's Philosophy of Right* (Oxford: Oxford University Press,1967), p. 13.

SELECTED PAPERS FROM
THE XXII WORLD CONGRESS OF PHILOSOPHY

To What Extent Are Philosophers Tolerant?

JEAN GRONDIN
UNIVERSITÉ DE MONTRÉAL

ABSTRACT: In a world allegedly lacking a moral compass, tolerance has become the major virtue of our time. All profess to be tolerant, but how tolerant are we in reality? As a case in point, how tolerant are philosophers themselves? A short overview of philosophy seems to suggest that they are less tolerant than one might imagine. A few reasons for this are provided : on the one hand, their commitment to issues of truth, logic and argument makes them perhaps intolerant of what they view as blatantly absurd or flawed views; on the other hand, the often very ideological nature of philosophy itself does its part to make philosophers less open to differing or opposite points of view.

In a world allegedly lacking a moral compass, one has to be impressed by the universal acceptance of the virtue of tolerance. Nobody is against it, at least on the level of virtuous assurances of one's good faith. Bequeathed to us through Enlightenment thinkers such as Locke and Voltaire, it has become the major virtue of our time.

It is not my intention to call into question this rare unanimity in ethical matters, but what strikes me is that there remains a gap between tolerance as a publicly recognized virtue and the practice of tolerance. Are we as tolerant as we claim we are? When our neighbors stage a loud party until the wee hours of the night, strangle a lamb and do so almost every day, or night, are we tolerant? If our daughter dates a guy with a razor blade hanging from his ear, how tolerant are we in practice? How do we react if someone murmurs or waves all the time when we give a public lecture? Or if we have to stand in line forever, if our plane is delayed, etc. This is the classical abyss between theory and practice. One doesn't necessarily have to entertain a misanthropic view of things to ask if we are as tolerant as we boast we are. It also strikes one that it is always the others that one accuses of being intolerant.

Special Supplement, *Journal of Philosophical Research* pp. 197–201
DOI: 10.5840/jpr201237Supplement36

We are accomplished moralizers when it comes to others. But how about us? How tolerant are we? As a case in point I would like to ask:

ARE PHILOSOPHERS TOLERANT?

The question is seldom asked. One would be inclined to think that philosophers are tolerant, especially in the context of a "World Congress of Philosophy" like this one, where one listens to papers on a wide variety of subjects, from all sorts of perspectives and from many continents. Such a diverse congress would seem to be the epitome of tolerance. On this, we could pad ourselves in the back: yes, we are tolerant, we open ourselves to views that are different from ours without becoming violent.

Yet, I somehow have the feeling that philosophers are not as tolerant as they might profess. To be reminded of this, one needs only to look at the history of philosophy as well as its present state:

In their history, philosophers have been more often than not famous for their feuds, rivalries and arguments. To recall but a few : was Plato tolerant of the sophists? or of the poets for that matter? What about the tolerance of Aristotle vis-à-vis Plato, or of saint Augustine towards the Donatists and Pelagians, Averroes with respect to al-Gazali, Albert the Great concerning Averroes,[1] Leibniz compared to Locke (two avowed champions of tolerance), Voltaire toward Rousseau, Kant toward Fichte, Fichte with Schelling, Hegel and Schelling, Nietzsche contra Schopenhauer, Heidegger with Husserl and Husserl with Heidegger, Adorno and Carnap vis-à-vis Heidegger, and so on. I have no time, nor space to go into the details, which could fill libraries, but I would argue that it was seldom the case that philosophers appeared really tolerant towards the point of view of others, especially their rivals, but they also appeared quite intolerant about those who claimed to follow in their footsteps, as Fichte claimed with regard to Kant and Heidegger with respect to Husserl.

This has remained true in the present, even if our debates appear more polite and subdued: but are analytic philosophers *really* tolerant toward continental philosophers, and vice versa? Communitarians vis-à-vis liberals? Husserlians and Heideggerians? Actually, some Heideggerians are very intolerant about other Heideggerians, and these types of divisions occur in almost every school.

I might evoke an example of this in the figure of my teacher Hans-Georg Gadamer. He professed a most tolerant philosophy, even claiming that the "soul of his hermeneutics" lied in the acknowledgment that "the other could be right." This sounds fine and Gadamer is indeed one of the most tolerant philosophers and persons one can think of, but did he actually live up to this in his epic debates with contemporaries such as Habermas, Betti or Derrida? I am not sure, since in all his debates, his first instinct, as is probably human, was to defend his own views. As far as we are concerned: how tolerant are *we* about our dear "colleagues" when they endlessly raise their hair-splitting points in our faculty meetings? Do we survive these without headaches?

SOME REASONS FOR THE RELATIVE INTOLERANCE OF PHILOSOPHERS

Assuming my all too swift survey does point to a possible gap between the theory and practice of tolerance on the part of philosophers, one can inquire as to the reasons for this relative intolerance.

1) *Truth and logic would seem to be intrinsically intolerant.* Philosophers have always dealt with issues of reason, truth and error. To be sure, there are many different views of reason and knowledge, but truth has something "intolerant" about it: something, a statement, is true or not. *Tertium non datur.* One can provide examples of this, starting with the most simple:

"2 + 2 = 4." This is true, and to claim otherwise would be insane. Philosophers can hardly "tolerate" this insanity (other than by recognizing it as an illness of sorts). The same would probably hold for the basic tenets of logic: either one thinks rationally, cogently, or one doesn't. A *non sequitur* is a *non sequitur.*

Matters of fact are also a rather stubborn lot. Can one tolerate the view that the sun revolves around the Earth? Of course not, even if at times it was the opposite view which sparked intolerance, often times a rather violent one at that.

We tend to be more tolerant regarding "world views." But here too a modicum of intolerance seems inevitable: how tolerant should we be toward those who believe in astrology or alchemy? How tolerant are liberals towards Marxism? Some believe that Marxism is akin to astrology, because it would be a view with no basis in reality, or which would have been refuted by it.

How tolerant are some philosophers about religion? Some, if not most, are religious, but others believe religion is nothing but an illusion which can be fought by science and should not be tolerated (after a host of others, Dennett and Dawkins recently wrote two rather intolerant books on religion).[2] Hans Albert in Germany argues that all theology or divinity faculties at German universities should be closed. To what extent is tolerance here possible?

2) *The argumentative nature of philosophy makes it intolerant of bad arguments.* Philosophy is about 90 percent argument and 10 percent vision (the exact proportion is open to debate). One can be open to various types of argument, but it is very difficult for a philosopher to accept an argument that is flawed: hogwash! a philosopher could exclaim when confronted with a baseless argument. In practice, one can pretend to respect the views of others, but inwardly it is difficult to accept an argument one doesn't recognize as valid. In this regard, philosophers are professional "nitpickers": they are trained to point out the flaws in arguments. How can tolerance flourish in such an environment?

3) *Philosophy and ideology.* In spite of its insistence on logic and argument, it is obvious enough that philosophy is in fact very dependent upon ideologies, which are not always (if ever) corroborated by reality, or logic. This should lead to more tolerance. But I would contend that, on the contrary, it makes philosophers less tolerant and more defensive concerning their basic convictions. Philosophers tend to defend their ideologies to the bone, come hell or high water. That might have

something to do with the fact that it is most difficult to validate a philosophical ideology. For all intents and purposes, there is indeed very little finality in philosophical discussions: there is no bottom line, hardly any *experimentum crucis* or empirical facts (except, of course, those put forward in the present paper). I would say here that the more ideological a discipline becomes, the less tolerant it tends to be. This is hopefully not always the case, but the danger is there.

TOLERANCE AS THE *ARÈTÈ* OF OUR TIME AND ITS RELATIVE SHORTCOMINGS

Why is it that tolerance has gained such a currency in our day and age? It certainly has everything to do with world history. The first obvious cause lies in the aftermath of the Second World War. After the senseless tragedies of two World Wars, the virtue of tolerance became the imperative of the hour: let's accept our differences instead of making war. It could be claimed that this was also true of the earlier promotion of tolerance in the works of Locke and Voltaire since it occurred in the footsteps of the Thirty Years War. The second cause lies in the demise of colonialism, especially in its underlying assumption that there is only one way to civilization, to which all other "inferior" societies should conform. This openness to the plurality of civilization was only reinforced by the process of globalization and the increasing linguistic, religious, cultural and ethnic diversity of all societies. A closed-knit community with a homogeneous identical set of beliefs doesn't exist anymore. Tolerance has thus become the paramount virtue if one wishes to avoid conflict and violence. Tolerance is better than war.

There is however a downside to this: tolerance has become the prime virtue of a rather "relativistic" age. There appears to be no one dominating truth nor value system anymore, except for the *koinè* or, in this case, *arètè* of tolerance. This has lead to our "postmodern" predicament with its nihilistic consequences. Besides the well-known aporiae of relativism, self-contradiction being one of them, this raises problems: (1) if there is no truth to be had, no real value to adhere to, why should tolerance be recognized as one? (2) doesn't this "universal tolerance" disregard the fact that some truths and values are better than others and that one cannot tolerate everything, in theory as well as in practice? Aren't there obvious limits to what one can and has to tolerate? To be sure, along with tolerance "otherness" has been celebrated as a value in itself. But this "otherness" must be specified if it is to have any content: the other of truth is falsehood, that of peace is war and that of good is evil, and one doesn't readily see why a premium should be put on them. Otherness and difference *per se* are not enough.

THE NOTION OF TOLERANCE CAN HAVE A PEJORATIVE RING

We all like to praise tolerance and proclaim ourselves tolerant, but this cannot hide the fact that tolerance can have a demeaning dimension to it. Usually, we "tolerate" things with which we don't agree and don't want to engage with. Voltaire was aware of this: I don't understand this or that culture, it is too remote from mine, but I will "tolerate" it as long as it doesn't do obvious harm and disturb my peace.

It is in this sense, I believe, that analytic philosophers will tolerate (?) continental philosophers, and vice versa, communitarians will tolerate liberals, fervent atheist will make do with believers, etc. What their opponents say, do or believe in, is for them a sham, but they will tolerate them nonetheless. This is also true in society at large. Some countries profess to be beacons of tolerance, yet they will decide to ban the burka, if not the head scarf, which is at best "tolerated," but viewed with suspicion. This shows the limit of tolerance in practice. Actually, more often than not, it is less a virtue than a way of coming to terms with views and practices one disrespects: I don't like what you do or say, but I will "tolerate" it. This is why the virtue of tolerance needs to be reinforced by others like those of respect and generosity. Respect must complement tolerance since it entails that we also honor what is distinct and perhaps superior in the other point of view. Generosity is also called for, even if it is also rare in philosophy. Maimonides said that generosity was the gift of goodness to those who are undeserving of it.[3] And he adds that it is only truly practiced by God. Such generosity can at least be imitated. I thank you for your generous tolerance.

NOTES

1. On this as well as other conflicts in the Middle Ages and Early modernity, see Kurt Flasch, *Kampfplätze der Philosophie. Große Kontroversen von Augustin bis Voltaire* (Frankfurt am Main: Vittorio Klosterman, 2008).

2. D. Dennett, *Breaking the Spell: Religion as a Natural Phenomenon* (New York: Penguin, 2006); and R. Dawkins, *The God Delusion* (London: Bantam, 2006).

3. Moïse Maïmonide, *Le Guide des égarés*, traduit par Salomon Munk (Paris: Verdier, 1979), 628 (3e partie, n° 53).

RELIGION, FOI, ET TOLERANCE

ALOYSE-RAYMOND NDIAYE
UNIVERSITÉ CHEIKH ANTA DIOP DE DAKAR, SENEGAL

RÉSUMÉ: L'intolérance religieuse qui alimente de nos jours de nombreux conflits contemporains nous conduit à repenser notre conception moderne de la tolérance, née des débats théologiques et philosophiques, qui ont accompagné ou qui ont été provoqués par les controverses doctrinales et les guerres politico-religieuses des XVIème et XVIIème siècles. Elle se définit par le respect des ordres distincts: celui de la conscience et celui de la loi, du privé et du public, celui de la foi et de la raison. Elle porte la marque de son origine, du religieux et du théologique, et renvoie à l'idée de dignité humaine à laquelle la doctrine de l'autonomie de Kant, au XVIIIème siècle, a apporté son fondement éthique. L'actualité nous apprend qu'aujourd'hui encore on tue, on persécute au nom de la foi, au nom de Dieu, au nom de la religion, pour avoir une opinion ou une croyance différente. Si la tolérance, fille des Lumières et de la raison critique, ne s'est pas imposée définitivement dans un monde rationnel et technique, il y a lieu de se demander si ce n'est pas pour avoir négligé la foi. Il ne suffit pas de déclarer la mort de Dieu pour faire disparaître la religion. Conclure de la distinction de la raison et de la foi à leur antagonisme n'a pas conduit à déraciner l'intolérance de l'esprit humain. Aurions-nous oublié que la paix est aussi l'affaire du religieux? Que faut-il attendre, que faut-il espérer du dialogue inter-religieux? La foi serait-elle l'antidote à l'intolérance? Que peut faire la foi?

L'intolérance religieuse qui alimente de nos jours de nombreux conflits contemporains nous conduit à repenser notre conception moderne de la tolérance, née des débats théologiques et philosophiques, qui ont accompagné ou qui ont été provoqués par les controverses doctrinales et les guerres politico-religieuses des XVIème et XVIIème siècles, que les historiens appellent «guerres de religion». L'expression englobe autant celles qui, en Europe, ont opposé les religions entre elles ou qui ont été menées en leur nom, au nom de la foi: les guerres médiévales, les Croisades,

Special Supplement, *Journal of Philosophical Research* pp. 203–215
DOI: 10.5840/jpr201237Supplement37

celles qui ont opposé les chrétiens entre eux, les catholiques et les Calvinistes, auxquelles l'Edit de Nantes, signé en 1598, mit momentanément un terme, guerres fratricides, qui duraient déjà depuis 1562 et qui devaient reprendre à la mort d'Henri IV, avant que les partisans des deux confessions acceptent, à la Paix d'Alès, de ne plus recourir aux armes pour résoudre leurs divergences religieuses. Sont également visées par l'expression «guerres de religion», celles qui ont été menées au nom du *Jihad* islamique, de même que les persécutions dont furent victimes, au XVème siècle, en Espagne, au Portugal, la communauté juive. C'est donc dans ce contexte marqué par l'intolérance que naît le concept moderne de tolérance.

Parmi les penseurs de la tolérance, on ne peut manquer de citer Locke et Bayle. Elle se définit par le respect des ordres distincts: celui de la conscience et celui de la loi, du privé et du public, celui de la foi et de la raison. Elle porte la marque de son origine, du religieux et du théologique, et renvoie à l'idée de dignité humaine à laquelle la doctrine de l'autonomie de Kant, au XVIIIème siècle, a apporté son fondement éthique.

L'actualité nous apprend qu'aujourd'hui encore on tue, on persécute au nom de la foi, au nom de Dieu, au nom de la religion, pour avoir une opinion ou une croyance différente, comme aux XVIème et XVIIème siècles, avec la même barbarie, même si les motifs religieux, c'est ce qui est nouveau, ne sont pas toujours clairement avoués. Tout se passe donc comme si la religion conduit ou prépare à la guerre, comme si guerre et violence sont consubstantielles à la religion et que, pour avoir la paix dans le monde, il convient soit de réformer la religion soit de l'exterminer comme le suggérait déjà Rousseau qui consacre le dernier chapitre du *Contrat social* à la religion civile, convaincu que l'esprit de religion est naturellement insociable et représente un danger pour les fondements de l'État.

L'on ne peut pas dire que les conflits contemporains, qui ont un lien avec la religion, servent les intérêts de la religion déjà fortement ébranlés par les avancées des Lumières et de la science. L'appel des autorités religieuses au dialogue interreligieux est peut-être le signe qu'elles ont pris conscience de leur responsabilité dans l'avenir de la paix dans le monde. L'Eglise catholique n'a pas manqué l'occasion, ces derniers temps, d'insister sur son désir de mener le dialogue avec toutes les cultures et toutes les religions. Elle a reconnu officiellement les valeurs spirituelles, morales et socio-culturelles des autres religions comme le Judaîsme et l'Islam et invité leurs représentants à un dialogue «franc» et «sincère», comme on peut le lire dans la déclaration suivante:

> Si, au cours des siècles, de nombreuses discussions et inimitiés se sont manifestées entre les chrétiens et les musulmans, le Concile les exhorte tous à oublier le passé et à s'efforcer sincèrement à la compréhension mutuelle, ainsi qu'à protéger et à promouvoir ensemble, pour tous les hommes, la justice sociale, les valeurs morales, la paix et la liberté. (Aucante 2008,19)

Cette orientation a été plusieurs fois confirmée et illustrée par les discours pontificaux.

Les réactions des autorités religieuses et des intellectuels musulmans au discours de Benoît XVI, prononcé le 12 septembre 2006, à Ratisbonne, bien que critiques, ont été assorties de déclarations en faveur d'un dialogue vrai, comme celle des auteurs de la «Lettre ouverte au Pape Benoît XVI, du 13 octobre 2006»:

> Nous partageons votre désir du dialogue franc et sincère, et nous reconnaissons son importance dans un monde de plus en plus interconnecté. Sur ce dialogue sincère et franc, nous espérons continuer à construire des relations paisibles et amicales basées sur le respect mutuel, la justice et le fondement commun de la tradition abrahamique que nous partageons. (Aucante 2008, 127)

La question est donc de savoir: que faut-il attendre, que faut-il espérer du dialogue inter-religieux? Si la tolérance, fille des Lumières et de la raison critique, qui repose sur la distinction des ordres, celui de la raison et celui de la foi, ne s'est pas imposée définitivement dans un monde rationnel et technique, il y a lieu de se demander si ce n'est pas pour avoir négligé la foi. En d'autres termes, la paix est aussi l'affaire du religieux. La foi serait-elle donc l'antidote de l'intolérance? Conclure de la distinction de la raison et de la foi à leur antagonisme n'a pas conduit à déraciner l'intolérance de l'esprit humain. Que peut faire la foi?

Nous nous interrogerons d'abord sur ce qu'est la religion, ensuite nous rechercherons dans l'histoire s'il y a eu des périodes où, ensemble, les religions ont été facteurs de progrès et de paix, pour enfin examiner comment la foi peut vaincre l'intolérance religieuse.

I

Qu'est-ce que la religion? Je ne m'étendrai pas longuement sur la définition de la religion qui est par ailleurs bien connue. Je m'inspirerai donc d'un texte de Claude Lévi-Strauss, au Chapitre XV de *Tristes tropiques* et qui a pour titre: «La terre et les hommes». L'ethnologue qui se trouve en Inde nous décrit les villes visitées. Il est impressionné par la multitude, la foule nombreuse, une foule dense, qui emplit les rues, que le grand nombre n'empêche pas de vaquer aux activités courantes et variées de la vie ordinaire. Il se demande alors comment exister avec si peu d'espace. La vie, ici, c'est la vie dans «un mouchoir de poche». Qu'est-ce qui la rend possible? Seule une vie spirituelle intense peut l'expliquer. Son observation le conduit à mettre, ainsi, en évidence des valeurs hautement spirituelles de cette population comme l'hospitalité et la convivialité, le respect d'autrui. D'où lui viennent de telles valeurs?

> Comment interpréter autrement l'aisance avec laquelle ces gens prennent place dans le cosmos? Voilà bien la civilisation du tapis de prière qui représente le monde, ou du carré dessiné sur le sol qui définit un lieu de culte. . . . Pour pouvoir résister, il faut un lien très fort, très personnel avec le surnaturel, et c'est là que réside peut-être un des secrets de l'Islam et des autres cultes de cette région du monde, que chacun se sente constamment en présence de son Dieu. (Lévi-Strauss 1955, 161)

La religion est ici définie par le lien très personnel avec le surnaturel. Elle est un lien, ce qui relie le croyant avec son Dieu, par la prière, sans intermédiaire, avec l'au-delà, la Transcendance. Ce caractère est essentiel. Un simple tapis de prière suffit. C'est le seul espace sacré qui convient à Dieu, un tapis de prière ou un carré dessiné sur le sol. L'espace du tapis de prière n'est pas celui de nos activités de survie quotidienne. Cet espace-là appartient à tous. Il est le lieu où se déploie la vie mais aussi les guerres. Dieu ne demande qu'un tapis de prière. Il se contenterait aussi bien d'un Temple, d'une Synagogue, d'une Mosquée, d'une Eglise pour y recevoir le culte qui lui est dû. L'espace du tapis de prière n'est pas l'espace de la conquête, de la domination, du pouvoir, de la guerre, mais plutôt de la paix, de la fraternité. En ce texte de *Tristes tropiques*, l'Islam est défini comme la civilisation du tapis de prière. C'est dire que la religion est culture, elle est la première expression de la culture qui représente le monde.

Qu'est-ce que le monde? Le monde, comme le rappelle Jacques Derrida, est tout ensemble la terre et toute l'histoire, l'humanité de l'homme, les droits de l'homme, les droits de l'homme et de la femme, l'organisation politique et culturelle de la société, la différence entre l'homme, le dieu et l'animal, la phénoménalité du jour, la valeur de la vie, le droit à la vie, le traitement de la mort. . . . C'est la culture. L'ensemble des valeurs de civilisation. La religion n'est donc pas indépendante de la civilisation. Présente, dès l'origine, dans les relations entre les hommes, entre les hommes et la nature, entre les hommes et l'environnement, elle leur dicte des règles de conduite, façonne leur représentation du monde. Elle imprègne leur vie. Elle est un fait social, une institution sociale qui dispose d'une administration plus ou moins complexe, de rituels, d'une organisation de cultes, des dogmes et de commentaires théologiques, d'un art. L'ensemble de ces éléments contribue à créer une communauté et un esprit de communauté

L'on pourrait conclure de là en indiquant que la religion est le lien qui unit l'esprit de piété, la croyance en Dieu, la foi en Dieu, et l'esprit de communauté, c'est-à-dire l'organisation sociale et historique du culte. Ces deux caractères sont essentiels de sorte que l'on ne peut pas appeler religion une croyance en Dieu qui n'est pas incarnée dans une institution, une communauté religieuse. Mais, allons plus loin et abandonnons, pour un moment, le texte que nous venons de citer. Toutes les religions ne sont pas identiques. Edmond Ortigues, se référant à la classification adoptée par les historiens des religions, distingue les religions du Livre et les religions de la Coutume. Cette classification repose sur la manière dont les religions se communiquent ou se transmettent.

Les religions du Livre sont les religions monothéistes: le Judaïsme, l'Islam et le Christianisme. Ce sont des religions missionnaires, fondées sur la croyance, la foi en un Dieu révélé dans les Ecritures, sur des dogmes, des vérités appelées à être commentées et communiquées par voie de prédication, diffusées à toutes les nations. Pour chacune de ces trois religions monothéistes, l'Ecriture demeure le lieu de l'Autorité. Chacune se prétend la religion d'un peuple avec lequel Dieu a noué une alliance, ce que recouvre les expressions: «peuple élu», «peuple des baptisés», «peuple des croyants», par opposition ou par exclusion des autres, les infidèles, les athées, les païens. La notion même de peuple élu ou de baptisés ou de croyants introduit, mentalement, pour reprendre le mot de Régis Debray, une idée de «clôture» sur soi, comme différent du voisin, donc l'idée de «territorialité», de «frontière mentale» (Debray 2003, 131).

Cette idée de «territorialité», même mentale, associée au caractère missionnaire du monothéisme, sur quoi repose sa prétention à l'universalité, représente un ensemble qui s'accompagne du risque d'intolérance, donc de violence. Le monothéisme affirme, en effet, l'existence d'un Dieu unique conçu comme le dieu d'un seul peuple qui, par la prédication de ses fidèles, étend sa domination sur les autres. Il y a risque d'intolérance et de violence si le peuple élu en vient à confondre, à identifier la cause de Dieu avec ses intérêts propres, considérant, dès lors comme ennemis de Dieu, ceux qui se réclament d'une autre croyance.

Les religions de la coutume sont par opposition les religions ethniques, les religions du foyer qui se transmettent par voie de coutume ancestrale. Elles se distinguent des religions de salut, du salut individuel qui, nous venons de le voir, se transmettent par voie de prédication doctrinale à vocation universelle. Les religions de la coutume se caractérisent au contraire par le culte des ancêtres, c'est-à-dire la continuité de la vie, la continuité d'une société. Elles relient les vivants et les morts. En sacrifiant aux ancêtres, ce que recherche l'individu, ce n'est pas l'immortalité individuelle, le salut personnel. Il cherche plutôt à s'unir aux ancêtres. Il y a, en effet, un lien de parenté avec l'ancêtre. Un lien affectif. La piété religieuse est d'abord, on le voit clairement, ici, un sentiment filial qui nous attache aux parents, aux ancêtres, avant de s'adresser à Dieu, par détournement. L'ancêtre n'est pas le dieu. Le lien affectif et religieux est premier par rapport à l'esprit de piété qui nous lie à Dieu, au Dieu unique.

Ce qui est donc universel, le seul fait absolument universel et que l'on retrouve dans toutes les sociétés, ce sont les religions de la coutume, religions ethniques, le culte des ancêtres, les religions du foyer telles que sont la plupart des religions africaines. Elles continuent à nourrir de leur sève populaire les grandes religions missionnaires qui n'auraient pu longtemps subsister sans elles, parce que la religion est ce qui unit les vivants et les morts. (Ortigues 1999)

Il nous faut cependant ajouter, avant d'aller encore plus loin, que les religions de la coutume se différencient des religions du Livre en ceci qu'elles n'ont pas de *credo*. C'est un élément important qui signifie que la religion des ancêtres n'est pas «exportable» comme l'est une doctrine. De ce fait et par rapport à notre problème, elle ne nourrit pas en elle le risque d'intolérance, de violence, de domination, risque qui est par contre bien présent, de façon consubstantielle, dans les trois religions missionnaires, les trois monothéismes. Parce qu'elle est du foyer, de la famille, du clan ou de l'ethnie, la religion de la coutume n'a pas, en tant que telle, vocation à s'exporter et à s'imposer aux autres comme seule vraie. Par contre, elle révèle paradoxalement l'essence universelle de la religion qui est d'unir tous les hommes, non pas sur la base d'une doctrine, du dogme, mais sur la reconnaissance mutuelle de leur appartenance à la même humanité, parce que la religion, comme le souligne Edmond Ortigues, est ce qui unit les vivants et les morts. Elle est universelle, non seulement parce qu'elle existe dans toutes les sociétés mais aussi parce qu'elle est porteuse de l'idée de communauté universelle des hommes, lien entre les vivants et les morts, entre ce monde-ci et l'au-delà. Bien que les religions du Livre aient une prétention à l'universalité, en tant que religions missionnaires, avec l'ambition de s'étendre à tous les hommes, cette prétention semble reposer aussi sur l'exclusion des autres religions.

II

La question qu'il faut maintenant se poser c'est celle de la coexistence des religions dans les périodes de l'histoire où ensemble elles ont été facteurs de progrès et de paix. Ces périodes ont existé, même si elles ont été de courte durée. Revenons au texte de *Tristes tropiques*. L'Islam y est présenté comme une religion qui coexiste avec d'autres cultes de la région, l'Hindouisme, le Bouddhisme. . . . Ces religions de l'Inde obéissent, en effet, à une autre tradition. Elles témoignent de «révélations». Elles ont donné naissance à des écritures sacrées. Mais elles ne sont pas identiques aux Ecritures des religions monothéistes, en ce sens que la source, l'origine absolue de ces écritures sacrées ne nous est pas accessible. Dans les religions monothéistes, les religions du Livre, Dieu est à la fois objet d'adoration et source de révélation. Il nous est difficile,par exemple, pour l'Hindouisme, dont les origines nous sont très lointaines et s'étalent sur des millénaires, de trouver un commencement absolu, soit sous forme d'une écriture, soit sous celle d'une prédication prophétique fondatrice. Les trois religions monothéistes nous renvoient chacune à un fondateur. Elles sont capables de remonter la lignée de leurs prophètes, d'identifier leur commencement absolu. Ce n'est pas le cas des religions de l'Inde.

Ce que note l'ethnologue et qui nous intéresse, c'est la cohabitation de l'Islam monothéiste avec les religions locales. Elles sont en parfaite convivialité. Elles partagent, précise-t-il, le même «secret», une règle commune: «que chacun se sente constamment en présence de son Dieu.» C'est le respect de cette règle qui garantit la coexistence conviviale entre les religions, donc la paix, la liberté de culte, la liberté de conscience. Il ne s'agit pas, ici, d'une coexistence dans l'indifférence qui ne serait alors qu'une intolérance déguisée. La coexistence conviviale implique sympathie avec autrui, compréhension de l'autre, amour de l'autre. C'est ce qui caractérise la tolérance. Elle demande, en effet, que l'on dépasse le fait d'admettre l'existence de l'autre vers la reconnaissance de ce qui le fait être différent, c'est-à-dire de ce qui le fait être d'une autre pensée, d'une autre croyance, d'une autre foi, d'une autre origine que soi. Elle implique la nécessité de dépasser la simple coexistence indifférente pour accéder à la reconnaissance et à l'accueil de l'autre. Qu'est-ce alors que la tolérance? Concrètement, être tolérant c'est reconnaître la pluralité des fois. C'est admettre que d'autres fois sont possibles et que l'on n'est pas le seul à détenir la seule vérité.

Le fameux axiome souvent invoqué: «La vérité a des droits, l'erreur n'en a pas» doit être corrigé. Il a servi dans le passé à nourrir l'intolérance. Refuser le droit à l'erreur c'est dès lors considérer, en matière de théologie, toute pensée nouvelle, toute interprétation nouvelle, toute nouveauté comme hérésie, et l'hérétique comme l'ennemi de la foi, l'adversaire qu'il faut combattre. Or, la vérité et l'erreur n'existent que dans un jugement. La personne morale seule est donc sujet de droit, non pas une vérité en soi séparée de la libre démarche humaine pour la conquérir. La vérité et l'erreur n'existent que dans un jugement, l'affirmation ou la négation d'une réalité par un sujet. Si nous sommes faits pour la vérité, il convient alors de conférer au sujet les droits nécessaires à l'exercice de son intelligence. C'est lui reconnaître le droit à la vérité mais aussi le droit à l'erreur. Les lui refuser c'est l'écarter du chemin de toute espèce de vérité.

Ce qui ressort de ce texte, c'est bien la culture de l'hospitalité de cette région du monde surpeuplée. Bien qu'il y ait trop d'habitants et peu d'espace, il n'y a, par contre, ni haine ni peur de l'étranger. Bien plus, ce que remarque l'ethnologue au passage de l'étranger, «c'est, nous dit-il, la courtoisie des sourires . . . accompagnés souvent, en pays musulman, d'un «salaam», la main portée au front». La main portée au front a une valeur supérieure, spirituelle. C'est le signe de reconnaissance de notre appartenance à une même famille, à une même communauté spirituelle et religieuse, ou simplement humaine, un signe de respect dû à tout homme. Ce sens de l'accueil, de l'hospitalité, cette disposition bienveillante à l'égard de l'étranger, de l'autre, est ici reconnue comme une valeur fondamentale de la culture islamique

Ainsi, le «secret» que l'Islam partage avec les religions de la région leur assure cette coexistence conviviale. Il correspond à l'opinion couramment admise, par exemple, dans l'Antiquité: «que chaque peuple vénère les dieux de ses ancêtres». Ainsi, l'interdiction de sacrifier aux «dieux étrangers», peut être une question de vie ou de mort. Elle n'implique pas pour autant que les «dieux étrangers» sont de faux dieux. C'est par là que la monolâtrie se distingue du monothéisme. La monolâtrie est le culte exclusif du dieu national. Le monothéisme est le culte exclusif d'un seul vrai Dieu. C'est, encore une fois, la question de la vérité qui sépare le monothéisme des autres religions, qui se définit par exclusion des dieux étrangers, en exaltant la transcendance de Dieu, en mettant l'accent sur le peuple élu, peuple choisi à part de tous les autres. Mais, l'Islam, bien que religion monothéiste, comme on peut le noter dans ce texte, a su être tolérant avec les autres religions de la région par respect de sa propre tradition de l'hospitalité. Dans cette région du monde, les religions ont été donc des facteurs de concorde. Il en est de même dans d'autres régions du monde. Vincent Monteil, qui a longtemps vécu en Afrique, particulièrement au Sénégal, dans son livre *L'Islam noir*, décrit la rencontre de l'Islam et des religions coutumières africaines. Il rappelle que, passée la période du Jihad, cette rencontre s'est faite, même dans le cas de conversion, dans le respect des croyances coutumières. Il conclut de ses analyses que l'Islam n'est pas senti, en Afrique, comme une religion «étrangère». Il est pour la plupart «la religion du cœur».

Notre texte de *Tristes tropiques* privilégie l'exemple de l'Islam. Mais en survolant l'histoire des trois religions monothéistes, l'on s'aperçoit qu'elles ont connu aussi des moments exceptionnels où elles ont été conjointement facteurs de progrès, entretenant des relations d'hospitalité et de convivialité. Ces périodes sont peut-être rares. Elles ont cependant existé bien que de courte durée. Michèle Gendreau-Massaloux, dans ses *Réflexions d'une hispanique*, nous décrit l'un de ces moments quand la ville de Tolède, en Espagne, était devenue un lieu de rencontres où érudits arabes, avec l'aide de traducteurs chrétiens, entreprirent de donner accès aux textes hindous, perses, coptes, grecs, et surtout de diffuser le savoir d'Isidore de Séville dans le monde islamique en le faisant passer du latin à l'arabe, langue philosophique. Il y avait là, dit-elle, une véritable interpénétration entre l'Orient et l'Occident. Cette cohabitation a produit une culture brillante dans tous les domaines, métaphysique, astronomie, astrologie, les sciences du corps et de la nature. Tolède a donc été un lieu privilégié d'un brassage des peuples et des cultures.

Dans l'histoire de cette région méditerranéenne, l'on peut citer un autre exemple de villes qui, de l'autre côté de l'Espagne, ont pu avoir le même rôle que la ville de Tolède. Il s'agit d'Alexandrie, d' Hippone qui furent aussi, à une époque antérieure, des lieux privilégiés d'un brassage des peuples et des cultures. Mais le rayonnement de Tolède qui se situe plusieurs siècles plus tard est spécifique. Il a la particularité de montrer la coexistence des trois religions monothéistes. Ce moment historique unique de coexistence et de dialogue entre les trois religions monothéistes allait être emporté par un violent séisme entraînant l'Espagne, qui aurait dû être le lieu où aurait pu naître la possibilité d'une Europe, aujourd'hui, ouverte et tolérante, à renoncer à sa mission en prenant la tragique décision, en 1492, d'expulser ses Juifs. Cette évolution est bien rappelée par Michèle Gendreau-Massaloux dans ses «Réflexions». L'Espagne mettait ainsi un terme, par la radicalisation de l'intolérance, à ce moment historique et unique de coexistence et de dialogue entre les trois religions monothéistes. Elle porte la responsabilité d'avoir introduit l'intolérance dans les Amériques où elle débarque, en effet, cette année 1492, transportée par le triomphe absolu de la catholicité castillane. C'est bien, en cette année 1492, que Christophe Colomb découvre l'Amérique. Nous savons comment furent traitées les populations locales qui furent entièrement décimées quand elles n'ont pas été contraintes à la conversion.

La décison de 1492 a été préparée par des processus antérieurs caractérisés par des conversions au catholicisme après les «progroms» de 1391, des migrations de Juifs vers d'autres pays, le Portugal, le Maghreb, la France. Quelques années auparavant, en 1480, venait d'être instituée l'Inquisition qui traquait, pour les démasquer, ceux que l'on a appelés les «conversos» judaïsant en secret. Expulsés d'Espagne, les Juifs le seront aussi du Portugal, 1496. Ils vont se répandre, non seulement dans le monde méditerranéen, mais aussi en Angleterre, en Europe du Nord et en Amérique. Ils faut noter qu'ils seront accueillis en Afrique du Nord islamique et par les gouvernants Ottomans. Ils jouiront, comme à Salonique, devenue nouvelle capitale séfarade, de libertés et d'autonomie.

Ces exemples nous montrent que les religions du Livre ne sont pas congénitalement incapables de tolérance. Elles ont su, dans de brefs moments de l'histoire, montrer qu'elles pouvaient être facteurs de progrès, de solidarité, de paix entre les hommes.

III

Comment dès lors comprendre que ces religions puissent, encore aujourd'hui, rivaliser entre elles au point d'être des facteurs d'intolérance et de conflits? Comment comprendre que des religions, qui font de l'amour et du pardon leur idéal, aient pu commettre et permettent encore aujourd'hui que l'on commette en leur nom les pires crimes? Elément nouveau et que relève avec pertinence Jacques Derrida, dans leur rivalité aucune ne néglige le recours aux puissants moyens modernes de communication. Nous sommes en présence d'une situation inédite, que Derrida considère comme une «nouvelle forme de guerre de religion». Il estime, en effet, que, ce qui se joue derrière la concurrence que se livrent les grandes entreprises de communication, est une nouvelle forme de guerre de religion entre les trois religions monothéistes pour le contrôle et la domination du monde: elles se déchaînent, dit-il,

> sur la terre humaine (qui n'est pas le monde) et luttent même aujourd'hui pour contrôler le ciel au doigt et à l'œil, système digital et visualisation panoptique virtuellement immédiate, «*espace aérien*», satellites de télécommunication, autoroutes de l'information, concentration des pouvoirs capitalistico-médiatiques en trois mots *culture digitale, jet et TV*, sans lesquels il n'est aujourd'hui aucune manifestation religieuse, par exemple aucun voyage et nulle allocution du pape, aucun rayonnement organisé de culte juif, chrétien ou musulman, qu'ils soient ou non «*fondamentalistes*», qui ne soit relayé par ces outils modernes de communication. (Derrida 1996, 35)

Le récent discours de Benoît XVI, du12 septembre 2006, à Ratisbonne, en est une illustration. Cette conférence controversée n'aurait pas connu un tel retentissement mondial si elle n'avait été amplifiée par les médias. Son prédécesseur, Jean-Paul II, a su utiliser avec efficacité, une technique parfaitement maîtrisée par les régimes des pays de l'Est, à l'époque du Communisme, d'où il était originaire. Le succès de ses voyages est à mettre autant au compte des médias qu'à celui de la ferveur des fidèles. Les médias ont été attirés à leur tour par le succès qu'ils ont contribué largement à créer. Le succès mondial des «JMJ», Journées Mondiales de la Jeunesse, initiées par Jean-Paul II, est, encore aujourd'hui, inséparable de leurs relais médiatiques. Analysant cette situation inédite de l'alliance de la religion et de la télé-technoscience, Derrida la compare au «mal radical». La religion est d'une part «la mondialatinisation; elle produit, épouse, exploite le capital et le savoir de la télé-médiatisation: ni les voyages et la spectacularisation mondiale du pape, ni les dimensions inter-étatiques de l'«affaire Rushdie», ni le terrorisme planétaire ne seraient possibles, à ce rythme, autrement . . . ». Mais, d'autre part, elle résiste, réagit contre cette alliance qui, en lui conférant ce nouveau pouvoir, la protège en la renforçant, mais en même temps la menace, en la contraignant à réagir, à se défendre. Il y a là, empruntant la métaphore à la biologie, comme une double structure contradictoire: immunitaire et auto-immunitaire, que la religion doit assumer. (Derrida 1996, 62)

Dans le texte de *Tristes tropiques* que nous avons cité, c'est l'Islam que l'ethnologue présente en parfaite cohabitation avec les religions de la région. Mais dans les derniers chapitres du livre, Claude Lévi-Strauss, revenant sur les rapports de l'Islam et du Bouddhisme, observe que ces deux grandes religions prétendent l'une et l'autre à l'universalité. Mais, l'une de ces deux religions, au fur et à mesure qu'elle s'universalise, donc atteint son but, devient dogmatique et sectaire. L'autre, le Bouddhisme, par contre, parce qu'il accepte que l'on puisse être bouddhiste et autre chose, échappe à l'intolérance. L'Islam au contraire n'y échappe pas. Pourtant c'est bien l'Islam qui, dans le Proche Orient, fut l'inventeur de la tolérance. Souvenons-nous de l'accueil réservé aux Juifs expulsés d'Espagne et du Portugal, mais aussi aux chrétiens, par les pays et gouvernants musulmans.

Que l'intolérance religieuse alimente de nombreux conflits contemporains est la preuve que, malgré les Lumières, la tolérance n'a pas entièrement et définitivement triomphé. C'est un point qui n'échappe pas à Régis Debray et à Jean Bricmont et qu'ils soulignent au cours de leurs entretiens qu'ils publient sous le titre: *A l'ombre des Lumières. Débat entre un philosophe et un scientifique.*

> J'avais été frappé, reconnaît Régis Debray, dans les années 70, en parcourant le monde arabo-musulman, du fait que les fondamentalistes, les intégristes, se recrutaient essentiellement dans les facultés des sciences et des techniques. Il en allait ainsi au Caire, à Tunis, à Alger, à Damas. Et c'était dans les facultés de lettres, d'histoire, de sciences humaines et de théologie que les progressistes se trouvaient. Comme à fronts renversés. Dès que l'on rencontrait un littéraire, il était rationaliste. Ce chassé-croisé s'est vérifié depuis. On le sait, les cadres des partis intégristes sont passés par le MIT, Harvard et autres grands instituts voués au performant et à l'exact, de même que les informaticiens de Bombay votent en masse pour le BJP hindouiste. (Debray 2003, 149)

Comment expliquer qu'un esprit, nourri de science et formé à la rationalité moderne, puisse avoir des comportements aussi irrationnels au nom de la foi? Jean Bricmont, le physicien, nous donne une explication. L'enseignement de la technologie, selon lui, peut se faire en insistant sur «ce qui marche» et en omettant ainsi ce qui est subversif dans la démarche scientifique par rapport à la religion, à savoir la notion de vérité et la nécessité de tester empiriquement ses opinions. Jean Bricmont met ici l'accent sur l'éducation, sur la formation des scientifiques qui trop souvent vise ce qui est utile, les compétences technocratiques et matérialistes, et néglige l'apport essentiel de la science à l'esprit, la critique, le goût de l'évidence, la recherche de la vérité et la nécessité de tester par l'expérience toute opinion, le refus de l'argument d'autorité.

Descartes faisait le même constat lorsqu'il déplorait, dans la première partie du *Discours de la Méthode*, «la faillite de la culture» de son temps, en regrettant que sur une science aussi certaine, «aux fondements si fermes et si solides», que les mathématiques, l'on n'ait rien bâti de plus relevé que ses applications pratiques comme l'art des fortifications, l'art d'arpenter, de tirer des plans. . . . Ne nous trompons pas sur la déception de Descartes. Ce n'est certainement pas celle d'une conscience avide de technique mais bien d'autre chose de plus relevé, et qui rejoint l'observation de Jean Bricmont. Sa remarque est en réalité une critique sous-jacente de l'enseignement des sciences aux scientifiques, comme Descartes critique l'enseignement des mathématiques dans les écoles des jésuites. Mais, elle peut vouloir dire aussi, de mon point de vue, qu'une raison trop orgueilleuse et triomphante, trop sûre d'elle-même, au point de se détourner, avec mépris, de la foi, obtient le résultat contraire auquel elle s'attend. A force de se convaincre que le débat entre la science et la foi est définitivement tranché à l'avantage de la raison, l'on a plutôt favorisé le retour de l'irrationnel, de l'intolérance religieuse.

Lorsque Descartes, le scientifique et métaphysicien, démontrait l'existence de Dieu, l'on a pu penser qu'il mettait, mais à son insu, «le ver dans le fruit». S'il a distingué la raison et la foi, leur distinction n'a jamais signifié chez lui leur opposition, ni leur exclusion. La distinction signifie autonomie et non indépendance. Le Grand Arnauld, l'auteur de la *Logique de Port Royal*, l'avait bien compris, pour avoir défendu avec beaucoup de vigueur, dans ses controverses philosophiques et théologiques, l'orthodoxie cartésienne, principalement, contre les audaces métaphysiques de Malebranche dont la conception fusionnelle et unificatrice de la raison et de la foi reposait précisément sur le non respect de la distinction des deux ordres comme Descartes l'avait pensée, compromettant ainsi les avantages que la religion pouvait tirer du cartésianisme. A ceux qui condamnent la raison à l'égarement, même dans les mathématiques, si elle n'est pas «disciple de Dieu», Arnauld recommande de renoncer à attribuer à l'Eglise «par une piété mal entendue . . . , une autorité de juger des choses qui ne sont pas de son ressort . . . » (Arnauld 1775–1763, t.38: 98). C'est tout naturellement que, dans l'affaire Galilée, dont il prendra le parti, Arnauld se range du côté de l'héliocentrisme, faisant «preuve de libéralisme et de clairvoyance». Il partage le même sentiment que Pascal et Malebranche. C'est le signe du triomphe de Copernic, victorieux du conflit entre la théologie et la cosmologie. Cependant, sur la question de la distinction de la raison et de la foi, nos trois classiques, Arnauld, Malebranche et Pascal, n'accordent pas à la distinction la même signification. Sur ce point, le Grand Arnauld est le plus cartésien.

Héritiers du XVIIème siècle, les philosophes des Lumières ont pensé, pour mettre un terme à l'intolérance religieuse, qu'il suffisait de se contenter d'une «religion naturelle», rationnelle, indépendante de tout support institutionnel, donc, pour reprendre les propres termes de Rousseau, «sans temples, sans autels, sans rites, bornée au culte purement intérieur du Dieu suprême et aux devoirs éternels de la morale.» L'un des précurseurs du déisme en France, Robert Challe, également connu, pendant longtemps, sous son pseudonyme du Militaire philosophe, dans ses *Difficultés sur la religion proposées au Père Malebranche*, reproche aux métaphysiciens leurs extravagances métaphysiques qui conduisent à l'athéisme, favorisent les disputes interminables et les violences. Ses critiques anticipent celles de Rousseau qui s'accordera avec le Militaire philosophe pour mettre en cause les dogmes sur lesquels repose la religion en tant qu'institution. Les philosophes des Lumières, en s'attaquant à cette dimension de la religion, la foi dogmatique, ont bien vu que là était l'élément par quoi l'intolérance pouvait prendre racine. Aussi, ont-ils cherché à construire une religion naturelle sans support institutionnel. Ce faisant, ils manifestaient une certaine méconnaissance de ce qu'est la religion qui ne peut exister, comme nous l'avons vu, sans son caractère institutionnel, c'est-à-dire historique et social. L'échec des philosophes des Lumières était donc inévitable.

Pour conclure, l'on avait cru, en effet, qu'avec les Lumières et les promesses d'un monde meilleur, un monde de progrès dont elles étaient porteuses, la religion allait progressivement disparaître, victoire de la «lumière» sur l' «ombre». Après quelques périodes de «désenchantement» dans quelques parties du monde, voilà que l' «ombre», le religieux, que l'on a qualifié de «sottise et baliverne», de «mystification», revient et est toujours présent. Régis Debray, auteur de cette critique, reconnaît néanmoins, malgré son jugement sévère, que «l'important est de comprendre, pourquoi cette incongruité fait aujourd'hui retour au rebours du dépérissement radieux qu'avaient annoncé nos grands aînés.» C'est une nouvelle aventure dans les rapports de la raison et de la foi qu'il s'agit donc d'entreprendre. Comprendre c'est remonter au principe, c'est rechercher un modèle explicatif qui corresponde aux faits d'observation et d'expérience.

Claude Geffré, un théologien contemporain, conscient de l'enjeu, souligne avec pertinence, dans ses *Entretiens avec Gwendoline Jarczyk* (1999), la responsabilité des religions dans l'avenir de la paix dans le monde:

«Il importe, dit-il, que les traditions religieuses, au lieu de rivaliser les unes avec les autres en vue d'étendre leur influence, prennent conscience de leur responsabilité historique commune par rapport au destin de l'homme. Au-delà des institutions internationales, des médiations d'ordre politique et culturel, les religions se doivent, en effet, de mettre leurs ressources spirituelles au service d'une convivialité entre les hommes en favorisant en particulier un esprit de paix, une éducation à cette paix, condition de la coexistence pacifique.» (Geffré 1999)

L'esprit de paix, c'est l'esprit d'unité, c'est l'esprit de dialogue que les religions ont le devoir de défendre contre la guerre, contre l'intolérance, au risque de se renier elles-mêmes en leur essence de communion spirituelle si elles venaient à manquer à leur mission. Les religions monothéistes devront auparavant surmonter une difficulté qui résulte de la contradiction entre la portée universelle de la révélation et l'acceptation de la pluralité des fois. A cette condition un véritable dialogue inter-religieux est possible. Organiser ce dialogue, c'est déjà se mettre dans la disposition d'écarter toute idée de conversion et de rendre inéluctable le nécessaire approfondissement interne et critique de chacun dans sa propre foi. Quelle serait, en effet, la portée d'un dialogue inter-religieux si une seule des traditions religieuses concernées n'accorde pas, en son sein, d'espace pour un dialogue critique entre ses fidèles? A la base du dialogue inter-religieux, qui ne doit exclure aucune tradition religieuse, il y a l'affirmation de la liberté de conscience, la liberté de l'esprit qui n'est pas une simple prétention rationaliste, mais qui s'identifie, aujourd'hui, aux espoirs de la communication, de la circulation spirituelle entre les hommes.

L'humanité, en effet, est cela même qui circule de l'homme à l'homme, qui s'accomplit dans cette circulation même, qui n'est le monopole de personne, car en chacun elle appartient à tous et à tous en chacun. C'est la loi de la Parole, au sens le plus noble du mot, loi de la communication, de la circulation spirituelle entre les hommes, la loi du logos, de la raison. Que la religion y renonce, c'est non seulement s'interdire de se définir elle-même en son essence de communion spirituelle, mais, plus grave encore, réduire la foi à une simple opinion. Le dialogue doit être un dialogue de raison. Seule une foi réfléchissante et interrogative en chacun, interrogative et publique, peut, en réponse à notre question du départ, être l'antidote à l'intolérance.

BIBLIOGRAPHIE

Arnauld, A. 1775–1783. *Oeuvres* t. 38. Paris et Lausanne: G. Du Pac de Bellegarde et J. Hautefage.

Aucante, V. 2008. *Benoît XVI et l'Islam.* Paris: Parole et Silence.

Challe, R. 1970. *Difficultés sur la religion proposées au Père Malebranche par M . . . officier militaire dans la marine.* Bruxelles: Roland Mortier.

Debray, R., and J. Bricmont. 2003. *A l'ombre des Lumières. Débat entre un philosophe et un scientifique.* Paris: Odile Jacob.

Delumeau, J. 1993. *Le fait religieux.* Paris: Fayard.

Derrida, J., and G. Vattimo. 1996. *La religion.* Paris: Le Seuil.

Geffré, C. 1999. *Profession théologien. Quelle pensée chrétienne pour le XXIème siècle? Entretiens avec Gwendoline Jarczyk.* Paris: Éditions du Cerf, 1999.

Gendreau-Massaloux, M. 2000. "Réflexions d'une hispaniste." *Etudes littéraires: Théories, Analyses et Débats* 32, nos. 1–2: 201–210.

Kung, H. 1991. *Projet d'éthique planétaire.* Paris: Le Seuil.

Lévi-Strauss, C. 1955. *Tristes tropiques.* Paris: Plon.

Méchoulan, H. 1992. *Les Juifs d'Espagne: histoire d'une diaspora, 1492–1992*, Préface Edgar Morin. Paris: Liana Lévi.

Monteil, V. 1971. *L'Islam noir.* Paris: Le Seuil.

Ortigues, E. 1999. *Religions du Livre et religions de la Coutume.* Paris: Le Sycomore.

Puech, H-Ch. 1970. *Histoire des religions.* Paris: Gallimard.

Viaud, P. 1991. *Les religions et la guerre.* Paris: Le Cerf.

SELECTED PAPERS FROM
THE XXII WORLD CONGRESS OF PHILOSOPHY

Conflicted Modernity: Toleration as a Principle of Justice

DAVID M. RASMUSSEN
BOSTON COLLEGE

Abstract: This paper will begin by clarifying the kind of context, which requires toleration. My point of departure is a characterization of modernity that both departs from the classical modern theory of secularization and draws from the current research on multiple modernities. Because of the more or less recent resurgence of religion we can no longer characterize toleration on the basis of a theory of secularization. This will lead to the definition of conflict and tolerance within the confines of a post-secular society. The philosophical component of the concept of toleration will be taken from both Aristotle and Kant in the sense that toleration is not only a necessary virtue in modern society, it is also a normative notion based on respect for the law. Finally, the paper concludes that toleration must be conceived of as a principle of justice in a society that requires respect not only for the rights of others but for their cultures as well.

I. THE CHANGING CONTEXT FOR TOLERATION

The context for the consideration of toleration as a solution to political conflict has changed. John Rawls presented us with the most radical and far-reaching perspective on toleration when he coined the phrase, "philosophy must apply the principle of toleration to itself."[1] When presenting this thesis Rawls had a very schematic view of the development of religion and politics from the time of the Protestant Reformation on.

Moving from a comprehensive framework in which religion and politics were conceived as a unity, the earliest form of toleration was conceived of as a *modus vivendi* in which religious groups were willing to lay down their arms in order to reach a political agreement, which avoided war. It was only a matter of time until a plurality of forms of religious belief could find political representation in an emerging culture that began to learn how to tolerate, however hesitantly, plurality.

Special Supplement, *Journal of Philosophical Research* pp. 217–222
DOI: 10.5840/jpr201237Supplement38

With the acceptance of plurality on the one hand and a uniform notion of legality on the other the path was laid open for forms of constitutionalism which would inaugurate a division of labor between the political and the religious resulting in an ability to accept plurality of religious expression while at the same time finding a uniform notion of politics. Toleration would play an ever stronger role in this process of separation of religious expression and practice from political justification. It is from this historical process that we can distinguish stronger and weaker modalities of toleration.

II. THE RESURGENCE OF RELIGION[2]

In some ways Rawls anticipated what would be central to any discussion of toleration and conflict, namely, how to accommodate the resurgence of religion. At the same time he presupposed a scheme which was from an historical point of view, Western, and from a cultural point of view, American. On the positive side he did not construe public reason which is the reason of politics for him in purely secular terms. Given his distinction between the comprehensive and the political a secular position could be and was as comprehensive as any religious position and was characterized by him as comprehensive. Hence, the secular point of view would *not* be sparred the burden of having to translate its own views into terms that could be comprehended by the religious citizen. At the same time Rawls's view would depart from positions popular among sociologists and philosophers in the West by not conceiving secularization as the counterpart of modernization. He did not view the task of the political philosopher to be on the side of the secularist. Rather, in the fashion of Wittgenstein he preferred to leave things as they are.

III. MODERNITY AND SECULARIZATION

Although the work of Rawls may be an exception, the concept of toleration within Western thought has generally been linked to a scheme that associates modernization with secularization. Certainly, a strong case can be made for that connection. The great developments in the natural and social sciences made possible a certain disenchantment with the world and the emergence of a human-centered perspective which replaces a more divinely oriented worldview. One might observe that from the writing of Locke's *Letter on Toleration* religious institutions began to loose control over the domains of law, politics, education, culture and science. And as Marx's *On the Jewish Question* so brilliantly illustrated, as the secular state emerged religion began to be relegated to the private sphere. In this scenario the secular point of view triumphs over religion and toleration exists as a kind of acknowledgement of the limits of religious belief on the one hand and the predominance of secular discourses on the other. However, the resurgence of religion has changed all that. While one could apply the model of progressive secularization to Western Europe, Australia and New Zealand, religion has been on the advance in the rest of the world. Missionary expansion, fundamentalist radicalization and the new use of religion as a force for conflict and violence in the world constitute the distinctive mark of religion on the rise in the world today. Although there is much to be said for the link between secularization and modernization the secular can no longer sustain the triumphal position that it had in the recent past.

IV. FROM MODERNITY TO MULTIPLE MODERNITIES: POST-SECULAR SOCIETY

For those of us whose experience has included being part of a secular state we can characterize the new situation as essentially *post-secular*. This term, post-secular, which I take from Jürgen Habermas not only pertains to the descriptive account of the recent past, it also suggests the kind of normative attitude one must take toward one another in this current context if stability is to be achieved not only on the level of domestic society but in the international arena as well. I take this to be the project Rawls was working on in his latest writings. The ideal, that philosophy must apply the concept of toleration to itself, resulted in a reconfiguration of the project of political philosophy. At the center of Rawls's later work one finds the problem of reconciling pluralism with global justice. The issue fundamental to the development of a post-secular society is not simply developing different principles of justice for a national and an international scene, but rather one of trying to be open to the legitimacy of other societies and their respective claims to justice while at the same time trying to find norms that will work on the international level.

In a post-secular society one cannot count on every society, every civilization, having shared the same historical experience as the modernization/secularization thesis does.

This assumption does not necessarily lead to the idea of a clash of civilizations but it does create significant space for difference. Instead, I take the perspective developed by Eisenstadt[3] and Arnason among others, namely, that although modernity is a more or less shared phenomenon there are various ways in which societies, cultures and civilizations have adapted to it. According to Arnason[4] "there can only be multiple modernities if there are multiple *components* of modernity—economic, political, cultural, etc.—unfolding according to their own logics and capable of different combinations in different settings." The variations can be significant, not only on a national level but on a regional one as well. In this view, modernity would be the common area in which different civilizations encounter one another. This would mean that civilizations and cultures have to contend with differing self-interpretations of modernity. And these differing self-interpretations of modernity will in some cases clash leading to conflict and violence. However, global justice, the code word for international stability would somehow come to terms with this *conflicted modernity*. At this point it is toleration itself that must be conceived as a principle of global justice.

V. DEFINING TOLERATION[5]

My account of modernity separates the concept of secularization from modernization opening the way for a concept of toleration that does not require merely the accommodation of the practicing religious citizen to secularism. One can be much more precise about the notion of toleration. As I suggested a moment ago, toleration, at the most elemental level can be conceived as a *modus vivendi* which I can define negatively as toleration without respect. This, of course, is a pure conceptual definition which in reality would do little to assure political stability. The examples of a *modus vivendi* are generally taken to be treaties arrived at when long conflicts have been terminated in which the interest of the parties is more or less instrumental in the sense that the parties enter into the agreement in their own self-interest. However, even the most elemental *modus vivendi* presupposes a rule or norm which has to be respected. However, in this case the notion of respect is based on self-interest alone.

The notion of toleration can include a much more nuanced notion of respect which "allows" for the existence of the other without giving that other equal rights. The example is the toleration of a minority by a majority as in sixteenth-century France with the Edict of Nantes or the complex arrangement worked out by the Ottoman Empire with its millet system where Greek Orthodox and Armenian Orthodox Christians and Jews were tolerated and given representation in the legal system without being given full equal rights. This model, as interpreted by Walzer and then Rawls[6] gave rise to the ideal state of Kazinistan in which there is a system of law, legal representation for all groups, and a respect for basic human rights.

A third model of toleration exists within the Kantian definition of right, which includes at its foundation a notion of respect that is grounded in a specific conception of law. Kant's idea of the self-legislating subject contains a notion of equality within it in the sense that the notion of freedom entails the idea that everyone has the equal right to exercise political coercion on others in accord with the law that the body politic has created. His famous formulation was the following:

> ***Right*** is the limitation of each person's freedom so that it is compatible with the freedom of everyone, insofar as this is possible in accord with a universal law; and ***public right*** is the totality of ***external laws*** that makes such a thoroughgoing compatibility possible.[7]

This would lead to the idea of toleration as mutual recognition in which a certain moral assumption regarding the incomparable dignity or worth of every individual is combined with a basic political acknowledgement of the mutual power to coerce.

VI. TOLERATION AS A PRINCIPLE OF GLOBAL JUSTICE

The kind of notion of toleration which is appropriate to a world shaped by multiple modernities has to be defined politically. Here, I make the distinction between the comprehensive and the political first made by Rawls. Although such a notion requires mutual recognition it need not be based on a comprehensive notion of reason. It is enough to conceive persons as having the capacity to be reasonable. Reasonableness simply means that a citizen has the capacity to make the distinction between the comprehensive and the political and to be able to conceive other comprehensive positions as reasonable without sharing belief in their respective positions. In this context toleration can be conceived of as a *virtue* (Aristotle) practiced by those who participate in the political process. Equally, such a view of toleration requires that this virtue be practiced on the basis of *respect* (Kant) for the other person and the other's reasonable comprehensive position. In this sense toleration is a principle of global justice because it grants a certain validity to the views of others without having to measure that belief on the basis or certain assumptions regarding secularization.

The background idea for this notion of toleration is Rawls's notion of the "duty of civility."[8] The idea is that in a democracy individuals take on the responsibility of being able to translate their comprehensive religions and secular ideas into discourses that can be understood by others who do not share a particular comprehensive view. This more or less presupposes that within each comprehensive position there is a corresponding political discourse that has been integrated into that position over time. The language for the practice of the duty of civility on a global scale could be modeled on public reason. Whether it has to be identical to what goes for public reason in democratic societies is another question. Communication on the international level must be something like a public discourse which serves not only as third kind of discourse along side of religious discourses on the one hand and secular discourses on the other. It presumably mediates the potential conflict that the various alternative appropriations of modernity manifest. Whether or not we can call this public reason or perhaps to use a term recently introduced by An-na'im,[9] civic *reason*, on an international scale depends on whether it is possible to build an overlapping consensus on matters of international political concern. The achievement of some kind of overlapping consensus is our last best hope. The alternative is to conceive of politics as a continuing battle between them and we, which would lead, indeed, to a clash of civilizations. In this context toleration must function as a principle of global justice.

VII. CONCLUSION

I began by stating that the context for consideration of toleration as a way of meeting the challenge of political conflict has changed. Given the recent rise of religion we can no longer conceive of toleration as the end of a long process that began with a religious consciousness and ends with a secular one. Hence, we can no longer think of modernization as the correlative with secularization. Modernity itself is a plural term. Hence, the scope of toleration has changed. One must concede that there is no one correct way in which to conceive modernity. And it is in this context that we are challenged to expand our notion of toleration to include all reasonable religious and secular positions. To be sure, in world of violent conflict this is an optimistic position. However, it remains to be concretized through the developing discourses of international law.

NOTES

1. John Rawls, *Political Liberalism* (New York: Columbia University Press, 1996), p. 10.

2. On the analysis of the resurgence of religion and the idea of a post-secular society I am particularly indebted to two recent unpublished papers by Jürgen Habermas. They are entitled: "The Resurgence of Religion—a Challenge for a Secular Self-Interpretation of Modernity?" and "A 'Post-secular" Society—What Does That Mean?"

3. Shmuel Eisenstadt, "Multiple Modernities: A Paradigma of Cultural and Social Evolution," *ProtoSociology* 24 (2007). I should note that this issue is devoted entirely to Eisenstadt's writings.

4. Johann Arnason, "East Asian Modernity Revisited" (Unpublished paper), p. 1.

5. For one of the best discussions of toleration, see Rainer Forst, *Toleranz im Konflict. Geschichte, Gehalt und Gegenwart eines Umstrittenen Begriffs* (Frankfurt am Main: Suhrkamp, 2003).

6. Michael Walzer, *On Toleration* (New Haven: Yale University Press, 1997); John Rawls, *The Law of Peoples* (Cambridge, MA: Harvard University Press, 1999).

7. "On the Proverb: That May Be True in Theory, But Is of No Practical Use," in *Perpetual Peace and Other Essays* (Indianapolis: Hackett, 1983), p. 72.

8. Rawls, *Political Liberalism*, p. 217.

9. Abdullahi Ahmed An-Na'im, *Islam and the Secular State* (Cambridge, MA: Harvard University Press, 2008). On the question of tolerance and civic reason he writes: "Does this model of founding public policy and legislation on civic reason unfairly deny those Muslims who believe in the unity of Islam and the state (the Islamic state model) the right to live by their convictions? . . . The basic answer is that since no person or group has the right to violate the rights of others, the issue is one of balancing competing claims. In my view, a successful mediation of this basic paradox of all social life would seek to create a process of negotiation, whereby each side to an issue would find the process sufficiently beneficial to want to work with others in protecting and implementing it" (p. 94).

SELECTED PAPERS FROM THE XXII WORLD CONGRESS OF PHILOSOPHY

The Principle of Toleration: Under What Conditions?

RUBEN APRESSYAN
RUSSIAN ACADEMY OF SCIENCES (MOSCOW)

ABSTRACT: As a moral principle toleration is universal, but only in the sense that potentially it is addressed to every rational and moral agent. The question is whether this principle is appropriate in all situations and what are those moral agents who recognize its practical actuality for them? Toleration is not an absolute ethical principle, but one among others in the context of a particular moral system. It should be given a proper place in the hierarchy of principles. Understanding toleration as the absolute or even overriding principle may lead in the face of obvious and directly threatening wrong to its use as an umbrella for adoptive or escapist behavior. The limits to toleration are given by basic and minimal ethical task to resist evil. The principle of active opposition to evil by all possible means is prior to the principle of toleration.

In discussion on toleration I'm interested in some normative-ethical ideas significant for understanding the place of toleration as value and principle within the framework of morality. My consideration is a kind of reflection on a specific socio-cultural situation, which has appeared in many Russian cities and settlements as a result of massive immigration (not infrequently illegal) into Russia from the southern states—the members of the former Soviet Union, as well as China in the Far East during the last fifteen to twenty years.

1. The limits of the principle of toleration. Toleration is a moral principle. As a moral principle it is universal, but only in the sense that potentially it is addressed to every rational and moral agent. The question is whether this principle is appropriate in all situations and what are those moral agents who recognize its practical actuality?

According to Michael Walzer, as he put this in his book *On Toleration* (New Haven, CT: Yale University Press, 1997), toleration is closely associated with

Special Supplement, *Journal of Philosophical Research* pp. 223–227
DOI: 10.5840/jpr201237Supplement39

peacefulness, specifically, with peaceful coexistence. In the context of democratic society it is the coexistence of citizens equal in rights; in the multicultural context it is the coexistence of individuals as representatives of different ethnicities, confessions, cultural traditions. Basing on a broad concept of 'open society' we can associate toleration with openness to differences. According to Catriona McKinnon, to be tolerant means putting up what one opposes to, or not to interfere with or suppress a practice or belief that one could if one wanted to (having the power or influence) (*Toleration: A Critical Introduction* [London and New York: Routledge, 2006]). This is a descriptive definition of toleration; it says nothing about moral propriety of the corresponding practices. We know about broad debates on 'headscarves affair' in France (a similar discussion in less scale occurred in Russia, when some Muslim women insisted on their true right to be with capped head on the passport photo), female circumcision or, what is quite different, artistic expression (which merit and creed always can be questioned). These cases show that people and communities need to negotiate on moral propriety of practices and how broadly they may be tolerated.

Under a behavioral approach, an important aspect of toleration is one's recognition of the other's right to maintain his/her otherness. The ethics of virtue would probably also point to one's ability to self-regulate one's negative feelings towards otherness as such, whatever it might be (skin color, appearance, manners, tastes, beliefs, modes of life, etc.). This ability is important for practicing toleration, but it is not essential for the concept of toleration.

So, there is a certain condition of toleration which is performed through the evidence of differences and one's entire readiness to put up with differences. There is no need in toleration, when one is ignorant of differences or does not care differences. And there is no case of toleration, when one has neither power nor energy to express one's prejudice towards that, what is different or to oppress it. The arguments to discriminate so called *active* and *passive* toleration proposed in current literature do not seem convincing. What is called passive toleration is associated with nonchalance, indifference, or aloofness towards others, with timidity and cowardice in self-expression. As personal virtue toleration implies one's willingness and ability to coexist with those, whose opinions, attitudes, and modes of life differ from one's own. To my mind, this is a sufficient description of toleration.

In this respect the principle of toleration is like the principle of nonviolence. The latter has no practical sense related to those, who are weak, powerless, passive, and timid. In the same manner, though in the opposite modality, the principle of toleration—from the point of view of disinterested observer—is actual for those, who are able to be aware of differences between individuals and groups, biased and have will and power to express their bias in their behavior towards others.

Besides openness to differences, Michael Walzer distinguishes one's curiosity to differences and one's recognition of constructive potential of social and cultural varieties. However, curiosity is a positive attitude and recognition of constructive potential of varieties also presupposes belief in the worthiness of that what is different. Toleration is needed, when for some reasons or owing to psychological inertia differences are perceived as threatening and deterrent.

To clarify the problem of the object of the principle of toleration it is worth looking again into "A Letter Concerning Toleration," by John Locke. Lockean discourse on toleration may be interpreted in a way that he was addressing this principle to the average member of civil society. And thus this principle was accepted by Modern political culture. However, speaking on toleration Locke was obviously concerned mainly of rulers and clerics, or those, who were at the top of social hierarchy and powerful enough not only to express their disagreement and distaste regarding others, but even to demonstrate their attitudes and realize them in direct action against those, who provoked their discontentment. At the same time, although Locke in his normative thinking was open to the principle of universalizability, and for him toleration was a universal principle in the society, based on natural law, he set up certain limitations upon the principle of toleration. These limitations were regarding wrongdoers, or those—I'm omitting here Lockean specification of wrongdoers—who were dangerous to the social order, which warranted the efficacy of this principle of toleration. In other words, there are limits for the principle of toleration and they are set up by the very *regime of toleration* (to use the term proposed by Michael Walzer).

So, following Locke, toleration is not a paradigmatic ethical principle and it is not absolute ethical principle as it is often presented in popular philosophical and political discussions. It is one among others in the context of a particular moral system. In liberal thought toleration is correlated with such ethical concepts as respect, dignity, human rights, autonomy, etc. Toleration as an imperative should be given a proper place in the hierarchy of principles. Understanding toleration as the absolute or even overriding principle may lead in the face of obvious and directly threatening wrong to its use as an umbrella for adoptive or escapist behavior. The limits to toleration are given by morality itself—by its basic and minimal task to regulate individual and collective behavior to resist evil. The principle of active opposition to evil by all possible means is prior to the principle of toleration.

2. The division of moral responsibility. Basically, Lockean approach towards relations between confessions could be considered as quite original against the background of long interfaith oppositions of his time. But in broad ethical context of Judeo-Christian tradition it should be familiar indeed for his contemporaries. An early version of the Commandment of Love, given in the Book of Leviticus reads: "When an alien lives with you in your land, do not mistreat him. The alien living with you must be treated as one of your native-born. Love him as yourself, for you were aliens in Egypt" (Leviticus 19:33–34). Two points are worth rethinking in this verse. First, unlike current literature, which discusses toleration mainly in the context of justice, the author of Leviticus proposed a different context for tolerance. This context—is the ethics of merciful love or, in modern terms, ethics of care. Second, the normative logic of moral thinking proposed in this passage is similar to the one developed by Locke: from one hand, the natives were considered as those who were well established, were belong to the existing communal traditions, knew and maintained those traditions, from the other—the strangers, or aliens were considered as less incorporated into the community, in this sense socially and culturally detracted and hence powerless, not speaking about the probable lack of property.

The reasons why the author of Leviticus cautioned against mistreatment of aliens are clear. Aliens, especially when they appear all of a sudden as neighbors, are usually perceived as a threat, as a factor of fright and psychological discomfort. As a result they become an object of intoleration, injustice, mistreatment, and repression. It may seem that intoleration causes conflicts. It is certainly so. But at the same time intoleration often becomes a sequence of spontaneous conflicts, starting with identity conflict. That is why a Biblical author argued that although aliens look different in their performance, one should treat them like one treats one's neighbors, one's companions, and friends. Locals should be tolerant to newcomers. At the same time, from Biblical books as from many other ancient texts, we know that particular behavior was expected from the party of newcomers. A well known old saying: "When in Rome, do as the Romans do" speaks about just this. One can discover the like proverbs and edifications in the eldest texts of the Bible as well as in various other cultural traditions. So natives, or locals, should be tolerant and, according to the above quoted text from Leviticus, careful towards newcomers, while newcomers should be adaptive to the existing traditions and rules and respectful to their holders. Sometimes newcomers are not adaptive for various reasons: say, because of experiencing uncomfortable intercultural differences or circumspection from the side of locals or because they do not feel themselves as a part of local community, and even keep themselves apart from the local community. But inadaptability of newcomers is absolutely not a reason for mistreatment towards them. They anyway should be treated adequately and fairly and first of all with indulgence and mercy.

In the terms of today political realities, these are immigrants, who are aliens. They leave their houses and families and move to other regions or countries with better economic conditions in search of jobs and business. Sometimes the scale of immigration becomes so high that it influences the local labor market with negative results for local population. Sometimes newcomers appear to be more industrious comparatively with locals, they work more sufficiently, their businesses are more ambitious and successful, they earn more money and they make better profits, or they just agree to do the same job for lower remuneration. Often they are not aware of local traditions or do not care of them. Massive immigration is usually followed with social-demographic imbalances, which cause problems in public sphere, education, health care, etc. They show that besides trivial xenophobia there are also severe social conditions for growing intoleration.

Many of such problems, though not all, are the result of incompetence at the level of provincial, municipal, and communal policies and generally speaking the lack of public awareness of toleration as public virtue as an indication of the quality of communal and public life, a feature of good society.

In regard to this we need deeper discrimination of moral and political aspects of toleration. The difference between these aspects is rather vague. From a political point of view toleration is seen as a factor promoting civil order and public stability, and from an ethical point of view toleration is perceived as a kind of normative restriction for individuals to interfere and oppress the beliefs and practices they dislike or hate. There is certainly some theoretical sense in such differentiation. But the point is that toleration should be understood and accepted as a public virtue, as one of the basic communitarian and civic values.

Above mentioned term proposed by Michael Walzer, 'toleration regime,' represents, to my mind, an important conception, according to which in different societies toleration is established through appropriate public structures and procedures specific to the given society. To be fully implemented, toleration as a practical ethical principle requires adequate political and legal instruments, owing to which the community shares responsibility for keeping the spirit and ethos of toleration in order to maintain stability and provide constructive opportunities for differences.

SELECTED PAPERS FROM THE XXII WORLD CONGRESS OF PHILOSOPHY

Globalization and Cosmopolitanism in the Context of Modernity

ALEXANDER N. CHUMAKOV
INSTITUTE OF PHILOSOPHY OF THE RUSSIAN ACADEMY OF SCIENCES

ABSTRACT: Globalization and cosmopolitanism, on the one hand, and autarchy and nationalism, on the other, are two extremes between which humankind is destined to balance constantly, due to diversity and the natural confrontation of various cultural and civilizational systems by which it is represented. At the same time, globalization and cosmopolitanism are natural phenomena and are the most important characteristics of social development. That is why we should not put obstacles in the way of their dissemination and rooting in social life, but to aim at deeper understanding of their essence and what is hidden behind them in order, preventing ourselves from rash evaluations and one-sided conclusions, to contribute to the formation of a stable and just global world.

First of all, it needs to be mentioned that the World Philosophical Congress takes place for the first time in Asia, whose role in global politics and economy has grown steadily in the last decades, and many problems and foundations of social life, for example Western values, look a bit different from here. It needs to be stressed, because globalization and cosmopolitanism are broadly understood in the world: from nearly full coincidence of their meaning to serious confrontation. And relation to them is varied from positive to strictly negative.

Positive evaluations are typical for a specific kind of world outlook, endemic, for example, for many philosophers and scholars and for people associated with the "golden billion," who, due to their mentality and world vision, are already cosmopolitan because of their way of life and broad opportunities for using the goods of the global civilization.

However, most of the Earth's population is at the low level of socioeconomic development. Poverty, misery, and absence of perspectives move the majority of

Special Supplement, *Journal of Philosophical Research* pp. 229–237
DOI: 10.5840/jpr201237Supplement40

countries and nations to the roadside of world processes, when their role, meaning, position, their dignity, at last, are mostly not interesting for anyone. This is the most important reason why negative evaluations of globalization and, at best, cautious relation to cosmopolitanism, evidently prevail in practically the whole world.

Globalization is usually seen as a threat to national interests, first of all, in the spheres of economy, politics, culture, and language. In *cosmopolitanism* its various facets are often emphasized and exaggerated as to what is harmful for a general humanistic direction of the idea of world citizenship.

Of course, those who receive benefits from globalization by word and by deed promote it, while the others, remaining objective observers or feeling themselves the objects of manipulation, undertake all sorts of attempts to oppose globalization, proclaiming demands to make it governable and held in the interests of the whole humankind.

The situation is the same with *cosmopolitanism*. It is confronted, as a rule, by nationalists of all sorts and practically by all authoritarian, totalitarian, and despotic regimes. Cosmopolitanism is proclaimed "rootless," torn from real life; the supporters of such ideas are often treated with suspicion or, at best, with indifference.

The weak side of the existing approaches is the prevalence of subjective evaluations and politically engaged statements. As a result, the fact remains neglected that cosmopolitanism and globalization are not someone's invention, but reality, which from various sides reflects a single human nature and general patterns of human evolution.

That is why to understand the modern situation and the prospects of social development it is important to define properly, and to correlate adequately, these notions, having found for each of them its own place in the system of categories reflecting the modern world. It is a principal and, moreover, needful step on the way to understanding globalization not primarily in the negative light, and to replacing fear for it with constructive analysis of objective and subjective factors being the foundation of the global processes and their consequences.

There is no doubt that the ideas of cosmopolitanism, their directedness towards understanding the common destiny of humankind, will also become more attractive and acquire a broader audience if we concentrate attention not on the extravagant behavior, for example, of the first "world citizens"—cynics or contemporary "anti-globalists"—but on their concern for the reduction of human rights and dignity. That is why if we analyze the performances of antiglobalists as protest movements, which they deserve, we should admit that in their essence the participants of the antiglobalist demarches are no less cosmopolitan than those whom they confront. The difference is that both look at the same phenomena from different positions and conduct themselves differently.[1]

We can only resolve these problems by analyzing what exactly are globalization and cosmopolitanism. And the first thing to pay attention to is the fact that although these phenomena are seen as tightly connected, they are, nevertheless, related to different spheres of social being.

For example, if *globalization* is, first of all, an objective historical process, *cosmopolitanism* is a philosophical position. Besides, if *globalization* looks like universalization of all connections and relations, the emergence of single structures in various spheres of social life at the planetary level, *cosmopolitanism* is a state of mind, ideology, creed, or, finally, a specific system of philosophical vision of the world and human place in it.

Let us also mention, that globalization and cosmopolitanism emerged in different historical epochs. They are engendered by different reasons and express different sides of social life.

Cosmopolitanism is a cultural phenomenon, characterizing human world outlook, while *globalization is a trend of social development*, directed towards the emergence of the holistic world.

And still there are serious reasons for speaking about real interconnection and mutual correlation between these phenomena. It is especially clearly seen in contemporary conditions, when humankind faces global problems and looks for ways of overcoming them; and tries to formulate philosophical principles, on the basis of which different nations and states could act in coordination. Due to this fact we need to briefly analyze the nature and reason for the emergence of cosmopolitanism and globalization.

Cosmopolitanism, as rejection of national isolation, is broadening the idea of fatherland to the whole world and striving for the world without state borders that emerged in the Ancient Times. People in that period did not know the real construction of the Earth, and the limits of the world they inhabited correlated not with a globe but with a cosmos. That is why the emergence of the cosmopolitan ideas in that time can and should be understand as the first symptom, the first sign, of globalization, which at the level of rationality revealed itself when in reality there was, of course, no globalization.

Ancient India, Ancient China, and the Ancient Mediterranean, where the first philosophical schools emerged, lived in that period exclusively within the borders of their eucumenas. But the strength of philosophical reflection means that it penetrates the essence of things, sometimes being many ages and even millennia ahead of its time. For example, together with the ideas of cosmopolitanism, the Ancient philosophy engendered other speculative constructions, absolutely not evident in that time, such as the idea of atoms (Leucippus, Democritus, Epicure), ruminations about the universal interconnection of events and phenomena (Heraclites), and even guesses that the Earth is a rotating globe (Eratosthenes, Philolaus, Nikita of Syracuse, Ekphant).

It should be specially emphasized, that cosmopolitan ideas have been formed not accidentally and not in a vacuum. Their emergence was determined by both the historical development itself and the rational type of thinking of that era, which was called "axial time" by K. Jaspers. It was the period of emergence of the world religions and philosophical teachings, of the famous campaigns of Alexander the Great and the dissipation of the traditional world order; when mass migrations of large numbers of peoples, coming into interaction with other peoples and cultures, led to the loss of the customary way of life, engendering the crisis of the Antic polis. As a result, the philosophical conceptions of the Hellenes, passed on the system of values of a polis, were being destroyed and penetrated the limits of the isolated city-states. Man, thus, found himself in the world of uncertainties, where the future no longer corresponded to the past well known by him. Deprived of the customary way of life, the Ancient Greeks tried to find support in their belonging to a single humankind, feeling and proclaiming themselves the citizens of the cosmopolis—world state. Late, in the Roman epoch, the universal nature of the Roman state itself contributed to the spread and development of cosmopolitan ideas.

Socrates, Antisphenes, Diogenes, Cicero, Seneca, Epictet, Mark Aurelius, and many others are bright representatives of the Antique cosmopolitanism, which took on different meanings depending on the concrete historic conditions and philosophical position of this or that thinker. For example, while the term "cosmopolitan" was invented by Stoics, the very idea of world citizenship was produced earlier by their predecessors, the Cynics. They were the first to proclaim themselves "world citizens," because they felt their belonging not only to the polis isolated in its space, but to the open and endless "cosmos," the whole world, the laws of which they put higher than the conventional laws of a polis.

In the next centuries we will also find many bright thinkers, whose outlook and basic ideas were in their essence cosmopolitan. These are representatives of Christian Philosophy: Tertullian, Eriugena, and Humanists of the Renaissance: Dante, Erasmus, Thomas More, Monten, Campanella, and many others whose names we can list up to modernity.

But the topic of my presentation requires that I pay special attention to the rise of interest to cosmopolitanism in the epoch of the Renaissance. It was an important historical boundary for understanding the problems in question, because from here *real globalization* begins, and cosmopolitanism becomes really planetary, i.e., not cosmic already, but global.

There is no doubt, that such a turn of events was provoked by rethinking the Antique heredity and discovering the real scale of the real human environment. And the most important role here was played, of course, by the "Copernican revolution," in the understanding of the world and the Great geographic discoveries, which firstly confirmed that the Earth is a globe. By this, the fundamental corrections were made in human outlook, when the final sphere of interaction between man and nature was not "cosmos," but "globe." With a share of conventionality, one can say that from that period the notion of the "globe" changed what the Ancient Greeks associated with the "eucumena," or, more generally, with the "cosmos."

At the same time the discovery of America and then the first circumnavigation of F. Magellan put a beginning for real globalization, which, having begun from discovering and exploring new territories, i.e., in the sphere of geography, very soon pulled into its orbit the spheres of economy, politics, culture. And cosmopolitan views for the first time acquired a principal opportunity to transcend the boundaries of abstract speculation and to be realized in the sphere of practical activity.

Now, in the beginning of the twenty-first century when the world has become a holistic system according to practically all basic parameters of social life, some countries and peoples in fact have no choice whether to take part or not to take part in globalization. They are determined to take part due to a natural course of events, which for them not only cannot change their place of living or neighbors, or to avoid integrating into the world community. Theoretically it is, of course, possible, but those who do not fit economic, political, and cultural processes of globalization, who confront cosmopolitanism, putting their national sovereignty above all, are condemned to isolationism and backwardness. And this, apart from a series of negative consequences for such a people, creates also a threat to world stability, because in such countries the most suitable conditions are for interethnic conflicts, organized crime, and international terrorism.

So, being a natural process, globalization itself is neither good or bad, but it influences differently on different people. For less developed countries and deprived strata of population it really conceals more threats than positive solutions, while rich and developed countries win more from it. But the cause is not globalization, but the sociopolitical and economic condition of modern humankind, its disunity and uneven development. Cosmopolitan ideas are not someone's engineering, but normal and needful conditions for common living of different people in the global world.

That is why we should fight not globalization and cosmopolitanism, but the existing bad world order and unjust social relations.

What I've said demonstrates some vector for resolving the problems set. Namely, if *cosmopolitanism* is a child of *culture* and *globalization*—a result of *civilizational development* of a society—our further analysis of cosmopolitanism and globalization should be directly connected with the analysis of these spheres of social life.

It is important to emphasize that at the verge of culture and civilization the dualistic, contradictory nature of social development, confrontation between cosmopolitanism and nationalism, globalization and autarchy, reveals itself most acutely and openly.

Indeed, if we understand *culture* not only as creative activity of man and its results, but first of all as a complex of customs, traditions, beliefs, values, making the spiritual basis for human living activity, and if we understand *civilization* as a historically defined step in social development, which is characterized by a level of development of state, urbanization, technosphere, finally, civil society and law, then *culture* should have been named the soul and *civilization*—the body of a society.

But why do we talk about it discussing, it seems, another topic—cosmopolitanism and globalization? The answer is, that under the influence of the objective global processes humankind moves in its development from local manifestations of civilization to civilizational unity, engendering simultaneously not only a single global civilization,[2] but also what can be called global, universal, mass culture. And here newly understood ideas of cosmopolitanism become not just mind play or philosophical position, but a needful condition for human survival in the global and interdependent world. In other words, as far as globalization increases, cosmopolitanism also gains force, because it is directly connected with global world outlook and is an attribute of social life in the global world.

But this is only a part of the reality. The point is that globalization, leading to some unification of social life, nevertheless does not exterminate cultural diversity, which has existed always, exists now, and will exist in the future, because every people, as well as every individual person, is absolutely unrepeatable and in a way unique. One cannot sit in several chairs at one moment, and one cannot exist in several cultures, for even more than two thousand years later a well-known saying by Confucius has not become less true: "People are close to one another in their nature, but they are far from one another in their habits."[3] That is why cultural development of any people, deeply connected with its language, traditions, religion, mentality, etc. presupposes cultural autonomy and, hence, the defense of nation-state, striving for self-determination and independence. As the well known Polish philosopher Tadeus Kotarbinsky accurately mentioned: "It is enough to be a cosmopolitan, to become a stranger in every point of the modern world."[4]

But in this case it is cultural context where one should look for the roots of nationalism, isolationism, chauvinism, and everything that, being brought to its extremes, is opposed to cosmopolitanism, global outlook, single humankind, i.e., to what, in its turn, civilizational development of both separated nations and the whole humankind leads. Let us mention, that globalization, now multi-aspect, is a concrete form of such a development, which, independent on will and wishes of separated people with necessity, forms the world civilization.

Summing up, one can say, that *civilization* is a basis for cosmopolitanism and the unity of the world community. It is the uniting element, the moving engine of the integration processes. At the same time, *culture* is a basis for individualism and difference. It separates and, in a way, disunites peoples, i.e., it is a basis for differentiation of the global humankind. And this state of things should not be evaluated in terms of "good" and "bad." It is a reality that we should recognize and learn to live with. It is also important to understand that absolutization or exaggeration of the role of one of the social development factors—cultural or civilizational—engenders extremes and not needful social tensions. One can bring a lot of examples, including ones from the modern life, to confirm that where culture is exaggerated, good soil for nationalism and chauvinism emerges. Where we worship civilization and exaggerate the meaning of globalization—we deal with naked, abstract cosmopolitanism.

In this regard we should state that a complex symbiosis of the cultural and civilizational development engenders, and as far as globalization increases, enforces and aggravates the fundamental contradiction between the national and the international, between patriotism and cosmopolitanism. Now this contradiction has transcended the boundaries of pure consciousness and become a distinctive characteristic of social life in the age of globalization.

But the age of nation-states is not over and that is why I would compare modern humankind with a man standing on two ice-floes, when one of them gravitates to one bank, and the other to another bank. And in order not to be drowned he should constantly apply efforts to make these ice-floes not distance from one another too much. And the world community is also determined to find the "golden mean," which would allow it to most firmly balance between the global and the local, the international and the national, and, finally, between cultural and civilizational development of both separated peoples and the whole of humankind.

But to analyze this new reality we need another categorical apparatus. The set of categories we use now is badly equipped for the adequate description of the global world. We should change not only our vision of the world, but the means of its expression if we want to manage the global problems we face.

That is why, discussing globalization and cosmopolitanism in the context of modernity, we cannot avoid a customary notion of "civilization" because it not just inadequately reflects reality, but mixes things up if being used while discussing contemporary world processes. In particular, the talks about multiplicity and diversity of civilizations is a myth, which we should get rid of as soon as possible, for it is only what seems to exist, an aberration of our visions, when we are not able to see civilizational development in the cultural context, while tearing cultural context from civilizational development.

In fact, when in this or that society the first signs of civilization emerge, we cannot divide its civilizational development from the cultural one. They, like two sides of one coin, are from this moment in unbreakable unity. And we should speak in this case not about culture or civilization separately, what at best would correspond some abstraction, but about *cultural and civilizational* development of this or that social organism. In other words: in the face of various social entities, separate states, and now in the conditions of globalization already world community as a whole, we deal not with different civilizations or cultures as such, but with different *cultural and civilizational* systems.

On this evidence, cultural and civilizational components of such systems should be considered from the position of the complimentarity principle.[5] That means what in one context we would call culture will be nothing but civilization in the other context, and vice versa. Let us only mention, that if civilizational principles are common for all social systems, cultures are many. And separately taken cultures are not better or worse than the others. They are simply different. From here proceeds the multiplicity of cultural and civilizational systems, which can be classified by different foundations. For example, not only separate countries and nations can be different cultural and civilizational systems, but also some regions, continents, or for example, religions. Europe, Latin America, or Africa, along with Christianity, Islam, or Buddhism, also can and should be considered as distinct cultural and civilizational systems.[6]

And all of them, being different, having their own tasks and reaching their own goals, defended, defend, and will always defend their own interests. That is why conflict and confront not some sort of mythical civilizations or separately taken cultures, but absolutely concrete cultural and civilizational systems where achievements of civilization, norms or values, interwoven into different cultural contexts, seeming the same, produce an unrepeatable and unique fusion of what we conventionally call soul and body of this or that concrete society.

That is why the East will never become the West, and the West—the East. Ecumenist ideas will not replace multiplicity of religious beliefs, and cosmopolitanism will not become unconventional value and the only regulator of social relations for all people even when the world will be fully formed as a single system according to the basic socioeconomic parameters. In other words, we are condemned to live at the same time in the conditions of not only a global, but a locally constructed world with its diversity of cultures. Hence, although humankind develops in the direction of a global civilization, the future cosmopolis will necessarily remain culturally diverse and heterogeneous. And it is fully evident, that sensibility to cosmopolitan ideas, their spread will directly depend on the level of development of civil society at the global scale—the way on which only the first steps are made.

World community has to make a correspondent system of governing world economy, which is practically impossible if we do not follow the way of making global civil society and global democracy. Some results are already visible in this way. For example, we objectively become world citizens when, say, we express concern about environmental problems of the world's oceans or climate change of the planet, when we formulate our attitude to the situation in Iraq or in the Balkans. We also behave as citizens of the world when we are guided by universal norms of conduct outside our country. In fact, we already live in the global world and continue to discuss cosmopolitanism, which has become equal to global world outlook and global world feeling, which we have in this or that way.

Time has come to clean the notion of "cosmopolitanism" from its fully negative connotations and to say that cosmopolitanism does not mean rejecting the national, just as adherence to universal interests does not reject patriotism. The problem is in the correct placing of the emphasis. Hence, a cosmopolitan is not the one who has no Fatherland of his own, but the one who correlates his duty to the Fatherland with the interests of the world community. It would be naïve to assume that all people, even in the distant future, will take this position. But humankind will simply have no future without transformation of social consciousness in this direction, or at least not a good future.

As for us, the representatives of philosophy, if we really want to influence historical process, we should look at ongoing events not only as observers, but as participants. Of course, philosophy cannot directly influence the decisions of national governments or the activity of international organizations. However, we philosophers, as Richard Rorty justly says, are good for making bridges between peoples, for initiating cosmopolitan initiatives, for if philosophers do not become internationalists, no one will.[7] Who, if not philosophers, he reasonably mentions, must formulate and defend "a clear image of a specific cosmopolitan human future: the image of the planetary democracy, a society where tortures, or closing a university or a newspaper in the other end of the world will provoke the same rage as if it has happened in the Motherland."[8]

In fact, Derrida says about it, who "does not want philosophy to be a judge, but rather a traveler and vagabond, having no place to dwell, hurrying here and where when it hears the call of the 'other' for action."[9] And this is right. Philosophy is cosmopolitan already because it lives behind "the city walls," out of this or that polis. But in this case we should also agree with K. Marx, according to whom the task of philosophers is not only to explain the world, but to change it.[10] And if it is so, the time has come when we should seriously make the most important step in this direction: to start thinking over problems of globalization and the ideas of cosmopolitanism, to change them from bogey into, finally, the instrument of building a just, sustainable, and more secure global world.

NOTES

1. See *Global Studies Encyclopedia*, ed. Alexander N. Chumakov, William C. Gay, and Ivan I. Mazour (Moscow: Raduga Publishers, 2003), pp. 27–29.

2. Global civilization should not necessarily be associated with global state.

3. Confucius, *Uroki mudrosti: Sochinenia* (Moscow: Izdatelstvo Folio, 2005), p. 109.

4. See http://www.aforism.ru/html/k/kosm/00001.htm.

5. The complimentarity principle, formulated by N. Bore to explain corpuscular-wave nature of light and elementary particles, can be applied to social phenomena, of course, with some level of conventionality.

6. See A. N. Chumakov, *Metafizika globalizatsii. Kulturno-tsivilizatsionnyi kontext* (Moscow: Canon+, 2006).

7. Richard Rorty's *Pragmatism and the Russian Context* (Moscow: Tradition, 1997), p. 110.

8. See Richard Rorty, "Filosofia i budushchee," *Voprosy Filosofii* 6 (1994): 29–34.

9. *Deconstruction in a Nutshell. A Conversation with Jacques Derrida*, ed. J. D. Caputo (New York: Fordham University Press, 1997), p. 51.

10. See: K. Marx, "Tezisy o Feierbakhe" [text 1888 goda]; K. Marx and F. Engels, *Sochinenia*; *Izdanie vtoroe*; *v piatidesiati tomakh*. T. 42 (Moscow: Izdatelstvo politicheskoi literatury, 1974), pp. 264–266.

Mondialisation et cosmopolitisme

CYRILLE KONÉ
OUAGADOUGOU UNIVERSITY

ABSTRACT: Capitalism generates globalization which, through the steady growth of trade, the internationalization of economic production, and changes in communications technology, reduces the importance of micro-states by pushing for the establishment of international economic structures. Globalization increases the separation between rich and poor. We will investigate, on the one hand, "internationalization" as a process of global unification of States to overcome the fragmentation and the competition between countries that is accentuated because of economic and financial globalization. On the other hand, the idea is to think about the possibility of cosmopolitanism, namely the conditions of universal brotherhood, of the union of men beyond their condition.

INTRODUCTION

La mondialisation s'enracine dans l'histoire du capitalisme dont elle reflète et traduit le développement le plus accentué. Le capitalisme sort du cadre purement national et continental pour adopter une dimension cosmique, puisqu'avec le triomphe du système économique de production libérale, consécutif à l'échec du modèle communiste de développement, la terre entière est devenue son aire de jeu. Il engendre la mondialisation qui, grâce à la croissance continue du commerce, à l'internationalisation de la production économique, aux mutations des techniques de l'information et de la communication (T.I.C.), réduit de façon inédite l'importance des États en poussant à la mise en place de structures économiques internationales. Mais si la mondialisation favorise le rapprochement des individus, l'intégration à la communauté mondiale; elle reste fondée dans le libéralisme, c'est-à-dire orientée vers la recherche du profit. Le respect du dogme de la privatisation du capital débouche assez souvent sur la précarisation de l'emploi et accroît le chômage, la pauvreté. La mondialisation nourrit de ce fait le conflit sociopolitique à travers les jeux sans fin de comparaison entre les riches et les pauvres, les dominants et les

Special Supplement, *Journal of Philosophical Research* pp. 239–250
DOI: 10.5840/jpr201237Supplement41

dominés. Loin donc de contribuer au processus d'unification des peuples du monde, elle les divise en zones développées, prospères et, en régions sous-développées, rongées par la pauvreté.

Son concept semble contredire l'idée de cosmopolitisme sous-tendue par l'édification d'une communauté homogène vivant sous le même régime juridique, unie par le droit et l'intérêt commun. La mondialisation accentue plutôt la séparation entre les riches et les pauvres. Comment se la représenter dans ces conditions comme une mise en œuvre du cosmopolitisme qui prétend abolir les vieilles querelles fratricides et sceller les retrouvailles entre les hommes par-delà les frontières étatiques? Et comment ne pas douter du possible ordre cosmopolitique face à la multiplication des revendications identitaires, à la montée des concurrences due à la mondialisation? Est-on condamné à vivre dans un monde toujours plus inégalitaire, plus «dur» pour les perdants, les faibles? Quel espace reste-il à la philosophie pour penser la solidarité nouvelle?

C'est à esquisser quelques réponses aux questions posées que l'on s'essayera ici en enquêtant d'une part sur la «mondialité» comme revers de la mondialisation économique et financière qui se détourne de l'idéal cosmopolitique au lieu de s'en rapprocher, et d'autre part en examinant la possibilité du cosmopolitisme, à savoir les conditions de la fraternité universelle, de l'union des hommes par-delà leurs appartenances.

I. ABANDON DE L'IDÉAL COSMOPOLITIQUE À L'ÈRE DE LA MONDIALISATION

La mondialisation prend source dans l'histoire du capitalisme qui s'est épanoui en Europe dans les conditions historiques, socioculturelles principalement marquées par les avancées de la science désireuse de «soumettre la planète à l'homme» et par l'idéologie du gain avec comme corollaire la domination, l'exploitation de l'ensemble des ressources humaines et naturelles existantes. L'industrialisation avec l'expansion du machinisme pousse les forces de production à sortir du cadre des frontières étatiques, régionales et continentales, devenues trop étroites, pour exporter les produits, trouver de nouveaux débouchés économiques, des espaces de développement de l'activité et chercher des matières premières à coût réduit (bois, gomme, poudre d'or, peaux, etc.) afin de fructifier les gains. C'est dans cette perspective que s'est institué l'esclavage qui réalisa pendant plusieurs siècles la connexion économique de l'Europe, de l'Afrique et de l'Amérique. Selon Makhtar Diouf, l'intégration de l'Afrique subsaharienne au système capitaliste commerçant s'est effectuée par le biais de la traite négrière.[1]

Le reste des régions du monde (Afrique maghrébine, Amérique latine, Asie, Australie, Nouvelle-Zélande) entre dans l'économie capitaliste à la faveur de la colonisation qui sous le prétexte d'apporter la «civilisation», de répandre l'esprit des Lumières européennes à l'ensemble des peuples du monde, implante le capitalisme dans les zones colonisées. La colonisation est donc la fille du capitalisme. C'est le phénomène majeur qui a étendu au monde entier le système économique fondé exclusivement sur le profit pécuniaire. Il est historiquement infondé, injuste de l'appréhender comme humaniste car il est impérialiste, établi dans le sillage du capitalisme dont il prépare la perpétuité. Avant la fin du 19e siècle la quasi-totalité des populations non occidentales du globe terrestre est annexée par les puissances européennes de l'époque (France, Angleterre, Hollande, Espagne, Italie, Portugal). Paul Valéry décrit le phénomène en ces termes: «Toute la terre habitable a été de nos jours reconnue, relevée, partagée, entre des nations! . . . Le temps du monde fini commence. Le recensement général des ressources, la statistique de la main d'œuvre, le développement des organes de relation se poursuivent. Quoi de plus remarquable et de plus important que cet inventaire, cette distribution et cet enchaînement des parties du globe?»[2] Le monde, dorénavant soumis à la logique du capital, est organisé économiquement pour soutenir l'ordre capitaliste et consacrer la division coloniale du travail, du commerce entre le Sud producteur de matières premières et le Nord transformateur de ces produits. Les différentes parties de la terre sont alors liées par l'économie et la finance. Le système économico-financier mondial est bien constitué pour qu'aucune zone ne puisse être une «île déserte». Le monde est enchaîné, entraîné plus encore par le mode économique capitaliste depuis la chute du Mur de Berlin.

L'émancipation politique des nations colonisées ne change pas fondamentalement la donne puisque le nouvel ordre économique néocolonial est placé sous le diktat du système politico-économique dominé par les pays Occidentaux à travers l'Organisation des Nations Unies (O.N.U.), les institutions du système de l'O.N.U. et celles de Breton Wood comme le Fonds Monétaire International (F.M.I.), la Banque Mondiale (B.M.), etc. Les pays souverains se trouvent dans l'impossibilité de prendre leur distance avec le système capitaliste. Par exemple, la voie africaine du socialisme et du développement a vite été abandonnée en Tanzanie, en Guinée Conakry et au Sénégal où le président Léopold Sédar Senghor, célèbre théoricien de la doctrine, n'a pas voulu ou pu l'expérimenter. Il reste de nos jours, les cas de la Corée du Nord et de Cuba, sortis de l'histoire moderne et coupés du monde pour leur refus de l'économie de marché, de la démocratie et du respect des droits de l'homme qui s'affichent comme le seul horizon concevable ayant remplacé l'affrontement Est/Ouest. Cela a pour conséquence de placer les populations sous contrôle, de les priver de droits élémentaires, sociaux, civiques, politiques, d'accès aux techniques d'information et de communication (T.I.C.). C'est dire que la mondialisation est devenue la réalité des temps modernes avec laquelle compter. En effet elle consacre le succès planétaire de l'économie de marché. Il faut donc s'y adapter ou périr. Il n'y a pas d'autres choix responsables tant elle paraît naturelle et parée des plus belles vertus. Le capitalisme est de nos jours sans rival sérieux. C'est ainsi qu'il s'est imposé comme panacée au développement, pour l'instant, il semble qu'on n'ait pas d'alternative au néolibéralisme qui gagne de plus en plus les esprits au point de convertir l'université, le monde entier à la vision productiviste et mercantile. Les principaux facteurs qui ont concouru à la mondialisation sont:

1) l'augmentation du volume du commerce international et sa planétarisation,
2. l'internationalisation de la production économique,
3. les mutations qualitatives des Nouvelles Techniques d'Information et de Communication (N.T.I.C.) qui facilitent et accélèrent les échanges.

On peut décrire ce phénomène marquant de l'époque contemporaine comme «l'extension à l'échelle de la planète d'un processus complexe et inégal d'unification, sous l'égide exclusive de l'économie de marché, de tous les segments des activités traditionnelles des nations et des États: commerce, flux financiers, organisation et production économiques, communication, culture et environnement.»[3] Comme processus d'unification économique, d'universalisation de normes sociopolitiques, la mondialisation peut être appréhendée comme une transition vers une «cosmo-civilisation pan humaine». Elle peut aussi s'entendre comme l'expérience d'un monde conduisant à l'éclatement, au renforcement des oppositions entre riches et pauvres ou encore à la constitution d'un «empire-monde», contrôlé par une «hyper puissance» qui serait garante de son ordre impérial. Nul en fait ne peut dire rigoureusement à quoi s'attendre avec la mondialisation. Il faut donc se garder de considérer l'opinion des élites sur cette question comme une pensée rigoureuse.

Pourtant pour les institutions internationales comme le Fonds Monétaire International, la Banque Mondiale, l'Organisation Mondiale du Commerce (O.M.C.), la mondialisation est le talisman permettant d'accroître continuellement les richesses, de lutter contre la pauvreté, le sous développement. C'est dire qu'elle comporte bien des aspects positifs qui sont entre autres:

1) la possibilité d'avoir une croissance rapide à condition de développer une stratégie économique et commerciale adaptive,
2) l'accès au marché mondial qui serait en principe moins soumis au protectionnisme,
3) la relative facilité d'accès aux technologies nouvelles avec une circulation multidirectionnelle de l'information,
4) la démocratisation du savoir.

Mais loin d'être porteuse d'avenir, la mondialisation est plutôt synonyme d'amplification des inégalités, de la pauvreté, des désordres éco-systémiques pour la majorité des êtres humains. Plus encore l'accentuation de la concurrence entre les États et à l'intérieur des États fait rage au point que les individus, les pays qui ne peuvent produire suffisamment et entrer en compétition avec les autres sont menacés de disparition à long terme. Les migrations massives, l'affaiblissement du rôle des États, la menace sur la démocratie avec la constitution des multinationales montrent qu'à l'ère du «tout capital» ce sont les puissances financières qui gouvernent, l'on vit sous la tyrannie du marché. La citoyenneté ne signifie plus grand-chose dans la mesure où les citoyens n'ont plus le pouvoir véritable.[4] Les «marges de manœuvre» des gouvernements au plan économique sont réduites. La mondialisation rétrécit l'espace de la délibération collective au profit de décisions imposées, elle développe le sentiment d'impuissance et contribue au renforcement des rivalités locales et planétaires. En somme elle ne réconcilie pas les hommes[5] car elle remplace l'opposition Est/Ouest par celle Nord/Sud. Elle entretient de ce fait les vieilles querelles entre les peuples (les déchirements au Liban, au Proche-Orient, en Afrique, etc.) et ravive les antagonismes anciens entre les classes, les générations. Dans le contexte de l'irruption des revendications communautaires, filon des investissements mercantiles, les hommes s'entredéchirent comme des bêtes. Par certains aspects ignobles de la mondialisation, l'espèce humaine perd son piédestal.[6] On le voit, la mondialisation fait douter du possible ordre cosmopolitique en détournant l'humanité de l'idéal de paix, d'unité et de bonheur. Comment se représenter dans ce contexte le cosmopolitisme de la citoyenneté, le dialogue des cultures, la fraternité universelle comme produit de la loi commune? Que faire pour favoriser l'avènement de l'ordre cosmopolitique?

II. CONDITIONS DE RÉALISATION D'UNE COSMOPOLITIQUE DE LA CITOYENNETÉ ET DE LA PAIX

Comme alternative à la mondialisation, on peut proposer de construire une «cosmo-civilisation pan humaine» capable de corriger les insuffisances de la mondialisation dans le but de pallier la crainte humaine de la misère. La réalisation d'une telle civilisation pour arrêter l'éclatement du monde, le renforcement de l'opposition riches/pauvres vise entre autres l'humanisation de la mondialisation, la réorientation de son cours pour permettre l'édification d'une communauté mondiale. La mondialisation actuelle est principalement un processus d'unification des capitaux économiques et financiers. Comme consécration de l'économie de marché, elle s'impose au monde entier sans que sa gestion ne relève d'une structure démocratique. Revoir sa gestion donnera aux citoyens, aux États le droit de délibérer sur les questions qui les concerne. Par-delà l'ajustement de la gestion, il importe de la recentrer sur les aspects fondamentaux de la vie sociopolitique, scientifique, culturelle, intellectuelle, environnementale qui ont été délaissés à tort alors qu'ils conditionnent l'équilibre du monde. D'où l'urgence de rectifier le cours de son évolution en articulant les dimensions oubliées aux aspects économique et financier afin qu'elle appuie le développement durable de l'humanité.

La cosmo-civilisation doit être la résultante du dialogue des cultures et non la traduction d'une domination sociopolitique et économique comme dans le projet cosmopolitique kantien. Cela signifie de remettre en cause la «dictature uniforme de ce que les Occidentaux croient être la modernité» pour refonder l'universel qui coïncide mal avec l'occidentalisation du monde. Il s'agit par conséquent de doter l'humanité d'une éthique universelle fondée sur les valeurs cardinales: liberté, égalité, solidarité, justice et responsabilité. Comment soutenir dans ces conditions le modèle européocentriste qui est au fondement du cosmopolitisme de Kant? Il semble plus judicieux de repenser l'universel autrement comme irréductible aux valeurs des dominants dans la mesure où l'approche occidentale du monde et du développement qui a jusqu'ici prévalu est source des difficultés que l'on connaît au plan socio-économique et environnemental avec l'augmentation de la pauvreté, du chômage, le réchauffement de la terre avec ses conséquences désastreuses.[7] Le modèle de l'«empire-monde» expose l'ensemble des individus, des peuples et des États du monde à la volonté hégémonique de l'hyper puissance et des capitaux.[8] Les valeurs essentielles au respect de la dignité humaine sont ainsi remises en cause et le développement de la plupart des États est contrarié du fait de l'unilatéralisme et de l'attitude anti démocratique des puissants. La conception du monde fondée sur le profit, le capital débouche sur une division des êtres humains en riches et en pauvres; elle sépare les hommes en mettant l'accent sur une caractéristique accidentelle. Son esprit qui est contraire à l'idéal de la société cosmopolitique ouverte conduit à explorer du côté d'une vision du monde comme celle subsaharienne, fondée sur l'éthique de la solidarité et le respect de l'environnement afin d'assurer l'épanouissement de la communauté entière. La vie en sympathie avec la nature[9] n'est pas l'expression d'un archaïsme, d'un conservatisme rétrograde mais l'invitation à se servir avec mesure de la nature pour assurer les besoins et préserver l'héritage commun. En effet le temps est venu pour l'homme de répondre aux besoins du présent sans compromettre la capacité des générations futures à satisfaire leurs propres besoins. Cela revient pour l'homme à penser un développement durable solidaire.

La civilisation pan humaine à réaliser ne saurait être une association civile des États puissants mais une fédération des individus, des pays du monde entier. Cela suppose de sortir de la violence et de la misère de l'état de nature pour entrer dans une «société des Nations» dans laquelle les droits et la sécurité de chaque individu, de tout État sont reconnus, ce quelle que soit sa taille, son importance. Dans pareille société, les lois qui sont le fruit de l'accord des hommes, des États sont respectées et assurent la paix. C'est en renonçant à la liberté sauvage pour celle civile que l'humanité peut être en droit d'attendre l'épanouissement dans la société conforme aux lois.[10] L'acceptation par les individus et les États de règles valables universellement assure à chacun des contractants la liberté, cela favorise en outre le développement des dispositions humaines naturelles. En somme, la fédération suppose l'autonomie, l'interdépendance des États, le bannissement de la violence dans les rapports interindividuels. L'entente est donc l'exigence fondamentale. «Il ne doit y avoir entre nous aucune guerre, car nous voulons ne former qu'un État, c'est-à-dire instituer un pouvoir suprême législatif, exécutif et judiciaire qui règlera pacifiquement nos conflits.»[11] L'État confédéral favorise l'expression des identités, des cultures; il ne saurait être le monstre tyrannique, négateur des spécificités. En effet leur protection est fondamentale car il faut reconnaître à l'individu, à chaque peuple ce qui lui est propre. La reconnaissance des particularités culturelles ne peut déboucher sur le conflit, le choc des traditions car celles-ci ne doivent pas être contraires aux exigences de la démocratie; la tolérance et le respect mutuel restant au cœur de la communauté mondiale. Les fragmentations nationalistes, ethniques cessent de valoir dans une telle société parce qu'elle réalise l'espérance, le bonheur auquel l'homme est naturellement attaché.

L'exercice des différences, le déploiement des traditions particulières dans le respect des valeurs communes est la règle qui permet de constituer l'État des peuples de la terre dans la fraternité par-delà les conditions. En outre, le monde commun exige de bannir les entraves à la libre circulation des personnes et des biens. Il va plus loin dans la garantie du principe de libre circulation puisqu'il reconnecte la libre circulation des biens, des services avec celles des individus qu'on ne respecte pas assez dans le cadre de la mondialisation économique et financière.[12] C'est dire qu'un tel État est hospitalier car il aide et manifeste de la bienveillance, de l'amitié envers les individus qui le sollicitent. «Le droit cosmopolitique doit se restreindre aux conditions de l'*hospitalité universelle*.»[13] En tant que fondé sur l'hospitalité, il accorde aux individus le droit à la terre. «La nature a renfermé tous les hommes ensemble (au moyen de la forme sphérique qu'elle a donnée à leur séjour, en tant que *globus terraqueus*) à l'intérieur de certaines limites; et dans la mesure où la possession du sol sur lequel peut vivre l'habitant de la Terre n'est jamais concevable que comme possession d'une partie sur laquelle chacun a originairement un droit, tous les peuples disposent originairement d'une communauté du sol—non pas toutefois au sens de la communauté juridique de possession (*communio*), ni non plus, par conséquent, d'usage ou de propriété de ce sol, mais au sens de la possibilité d'y exercer une action réciproque physique (*commercium*), c'est-à-dire d'y entrer dans une relation continuelle de chacun avec tous les autres consistant à se prêter au commerce réciproque, et ils ont un droit de faire cette tentative avec chacun, sans que l'étranger soit pour cela légitimé à traiter chacun d'eux pour cela comme un ennemi. Ce droit, dans la mesure où il tend à la réunion possible de tous les peuples par rapport à certaines lois universelles de leur commerce possible, peut être nommé le droit cosmopolitique (*jus cosmopoliticum*).»[14] La reconnaissance du droit de tout être humain à circuler librement, à jouir de la planète et de ses ressources en tant qu'héritage de toute l'espèce est par excellence le principe fédérateur de l'humanité. L'institution du droit de visite et/ou de séjour assure à l'homme de vivre librement partout sur la terre sans être traité en ennemi. L'individu peut dès lors voyager de cité en cité à la manière des Sophistes pour exercer son métier, visiter le monde plutôt que de vivre enfermé dans les limites étroites des frontières nationales.

Les guerres multiformes (commerciales, diplomatiques, préventives, etc.) que se livrent les États dans le cadre de la mondialisation économique et financière n'ont pas droit de cité dans la cosmo-civilisation pan-humaine. «La misère produite par les guerres constantes par lesquelles les États cherchent, tour à tour, à s'amputer et à s'assujettir mutuellement, doit finalement les pousser soit à prendre la résolution, même contre leur gré, d'entrer dans une Constitution civile, soit, si un tel état de paix universelle est encore plus dangereux, d'un autre côté, que la liberté, parce qu'elle amène le despotisme le plus effroyable (comme c'est arrivé effectivement plus d'une fois avec des États trop puissants), cette même misère doit pourtant les contraindre à entrer dans un état qui, certes, n'est pas une communauté cosmopolitique soumise à un chef, mais n'en est pas moins un état fédératif de droit réglé par un droit des gens dont ils ont convenu en commun.»[15] Dans la société cosmopolitique, les rapports interindividuels et interétatiques sont pacifiquement régis par le droit pour garantir non l'intérêt du dominant mais celui de tous. Cela suppose une «société civile administrant le droit de façon universelle»[16] pour en finir avec l'état de liberté sauvage des individus, des États enclins à user de la force pour assurer leurs intérêts égoïstes. Par conséquent un contrat doit être institué entre les individus ou leurs représentants d'une part et d'autre part entre les États en vue de la cordiale entente, de la sauvegarde des intérêts individuels et collectifs. En effet il permet de garantir une existence humaine digne en régulant l'ensemble des rapports sociopolitiques et économiques dans le sens des intérêts de tous.

Le problème fondamental qui se pose dans le cadre du monde commun c'est de déterminer l'autorité commune aux hommes. À quelles exigences les hommes accepteront-ils de se soumettre? Il semble que l'organisation du vivre-ensemble requiert de mettre en place et de respecter les règles en vue d'assurer la paix, l'intérêt général. «Le problème de l'établissement d'une constitution civile parfaite est lié au problème de l'établissement de relations régulières entre les États, et ne peut pas être résolu indépendamment de ce dernier.»[17] C'est dire toute l'importance du droit devant régir les rapports interétatiques dans un esprit d'équilibre, de justice et d'équité. Les êtres humains en dépit de leurs diversités (socioculturelles, intellectuelles et idéologiques, etc.) peuvent accepter de se soumettre au droit qui est reconnu comme étant au fondement des sociétés. En effet en tant que disposition contraignante, le droit peut être une des exigences communes aux hommes. Il est l'autorité à laquelle les hommes rendent aujourd'hui hommage, se réfèrent dans toutes les tentatives sérieuses d'organisation de la vie sociale. «Le mot droit ne viendrait sinon jamais à la bouche des États qui veulent se combattre, à moins de le tourner en ridicule.»[18] Si on peut tenter de rassembler les êtres humains sous la loi commune, il est toutefois vrai de dire que le droit est lui-même l'expression de la culture, d'un rapport de forces. Dans ce cas comment assurer le droit des individus et amener les nantis, les pays puissants à vivre sous le même régime juridique que ceux moins forts, à ne pas s'en écarter en vue de la constitution de la société cosmopolitique? Comment garantir le respect du droit de tout individu, de chaque État, la validité universelle du contrat qui établit la communauté pan humaine? Il paraît important d'organiser le vivre-ensemble au niveau de l'humanité toute entière, de penser les conditions de possibilité de la communauté universelle à l'aune de la démocratie, du respect des droits de l'homme pour garantir les droits des individus et des États. Avec la constitution de la communauté cosmopolitique cohérente, on ne pourra plus exhorter au respect des règles démocratiques et se comporter en dominateur, en violateur de droits. La menace de malheurs à l'horizon du monde divisé en groupes antagoniques, la détresse du monde soumis à la dictature d'une super puissance et la capacité de l'homme à comprendre que l'humanité ne peut réaliser le bonheur que dans l'union, l'interdépendance, inciteront les individus, les États à mettre en accord leurs inclinations avec la recherche du bien commun. «L'idéal politique d'une Fédération d'États libres et républicains, qui seule conduit à la paix universelle, doit coïncider avec l'intérêt bien compris des États et c'est pourquoi l'histoire doit pouvoir le voir réalisé.»[19] Cela signifie que l'éclairage de la raison est suffisant pour permettre d'appréhender les inconvénients d'un monde divisé par rapport aux avantages du cosmopolitisme, fondateur de la communauté heureuse.[20]

CONCLUSION

Au total la mondialisation consacre le triomphe planétaire du capitalisme qui préconise la libéralisation des échanges, la privatisation de l'économie pour favoriser la croissance de la richesse. Mais si celle-ci augmente c'est assez souvent au profit des riches, des multinationales auxquels les gouvernements sont de plus en plus soumis. L'unification économique et financière n'apporte donc pas les bienfaits escomptés aux individus, aux États. Elle ne parvient pas à juguler l'exclusion, le développement des inégalités. On assiste au contraire à l'accentuation de la misère avec l'accroissement du phénomène des travailleurs pauvres du fait de la précarisation de l'emploi. Cela maintient non seulement les hommes dans l'affrontement des classes mais surtout perpétue la violence en les détournant de l'idéal de l'ordre cosmopolitique, tendu vers la construction d'une communauté mondiale unie par le droit et qui garantit aux êtres humains la sécurité, la liberté et l'épanouissement. Le monde commun, la «société des Nations» apparaît donc comme la forme achevée de l'accomplissement humain qui permettrait à l'humanité d'atteindre la maturité.

NOTES

1. Diouf 2002, p. 30.
2. Cf.: *Regard sur le monde actuel.*
3. Samb 1999, p. 135.
4. Voir Koné 2007.
5. Selon Francisco Naishtat dans «La réactivation philosophique du cosmopolitisme», *Philosophie politique et horizon cosmopolitique*, Journée de la philosophie de l'UNESCO, 2004, N°10, 18–19, «La mondialisation actuelle se caractérise, à la suite de la chute du Mur de Berlin, par la substitution de la coupure Nord-Sud à la coupure Est-Ouest, en vigueur après les accords de Yalta, ce qui introduit un sens très différent dans la ligne du partage du globe, non plus définie en termes de régime politique mais en termes d'inclusion-exclusion au marché global. Ce déplacement introduit en même temps une nouvelle donne dans la question des étrangers: il ne s'agit plus seulement ni même principalement du mouvement individualisé et personnalisé caractéristique du traitement de l'asile politique à l'époque de la Guerre Froide, mais du mouvement en bloc des populations désespérées par la misère et l'exclusion et disposées à périr dans la recherche de nouvelles possibilités et opportunités de survie sur d'autres territoires. Cette situation a amené les États à combiner le traitement policier en termes du contrôle radioscopique des frontières avec l'assistance humanitaire, laquelle, recouverte par un catastrophisme naturaliste, est destiné à mettre le mouvement des populations dans le circuit médiatique.»

6. Kant déplore la sauvagerie des rapports fondés sur la force en ces termes: «Pas un instant, l'autonomie et la propriété d'un État ne sont garantis contre un autre État. On constate en tout temps la volonté d'assujettir l'autre ou d'amputer son territoire; et on ne peut jamais relâcher l'effort militaire de défense qui rend la paix plus oppressante et plus destructrice du bien-être intérieur que la guerre elle-même. Or le seul moyen de s'y opposer est un droit des gens fondé sur des lois publiques accompagnées par la force auxquelles il faudrait que chaque État se soumette (par analogie avec un droit civil ou politique régissant les particuliers).» Voir «Du rapport entre la théorie et la pratique dans le droit des gens. Considéré d'un point de vue universellement philanthropique, c'est-à-dire cosmopolitique (contre Moses Mendelssohn)», *Théorie et pratique*, p. 92.

7. C. Koné, «Repenser l'action des sciences sociales», L'action des sciences sociales en question, *Repères*, Année 2000, N°1, pp. 95–101.

8. Les USA, dirigés par le président Georges W. Bush, ne montrent pas toujours leur disponibilité à réaliser le consensus avec les autres pays sur les questions politiques, commerciales et environnementales. Ils paraissent obnubilés par leurs intérêts égoïstes. Mais l'unilatéralisme de l'Union Européenne qui tente d'imposer aux États africains les APE (Accords Afrique, Pacifique, Union Européenne) est tout aussi critiquable car pareille vision renforce l'éclatement du monde et ne favorise pas le rapprochement des êtres humains.

9. Voir L. S. Senghor, «Ce que l'homme noir apporte», *L'homme de couleur* (Paris: Plon/Présence Africaine, 1939); et *L'esprit de la civilisation ou les lois de la culture négro-africaine* (Paris: Présence africaine, 1956).

10. E. Kant, «Idée d'une histoire universelle au point de vue cosmopolitique», pp. 79–80.

11. Ibid.

12. Alain Badiou (1997, p. 10) écrit en effet dans: «À l'heure de la circulation généralisée et du fantasme de la communication culturelle instantanée, on multiplie partout les lois et règlements pour interdire la circulation des personnes. C'est ainsi qu'en France, il n'y a pas eu aussi peu d'installation d'étrangers que dans la dernière période! Libre circulation de ce qui se laisse compter, oui, et d'abord des capitaux, de ce qui est le compte du compte. Libre circulation de l'incomptable infinité qu'est une vie humaine singulière, jamais!»

13. Kant, *Vers la paix perpétuelle. Que signifie s'orienter dans la pensée? Qu'est-ce que les Lumières*, p. 93.

14. Kant, «Doctrine du droit», pp. 179–180.

15. Kant, «Du rapport entre la théorie et la pratique dans le droit des gens. Considéré d'un point de vue universellement philanthropique, c'est-à-dire cosmopolitique (contre Moses Mendelssohn)», p. 90.

16. Kant, «Idée d'une histoire universelle au point de vue cosmopolitique», p. 76.

17. Kant, *Opuscules sur l'histoire*, p. 79.

18. Kant, *Vers la paix perpétuelle. Que signifie s'orienter dans la pensée? Qu'est-ce que les Lumières*, p. 91.

19. Kant, «Du rapport entre la théorie et la pratique dans le droit des gens. Considéré d'un point de vue universellement philanthropique, c'est-à-dire cosmopolitique (contre Moses Mendelssohn)», p. 179.

20. Kant, *Opuscules sur l'histoire*, pp. 76–77.

BIBLIOGRAPHIE

Badiou, A. 1997. *Saint Paul La fondation de l'universalisme*. Paris: PUF.

Balibar, E. 2001. *Nous, citoyens d'Europe? Les frontières, l'État, le peuple*. Paris: La Découverte.

Bayart, J. F. 1996. *L'illusion identitaire*. Paris: Fayard.

Bourdieu, P. 1998a. *Contre-feux Propos pour servir à la résistance contre l'invasion néo-libérale*. Paris: Raisons d'agir.

———. 1998b. «L'essence du néolibéralisme». *Le Monde diplomatique* (March 1998).

Defarges, P. M. 2001. *La mondialisation*. Paris: PUF/ «Que sais-je?» N° 1687.

Diouf, M. 2002. *L'Afrique dans la mondialisation*. Paris: L'Harmattan.

Forrester, V. 1996. *L'horreur économique*. Paris: Fayard.

Frémeaux, P. 1998. *Sortir du piège. La gauche face à la mondialisation*. Paris: Éditions La Découverte et Syros.

Habermas, J. 1995. *La paix perpétuelle. Le bicentenaire d'une idée kantienne*. Paris: Cerf.

Hardt, M., et A. Negri. 2004: *Multitude. Guerre et démocratie à l'âge de l'empire*. Paris: La Découverte.

Kant, E. 1990. «Idée d'une histoire universelle au point de vue cosmopolitique». *Opuscules sur l'histoire*. Présentation par Philippe Raynaud, traduction par Stéphane Piobetta. Paris: GF-Flammarion.

———. 1991. «2e article définitif en vue de la paix perpétuelle. Le droit des gens doit être fondé sur un fédéralisme d'États libres». *Vers la paix perpétuelle. Que signifie s'orienter dans la pensée? Qu'est-ce que les Lumières?* Présentation par Françoise Proust, traduction par Jean-François Poirier et Françoise Proust. Paris: GF-Flammarion.

———. 1994a. «Doctrine du droit», Deuxième partie, deuxième section, *Métaphysique des mœurs* II. Traduction, présentation, bibliographie et chronologie par Alain Renault. Paris: GF-Flammarion.

———. 1994b. «Du rapport entre la théorie et la pratique dans le droit des gens. Considéré d'un point de vue universellement philanthropique, c'est-à-dire cosmopolitique (contre Moses Mendelssohn)». *Théorie et pratique. D'un prétendu droit de mentir par humanité. La fin de toutes choses*. Introduction, traduction, notes, bibliographie et chronologie par Françoise Proust. Paris: GF-Flammarion.

Ki-Zerbo, J. 2003. *À quand l'Afrique? Entretien avec René Holenstein*. Paris/Ouagadougou: Éditions de l'Aube/ Éditions d'en bas.

Koné, C. 2007. «Mondialisation et idéologie». *Cahiers du CERLESHS*, N° 28.

Lafay, G. 1999. *Comprendre la mondialisation*. Paris: Économica.

Maalouf, A. 2001. *Les identités meurtrières*. Paris: Le Livre de Poche.

Manière de voir 32: *Scénarios de la mondialisation*. 1996, Novembre.

Manière de voir 41: *Un autre monde est possible*. 1998, Sept.–Oct.

Ndaywel E Nziem, I., et J. Kilanga Musinde. 2005. *Mondialisation, cultures et développement*. Paris: Maisonneuve & Larose.

Philosophie politique et horizon cosmopolitique. N° 10. Journée de la philosophie à l'UNESCO 2004. Paris: UNESCO 2006.

Pisani, E. 1996. «Tous contre la mondialisation». *Le Monde diplomatique* (Janvier).

Rancière, J. 2005. *La haine de la démocratie*. Paris: La fabrique éditions.

Rue Descartes, 2002. *L'Étranger dans la mondialité*. N° 37. Paris: PUF.

Samb, D. 1999. «Civisme, communication et mondialisation». *Comprendre Abdou Diouf*. Dakar: Horizon 2000.

———. 2002. «Mondialisation et rencontre des cultures: le dialogue est-il possible?». *Mondialisation et rencontre des cultures: le dialogue est-il possible?* Actes du Colloque du 21 juin 2002. Saint-Louis: Éditions Xamal.

Stiglitz, E. J. 2002. *La grande désillusion*. Paris: Fayard.

———. 2003. *Quand le capitalisme perd tête*. Paris: Fayard.

Tassin, E. 2003. *Un monde commun. Pour une cosmopolitique des conflits*. Paris: Seuil.

SELECTED PAPERS FROM
THE XXII WORLD CONGRESS OF PHILOSOPHY

Globalization and Cosmopolitanism: Claims, Attitudes, and Experiences of Friendship

PETER MCCORMICK
INSTITUT INTERNATIONAL DE PHILOSOPHIE (PARIS)
FELLOW OF THE ROYAL SOCIETY OF CANADA

Abstract: This paper focuses on four brief points only: first, the general character of today's understandings of globalization; then, one substantive danger that arises from this general understanding of globalization; third, by contrast, the universal character of just one of the most important traditional understandings of cosmopolitanism; and, finally, on what might bring together a certain globalization and a certain cosmopolitanism into something more than either just a so-called European or African "anthropocentric ethics." The key conceptual resource highlighted is that of friendship.

My suggestion here will be that many understandings of today's globalization give rise to at least one major problem. And I would also like to suggest that what might help solve that problem is focusing fresh philosophical attention on a cardinal conceptual innovation in yesterday's cosmopolitanism.

Such help would be important. For, as Korea's Ban Ki-moon, the United Nations Secretary General, observed in his speech, "The Bonds that Unite Us," on the eve of the G8 summit just weeks ago in early July 2008 at Lake Toyako in Japan's Hokkaido, we must recognize that today's radically new problems are global and require global solutions.[1] But among these problems might also figure a still insufficiently critical understanding of what today's globalization itself is. My suggestion will be that a still almost forgotten understanding of cosmopolitanism yesterday may help us articulate a less unsatisfactory notion of globalization today. The bonds that unite us, I believe, are not so much Ban Ki-moon's global concerns; they are our own ancient cosmopolitan natures as human beings.

Special Supplement, *Journal of Philosophical Research* pp. 251–261
DOI: 10.5840/jpr201237Supplement42

By way of introduction, here are several usage stipulations about how I will be using in what follows our key terms, 'globalization' and 'cosmopolitanism.'

In what we may call "Oxford English," that is, in contemporary British usage of English as recorded in the most recent Oxford dictionaries,[2] "globalization" is a relatively recent English word. This is also the case for its equivalents in other languages. In common English usage, the word "globalization" goes back no farther than to the mid-twentieth century.[3] And, today, the word "globalization" refers to "the action of globalizing" in the sense of doing something whose scope encompasses the whole world. Thus, the emphasis of the English word "globalization" falls heavily on generalization.

By contrast, in Oxford English "cosmopolitanism" is a relatively older word. Its common English uses go back to the mid-seventeenth century. Today, the word "cosmopolitanism" generally refers to a quality some persons and groups may have. Some dictionaries call this quality "being at home." That is, some are at home not just in their countries of origin but almost anywhere in the world. Such persons or groups are understood as no longer confining themselves to all the attachments of their countries of birth. Here the emphasis falls more on universality rather than on generality.[4]

When viewed from the perspective then of common Oxford English usage today, a philosophical seminar entitled "Globalization and Cosmopolitanism" might seem to be about inviting renewed philosophical reflection not just on some everyday particular matters like the world-wide spread of information, communication, and financial technology. Rather, the title of such a seminar might suggest a focus on two rather abstract matters, on, say, generality and universality. And indeed our colleagues in this seminar have mainly pursued the general and the universal.[5]

With these initial remarks in mind, let me now reflect with you briefly on four brief points only: first, the general character of today's understandings of globalization; then, one substantive danger that arises from this general understanding of globalization; third, by contrast, the universal character of just one of yesterday's understandings of cosmopolitanism; and, finally, on what might bring together a certain globalization and a certain cosmopolitanism into something more than either just a so-called European or African "anthropocentric ethics"[6] or just a so-called East Asian "eco-centric ethics."[7]

1. TODAY'S GLOBALIZATION AS THE GENERALIZATION OF SYSTEMATIC COGNITIVE KNOW-HOW

We are already aware of course that globalization is not one thing. For in addition to the spread of the sciences and technologies across the entire world, other important areas of human activity have also become increasingly uniform on a global scale. This has been especially the case in the course of the last several generations.

Thus, some cultural activities are now to be found almost everywhere, such as the dominance of certain forms of popular Western music. Similarly, certain industrial practices are also now to be found almost anywhere, such as the dominance of East Asian just-in-time manufacturing and ware-housing techniques. Still another example of globalization can be found in the accounting practices of the World Trade Organization which now uses widely harmonized methods for primary, secondary, and tertiary goods and services. So, far from being just one thing, globalization includes different scientific, technological, financial, industrial, political, and cultural forms—to give a partial list only.

Moreover, globalization in this sense of the world-wide generalization of certain human practices has occurred many times in human history and not just within the limits of our own daily experiences and memories today.

To take but one example, recall that at the end of the nineteenth century and up until the outbreak of the twentieth-century's ominously entitled First *World* War, the industrial revolution had already spread—at least in theory—across the entire world. This movement has been called the first modern globalization. That is, countries around the world were already beginning to profit everywhere from the application of efficient manufacturing practices that previously had been confined to one part of the world only. Contemporary world historians point to many other examples in the ancient, the medieval, and modern eras across the globe, such as the spread of Alexander the Great's Hellenistic culture across the ancient world, or, in the medieval period, the spread of Chinese maritime trade, and so on.

Many world historians would even appear to have reached provisional consensus on at least two aspects of globalization. Thus, many historians today seem largely to agree, first, that the most important period of extensive and truly pervasive globalization is the present era. And they also seem largely to agree, second, that the most salient kind of globalization is the globalization of today's science and technology. In this second respect we may speak of globalization in Imamichi Tomonobu's felicitous terms as "the technological conjuncture," that is, as the now historically most important era of the global interconnectedness of informational and communicational technologies.

If globalization today is neither uniform in kind nor unique in number, can we briefly specify globalization further in terms of several of its most striking properties? Recall for now several elements only from just one of many such contemporary analytic attempts to do so.

Thus, we might reasonably characterize globalization thematically as a set of at least six theoretical features we need not take here in any certain order.[8] That is, at the worldwide level globalization would seem to exhibit the systematization and generalization first of economic realities, then of social relationships, and third of political unions. And, similarly at the world wide level, globalization would also seem to exhibit, fourth, the generalized contraction of diversity, fifth the collapse of various dichotomies between the particular and the universal, and finally a generalized mixture of trust and risk. Very schematic characterizations like these of course call for careful qualifications. Nonetheless, something like this recent thematic characterization of globalization is highly representative of contemporary expert opinion.

If we now go on to reflect on the current working consensus among historians and theorists of globalization, perhaps we can discern at last one very prominent and perhaps even fundamental feature of globalization today. May I suggest that such a feature might not unreasonably be taken in summary as globalization's essential tendency today to generalize at the world level that particular kind of practical knowledge English speakers call "know-how"—the specific cognitive mix of imaginative power and technical expertise? For our present purposes then, we might take globalization here as the planetary generalization of systematized practical know-how. Perhaps we may call the generalization of this kind of knowledge "cultural globalization."

2. A PROBLEM WITH TODAY'S GLOBALIZATION AS THE COGNITIVE GENERALIZATION OF MAINLY TECHNICAL KNOW-HOW

I come now to a second point, an important problem with today's generalized understanding of globalization as mainly cultural globalization in the sense of the generalization of knowledge understood as mainly technical know-how.

The difficulty is that this insufficiently critical understanding of globalization all too often results in devastating cultural consequences. Among these consequences, I think, are often the rather thoughtless Western criticisms of most Asian so-called "ecocentric" ethical reflections, of so-called "Asian values" and of the absolute primacy of the value and worth of nature. And, conversely, among these negative consequences also are the often rather thoughtless Asian criticisms of most European and African so-called "anthropocentric" ethical reflections, of so called "humanistic values" and of the absolute primacy of human beings.

But perhaps the most important negative consequence of the overly narrow yet dominant understandings of globalization today in terms mainly of cultural globalization is the gradual subjection of the entire planet to a generalized and largely uncritical notion of knowledge and understanding.

This notion is the idea of knowledge and understanding as pre-eminently systematized practical know-how, as contrasted with the idea of knowledge and understanding as also an always incomplete approximation to less inadequate knowledge of oneself and of others.[9] This subjection of the reflective pursuits of genuine self-knowledge—artistic, philosophical, and spiritual—in turn leads inexorably to the instrumentalization of nature itself, including human nature, whether in the smoggy skies today above Beijing or in the smouldering forests of Borneo or in the depleted fisheries of the Mediterranean or in the now virtually completed hyper-development of the Italian, French and Spanish coastlines.

This quite serious problem, however, may also be taken as including in part some elements for a serious solution. For the very cultural *imperium* today that has globalized an overly practical interpretation of knowledge and understanding as systematized cognitive know-how conceals within its origins a still fruitful philosophical view. That view is an understanding of a reflective cosmopolitanism in terms of a stable yet dynamic equilibrium between fundamental self-directed and other-directed primary impulses at the centre of human nature itself.

Besides the generalization of systematized practical know-how, then, globalization now needs to incorporate a certain critical cosmopolitanism. Such a critical cosmopolitanism would be a universal and not just general consciousness of human nature as so constituted that both natural self-interest and natural affinity with others and with all living beings are equally primordial for all human beings.

But on such a view of globalization and cosmopolitanism, neither human nature's instrumentalization of nature as a whole, nor the deification of cosmic nature as a whole, is finally satisfactory. The simple truth we already recognize everywhere is that neither human kind nor nature is divine. Neither an anthropocentric ethics nor an ecocentric ethics can finally satisfy us. The differences are too profound.

To begin to appreciate how profound, imagine for just a moment another one of those tiresome so-called "dialogues" between still another European sometime political leader visiting East Asia and trying to suggest all too politely to his East Asian host that the continuing violation of human rights in his country is ethically unacceptable everywhere. And imagine a similarly tiresome dialogue between still another sometime East Asian political leader visiting Europe and insisting just as overly politely to his European host that the continuing violation of the natural environment in his country is ethically unacceptable everywhere.

In Europe, the European leader could well respond to his East Asian guest's criticism by questioning the absolute primacy many East Asians seem to place on the value of nature in the light of the finally more important priority human beings have of needing reasonably to use nature for their legitimate development. And in Asia, the East Asian leader could well respond to his European guest's criticism by questioning the absolute primacy many Europeans seem to place on human rights in the light of the fundamentally more important priority over human rights for any truly humane government to guarantee natural communal harmony. The basic difficulty is how to mediate thoughtfully enough the quite fundamental differences here in such a way as to preserve the genuine insights of each quite basic worldview while finding a mutually acceptable way of reconciling their incompatibilities.

We must be careful not to underestimate the profound nature of differences like these, differences between which of two primary values is taken as finally absolute in the sense of being primordial. For behind such fundamental differences between nature as absolute value versus human beings as absolute value lie still more fundamental cultural presuppositions. Such presuppositions subsist not just at the level of countries nor of languages nor of religions, but at the level even of entire civilizations where greatly different comprehensive worldviews have held sway for many centuries.

Thus, for many European philosophers today, often marked beyond their conscious realizations by their Hebrew, Greek, Roman, and Christian heritages, who might argue the absolute priority of human beings over that of nature itself, one profound assumption is necessarily the presupposition of meaningfulness and, still more deeply, of reason in its guise of Greek *logos.*[10] By contrast, for many East Asian philosophers today, often marked equally beyond their full comprehension by a Buddhist heritage in whatever its Indian, Chinese, Tibetan, Korean, or Japanese lineages, who might urge the absolute priority of nature over human beings, one profound assumption would be the presupposition of action and, even more deeply, of suffering in its guise of Sanskrit *dukkha.*[11] How could any clear-headed European philosopher argue out of the fundamental cultural presuppositions of a universal cosmic reason in any finally mutually satisfactory way with any right-minded East Asian thinker reflecting out of the fundamental cultural presuppositions of a universal cosmic suffering?

For an all-too-partial response, if not a solution to this difficulty with today's overly narrow construals of globalization, may I direct our attention briefly to several elements from one of yesterday's reflective cosmopolitanisms?

3. YESTERDAY'S REFLECTIVE COSMOPOLITANISM AND THE CONSCIOUSNESS OF UNIVERSAL AFFINITIES

If we might agree tentatively, then, on taking the problematic nature of today's globalization as mainly the planetary generalization of systematized practical know-how only, just how are we not unreasonably to understand further the sense and significance here of "cosmopolitanism?"

Like globalization, cosmopolitanism is neither uniform nor unique. That is, cosmopolitanism is neither essentially any one thing nor has it historically appeared at only one time. Rather, I think that, on similar kinds of historical and thematic investigations that we just rehearsed with respect to globalization, cosmopolitanism is also more than one thing and has also appeared historically more than once. This is especially the case for what we might call generally a reflective or philosophical cosmopolitanism. And it is particularly for at least one cardinal conceptual feature of ancient Western Stoic cosmopolitanism.

In short, I would now like to follow up on Alexander Chumakov's evocation in our Round Table of the ancient Greek Stoics. And I would like to suggest that a cardinal conceptual element on exhibit in, specifically, late Stoic cosmopolitanism in one of the major originating moments of Hebrew, Greek, Roman, and Christian Europe may still prove fruitful even today in other parts of the world. For this Stoic notion in yesterday's cosmopolitanism may offer an important conceptual resource for reconfiguring less unsatisfactorally the generally one-sided and insufficiently critical understandings of today's globalization.

That almost forgotten conceptual feature was what later Greek and early Roman Stoics termed, with a now barely translatable expression, *oikeiôsis* or *oikeiôusthai.* Very roughly in English, the noun form, *oikeiôsis*, means something close to "orientation," or "appropriation," or "affiliation," or "the recognition of something as belonging to one[self]." And in its more frequent occurrences in its verbal form as *oikeiôusthai*, *oikeiôsis* means, again very roughly, something like "coming to be (or being made to be) well-disposed towards something."[12]

Stoic philosophers began their reflections with a shared conviction that the nature of human beings was part and parcel of the nature of the universe.[13] Accordingly, cosmic nature and human nature, although evidently quite different in scale and in many other respects, are, on Stoic views, unified in the ways in which the whole is unified with its parts. Stoic thinkers investigated cosmic nature mainly in the contexts of their logic and physics. And they investigated human nature mainly in the related contexts of their logic and their ethics.

In particular, many Stoic thinkers believed that they could most reliably investigate human nature by beginning empirically with careful observations of the newly born human being, and then by confronting their own observations argumentatively with those that eminent non-Stoic thinkers had also made of newborns. Thus, sets of fundamental observations were to be opposed and their oppositions resolved wherever possible through reasoning.

In particular, some Epicureans believed that observations of the newborn human being show that it naturally and above all primarily and originally endowed with a basic inclination towards pleasure. By contrast, some Stoic thinkers held that the most basic, original, natural, and primary impulse of the newly born human being (just as with newborn animals and newly burgeoning plants) was not towards pleasure but towards self-preservation.

These Stoic thinkers held, further, that in all cases this primary impulse was directed to the way the human being, animal, or plant is so-to-speak "constituted." This constitution while remaining generally fixed nonetheless changes with time. In the specific case of the human being, the generally stable character of one's constitution is the natural basis for one's ego-centric dimension, the self-regarding pole. And the particular evolving character of one's constitution is the natural basis for one's "allo-centric" dimension, the other-regarding pole.

Thus, on many late Stoic accounts, a human being retains a fundamental affiliation with its own natural constitution, with itself. Yet as its natural constitution develops, a human being also develops a consciousness of a just as natural fundamental affinity with others. That is, a human being has a natural affiliation both with himself or herself and with all other human beings as well.[14]

In short, late Stoic teachings on *oikeiôsis* comprise a set of carefully argued both empirical and philosophical views. On these views, all human beings are naturally endowed with a stable and yet dynamic natural constitution. All human beings bear an inalienable affinity to their natural constitutions which their primary impulse is to preserve. And they also bear a natural affinity to all other human beings in that all other human beings have exactly the same natural constitutions. This human nature of all human beings strongly impels human beings to appropriate consciously and reflectively their double affinity, both to themselves as singular individuals and to all other human beings a well, by leading thoughtful, reasoned, and virtuous lives in the interest, one may say with Cyrille Koné in our Round Table, of promoting a new solidarity.

So much then for several brief reminders about one of yesterday's reflective cosmopolitanisms, a truly critical cosmopolitanism refined in both continuing empirical inquiry and in continuing philosophical argument, an almost forgotten resource today for thinking second thoughts about the nature of globalization.

4. CLAIMS, ATTITUDES, AND PHILOSOPHICAL FRIENDSHIPS

I would now like to conclude with a fourth and final remark about mediating profoundly opposed philosophical attitudes such as those often underlying some of today's most intractable ethical disputes about absolute values. This final point can be no more than a speculative proposal. Such a proposal arises not from further reflection on the uncritical globalization of systematized practical know-how. Rather, the proposal comes from trying to retrieve the old ideal, remarkably present in both traditional East Asian as well as in traditional European reflective cultures, of pursuing the virtues of cosmopolitan philosophical friendships. Please allow me to offer you this concluding suggestion not in the typical European form of an extended philosophical argument such as those between Greek Epicureans and late Roman Stoics, but in the looser and larger form of a brief personal reminiscence.

Thus, the bare fact is that in concluding I have no theories to urge on you as to how finally to mediate today such profound differences as those that hold between contrasting basic cultural presuppositions. However, like so many others of us both in Asia and in Europe, I do have several exemplary teachers whom I often remember. And, again like so many others, I also have the experiences of philosophical friendship to reflect on. I would like then to draw on those experiences now in an informal way to bring some of these perhaps overly abstract reflections a little more down to earth. And I would also would hope to remind some of you here today of presumably very similar experiences which perhaps you have had yourselves.

With deep gratitude I often remember a most demanding teacher. He was at home in the bi-lingual, multi-religious Alsatian culture of France, my maternal grandmother's culture, but almost everywhere else as well. He had not just generalized but universalized certain reflective views about the proper appropriations of true self-knowledge in the ongoing recognition of one's true affinity with others—"*soi-même comme un autre*" he would say. And in speaking of the profound reflections of the truly great philosophers, he also often said,

> Do not keep looking for mistakes. Even in the finest works of the finest philosophers there are always far too many mistakes. Rather look always for what is good in these thinkers. And then strive over and over again to re-articulate that good ever less unsatisfactorily.

After some years working together yet always independently, we became friends, philosophical friends.

And with deep gratitude I also remember a most challenging colleague. He was at home in the culture of Japan, the culture of my father's mortal enemies, but almost everywhere else too. For like my French philosophical friend, he too had not just generalized but universalized certain reflective practices, especially those arising from the relationships between *jiriki* and *hariki*, between self-power and other-power. While discussing with each other the successes and failures of different philosophical attempts to articulate the good, he often would stop and then say nothing. He simply sat there, and he sat there silently. Like many Western persons I was both increasingly disquieted by this behaviour and yet unwilling to risk offence by breaking such silences. And after awhile my colleague would start talking again. Then, the pauses became longer. Eventually, I was less disquieted with his now protracted silences. And after some years meeting together, we became friends, philosophical friends.

In the case of my European philosophical friend, speaking together as long as possible both in his own language, French, and in my language, English, while trying to articulate what is good, was at the very basis of this friendship. Putting together less unsatisfactory words in the order of reasons enabled us, I believe, to open ourselves out sometimes onto fresh philosophical reflections which we now shared in a feeling of profound respect, gratitude, and freedom. And, in striving to articulate what is good, I also believe we came to realize more fully a fundamental affinity between perhaps some small goodness in ourselves and finally one that subsists in ever human being. Thanks to my friend, I sometimes think perhaps mistakenly, I am now a little more like him, a little more at home almost anywhere, at least for awhile.

In the case of my East Asian philosophical friend, however, I discovered that trying together to articulate what is good was not a matter of speaking for as long as possible about such dark matters; it was rather a matter of letting certain silences protract themselves. For although he alternated speaking English and German, my friend could not speak his own language with me because I neither understood nor spoke Japanese. We were often silent.

Meditating these initially frustrating silences, however, eventually became the basis of this different philosophical friendship. Letting the silences gather gradually made room, I now believe, for intimations of very much larger contexts which we learned to share. And, in struggling repeatedly to let myself be silent while my friend was silent, I also believe I sometimes succeeded not so much in opening up a set of philosophical claims about what is good that each of us together could reasonable come to endorse. Rather, I came to believe, again perhaps mistakenly, that my friend and I had allowed ourselves to come to recognize perhaps some of those much larger contexts that underwrite no particular set of philosophical claims yet sustain some of our most fundamental philosophical attitudes, the complex contexts of our shared humanity.

These two personal experiences of philosophical friendship—so similar I am sure to what so many here today from both Asia and the West have also experienced—give rise to my concluding suggestion. The suggestion is that exploring the universalization of the reflective cosmopolitanism we find in traditional understandings of philosophical friendship can help counter the often dangerous consequences of most understandings of globalization today only in terms of the generalization of systematic practical know-how. This reflective cosmopolitan attitude that philosophically interiorizes a critical re-appropriation of Stoic doctrines of *oikeiôsis* is part of what makes for true philosophical friendship. And this reflective cosmopolitanism is also what can motivate the striving for a dynamic equilibrium between egocentric self-regard and altruistic concern for others, between self-power and other-power, between a merely anthropocentric ethics and a merely ecocentric ethics.

NOTES

This is the revised version of an invited plenary session symposium paper presented during the XXII World Congress of Philosophy, Seoul National University, South Korea, July 30–August 5, 2008. I thank the Organizers for their invitation and the Plenary Round Table participants, Francis Cheneval (Switzerland), Cyrille B. Koné (Burkina Faso), and Alexander Chumakov (Russian Federation), for their comments. Note that the original paper appeared in Russian translation in the journal *Age of Globalization: Journal of Global Studies* 2, no. 4 (2009): 61–70.

1. Cf. the French version of his speech, "*Ces liens qui nous unissent*," in *Le Figaro*, July 3, 2008.

2. These new dictionaries are all based on the extraordinary resources of the British National Corpus of the English Language database, the Oxford English Corpus database, and the Oxford Reading Programme database.

3. I rely here and throughout on the two-volume *Shorter Oxford English Dictionary*, 6th edition, 2007.

4. More specific nuances may be found notably in *Roget's Thesaurus of English Words and Phrases*, 150th Anniversary Edition, ed. G. Davidson (London: Penguin Reference, 2002).

5. Cf. F. Cheneval's Chairman's remarks about three contemporary uses of "cosmopolitanism" and recent criticisms of cosmopolitanism, C. Koné's paper, "Mondialisation et cosmopolitanisme," and A. Chumakov's paper, "Globalization and Cosmopolitanism in the Context of Modernity."

6. See, for example, Park Ynhui's "Human Nature and Human Worth," in his *Man, Language and Poetry* (Seoul: Seoul National University Press, 1999), p. 41.

7. See, for example, Imamichi Tomonobu's critiques of such merely "eco-eccentric" views and the elaboration of his alternative account of an "eco-ethics" in his influential book, *Eco-Ethica* first published in Japanese in 1990, shortly thereafter translated into Korean by Jung Myong-Hwan, and then recently translated into German by Stefan Döll "(München: Iudicium, 2006), and into English by Judy Wakabayashi (Lanham, MD: University Press of America, 2009).

8. Among many others, see notably M. Waters, *Globalisation*, 2nd ed. (London: Routledge, 2001), pp. 15–16. I owe this reference to Cheikh Mbacké Gueye. See his discussion in his important book, *Late Stoic Cosmopolitanism* (Heidelberg: Universitätsverlag Winter, 2006),

pp. 147–159. Note, however, that my discussion of *oikeiôsis* is independent of his views (cf. notes 12 and 13 below).

9. See, for example, J.-P. Delahaye's paper on undecidability and incompleteness in recent work on Gödel, "Presque tout est indécidable!" *Pour la Science* 375 (January 2009): pp. 88–93.

10. See, for example, the unusual Japanese perspective of Seizô Sekine's *A Comparative Study of the Origins of Ethical Thought: Hellenism and Hebraism*, trans. J. Wakabayashi (Lanham, MD: Rowman and Littlefield, 2005).

11. For example, see the non-Asian American perspective of Glenn Wallis's new compilation, translations, and notes in his *Basic Teachings of the Buddha* (New York: Modern Library, 2007).

12. The first translation is that of B. Inwood in his *Ethics and Human Action in Early Stoicism* (Oxford: Oxford University Press, 1985); the second that of A. A. Long and D. N. Sedley in their standard collection of texts and translations in English, *The Hellenistic Philosophers*, 2 vols. (Cambridge: Cambridge University Press, 1987); the third that of B. Inwood and P. Donini in their comprehensive article, "*Oikeiôsis* and Primary Impulse," in the authoritative *Cambridge History of Hellenistic Philosophy*, ed. K. Algra et al. (Cambridge: Cambridge University Press, 1999), pp. 675–738; and the fourth that of G. Stricker, "The Role of *oikeiôsis* in Stoic Ethics," in her collection, *Essays on Hellenistic Epistemology and Ethics* (Cambridge: Cambridge University Press, 1996), pp. 281–297.

13. In this general summary here I mainly follow Inwood and Donini, "*Oikeiôsis* and Primary Impulse."

14. Note that later Epicureans tried to explain how in friendship our own pleasure is more desirable than our friend's and yet how our own pleasure in friendship cannot be more desirable than our friend's without taking our friend's pleasure fundamentally into account. For experience shows that taking our friends as no more than means to our own pleasure finally subverts the friendship itself. Yet taking our friends as ends in themselves would subvert the basic Epicurean doctrine of the primacy of one's own pleasure. Addressing this problem in Book I of his *De finibus*, Cicero distinguished. He argued (at least on one authoritative reading) that "although our friends' pleasures and wellbeing are not intrinsically as important as our own, we must love them as though they were. And the only way someone can do that is actually to feel the same towards his friend as he does towards himself. . . . Hence the [Epicurean] theory [of friendship] is made to yield to treat friends altruistically" (I.67–68). The ms. text is to be found in *Sent. Vat.* 23. This translation incorporates, however, a strongly supported textual emendation of *airetê* (choice-worthy) for *arête* (virtue). See M. Erler and M. Schofield, "Epicurean Ethics," in *The Cambridge History of Hellenistic Philosophy*, ed. K. Algra et al. (Cambridge: Cambridge University Press, 1999), p. 668, note 61, whose discussion I follow here.

SELECTED PAPERS FROM
THE XXII WORLD CONGRESS OF PHILOSOPHY

Mind the Gap: Introductory Thoughts on Globalization and Cosmopolitanism

FRANCIS CHENEVAL
UNIVERSITY OF ZURICH

Abstract: Globalization stands for systemic integration, mainly economical and technological. It is related to the expansion of the free market economy, trade, and the global integration of systems of communication and information technology. As such, globalization co-exists with strong cultural affirmations of individual and collective difference and with political fragmentation. Cosmopolitanism needs to take into consideration cultural and political conditions of human existence. The cosmopolitan imperative to form a political community beyond the nation state is a process-guiding principle or regulative ideal, not an institutional blueprint. Cosmopolitanism needs to stress the voluntary character of integration among self-governed peoples who are willing to enhance the transnational rights and freedoms of their citizens while accepting institutional constraints.

The topic of this symposium unites two concepts that are of often used and abused in our times and that provoke controversial discussions in philosophical as well as public discourse. Especially "Globalization" has become a "buzzword," a general term to explain a myriad of phenomena in economic, social and political life. "Cosmopolitanism" is an age old concept of philosophy that has known an impressive renaissance in recent decades.

I suppose the organizers of this congress put these concepts together because they seem to be so closely related: Globalization can be conceived as the general economic, social and technological process which liberalizes trade, generalizes economic rationality, promotes world wide communication, and triggers increased migration and interaction. In other words, globalization integrates humanity systemically. Seemingly, many people seem to believe that globalization makes humanity ready for a cosmopolitan structure of government and turns people into citizens of the world before they know it.

Special Supplement, *Journal of Philosophical Research* pp. 263–267
DOI: 10.5840/jpr201237Supplement43

Globalization is to be conceived as a phenomenon of systemic integration, mainly economical and technological. It is related to the expansion of the free market economy, trade, and integration of systems of communication and information technology. It is often presupposed that it leads to cultural homogenization. But this is true only on the systemic-technological level. It does not apply to the levels of culture and politics. Globalization is actually a phenomenon that co-exists with strong cultural affirmations of individual and collective difference and with political fragmentation: in our age of globalization the number of independent sovereign states has increased considerably and continues to do so.

We are thus called upon to reflect on this seemingly paradoxical phenomenon of globalization and fragmentation and its relation to cosmopolitanism. And, the conception of the relation of globalization and cosmopolitanism also depends on the concept of cosmopolitanism which we might want to adopt. Cosmopolitanism is a very rich concept with a history as old as philosophy itself, at least as far as western philosophy is concerned. Without simplifying too much, I think that the contemporary discussion of cosmopolitanism and anti-cosmopolitanism uses three different concepts:

1. Some use the term cosmopolitanism to refer to the imperative of creating a world state or world government, in order to guarantee human rights and to address global challenges such as global security and climate change.
2. Some use the term cosmopolitanism to refer to a Kantian model: ie. cosmopolitanism is a regulative idea to put all human relations under the rule of law and to enforce this law through a cooperative structure of domestic, international and supranational institutions. In this model, no definite political structure such as a world state is explicitly anticipated in a counterfactual manner. Cosmopolitanism is seen as a civilizational process underpinned by political institutions at different levels, but the final nature of these institutions is not determined and should not be determined.
3. Some use the term cosmopolitanism to refer to a strictly moral reality: i.e., a critical concept used to evaluate all worldly political institutions, be they national or global, a concept that considers all human beings as beings of equal value or a concept that puts all positive law under the guidance of morality or an eternal law of nature. In this vein of thought, cosmopolitanism can actually become an anti-political concept, a concept that refers to the *forum internum* of human conscience and establishes a dual concept in which we are always citizens of two polities, the worldly political polity we live in and the universal polity of moral ends.

Critics of cosmopolitanism usually invoke:

1. The essentially local nature of all politics
2. The difference between systems and life worlds, and the fact that politics has as much to do with the historical and hermeneutic condition of people as with the technical realities of systemic integration. There is thus no

necessary link between systemic integration of globalization and the political organization of people.

3. The excessive abstraction of cosmopolitanism's disregard for difference: the cultural world is anything but flat
4. The excessive repression and bureaucracy needed to achieve the finalities of global distributive justice
5. They invoke the fact of democratic peace which contradicts the Hobbesian argument in favor of a world state as the only way to guarantee peace among nations.

Given the complex nature of globalization and given the non-analytical nature of the concept of cosmopolitanism, the thinking of the relation between globalization and cosmopolitanism is a matter that requires a high degree of differentiation and analytical work. This symposium and many of the sessions in our program address this issue which I think is of great importance for the well-being of humanity.

However, critical philosophy has to acknowledge the bounds of reason regarding teleological conceptions of global government as proposed by the first school of cosmopolitanism stated above. The direction the debate on this issue takes depends on how one conceives of such a global political community or global basic structure as the ideal and end point of political development. Given the bounds of reason regarding the *telos* of history, a legal or political community beyond the nation-state ought to be conceived in a constructivist manner respecting existing self-governed peoples. Political units have to form voluntarily and in a process in which every step is based on the ownership of the peoples involved. These points can be argued from two perspectives: the perspective of the individual and the perspective of the self-governed people. On the one hand, a legitimate political and legal construction cannot be conceived uniquely based upon the will of states. Citizens as individuals must be granted institutionally guaranteed voice, participation and exit in any law-enforcing polity. On the other hand, the individualist dimension cannot be taken as the only normative reference of politics beyond the nation state, given that the principle of self-government applies to the collective will of individuals organized as peoples. It is up to people to deliberate, negotiate, and decide at what level they want to constitute a "self" that governs and defends itself. Individuals organized as particular peoples form a realm of justice, and they have the right to preserve self-government as a people. Self-determination is a collective strategy of guaranteeing non-domination. Political justice is ill served if this dimension is totally disregarded in the name of an abstract, context-detached, individualistic cosmopolitan liberal democracy underpinned by globalization. Given the person- *and* people-centred normative foundation of political organization, political constructivism applied to the post-national realm leads to a position which considers the individuals *and* the peoples as normative references.

Furthermore, the constructivist approach presupposes an initial context of peoples engaged in the common realization of rights, freedoms, and life chances for their citizens while seeking to preserve a maximum of self-government and democratic self-determination. Abstract cosmopolitanism thus faces the difficulty that, while advocating the obligation to form a global political community, it has to recognize the peoples as separate realms of self-government. Normative theory for political organization beyond the nation state has to be based on the principle of non-domination of peoples, not just of individual citizens. This is not an argument against political integration of peoples, but it is an argument for the subordination of political integration of peoples to the collective political will of citizens of individual peoples. Above the minimum of human rights and *ius cogens*, peoples have to be given the freedom to engage (or not to engage) in systemic and political integration.

The problem political philosophy has to focus on is thus not the counterfactually assumed validity of an abstract and elusive concept of world republic, but on the conditions of realization of incremental institutionalized cooperation among statespeoples. It has to weigh the intended and unintended consequences of every step of integration without presupposing that the morally justified end of forming a world republic will necessarily justify the means of promoting such an end. If the claim to form a global political community is made concrete without giving attention to the conditions and intermediate consequences of realization, cosmopolitanism turns form a noble ideal into an oppressive practice very easily. The primary goods of politics being peace, security, and freedom, the formation of a global political community has to be contemplated in the light of the normative difficulties any cosmopolitan theory faces regarding the realization of these primary goods. The counterfactual anticipation of an ideal world state offers little to no guidance on how it could be legitimately realized under adverse conditions in which not all states adhere to republican principles and pursue strategies of domination and oppression. This is in fact the essence of Machiavelli's political theory: instead of conceiving the ideal state, political theory ought to determine the conditions of preservation of the republic given the fact of its ever possible "death" due to internal and external threats.[1] One might add to Machiavelli's observations that real threats are as dangerous for the republic as threats stemming from the paranoia about threats. But in any case, given the primacy of the process of realization and preservation of freedom, the counterfactual anticipation of an ideal state of world affairs does not give the normative guidance it pretends to give and it carries a heavy teleological burden of proof. Do we really have a way of knowing whether the world republic is the ideal state of world affairs for all possible worlds and possible futures? If we answer the question in the negative, which we humbly should, a normatively guided political constructivism is the adequate approach to the shaping of an argument on how to institutionalize political cooperation beyond the democratic statespeople. Cosmopolitanism has a place in this design as a regulative ideal containing no more than the abstract idea of the *conctractus originarius* holding that any political arrangement ought to follow the ideal of the coexistence of free and equal individuals and their free associations. Furthermore, if the right to self-government is taken seriously, republicanism has to refrain from any generalization and imposition of culture, lifestyle and political organization on existing collective political "selfs" against the will of their members. The areas in which such an imposition can take place ought to be limited to the most basic human rights and *ius cogens*.

Cosmopolitanism's imperative to form a political community beyond the nation state, i.e., cosmopolitanism as process-guiding principle or regulative ideal, cannot directly be understood as the imperative to the formation of a world republic without a careful normative analysis of the consequence of every step of integration taken along the way. Kant himself pointed out that the anticipation of the ideal of the world republic should not be confused with the normative guidance for gradual integration, and it is certainly not to be taken as a general justification for the aggressive use of force against states, or as an argument against the voluntary character of the integration process among statespeople.

NOTE

1. See Machiavelli, *Discorsi*, III.41, ed. S. Bertelli (Milano: Feltrinelli, 1960), p. 495.

La communauté morale et son extension

JEAN-YVES GOFFI
UNIVERSITÉ PIERRE MENDÈS FRANCE

RÉSUMÉ: On se propose de fédérer les questions relevant de la bioéthique, des générations futures et de l'éthique environnementale autour du thème de la communauté morale. On examinera certains problèmes théoriques posés par l'élargissement de celle-ci. On soutiendra qu'il n'est possible d'y faire face qu'en se ralliant à une forme d'anthropocentrisme. Toutefois, il s'agit d'un anthropocentrisme méta-axiologique, pas d'un anthropocentrisme normatif: il ne saurait être question de soutenir que les intérêts des être humains ont, toujours et partout, priorité sur les intérêts des autres créatures.

Il existe deux façons de définir la bioéthique Au sens étroit, il s'agit de l'éthique biomédicale dans un contexte où la médecine n'est plus seulement une relation de face à face entre un médecin et son patient, mais prend des formes multiples et variées: médecine préventive, médecine palliative, médecine transformatrice, médecine expérimentale, médecine méliorative, etc. Au sens large il s'agit d'une forme prise par l'éthique dans un contexte où les technologies accroissent sans cesse leur emprise sur le vivant. Elle est l'éthique de cette emprise, l'éthique des technologies du vivant, bien sûr, mais, plus généralement, l'éthique de l'interface entre les technologies et le vivant, l'éthique de l'interface entre l'ordre vital et l'ordre technologique.

Selon la première définition, la finalité de la bioéthique est d'élargir ou d'adapter la sagesse immémoriale de la médecine (appelons là, pour faire simple: la sagesse hippocratique) à des situations inédites. Les bioéthiciens qui l'adoptent sont généralement conscients, mais pas toujours, du fait que le caractère radicalement inédit de ces situations les met dans des situations souvent inconfortables. C'est pourquoi les bioconservateurs—dont Leon Kass est le représentant le plus connu—tentent de réduire la médecine à sa seule dimension thérapeutique.

Le caractère inédit des situations induites par les technologies contemporaines est, au contraire, envisagé d'emblée par ceux qui considèrent la seconde définition

Special Supplement, *Journal of Philosophical Research* pp. 269–278
DOI: 10.5840/jpr201237Supplement44

comme plus appropriée: les biotechnologies et (de façon générale) les technologies de l'hyper-modernité ne s'inscrivent pas dans le prolongement des savoirs et des savoir-faire ancestraux (ceux des éleveurs, ceux des cultivateurs ou même ceux des médecins). À des défis absolument nouveaux, il convient d'apporter des réponses absolument nouvelles. Telle est l'intuition qui semble, par exemple, sous-tendre l'ouvrage majeur de Hans Jonas: *Das Prinzip Verantwortung* (1979).

Il me semble que c'est la définition large qui permet, sinon de penser un objet aussi vaste que «Bioéthique, éthique environnementale, générations futures», du moins d'opérer quelques distinctions pertinentes à propos de cet objet. C'est ce que je me propose de faire ici

En un premier temps, je préciserai ce que j'entends par communauté morale et je montrerai que c'est un concept qui agit déjà, de façon plus ou moins inaperçue, dans la tradition de la philosophie morale occidentale. En second lieu, j'indiquerai dans leurs grandes lignes ce que sont les principales reconfigurations contemporaines de la communauté morale et leurs limites. Pour conclure, je dirai en quel sens nous ne pouvons pas échapper à une perspective anthropocentrée et en quel sens nous ne pouvons pas non plus nous en contenter. En cela, nous avons affaire à un programme de recherches en philosophie morale appliquée pour le vingt-et-unième siècle.

Je partirai de ce qui me paraît être la difficulté majeure pour qui adopte, comme je le fais, la seconde des deux définitions que je viens de rappeler: la reconnaissance du caractère inédit de la situation contemporaine s'accompagne, à première vue, d'une absence de précédents, ce qui la rend particulièrement difficile à penser (sauf à croire, naïvement, que l'on peut repenser la philosophie, et d'ailleurs quoi que ce soit, à partir de rien).

Par Exemple L''éthique biomédicale, la bioéthique au sens étroit, s'apparente à l'éthique médicale; mais ce n'est pas la même chose; l'éthique environnementale s'apparente aux philosophies de la nature; mais ce n'est pas la même chose. La question philosophique des générations futures ressemble, en quelque façon, à la philosophie de l'éducation; en quelque façon également, à la philosophie de l'histoire. Mais ce n'est pas, non plus, la même chose.

Donc, par où commencer? J'ai presque envie de m'excuser de rappeler cette banalité, mais la bioéthique est, comme son nom l'indique, une partie ou un branche de l'éthique. Ce rappel élémentaire pourra fournir le point de départ recherché:

Je définirai l'éthique (sans distinguer ici ce terme de celui de «morale») comme le fait, pour un agent moral, d'admettre des restrictions normatives directes pesant sur son agir. J'oppose des restrictions de ce type aux restrictions prudentielles, visant, par exemple, la seule autoconservation de l'agent, ou la seule promotion de ses intérêts. L'admission de ces restrictions se traduit concrètement par la reconnaissance d'interdictions et d'obligations. Je laisse de côté, pour l'instant, la question de déterminer ce qui les justifie. La question se pose également de savoir aussi si l'agir dans sa totalité est concerné par de telles restrictions, autrement dit, de savoir s'il existe des actes éthiquement neutres et donc simplement permis. La réponse de bon sens et qui fait l'objet d'une sorte de consensus chez les philosophes, c'est qu'il existe, en effet, de tels actes.

On pourra donc définir la communauté morale, sous sa forme la plus générale comme la classe des êtres envers lesquels les agents moraux se reconnaissent des obligations directes, ou des devoirs directs. Les obligations directes—ou les devoirs directs—peuvent être caractérisés comme ceux qui sont corrélés à des droits-titres—peu importe qu'il s'agisse de droits conférés par la nature ou bien de droits résultants d'une convention. Par exemple, X a une obligation directe d'accomplir l'action Φ si et seulement si il existe un Y qui peut faire valoir un droit-titre dont le contenu est que X accomplisse l'action Φ (il n'est pas nécessaire que Y fasse valoir ce droit par lui-même: Y peut être représenté). Le point crucial est alors le suivant: les systèmes éthiques qui mettent l'accent sur l'autonomie du sujet (comme, par exemple, l'éthique d'inspiration kantienne ou certaines formes de contractualisme) ont tendance à identifier la communauté morale et l'ensemble des agents moraux. Leur formule d'inclusion dans la communauté morale est alors la suivante:

X fait partie de la communauté morale si et seulement si X est un agent moral.

Cela pose toutes sortes de problèmes, au premier rang desquels la question très discutée des devoirs envers soi-même. Mais d'abord, que faut-il entendre par agent moral? Les agents moraux sont, typiquement, les êtres capables de faire valoir leurs droits-titres dans un espace particulier, typiquement l'espace juridico-politique ou l'espace éthique, ce qui suppose de leur part un certain nombre de compétences, diversement décrites: rationalité, autonomie, aptitude à se fixer des buts, à organiser son existence en fonction de valeurs, à entretenir l'estime de soi, à instaurer une relation dialogique avec d'autres agents moraux, etc.

Ceci étant, d'un point de vue conceptuel, il n'est pas du tout nécessaire que la communauté morale se compose des seuls agents moraux. En d'autres termes, il n'est pas nécessaire que la classe des agents moraux soit extensionnellement équivalente à la classe des membres de la communauté morale. Il est, par exemple, possible de considérer que la communauté morale est plus étroite que la classe des agents moraux. En général, ce genre de considération a été lié à des entreprises d'exclusion ou de discrimination: elles ont visé à séparer de la communauté morale des membres qui appartenaient en réalité de façon plénière à celle-ci (les motifs invoqués ont été le plus souvent liés au sexe, à la race ou au statut social). Je laisserai de côté ces tentatives. On peut considérer également que la communauté morale est plus large que la classe des agents moraux. Pour prendre un exemple évident, c'est bien ce que font les contractualistes et les kantiens, même les plus orthodoxes (et en tout cas c'est ce que fait Kant lui-même) lorsqu'ils réfléchissent à l'éducation des enfants (et, de façon générale, au statut éthique de l'enfant). C'est d'ailleurs, et il est heureux qu'il en soit ainsi, un fait qui n'a rien à voir avec la réflexion philosophique. Nous attribuons spontanément des droits moraux ou juridiques à des êtres humains qui ne sont pas ou plus des agents moraux: nouveaux-nés, blessés ou malades dans le coma, déments, etc. Cela revient à dire que nous acceptons spontanément la distinction (due à Tom Regan) entre «agents moraux» et «patients moraux».

Maintenant, qu'il y ait des obligations directes envers les membres pléniers de la communauté morale n'implique pas qu'il n'y ait aucunes obligations envers les êtres qui n'appartiennent pas à cette communauté. Simplement, elles seront des obligations indirectes: cela ne signifie pas, comme on a tendance à le penser, qu'elles sont nécessairement moins contraignantes. Cela signifie qu'elles sont une fonction des obligations directes légitimement reconnues et qu'elles ne tiennent que par elles. Par exemple, si j'ai une obligation directe de ne pas causer de dommage à autrui, il s'ensuit que j'ai une obligation indirecte de ne pas endommager les biens dont il est propriétaire. Mais je n'ai pas pour autant d'obligations envers ces biens qui n'ont pas de droits-titres à faire valoir.

Au total, si on prend en compte la perspective que je viens d'esquisser (c'est-à-dire si l'on admet qu'il est possible de poser les questions éthiques en termes d'appartenance à la communauté morale) on s'aperçoit du même coup qu'il existe un grand nombre de précédents. J'en donnerai trois exemples, concernant la question des générations futures.

Aristote (*Éthique à Nicomaque*, 1097 b 7–14) se demande comment il faut comprendre l'autosuffisance du bien parfait. Sa réponse est bien connue: c'est non seulement ce qui suffirait à un individu menant une vie solitaire, mais également à ses enfants, à sa femme, à ses amis et à ses concitoyens en général. Cependant, le Stagirite refuse explicitement d'étendre cette énumération aux grands-parents, aux descendants et aux amis d'amis, au motif que l'on devrait alors aller à l'infini. Ce qui justifie l'élargissement de la communauté morale, c'est la politicité de l'être humain; ce qui justifie le caractère limité de cet élargissement, c'est le refus typiquement grec de l'illimité.

L'épicurien Diogène d'Oenoanda (fr. 3) raisonne de façon assez différente. Il considère que l'enseignement qu'il se prépare à (faire) graver dans la pierre consiste à rendre publics les remèdes du salut. Et il ajoute que doivent en bénéficier aussi ceux qui ne sont pas encore nés, car ils sont des nôtres. Il justifie l'élargissement de la communauté morale aux générations futures par une analogie: ceux qui ne sont pas encore nés sont comparables aux étrangers qui vivent chez nous, auxquels s'applique une exigence générale de philanthropie. Il est d'ailleurs remarquable que l'élargissement de la communauté morale ne comporte, en droit, pas de limites. Pour un instant quelconque donné, le nombre d'étrangers domiciliés doit être limité (autrement la distinction entre nous et ceux qui vivent chez nous n'aurait plus lieu d'être). Mais le nombre de ceux qui ne sont pas encore nés est, en principe, illimité; quant au bien que la philanthropie nous commande de leur transmettre, il est, par sa nature inépuisable (puisqu'il s'agit de la vérité).

Cicéron (*De Finibus*, III, 19, 64) voulant exposer la doctrine des stoïciens, explique que le monde est la résidence commune des dieux et des hommes, la cité dont chacun constitue une partie. Or, c'est un devoir civique que de faire passer l'intérêt de la cité avant son intérêt personnel. D'où il suit que les générations qui doivent nous succéder méritent que nous nous intéressions à elles et pour elles-mêmes. En effet, là encore une analogie commande l'élargissement de la communauté morale (et les limites de cet élargissement). Comme les bons citoyens doivent s'intéresser à la formation civique de ceux qui assureront la pérennité de la cité, de mêmes les êtres humains comme tels doivent s'intéresser, s'ils veulent être tenus pour bons, au sort de ceux qui prendront un jour leur place sur terre.

On sait bien que la question des générations futures est devenue, à l'heure actuelle, la question de la justice intergénérationnelle: le débat concerne la répartition des charges et des bénéfices à travers le temps. Nécessairement, cette question est devenue très technique: quand, par exemple, on essaie de mesurer la préférence pour le présent qu'exprime le choix des taux d'actualisation c'est, de toute évidence, une question qui ne concerne plus la seule spéculation philosophique. Mais, puisque l'on est dans le contexte de la bioéthique, au sens large, on parle «seulement» de l'élargissement de la communauté morale aux vivants comme tels. La pensée contemporaine est riche en tentatives allant en ce sens.

On peut mentionner, par exemple, les pensées dites «pathocentrées», comme celles de Peter Singer. Ce dernier définit, en première analyse, la communauté morale comme celle dont les membres acceptent certains principes ou droits moraux fondamentaux comme règles de conduite gouvernant leur relations mutuelles, règles de conduite susceptibles d'être imposées par le droit. La question se pose de savoir si cette communauté morale se limite à ceux de ses membres qui sont conscients de ces principes. Comme on sait, Peter Singer va répondre par la négative, et ce pour plusieurs raisons qui tiennent à la théorie éthique à laquelle il adhère (à savoir une forme de conséquentialisme).

Parce qu'il est conséquentialiste, il pense que la correction morale d'un acte (ou d'un type d'acte) ne tient pas à la nature de celui-ci, mais à ses conséquences. Parce qu'il considère que l'exigence d'impartialité est non seulement indissociable de la posture morale, mais encore constitutif de celle-ci, il estime qu'un agent authentiquement moral doit prendre également en compte tous ceux qui seront affectés par les conséquences de ses actes. Parce qu'il refuse une conception volontariste des droits moraux, il pense que l'agent moral doit prendre également en compte les intérêts de tous ceux qui seront affectés par les conséquences de ses actes. Parce qu'il se rattache ultimement à une tradition empiriste, il juge que la possession d'intérêts est étroitement liée à la *sentience*, c'est-à-dire à la capacité d'éprouver du plaisir ou de la peine. Ce qui veut dire que les intérêts dont il vient d'être question doivent être subjectivement éprouvés pour être des intérêts dignes de ce nom. Par conséquent, puisque les agents moraux peuvent améliorer le bien-être des êtres capables d'éprouver du plaisir ou de la peine, en augmentant leurs plaisirs et en diminuant leurs peines, l'élargissement de la communauté morale doit donc se poursuivre jusqu'à ce qu'elle en vienne à inclure la plupart des animaux (à titre de patients moraux, bien entendu, pas à titre d'agents moraux).

Je voudrais mentionner très rapidement et sans m'étendre plusieurs points qui posent problème chez Peter Singer. Ainsi, il va chercher une justification de l'élargissement de la communauté morale du côté de la sociobiologie et de la théorie darwinienne de l'évolution (*The Expanding Circle*, 1983). L'élève de R. Hare qu'il est ne saurait, bien entendu, adhérer à une forme quelconque de naturalisme: il est parfaitement conscient des limites de l'entreprise et son interprétation de l'altruisme de parentèle et de l'altruisme réciproque donne des éléments pour la genèse de la posture morale, pas des éléments pour la justification de jugements moraux à portée normative universelle. Ceux-ci ne sont, en définitive, admis qu'à la suite d'un acte de foi selon lequel il existe une dynamique des énoncés de l'éthique, analogue à celle des énoncés des mathématiques. Ensuite, les conséquences de sa théorie pour le statut des êtres humains semblent très difficile à admettre: en gros, il s'agit de remplacer une perspective classiquement personnaliste par une perspective personniste. C'est une affaire qui a une longue histoire. Tout dépend de la question de savoir si la réalité de la personne est substantielle ou non. Boèce défend une conception aristotélicienne et distingue nettement la substance de ses accidents. En conséquence de quoi, il fait de la personne une substance individuelle de nature rationnelle (il n'y a pas de personnes des propriétés que l'on peut prédiquer accidentellement, il n'y a pas de personne des entités collectives et les êtres dépourvus de raison ne sont pas des personnes). Pour Locke, au contraire, nous n'avons pas d'idée de ce qu'est une substance mais seulement une idée de ce qu'elle fait (encore cette idée est-elle obscure et confuse). Cette insistance va avoir des conséquences décisives lorsqu'il s'agira de définir la personne: Locke fait de la personne un être pensant et intelligent qui a raison et réflexion, et peut se considérer soi-même comme un soi, la même chose pensante en différents temps et lieux; ce qu'elle ne fait que par cette conscience qui est inséparable de la pensée et qui lui est essentielle. Le point est le suivant: dans une perspective inspirée d'une définition à la Boèce, aussi longtemps qu'on a affaire à la même substance (individuelle, de nature rationnelle), on a affaire à la même personne: qu'elle ait ou non conscience d'elle-même ne change rien à l'affaire. Pour J. Locke, on est la même personne aussi longtemps que l'on a la même conscience d'être soi. Il s'ensuit que l'on peut cesser d'être une personne, cesser d'être la même personne et être plus ou moins une personne, selon que l'on a plus ou moins accès à la conscience de soi. P. Singer va radicaliser une analyse de ce type en extrayant complètement la personne de son substrat naturel ou biologique: il peut exister des personnes non-humaines, il peut exister des êtres humains qui ne sont pas des personnes. Comme ce sont les accomplissements effectifs de la personne qui ont une portée et une signification morales pas l'espèce biologique à laquelle cette personne se trouve appartenir (de façon contingente), il s'ensuit qu'une plus grande considération morale (il s'agit ici simplement de la prise en compte des intérêts, pas du respect ou de quoi que ce soit d'approchant) doit être accordée à une personne non-humaine qu'à un être humain qui n'est pas une personne. Lié au problème précédent est celui de l'articulation d'un conséquentialisme hédoniste (en ce qui concerne les êtres simplement conscients—les personnes imparfaites si l'on veut) et d'un conséquentialisme de la préférence (en ce qui concerne les êtres conscients d'eux-mêmes—les personnes au sens plénier du terme).

Laissant toutes ces difficiles questions de côté, je voudrais simplement faire observer qu'une éthique pathocentrée ne constitue une éthique environnementale que par défaut. En effet, même si la communauté morale s'est élargie, elle ne comporte pas tous les êtres vivants: elle n'est peuplée que par les êtres sensibles.

Par conséquent, les seules obligations qui existent envers les êtres vivants mais non sensibles sont des obligations indirectes (dont j'ai observé qu'elles sont des obligations dérivées des obligations directes).

Les éthiques biocentrées se proposent, parfois, explicitement de remédier à un tel défaut. Une éthique biocentrée, comme son nom l'indique, inclut dans la communauté morale tous les êtres vivants, quelles que soient les performances mentales dont ils sont capables. C'est donc ici le simple fait de la vie qui est valorisé. Albert Schweitzer, au début du siècle dernier, a articulé une éthique de ce genre; elle a le grand mérite de s'adosser à une réflexion critique sur la croissance et les effets de la technologie. S'inspirant vraisemblablement de l'historien et penseur suisse Jacob Burckhardt, il estime que le projet de la modernité est le suivant: les européens ont voulu, en développant une civilisation technicienne, créer des valeurs spirituelles et matérielles au service du développement supérieur de l'individu et de l'humanité. Mais le monde de la machine, instauré à cet effet, est venu s'interposer entre son auteur et le but visé par lui. Les hommes se sont mis, à leur insu, au service des machines: exclusivement préoccupés d'agir sur la nature, ils en sont venus à développer une illusion d'insularité et à se croire à part dans l'univers. Ils ont perdu le sens de la solidarité cosmique entre tous les vivants: hors de tout projet de maîtrise et de possession de la nature, un être humain, en effet, n'est pas un sujet pensant, mais avant tout une vie qui veut vivre parmi la vie qui veut vivre. Ce vouloir vivre, d'inspiration évidemment schopenhauerienne, est le fond insondable de toute réalité et de toute existence: il s'étend aux plantes et, de façon générale, à tout être vivant. Qui est saisi par cette volonté infinie éprouve le respect de la vie. Pour autant, nul ne peut vivre en respectant toute vie. Même celui qui cherche à adopter une attitude de non-violence radicale sera amené à faire des choix déchirants: le caractère tragique de la vie lui vient de ne pouvoir se maintenir et se perpétuer qu'aux dépens d'autres vies. A. Schweitzer ne cherche pas à déterminer des règles qui permettraient de résoudre les dilemmes prévisibles (quelle(s) vie(s) préserver? quelle(s) vie(s) sacrifier?), peut-être parce qu'il estime que, s'il existait réellement des règles permettant de résoudre de façon infaillible les dilemmes moraux, cela signifierait que ces dilemmes sont seulement apparents et non réels. Concrètement, dans le biocentrisme de Schweitzer, il n'y a pas de place pour des règles substantielles ou même procédurales qui permettraient d'arbitrer lorsque des vies sont en jeu: toute vie en vaut une autre et ne peut être détruite, par celui qui a été touché par le respect de la vie, que sous l'effet d'une nécessité à laquelle il ne consentira jamais intérieurement. Nous avons donc là un biocentrisme fort qui débouche, dans ses applications pratiques, sur une sorte d'éthique de la situation.

D'autres formes de biocentrisme attachent une grande importance à la dimension téléologique des vivants. Un organisme vivant est un centre vital téléologique à la recherche d'un bien qui lui est propre, selon un mode qui lui est propre. En l'absence de raisons impérieuses d'agir en sens contraire, cette orientation téléologique des vivants doit être respectée. Cependant, une objection se présente: du fait qu'un être a un bien qui lui est propre, peut-on conclure que la recherche de ce bien soit, en elle-même, une entreprise qui mérite le respect? Il semble bien que non, car encore faut-il que ce bien ait lui-même une valeur inhérente. Et les contre-exemples ne viennent que trop facilement à l'esprit: le psychopathe—c'est-à-dire comme on disait naguère: «le pervers»—qui cherche à humilier ses victimes recherche son bien propre. Mais il est difficile d'estimer que cette recherche se recommande. Il convient toutefois de relever que dans cette version du biocentrisme on raisonne en termes d'organismes alors que le contre-exemple qui vient d'être donné met en jeu des agents humains. Il est toujours possible de considérer que l'élimination brutale ou insidieuse d'organismes par d'autres organismes qui recherchent leur bien propre (celle de la proie par un prédateur; celle d'un organisme sain par un parasite) se justifie dans le cadre d'une économie générale de la nature. L'idée sous-jacente est alors la suivante: un monde comme totalité organisée au sein de laquelle des êtres cherchent à réaliser des fins, peu importe lesquelles du moment qu'elles s'ajustent les unes aux autres et maintiennent l'intégrité du tout, a lui-même une valeur inhérente; ou, à tout le moins, une valeur supérieure à celle d'un monde où de tels êtres n'existeraient pas. Mais on aborde ici des problèmes qui excèdent largement le champ de l'éthique et qui relèvent plutôt de la théodicée classique.

Les considérations qui viennent d'être évoquées m'ont conduit d'une perspective biocentrée jusqu'à une perspective écocentrée. Il est possible d'adresser, *mutatis mutandis*, aux éthiques biocentrées les mêmes critiques que celles qui ont été adressées aux éthiques pathocentrées: elles ne dessinent que des obligations indirectes à l'endroit de l'environnement comme tel. C'est pourquoi on a vu apparaître également des éthiques cherchant à corriger ce défaut: ce sont les éthiques écocentrées. Elles s'orientent vers deux grandes directions.

Les uns insistent sur les capacités d'auto-organisation des vivants, mais aussi de leur environnement: ils sont capables de s'organiser, de se régénérer, de se reproduire, de s'adapter et se développer à travers le temps. Il s'agit, en gros, des thèses développées par Holmes Rolston et Laura Westra. Bien entendu, il existe d'importantes différences entre ces auteurs et je les laisse ici de côté. Le point commun est évidemment le suivant: en l'absence de raisons impérieuses d'agir en sens contraire, cette capacité doit être préservée ou restaurée.

D'autres adoptent une posture communautarienne et insistent sur l'apport de l'écologie et de la théorie de l'évolution comme sciences. Cela leur permet d'affirmer que la communauté à laquelle l'individu appartient est celle des vivants à l'échelle de l'évolution et que ses frontières doivent être étendues jusqu'à inclure la terre (les sols, les eaux, les plantes, les animaux). Il s'agit de thèses que l'on trouve chez J. B. Callicott et qui trouvent leur origine chez Aldo Leopold.

Le défaut de la version communautarienne des éthiques écocentrées est qu'elle est tributaire d'états de la connaissance scientifique qui, du fait que la science évolue et progresse, sont en principe susceptibles d'être remis en cause. À supposer même qu'elle ne succombe pas aux objections classiquement dirigées contre le paralogisme naturaliste, elle apparaît trop instable pour fonder une éthique. Il est d'ailleurs révélateur à cet égard de constater que J. B. Callicott semble actuellement diriger son attention vers les sagesses écologiques spontanées des peuples premiers—par une mise en relation audacieuse du post-modernisme et du primitivisme; et que certains de ses continuateurs (C. and R. Larrère) interprètent l'éthique de la terre à la lumière du contrat naturel.

Puisqu'il s'agit de repenser la philosophie en ce siècle qui commence, je voudrais conclure par quelques considérations prospectives. Ce que j'ai décrit, c'est un processus visant à élargir la communauté morale. Il peut être représenté par l'image des cercles concentriques (P. Wenz, *Environmental Justice*, 1988. Mais l'idée de représenter ainsi les chose est bien plus ancienne: on la trouve, par exemple, chez Cicéron, *De Officiis*, I, 17, 53). Au centre de la communauté morale se trouvent les agents moraux classiques, à savoir les sujets—qui, dans une perspective laïque ne sauraient être que les êtres humains. À l'extérieur de la communauté morale, on trouve ce qui n'est pas censé être directement pris en compte au point de vue moral—les simples choses, par exemple, dont on peut disposer à sa guise. Ce qui va résulter de l'élargissement de la communauté morale, c'est la prise en compte directe par les agents moraux de plus en plus de ces êtres qui ne sont pas des agents moraux comme eux. Et ici, il faut distinguer: on a intégré relativement tôt dans la communauté morale des êtres qui étaient effectivement des agents moraux mais dont on ne se rendait pas compte qu'ils l'étaient à cause de divers préjugés: esclaves, femmes, etc. Mais ce qui se passe avec les tentatives contemporaines est assez différent: il s'agit d'intégrer dans la communauté morale des êtres dont on sait qu'ils ne sont pas des agents moraux et dont il y a lieu de penser qu'ils ne le seront jamais: végétaux, environnement, etc. (Le cas des grands singes anthropoïdes est à part).

L'idée même d'élargir le cercle a été contestée (au nom de la dignité humaine, par exemple). Mais ce qui a été aussi contesté, c'est la pertinence même de la métaphore du cercle: certains, comme J. B. Callicott, pensent qu'elle est l'expression d'une perspective fondamentalement égoïste (au sens moral et au sens non-moral du terme). D'autres, comme F. Matthews, estiment que cette métaphore est tributaire d'une métaphysique inadéquate, destinée à être remplacée par une sorte de panpsychisme visant à réenchanter le monde.

Comme John Baird Callicott je pense qu'un jour viendra sans doute où le sujet, au sens de la métaphysique de la subjectivité, sera une curiosité historique au même titre que l'intellect agent des averroïstes médiévaux. Comme Freya Matthews, je pense que ce serait une bonne chose si on pouvait en appeler à une métaphysique respectable.

Pour autant, réenchanter le monde est le type même du programme au mieux utopique, au pire régressif: le monde est désenchanté depuis la révolution galiléenne-cartésienne et toutes les incantations imaginables seront impuissantes à provoquer un retour en arrière. Quant à la métaphysique de la subjectivité, même si son défaut constitutif c'est de chercher l'autofondation de l'ordre du monde dans la conscience du sujet, il n'est pas certain qu'elle soit si active dans cette toute affaire: c'est le sens commun, philosophiquement naïf et non éduqué, qui distingue les personnes et les choses et organise le monde en conséquence.

Il me semble donc que le projet de reconstruire de fond en comble notre interprétation métaphysique du monde pour parvenir à penser de façon satisfaisante notre rapport à celui-ci est quelque peu vain.

Maintenant, lorsqu'on prétend élargir le cercle par intégration de nouveaux hôtes dans la communauté morale, on ne prétend pas seulement modifier à la marge nos obligations en accordant quelques avantages à des êtres qui, autrefois, n'en bénéficiaient pas. On prétend, comme je l'ai rappelé, qu'il existe des obligations morales directes à leurs égards. Ce qui est profondément gênant dans l'image des cercles concentriques, ce n'est pas tant qu'elle repose sur une mauvaise métaphysique ou sur une conception inadéquate de la subjectivité: c'est plutôt qu'elle conçoit l'éthique essentiellement en termes d'obligations et de droits. Je ne prétends pas, bien sûr, qu'il n'existe aucun rapport entre ces trois reproches, mais c'est une autre question. Or, se représenter l'éthique principalement en termes d'obligations et de devoirs corrélatifs, c'est l'envisager de façon singulièrement restrictive. Étendre au-delà de l'humanité une éthique aussi étroitement conçue me paraît presque une contradiction dans les termes; en tout cas, le monde non-humain n'a pas grand chose à attendre d'une éthique qui figure parmi les plus pauvres que les humains aient jamais conçu.

Mais une conclusion aussi négative ne saurait être qualifiée de prospective. Ce que je souhaiterais faire, c'est suggérer en quel sens on peut, et en quel sens on ne peut pas, s'en tenir à une perspective anthropocentrée. Le terme est à ce point honni qu'il fait presque figure d'injure. Et s'il est vrai qu'il signifie que les êtres humains sont les maîtres du monde et que leurs intérêts ont partout et toujours priorité sur ceux des êtres non-humains, cela se comprend. Mais il peut indiquer simplement qu'il n'existe pas de valeur intrinsèque qui s'attacherait aux êtres comme si elle faisait partie de leur équipement ontologique. Ceci étant, pourquoi vouloir à tout prix détecter des valeurs intrinsèques? Bien sûr, pour établir autour d'elle une sorte de périmètre protecteur destiné à les mettre hors d'atteinte. À cet effet, le recours à la valeur intrinsèque ne me paraît ni nécessaire, ni suffisant. Ce que je veux dire, au contraire, c'est qu'avoir une valeur, c'est avoir été valorisé: à ce titre, la façon dont les êtres autres qu'humains constituent leurs valeurs nous restera à jamais opaque et notre éthique restera à jamais anthropocentrée. Mais, comme l'a bien vu J. B. Callicott, cela n'empêche en aucune façon que les êtres non-humains soient valorisés pour ce qu'ils sont. En d'autres termes, que la source de la valorisation soit humaine n'implique pas que les seuls êtres valorisables soient les êtres humains. J'ai suggéré que les capacités d'organisation des vivants et de leur environnement constituent une bonne raison pour retenir notre attention et mettre en œuvre nos capacités de valorisation. Et qui a valorisé dans la mesure où il convient ce qu'il convient de valoriser n'aura aucune inclination à l'utiliser comme une ressource dont on peut disposer à sa guise.

Le siècle qui vient n'a rien à gagner, ni philosophiquement ni pragmatiquement, à abandonner l'anthropocentrisme comme tel. Il a tout à gagner à encourager certaines formes d'anthropocentrisme. Il a pour priorité de décourager l'anthropocentrisme consumériste qui valorise ce qu'il ne convient pas de valoriser.

SELECTED PAPERS FROM THE XXII WORLD CONGRESS OF PHILOSOPHY

Why Does the Environmental Problem Challenge Ethics and Political Philosophy?

VITTORIO HÖSLE
UNIVERSITY OF NOTRE DAME

Abstract: This essay discusses the challenges that the problem of environmental destruction represents for both ethics and political philosophy. It defends universalism as the only ethical theory capable of dealing adequately with the issue, but recognizes three limitations of it: First, its strong anthropocentrism (as in Kant); second, the meta-ethics of rational egoism (Spinoza and Hobbes); and, third, the reduction of ethics to symmetric relations in the mores of modernity. With regard to political philosophy, universalism rejects the idea that consensus is a necessary and sufficient condition for morality; it points out that democratic rule is rule by majority, only rarely by unanimous consensus, and insists on the fact that even a unanimous consensus does not guarantee justice if the people affected by a decision are not identical with those entitled to make it. The latter is the case in issues of intergenerational justice. The essay ends by opposing a formalist and proceduralist concept of democracy with one that understands democracy as one reasonable tool for achieving a substantive concept of justice.

On the one hand, philosophy enjoys an enviable immunity from historical change. That its truths are not subjected to time is hardly a remarkable property, for it holds for all truths. After all, the truth value of the proposition that Caesar was murdered in 44 BC does not change with time, although the content of the latter truth is a temporal state of affair. Philosophy, however—in its core disciplines—does not deal with temporal states of affairs. Certainly an ethicist or political philosopher may try to argue that Brutus's participation in the conspiracy against Caesar was morally right or wrong. But his argument will be a philosophical argument only if it relies on general principles that are as such not subject to historical constraints, for example, that one should never kill one's benefactors; that one should not

Special Supplement, *Journal of Philosophical Research* pp. 279–292
DOI: 10.5840/jpr201237Supplement45

engage in behavior conducive to civil war, etc. Even if someone thinks that there are certain morally relevant features of the situation that have to do with specific historic circumstances, they have to be formulated in such a way that they are in principle applicable to other situations (even if the situation at stake may be the only known instantiation). Such a principle might be that one should act according to the ideas of political legitimacy shared by one's contemporaries and peers—in this case one has to look at the contemporaries' ideas in order to judge whether the act was morally right or wrong, and these ideas are inevitably temporal. But the principle that these ideas determine the moral quality of one's action is no more temporal than the Lorentz transformations are.

On the other hand, the *discovery* of philosophical truths is indeed temporal, and there is little doubt that there are historical factors that facilitate, or render difficult, such a discovery. Let me give one example. The basic difference between classical Greek and Hellenistic ethics and political philosophy consists in the expansion of the horizon within which people feel morally responsible for other human beings. In the classical world, it is mainly the *polis* that demarcates this horizon. Hellenism expands the domain and moves in the direction of universalism, i.e., the idea that it is an essential property of an ethical norm that it be valid for all rational beings. This idea was further strengthened by universal religions, particularly Christianity, and later by modern Enlightenment. It is quite obvious that the change represented by Hellenism was determined by the collapse of the political world based on the *poleis* and the emergence of territorial states, the conquest of the Orient by Alexander the Great, and the formation of the Roman Empire. Needless to say, those who regard universalism as the core of any rational ethical theory will not claim that with the collapse of the *polis*, new principles of ethical evaluation evolved; for principles of ethical evaluation are not temporal. They will only claim that certain ethical principles were grasped for the first time.

It is in a similar vein that the question of my lecture has to be taken. The environmental problem does not create new ethical principles; but it obliges us both to draw new consequences from age-old principles, and to re-conceive our moral principles in a way that allows us to justify moral intuitions that the environmental problem forces upon us. I want to focus mainly on issues of political philosophy, but since political philosophy cannot be detached from ethics, I have to touch upon ethics. Let me state, by the way, that I regard it as unfortunate that, in the Anglo-American world, political philosophy is mainly done outside of philosophy departments, namely within the field of political theory in political science. Certainly, the subdivision of knowledge in departments is inevitable, even if knowledge forms far more of a continuum than its institutional departmentalization suggests. But not all subdivisions are equally reasonable, and the one practiced by most Anglo-American departments tends to render philosophers more apolitical than necessary, and political science less informed by ethical reasoning than is desirable. Similarly, the separation of comparative and American politics in US political science tends to render Americanists less aware of the rest of the world than befits the scholar of a hegemonic power. In Germany, by contrast, the German political system is always studied by comparatists. In what follows, I want to focus, first, on the challenges for ethics, then for political philosophy. For ethics lays the foundation for political philosophy. However, the reverse holds to a certain degree as well, even if in another sense. Not ethical propositions, but the moral convictions people have regarding the truth of certain ethical propositions are influenced by the political structures within which they live. For these structures necessarily try to shape moral convictions in order to achieve a degree of legitimacy essential to their survival.

I

Modern ethics is distinguished from ancient ethics by its universalism.[1] Traditional societies are characterized by the assumption that there are different sets of norms for different ranks. Particularly the idea of universal human rights, as elaborated by the Enlightenment and developed as the basis of modern legal systems, is alien to them. Still, it is extremely important to understand that it is a reduction of universalism to define it as the belief in universal *rights*. The ethics of Kant and Fichte are perhaps the purest manifestations of universalism, and their basic category is that of *duty*, not of right. Universalism believes that *if* something is permissible, obligatory, or forbidden to a person, it is, ceteris paribus, permissible, obligatory, or forbidden *to all persons*. It does not in itself favor rights over duties. I have no doubt that universalism is the core of ethical reasoning and that all valuable ethical insights have to be compatible with it.

The concept of virtue, for example, is a decisive ingredient of a complete ethical theory, for we need habits in order to render our behavior stable and predictable to others. But it is the idea of the good that allows us to choose among the many, partly reciprocally contradictory habits that different cultures have proposed as virtuous. Only reason and justice allow a universal answer to the question: which virtues and whose traditions? In particular, it is profoundly misleading if the attempt to rehabilitate the concept of virtue is proposed in terms of an Aristotelian virtue ethics, usually in ignorance of the fact that the most elaborated modern doctrine of virtues stems from Kant himself. For Aristotle's ethics is pre-universalistic, as is proven by his defense of slavery and his account of what constitutes a just war. When, in the sixteenth century, Juan Ginés de Sepúlveda defended the enslaving of the Native Americans, he supported his position by arguments from Aristotle, whom he understood basically correctly,[2] and it was his fellow Christian, Bartolomé de Las Casas, who opposed him in the name of the Gospel. It would be a valuable enterprise to write another short history of ethics in which it could be shown how ethical universalism slowly emerged through Hellenistic philosophy and matured within the Christian tradition. Also the re-appropriation of Aristotle by Thomas is subtly different from his Greek model, and in particular, there can be no doubt that only Kant's ethics brings to completion central Protestant, and thus Christian, intuitions still alien to the Greeks. I have in mind Aristotle's second limit, namely that the primary motive in moral behavior is the search for one's own happiness.

My defense of universalism is compatible with the recognition of problems peculiar to modern ethical theory. Universalism necessarily favors symmetric relations (for asymmetric relations cannot hold for both sides), and this has led to the formation of a society deeply characterized by reciprocity. Reciprocity is certainly something which all human societies have known, but the decisive point is that earlier societies acknowledged, besides this type of relation, vertical, asymmetric relations: towards the gods, the priests, the king, the elders, the teachers, etc. It is the slow erosion of the ability to maintain a vertical relation that defines the moral sensibility of modernity. It is not universalism as such that excludes vertical relations; for universalism is thoroughly compatible with the norm that each person should try to perfect herself, and that, in order to do so, she should try to imitate persons morally superior to her—as long as the moral superiority is not defined by appealing to an external quality such as rank, status, gender, age, etc. Still, those critics of modernity who lament that, in the last centuries, an erosion of that ability has occurred are right. And it has occurred on both sides—the superior as well as the inferior. For it is not at all easy to maintain authority: traditional priests or monarchs had to deny themselves certain vulgar pleasures and cultivate a complex sense of forms in order not to lose their ascendancy. And the inferior side often succeeded in the amazing feat of avoiding servility while sincerely admiring those persons whose culture they experienced as superior. The institutions most informed by the new egalitarian spirit are: First, a contractual marriage bond among equals that can be dissolved when one of the partners finds the equality of the relation violated; secondly, a generalized market; thirdly, democracy; fourthly, an army of paid volunteers; and fifthly, a religious community that hires and fires its own ministers.

The theoretical fascination for, and the spread of, these institutions can now lead to something which is not entailed by universalism, but which is compatible with it: the meta-ethical idea that one should opt for symmetrical relations *because* it is in one's own egoistic interest. Rational egoism is the meta-ethical theory of several of the leading ethicists of early modernity, such as Hobbes, Spinoza, and Locke. (For the latter, this applies only to the *Essay Concerning Human Understanding*, not to the *Two Treatises of Government*, whose doctrine of natural law is hardly compatible with *Essay* II 21.) It is, however, important to see that this in itself is not really a break with pre-modern ethics (for after all, as we have seen, eudemonism was the leading meta-ethical position of the ancients). The difference does not consist in the egoistic starting-point, but in the content of the satisfaction of the self. Happiness was understood by the ancients in a far more comprehensive way than it is in modern ethics. It culminated in contemplation and encompassed friendship, both private and political. It was thus open both to a transcendent and communal dimension. It is the loss of these two features which renders the modern meta-ethics of rational egoism far less attractive than the ancient quest for self-perfection, as egoistic as it was, and which renders the modern welfare-state aiming at the satisfaction of these rational self-interests far more vulgar than the ancient *polis* with its aesthetic wonders. At least this seems true as long as we forget that its beauty was only possible thanks to slavery.

But not only is the rational egoism of early modernity in formal continuity with the ancient world; it has been modern, not ancient, ethics that has brought forth the greatest challenge to both eudemonism and rational egoism. I have in mind, of course, Kant. Perhaps the peculiarity of his ethical mindset can be characterized thus: he has introduced the most awe-inspiring form of vertical dependency in order to justify symmetric relations. What I mean is that the content of Kant's ethics, the categorical imperative, is an abstract formulation of the leading intuitions of early modern ethicists favoring symmetric relations. But it is a *categorical imperative*, and this means that I have to accept it independently of my interest, even the interest in my own happiness. I am subject to it with an absolute force that goes far beyond the submission elicited by ancient kings, priests, or even gods. For they all were, even if superior to me, amenable to some compromises by flattery, bribes, prayers, etc. It is the impersonal nature of the moral law that eliminates all these alternatives, while at the same time avoiding the humiliation that the absolute power of another person would entail. For as much as the higher faculty of desire, according to Kant, is irreducible to the lower one, it is not something alien to me, but my own core. The capacity of recognizing and submitting to the categorical imperative is the only thing in the world that carries intrinsic value, which is thus limited to the good will of persons (who need not be humans).

What has all of this to do with the environmental problem? My thesis is that it has challenged, although in different degrees, three basic features of modern ethics: First, its anthropocentrism; secondly, the meta-ethics of rational egoism; and, thirdly, the reduction of ethics to symmetric relations. The first point is the most controversial one, for one might well argue that the environmental problem can, and ought to, be understood within anthropocentric premises alone. No doubt a large part of the immoral behavior connected to environmental destruction consists in harming the life, health, and property of other human beings, be they our own contemporaries or members of future generations. It should indeed not be doubted that the life of humans is of a higher value than that of the life of other organisms not endowed with reason. We can call this position "weak anthropocentrism," and it does not seem wise to challenge it. Particularly, it is of no avail to appeal to a pantheistic "deep ecology" that sees in nature as such the only value. For nature as such is always there, even after the extinction of higher species, including humankind. Thus this is no ground for limiting our environmentally harmful behavior. But my option for weak anthropocentrism does not entail that human goods are the *only* entities with intrinsic value (a position one could call "strong anthropocentrism"), and indeed the more we study ecology, the more doubtful this thesis becomes. I do not simply mean that ecology teaches us that humankind can only thrive in an environment of astonishing complexity; for this could only prove that the extra-human environment has an instrumental value for the survival or flourishing of humankind. No, the study of the interdependency between humans and other living beings manifests so many resemblances between us and our organic relatives that it seems absurd to deny any value to what is in many respects (e.g., in its cognition, its emotions, its behavior) more similar to us than we believed 150 years ago. For those who do not simply accept values as fortuitous events occurring mysteriously in nature with the emergence of humankind, and for those who on the contrary cherish the surprising idea that ontology is grounded in axiology,[3] it is far more plausible to ascribe value from the beginning to nature and assume a slow increase in the intrinsic value of sentient beings with the evolution of increasingly complex organisms.

Rational egoism has become such a widespread meta-ethical theory because modernity has created a form of life in which such a theory does not seem to contradict our most basic moral intuitions. The average rational egoist does not teach that one should engage in the most shocking behavior, if this helps one's pleasure or career (the Marquis de Sade is, after all, quite an isolated exception in the discourse community of the Enlightenment). On the contrary, the Enlightenment teaches that most of the norms of traditional ethics are reasonable with regard to their content, even if the tradition did not understand the grounds for obeying them, namely, that they are ultimately in our own rational interest. However, the Enlightenment adds that we moderns should change certain parameters of society. In particular, we should create a universal market in order to guarantee a harmony between selfish interest and the needs of society. The discovery of the economic sphere as its own autonomous region clearly helped the articulation of this view.[4] And one cannot deny that the amazingly quick triumph of modernity's value system was enormously facilitated by this appeal to rational egoism.

The first objection to the creation of a social world characterized by the equilibrium of rational egoism and social benefit is that it betrays everything which is noble and heroic in human nature. A figure like Carlyle, echoed by Dickens in *Hard Times*, is a symptomatic expression of this revolt. On the one hand, those who do reject the meta-ethics of rational egoism will agree with the driving motive behind this revolt. It is not only a theoretical error to think that the convergence of rational egoism and morality is conceptually necessary; for it is very easy to conceive situations (they do not even have to be counterfactual) where this harmony does not occur. The theoretical error unfortunately also tends to corrode the human capacity to sacrifice oneself, for the theorist has not prepared herself or her disciples to the possibility of a divergence between the two. And even where this conflict does not occur, the maxim of the person remains morally dubious—for it is unclear to others, and usually also to himself, whether he acts selfishly because it is beneficial to society, or for other reasons. On the other hand, it is extremely important to see that, not only the belief in the pre-established harmony between private and social good is morally detrimental, but also the generic revolt against it. For there may be vast areas of social life where there is indeed such a harmony, and acting against it solely to convince oneself of the purity of one's motives is on a higher level itself selfish and thus morally unacceptable. I have my doubts as to whether engaging in life-endangering sports with no other end in view than fun is morally permissible, but I have no doubts whatsoever that it is forbidden to risk other people's lives in order to prove to oneself one's heroic disposition. This is, by the way, not only a theoretical problem. One cannot understand the enthusiasm for the First World War and the attraction to bolshevism without appealing to the need for senseless heroism that so often dominates young males.

The second objection against the belief in the harmony between private and social goods is not based on its corrupting effect on the human soul, but on the fact that this harmony does not hold in reality. As I said, there are not only counterfactual cases (as those proposed by Plato at the beginning of the second book of the *Republic*), there are also many real life cases in which a person, particularly at the end of his life, may commit a crime without fear of ever being punished for it and, if he is shameless enough, without fear of being tormented by his conscience. But one might say that these are only exceptional cases. The importance of the environmental problem, however, is that it proves a systemic failure of this harmony. This is a consequence of the fact that the environmental problem is to a large extent a problem of intergenerational justice. I say "to a large extent," because I have already suggested that it is also a problem of our refusal to recognize intrinsic value in nature. And of course the question of intergenerational justice encompasses more than just the environmental problem (e.g., fiscal policy). I am afraid that the price for the environmental disaster towards which we are heading will be paid by the younger generation, i.e., by people who are already born; it is no longer future generations that will have to struggle with dwindling resources and face a pollution that will destroy more and more human lives. Yet the persons who made the relevant decisions twenty years ago could reassure themselves that the consequences of their decisions would not fall upon them, but upon their descendants. It is easy to see why intergenerational justice is so much more difficult to implement than justice between classes: the members of different classes are contemporaries, they need each other, and can take revenge against each other. International justice is realized to a lesser degree than inter-class justice. This has to do with the fact that different nations are not under the umbrella of the same legal system, and a nation hurt by the decision of another nations cannot vote the politicians responsible for this behavior out of office. Still, there is international law, and international public opinion allows nations victimized by others a voice. But future generations are voiceless both in the market and in democracy, the two leading economic and political institutions of modernity.

Universalism obliges us to recognize (conditional) rights to future generations. And since there is no way to conceive these rights according to the model of the harmony between selfish and public interest, the environmental issue is of decisive importance in demonstrating that universalism is incompatible with a meta-ethics of rational egoism. I do not claim at all that it is the only, or the philosophically strongest, argument in favor of this incompatibility. I only say that it is the most *visible* one, the one most capable of convincing a layperson that the belief in such a pre-established harmony is a superstition. This is, incidentally, the reason why Hans Jonas's theory of intergenerational justice[5] is superior to that of John Rawls.[6] No doubt, their theories in the field of intergenerational justice have been the most influential ones of the last decades; the first in Germany and increasingly in the whole of continental Europe, the latter in the Anglo-American world. Rawls's theory antedates Jonas's; it is developed within a framework that constructs an original position in such a way that the principles of justice that Rawls considers morally justified appeal even to rational egoists. I have argued elsewhere[7] that Rawls's procedure is circular: one may construct different original positions and then come to different principles of justice. The whole desire to reduce principles of justice to fictional principles of prudence is an unwholesome compromise between the Hobbesian starting point from rational egoism and the Kantian commitment to ethical principles irreducible to selfishness, a pointless compromise in my view. The greatness of Jonas's theory, on the other hand, is to recognize the categorical nature of the obligation to practice intergenerational justice and to connect it with an account of the nature of being that renders justice to the peculiar nature of organisms.[8] My own philosophical work was strongly influenced by Hans Jonas, both by his philosophy of biology and by his ethics. I have developed it in two directions: First, I have tried to move beyond the phenomenological foundation of ethical norms and replace it with transcendental arguments; secondly, I have attempted to elaborate the basic idea of intergenerational justice into a complex material ethics and philosophy of law, addressing in detail issues like the right to property, liability law, the right to reproduction, as well as questions of the right economic and political order. I do not want to repeat here what I have elaborated in *Morals and Politics*. Rather, I want to limit myself to saying that it should be a decisive part of a rational economic order to render it profitable to save the environment. This can occur through eco-taxes that say the ecological truth by anticipating the needs of future generations and raising the prices of scarce commodities in such a way as to create an incentive to using them parsimoniously, increasing efficiency, and developing alternatives. Still, the decision to create an economic order in which there will be greater harmony between private and public good cannot itself appeal to rational interest; it needs purer moral motives.

Instead of pursuing this issue in detail, I want to focus on the third challenge the environmental problem presents for modern ethics: the focus on symmetric relations. The appeal of Jonas's book to a broader public was grounded in his phenomenologically dense elaboration of the category of responsibility. His main examples involve the responsibilities of parents and statesmen. As much as he has been criticized for engaging in a paternalist understanding of responsibility[9] and his deep mistrust against democracy, he rightly elucidates that the notion of care for persons either not yet able to reason (e.g., the newborn baby) or not yet existing (future generations) can hardly be approached according to the model of symmetric relations. For future generations will not be able to reciprocate what we do to them. Our duties towards them are not corresponded by their duties towards us, but only towards even later generations. (Jonas even denies that they have rights, since he does not seem to have the concept of conditional rights.) While the "discourse community" of Habermas is the archetypal model of a society based on equality and symmetrical relations, Jonas points to the persistence of asymmetric relations, which the modern mindset is less and less able to grasp in their peculiar nature. I have already said that the concern for future generations is only an extension of the universalistic commitment of modern ethics—if we want to grant basic rights to everybody, we do not have the right to exclude future generations. Pre-modern societies recognized a concern for their immediate descendants, but it was limited to one's own family or one's own nation; the concern for the future of humankind at large presupposes a universalistic ethics. This proves again that universalism, even if does not favor asymmetric relations, is not incompatible with them. Jonas argues that such relations are due to our natality and mortality, which are themselves grounded in the temporality of the organic mode of being.

II

This persistence of vertical responsibility has important consequences for political philosophy. The decisive model of political legitimacy that has evolved in the modern age and gradually conquered the whole planet is that of popular sovereignty. Usually it is acknowledged that a people cannot govern itself directly, but needs some form of representation. The modern idea of representation is distinguished from the medieval one by the fact that the representatives do not stand only for their constituency but represent the people as a whole and thus are not bound by an imperative mandate. Still, there is little doubt that in the overwhelming majority of cases a member of parliament wants to be re-elected, and thus is well advised to satisfy the desires of his electors. On the other hand, since he needs money to convince people to elect or re-elect him, he is also well advised to be kind to those persons or institutions that support him financially. Thus, his loyalty will shift between the electorate and the lobbyists that finance him. But is there a comparably powerful institutional mechanism that obliges him to be dedicated to the common good? In a proportional system, party discipline can be enforced more easily, which may or may not be conducive to the common good. The reciprocal dependencies of the different members of parliament on each other will lead to some form of compromise that may come close to the common good.

But here one question imposes itself: who represents future generations? They do not have an impact on the market by presenting their demand, nor can they elect their representatives. In earlier forms of representative rule, where there was no universal suffrage for the adult population, there was sometimes an institution of a protector of those who were not represented—for example, of the aboriginal people in Australia. Needless to say, such an arrangement is inferior to the granting of voting rights, which were given to the native population of Australia for the Commonwealth elections only in 1962 irrespective of their voting rights at the state level. But there is one thing which is even worse than having a protector instead of political rights: having neither political rights *nor* a protector. That is exactly the situation that future generations face. I do think it will be one of the main tasks of democracy in the twenty-first century to devise an institution that corresponds to the protector, or guardian, of future generations. In my book aforementioned, I have proposed such an organ. It should be analogous to a constitutional court, which also has the right and duty to protect the rights guaranteed by the constitution from encroachments by the majority.

But I do not want to pursue this technical idea here. Rather, what I want to consider is something more general. Democracy can be, and has been, justified in very different ways. Oversimplifying, one can order the various attempts at justifying democratic rule according to a spectrum extending from one extreme which accepts democracy as a mere result of a natural power distribution to another which declares the result of a democratic decision as by definition morally right. According to the first position, the majority is simply stronger than the minority; therefore it is wise to submit to the principle of majority rule. The argument may hold for contemporary societies; it certainly did not apply to earlier social formations, in which a minority often maintained all of the military power and in which the majority was sometimes inimical to majority rule because it mistrusted its average fellow human beings far more than a ruling dynasty or aristocracy. In any case, the argument for democracy based on the power of the majority is utterly unsatisfying. For might is not right; and it can lead to no more than a prudential submission to democracy, but never to its support out of moral conviction.

On the other end, we find the naturalistic definition: The political good is what is decided upon by the majority in an election with universal suffrage. Here it is not sheer power that asks us to submit to democratic decisions; it is the authority of pure morality embodied in the sovereignty of the people. It is not difficult to show that this position is as unsatisfying and untenable as the other, even if it is easy to understand why democratic politicians sometimes embrace it: It renders their rule, even if only temporarily, immune from moral criticism. Why does this doctrine not work theoretically, and why is it a grave danger to democracy itself?

First, one may have strong doubts whether consensus is a sufficient, or even a necessary, condition of morality. Not all relations agreed upon by two people are respectable—consider the bond between a sadist and a masochist. Certainly, in this case, at least there is no violation of another's will. But there is no reason to believe that this is the only value that counts. One might even object that in the case of the submission to, and internalization of, immoral demands, more important values are violated: not the will of the victim, but her dignity, which is maintained when her will has still to be broken. But is consensus not at least a necessary condition of morality? That depends on how one understands consensus. The legitimacy of punishment cannot depend on the assent of the person to be punished. Even if an assent is desirable, it rarely occurs, and almost never with the worst criminals. However, one might argue—as Hegel famously does[10]—that the criminal has given his consent by his own deed, for as a rational being he has created a new rule, which in retributive punishment is directed *against him*, but *in his own spirit*. Hegel's argument is ingenious, but it clearly stretches the concept of consensus. And even if we follow him, there are cases in which even the harming of an innocent person may be justified in order to save a higher good, even if consensus in such cases seems hardly possible. One might say that he *should* have assented to such a principle, since it is a rational principle. But if consensus is supposed to mean, not the factual, but the rational, consensus, then we can immediately settle with the demands of reason and renounce the search for consensus.

But even if we grant that consensus is a necessary and sufficient condition for morality, it is quite clear that such a consensus is almost never achieved in a democracy. *There is almost always a minority overruled by a majority*, and it is not clear why they should accept this overruling. We might appeal to the power of the majority; but then we would fall back on the standard of prudential advise, and this would not give a moral justification of the duty of obedience. (There is a moral argument for the prima facie obligation to obey the laws of one's country, namely, that it allows us to avoid anarchy and the evils inherent in it, even if they do not fall upon oneself; but this argument holds for all governments and does not favor democracy.) Usually one hears that one should obey the majority because everyone has agreed to the principle of the majority rule. I am not sure that such an agreement has been explicitly given by everyone. But one might argue that it has been given implicitly by remaining in a country whose constitution acknowledges the rule of the majority. (It would be valid also for those who remain in non-democratic countries.) The argument, by the way, presupposes a right to emigration, which must be antecedent to majority rule and thus cannot be subjected to it, if the argument is to hold. But even where such a right exists, not everyone has the economic means to emigrate and not everyone willing and able to emigrate can find a country willing to let him immigrate.

Usually people prefer to submit to the majority rule of a given country than to an autocratic rule because they anticipate that, even if they have been overruled in some issues, they will have a chance to be on the winning side of other issues and because they regard this alternation as fundamentally just, empowering all persons and giving them the right to be taken serious politically. (Universal suffrage, by the way, does not lead automatically to such an alternation, since a group may find itself always in the position of minority.) Furthermore, people trust that the collective decisions will be made only in those fields in which it is indispensable to have a collective decision (as with regard to taxation), leaving untouched, and even protecting, the private sphere of each citizen. That is, they combine their recognition of the democratic principle with the belief in a series of antecedent rights that are not at the mercy of majority rule. What I have just said of the right to emigration holds analogously of other basic rights. The intelligent democrat is a liberal, i.e., he believes that there are limits to majority rule and that we need a complex system of separation of powers (including the judicial review of laws) in order to prevent the rule of majority from becoming tyrannical. Of course, it is both morally and politically wise to hope that the principles of the liberal state are accepted by as many people as possible. But if these principles are not to be at the majority's mercy, then it cannot be the popular consensus that *gives* them legitimacy. It *recognizes* their legitimacy, but the latter does not stem from the people.

But even if we grant that consensus is, first, a necessary and sufficient condition for morality and, secondly, that democratic decisions are supported by an unanimous decision, they might still be wrong. Why? The answer is simple: *the persons who make the decisions may not be the only ones who are affected by them.* This is true in both a spatial and a temporal dimension, since a state has both a limited territory and a limited people whose members live in a given time. If the German people had unanimously supported the attack against Poland in 1939, it still would have been an unjust war and would have shown even more injustice on the German side. And—to give a less dramatic, but more widespread example—if a nation unanimously engages in a behavior that leads to more emissions of greenhouse gases, and thus to higher temperatures and greater desertification, depriving people in distant countries or distant generations of the means of livelihood, they act unjustly. And they increase their injustice, if they refuse, even if unanimously, to pay compensation.

We now see why the environmental problem radically challenges democracy. The political intractability of the problem has much to do with the fact that the decisions are made by people who do not have to suffer the repercussions of those decisions (or at least not to the same degree as their descendants, who, furthermore, no longer will enjoy the short-term benefits of their ancestors). If we assume that people act according to their selfish interest, it is not likely that an earlier generation will renounce anything for the sake of a later generation. We have already seen that democracy is acceptable only if the basic rights of people are respected. But now we realize that there is no egoistic incentive to respect these rights in the case of future generations and analogously distant nations. This endangers the claim to universalistic justice that has given legitimacy to democracy—for indeed, it was a universalistic ethics that led the political development towards universal suffrage.

Again, I do not want to repeat here the details of the institutional idea of a state organ with the duty to protect future generations. I regard this idea as more likely to limit the worst forms of intergenerational injustice than the proposal, discussed in several countries, to extend the suffrage to every born citizen (since this obviously does not work in the case of small children, one would have to give it to their parents, not knowing what to do when the parents of an odd number of children cannot agree). The issue I want to discuss is the more theoretical one concerning whether such an institution would not be antidemocratic. The answer is to a large extent terminological. If we understand by "democracy" the principle that the majority should have absolute power, then such an organ is antidemocratic. But so is the constitutional court, as well as the fact that the norms of a constitution cannot usually be altered by simple majority. If, however, we do think that the right political order is based on a universalistic ethics, and we want to call this commitment "democracy," then a truly democratic constitution will guarantee basic rights to everybody, including future generations. Since these rights have to be applied to concrete situations, we need the determination of procedures that guide the legislative processes. Universalism entails that, in the legislative process, all people, either directly or indirectly, have a say, and thus universal suffrage is an important feature of a just political system. But universalism also demands that the antecedent rights of persons not be violated. Thus it asks for mechanisms that defend these rights, such as independent courts (including a constitutional court) and other mechanisms that render it more likely that the persons who come to legislative and executive office are as morally and intellectually qualified as possible in order to defend those rights by concrete policies. The balance that has to be found between the demands of material and procedural justice doubtless asks for intellectual complexities that are not required by the simple transposition of Hobbes's doctrine of sovereignty to democracy; but this hardly recommends the latter.

We can therefore oppose two ideal types of democracy: A democracy that is a natural outgrowth of a commitment to a universalistic ethics, and thus morally obliged to protect the basic rights of future generations as well as of persons in other countries; and a democracy that is a means of channeling power in such a way that those who happen to form the majority by appealing to the more direct needs of their voters can legislate whatever they want, even declaring as per definition just whatever the majority happens to pass. Needless to say, I do not deny the necessity of procedures based on majority rule. I only insist that, as such, they do not lead to just results, particularly in the field of intergenerational justice, but have only a chance to do so if they are inspired by the quest for a material concept of justice. Perhaps it is the lasting merit of the environmental problem for political philosophy that it has shed more and more doubts on the moral acceptability of a purely formal concept of democracy.

NOTES

1. On the slow implementation of universalist ideals in European societies, see Jonathan Israel, *Radical Enlightenment* (Oxford and New York: Oxford University Press, 2001).

2. This does not mean that Sepúlveda did not somehow mitigate Aristotle with Stoic and Christian elements. His "servus natura" is a slave due to a kind of second nature, which is in principle modifiable by the colonial process—an idea alien to Aristotle. But for the near future, the enslavement of the native Americans is justified. See Hans Schelkshorn, *Entgrenzungen* (Weilerswist: Velbruck Wissenschaft, 2009): pp. 330ff.

3. See John Leslie, *Value and Existence* (Totowa, NJ: Rowman and Littlefield, 1979).

4. See Alexander Pope, *Essay on Man*, IV 396: "that true Self-love and Social are the same." Cf. Charles Taylor, *A Secular Age* (Cambridge, MA: Belknap, 2007), pp. 176ff.

5. Hans Jonas, *Das Prinzip Verantwortung* (Frankfurt am Main: Insel-Verlag, 1979).

6. John Rawls, *A Theory of Justice* (Cambridge, MA: Belknap, 1971), pp. 128–129, 136ff., 284ff.

7. *Morals and Politics* (Notre Dame, IN: University of Notre Dame Press, 2004), pp. 640ff. Most of what I say in this paper is further developed in this book, and in my essay "Ethics and Economics, or How Much Egoism Does Capitalism Need?," *Archiv fur Rechts- und Sozialphilosophie* 97 (2011): 425–440.

8. See my analysis: "Hans Jonas' Position in the History of German Philosophy," in *The Legacy of Hans Jonas. Judaism and the Phenomenon of Life*, ed. Hava Tirosh-Samuelson and Christian Wiese (Leiden/Boston: Brill, 2008), pp. 19–37.

9. See Richard Bernstein, "Hans Jonas: Rethinking Responsibility," *Social Research* 61 (Winter 1994): 833–852.

10. G. W. F. Hegel, *Grundlinien der Philosophie des Rechts*, §100.

SELECTED PAPERS FROM
THE XXII WORLD CONGRESS OF PHILOSOPHY

Towards an Ethic of Technology? Nanotechnology and the Convergence of Applied Ethics

MARIE-HÉLÈNE PARIZEAU
LAVAL UNIVERSITY, QUÉBEC

ABSTRACT: The hypothesis I develop involves that we have been witnessing, during the last ten years or so, an interpenetration in the area of applied ethics of certain concepts originally belonging to different areas of ethics, namely bioethics, environmental ethics, and also business ethics. Certain concepts such as "future generations," "consent," "precautionary principle," "intrinsic value," "global governance," "sustainable development," or "scientific uncertainty" are becoming "thick ethical concepts," in the terminology of metaethics; or in the terminology of American pragmatism: "living beliefs." They are now charged with strong moral contents that unfolds a new horizon of meaning at the heart of Western Modernity, a horizon largely defined by science and technical actions. Nevertheless, is this conceptual convergence in the area of applied ethics the sign of the coming of a new ethic of technique? I will discuss this topic taking as an example the case of nanotechnology.

The hypothesis I wish to develop here involves that we have been witnessing, during the last ten years or so, an interpenetration in the area of applied ethics of certain concepts originally belonging to different areas of ethics, namely bioethics, environmental ethics, and also business ethics. Certain concepts such as "future generations," "consent," "precautionary principle," "intrinsic value," "global governance," "sustainable development," or "scientific uncertainty" are becoming "thick ethical concepts," in the terminology of metaethics; or in the terminology of American pragmatism: "living beliefs." They are now charged with strong moral content that unfolds a new horizon of meaning at the heart of Western Modernity, a horizon largely defined by science and technical actions. Nevertheless, is this

Special Supplement, *Journal of Philosophical Research* pp. 293–302
DOI: 10.5840/jpr201237Supplement47

conceptual convergence in the area of applied ethics the sign of the coming of a new ethic of technique? I will discuss this topic taking as an example the case of nanotechnology.

1. NANOTECHNOLOGY: THE CONVERGENCE OF SCIENTIFIC DISCIPLINES AND AN EFFICIENT SCIENTIFIC POLICY

Here are some key pieces of information concerning nanotechnology in order to better understand the phenomena of convergence of applied ethics that occur simultaneously.

If many definitions of nanotechnology are available, let us consider that they are generally defined according to the size of their object—the nanometer— and their main goal, which is to build machines from atoms; the construction of devices on the scale of molecules with superior (or completely new) capacities compared to the existing devices we know of. Consequently, the goal is to develop new technical abilities, a task more related to a very small scale engineering project than to the development of a new knowledge, although it is clear that new properties of matter can be discovered. Nanotechnology is oriented towards the creation of useful devices with implications in different fields of activity such as the military, economics, and biomedicine. We can affirm that nanotechnology's goal is more to create machines and devices in order to create more well-being in the context of a market economy, and much less to push forward scientific knowledge as an understanding and control of natural phenomena. Nevertheless, nanotechnologies are characterized by a key feature: they are a converging point of many classical disciplines—physics, chemistry, biology—also coupled with other technologies such as computer science and other techniques such as engineering. This convergence is the result of a multidisciplinary and interdisciplinary approach which is supported by very precise scientific policies.

The success in the development of nanotechnology is also the result of a variety of external factors. First, there is a real political will, initiated in the United States, to promote nanotechnology in order to launch a new economical and industrial revolution. Thus, since 2001, a colossal funding for scientific research has been put into place in the United States, quickly followed by the European Union and Japan, and then by Canada and Korea. In the United States, the coordination of the different federal agencies was started as early as in 1996, then followed in 2001 by the *National Nanotechnology Initiative* (NNI). The NNI developed an efficient political strategy which, on one side, funds the research, and on the other, promotes the organization of researchers into areas of expertise and the networking of researchers, universities, funding parties, and business organizations. Finally, the policies have also worked on the social acceptability of nanotechnology following different strategies: public education, the ideology of post-humanism, and the funding of social science research which, since 2004, was oriented towards risk assessment, social acceptability, and the public perception of nanotechnology.

Nevertheless, a political opposition has also emerged. Powerful and well established environmental NGOs took up a stand in the United States as well as in Europe. For example, in 2004, the *Berkeley Community Environmental Advisory Committee* protested against the construction of a laboratory facility capable of producing carbon nano-tubes. What was targeted there was not even the industry itself, but what preceded it—that is—the research facilities. NGOs like Greenpeace perceive nanotechnology as a direct threat to the ecosystems. *Canada's Action Group on Erosion, Technology, and Control* (ETC), an organization linked to an NGO well known for its stand against the use of GMOs (Raffi), called for a moratorium on the commercial production of nanoparticles (Preston 2005). In France, public consultations on nanotechnology in 2010 were stopped following the action by different groups, such as "Pièces et main d'oeuvre." For many, there is a similarity between the cases involving nanotechnology and GMOs (genetically modified organism), and the only way to prevent a widening of the gap (A. Mnyusiwalla, A. Daar, and P. Singer 2003) between the public opinion and nanotechnology is to initiate different strategies of ethical reflection. In its 2007 document, *The National Nanotechnology Initiative Strategic Plan*, the NNI calls for an ethics of nanotechnology based on responsibility, economical gains, State security and the increase of the citizen's quality of life.

2. A CALL FOR ETHICS AND THE CONVERGENCE OF APPLIED ETHICS

2.1 A Call for Ethics

This call for a wide ethical debate aims at overtaking the prophetical claims of the posthumanist movement that defined the early years of the discourse (*champ discursif*) on nanotechnology. This reflection, more complex and more specific to the present and future practical issues of nanotechnology, focuses on many ethical questions already well identified in the literature. The American context concerns six main ethical issues:

1) *The issue of equity:* how these techniques, or their production, are available to poor countries.

2) *The issue of privacy and security:* as much for the individual as for the State. Here the classic question arises again: what are the limits of the State's intrusion in one's private life. This question is viewed from two angles: security of the workplace and military usage.

3) *Environmental and public health issues* are more than ever identified as central to the problem of nanotechnology.

4) Philosophical issues, here the question of the *hybridization of humans and machines*, with the possibility of a co-evolution of the human specie with technology. What is at stake here is not only the social acceptability of

certain scenarios of enhancement devices put into place, but the specific problem of the definition of the normal and the pathological, the normal and the enhancement of human performances.

5) *Issues of economical development* are central in a very competitive globalization context that raises the problem of competition versus ethical behavior. Asian competition is considered as the main threat to the US economy as it relies on a fast development strategy sometimes lacks or simply ignores ethical and environmental issues.
6) *The issues of education and public participation* in the orientation and the choice of nanotechnology potentially beneficial to society.

In the light of these ethical issues, it is easy to see how, in the US, different branches of what is called applied ethics are summoned to answer to a position often considered as anti-science, anti-progress and anti-modern held by active environmental NGOs. In the last thirty years, applied ethics—bioethics, environmental ethics, business ethics and professional ethics—have developed in a sectional fashion in relation to the different activities or institutions of Western society. They adapted the American model to their reality. These applied ethics have held, and are still holding, a major role in the production of norms and in the social regulation in the face of multiple scientific and technological developments. In the biomedical field, bioethics, with its bioethics committees, its clinical ethicists and its biolaw, is probably the most accomplished western model of this normative regulation of techno-scientific progress.

In front of the six main ethical issues of nanotechnology, how do applied ethics answer? Is it possible to observe convergences or splits in the analysis and moral contents? In the literature, it is mainly in bioethics and in environmental ethics, although also somewhat in business ethics, that we find the analysis of these issues. My hypothesis is that this analysis is putting together an ethic of technique through the interpenetration of certain ethical concepts now "thick" or considered as "living beliefs." This is what I shall try to demonstrate briefly.

2.2 The Convergence of Applied Ethics and Nanotechnology

From a survey of the literature, I identified certain recurring ethical concepts in the fields of environmental ethics, bioethics, and business ethics which are presently used in the debate concerning the discourse (*champ discursif*) on nanotechnology.

2.2.1 Environmental Ethics and the Precautionary Principle

On account of environmental risks, environmental ethics are directly concerned in the debate on nanotechnology. These risks are a major societal issue. The current applications of nanotechnology are nanomaterials, and two main environmental risks are associated with them. The first would be a possible dissemination of nanoparticles in the environment which could interact with the atmosphere. The second risk consists of the absorption of nanoparticles by living organisms, including humans, which could induce lethal modifications to the organisms, certain forms of cancer, and DNA modifications. This question is raised particularly in the field of novel foods where nanotechnologies are increasingly used without any international regulations (Centre for Technology Assessment, Switzerland 2009).

Nevertheless, nanotechnologies are interesting to the environmentalists because they could help to detect certain forms of pollution. They could also be useful to decontaminate certain sites and make a better use of energy. The environmentalists are all concerned by these risks as they are sensitive to their promises.

Environmental ethics includes a variety of theoretical positions, from a rational management of the environment to an almost absolute protection of Nature, a position held by some deep ecologists. But as explained by Brian Norton (1991), a certain unity exists in this intellectual movement. The core philosophical point of view is that Nature possesses an intrinsic value, independently of human beings. For this reason, Nature deserves moral consideration because of the biotic community which includes human beings (Aldo Leopold 1949). This biotic community results from a historical development over millions of years that generated a living system, both diversified and complex. This natural and historical process holds moral signification that is distinct from the production of human activities. There lies the moral intuition shared by environmentalists. The moral respect of this historical process needs not to be absolute, but it clearly questions, or blames, those who wish to modify the natural process or certain living organisms. The burden of the proof is on the shoulders of those who wants genetic transformations of living beings, for example. Nature is now seen as "vulnerable" to human technical intervention.

Concretely, because nanotechnologies claim to be able to create radically new materials, they should be the object of a serious risk assessment study. The environmentalists demand substantial studies on the risks involved by nanotechnology on health and ecological security. Many call upon the "precautionary principle" (European Commission 2007), exposing for example, certain American administrative decisions which promote an evaluation method of the risks of nanomaterials based on the methods used for standard macromaterials. Hence, nanotubes fall in the same category as graphite. Such an analogy is dangerous and illogical for it does not distinguish between the different types of materials. The environmentalists denounce the economical arguments hidden behind these decisions. Clearly, as it is now impossible to adopt the same behavior as was done concerning GMOs, a more responsible stand must be adopted in the face of possible consequences on environment and human health. Europe is given as an example in the way it applies the "precautionary principle": "no data, no market."

The "precautionary principle" brings into light a new method of risk management by introducing: (1) a responsibility of proof placed on the developers, (2) an effort of scientific knowledge concerning the global risks; (3) an introduction of temporality (long range risk assessment); (4) the knowledge of risks as a condition to the economic development for a given technology.

2.2.2 Bioethics and Human Dignity

In the field of bioethics, two topics of discussion can be identified as relevant in the case of nanotechnology. The first one concerns the ethical evaluation of nanotechnology, and in particular, nanomedicine. Many ethicists, inspired by the main American bioethical theory of Childress and Beauchamp (2009)—autonomy principle of the person, the principle of justice, and the principle of beneficence and non-malfeasance—consider that the tools for the ethical evaluation of research have been perfected enough over the last thirty years to answer the challenge that certain biomedical innovations might represent.

The second issue revolves around the problem of post-humanism, and therefore on the possible modification of the human being in terms of a reconstruction or an enhancement of human performances. It is the question of the hybridization of humans and machines, with the possibility of a co-evolution of the human species with technology, a radical modification of the natural evolutionary process of the living. The philosophical ground of this debate is far different from the ground of environmental ethics.

As a prophecy of hope, a utopia of the New Man, of transformation and mastering over matter, the post-humanist view flourishes with the arrival of nanotechnology, but this view was already discussed in the field of bioethics since the 1990s. These discussions were about the possibility, and the morality, of a modification of the human genome, no longer for therapeutic goals, but for the sake of personal enhancement. Let us remember that in 2003 the American *President's Council on Bioethics* published a document titled, *Beyond Therapy*, in which it is stated that the modification of the human genome is morally acceptable because it is legitimate to desire to have "healthier children, to be more efficient, to desire an ageless body, to have a healthier spirit."

Nanotechnologies are not the starting point of post-humanism, but they put into place oppositions between the proponents of the "hybridization of human and machines" (the cyborg), and the defenders of "human dignity." The latter, although they base human dignity on the autonomy principle or on rationality, share with the environmentalists the idea that the rules of evolution are not to be changed when it comes to living organisms. Jurgen Habermas's thesis in *L'avenir de la Nature humaine* (2002), is a good example of this position.

By introducing the issue of a transformation of the human being—both body and spirit—the discourse on nanotechnology radicalizes the debate on the normal and the pathological, and also on the criteria of therapy and enhancement. Ethical concepts such as "human dignity," "personal autonomy," and "consent," that built a certain definition of the human being, are imported from bioethics to the discussion field of nanotechnology.

2.2.3 Business Ethics and Global Governance

Business ethics has been actively developed in the US over the last fifteen years. The fast evolution and multiplication of professional activities related to the phenomena of bureaucratization that is part of our societies has created complexity in the social structures and thus have made social interactions more difficult. Hence, a certain number of ethical questions specifically related to the different professions have crystallized into "professional ethics." For example: in business ethics, problems discussed are related to topics such as: the loyalty of the employee to its employer and, inversely, confidentiality and respect of the private life, business fraud, transparency of administrative decisions, and social responsibility of enterprises, etc. The concept of "global governance" became central in business ethics in the late 1990s. This ethical concept was imported into the discussion field of nanotechnology around the year 2004.

Governance is defined thus:

> Governance is the sum of traditions and institutions through which power is exercised in a given country for the common good. This includes procedures by which rulers are chosen, controlled and replaced (political aspect); the government's capacity to manage efficiently its resources and apply the right policies (economical aspect); and the respect of the national institutions by the citizenry and the State (institutional aspect). (Kaufmann 2005, 41)

This concept of governance does not limit itself to public administration, but also includes the private sector, civic organizations, NGOs, and international institutions. Governance aims at examining, in a wide fashion, the distribution of rights and obligations as well as power structures that define the specific structure of the organizations.[1] Global governance is interested in the conditions of the exercise of power.

In the discussion field of nanotechnology, global governance appears following three topics: the governance of risks, the social structures' adaptability, and the responsible development of nanotechnology.

Responsible development is directly referential to the notion of "sustainable development," including the issues of equity between the poor and the rich countries, the quality of life of human beings, and a care for the environment. This care is motivated by the risks involved by nanotechnology and obligates anticipation of issues concerning the environment, public health, and social consequences (Rocco 2008).

In the discussion field of nanotechnology, the concepts of global governance and sustainable development are treated through the field of business ethics, rather than from environmental ethics.

In the light of this exploration of the convergence of applied ethics in the field of nanotechnology, two issues are to be remembered. First, we can witness a selective appropriation of certain ethical concepts such as "the precaution principle" from environmental ethics, "human dignity" and "autonomy" from bioethics, "global governance" and "sustainable development" from business ethics, in the field of nanotechnology. Secondly, this ethics of nanotechnology which is appearing in the United-States, addresses, or will have to address one day, a core philosophical question—that is the progressive transformation of the human being and the environment by technology to the point where they will be co-evolutive to the phenomena of the natural evolution of the living. Thus, I believe that nanotechnology forces us to think, in all its consequences, an ethic of technology to which moral content will possess a variable content.

3. TOWARDS THE CONSTRUCTION OF A NEW ETHIC OF TECHNIQUE?

My hypothesis is that, through the convergence of applied ethics, a movement initiated by American policies, an ethic of technique is developing. This ethic of technique has, it seems, two main features.

The first is that the core method of this ethic of technique, as it appears in the field of nanotechnology, is related to the philosophy of American pragmatism. What I tried to demonstrate through the convergence of applied ethics is the construction of a discursive field of nanotechnology which is structured from "living beliefs," according to pragmatists, or, as I call them, ethical concepts. These beliefs are, as I described, variably in competition or sticking together, but also ready to be evaluated through an experimentation of reality. This evaluation of facts (*épreuve des faits*) is linked as a retroactive cycle, to the technical development of nanotechnology, which will result in the creation, or not, of certain machines or techniques. Thus, "living beliefs" will be validated or invalidated by an analogical process, therefore a test through reality.

But these "living beliefs," in conformity to American pragmatism, possess specific characteristics. They are *pluralist*, therefore potentially in contradiction or competition with each other. They are *meliorative*, that means expressing the potential of a moral superiority in opposition to "dead beliefs." They are *contextualized* in function of a given culture, attached to common sense, and finally, compatible with present day *religious convictions*. It seems to me that this moral frame works perfectly well with technological development. Nanotechnology are linked with this proof by facts that allow a continual readjustment in the process of action. In this sense, is the American pragmatic moral philosophy an ethics of technique? A philosophical framework unaware of itself as it sticks to the movement of technological development?

My second point concerns what I believe to be one of the core moral problems of modernity, which is the transformation of the human being and its environment by technology to the point where it will be co-evolutive to the phenomena of the natural evolution of the living. The tension between artificialization and naturalization of the human being and the world is obvious, for biotechnologies and nanotechnology offer real and manifold opportunities of transformation.

As Heidegger clearly stated: "technique in itself is not what is dangerous" (Heidegger 1958, 37). As a technique it exercises its power on humanity or nature, forcing it to manifest itself under the exclusive mode of production that danger appears. Lyotard (1979) also commented in this sense, technique is "the spirit of generalized performativity." "Performativity is understood as the best input/output account," it is also "efficiency, that is, the collection of the wanted effect." The result is an increase of power, not of what is true.

Is the potential co-evolution by technique the expression of the power of the modern Western world's dream of a world transformation? Is the ethics of technique being built through the American pragmatic framework simply applying furthermore this exclusive rule of performativity and enhancement? Or is it opened to other types of knowledge, thinking and existence in a plurality, inclusive of other cultures and civilizations?

These are the philosophical questions that are emerging through bioethics and environmental ethics and which responses engage future generations.

NOTE

1. See Gilles Paquet, "Introduction" in Mémoires de la Societé royale du Canada, *La gouvernance au 21ième siècle*, sixième série, tome X, 1999, pp. 14–15.

BIBLIOGRAPHY

Bawa, R., and S. Johnson. 2007. "The Ethical Dimensions of Nanomedicine." *Medical Clinics of North America* 91: 881–887.

Beauchamp, T., and J. Childress. 2009. *Principles of Biomedical Ethics*, 6th ed (New York: Oxford University Press).

Clarke, S. 2005. "Future Technologies, Dystopic Futures and the Precautionary Principle." *Ethics and Information Technology* 7: 121–126.

Commission de l'éthique de la science et de la technologie. 2006. *Éthique et nanotechnology: se donner les moyens d'agir*, Avis, Gouvernement du Québec.

European Commission. 2007. *Taking European Knowledge Seriously*. Report of the Expert Group on Science and Governance to the Science, Economy and Society Directorate, Directorat-General for research.

Ferré, Frederick. 1995. *Philosophy of Technology* (Athens, GA: The University of Georgia Press).

Fleischer, T., and A. Grunwald. 2008. "Making Nanotechnology Developments Sustainable. A Role for Technology Assessment?" *Journal of Cleaner Production* 16: 889–898.

Grunwald, A. 2005. "Nanotechnology—A New Field of Ethical Inquiry?" *Science and Engineering Ethics* 11: 187–201.

Gwinn, M., and V. Vallyathan. 2006. "Nanoparticles: Health Effects—Pros and Cons." *Environemnetal Health Perspectives* 114, no. 12: 1818–1825.

Habermas, Jürgen. 2002. *L'avenir de la nature humaine. Vers un eugénisme libéral?* (Paris: Gallimard).

Heidegger, Martin. 1958. *Essais et conférences* (Paris: Gallimard).

Hoyt, V., and E. Mason. 2008. "Nanotechnology Emerging Health Issues." *Journal of Chemical Health and Safety* 15, no. 2: 10–15.

Jonas, Hans. 1984. *The Imperative of Responsibility. In Search of an Ethics for the Technological Age* (Chicago: The University of Chicago Press).

Kaufmann, Daniel. 2005. "10 idées reçues sur la gouvernance et la corruption," *Finance et développement* 42, no. 3.

Kulkarni R. 2007. "Nano-bio-genesis: Tracing the Rise of Nanotechnology and Nanobioetchnology as 'Big Science.'" *Journal of Biomedical Discovery and Collaboration* 2, no. 3: 1–16.

Leopold, Aldo. 1949. *A Sand County Almanac* (New York: Oxford University Press).

Lewenstein, B. 2005. "What Counts as a 'Social and Ethical Issue' in Nanotechnology?" *International Journal for Philosophy of Chemistry* 11, no. 1: 5–18.

Lyotard, Jean-François. 1979. *La condition post-moderne* (Paris: Éditions de minuit).

Maynard, A. 2007. "Nanotechnology: The Next Big Thing, Or Much Ado about Nothing?" *Annals of Occupational Hygiene Advance* 51, no. 1: 1–12.

Mitcham C., and R. Mackey, eds. 1972. *Philosophy and Technology. Readings in the Philosophical Problems of Technology* (New York: The Free Press).

Mnyusiwalla A., A. Daar, and P. Singer. 2003. "'Mind the Gap': Science and Ethics in Nanotechnology." *Nanotechnology* 14: 9–13.

Moor, J. 2005. "Why We Need Better Ethics for Emerging Technologies." *Ethics and Information Technology* 7: 111–119.

Norton, Bryan. 1991. *Toward Unity among Environmentalists* (New York: Oxford University Press).

Pense, C. M., and S. Cutcliffe. 2007. "Risky Talk: Framing the Analysis of the Social Implications of Nanotechnology." *Bulletin of Science Technology Society* 27, no. 5: 349–366.

Preston, Christopher. 2005. "The Promise and the Threat of Nanotechnology. Can Environmental Ethics Guide Us?" *International Journal for Philosophy of Chemistry* 11, no. 1: 19–44.

Rapp, Friedrich. 1974. *Contributions to a Philosophy of Technology* (Dordrecht: Reidel Publishing Company).

Resnik, D., and S. Tinkle. 2007. "Ethical Issues in Clinical Trials Involving Nanomedecine." *Contemporary Clinical Trials* 28: 433–441.

Rocco, Mihail C. 2003. "Broader Societal Issues of Nanotechnology." *Journal of Nanoparticule Research* 5: 181–189.

———. 2008. "Possibilities for Global Governance of Converging Technologies." *Journal of Nanoparticule Research* 10: 11–29.

Rocco, M. C., and W. S. Bainbridge. 2002. "Converging Technologies for Improving Human Performance: Integrating from the Nanoscale." *Journal of Nanoparticule Research* 4: 281–295.

Schulte, P., and F. Salamanca-Buentello. 2007. "Ethical and Scientific Issues of Nanotechnology in the Workplace." *Environemental Health Perspectives* 115, no. 11: 5–12.

Sweeney, A. 2006. "Social and Ethical Dimensions of Nanoscale Science and Engineering Research." *Science and Engineering Ethics* 12: 435–464.

Swiss Centre for Technology Assessment, Switzerland. 2009. *Information about the Study "Nanotechnology in the Food Sector."* www.ta-swiss.ch.

NOWHERE IS ALWAYS NOW AND HERE

BENGT KRISTENSSON UGGLA
ÅBO AKADEMI UNIVERSITY

ABSTRACT: This paper presents a critical reflection on the attempts to determine the historical meaning of the present situation as a philosophical topic. To determine the specific interpretative character of the diagnostics of our contemporary situation—beyond both absolute knowledge and arbitrary thinking—this paper argues that "now" and "here" need to be defined in accordance with the concepts of "historical time" and "inhabited space." This has been made possible as a result of the recent metamorphosis within the hermeneutical tradition.

More than four decades after we first listened to Bob Dylan telling us that "the times they are a-changing," we are inevitably confronted today with "[t]he end of the world as we know it."[1] The reasons for talking about paradigmatic transformations seem to be more convincing than ever, and in our current situation it has almost become a truism to say that we are living in a time of great change. However, as always when experiencing dramatic change, we need to resist "epochal hubris," a tempting egocentrism which places ourselves in an unfeasibly privileged position at the centre of history and the world.

There is a profound philosophical tradition, mainly stemming from Immanuel Kant, which has tried to cope with the task of determining the historical meaning of the present situation as a philosophical topic. Although as philosophers, we sometimes think we are "nowhere," if truth be told—and if we listen carefully to the ontological philosophical tradition stemming from Heidegger and others—we recognize that we are always already embedded in the same world we are attempting to comprehend—"now" and "here." For more than two centuries, this has been taken up as a serious philosophical task: from Kant's attempt to answer the urgent question "Was ist Aufklärung?" and the historization of this question in Hegel's *Geist*-philosophy, via Arendt, Foucault, Beauvoir, and the later humanistic works

Special Supplement, *Journal of Philosophical Research* pp. 303–312
DOI: 10.5840/jpr201237Supplement48

by von Wright and die neue Unüberblickbarkeit of Habermas, to more recent contributions from Hart and Negri, Nussbaum, and Žižek.

With time the task has migrated, the perspectives have been extended and a new kind of expert, with a mixed generalist-specialist competence, mainly based in the social sciences, has emerged.[2] Over the last few decades, we have also gradually been confronted with a web of new notions conceived in an ambition to cope with our turbulent world, and aimed at naming the present. In point of fact , the quest for orientation in an ever changing, runaway world framed by the race for competitive advantages has turned into huge business, associated with a variety of labels—business intelligence, scanning, geo-strategy, contemporary diagnostics—including expectations of receiving specific predications about the future.

In this situation, we need to ask ourselves what kind of particular contribution philosophy might offer. Could it be a more comprehensive understanding of our present circumstances originating from a capacity to develop a bird's-eye view in combination with more accurate concepts, or a more thorough historical contextualization of the current transformations, or a critical philosophical reflection, which turns the world upside down, thus further fostering the idea that "another world is possible"? Valid as these contributions are, nonetheless, according to my opinion a more decisive contribution from philosophy would be to cope with the exceedingly vague theoretical status of these diagnostics of our contemporary situation, and the serious hermeneutical deficit of these often allegedly objectivistic statements; to be precise, to determine the specific interpretative epistemological character of these attempts to name the present, as well as their ontological indications in terms of interventions in an emerging reality.

However, first we need to contextualize our reflections according to the intellectual scene denoted by the title of this symposium.

POST, POST, POST

Beginning in the last decades of the twentieth century, a web of "post-concepts" emerged on the intellectual scene, this caused enduring conflicts concerning the normative status of modernity in a variety of fields with the epicenter in the postmodernism-debates. Thus, when modernity was no longer able to be conceived as uncomplicated, questions were raised as to what extent modernity should be recognized as a problematic, unfulfilled or even more seriously a dangerous and failed project. Already controversial in themselves, if grouped together the inherent complexity of notions such as Tradition, Modernity, and Postmodernity promptly increased. The fact has to be considered that the recognition of a tradition, the authority of which is opposed by the modern quest for *Mündigkeit*, is in itself an innovation of modernity—moreover, today, the same modernity is concurrently one of our most important traditions. In point of fact, due to our embeddedness in the world and the inevitable selective character of our ways of coping with reality and the past, we are *always already* part of traditions (due to more or less critically reflected agreements), and there will *always already* be some kind of canon governing our intellectual interests and preferences (we do not have the capacity to read everything, selection is inevitable).

Nevertheless, one important outcome of the controversies about postmodernism is the inducing of a self-critical instance within modernity itself, also perceived as a kind of self-confrontation in accordance with a "second age of modernity."[3] The recognition that the slaves in America were perhaps the first human beings who experienced what modernity really means, reveals a dark side of modernity, a hidden agenda of racism, eurocentrism, US-centrism, androcentrism and logocentrism—as well as the inherent barbarism which seems to dwell unconsciously in every civilization.[4] It is a known fact that only an emperor in the early twentieth century had a comparable living-standard with any ordinary man from a developed country at the end of the same century—and yet during this century more people where murdered than in the entire previous history.[5] The contradictions of this century—also increased by taking into consideration the contrasting experiences and extraordinary progress of democracy and human rights—were in many ways anticipated by Nietzsche, the philosopher who died on its threshold, and yet who determined much of its postmodern philosophical agenda.

However, sometimes the word "postmodern" has appeared as a buzz-word meaning anything and referring to everything—hence signifying nothing. This has made it appropriate to ask if postmodernism is just a new kind of transcendental idealism or the return of a Hegelian specter, which once more haunts our orientation in history. Nevertheless, the philosophical reflections often presented under the title postmodernism must, in effect, be understood in association with some momentous and irreversible changes already transforming our world in profound ways. These include the dramatic geopolitical shift, which is transforming a former Eurocentric world order and a subsequent American dominance into an emerging three-polar world order due to the rise of the East Asian super powers in the aftermath of decolonialization. Language is never to be seen as an innocent and pure instrument, thus the fact that modern philosophy has mainly been articulated in three languages of European origin—English, German and French—might have had tremendous impact on our philosophical thinking, as to its form as well as matter, and on issues of access and influence. Certainly, a World Congress of Philosophy located in South-Korea is a sign which seriously urges us to "re-think philosophy" in fundamental ways. Philosophy, together with other disciplines, is in this situation forced to confront and revise the actual particularity of many of its universal claims, as well as the fact that so many "discoveries" have turned out to be inventions, thus disclosing its actual prerequisites. The solution is not to erase these traditions, as if trying to start the philosophical reflection from zero without any prerequisites, nor to develop that kind of self-contradictory philosophy, which is being manifested in such philosophical positions as "anti-Eurocentric eurocentrism."[6] Philosophy is solidly fabricated upon traditions, but traditions must always be handled and nurtured in a critically reflected way.

THE NEW AGENDA DEFINED BY GLOBALIZATION

After the fierce debates about modernity and postmodernity on the cusp of the millennium—in philosophy, we acquired post-structuralism as well as post-analytical philosophy—the number of "post-concepts" has decreased as has the intellectual energy in the controversies concerning modernity. Subsequently, the agenda has changed dramatically. A new predominantly epochal concept has emerged, challenging philosophy to cope with new realities—globalization.

To define globalization in vague terms referring to a general interdependency around the globe does not seem sufficient. Instead, in accordance with Manuel Castells, I understand globalization as something more specific referring to the synergic and centrifugal effects of a de-regulated world economy with increasing trans-national features and the rise of a new networked, digitally convergent information systems operating in real time. Increasingly, over the last three decades, the dominant activities in our world have begun to be organized around information technology-powered networks and for the first time in the history of humankind, we are experiencing a global simultaneity and a market operating in real time, with all its unpredictable consequences.[7]

Globalization has brought about incomparable economic growth and increased standards of health in the world—but simultaneously produced a dramatic growth in the inequalities between states and individuals. Due to the one-sidedness of the development, in which the technological and economical dimensions of the globalization process are so well-developed when compared with the weak socio-cultural and political infrastructures, the risk of a cultural back lash is overwhelming. Certainly, we need to be reminded that there are many different and divergent narratives about globalization, which are gradually generating a clash of globalizations.

Without any doubt, today this transformation process is also determining a great deal of the current philosophical agenda; however, we also need to ask ourselves seriously, not only what globalization means to philosophy, but what kind of contribution philosophy might offer to the challenges raised by the globalization process.

Furthermore, a global policy consensus now seems to have been established about the most appropriate strategy to successfully cope with the challenges of globalization, namely by supporting a rapid transition to a knowledge-based economy. This is probably articulated most clearly in the Lisbon Agenda, with its strong focus on global competitiveness by developing a knowledge-based economy. Accordingly, in the newly emerging informational society, which has replaced industrialism, knowledge is increasingly identified as a key factor with utopian expectations; hence it is conceived as the engine powering economical development. Re-reading the "postmodern classics" *La condition postmodern* (1979) within this current context, we may recognize Jean-François Lyotard's foresight in his work on the strategic importance of knowledge in the emerging knowledge economy.[8] Three dominant aspects may be distinguished in this new cognitive capitalism (Yann Moulier-Boutang), configured according to the virtue of flexible order in an organization; competence (lifelong learning as the new life script), evidence (the new focus on measurement, efficiency, accounting) and innovation (creative industries). However, the predominant virtue of flexibility, in these new discourses concerning knowledge, also risks ruining the cultural prerequisites for a vibrant philosophical discourse. In addition, this new predominant, flexible mode of knowledge organization does not seem at all sufficient to support the cultivation of meaning and identity. Consequently, in order to resist the evolvement of a flexible man—a man without memory, conviction, and responsibility—we turn to the intellectual resources provided by hermeneutics.

THE METAMORPHOSIS OF HERMENEUTICS

From a historical point of view, it is certainly relevant to ask if globalization has anything at all to do with hermeneutics, because traditionally, hermeneutics has not been in any way compatible with the areas in which globalization is associated. However, recent transformations within the hermeneutical tradition have exposed new opportunities to link together the problematic of hermeneutics respective globalization.

The echo from German hermeneutics of understanding (and later pre-understanding) has been constantly present in every dialogue on interpretation during the twentieth century. It is hardly possible to overestimate the significance of the fact that hermeneutics from its very entry into the epistemological discourse established a radical dichotomy between "understanding" (*Verstehen*) in the human sciences and "explanation" (*Erkärung*) in natural sciences (Wilhelm Dilthey). However, it is also impossible to disregard the turn towards an elaborated phenomenological conception of time and the finite horizons of understanding of Martin Heidegger and Hans-Georg Gadamer, who put universal ambitions behind the defense of a comparable ontological domain.[9]

To be able to deal with globalization, and thus connect the globalization process to the hermeneutical experience, we need to find a way out of this blind alley of the predominant German tradition. Although Paul Ricoeur is confusingly often integrated into this "canonized" narrative of German hermeneutics, it must be emphasized that Ricoeur's hermeneutics cannot be fully understood as merely an augmentation of German hermeneutics. Ricoeur, by defiantly pointing out "the hermeneutical function of distanciation in all communication," has brought about a profound metamorphosis of hermeneutics, which has extended the concept of interpretation to embrace understanding (*Verstehen*) as well as explanation (*Erklärung*). According to this hermeneutical perspective, ontology must be developed *with the help of* epistemology (as an alternative to Martin Heidegger's fundamental ontology) and truth must be reached *through* method (instead of Hans-Georg Gadamer's "truth or method").[10]

GLOBALIZATION AND THE AGE OF HERMENEUTICS

Instead of trying to bring all sciences and experiences back to a more primordial ontological *Dasein*-domain, or to limit hermeneutical experience exclusively to an epistemology of understanding or an aesthetic sphere, philosophers in the vein of Gianni Vattimo and others have pointed out how the internal development within science and technology themselves has prepared the way for hermeneutics; a situation in which there are no stable facts, only variable interpretations. From this perspective, hermeneutics seems in a startling way to be inscribed as an integral part of the discourse on globalization. Through the digitalized, global information system, the old stable hierarchies of meaning, identity and truth are being eroded, dissolving traditional canons of art, values and knowledge. When all information is increasingly ordered horizontally and when the networks of relationships on the Internet (as a convergent technology of information) are constantly changing, when everything is continuously re-contextualized and re-interpreted as new links are added, which give our knowledge a center-less and historically contingent character, causing a multitude of conflicting interpretations to be released. The loss of a stable center and hierarchy in the world due to the use of computer technologies and the reception of the many voices in the mass media paves the way for a culture of knowledge far removed from Platonic essentialism and a "foundationalist" quest for an underlying nature. Vattimo brings this all together with the profound consequences of the geopolitical transformations in the aftermath of de-colonialization, Nietzsche's philosophical reflections on "the erosion of the very principle of reality" and Heidegger's critique against the strong and violent thoughts of Metaphysics into an ultimate conclusion of a history of nihilism as a weakening of the strong and violent thoughts of Metaphysics. This has altogether dissolved the conception of a single and stable Reality into a multitude of interpretations among which there is, in the end, no correct interpretation.[11]

From this background, we may state that globalization has also contributed to a situation that might be defined as an age of hermeneutics.[12] The circumstances today that allow interpretation be found everywhere, as a non-reflected, generalized experience of variations and an endless plurality of perspectives, together with the rise in the number of conflicting interpretations, are to be precise essentially abetted by the main economical and technological transformation of the world—the globalization process.

RE-THINKING PHILOSOPHY AS A CONFLICT OF INTERPRETATION

Today, as a combined outcome of the globalization process, an emerging knowledge economy and profound geopolitical transformations in a "flat world"[13] Reality tends to disperse into a multitude of interpretations. However, it is obvious that the many different visions of the world today do not automatically coexist peacefully, on the contrary they tend to generate violence and in a worst-case scenario a war of all against all. In many ways, we might say that we are challenged by the cultural aspects of an "armed globalization"[14] where people, just by imposing their own perspectives on others, generate ever new "reality battles" and "knowledge massacres." One of the immediate major challenges in this situation is to transform the conception of a threatening clash of civilizations[15] into a conflict of interpretations, i.e., to configure a peaceful model for conflict resolutions where all convictions are critically and self-critically reflected upon and where all perspectives are legitimized and "founded" by being limited. The hermeneutical alternative to both a fearful "war of interpretations" and a philosophical resignation of non-communication is a conflict of interpretations, but this presumes an awareness of the interpretative character of ones own perspective. The reason being, that the strong and violent thoughts of Western metaphysics threatens our conversations by not recognizing themselves as interpretations, Vattimo has argued for an understanding of hermeneutics as "weak thought"—*pensiero debole*—a critical as well as self-critical approach informed by the intention to carefully relate ones own interpretations to other interpretations.

Globalization is today generating a mould for interpretations configured as an unreflected, generalized experience of variations and an endless plurality of available perspectives. However, hermeneutics may also offer resources to develop a more pro-active, critically reflected strategy to cope with this experience of a plurality of perspectives in a responsible way by conceptualizing conflicts in terms of conflicting interpretations. At the same time, this ability to articulate conflicts in terms of conflicting interpretations is also a safeguard against the risk of transforming hermeneutics into arbitrary thinking. Within hermeneutics, text and interpretation are mutually defined concepts, a correlation in which both the possibility and the limitations of all interpretations are determined. Interpretation can therefore not be considered as free imagination, but as regulated imagination bound to external determinations.

Thoroughly conscious of the need to combine the act of taking a stand with the need to respect the legitimacy of other interpretations, hermeneutics, as such, is probably the most appropriate intellectual resource for a society framed by pluralism and democracy.[16] Furthermore, hermeneutics may remind democracy, suffering from a "hermeneutical deficit," about both the possibility and the necessity of a multitude of perspectives—while democracy may remind hermeneutics that all interpretations are inevitably controversial and inscribed in power-relations. Hermeneutics as well as democracy urges us to live without Absolute Knowledge, to cope with incomplete solutions, endure fragility—and simultaneously they both intend to resist being reduced to arbitrary relativism. Nevertheless, in order to be able to succeed in living together in polis with preserved differences (Hannah Arendt), constantly striving for better interpretations (Paul Ricoeur) and through processes framed by the preserved tension between the ideal and the real community of communication (Karl-Otto Apel), we sometimes need to remind our anxiety that as a matter of fact only a democratic society recognizes itself as not being democratic enough (Jacques Derrida, Zygmunt Bauman).

HISTORICAL TIME AND INHABITED SPACE

Confronted with the task of defending the truth claims of interpretation—and at the same time renouncing the hubris of a Total Reflection—we are asked to account for a hermeneutical situation where the "fact" that everything is interpretation needs to be recognized as an interpretation itself. As the concept of interpretation seems to have the same amplitude of application as that of the concept of truth, Vattimo has requested that we situate our philosophical reflections historically, thus defining hermeneutics as being the accomplished history of nihilism.

History holds a paradigmatic function for knowledge and truth in an age of hermeneutics, however, it does not seem sufficient to achieve the transition from a vague "nowhere" to a concrete determination of "now" and "here" by exclusively applying the phenomenological conceptions of time and space (thus by an approach to time where no watch, no calendar and no examining of the archives are necessary). In order to present an alternative to the predominant concept of flexible man, our philosophical anthropology needs to be situated properly in space and time, which presumes an understanding of the human as someone being capable of memory, conviction and responsibility,

In one of his later works, Ricoeur stated the problems connected with a phenomenological approach by asking: "up to what point can a phenomenology of dating and localizing be constituted without borrowing from the objective knowledge of geometrical—let us say, Euclidian and Cartesian—space and from the knowledge of chronological time?"[17] Ricoeur himself has, moreover, proposed an alternative dialectical model for hermeneutics, where temporality is not solely identified as a lived (experiential—phenomenological) time in opposition to cosmic time, but as a "third," historical time, constituted by the dialectical connections between lived and cosmic time. In a similar way, it is not sufficient to define spatiality solely as a lived space, in opposition to geometrical space, but rather as an inhabited space, constituted by the connections between these two conceptions of space.[18] However, this parallel constitution of temporality and spatiality as a hetereogeneous synthesis indicates a "mixed" mode of thinking, which incorporates objective as well as subjective approaches, making it possible not only to distinguish hermeneutics from absolute knowledge, but also from a relativism which risks transforming interpretation into arbitrary thinking. A naming of the present, situated and contextualized in historical time as well as inhabited space, does not only influence broader epistemological perspectives, it also involves ontological implications, placing the whole problematic of our world orientations on the hermeneutical edge between discovery and innovation. The interpretative character of our interventions in the world may be understood according to a mimesis-process where our configurations continuously reconfigure the world we try to understand.[19] Consequently, instead of posing the question whether our knowledge and diagnostics—as well as such phenomena as language, science, history and media—are discoveries or inventions, hermeneutics invites us to explore the landscape that opens up upon the distinction itself as an emerging reality. This being exactly the place where interpretation resides.

NOTES

1. Immanuel Wallerstein, *The End of the World as We Know It. Social Science for the Twenty-first Century* (Minneapolis: University of Minnesota Press, 1999).

2. Among this new generalist-specialists we might identify such authors as Ulrich Beck, Anthony Giddens, Zygmunt Bauman, Saskia Sassen, David Held, and many others.

3. Ulrich Beck, *Rissikogesellschaft. Auf dem Weg in einen andere Moderne* (Frankfurt: Suhrkamp, 1986); *Macht und Gegenmacht im globalen Zeitalter* (Frankfurt: Suhrkamp, 2002).

4. Cornel West, *The American Evasion of Philosophy. A Genealogy of Pragmatism* (Madison, WI: The University of Wisconsin Press, 1989); *Beyond Eurocentrism and Multiculturalism I–II* (Monroe, ME: Common Courage Press,1993).

5. Eric Hobsbawn, *Globalisation, Democracy and Terrorism* (London: Abacus, 2007), p. 15

6. Immanuel Wallerstein uses this notion in *The End of the World as We Know It.*

7. Manuel Castells, *The Information Age I–III* (Oxford: Basil Blackwell 1996, 1997, 1998) including later revised editions and other works. Although we have experienced a web of literature on globalization, I find Castells works still as a milestone in connection with the task to define what globalization really means.

8. Jean-François Lyotard, *La condition postmoderne. Rapport sur le savoir* (Paris: Minuit, 1979).

9. Wilhelm Dilthey, "Die Entstehung der Hermeneutik" (1900), in *Gesammelte Schriften*, band 5 (Leipzig: Verlag von BG Teubner, 1924), pp. 317–331; Martin Heidegger, *Sein und Zeit* (Tübingen: Max Niemeyer Verlag, 1927/1993); Hans-Georg Gadamer *Wahrheit und Methode. Grundzüge einer philosophischen Hermeneutik* (Tübingen: J. C. B. Mohr, 1960/1975).

10. Paul Ricoeur, *Le conflit des interprétations. Essais d'herméneutique* (Paris: Seuil, 1969); *Du texte á l'action. Essais d'herméneutique, II* (Paris: Seuil, 1986).

11. Gianni Vattimo, *Beyond Interpretation: The Meaning of Hermeneutics for Philosophy* (Stanford, CA: Stanford University Press, 1994/1997); *Nihilism and Emancipation: Ethics, Politics and Law* (New York: Columbia University Press, 2003/2004); *Dialogue with Nietzsche* (New York: Columbia University Press, 2000/2006); and other works.

12. Jean Greisch, *L'âge herméneutique de la raison* (Paris: Cerf, 1985); Gianni Vattimo *Beyond Interpretation: The Meaning of Hermeneutics for Philosophy* (Stanford, CA: Stanford University Press, 1994/1997); and Bengt Kristensson Uggla, *Slaget om verkligheten. Filosofi, omvärldsanalys, tolkning* (Stockholm: Symposion, 2002).

13. Thomas Friedman, *The World is Flat: A Brief History of the Globalized World in the 21st Century* (New York: Penguin, 2005).

14. Michael Hardt and Antonio Negri, *Multitude: War and Democracy in the Age of Empire* (New York: Penguin Books, 2005/2006), pp. 231–237.

15. Samuel Huntington, *The Clash of Civilizations and the Remaking of World Order* (Clearwater, FL: Touchstone Books, 1998).

16. This is one of the main theses in Gianni Vattimo, *Beyond Interpretation: The Meaning of Hermeneutics for Philosophy* (Stanford, CA: Stanford University Press, 1994/1997).

17. Paul Ricoeur, *Memory, History, Forgetting* (Chicago: University of Chicago Press, 2000/2004), p. 41.

18. Ibid., pp. 147–161.

19. Paul Ricoeur, *Temps et Récit I* (Paris: Seuil, 1983), 85–129. Peter Kemp has elaborated on this threefold mimesis process as a process of cultivation, in *Världsmedborgaren. Politisk och pedagogisk filosofi för det 21 århundradet* (Göteborg: Daidalos, 2005). English translation by Russell L. Dees as *Citizen of the World: Cosmopolitan Ideals for the Twenty-First Century* (Amherst, NY: Humanity Books, 2011).

Overcoming Dichotomies

ELMAR HOLENSTEIN
PROFESSOR EMERITUS FROM BOCHUM, ZÜRICH

ABSTRACT: A symposium with the title "Tradition, Modernity and Postmodernity: Eastern and Western Perspectives" is in need of a subtitle auch as "Overcoming Dichotomies." Societies, as well as historical epochs, are complex and overlapping phenomena. A clash between complex civilizations will naturally be a complex encounter. The conflicting parties will always find kindred souls on the other side, motivated by converging interests and values. Modernity and secularism are not inseparable, and tradionality and secularism are not incompatible (see Confucian politology). Two main philosophical reasons for the complexity of civilizations are the heterarchical structure of the human value system and the creative potential of human individuals. These highest values cannot be optimally realized at the same time. The potential for self-fulfillment that every human being has, thanks to his mental structures, excedes the potential for self-fulfillment a singular culture can provide.

Let me welcome you to the symposium "Tradition, Modernity, and Postmodernity: Eastern and Western Perspectives." To be honest, I feared the title of the symposium would not be overly inviting, that it was too reminiscent of the somewhat stale debates from the past century. I therefore assume that, like me, you spontaneously appended a super- or subtitle, such as "Overcoming Dichotomies." The objective is not to enlarge on the concepts of *Tradition, Modernity, and Postmodernity, East and West* but rather to break them down and perhaps even to strike them off the list of philosophical concepts.

I have the honor of moderating a panel with three distinguished scholars, but reading their names made me think twice, naturally not because of the persons themselves but because of their origins. All three and I myself are at home in the northern half of the Northern Hemisphere. (I'm the only one at this table who lives outside that region—south of Seoul by about 100 miles, in Yokohama, Japan.) No one comes from South Asia, South America, or Africa. That, too, should stimulate

Special Supplement, *Journal of Philosophical Research* pp. 313–316
DOI: 10.5840/jpr201237Supplement49

our debate. There are not only Eastern or Western perspectives, foreshortened to Northeastern and Northwestern ones, but also manifold Southern perspectives.

We are all familiar with the opening lines of Rudyard Kipling's "Ballad of East and West"; we have heard them quoted untold times:

> Oh, East is East, and West is West / and never the twain shall meet.

Few know the closing lines of the ballad and even fewer people quote them:

> But there is neither East nor West, / Border, nor Breed, nor Birth,
>
> When two strong men [read: humans] stand face to face /
> though they come from the ends of the earth!

It is not a question of one assertion being true and the other false. The truth of both is obviously limited: East and West, border, breed and birth, genes and genders, caste and "race," region and religion, cultural background and intellectual orientation, traditional roots and contemporary rootlessness—happily, there are more and more, and even enduring situations, where such distinctions have become irrelevant. Nonetheless, there are quite enough opportunities for encounters among people, even from the far-flung corners of the earth, who delight precisely because the others are different, feel different, think differently and behave differently. We appreciate having our attention drawn to something we would otherwise have neglected and perhaps even mistakenly considered inferior. Or we are grateful to have found a partner who has something to offer that compensates for our own insufficiencies. There is so much that is only possible by cooperating with others who take a different approach.

These are common experiences when it comes to encounters between individuals from the same culture. But they meet with disbelief when individuals and, even more so, entire groups come from different cultures, some from so-called traditional, others from so-called modern and still others from so-called postmodern ones. The question that concerns us as philosophers is whether disbelief in the compatibility of these cultures can be supported by cogent and compelling philosophical arguments. The causes of this stubborn disbelief may possibly be instilled or even innate, in which case it ought to be corrected or at least kept in check by social measures.

One of the maxims of comparative linguistics states: Never compare only two languages but always a minimum of three or, still better, several. This obviates trading in precocious absolutes, making claims to uniqueness and to mutual exclusion: typically traditional and typically modern, typically Eastern and typically Western. Obviously, contrasts can be observed between certain articulations of traditional and modern, Eastern and Western civilizations, social systems and nations. But the moment one considers several civilizations, social systems and nations in concert, all kinds of crisscrossing connections emerge in one respect and dividing lines in another. Cross-classifications surface and create a mesh of intertwined alliances. They cannot be untwined without causing the formation of new knots elsewhere or, worse yet, tearing the strings and the threads.

The mesh turns into a tangle in view of the fact that (1) all societies and civilizations are complex and that (2) they are all subject to historical change—the so-called traditional ones included. Over are the days of believing in homogeneous cultural areas and of equating "prehistoriographic" with "prehistoric" (i.e., static). All societies make distinctions of age, gender, kinship, and marital status; many also make social distinctions based on occupation, property, and education as well as center and periphery, town and country. A clash of civilizations inevitably proves to be a clash of *complex* civilizations. A uniform front line in the clash between two richly varied cultural societies (traditional and modern or Eastern and Western) is not to be expected. Time and again the conflicting parties will find kindred souls and sympathizers on the other side, motivated by converging interests and values.

Talk of "multiple modernities"[1] has speedily become commonplace. Postmodern societies are diverse *per definitionem*—they, however, sometimes think that modern and premodern ones are not. Anthropologists have always been aware of the multiplicity of traditional societies. In the nineteenth century they managed at least to distinguish between "savages," "barbarians," and "ancient high civilizations." Only some philosophers still speak sweepingly of "traditionally defined civilizations."[2]

The breakdown of "modernity" as a concept is recently illustrated by the belated insight that modernization and secularization are not inseparable processes. A state can fulfill the classical criteria of a modern state (democracy, separation of powers, separation of church and state, individual human rights, equality of the genders, bureaucracy, industrial and post-industrial economy, appreciation of the Enlightenment, etc.) and still have a largely religious population. In fact, a number of modern states rely on a religiously defined party as one of their main pillars.

To all appearances, however, leading philosophical analysts of modern "Western" secularity do not seem to realize that secularity (separation of both church and state as well as theology and morals) is not an exclusively modern phenomenon. Nor is it applicable only to the affluent societies of the North Atlantic and South Pacific (Europe, U.S.A. and Canada, Australia, and New Zealand). China was a secular empire long before coming into contact with European Enlightenment and, at the same time, it was a civilization with characteristically traditional structures (estimation of tradition, belief in fate, a communitarian and family-centered social order, monarchy, no separation of powers, inadequate individual rights, legal and social inequality of women and an agricultural and craft-oriented economy, to mention but a few). Individual religious freedom was taken for granted in traditional China and, at least among the literati, the attitude towards all questions regarding a divine sphere and the "hereafter" was predominantly agnostic.

In a philosophical discussion of our subject matter, the question arises: are there, apart from the predictable economic and social factors, philosophical reasons for the complexity of civilizations, especially those in which modern and traditional traits are intertwined?

There is one important and obvious reason: human civilizations are not the only entities with great inner tension. The same applies to human value systems.

The values that are by nature dear to human beings do not yield neat pyramids of single values arranged above, under, or next to each other in harmony and without conflict. The optimal realization of one value does not, at the same time, contribute to the optimal realization of all other values. Value dilemmas and the far-reaching consequences of choosing not only between good and evil but also between various goods are inescapable. Optimal individual freedom is not compatible with optimal social justice, just as the principle of "everyone according to their needs" is not compatible with the principle of "everyone according to their performance." Contingent factors play an unpredictable role in making decisions. For this reason, in every democracy, some parties believe they attain the greatest happiness for the greatest number of people by granting more individual freedom and others call for a more regulated solidarity to achieve that same goal. The prosperity of a civilization is also always dependent on its numbers. What is more important for a member of a threatened civilization: the right to self-fulfillment exercised by moving away, by a mixed marriage, or by a technical profession, or the obligation to adhere to a language and a culture that is threatened with extinction? Universal agreement when faced with such dilemmas is simply not possible. People will, in future, continue to be traditionalist, modernist and postmodernist and, what's more, in different ways within each.

The potential for self-fulfillment that every human being has due to his mental structures is more comprehensive and more varied than the potential for self-fulfillment that a singular civilization (be it modern or traditional, Eastern or Western or Southern) provides. The various natural dispositions with which a human being is born are not all optimally realized in a singular cultural tradition, be it pre-modern, modern or post-modern.

NOTES

1. Shmuel Eisenstadt, "Multiple Modernities," *Daedalus* 129, no. 1 (2000): 1–29.
2. Cf. Jürgen Habermas, "Die Dialektik der Säkularisierung," in *Blätter für deutsche und internationale Politik* (April 2008): 33–46, 37.

BIBLIOGRAPHY

Holenstein, Elmar. 2004. *Philosophie-Atlas: Orte und Wege des Denkens*. Zürich: Ammann.

———. 2009. *China ist nicht ganz anders*. Zürich: Ammann.

SELECTED PAPERS FROM THE XXII WORLD CONGRESS OF PHILOSOPHY

Asian Naturalism: An Old Vision for a New World

HEE-SUNG KEEL
SOGANG UNIVERSITY

Abstract: Naturalism is a pan-Asian view of the world and way of life. Unlike the atheistic naturalism in the West, Asian naturalism, which rests upon an organic view of the world as represented by key concepts such as the Dao, Heaven, and Emptiness, is basically spiritual. Going beyond the traditional Western antithesis of naturalism and supernaturalism, matter and spirit, it can even be called "supernatural naturalism." As a living example of Asian naturalism, this article examines the ethics of threefold reverence: reverence toward Heaven, all human beings, and all beings, animate and inanimate. Threefold reverence constitutes the cardinal teaching of Cheondogyo or the Eastern Learning, a native Korean religio-philosophical movement which arose in the latter half of the nineteenth century. The ecological-environmental crisis of our age cannot be overcome without a fundamental change in our attitude toward nature. Recovering humanity's primal sense of reverence toward all beings in nature is a vital part of this change.

INTRODUCTION

In his great work, *Science and Civilization in China*, Joseph Needham characterized the Chinese world view as "organic naturalism,"[1] a naturalism that differs from the mechanistic view of the world which has dominated the Western approach to nature since the rise of modern science. Organic naturalism is a holistic way of understanding reality, according to which things in the world are not separate entities but are internally related to form organic patterns and unity; there is a fundamental "continuity of being" not only between individual entities but also between different categories and layers of being. All forms of existence are regarded as visible manifestations of the single primordial vital force called *yuan-qi* which constantly transforms itself into different modalities.

Special Supplement, *Journal of Philosophical Research* pp. 317–332
DOI: 10.5840/jpr201237Supplement50

I would not hesitate to call this dynamic holistic view of the world a "pan-Asian" (East Asian) world view that has dominated the Asian mind in nearly every aspect of life—from religion and philosophy to medicine, art, and architecture—not only in the high cultures of Asian countries but also in the daily lives of ordinary people. It is still a living tradition in Asian countries, considerably weakened as it has been under the influence of the modern scientific and technological way of thinking.

In this paper I will examine the nature of this Asian naturalism, its fundamental spirit and characteristics in contrast to the naturalism in the West. I will then introduce the ethics of "threefold reverence" (*samgyeong*) formulated by Haeweol (1827–1898), the third patriarch of Cheondogyo, a native Korean religio-philosophical tradition, as a prime living example of Asian naturalism. My paper concludes with some observations on the need and possibility of constructing a new metaphysics of Asian naturalism for today.

NATURALISM EAST AND WEST

Organic naturalism is by no means a monopoly of the Asian mind; it was a dominant view of nature in the West before the rise of the modern scientific world view. But nowhere has its influence been as pervasive and lasting as in East Asian cultures, and there is something unique in it which from the beginning distinguishes it from its Western counterpart. The Greeks viewed the world with its ceaseless motion as alive, that is, animated by the world-soul, and as intelligent and rational because of its orderly and regular movement, attributing this to a cosmic mind or intelligence. But the East Asian organic naturalism did not conceive of such cosmic intelligence; the world was regarded as essentially self-organizing and self-regulating.

The cosmic mind was initially thought by the Greeks to be inherent in nature, but later came to be regarded as outside of it under the Christian influence with the idea of a supernatural deity. The Western world eventually came to dispense with the idea of cosmic intelligence altogether as superfluous. The idea of God as cosmic intelligence and law-giver initially played a significant role in developing modern science, but the idea of a supernatural God who can at the same time intervene in the process of the world against the laws of nature enacted by himself was totally unacceptable for the scientific mind seeking mechanistic explanation of the natural world. As a consequence, naturalism, as a philosophical position which seeks to understand all phenomena and events occurring in the world without any reference to divine causality, came to be virtually synonymous with atheism in the West.

It is now widely recognized that the biblical belief in God as the supernatural creator of the world, with its sharp distinction between God and the world, formed an important ideological background for the desacralized view of the world in the modern West. By separating divinity from nature, and thus allowing the very possibility of understanding the natural world without reference to its supernatural author, Christianity ironically paved the way for its own demise in the modern world. In the ancient world dominated by the worship of the mysterious forces of nature and the magical efforts to influence them, the Christian faith in God cleared the ground for the rise of a purely naturalistic understanding of the world, resulting in the thorough disenchantment of the world such as we witness today. Is it a mere coincidence that "atheism" in its authentic sense, with all its negative connotations and consequences—skepticism, nihilism, and the sense of the meaninglessness of the universe and human life, and so on—first arose in the Christian West?

It is also a well-known fact that the Western intellectual tradition has long been dominated by a series of dualistic oppositions created by the biblical notion of the creator God: the transcendent and the immanent, the sacred and the profane, nature and grace, reason and revelation, church and state, and religion and culture—which in turn have been closely related to the dualism of spirit and matter, the soul and the body, the masculine and the feminine, and so on. These oppositions were basically alien to Asian thought and culture in general, which not only had no idea of supernatural deity in the first place but, more fundamentally, had no dual origin analogous to that in the West, the so-called Hellenic and the Hebraic.

Having no concept of divine revelation in the first place and hence no split between reason and revelation, Asian religions have been basically philosophical religions and Asian philosophies religious philosophies. Thus naturalism has not been defined in Asian tradition in terms of its opposition to supernaturalism. Asian naturalism is accordingly not antagonistic to religious spirituality at all. Simply stated, there is a "sacred depth" to nature[2] in Asian naturalism, hence a religious or spiritual naturalism. Just as the Asian concept of "nothingness" (*wu*; Kor.: *mu*) goes beyond the Western antithesis of being and non-being, Asian naturalism defies the opposition of theism and atheism predicated upon the sharp distinction between the natural and the supernatural, and the spiritual and the material, in the Western tradition.

This is borne out by the fact that matter itself has not been understood in the Asian naturalistic tradition as purely "material," or the spirit purely as "spiritual" either for that matter. The best evidence for this is the concept of *qi/ch'i* (Kor.: *gi*), the vital force or energy—the key concept underlying Asian organismic view of the world and one of the common vocabularies in daily use in Asian countries, but often very elusive for the Western mind to grasp, because it does not fit nicely into either of the two categories, spirit and matter. Asian naturalistic world view has never been dominated by the dualism of spirit and matter that has defined the Western attitude toward the material world and spirituality. Unlike "Europeans who could only think in terms either of Democritean mechanical materialism or of Platonic theological spiritualism,"[3] Asian naturalism understood the world and the human being in a holistic way. Far from viewing the material world as purely inert and passive, and hence as the object that can be made completely transparent to human mind and mastered by it, Asian naturalistic mind always regarded the world of nature as inexhaustibly vibrant and creative, and full of spiritual meaning and message for humans to read. Accordingly, the metaphysical depreciation of the material world and the human body is essentially foreign to Asian naturalistic spirituality, which is very much "earthly" and "bodily."

Nature is simply everything in Asian naturalism, and there is no other reality which is responsible for its existence and operation. The modern East Asian word for nature, *ziran* (Kor.: *jayeon*), which literally means "so of itself," was originally not used as a noun referring to the natural world but as an adjectival and adverbial term referring to the spontaneous way nature works by its own power and principle, with no further cause beyond it. The Asian mind did not recognize the need to postulate cosmic intelligence in order to account for its harmonious order. The world is simply self-organizing and self-regulating, having no creator or the law-giver.

This does not suggest, however, as some erroneously believe, that the Asian mind lacked any metaphysical interest in exploring the ultimate ground of reality—the search for the *arche* of the natural world or its *prima causa*. The biblical notion of creation Asian naturalism certainly did not have, but it did not avoid metaphysical speculation on the ultimate reality of the world; it is only that it was sought within nature itself. This distinguishes Asian naturalism from Christian supernaturalism, on the one hand, and from the atheistic and anti-metaphysical naturalism of the West, on the other hand.

THE DAO AND HEAVEN

The first concept that comes to our mind in this regard is the famous term Dao (Kor.: *do*). It literally means "way," and it has often been rendered as the Way in the West. While certainly legitimate in denoting the aspect of the Dao as the way nature works spontaneously, it does not, on the other hand, do full justice to its metaphysical dimension. For the Dao, like the Hindu concept of Brahman, has at the same time the ontological meaning as the ultimate reality of the world—the source from which the myriad things of the universe originate and to which they return. Thus I regard the Dao as a metaphysical concept without any reservation, notwithstanding some tendency to interpret it otherwise today. Eternal and infinite, the Dao is self-subsisting, having "its own souce: and "its own root."[4] Formless and nameless, it is not a being but rather "nothingness"—not as pure nonbeing, but as the ever-creative matrix of the infinite varieties of beings in the world.

The Dao is not the creator of the world in the sense of making the world as its handiwork, nor is it understood as its law-giver who is responsible for its rational order. As mentioned before, the world is basically self-organizing for the Daoist; the very word Dao refers to this self-organizing power of the world. As such, it is thoroughly immanent in the changing world and does not constitute a "separate" reality distinguished from it by its immutable eternity. Much like Spinoza's *natura naturans*, the Dao is not merely immanent in the world, but the world is its manifestation. Thus it is present even in the most insignificant things of the world, such as tiles and feces, as *Zhuangzi* says. Daoism is unabashedly "pantheistic" in this respect, if we may still use a theistic term.

There is no concept of creation *ex nihilo* in Daoism, and in Asian tradition as a whole for that matter; the nothingness (*wu*; Kor.: *mu*) of the Dao refers to the inexhaustible creative matrix of the universe, not the pure and simple nonexistence of the world. The world is not created *ex nihilo* but formed out of the primeval chaos (*hun-dun*; Kor.: *hondon*) of the Dao as the primordial vital force (*yuan-qi*; Kor.: *weon'gi*) of the universe. This means that there is no absolute beginning of things nor their absolute end; they only change forms. Everything in the world is explained in terms of the ceaseless movement of the primordial vital force *yuan-qi*, the ever-shifting interplay of its two polar powers, *yin* and *yang*, and by its condensation and dilution.

Unlike God, whose will as the law-giver of the universe has been rationalized in the Western tradition through the concept of divine logos or reason, Dao's operation is considered essentially "dark" and mysterious, escaping our rational comprehension. Our intellect and discursive thought are said to be unable to plumb its infinite depth and creativity nor capture its lively movement. Using Bertrand Russell's expression, "the combination of mathematics and theology"[5] did not have a parallel in Asian naturalistic tradition. It did not particularly strike the Asian mind that nature has a mathematical structure—a rational order intelligible to human mind. While this may have had negative effect for Asian naturalism to develop modern physics operating with mathematical formulations, at the same time it prevented the Asian mind from viewing the natural world as a closed system strictly governed by causal laws. Full of inexhaustible vitality and shrouded in the mystery of the inscrutable Dao, nature was never viewed by the Asian mind as fully transparent to human intellect and amenable to its rational comprehension through quantifying and mechanistic approach. The Daoist universe is not a closed system. Ever-creative and open, new things and unpredictable events can always happen in it. Surely the world is orderly for the Daoist as well, but its order is by no means considered pre-given or predetermined; it is emergent with the spontaneous movement of the Dao itself.

An essentially similar view of the world emerges when we examine another key concept in the Asian naturalistic tradition, namely Heaven (*tian*; Kor.: *cheon*), a term equally at home in Daoism and Confucianism. Often virtually synonymous with the Dao, Heaven also refers to the invisible and infinite source of the universe from which "ten thousand things" originate, each with its proper nature, and to which they all return in due time, following the Heaven's way (*tian-dao*; Kor.: *cheondo*) or its principle (*tian-li*; Kor.: *cheolli*). The *Zhuangzi* calls it the Gate of Heaven (*tian-men*; Kor.: *cheonmun*)[6]—the "absolute nonbeing" (*wu-you*) as the creative matrix of all beings like the Dao. Although often conceived at the popular level as possessing human will like a personal God, the more philosophical mind, whether Daoist or Confucian, has always understood Heaven in transpersonal and cosmic terms.

One crucial element, however, that distinguishes the Confucian view of Heaven and the Dao from the Daoist, comes from the fact that the former extends the way of

Heaven and the Dao beyond the natural world to embrace the human realm as well, its moral and social order. It is this holistic vision, in which nature and culture, and the way of nature and the way of humans, are not separate but form a single order, that is characteristic of the Confucian view of reality. Nevertheless we should not overlook the fact that the Confucian view is equally naturalistic in that it seeks to ground human order upon the natural order. One could say that nature is human and morality natural in Confucianism—the Confucian way to secure ontological foundation for moral order. After all, Heaven, like the Dao, is the all-comprehensive ultimate reality which defies the distinction of nature and culture, the natural order and the human order.

Heaven's way or principle is considered perfectly immanent in the natural world as well as in the human nature endowed by Heaven—hence the complete unity of Heaven and humans (*cheonin habil*) as the Confucian ideal of sagehood, which is to be attained through a perfect realization of one's own nature. This in turn is believed to lead to the realization of the natures of other people as well as other things. This cosmic ideal of human perfection represents the Confucian spirituality as its highest, which, along with the Daoist ideal of nonaction, has inspired the Asian mind for thousands of years. And it has not completely lost its appeal among Asian peoples even today. The content of morality may change according to the circumstances; but it remains the unchanging core of the Confucian naturalistic vision that morality should be securely grounded upon nature, inner and outer, given by Heaven and the Dao.

Although the Confucian tradition did much to "rationalize" the concepts of Heaven and the Dao by moralizing them, the Asian mind, including the Confucian, has always held deep reverence (*gyeong*) toward the Dao and Heaven and their ways. As the ultimate reality of the universe, they are considered essentially mysterious and beyond our full comprehension. Ontologically, they are thoroughly immanent in the world, but epistemologically transcendent in that our mind is not capable of fully understanding their ways and our language can never capture their infinite depth and creativity. As the famous first line of the *Daodejing* declares—"the Dao that can be spoken of is not the constant Dao"—the Asian mind never forgot the ineffable nature of the Dao and Heaven. In this respect, the Asian thought and its spirituality can certainly be designated "mystical." Ever mindful of the fundamental inadequacy of human language and discursive thought to grasp the reality of the world, Asian philosophy can hardly be characterized as logocentric. In Asian naturalism language and reality never enjoyed an intimate marriage as in Western philosophy—at least in its classical tradition, before the barrage of today's fashionable antirationalism.

One may even say that the Asian naturalistic mind and spirituality had an infinite "faith" in nature with its sacred dimension, but not in its own rational capacity to grasp the ultimate reality. Deeply aware of the alienating and reifying nature of human language and intellect, and their inherent limitations in grasping the infinite world of the Dao, the highest aspiration of Asian naturalistic mind has always been directly to embody a perfect unity with the Dao or Heaven in one's own being—not to be engaged in philosophical discussions about them as the object of intellectual concern. The Dao is primarily to be lived, not studied, in Asian naturalism. This accounts for its ultimate practical, spiritual, and mystical character.

One final consideration. If nature is everything in Asian naturalism, some ultimate but speculative questions may be raised regarding this naturalistic outlook: Can we ask in Asian naturalism why the world is as it is? Whence its order and regular patterns? Yes, we can ask, and the answer is that everything is "natural" in the sense that it follows the spontaneous operation of the Dao or Heaven; but the order is not considered preordained or predetermined but emergent with the natural movement of the Dao itself. Can we then ask why the Dao is as it is, particularly its ordering nature? No, because the Dao is considered ultimate, with no further reason or reality behind or beyond it, like the God in Christianity except that the Dao or Heaven is considered thoroughly immanent in the world and constantly changing with it, or even prior to its formation, due to its dynamic creativity. Further yet, can we ask in Asian naturalism why the world exists in the first place—the famous question of Leibniz, why is there something rather than nothing? Yes, we can, but the Asian naturalistic answer would be that everything originates from the Dao or Heaven, and we cannot further ask why the Dao exists in the first place, because it is considered primordial and self-existing like God in Christian theology, except that Asian naturalism did not have the notion of necessary being or develop the ontological proof for the existence of the Dao!

BUDDHISM AND NATURALISM

One may argue that Buddhism, another important strand of the East Asian religio-philosophical tradition, does not share the naturalistic view of the world outlined above. It may appear that Buddhism, with its doctrine of karmic retribution and "world-denying" attitude, is basically incompatible with the calm and yet cheerful naturalistic affirmation of the world and human life. On closer examination, however, it turns out that Buddhist thought never seriously challenged or went out of the boundary of the naturalistic outlook we have outlined above. On the contrary, Buddhism, at least in its Sinicized Mahāyāna form, has essentially moved within the naturalistic framework broadly considered. Three points of their basic consonance should be pointed out here.

To be noted first is the fact that the Mahāyāna Buddhist vision of the world is not predicated upon a dualistic view of reality such as we find in the Theravāda concept of *nirvāṇa* as opposed to *saṃsāra*. In the Mahāyāna vision, *nirvāṇa* does not form a separate order of reality apart *saṃsāra*, the world of birth-and-death, and liberation is to be sought in the very midst of the ordinary world. The Mahāyāna ontology recognizes only one world, as naturalism does, not two separate realms of reality. Depending on how we view it—through wisdom or ignorance—the world appears either as it is in its true empty nature (*tathatā*, Suchness) or in its delusory aspect. In other words, the world of birth-and-death, correctly viewed, is none other than the world of liberation. Hence the famous Mahāyāna dictum that *saṃsāra* is none other than *nirvāṇa*, and *nirvāṇa* none other than *saṃsāra*. What this suggests is that East Asian Buddhism, like Confucianism and Daoism, is essentially a "world-affirming" religion seeking redemption *in* the material world, not *from* it as in Theravāda Buddhism or other schools of soul-oriented Indian philosophy. As is well known, Chan (Kor.: Seon; Jap.: Zen) Buddhism, commonly regarded as the flower of Chinese Buddhism formed under the influence of Daoist philosophy, best represents this "worldly" spirituality.

Secondly, East Asian Buddhism shares with Daoism and Confucianism the holistic and organismic "process" view of the world, according to which each and every entity in it is intrinsically related to others. The Buddhist theory behind this view is the famous doctrine of dependent-arising (*pratītyasamutpāda*), according to which things in the world are without exception dependent upon each other, and nothing can exist as an independent substance with its own distinct and fixed nature (*svabhāva*). The native Chinese naturalistic vision of the world and the Mahāyāna Buddhist philosophy share a dynamic view of reality which sees the world as ceaselessly changing—a flow of cosmic energy where things do not constitute separate individual entities but are in constant transformation in mutual dependence. True, Buddhism does not talk about such cosmic energy, but it is equally naturalistic in that it does not seek any other reality separate from the changing world itself. From the interdependent nature of things the Buddhist wisdom derived its core insight into the nature of reality: Emptiness (*śūnyatā*; Kor.: *gong*) as the true nature of things lacking fixed natures corresponding to their names and concepts. Once we realize that things lack their own being and nature, we can affirm and enjoy the myriad things of the world as they are in their rich diversity. Emptiness is not a desolate world devoid of forms but an exuberant display of multifarious forms and characteristics. Once desubstantialized by our insight into their Emptiness, they reappear as subtle beings (*myoyu*) in a plethora of forms and names. This is the philosophical background for East Asian arts such as landscape painting and poetry inspired by the Daoist and Zen naturalistic spirit.

Thirdly, closely related to the above, the Mahāyāna Buddhist theory of causality, which does not recognize the existence of individual entities separate from other entities, is basically consonant with the Chinese indigenous organic naturalism in that both represent a holistic and non-atomistic understanding of reality, according to which things are not grasped merely in their linear causal relationships but viewed as interrelated from the beginning in such a way that they respond and resonate with each other in systemic patterns forming organic unity. The Huayan vision of reality which sees "one in all, and all in one" is typical of this holistic understanding of the world.

Lastly and most importantly, all three philosophical traditions—Daoist, Confucian, and the Buddhist—converge in pointing out the inherent limitations of human language and discriminative thought in revealing the nature of the ultimate reality, whether it is called the Dao, Heaven or Emptiness. Thoroughly and universally immanent in the world, humans can never depart from it even for a moment. Yet our intellect and discursive thought are considered unable to grasp its subtlety and depth. Accordingly, the highest goal of life for Asian naturalism has been to realize and embody a perfect unity with the ultimate reality in one's own being and life through a direct intuitive access to it without conceptual mediation. In other words, all three traditions espouse mystical approach to the ultimate reality as the last resort, which they regard as lying beyond our linguistic construction.

In view of these basic agreements between Mahāyāna Buddhist view of the world and the naturalistic philosophy of Daoism and Confucianism, it is not without reason that in East Asian cultures, people have had no qualms about following all three religions at the same time—an unintelligible anomaly for the Western mind. Some thinkers even went as far as asserting their essential unity.

HAEWEOL'S ETHICS OF THREEFOLD REVERENCE

I have thus far broadly outlined what I believe to be the fundamental spirit of East Asian organic naturalism, a holistic vision of the world which cannot be understood in terms of the dichotomy of naturalism and supernaturalism, theism and atheism, in the Western tradition. It has its own spirituality which is not predicated upon the antagonism of spirit and matter, so characteristic of Western and Indian spirituality, and its own form of redemption which does not seek the liberation from the world but a perfect unity with the Dao and Heaven as manifested in the way of nature. As mentioned before, this naturalism is pan-Asian. Accordingly I did not dwell on the differences found among East Asian philosophical schools and traditions; nor was it my intention to highlight the peculiar characteristics of Korean philosophical thought in particular. Let me, however, conclude this paper with a brief discussion of the case of *Cheondogyo*, literally the "Way of Heaven," a native Korean religion that arose in the latter half of the nineteenth century, as a typical and yet highly creative exemplification of the spirit of Asian naturalism still well and alive today.

As indicated by its name consisting of two Chinese words, "Heaven" (*Cheon*) and "Dao" (*Do*), its fundamental spirit is naturalistic through and through, yet its practice very revolutionary. Of particular interest to us is its idea of threefold reverence (*samgyeong*) formulated by Haeweol (Choe Si-hyeong, 1827–1898), the second patriarch of the *Donghak* (Eastern Learning), the original name of Cheondogyo. Threefold reverence represents reverence for Heaven, reverence for human beings, and reverence for all things, animate as well as inanimate.

In view of our discussion of the fundamental spirit of Asian naturalism thus far, Haewol's teaching of threefold reverence should not need much explanation. The idea of revering Heaven was a commonplace in Haewel's times, as it still is today. More significant was his emphasis on revering human beings and its inseparability from revering Heaven, as epitomized by his teaching of "serving humans like Heaven" (*sain yeocheon*), one of the cardinal teachings of Cheondogyo. The idea of serving all human beings like Heaven, regardless of their gender, class, and age, was truly revolutionary in the heavily class-oriented Korean society of Haeweol's times, as was demonstrated by the massive peasant uprising of 1884 that occurred under the influence of Eastern Learning. Yet even more striking and revolutionary from today's perspective was Haeweol's idea of universal reverence toward all things, animate and inanimate. Let me elaborate on this.

Haeweol declared, "we cannot reach the ultimate of the Way and its virtue by merely revering human beings."[7] This may well be, as far as I am aware, the first open declaration in human history of the need for our moral obligation to go beyond anthropocentric boundary. It is premised upon the holistic view that Heaven, as the source of the primordial vital energy of the universe, constitutes the cosmic womb from which all beings, including inanimate things, originate. Hence his remark that I and others, as well as I and all things, are of the same womb, that is, of one family.

The world as envisaged by Haeweol is filled with "one chaotic and primordial vital energy" of Heaven.[8] It is a vast organic community of beings sharing the same energy originating from Heaven. "Each and every thing is Heaven, and each and every affair Heaven," says Haeweol.[9] It is this "pantheistic" vision that underlies his teaching of universal reverence toward all things, even toward inanimate beings. Permeated by the same primordial energy of Heaven, everything that exists in this vast organismic world is considered sacred and nothing insignificant. Haeweol would have readily endorsed our contemporary idea of the "intrinsic value" of all living beings, but he would have extended it further to embrace even inanimate beings. He would have undoubtedly sided with Albert Schweitzer's ethics of reverence (*Ehrfurcht*) toward all living beings, but he would have pushed it further to include inorganic beings as well. For all things, animate and inanimate are "alive" in his eyes because they all partake of the sacred energy emanating from Heaven.

Haeweol's universal reverence is directed above all to the earth. There is an interesting episode about this. Once he happened to hear a child passing by him fast on his wooden clogs. Frightened at the sharp sound of them striking the ground, he jumped to his feet. Stroking his chest, the story goes, he uttered: "At the sound of this child's wooden clogs, I felt pain in my chest."[10] He then told people to cherish the earth like the skin of their mother. In a similar vein, he taught people not to throw water wildly on the ground, or to spit or blow their noses on it. This reminds us of the well-known story of a native American tribal chief who refused to sell his land to a white man, saying that we cannot buy or sell our mother's skin. The earth was for Haeweol literally "Mother Earth," to be treated with care and caution. Never perceived merely as the resource for human life, not to mention a great mass of inert matter, the earth was for Haeweol an organic body full of vital energy ceaselessly producing the myriad forms of life, all sacred.

Haeweol literally regarded grains as the milk from the earth. Not surprisingly, he taught people not merely to be grateful to earth, but to revere heaven and earth as their parents. The simple ritual of *sikko*, "announcing eating" to heaven and earth, which he enjoined his disciples to practice before eating, was a ritual expression of this feeling of gratitude and reverence toward heaven and earth as our living parents.[11] If you know the principle of *sikko*, says Haeweol,[12] a perfect knowledge of the Way (*dotong*) is there. Eating was a sacramental act for Haewol.

This was so not just for human act of eating alone. For Haeweol, the whole world of living beings formed a vast sacramental community of "Heaven eating Heaven" (*icheon sikchoen*)—his version of our idea of the food chain or the web of life in which organic beings live on other organic beings. Since all beings are manifestations of Heaven's vital energy and live by eating other beings, "Heaven eating Heaven" was literally true for Haeweol. He observes that beings of the same species live by solidarity and mutual support, whereas beings of different species live by eating other species. Human prejudice, Haeweol points out, may tell us that the idea of Heaven eating Heavens is not rational; we may think that everything exists for humans! From Heaven's universal perspective, however, Heaven eating Heaven is the way Heaven nourishes all beings without discrimination, says Haeweol.[13] Nature is for him a truly cosmic community of universal love, a community of mutual giving of life. To quote Gary Snyder: "To acknowledge that each of us at the table will eventually be part of the meal is not just being 'realistic.' It is allowing the sacred to enter and accepting the sacramental aspect of our shaky temporary personal being."[14]

Haeweol lived in an age when the environmental crisis was not a major threat to our way of life, and it may be anachronistic to talk about his "environmental ethics." If he were living today, however, and joined our conversations on environmental ethics, he would warn us that our environmental problem is not just an ethical issue. His idea of universal reverence goes far beyond moral approach to environmental problems. He would argue that without a profound sense of reverence toward all beings in nature, overcoming our deep-rooted anthropocentrism is not possible. Unless humans learn to be humble enough to revere even insignificant objects in nature as sacred manifestations of Heaven's primordial energy, Haeweol would say that ethical approaches to our environmental crisis will meet with only a limited success, if any. If what deep ecologists are saying is correct, the colossal disaster we are heading for can no longer be adequately dealt with on technological and resource-managerial level. It calls for our radical change of heart, along with an equally radical change in our way of life. Recovering the primal sense of nature's sacred depth and "re-enchanting" the world would constitute the essential precondition for this, and a serious engagement with the age-old Asian naturalistic vision would be an important step toward it.

CONCLUDING OBSERVATIONS: TOWARD A NEW METAPHYSICS OF ASIAN NATURALISM

One of the main causes of the spiritual plight of modern men and women stems from their failure to find human meaning in a radically despirited world. How to reclaim the right—virtually relinquished by modern philosophy—to interpret the world, and that in such a way as to find spiritual meaning in nature, constitutes in my mind the central challenge for the world philosophical community today. The whole Romantic enterprise which arose to heal the rupture between subject and object in the Enlightenment thought was a heroic attempt to do that. In Carlyle's word, it represented a "naturalistic supernaturalism" which sought to naturalize the supernatural and humanize the divine.[15] Yet the Romantic movement, as well as other reactions against modern industrial-technological civilization, have all been powerless to stem the tide of history. Nevertheless, we cannot give up such attempts without making philosophy virtually inconsequential today. We have to keep asking whether or not there still is a way nature can "speak" to us. Can nature be "human" again and send spiritual message to us? Conversely, can humans be "natural" again and humbly dwell in the world of "earth, sky, gods, and mortals," as Heidegger's Fourfold would have it?

Nothing is further from my intention than to propose Asian naturalism, or Haeweol's ethics of universal reverence for that matter, as a panacea for today's spiritual plight and civilizational crisis. Nor do I mean to ignore a host of serious philosophical issues confronting naturalism, Eastern or Western. To name a few: how does one secure universal human dignity and rights if humans are thoroughly "natural" and immanent in nature? How can we ground human free will and moral responsibility upon the naturalistic ontology? Can evolutionary theory of moral values, for instance, provide a satisfactory answer to these questions? And, closely related to them, how can we resolve the mind-body problem without the unhappy consequences entailed by various forms of naturalistic reductionism and determinism?

While it would undoubtedly be too facile a view to assume that Asian organic naturalism is exempt from these problems altogether, it is on the other hand worth pondering why Asian naturalism did not engender such problems in the first place. According to Asian naturalism, there is a fundamental continuity of being between the human mind and the material world—a primordial unity of man and nature in the depth of their being. For they are equally manifestations of the Dao or Heaven. The holistic vision of Asian naturalism could never conceive the human being as disembodied spirit or self; the dichotomy of subject and object, with the dualistic split of spirit and matter, was essentially foreign to it. From Asian naturalistic perspective, the epistemological turn of the modern Western philosophy has to be regarded as highly unnatural and unfortunate. Good or ill, Asian naturalism did not produce a thinker like Descartes, who led Western thought into the philosophy of overblown subjectivity (*res cogitans*) on the one hand, and paved the way to the purely materialistic and mechanistic understanding of the world (*res extensa*), on the other hand.

Let us not forget the fact that Asian naturalistic philosophies have fared remarkably well for more than two millennia without being trapped by the unfortunate choice between mechanical materialism and theological spiritualism, or between spiritually sterile naturalism and irrational supernaturalism, which has played such an important role in shaping the Western intellectual tradition and bringing about today's global crisis, spiritual and environmental.

Disenchanted with the Christian supernaturalism, many in the West have already "turned East," especially to Zen and Daoism, in their spiritual quest; and many Christian theologians are grappling with their own understanding of the Christian message in the face of the challenge from Eastern religions. The combined practice of Western medicine and the *qi*-oriented Chinese medicine is becoming a more commonplace and accepted as desirable—at least in Asian countries—apart from the popularity of acupuncture in the West, although the full integration of the two medical traditions at the theoretical level still has a long way to go.

Most significantly, the post-Cartesian and post-Newtonian science already transcended the atomistic, mechanistic, and deterministic understanding of the world that has long dominated the modern way of thinking. Relativity theory, quantum theory, chaos theory, Gaia theory, systems theory, and more recently, ecology as a new field of scientific concern are transforming our understanding of the material world in the direction of a relational and holistic view of reality, stimulating a new interest in Asian organismic view of the world. Many in the world's scientific community have turned their attention to what they consider as significant agreement in the ontological vision between traditional Asian philosophies and the post-Newtonian science. What Clarke observes on Daoism seems to be valid for Asian naturalism in general: "Daoism, with its dynamic conception of nature as movement, flow and change, its emphasis on energy (*qi*) rather than substance, its grasp of the web of interconnections that bind together all phenomena both human and cosmic, and its rejection of rigid laws and absolute boundaries, is especially close in spirit to modern physics, in spite of differences in empirical detail, methodology and overall aims."[16]

Isn't it time now for philosophical communities to take Asia's age-old holistic vision more seriously at philosophical level rather than leaving it to the hands of Sinologists or the historians of Asian philosophy, and to reexamine the fundamental presuppositions with which they have been working? More positively and ambitiously, if Asian naturalism is going to remain more than a source of poetic inspiration or mystical insights, it cannot neglect the effort to develop itself through continuous theoretical elaboration and cogent argument, in active dialogue not only with other philosophical thoughts as well as modern science. In other words, a new "metaphysics of Asian naturalism" is called for—new beyond the modern Cartesian split and the self-destructive postmodernist philosophy. It is noteworthy that already some works have already been done to construct a systematic and general view of the world and the human life from the perspective of Asian naturalism, especially the Daoist. Although not a systematic metaphysical work, Fritjof Capra's *The Turning Point: Science, Society, and the Rising Culture* is pioneering in this direction.

On the other hand, quite different from this constructive effort for a new metaphysics of Asian naturalism, many comparative studies have been made focusing on the anti-rationalistic spirit of Asian naturalism, especially the Daoist and Buddhist, and its similarity to Heidegger's "mystical" thought and Derrida's philosophy of deconstruction. Here the central question is whether or not it is still legitimate and possible to pursue a metaphysics of Asian naturalism in this age of the "end of philosophy." If a metaphysics of Asian naturalism is desirable, how can we do it in this age of metaphysical skepticism?—the skepticism which derives not only from the cognitive retreat of modern philosophy before science, but more radically from the loss of faith in the ability of human reason and language to grasp reality.

At the heart of the matter stands the problem of language in general as a philosophical problem, not just the metaphysical language alone. A new metaphysics of Asian naturalism can no longer simply disregard recent postmodernist assault on language and continue its business as usual. For skepticism concerning the representational value of language is raised not only by postmodernist philosophers, but also by the classical Daoist and Buddhist philosophers themselves. I have myself underscored the ineffable nature of the ultimate reality in Asian naturalism, its anti-rationalistic and mystical dimension, often exaggerated as it is. Thus the question: "What must be the nature of philosophical discourse that wants to announce the inability of thought and language to re-present reality?"[17] Or, the question Caputo raised regarding Heidegger's thought may as well be valid for Asian naturalist thought: "What interest can philosophy have in a thinker who thinks at the end of philosophy, who has moved beyond the sphere of influence of philosophical principles into the neighborhood of mystics and poets?"[18]

While I cannot go into a detailed examination of this important issue here, one thing though remains certain in my understanding of Asian naturalism: whatever affinities one may find between the Daoist and Buddhist approaches to reality and Heidegger's "mystical" thought or Derrida's philosophy of deconstruction,[19] the negative view of language and philosophical discourse in Asian naturalism always presupposed and claimed—not just postulated—a direct intuitive knowledge of the metaphysical absolute, a privileged access to the ultimate reality through "a transformed mode of experiencing the world."[20] To live and act in perfect accord with this intuitive knowledge is considered the highest form of spirituality in Asian naturalism. This is why Asian naturalism always understood all philosophical discourses as essentially heuristic, or as "skilful means" (*upāya*) in Buddhist terminology.

Whatever noble motivations or profound insights a philosophy may have, it cannot simply remain satisfied with negative discourses alone, nor can it afford to indulge in an endless play of signifiers without the sifnified. With due regard for and full awareness of the fundamental limitations of conceptual knowledge in grasping reality, a new metaphysics of Asian naturalism nonetheless has to find some way to secure the legitimate place for metaphysical discourse. One way to do this is to take recourse to the well-known theory of two levels of truth in Mahāyāna philosophy of Emptiness and the Indian Advaita Vedānta philosophy: the higher level of truth or the supreme truth, and the lower level of truth or the conventional truth.[21] According to this theory, all philosophical discourses, including the Buddhist and the Advaita Vedānta, belong to the level of conventional truth. They are to be taken merely as pointers to, rather than signifiers of, the ultimate truth, which is considered essentially ineffable. As far as the highest truth is concerned, all languages—philosophical or ordinary, representational or metaphorical, apophatic or kataphatic, subversive or constructive—are viewed as heuristic in Asian naturalism. It is in this spirit that the metaphysical discourse of Asian naturalism is to be undertaken in the future, as it was in the past. For, as Nāgārjuna reminds us, there is simply no way for us to arrive at the supreme truth without recourse to conventional truth. We should not overlook the fact that the Asian naturalist philosophers of the past did not abstain from rational argument at all, although its ultimate purpose was to disclose the reality beyond language.

A new metaphysics of Asian naturalism should not regard it as self-defeating or betraying its own spirit to make the effort to corroborate its vision of the world through rational argument and theoretical elaboration. Granted that philosophy can neither replace the living experience of the ultimate truth nor claim to do so, it still cannot relinquish what has been its prerogative from of old, namely the reflective activity a step removed from the stream of life, in order to construct a model understanding of the world in all its dimensions. In this age of global reign of instrumental reason, this constructive task is more urgently called for in Asian naturalism particularly.

If the present global crisis should in essence be attributed to human alienation from the world of nature, it is incumbent upon today's philosophers to formulate a new vision of the world which, boldly transcending the outdated dichotomy—still shackling our mind nonetheless—of matter and spirit, body and mind, fact and value, and science and spirituality, and overcoming the metaphysical timidity prevalent in the contemporary philosophical world, can lead to the "humanization" (or spiritualization) of nature and the "naturalization" of humans (or spirituality). For this, I believe, the holistic vision of Asian naturalism provides an important source of insight and inspiration.

Let me conclude with a reminder once again that naturalism has been more than a philosophical vision in Asia. It has been, and still is, a way of life for ordinary people today, seriously challenged and eclipsed as it has been by the onslaught of various other ways of thinking and forms of life in modern times. It is up to philosophers to capitalize on this in whatever way they can, before it is too late.

NOTES

1. In this paper I will be using this term in a more general sense than Needham does in his work; Needham seems to have particularly Leibnizian and Whiteheadian organicism in mind. I use the word "organicistic" to refer to the relational and holistic understanding of the world instead of viewing it as consisting of separate individual entities causally related in linear fashion.

2. See Ursula Goodenough, *The Sacred Depths of Nature* (New York: Oxford University Press, 1998).

3. Joseph Needham, *Science and Civilization in China*, vol. 2 (Cambridge: Cambridge University Press, 1956), p. 302.

4. Burton Watson, trans., *The Complete Works of Chuang Tzu* (New York: Columbia University Press, 1968), p. 81

5. Bertrand Russell, *A History of Western Philosophy* (New York: Simon and Schuster, 1945), p. 37.

6. Watson, *The Complete Works of Chuang Tzu*, p. 257.

7. *Cheondogyo Gyeongjeon* (Seoul: Cheondogyo Jungangchongbu Chulpanbu, 1992), p. 358.

8. Ibid., p. 305.

9. Ibid., p. 364.

10. Ibid., pp. 305–306

11. Ibid., p. 262.

12. Ibid.

13. Ibid., pp. 364–365.

14. Quoted from David Landis Barnhill, "Great Earth *Saṅgha*: Gary Snyder's View of Nature as Community," in *Buddhism and Ecology*, ed. M. E. Tucker and D. R. Williams (Cambridge, MA: Harvard University Center for the Study of World Religions, 1997), p. 189.

15. M. H. Abrams, *Natural Supernaturalism: Tradition and Revolution in Romantic Literature* (New York: W. W. Norton and Company, 1971), p. 68.

16. J. J. Clarke, *The Tao of the West: Western Transformations of Taoist Though* (London and New York: Routledge, 2000), p. 75.

17. David Loy, *Nonduality: A Study in Comparative Philosophy* (New York: Humanity Books, 1998), p. 255.

18. John D. Caputo, *The Mystical Element in Heidegger's Thought* (New York: Fordham University Press, 1986), p. 258.

19. See Clarke's summary review of this issue with regard to the Daoist Philosophy, *The Tao of the West*, pp. 166–193; regarding the Buddhist philosophy of Emptiness and Derrida, see Loy's critical discussion in his *Nonduality*, pp. 248–260.

20. Loy, *Nonduality*, p. 249. I agree with Loy that this is a decisive difference between the Buddhist philosophy of Emptiness and Derrida. The same observation can be made with regard to the Daoist philosophy.

21. I took this insight from Loy's *Nonduality*, pp. 248–260.

SELECTED PAPERS FROM
THE XXII WORLD CONGRESS OF PHILOSOPHY

Philosophy in Korea and Cultural Synthesis

YERSU KIM
THE GRADUATE INSTITUTE OF PEACE STUDIES, KYUNG HEE UNIVERSITY

ABSTRACT: This an attempt to present, in analytic-descriptive terms, the complex and multi-layered legacy of the way philosophy has been done in Korea throughout history. It is panoramic and selective, largely intended for colleagues who are encountering philosophy in Korea for the first time. This presentation will be carried out in four parts.

First, I examine how Korea's geographical location on the periphery of the Asian continent has made it imperative to make use of philosophical influences coming from the continent to solve the existential and political problematique faced by Korea. Second, I describe the encounter of Korea with the West, and particularly with Westernized Japan, as a clash of civilizations that has led to a century-long total rejection of the tradition in Korea. Third, I describe the present day philosophical scene in Korea, as it attempts to deal with direct exposure to Western philosophy and revival and renewal of the traditional philosophy. Finally, I advance the thesis that it is philosophy's task to forge a cultural synthesis adequate to deal with the problems facing humanity that will engage philosophy in Korea in the future.

I. INTRODUCTION

The day you forget your home
Is sadder and more painful
Than the day when your house is taken away.
When it is taken away, home sinks deeper into your heart.
When your home is forgotten, even the house of your heart is lost.
When taken away, it is just your house that disappeared.
But when forgotten, has not your self disappeared?
When you no longer have home, both Heaven and Earth are your home.
When you no longer have self, you have no place even in Hell.

Special Supplement, *Journal of Philosophical Research* pp. 333–342
DOI: 10.5840/jpr201237Supplement51

I begin my presentation to you by quoting a passage, freely translated into English, from *Korean History as Unfolding of Meaning* by Ham Suk-hun (1901–1989), one of the intellectual and spiritual leaders of modern Korea and to whom a series of special sessions are devoted in this World Congress of Philosophy. It expresses poignantly, in the symbolic language of home and self, the constant threat to its very existence, its dogged determination to overcome such existential precariousness, and its affirmation of the self as the locus of the struggle for survival and even prospering.

II. TRADITIONAL PHILOSOPHY

Philosophical thought cannot be separated from the existential field in which it has its origin and life. Situated as it is on the eastern periphery of the Asian continent and cut off by water on three sides from other countervailing forces, Korea was exposed from early on to the pervasive influence from the Asian continent. The influences and borrowings from China were to leave indelible marks on the philosophical, cultural and religious, linguistic, and social forms of Korean life. Among the most pervasive of these influences have been the three major religion-philosophic systems of the East—Taoism, Buddhism, and Confucianism. It was during the Three Kingdoms era (57 B.C. to 558 A.D.) that they began to make their way into Korean culture.

It is clear, however, that these influences from the Asian continent did not operate in a vacuum. Throughout more than two millennia of recorded history, the Korean people inhabited essentially the same geographical area, spoke a singular language of the Altaic family, and lived in an essentially homogeneous cultural milieu. Kochoson, with its shamanistic bronze culture, built up a polity strong enough to gain dominant control on the Korean peninsula and Manchuria, and developed the first ancient civilization east of China.

Though it was never systematized into an explicit conceptual scheme, shamanism was probably the first form of religious worship in terms of which the Korean people learned to come to terms with themselves and with nature. Even in the face of powerful and pervasive exogenous influences, the animistic view of human beings and nature remained a strong substratum of Korean culture, influencing and modifying more sophisticated religions and ideologies that found entry into Korea during the last two thousand years.

A close examination of the process of introduction and assimilation reveals a certain distinct pattern. The open and receptive attitude toward new religions and philosophical thoughts is almost always tempered by the wish to make them relevant to the concrete existential and political tasks at hand, seemingly opposed influences reconciled and sometimes developed into a viewpoint that, to a greater or lesser degree, does justice to the concrete problematique at hand. Such a process results sometimes in creative cultural synthesis, and sometimes in merely syncretic pattern.

III. TRADITIONAL PHILOSOPHY: BUDDHISM

Buddhism was accorded official recognition by the Three Kingdoms almost as soon as it was introduced. Three kingdoms, engaged in a fierce struggle for supremacy on the Korean peninsula and beyond, welcomed this new religion as an ideology that could serve the secular purpose of the state. Buddhist precepts, symbolism and rituals were used to "modernize" their respective societies by replacing widespread necromancy and divination practices. They were used to strengthen the centralized power of the kingship. It was , however, the Silla rulers who made the most effective secular use of Buddhism toward modernizing society and strengthening the power of the monarchy, and eventually succeeded in unifying the Three Kingdoms. Buddhism thus became the foundation the development of the brilliant Shilla culture in the seventh and eighth centuries, laying the groundwork for a long-lasting national culture.

Originally a philosophical formula for personal salvation through renunciation of worldly desires, Buddhism had, in its course of propagation, absorbed enough esoteric deities and forms of worship to constitute a new school, Mahayana, and it was this form of Buddhism that found ready acceptance in Korea. Its beliefs were, at the plebeian level, further mixed with native shamanism and integrated into a shamanistic polytheism. It is in this syncretic form that Buddhism struck deep roots in the minds of common people. It remains to this day the religion with the largest following in Korea. The syncretic naure of Korean Buddhism manifests itself at the philosophical level in a tendency towards a reconciliatory synthesis of opposing doctrines. Korean Buddhism produced a number of monk-philosophers, whose philosophical writings were influential beyond the boundaries of Korea. Some, such as Wonhyo (617–686) of Silla and Pojo Chinul (1158–1210) of Koryo, are on the agenda of this World Congress.

IV. TRADITIONAL PHILOSOPHY: CONFUCIANISM

Confucianism, ever since its introduction to Korea in the early centuries of the first millenium, has been a potent force in the political, social, and intellectual life of Korea. This has been true even in those periods in Korean history when Buddhism was accorded the status of state religion, and this is true even today, though in less explicit way. The remarkable resilience of Confucianism is all the more noteworthy when one thinks of its century-old de facto devaluation following what might be called a civilizational defeat in Korea's encounter with modernity—with Western powers and the newly Westernizing Japan.

The establishment in AD 372 of *Taehak*, a state-operated institution of higher learning in the Kingdom of Kokuryo, points to a well-established tradition of Confucian learning already in existence. Although Buddhism was the state religion in Unified Silla, Confucianism formed its philosophical and structural backbone. It provided the basis for training the high-level officials needed to ensure the functioning of the emerging monarchical system. The content of formal education in Korea consisted primarily of Confucian and other related Chinese classics, and this state of affairs lasted well into the nineteenth century.

It is perhaps one of the first instances in world history of a non-religious philosophical system of thought being consciously employed as an instrument of dynastic policy. Confuciansm was adopted by the founders of the Choson dynasty as the official philosophy of the state. Thus the establishment of the Choson Kingdom in 1392 represented not only a dynastic change; it also entailed a major intellectual transformation whereby the Buddhist conception of politics, culture and religion was replaced by the Confucian conception. Reform-minded Confucian scholars, who had criticized the corruption of the Buddhist based Koryo society and politics, instituted reforms, including land reforms designed to ensure greater equity. They were able to make the propagation of Confucianism a major program of the new regime and enacted Confucian rites and social norms into law. The encompassing character of these Confucian edicts was intended to regulate the life of people, particularly of the upper class, down to the smallest detail.

The civil service examination, *Kwago*, and the educational system were reformed as as to further facilitate the advancement of Confucianism. Mastery of Confucian classics was mandatory. At all levels of education, from education of kings and aristocracy down to secondary schools, the content of education consisted primarily of the Confucian classics and other Chinese literary and historical writings. All government officials above certain levels were recruited from these schools.

The Confucianism that flourished during the Choson period is Neo-Confucianism, a philosophical synthesis of original Confucianism, Buddhism and Taoism achieved by the Chinese philosopher Chu Hsi in the twelfth century. During the five hundred years of Neo-Confucian orthodoxy, a number of Korean philosophers suceeded in bringing philosophical speculation to new heights of originality and influence both at home and abroad. *Yi Hwang*, widely known under his pen name *Toegye* (1501–1570), and his younger contemporary *Yi I* (*Yulgok*, 1536–1584) deserve special mention, and they are still widely discussed in Korea today, as you have seen in this Congress.

Since the beginning of the seventeenth century, Christianity and Western thought began to trickle into Korea. They were received with great curiosity by a small group of intellectuals, by that time dissatisfied with Neo-Confucian philosophical thinking which was becoming overly speculative and impractical. Coupled with the pressing need for social, economic and administrative reforms subsequent to the Japanese invasion (1592–1597), these new stirrings gave rise to a group of Confucian philosophers who were collectively given the name Silhak. Despite their diverse interests and orientations, these thinkers were bound by their commitment to the spirit of practicality and utility as well as to seeking facts grounded in evidence in all scholarly endeavors. Nevertheless, they saw their intellectual efforts as return to the spirit of the original Confucianism, incorporating the new elements and tendencies into a new Confucian synthesis.

V. A NEW BEGINNING

The nineteenth century will go down in the annals of development of human civilizations as the century in which an encounter of civilizations with universalistic claims resulted in a clear-cut victory for one and an humiliating defeat for another.

When Japan began its Westernization drive with the Meiji restoration of 1868, following its forced opening by Comodore Perry a few years earlier, Korea denounced Japan's Westward orientation as a betrayal of the ecumenical Confucian cultural order and declared it a virtual pariah. For their part, the rulers of Korea chose a policy of seclusion and retrenchment in face of the challenge of the West. But in less than ten years, in 1876, Korea signed under duress an unequal treaty with Japan, thus bringing its traditional exclusively sinocentric orientation to an end. Six years later, Korea signed a treaty of friendship with the United States, opening its doors directly to the West for the first time history. Then, in rapid succession, signed treaties with Great Britain and Germany in 1883, with Russia in 1884, and with France in 1886.

The nation, thus thrust unceremoniusly into the modern world, was ill-prepared for it. Suddenly confronted with the vitality of the West, Koreans blamed their own political, social and philosophical tradition for the stagnation, ineffectiveness, poverty and injustice in their own society. Many associated the ignoble demise of the Choson kingdom with a Confucian tradition rendered defunct, as some intellectuals thought, by its empty formalism, regressive world view and political factionalism.

The exposure to Western ideas and institutions which the opening entailed coalesced into an ideological movement during the last two decades of the nineteenth century. For those Koreans who led the Gaewha movement, what seemed to be the overpowering military might and economic affluence of the Western nations and rapidly Westernizing Japan seemed to constitute the incontrovertible proof of the superiority of Western ideas, institutions, and values. Their eleventh-hour reform efforts were a case of too little, too late. With the annexation of Korea by Japan in 1910, which was to last thirty-six years, the final collapse of the valiant efforts to transform Korea into a strong modern nation brought a deep de facto devaluation and rejection of any part of what was perceived as a bankrupt tradition, while the desire to absorb whatever the West had to offer in all areas and walks of life became all the more intense.

It was during this period of all-encompassing civilizational transformation that Koreans came in contact with the word "cholhak," a Korean word for what was introduced as one among the many disciplines constituting academic horizon of the West. In retrospect, the first Korean contact with Western philosophy had come much earlier in the seventeenth century in the form of treatises written by Jesuit priests active in China at the time on various aspects of scholastic theology and other branches of Western learning. One such treatise introduces philosophia as a study of anima, a study of ultimate principles governing human being and nature.

There seems, however, to have been no realization of the match between *philosophia* and *dohak* (Study of Tao) or *ihak* (Study of Principles), terms current for centuries in Korea and other areas of the Chinese cultural sphere to designate the tradition of moral and metaphysical speculation in the East which consituted the proper domain of *philosophia*. It was Nishi Amane, a Japanese philosopher who coined a Chinese compound word to designate the discipline of philosophy. You will certainly have noticed that this World Congress of Philosophy is called *Segyee*

Cholhak Deahwai. Nishi's coinage remains to this day the *terminus technicus* for the discipline in those countries where the Chinese writing system had been the dominant scholarly medium.

In what must be one of the great discontinuities or detours in the history of civilizations, the circumstances of civilizational transformation contributed to the fact that, for many decades in the twentieth century, philosophy was simply equated with Western philosophy in East Asian countries, including Korea. When the first volume of the professional journal of philosophy was published by a small group of young Korean philosophers, it contained not a single article dealing with traditional philosophy. Judging that the ineffectiveness of the *Gaewha* movement and subsequent loss of national sovereignty was at least in part due to an inadequate and piecemeal understanding of the philosophical foundation of Western ideas and institutions, a number of young Koreans, perhaps not more than two dozen, went abroad to study Western philosophy first-hand during the first decades of the twentieth century, some to Germany, France, and the United States, and others to Japan. When the department of philosophy of the Kyong Song Imperial University, the forerunner of the very university where this Congress is being held, produced the first group of six graduates in 1928, some of these expatriates had returned and were engaged in teaching philosophy in the several colleges that were established by nationalistic and missionary initiatives.

It was a beginning of sorts for modern Korean philosophy, but a sad and stunted beginning. It was a beginning because it was radically shorn of the rich legacy of traditional philosophical thinking. We may be critical of this distorted beginning on the needs and predilections of the Japanese colonial administration and the philosophical orientation of the Japanese professors of philosophy, who were, now teaching in Korea, themselves steeped in the tradition of German idealism, not unrelated to the modalities of Japanese modernization and Westernization. But it would be amiss not to point out that traditional philosophical thinking at the core of the Confucian humanistic culture was inseparably bound up, in the minds of Koreans, with the ignoble demise of the Choson Kingdom and its traditional cultural order. Everything Western, even second-hand Japanized West were looked upon with reverential curiosity, looking there for inspiration and guidance. Even this distorted initial developments of philosophical studies in Korea was discontinued when Japan, as part of the mobilization efforts for its militaristic efforts in the late 1930s and 40s, imposed greater thought control and censorship.

VI. KOREAN PHILOSOPHICAL SCENE TODAY

The years following the liberation of Korea in 1945 from Japanese colonial rule were years of confusion and chaos, for the liberation brought in its wake not restoration of national integrity but a tragic division of the nation into two ideologically opposed political entities. Given the ideological nature, some of the brightest philosophers were drawn into this struggle and were lost to the task of giving form and substance to the fledgling philosophy in Korea. This ideological confrontation erupted into a three-year fratricidal war. The psychic wound inflicted on the Korean people can hardly be exaggerated. Confidence in human rationality and goodness, as well as in the future viability of the nation, was badly shaken. A suffocating sense of isolation from the Asian continent, which had also turned to the alien ideolology of communism, formed the subterranean sentiment of *angst*. For some years, existentialism in its bewildering variety gripped the minds and hearts of young Korean intellectuals.

The period of three consecutive decades beginning in the 1960s was a vital and creative period without parallel in modern Korean history. During this period the southern part of the Korean peninsula was dramatically transformed from a agrarian into an industrial society that can realistically expect become a part of the fully indusrialized international society sometime soon. Such an economic transformation was able to deal substantively with the centuries old problem of absolute poverty and move toward a more equitable society. All this was happening under the inspiration and guidance of the Western ideas and institutions in a geopolitical situation which for the first time history made South Korea effectively an island state, with nowhere to go but abroad to the world at large. This may be one of the fundamental reasons for the development of Korean economy in recent decades. But at the same time, the orientation toward the Asian continent which had been the cultural home for Koreans ever since dawn of history, and the maritime and aerial outreach toward the West and world which has brought so much good for South for last several decades sometimes play as opposing forces within the collective soul of South Korea. One sees this psychic split manifested in social, political, intellectual and philosophical discontinuities, conflicts and confrontations.

During this period of national resurgence, the Korean philosophical community grew almost exponentially, together with other sectors of Korean life. Although one talks about the crisis of the humanities in Korea in the wake of university reforms of neo-liberal provenance, Korean Philosophical Association, which represents the umbrella organization for this World Congress, numbers more than 1200 members as of 2005, a quantum jump from about two dozen when it was first organized in the early 1950s. Among close to 400 universities which exist in Korea today, about 80 universities have philosophy departments under various names and in different forms. They together produced 1200 college graduates, 196 MA, and 92 PhD degree holders in 2004 alone.

Reflecting perhaps this quantitative leap, one of the outstanding characteristics of Korean philosophical activity in recent decades is the sheer variety of philosophical interests. From a pervasive preoccupation with German philosophy in the earlier years, the focus of philosophical activity had widened to include all varieties of Western philosophy—analytic philosophy, phenomenology, social philosophy, classical Greek philosophy, recent French philosophy represented by post-modern and deconstructionist thinking and other currents of philosophy, as were prevalent in universities in Europe and America. Keeping steps with the general development of the Korean society, philosophy too was engaged in a great catch-up game. There began to emerge a small number of philosophers of Korean origin who were gaining prominence in European and American philosophical world, and you see some to them here at this Congress. Korean philosophers began to publish articles in the professional journals abroad.

A development of signal importance during these decades was the fact that the Korean philosophical community came into direct contact with Western philosophy, which came hitherto largely indirectly through Japan. A number of young scholars were returning home from Europe and America. A number of influential philosophers of international repute began to visit Korea for lectures and discussions with their Korean counterparts. These trends continue to strengthen today. Today we have more degree holders from European and American universities than we have places for in our academic institutions. For many of you from abroad who are with us in this Congress, this is probably not your first visit to Korea. As Korea lies somewhat outside the tourist orbit we philosophers made conscious efforts to invite you to visit Korea so that we may learn from your wisdom and expertise. These efforts are bearing fruits in a spectacular by the presence of thousands of you at this Congress.

Direct exposure to Western philosophy has been salutary for the development of philosophy in Korea. It gave Korean philosophers opportunities to assess the state of philosophy in contemporary Korea. While it enabled Korean philosophers the expertise and knowledge to engage in dialogue with practitioners of Western philosophy, it also contributed a normalization of the Korean view of Western philosophy prevalent during the first phase of modernization and Westernization. It did much to expose the extent to which the development of philosophy in modern Korea had been influenced by the Japanese reading and interpretation of, and Japanese needs and expectations from, Western philosophy. It enabled us to see Western philosophy in dispassionate and objective, each of us in his own fashion, way, without awe and mystification resulting from the circumstances of the civilizational transformation in the nineteenth century.

In retrospect, one unforeseen and yet inevitable outcome of this direct exposure has been the resurgence of interest in traditional Korean philosophy. There were to be sure other reasons for this phenomenon, but the first-hand encounter with Western philosophy brought into sharper focus the problem of identity for Korean philosophers. It provided opportunity to cast a fresh look at the traditional Korean philosophy badly bruised by the colonialist efforts to devalue it as of no intrinsic worth. It is clear however that it is a brilliant and complex legacy consisting of several layers of philosophical thinking. It must aim at laying bare the fundamental character of traditional Korean thought, how it was able to transform and synthesize various indigenous elements and exogenous influences into vital philosophical thoughts which are relevant and valid both within as well as beyond time-space coordinates. It must be able to show how these thoughts are related to the philosophical thoughts of today and how they are related to the concrete problematique which gives rise to philosophical reflection. If the encounter with Western philosophy has increased our consciousness of the problem of identity of Korean traditional philosophy, it has also brought about an enhanced awareness of the existence and worth of other hitherto neglected traditions of philosophy. This is perfectly consonant with this age of diversity and the spirit of the theme of this Congress: "Rethinking Philosophy Today."

VII. PROSPECTS: CULTURAL SYNTHESIS

I hope you will permit me to gaze a little into the future of philosophy in Korea, on the understanding such an exercise is a personal one. Of course everything I have said about philosophy in Korea is personal in the sense that what lies on the surface as historical facts are heavily colored by my personal points of view. Only the problem is a bit more serious when the time frame is the future. Philosophy, despite its strong claim to universality, is inextricably bound up with the civilization and its values in which it is embedded, and it is the civilizational transformation that we are going through today that I will base what I am about to say on the future of philosophy in Korea.

The world we live in today as we celebrate XXII World Congress of Philosophy is very different from the world which celebrated the first World Congress more than one hundred years ago in 1900 in Paris. We live today in a situation of extraordinary challenge and openness. Scientific and technological advances are creating new opportunities on a scale previously unimaginable, even as they threaten to destroy the very foundation of human life. The forces of a globalizing economy are creating new wealth, even as they widen the chasm between the rich and poor. Increasing global interdependence gives rise to ever more complex trans-border problems that defy traditional solutions. The rise of new global powers are creating new epicenters of power which come into ever sharper conflicts with the traditional center of power. Growing interdependence among cultures, instead of closer knitting together of world communities, is giving rise to a world in which conflicts and confrontations are the order of the day.

Why?

The ideas, values and institutions that had formed the backbone and motor behind the rise and development of Western civilization seem to be losing their once self-evident relevance and validity. It is becoming increasingly clear that signs of stagnation and even of relative decline are due to a tension and contradiction within and among ideas, values, institutions, and practices that had been at the core of a dynamic expansionistic civilization. They seem due not merely to an accidental configuration of factors. A growing sense of uncertainty and crisis has been evident now for a number of years, a sense that ideas and values underlying the Western synthesis that had served humanity so well in its tasks of survival and prospering seem now to be increasingly counter-productive and seem to be working at cross-purposes. There comes a point in the evolutionary process when and where certain ideas and values, because of their once proven efficacy and validity, assume a semblance of universality. With the changes in historical circumstances, they sometimes work to defeat the purposes they are intended to fulfill. The ideas and assumptions on which modern society was founded are no longer adequate to deal with many of the central problems facing humanity, such as environmental degradation, inequalities among individuals and among nations, and dehumanization of work and consequent deprivation of purpose and meaning of life.

I think the cultural arrogance that simply assumes the universality of the Western model of human survival and flourishing has prevented us from seeing its essential embeddedness in a larger historically conditioned context, from which there emerges a set of ideas, values, and practices that together constitute what might be called a conception of human flourishing. I have referred to such an emergent conceptions "cultural synthesis." I see cultures and civilizations of different times and places as striving to forge a synthesis of this kind, each in its own way, that would best enable it to deal with the problems it faces. Each of some two dozen civilizations identified by Toynbee was probably based on such syntheses of varying degrees of finesse and comprehensiveness. East Asia achieved such a synthesis from the fourteenth to nineteenth centuries. So, too, did the Islamic civilization from the twelfth to the middle of the nineteenth centuries, when the Ottoman empire was, for all practical purposes, incorporated into the Western world. Such a synthesis, when successful, provides a clear model for emulation, and sometimes a yardstick against which other culture's efforts at synthesis may be measured and evaluated, thus sometimes giving rise to claims of universality.

Existence of multiple cultural syntheses was perhaps a blessing when the interaction among cultures and civilization was relatively modest in scale. With modern means of technology and transportation, and particularly with the revolution in communication, a rather different situation emerges. East Asian civilization, abandoning its traditional role as the teaching civilization, became a willing pupil of the Western synthesis. In moments of doubt and uncertainty, one needed for the most part simply go to the ready-made cultural model provided by the Western synthesis. Today, in the early years of the twenty-first century, East Asia, a region where more than 1.6 billion live, has once again becoming one of the major poles of the world economy.

It is this task of cultural synthesis that I see as the future of philosophy in Korea. As we have reached a certain stage of economic and social development, there is no longer any ready-made source of inspiration and guidance as to where we shall go from here to construct a more humane, creative and flourishing society. Philosophy in Korea, after the great detour of the last century, must now be able to contribute creatively to this task. We will be harking back to the neglected recesses of our intellectual tradition for inspiration and instruction. Knowledge and insight thus gained will be chastened and enriched by what we have learned from from Western philosophy. But philosophy in Korea today and in the future will no longer be engaged in this task of civilizational transformation in isolation or in enforced transplantation from the forces from outside. It will be in cooperation with other vibrant philosophical traditions which are so well represented in the World Congress. It will be through a dialogue and mutual learning with many diverse traditions, through a philosophical conversation of mankind, that we hope to carry out the process of "Rethinking Philosophy Today," set in motion so auspiciously in this Congress.

SELECTED PAPERS FROM
THE XXII WORLD CONGRESS OF PHILOSOPHY

Heidegger's Seyn, Ereignis, and Dingen as Viewed from an Eastern Perspective

KWANG-SAE LEE
KENT STATE UNIVERSITY

Abstract: In *Being and Time*, Heidegger undertakes fundamental ontology. Heidegger conceives of Being as temporality. Being (*Sein*) is unconcealment which is replaced by be-ing (*Seyn*), that is, the disjunction between unconcealment and concealment. In the topological phase as in *Contributions to Philosophy* (*CP*), *The Thing* and *Building Dwelling Thinking* be-ing yields to enowning. "B-ing holds sway as enowning" (*CP* section 10). But be-ing holding sway entails that a being (*Seiende*) "is". Which means that a thing things. Enowning is Dasein's thinking-responding to the call of Be-ing. Hence be-ing historical thinking (*Seyns-geschichtes Denken*) which is enowned thinking. When a thing things, world worlds (*Die Welt weltet*). Be-ing-historical thinking is thinking-thinging, that is, thinking space-time or thinking gathering (*Versammlung*) of elements that "belong together". Thinging is the mirror interplay of the fourfold. In *Four Seminars,* Heidegger says: "There is no longer room for the very name of being. . . . Being is enowned through enowning. *Sein ist durch Ereignis ereignet*." But enowning means thinking thinging.

Heidegger moves away from metaphysics towards a nominalistic process philosophy. Heidegger's lifetime work is devoted to exorcizing the ghost of the monolithic design of Platonic metaphysic As H. W. Petzet observes, "His whole life is, he says, has been devoted to a freeing from this prison."[1] Heidegger is manifestly following in the footsteps of Nietzsche who excoriates the Christian faith-*cum*-Plato's doctrine of truth. Heidegger has tried to free himself from the prison of the monolithic design of Platonic realist, substantialist philosophy and move towards a nominalistic process philosophy. An integral part of this move is his polemics

Special Supplement, *Journal of Philosophical Research* pp. 343–351
DOI: 10.5840/jpr201237Supplement52

raised against Husserl's notion of self-consciousness as juxtaposed to object, or more broadly, the standard subject-object distinction as drawn by typical modern philosophers. In the early phase of his philosophical career (as in *Being and Time*) Heidegger undertakes fundamental ontology. Then in the middle phase (as in *Contributions to Philosophy*) and the later phase (as in "The Thing" and "Building Dwelling Thinking"), Heidegger yields beyng to enowning as thinging. We begin with fundamental ontology.

In fundamental ontology Heidegger begins with being (*Sein*) conceived as presence (*Anwesenheit*) which is the "transcendental condition of the possibility of objects" as he subsequently characterizes in *Contributions to Philosophy* the sense of being in *Being and Time*. Being is replaced, for example, in "On the Question of Being" by be-ing or beyng (*Seyn*) or being with a crossing out, the three equivalent symbols signifying the disjunction between presence (disclosure) and absence (withdrawal), or between presence and nothing ("what is yet unrevealed"). Talk of beyng is an explicitly pluralistic talk with respect to the framework question allowing for multiplicity of ways of revelation (multiplicity of the conditions of the possibility of objects). In regard to beings, beyng conveys the "the sense of the plenitude of all their facets," (to borrow the expression Heidegger, inspired by Rilke, uses in "What Are Poets For?"). Beyng signifies the Open. Just as the lighted side and the dark side only taken together are the whole of the globe, so what is present and what is now absent (that is, "what is yet unrevealed" and, to make the sense of absence or nothing fully explicit, what has already been disclosed and what has been) taken together give expression to the "sense of the plenitude" of beyng. Fossilizing presence as eternal being, the only possible disclosure of being, the only truth, sires metaphysics, more specifically, what is known in postmodernist circles as the metaphysics of presence. Metaphysics comes into being when the dark side of the globe (in the metaphorical sense) is forgotten, that is to say, when open-ended alternative ways of disclosure are forgotten. Hence the forgetfulness of being (better, the forgottenness of beyng). Ab-ground (*Ab-grund*) that Heidegger introduces in *Contributions to Philosophy* is designed to dispel the metaphysical notion of absolute, unique grounding, namely, Plato's Doctrine of Truth.

The forgetfulness of being (*Seinsvergessenheit*, still better, *Seynsvergessenheit*), based on the abandonment of being (*Seynsverlassenheit*) means the failure of questionableness. Thus in *BQP* Heidegger avers: "If we try to determine the present situation of man on earth metaphysically— . . . —thus not histographically and not in terms of world-view—then it must be said that man is beginning to enter the age of the total unquestionableness of all things and all contrivances."[2] The failure of questionableness means closure, determinateness, being locked up in the prison of metaphysics, falling prey to the block universe, and the failure of projecting-open in the perspective of beyng-historical thinking. Overcoming metaphysics is becoming open to the open-ended multiplicity of ways of disclosure. Scientism, which says that science is the measure of all things, as coupled with its inseparable companion, *Gestell* (the technological mode of thinking, which should be distinguished from technology) is the culmination of Platonic metaphysics. Any monolithic design claiming the monopoly of truth is metaphysics. In addition to science, religion and art, among others, are also ways of disclosure of beyng. Even in science, theories of physics, chemistry, biology, etc. are manifold ways of disclosure of beyng. Even within physics, there are alternative ways of disclosure (e.g., Aristotelian, Newtonian, Einsteinian, etc.). In art painting is one way, and music is another way of disclosure. Even in painting, Cezanne's paintings of Mont Sainte-Victoire and Van Gogh's paintings are different ways of disclosure of beyng . Even Van Gogh's paintings done in different periods are different ways of disclosure. When Heidegger contemplated Mont Sainte-Victoire at different times, beyng was disclosed to him differently. To anticipate a bit and to rephrase the point in unmistakably nominalistic parlance, on each occasion of Heidegger's contemplating Mont Sainte-Victoire, a thing thinged in a unique and unrepeatable fashion.

In *On Time and Being*, Heidegger gives expression to beyng in terms of temporality. He says: "The supposition appears to be fully confirmed when we note that absence, too, manifests itself as a mode of presence. What has-been which, by refusing the present, lets that become present which is no longer present; and the coming toward us of what is to come which, by withholding the present, lets that be present, which is not yet present—both made manifest the manner of an extending opening up which gives all presencing into the open."[3] Beyng is characterized as "all presencing." "All presencing" signifies not only the present, but also what has-been and what is-to-come. However, fully to give expression to the plenitude of beyng, we should also consider not only what are absent in terms of temporality (what has-been and what is-to-come) but also what are absent in terms of spatiality. Unlike the East Asians, Heidegger (the early Heidegger in particular of *Being and Time*) neglects spatiality. We post-Heideggeerian cosmopolitans who transcend the traditional East-West duality should be mindful of spatiality as well as temporality. Further, we should fully unfold the significance of the plenitude of beyng with regard to aesthetic, cognitive, moral, cultural, religious, and other relevant dimensions.

Fully to appreciate the significance of ab-ground (*Ab-grund*) we should unfold the fundamental way in which Heidegger creatively transforms Plato's notion of *chora* into the manifoldness of enownings.

For Plato, *chora* is what is absolutely not amenable to Reason. *Chora* is "absolutely unreal and unknowable " But Heidegger transforms Platonic Nothing into what is not present here and now and yet what has-been and what is to-come. Let us expatiate on the theme. For Plato, *chora* is "the absolutely unreal and unknowable."[4] *Chora* "is apprehended by some sort of bastard reasoning."[5] *Chora* "has some sort of existence . . . , but not real being . . . ,"[6] Form and *chora* "must forever remain distinct."[7] *Chora* "can never enter into the existence of Forms."[8] *Chora* is negative reality with shadow existence which constitutes otherness to Platonic

Reason and the rationally structured Reality. For Plato, the Reason/Unreason distinction is ontologically and epistemologically ultimate and immutable. The Platonic distinction is the source of binary opposition and dualistic thinking in the traditional Western mainstream Rationalistic thinking. *Chora* is alterity which defies the metaphysics of presence. But what defies the logic of Platonic reason and metaphysics only shows the limitation of Platonic logos and reprsentationalism. By the dexterous hands of Heidegger *chora* is transformed into Heideggerian absence, pointing to open-ended multiple ways of disclosure alternative to presence. What is "absolutely unreal and unknowable" is really what is resistant to the logic of monolithic Platonic Truth. The "bastard logic," if creatively recast pluralistically along the Heideggerian line of thinking, offers intimations of alternative ways of disclosure of beyng and thinking, points to the manifoldness of enownings and beyng-historical thinking.

Now let us move on to topology the way Heidegger does in his middle phase, as in *Contributions to Philosophy*, and in the later phase, as in *The Thing* and *Building Dwelling Thinking*. In his topological phase, be-ing yields to enowning (*Ereignis*). Focus shifts from be-yng to enowning. "Be-ing holds sway as enowning."[9] But when be-ing sways as enowning, "a being is." This is what Heidegger says: "Be-ing holds sway: a being is."[10] In the German original, the passage reads: "*Das Seyn west: das Seiende ist.*"[11] "Seiende" means a a particular thing (as in thinging). So Ereignis really means thinging, that is, particular, unique, and unrepeatable happening (event). Now the customary translation of "Ereignis" as "event" makes sense. Here I am adumbrating the Heideggerian project of nominalistic process philosophy.

"Be-ing needs man in order to hold sway; and man belongs to be-ing so that he can accomplish his utmost destiny. . . . The *counter-resonance* of *needing and belonging* makes up be-ing as enowning; and the first thing that is incumbent upon thinking is to raise the resonance of this counter-resonance to the onefold of knowing awareness and to ground the counter-resonance in its truth. "[12] That be-ing enowns Dasein means that be-ing historically unfolds itself in response to which Dasein projects-open by way of thinking. Here thrown projecting-open is en-owned projecting-open. Enowned projecting-open is inceptual thinking, that is, the inception of beying-historical thinking (*Seynsgeschichtes Denken*).

Unique, unrepeatable, particular historical happening is "time-space as ab-ground (*Die Zeit-Raum als Ab-grund*). "Ab-ground is the originary essential swaying of ground. . . . Ab-ground is the staying-away of ground. . . . The manner of non-granting the ground. . . . letting *be* empty—thus an outstanding manner of enopening. "[13] Particular happening is contingent. Ab-ground is a particular happening yielding and deferring to other unpredictable contingent particular happenings, "as yet unrevealed." Particular happening is not disclosure of being as a whole. Rather be-ing is the disjunction between presence and absence, that is, unpredictable, open-ended particular happenings. Be-ing (beyng) or being with a crossing out "shelters untapped treasures and is the promise of a find that awaits only the appropriate seeking."[14] Heidegger unfolds "time-space as ab-ground" thus: "Space is rendering ab-ground that charms-moves unto the encircling hold. Time is rendering ab-ground that removes unto the gathering. Charming-moving-unto is the encircling hold of gathering that holds to abground. Removal-unto is gathering unto the encircling hold that holds to abground."[15] "Time-space is the charming-moving-removal-unto gathering encircling hold , . . . , whose essential swaying becomes historical in the grounding of the "t/here [*Da*] through Da-*sein* (its essential trajectories of sheltering truth)."[16]

Spatializing (space) is coming to be present, moving-into, that is, unconcealing. Temporalizing (time) is becoming absent, that is, concealing. Be-ing is unconcealing and concealing, disclosing and self-sheltering. Hence time-space. Or spatializing-temporalizing. Still better, thinging-spatializing-temporalizing. For coming-to-be present and becoming-absent is coming to be present and becoming absent of things. And a thing things which unfolds unto the dynamical interplay of the fourfold. More of it later. Time-space as ab-ground is contingent, finite, historical , non-teleological "simultaneous" happening which is "unique and once only."[17]

"The relation of Da-sein to be-ing belongs in the essential sway of be-ing itself."[18] Dasein should be mindful of, and should not forget, "as yet unrevealed essence . . . of being with a crossing out" that "shelters untapped treasures and is the promise of a find that awaits only the appropriate seeking." Dwelling in the beingness of beings is "the forgetting of returnship."[19] The forgetting of returnship [*Rueckkehrerschaft*] is forgetting "the free-throw," forgetting that "every projecting-open is a thrown one, "how everything becomes an extant, orderable, and producable possession," and "how be-ing itself as machination sets itself into what is precisely not its own-most."[20] Which sires metaphysics and Plato's doctrine of truth.

But seeking be-ing as a whole is being capable of returnship. Experiencing returnship is being free from the beingness of beings, being disowned and disengaged from monolithic, Platomic truth. De-cision, that is, Dasein's manner of responding to historical, specific saying of be-ing, is beyng-historical thinking. The experience of returnship is ineluctably fused with be-ing's enowning-throw as onefold happening. To experience returnship is to turn from familiar saying to unfamiliar saying of be-ng. Be-ing's "grounding-attunement . . . "must remain fundamentally an unintended happening [*Zu-fall*]."[21] Heidegger calls this grounding-attunement of be-ing reservedness because be-ing's disclosure is staying-away, self-sheltering. Thinking is "projecting-open, i.e., the grounding enopening of the free-play of the time-space of the truth of be-ing."[22] If be-ing enowns Dasein, then enowned thrown Dasein that "belongs to" be-ing" enables the opening up (enopening) of the free-play, that is, the play freed from the constraint of the Platonic doctrine of truth, the play of time-space not directed by any preconceived design, of time-space. Thinging-spatializing-temporalizing (thinging-spacing-timing) is indeed a *Zu-fall*. "[The *leap*] is the enactment of projecting-open the truth of be-ing in the sense of shifting into the open, such that the thrower of the projecting-open experiences itself as thrown—i.e., as en-owned by be-ing. The enopening in and through projecting-open is such only when it occurs as the experience of thrownness and thus of belongingness to be-ing."[23] Thinking as enopoening is existential/ performative.

In *Four Seminars*, Heidegger says: "there is no longer room for the very name of being. *Letting* is then the pure *giving*, which itself refers to the it [*das Es*] that gives, which is understood as *Ereignis*."[24] On giving Heidegger says: that in "il y a" or "there is/it gives" ["*es gibt*"], " " the "it" that here "gives" is being itself. . . . The self-giving into the open, along with the open region itself. is self-giving."[25] But, as pointed out earlier, "being is enowned through enowning" [*Sein ist durch Ereignis ereignet*],"[26] and enowning, as already observed, is thinging. Just as being is appropriated (enowned) by enowning, so is enowning appropriated by thinging. Hence "self-givng" of being is "self-giving" of thinging. The "ground" of the thing which things is thinging itself.

"Angelus gave us the occasion to show that the principle of reason generally does not hold in the strict sense. The rose is without why, it blooms because it blooms. . . . "[27] "The rose is without why, but not without grounds."[28] What are the grounds? "Blooming is grounded in itself, it has its ground with and in itself. The blooming is a pure arising on its own, a pure shining ."[29] Here Heidegger lets the Leibnizian principle of sufficient reason or the Kantian notion of the "transcendental condition for the possibility of objects" wither away. Heidegger delivers a decisive blow to foundationalism. In fine, beyng as enownig is thinging. Blooming is groundless thinging, *Zu-fall.*

The jug (better, jugging, that is, the swaying of the jug) is an apt example of thinging. "The jug's swaying is the pure, giving gathering of the fourfold into a single time-space, a single stay. The jug sways as a thing. But how does the thing sway? The thing things. Thinging gathers.. Appropriating the fourfold, it gathers the fourfold's stay, its while, into something that stays for a while: into this thing, that thing."[30] A jug, when wine or water is poured from it, is a thing that things. The jug as a thing gathers the fourfold, earth, sky, gods, and mortals that belong together: they are "the same." "The jug-character consists in the poured off gift of the pouring out."[31] The jug is a thing that things. Thinging is gathering. "Our language denotes what a gathering *is* by an ancient word. That word is: thing."[32] A jug is a thing as a a mirror-play of the fourfold. The jug jugs. The world worlds. Jugging, thinging, is thinging-spacing-timing.

"The fouring sways (*west*) as the worlding of world. The mirror-play of world is the round dance of happening (*des Reigen des Ereignens*). Therefore, the round dance does not encompass the four like a hoop. The round dance is the ring that joins while it plays as mirror. As happening (*Ereignend*), it lightens the four into the radiance of their simple oneness. . . . The gathered sway (*Das gesammpte Wesen*) of the mirror-play of the world, joining in this way, is the ringing. In the ringing of the mirror-playing ring, . . . each one (of the four) retains its own nature. . . . they (the four) join together, worlding, the world."[33] The event of the "pure gift of pouring out"of wine is conditioned (*be-dingt*) by, *inter alia*, the brewing process of wine which involves the work of human beings (mortals), the growing process of grapes which also calls for human labor, earth (soil, for one thing), sky (the favorable weather and climate among others), and patterns of wine cultivation commensurate with cultural tradition (hence gods). The four "belong together" inseparably and inviolably. The fouring (*die Vierung*) is the dynamical sway of the mirror-play of the "betrothed." The mirror-play of the fourfold, mirroring one another, as enfolded by "the radiance of the simple oneness," while each of the four retaining "its own nature (*je eigenes Wesen*). In fine, the happening of wine being poured out of a jug gathers the fourfold in one unifying sway.

Thinking is gathering. To expatiate on the theme, let us talk of the bridge as an example. "The bridge swings over the stream "with ease and power." It does not just connect banks that are already there. The banks emerge as banks only as the bridge crosses the stream. The bridge designedly causes them to lie across from each other. . . . With the banks , the bridge brings to the stream the one and the other expanse of the landscape lying behind them. It brings stream and banks and landscape into one other's neighborhood."[34] Here the bridge as a thing is the center of gathering. The bridge enfolds the banks, the stream and the landscape. What makes the bridge the bridge is its relating to other related elements.

A thing things, And things are locations which allow for spaces. "Only things that are locations in this manner allow for spaces. . . . Space is in essence that for which room has been made, . . . That for which room is made is always granted and hence is joined, that is, gathered, by virtue of a location, that is, by such a thing as the bridge."[35] "The bridge is a location. As such a thing, it allows a space into which earth, heaven, divinities and mortals are admitted. The space allowed by the bridge contains many spaces variously near or far from the bridge."[36] A thing that gathers is a location which generates a space, just as Dasein is temporality. It is just that Heidegger should have said here that a thing is a time just as it is a space, just as he should have said in *Being and Time* that Dasein is spatiality as well as temporality. Thing is thinging-spacing. But thinging-spacing is thinging-spacing-timing. Thinging-spacing-timing is a center of gathering.

Let us come back to the example of the bridge. The bridge is the bridge in virtue of the way it plays the role as "a passage that crosses." The bridge bridges; it lets the banks emerge as banks. The bridge gathers into this particular world the stream and the landscape as well as the banks. The bridge is a thing because of its dynamically relating to and enfolding the banks, the stream, and the landscape. Does it also mean that the banks also gather and enfold the bridge as well as the stream and the landscape? Does it mean that the banks can also be a center of gathering? Heidegger does not say that the banks let the bridge emerge as the bridge. Nor does he say that the stream is a center of gathering just as the bridge is a center of gathering. For him, the bridge is the only center of gathering.

On place Heidegger says: "The essence of the place consists in holding gathered, as the present "where," the circumstance of what is in its nexus, what pertains to it and is "of" it, of the place . The place is the originally gathering holding of what belongs together and is thus for the most part a manifold of places reciprocally related by holding together, which we call a settlement or district [*Ortschaft*]."[37] In the case of the bridge, it does not seem to be the case that "a manifold of places is reciprocally related by belonging together." Belonging together is reciprocal relating. That is what "the same" means. Reciprocal relating clearly means the symmetry of relating. Yet reciprocality of gathering has lost meaning and relevance here. Here gathering is asymmetrical. Here Heidegger is manifestly uni-centric. The bridge enjoys privileged status. By contrast, Buddhists would say that centers are everywhere. They are genuinely and plur-centric and egalitarian. His avowal of pluralism notwithstanding, Heidegger is still laboring in the shadow of Platonic monolithic design. He has not quite succeeded in freeing himself completely from the prison.

NOTES

1. Heinrich Wiegand Petzet, *Encounter and Dialogues with Martin Heidegger 1929–1976*, trans. Parvis Emad and Kenneth Maly (Chicago: The University of Chicago Press, 1993), p. 176; *Encounter* hereafter.

2. Martin Heidegger, *Basic Questions of Philosophy: Selected "Problems" of "Logic,"* trans. Richard Rojcewicz and Andre Schwer (Indianapolis: Indiana University Press, 1994), p. 13; *BQP* hereafter.

3. Martin Heidegger, *On Time and Being*, trans. Joan Stambaugh (New York: Harper & Row Publishers, 1972), p. 17; *TB* hereafter.

4. Francis Macdonald Conford, *Plato's Cosmology: The Timaeus of Plato Translated with a Running Commentary* (London: Routledge & Kegan Paul LTD, 1956), p. 193; *Timaeus* hereafter.

5. Conford, *Timaeus*, p. 193.

6. Ibid., 194.

7. Ibid.

8. Ibid., 195.

9. Martin Heidegger, *Contributions to Philosophy*, trans. Parvis Emad and Kenneth Maly (Indianapolis: Indiana University Press, 1999), section 10, p. 22; *CP* hereafter.

10. Heidegger, *CP*, section 139, p. 183.

11. Martin Heidegger, *Gesamptausgabe Band 65 Beitrage zur Philosophie (Vom Ereignis)* (Frankfurt am Main: Vittotio Klostermann, 1989), 260; *BP* hereafter.

12. Heidegger, *CP*, section 133, p. 177.

13. Ibid., section 242, pp. 264–265.

14. "On the Question of Being" which is included in Martin Heidegger, *Pathmarks*, ed. William MacNeil (Cambridge: Cambridge University Press, 1998), p. 314; *PM* hereafter.

15. Heidegger, *CP*, section 242, p. 269.

16. Ibid., section 242, pp. 269–270.

17. Ibid., section 242, p. 269.

18. Ibid., section 135, p. 179.

19. Ibid., section 263, p. 319.

20. Ibid., section 263, pp. 318–319.

21. Ibid., section 6, pp. 16–17.

22. Ibid., section 1, p. 4.

23. Ibid., section 122, p. 169.

24. Martin Heidegger, *Four Seminars*, trans. Andrew Mitchell and Francois Raffoul (Indianapolis: Indiana University Press, 2003), p. 60; *Four Seminars* hereafter.

25. Martin Heidegger, "Letter on 'Humanism'" which is included in *PM*, p. 255.

26. Heidegger, *Four Seminars*, p. 60.

27. Martin Heidegger, *The Principle of Reason*, trans. Riginald Lilly (Bloomington and Indianapolis: Indiana University Press, 1993), p. 41; *PR* hererafter.

28. Heidegger, *PR*, p. 56.

29. Ibid., p. 57.

30. This passage is in "The Thing *(das Ding)*," which is contained in Martin Heidegger, *Poetry, Language, Thought*, trans. and intro. Albert Hofstadter (New York: Harper & Row, 1971), 174; *PLT* hereafter. Hofstadter translates "Der Krug west als Ding" as "This jug presences as a thing." His rendering of "west" as "presences" is infelicitous. I translate the German original to read: "The jug sways as a thing." "Sways" conveys the dynamic sense of "west" here. Similarly I have changed "das Wesen des Kruges" from "the jug's presencing" to "the jug's swaying." "Presencing" is a more fitting counterrpart of "Anwesenheit." Jugging (wine or water being poured from a jug) is a dynamic process. Wine or water being poured from a jug is thinging, that is, a dynamic event. For the German original, see Martin Heidegger, *GESAMPTAUSGABE BAND 7 Vortrage und Aufsatze* (Frankfurt am Main: Vittorio Klostermann, 2000), p. 182; *AG Band 7 VA* hereafter.

31. Heidegger, *PLT*, p. 172.

32. Ibid.

33. Ibid., p. 180. Again I change Hofstadter's rendering of "*west*" as "presence" to "sway," his rendering of "*Ereignen(s)*" as "appropriation" to"happening." his rendering of "Ereignend" as "Appropriating" to "As happening," his rendering of "*Wesen*" as "presence" to "sway." See *AG Band 7 VA*, p. 182. After "each one" I add "of the four" with brackets. After "they" I add "the four" within brackets.

34. This passage is in "Building Dwelling Thinking" which is in *PLT*, p. 152.

35. Heidegger, *PLT*, p. 154.

36. Ibid., p. 155.

37. Martin Heidegger, *Parmenides*, trans. Andre Schuwer and Richard Rojcewicz (Bloomington and Indianapolis: Indiana University Press, 1992), p. 117.

SELECTED PAPERS FROM
THE XXII WORLD CONGRESS OF PHILOSOPHY

Philosophy as Self-examination and Korean Philosophy

TAESOO LEE
SEOUL NATIONAL UNIVERSITY

ABSTRACT: The purpose of this paper is to clarify the issue of the meaning to be attributed to our talk of Korean philosophy. Of course, the answer to all the questions that can be raised concerning this issue depends on our conception of philosophy. I start by claiming that philosophy should be an *ars vivendi* aiming at making our life worth living. Drawing on Socrates's saying that the unexamined life is not worth living, I try to show that philosophical inquiry has to start with the reflection upon the belief-system underpinning our way of life. Through this reflective activity we are inevitably led to tackle the problem of cultural identity constituted by such belief system; there is no belief-system that is not culturally conditioned. Korean philosophy is an ongoing endeavor of the Korean people to renew their cultural identity—by way of philosophical reflection upon their cultural identity.

Among Korean philosophers the term 'Korean philosophy' is used mainly as a designation for the legacy of Confucian and Buddhist thought of the pre-modern era. Why don't we extend the meaning of the term to include the activities of contemporary Korean philosophers as well as past chapters of our history of philosophical thought? By raising this question I propose to face the problem about the possibility and legitimacy of Korean philosophy as ongoing concerns with our actual problems of life. I think Korean philosophers have been evading this problem using the term 'Korean philosophy' in the narrow sense mentioned above. It appears that some Korean philosophers of today want to proclaim themselves not specifically Korean philosophers but simply philosophers, that is, cosmopolitan philosophers, treating the adjective 'Korean' in the term 'Korean philosophy' as a sort of unnecessary appendage, completely irrelevant to the essential feature of philosophy; it is just as in the term 'a bald philosopher' baldness has essentially nothing to do with philosophical activities of the person in question.

Special Supplement, *Journal of Philosophical Research* pp. 353–360
DOI: 10.5840/jpr201237Supplement53

Given the violent break in our history at the end of nineteenth century and the overwhelming onslaught of Western civilization against our traditional culture, it is not difficult to see why those Korean philosophers do so. Indeed, it is very difficult for us to conceive of our history of philosophical thought as a continuous and coherent story and to take the adjective 'Korean' in the term 'Korean philosophy' as expressing an unbroken cultural identity. Nevertheless, I think the idea of Korean philosophy as an ongoing concern is not to be abandoned. I cannot show here exactly what constitutes the cultural identity to be expressed in Korean philosophy. I will, however, argue for the possibility and legitimacy of Korean philosophy that is alive today and will be alive in the future, that is, even at the time when the idea of world-citizenship is realized. My argument, I hope, will help throw light upon the real significance of Korean philosophy of the past era and revive it also from the state of being merely a museum-piece, a state of quasi-coma.

I start my argument by borrowing an idea from Richard Rorty. He once made a distinction between two radically different philosophical positions characterizing them with the interesting pair of terms 'the serious' and 'the playful.'[1] As we all know, Rorty had been vigorously propagating the idea of anti-realism for some decades, and the thinkers whom he approvingly called the playful are just those who side with him in the crusade against realism. By quoting Schiller's claim that "man is truly man only when he is at play" he made it clear why he had chosen this word.

Anyhow, on his interpretation, these playful thinkers don't believe in the reality which can be objectively represented by mirroring human mind. What philosophers used to call truth is basically nothing different from this kind of representation, whatever sophistication they may put in their epistemological explanation of knowing truths. The playful thinkers are therefore understandably very mistrustful when it comes to the talk of truths; they see truth as a dubious item in the inventory of philosophical concepts. Especially the so-called philosophical truths, which are supposed to be the correct answers to the allegedly perennial questions in (or outside of) the history of philosophy, are almost an anathema to them. Thus, for them, philosophy is not to be understood as a pursuit of universal truths that transcend all bounds of place and time, ethnicity, cultural differences, gender, etc. Philosophical problems and accordingly their solutions are specific to a certain period and place, always inseparably bound up with a particular culture, if there are such things as philosophical problems at all. (Some of the playful thinkers go so far as to contend that all the philosophical problems are in truth pseudo-problems.) In a word, they think that philosophy is more similar to art than to science. The value of philosophical thinking is to be appreciated in the same manner as artistic activities are appreciated as self-expression of individuality and of a cultural identity.

By contrast, the serious philosophers believe that philosophical activity is essentially a pursuit after truths, more precisely philosophical truths. They recognize fully the existence of truths in general and also that of distinctively philosophical truths; otherwise, they seem to think, philosophy would be an aimless enterprise. Most of them tend to take the realistic position. They think that some sort of realism is a necessity, that is, realism that postulates the reality and thus provides us not only with objects of knowledge, but also with a compelling framework of reason, along with its obligatory methods. They would object to the playful anti-realists that, without some kind of constraints provided by the reality, nothing would prevent the playfulness of anti-realist thinking from deteriorating into sheer arbitrariness. In a word, the serious philosophers prefer taking philosophical inquiry as modeled on scientific research to assimilating it to artistic activity.

Applying Rorty's typology[2] to the case of the possibility and legitimacy of Korean philosophy, we will find right off that, whereas a majority of playful thinkers are likely to acknowledge the possibility as well as the legitimacy of Korean philosophy, the serious ones will reject the idea of Korean philosophy. From the serious philosophers we can hardly expect such a kind of open-mindedness towards multiculturalism in philosophers' worlds as we find in the playful thinkers. They, wanting their work place to be cleansed from all elements that can be understood as indices of cultural differences, would regard Korean philosophy as nonsense on the same basis that the idea of Korean physics, claiming to study Korean-specific physical laws, should be rejected as nonsense. Or, if they take culture in a so wide a sense as to embrace all kinds of intellectual activities under its name, they will not hide their conviction that there is only one privileged culture that can rightly claim to include philosophy in its sphere, namely the culture of the West. Thus, from the perspective of the serious philosophers, philosophy other than the Western philosophy, be it Korean or whatever else, should be treated as a peripheral phenomenon, an inferior variant of philosophy proper.

Does this mean that the possibility and legitimacy of Korean philosophy presupposes the conception of philosophy as the activity of the playful thinkers? Is it imperative that Korean philosophy ally itself with the playful philosophy of the West? It is too hasty to say something conclusive about Korean philosophy only on the basis of Rorty's distinction between the two somewhat idealized extreme positions concerning the question about the identity of philosophy in general. We should not forget that there can be a wide spectrum of different conceptions in between. I guess that the majority of my Korean colleagues will disapprove of the extreme positions opposed uncompromisingly to each other. They are not very enthusiastic about the idea of emphasizing the affinity between philosophical thinking and artistic activity. In the land of art there prevails too much anarchy for their taste; there, uncontrollable intuitions and all sorts of whims are esteemed more highly than rules of strict argumentation. (Surely, this is a typical prejudice of most philosophers against art.) On the other hand, for various reasons they are no more attracted to the idea of assimilating philosophy and science. Some of them, perhaps, consider the scientific method in general to be too strict and rigid a procedure to be effective and useful in philosophy. Others, on the contrary, may have lost their belief in the role model of science—in the wake of Kuhn's study that showed what had been really happening in scientific research. At any rate, they generally don't like their position to be labeled simply that of scientism. I guess that the same situation applies even to those who are favorably disposed to a naturalistic revision of the important issues of traditional philosophy.

I agree with the majority of Korean philosophers and think that the proper place for philosophy is to be located somewhere between science and art. Now, to answer the question where exactly it is to be located, I propose to consider first the question of for what purpose do we philosophize at all. For, although the purpose of an activity is not to be identified with the activity itself, nobody will deny that it is one of the most important factors that determine the essential character of the activity in question; in most cases, if you know the purpose of an activity you know more than half of what the activity is. The problem is that there is not an answer to that question upon which all philosophers can unanimously agree. I will go back to the times of Socrates to find the answer in his saying that an unexamined life is not worth living. I am well aware that the answer I am going to give is one of many possible answers. The most I can do in such a case is to attempt to make my answer as plausible as possible.[3]

Now, what does Socrates's saying suggest? The first point to be made is quite plain. Socrates seems to take for granted that to live a life worth living is the ultimate aim of all our activities. Indeed, if someone, asked for what purpose he does this or that thing, gives the answer "to live a life worth living," you may complain that his answer is too imprecise, not particularly informative, and ask him further, for example, such a question as why he believes that he can live a life worth living by doing this or that thing. But you will never ask him the almost nonsensical question: "for what purpose do you live a life worth living?" or "why do you want to live a life worth living?" Likewise, to a philosopher claiming that the purpose of his doing philosophy is to live a life worth living we will ask no further question. So the case of doing philosophy is no different from other cases. Maybe there might be some philosophers among the adherents of the serious kind of philosophy who would claim that they are doing philosophy in order to discover truths. Do they really give a different account of the purpose of doing philosophy? In this case we can ask a further question about the purpose of discovering truths, which is not a nonsensical question, and we will not stop until we hear the answer that they are endeavoring to discover truths because they believe that endeavor makes their life worth living. Alternatively, they may declare solemnly that knowing truths, or the pursuits of truths, is the end in itself, period. But in this case we will hesitate to call them philosophers. A dedicated scientist can afford to give such an answer without further caring about the question of the meaning of life. But we cannot help doubting whether a person who declares that it is not his business to reflect upon the problem of what the meaning of life is or upon how to live a life is really entitled to be called a philosopher.[4]

The next point is not as plain as the first one. According to Socrates, what makes our life worth living is, in a word, self-examination. It will turn out in a moment that self-examination in this case is nothing different from philosophy. So he speaks as if doing philosophy suffices to make your life worth living. You do philosophy for the purpose of making your life worth living, as already said, and this purpose is already achieved if you begin philosophical pondering over your life. It seems that philosophy is deemed to be almost the end in itself or, in other words, the purpose of doing philosophy is philosophy. But Socrates's saying is neither vacuous nor circular, for there must be something concrete to be examined in your life. If in your life there were nothing that awaits Socratic examination, even such a wise teacher as Socrates could not do anything for you. In that case you would have no chance to live a life worth living in the Socratic sense; philosophy with nothing to examine cannot be philosophy.

Then, what is that something you have to examine? The whole body of ideals, values and norms and all sorts of beliefs about human beings and their surroundings, such as other human beings, society, and nature—in a word, the worldviews are the object of examination. They are the presumptions that determine the content of the narrative of the life you imagine for yourself. Because these presumptions are transmitted to you and implanted in you through the cultural tradition into which you are born, they are often very unclear and incompatible with each other. Thus, if you live your life without examining these presumptions, your life will very likely represent a poor narrative, confused and incoherent, almost schizophrenic in a worst case. In such a case, you cannot deny that your life or the narrative of the life you imagine for yourself is badly in need of philosophy as self-examination.

Now, I believe, it is clear enough what we should expect from Korean philosophy. Korean philosophy should be understood as self-examination of Korean people. When we try to articulate and assess critically our received, already internalized presumptions that determine the content of the life story of Korean people, we are doing Korean philosophy. To take a familiar example, if a Korean speaking scholar is reporting on American philosophers' debate about the mind-body problem, we cannot yet say whether he is doing Korean philosophy. If he does this job totally ignoring that the English words 'mind' and 'body' represent important concepts embedded in the culture of English-speaking people and without taking into account the implications the problem has possibly for the life of American people, he is not doing philosophy at all, not even American philosophy. If he, while talking about the mind-body problem, considers the possible influences this problem can have for the life of Korean people and the possibility of comparing the English words with their Korean equivalents 'maum' and 'mom,' for example, he is doing Korean philosophy.

So long as there are normative preferences and worldviews that underlie the narrative Korean people imagine for their life, whether at the individual or collective level, and they deserve to be the object of Socratic examination (I don't see how they don't deserve that), Korean philosophy is not only possible but is required.

It is a possible and legitimate intellectual undertaking to enable Korean people to live a life worth living. Whatever results a Korean philosopher produces in this self-examination can become a part of Korean culture to be examined, in its turn, by another Korean philosopher. To that extent Korean philosophy is thoroughly a cultural phenomenon. Of this aspect of philosophy, we can now admit, Rorty's playful thinkers give an adequate account.

However, there is another important aspect that needs emphasizing. All cultures have an inborn tendency to seek self-perpetuation through isolation; they tend to see in foreign cultures they encounter a potential threat to their identity. Philosophy, being a critical examination, cannot serve to strengthen such a tendency. What it aims at is not protection and preservation of cultural identity under all circumstances. Rather, it attempts to eliminate unclarity and incoherence in the belief system peculiar to a culture and amend it by developing some part of it or discarding some other part of it, if necessary, and adjusting the whole accordingly. In this way, philosophy brings about changes in the culture to which it belongs and contributes its enrichment.

To do this job, philosophers must be always sensitive to influences coming from outside of their own cultural tradition. If Korean philosophers are not responsive, or not receptive to elements of foreign cultures, they will not be able to do Korean philosophy properly. Otherness is just what invites or compels us to self-examination. I guess that it was because Socrates lived in the most multicultural place at that time, Athens, that he could be the first to urge us to self-examination. Now we live in a far more advantageous situation in this respect; we are far more exposed to all sorts of influences from outside. It seems that nowadays we are invited at every turn to examine our life and thereby to make it worth living, that is, to philosophize.

Koreans originally received Confucianism and Buddhism from outside and have integrated them as the most important part of our own culture. In the present also, we are fully occupied with receiving all kinds of cultural achievements of foreign origin and with trying to integrate them into our culture. Among them, it needs not be denied, sciences of the Westerners, along with their philosophy, particularly their political and social ideals like democracy, have been occupying Korean philosophers' minds most. It is the most urgent task for Korean philosophers to adjust the belief system of our culture in such a way that it squares with the knowledge of Western sciences and the Western ideals of human life.

However, we may not forget that philosophers' task is basically a critical examination. Korean philosophers should critically examine also what they are going to receive from outside. Before and after receiving something from other cultures, Korean philosophers should not stop examining them critically. Tolerant multiculturalism is not the whole story to tell in philosophy. To take a very simple example, a philosopher has to decide between Galileo's claim that the earth moves around the sun and that of an Asian sage that the earth stays unmoved at a fixed place in the universe. (In fact, the decision is already made.) What kind of life would someone live who allows such incompatibilities to coexist in his own belief system?

His life would represent an incoherent, hardly understandable narrative; needless to say, such a life is not a life worth living. One of the main tasks of philosophers consists in spotting instances of incoherence in our belief system and correcting them. Of this aspect of philosophy represented by the spirit of critical examination the serious philosophers have given a more adequate account than the playful thinkers. So we should take also the position of the serious philosophers seriously if we want to picture a desirable image of Korean philosophy.

I think Korean philosophy must be a playful cultural activity mingled with seriousness and at same time a serious intellectual activity mingled with playfulness. Concluding this paper I would like to recall how playful and serious Socrates was in the dialogue with his fellow human beings equipped with various presumptions about their life. He thought that it was necessary to mingle playfulness and seriousness to teach us how to live a life worth living. His loyal disciple Plato followed his teacher by saying that philosophy is an interplay of seriousness and playfulness.[5]

NOTES

1. Richard Rorty, "From Logic to Language to Play. A Plenary Address to the Inter-American Congress," *Special Reports*, 11th Inter-American Congress of Philosophy, 1985.

2. No doubt the distinction Rorty made has its place primarily in the context of Western philosophy. Yet I see no problem in making use of his distinction, along with many points made upon the basis of that distinction, in our discussion on Korean philosophy. I am aware that some Korean philosophers will reject the distinction as an inadequate oversimplification. Even those who willingly acknowledge the usefulness of such a typology might be uncomfortable with Rorty's terms for the characterization. But I want to note the fact that Korean philosophy, if some kind of intellectual activity can be legitimately called as such, is after all a hybrid formed on the basis of imported philosophy along with other sciences from the West.

3. I can give two reasons why I think it is appropriate to draw on Socrates in the search for the answer. First, it is from ancient Greek that the term 'philosophy' has originated and it is roughly during the lifetime of Socrates that the meaning of the term began to develop in the direction in which the later usage of the term was to be settled. Secondly, although Socrates is sometimes regarded as the founder of the tradition of dogmatic essentialism, he is the least dogmatic thinker, maybe next to thorough-going skeptics like Pyrrho—as far as I know. The minimum he recommends with his famous saying can serve, I believe, as the starting point from which a very wide range of various philosophical positions, extending from that of analytical philosophy to that of continental philosophy or that of such philosophers as Richard Rorty and even to that of the Indian philosopher Ashis Nandy, not to mention the yet-to-be-clarified position of the most Korean philosophers, can arrive at a consensus about the purpose of philosophical activity.

4. Philosophers of today are too much accustomed to the idea of partition of their task. Many of them show a tendency to behave like a professional who, acquiescing in the principle of division of labor, regards the problems of life just mentioned as a subject matter assigned to the academic field of other professionals specializing in ethics. This tendency

has been encouraged by the insight that an ought-sentence cannot be inferred from a set of sentences asserting a factual state of affairs. To this time-worn insight has been attributed too much of philosophical import. And the result is that the distinction of value and fact is largely perceived as a chasm between the two realms and the schism of philosophy into the theoretical and the practical philosophy.

5. Plato's 6th Letter 323d.

Modernization, Counter-Modernization, and Philosophy

IN-SUK CHA
SEOUL NATIONAL UNIVERSITY

Abstract: The ennobling vision of modernity asserts that the benefits of identifying individual citizens as subjectivity are realized only when each subject is aware of the self as free in decisions and actions. Modernization through industrialization and urbanization has been seen as a means by which society can, through market contractual relationships, allow each citizen to become a self-determining subject. In Korean society this self-awakening has already set in and ought to deepen through dynamic economic growth. However, the authoritarian political power combined by technocracy obstructs the emergence of mature subjectivity. This is what can be called a phenomenon of counter-modernization. Citizenship training through philosophical dialogue may find ways to resolve this impasse by reconceptualizing modernity's goals and means in terms of enabling the potentiality inherent in subjectivity.

BEYOND CULTURAL DIVERSITY

The philosophical dialogues which frame today's multicultural world usually revolve around comparisons of the varied traditions of world views which are said to characterize the regions concerned. Comparative approaches examine various philosophical traditions in terms of both commensurability and incommensurability. In these approaches there seem to be two opposing views. One view argues that no meaningful comparison of differences can be made because there is no basis for comparison to begin with. The other argues that the core content of any cultural tradition can be identified and it is essentially the same, no matter what the culture. In this paper, it is assumed that in spite of their seeming differences, diverse traditional thoughts invariably deal with the nature of reality, modes of knowledge and how people ought to live together and there can be found a great deal of commonality as well as elective affinity in many respects among them. Furthermore, it

Special Supplement, *Journal of Philosophical Research* pp. 361–374
DOI: 10.5840/jpr201237Supplement54

is here suggested that both new and advanced industrial societies today appear to be shedding or transforming certain aspects of their respective traditional cultural perspectives that are purportedly responsible for their worldviews. The result is a convergence of world views among different peoples especially with regard to how people sharing the same global environment ought to live together.

A comprehensive socio-historical, and I might add, hermeneutic, explanation for this convergence has been articulated in the United Nations' recent *Alliance of Civilizations* document which asserts that "civilizations and cultures reflect the great wealth and heritage of humankind; their nature is to overlap, interact and evolve in relation to one another.[1] All civilizations share a history of mutual borrowing as well as accommodation and assimilation of one another's ideas and customs. Because cultures and civilizations evolve through interaction with others, local customs, knowledge, and ideas are transformed in the processes of their transfer from one culture to another, around the globe. The narratives played out by the individual and collective lives in each culture are shaped by complex social, experiential interactions within the dynamics of histories, cultures, cultural identities, globalizations, self and selves. No one of these alone can claim to be the primary sculpting force of humankind's destiny. Neither can any one of them exist without the others. Indeed, the complexity of the interactions involved in the dynamic and ever constant developing of selves and cultures over time and space can only be hinted at, never charted precisely. All that can be said with a fair degree of certainty is that societal change, whether subtle or stark, recognized or unrecognized, is constant and multiple by its nature. Even Hegel, who gave us our present notion of historicism, and maintained that the meanings of change can only be understood or constructed at the end of an era, insisted that the complexities of change never ceased.

What better example of the complexity of change can there be than the newly industrializing societies in East Asia, long considered the region of timeless, changeless traditions and now, hailed as "emerging markets" in the global economy. They have been rapidly progressing in achieving greater scientific-technological renovations in production, thus creating material abundance and enhancing the quality of life for larger and larger numbers in their respective societies. As their economic structures become increasingly modernized, the daily lifeworlds of the metropolitan areas of Beijing, Seoul, Bangkok, Manila, Kuala Lumpur and Djakarta are becoming more and more immersed in the techno-scientific culture so that it is now impossible for citizens of such metropolitan areas to think of perceiving and negotiating daily life in this world without technology.

Indeed, for emerging markets, development, economic growth, science and technology have become vital appendages to each other. As science and technology move forward and encompass the globe, East and West, North and South are operating more and more in the same sphere of rationality, and thus the concepts of reality, objectivity and rationality can no longer be claimed as characteristic of only Western civilization. Both empiricism and rationalism, once considered to constitute the main developmental phase of Anglo-European intellectual history, are now merging seamlessly into the history of world philosophy. There is no doubt whatsoever that the legacies of these two schools of modern philosophy resonate deeply in the Zeitgeist of East Asia's new industrial societies, just as they resonate deeply in today's Anglo-European societies. Indeed, sometimes when I speak of Zeitgeist, or spirit of a grand, dominating idea in the context of today's modernity, I find myself thinking of the term much as it was used by Hegel, as something enduring and powerful, almost supernatural, guiding the human race. For Hegel, a Zeitgeist was conceived and then manifested itself, took hold, as it were, in the material life of a people but it did so in such a way that its purity was lost. Purity was lost because every idea has an oppositional idea and conflict ensues in some form or other until the conflict is resolved, the resolve is always soon challenged and the dialectical cycle continues. Hegel generally considered each resolve to be a synthesis of the spirit, providing for an expansion of its meaning, until it could be realized once again in a glorious, comprehensive purity. The idea itself, in all its ramifications, he sometimes called reason, sometimes freedom and sometimes, simply, idea. For Hegel, such Zeitgeists were universal and one could interpret some form, even if an antithesis, of them in the history of any culture in any era.

Freedom is a magnificently powerful notion. But Hegel's reasoning prompts us to recognize that many ideas have the same guiding, transforming power and some of these, as he pointed out, are in opposition to freedom. All of the ideas, in their opposition or not, belong to societal life. These ideas are developed expressed and sometimes, oppressed, in many and diversified, traditions, customs and rationales.

Because concepts like freedom are universal, they are transcutltural and so, when two or more cultures interact, the taking in of each others' cultural attitudes, customs or thought patterns is a natural opening or expansion of fundamental conceptual elements found in each of their homeworlds. In the case of an individual, the process of taking in widens the horizon of the individual's lifeworld. However, whether the taking in process is collective or individual, it is a "mundialization" of home."[2] In the mundializaiton process, ideas, beliefs, values and customs of different worlds interact and are transformed through the interaction and, altered, they come to roost again in their respective homeworlds, which, then, also change. What was once strange and unfamiliar transforms into something familiar and intimate. That is to say it is accommodated or assimilated into the homeworld. Through such mediation of common, universal elements found in the orientation schemata of two or more homeworlds, cultures and individuals change, becoming more complex, more capable of communicatively expressing humankind's multifaceted potential.

Traditional societies and modern societies share elements or orientation schemata. For example, the primary type of action in both agrarian societies and industrial ones is work or labor in which humans relate to nature. From time immemorial tilling arid lands, sowing seeds and tending them, or devising hunting spears, and other means of securing food have been planned actions, requiring observation and calculation, all in the interest of survival. In the long ago beginnings of human societal living, work came to be viewed as a way to release humans from their physical bond to nature and prompted them to contrive entities which were not part of nature. From this effort of contrivance arose science and technology whose principles are objectivity and rationality. Science is a form of knowledge about nature, and technology is a tool with which humans control nature to serve their needs. Science and technology spurred and assisted in the establishment of towns and cities, the building of dams and temples, and, most significantly, they spurred rationalization for constant productivity and the institutionalization of commerce and trade, thus generating whole civilizations. The ubiquitous propensity to work with tools is a strong common element in the orientation schemata of traditional homeworlds and modern homeworlds. Such elements act as mediators and resonate from one age or culture to another. As mediators, they are complex and intricate, but they are not mystifying.

CULTURAL CONTRADICTIONS

All labor is interactive in essence, even that which seems to be performed in isolation. Work is essentially communal, and its sociality is evident in the division of labor by gender. The product of work is always shared or traded. Working with others creates a sense of solidarity and communal purpose. From such collective solidarity stems the codes of morality for living together in peace. It is really not too far fetched to assert, as Hegel did in his *Phenomenology of Mind* that ideas such as mutual recognition, social justice and civil rights are derived from our awareness of the true collaborative, collective character of human labor. Indeed, the administrators of the current project of globalization often stress the power of collaboration in labor for successful development and for peace. Yet, for some time, the social nature of labor with its ramifications for peaceful co-existence has been denied in instance after instance during this current economic globalization, just as it had been in periods characterized by empire building and colonization. This denial is, of course, a contradiction of the goals for democratization that all nations participating in the globalization project claim to espouse. One of the most blatant examples of this denial is the practice of moving industries to locations where safeguards for laborers and the environment are weak or non-existent, rendering the promise of freedom through development. Advanced developed nations began to promote this practice within their own borders in the 70's, but for some years now they have been moving industries to developing countries which are often in competition regarding the lowest wages and lowest safety costs. What has ensued, of course, are growing pockets of impoverished and unemployed workers in the advanced developed nations and a guarantee of continued poverty in the developing nations and a concentration of extreme wealth in the hands of small numbers of citizens in both types of nations.

The new industrial nations of East Asia have not had modernization thrust upon them by the tides of history. On the contrary, they chose economic development so that they could enjoy the same human dignity, individual freedom and social justice that they perceived societies advanced in modernization practices to enjoy.

Yet one wonders if East Asia has not benightedly mistaken the counter or oppositional ideas of the past for the thesis or grand idea, and set up barriers to realizing modernity in their very modernization processes. It is no comfort to know that they are not alone in this venture. Most of the nations of the world today appear to have embraced the neo-liberal modernization scheme that favors plutocracy over democracy. How did this happen? How can nations who chose modernity end up with plutocracy and not democracy?

Both Kant and Hegel stressed the catalyst role of citizens' awakening to themselves as individuals in a collective for the achievement of modernity in advanced societies. It is generally believed that a high degree of social mobility is catalyst to developing an awareness of individuality in an expanding middle class. Modernization through industrialization and urbanization holds the promise of leading new industrial societies to acknowledge the rationality principle of the contractual relationships in a market economy and thus, of allowing every person to stand on his or her own merits, free from traditional bonds of caste. When modernization is seen in this light, it becomes essential to its success that each citizen become aware of being an individual and possessing a right to self-subsistence. For the people of East Asia, it can be said that the process of such self-awakening has already set in and ought to only deepen through its dynamic growth.

In Korean society, however, there are some great stumbling blocks lying ahead on the path to unfolding individuality. Despite the steady progress of science and technology in the instrumental rationalization of productivity, changes in traditional ways of thinking and perceiving proceed at a slower pace, and an unsettling discrepancy between modernity and tradition widens proportionally. While productive forces revolve on the axis of instrumental rationality, political and social consciousness still clings to traditional value systems. The process of rationalization does not appear to be accompanied by corresponding changes in the superstructures of society. Instead, we see patrimonial political and social consciousness guiding the rational direction of economic development. These entrenched patterns of thought strongly influence the orientation and disposition to action of those who make decisions and manage affairs at the level of rationalized formal institutions.

Historically, this phenomenon is understood as intrinsic to the very nature of society itself. Certainly, resistance to modernity has been recurring in one form or another in the West over the past two or three centuries, and in contemporary developing countries we witness its unmistakable signs again and again. It is the driving force of the divisive doctrine of cultural relativism. When modernization is deliberate, as it is in most developing countries, traditional sentiments counter reforms by seeking to absorb them into the old system. In this age of globalization, counter-modernization moves are often masked by an appeal to tolerance for feudalistic traditions in the name of various multicultural doctrines. Beseeching tolerance from the world at large, many East Asian political leaders espouse an ideology of development which is solely dependent upon their authoritarian and ultimately repressive rule. When traditional authoritarianism combines with modern technology, the result is an undemocratic technocracy. This form of government is most damaging to those societies wherein a civic culture has not yet experienced circumstances by which it could mature. As a result, those institutional structures credited with the capacity to foster the development of civic culture, such as a free press, which includes theater, and all of the arts, interest groups, and access to dissent and participation through the internet are stifled or nonexistent.

Political leaders purport to achieve a stable economic development through technocratic management in the belief that citizens with "full belies" will eventually be able to embrace the freedoms and responsibility of democracy. Such a rationale generally appears to yield results in the beginning. But, as time passes, it becomes quite clear that the process of self-awakening for citizens as individual subjects does not emerge simply because the quality of their lives has been enhanced by abundance. In the absence of self-awakened citizenry, authoritarian leadership encourages people to become consumers, concerned only with economic growth managed by an efficient government. For such a state as this, they reason, there is no need for democracy.

Surely, one of the greatest hindrances to the self-awakening of individual citizens as subjects of thought and action is consumerism. Consumerism is not new, nor does it necessarily have to stifle subjectivity, but when it is driven by the pervasiveness of high technology, it can hardly avoid becoming totalitarian. As Marcuse so aptly noted in his critique of modern technology and consumerism in the West,[3] illusory needs, fueled by techno-scientific innovations, are concocted by mass media and the consequence is that workers, who were supposed to have been freed by technological advances, are instead socially and psychologically forced to work harder and more in order to satisfy an insatiable need to possess. Technology is neutral. It is a tool. It is the rhetoric of a positive and idealistic view of modernization that technology should be used to support a good quality of life in every aspect for all citizens. In the less than utopian world we inhabit, technology has always been and, is still, a formidable instrument for political and social control. Consumerism, invigorated by endlessly refined information technology, paralyses the intelligence of even reflective citizens by glossing over reality and luring them with materials and convenience to a shallow, vacuous consciousness. This callow sense of individuality, described so well and lamented so vigorously by Marcuse, now pervades in emerging market societies. Material satiation alone does not foster subjectivity. Indeed, in the world Marcuse described, materialism encourages insensitivity to others and to one's environment, creating a numbed ignorance of life itself. Marcuse, of course, was describing consumerism in the age of post World War II renewed industrialization. That age, in the America he was writing about, also produced a strong middle class, but a contented one whose, progeny were characterized by the self-involvement of the "me" generation in the '80s.

ENDANGERED MODERNITY

Don Ihde, an eminent philosopher of technology of long standing, places the shift in technological paradigms from mega-industrial technologies to the information technologies of the cyberage in the 1980s.[4] This shift was certainly very apparent in advanced nations, but, even today, for most developing countries, such as those in East Asia, the two stages exist side by side. However, in the metropolitan areas of East Asia's newly industrialized countries, the cybercultural world of computers and the Internet, that is, the world of virtual, not actual, reality may already constitute the lifeworld of many an urbanite.

It may be needless to point out here that for those whose daily routines belong to cyberworlds, virtual communities will regulate their perceptions, thoughts and, consequently their actions, forming their identities. Not so very long ago, sociologists warned that cyberculture would eventually become the prime determining force in the lives of citizens in every country.[5] Today, we see that this is already true for a great many of the younger generations in East Asia. The United States still has the highest number of broadband users at 60 million, but China, with 56 million at last count is close behind. Japan is next, and South Korea is slightly behind Germany to place fifth in the world for its use of high speed internet, at the time of this writing at least. How did this occur in countries which have only recently become industrialized and are in the throes of that phenomenon? One might say the dangers have been divided among classes, with the lower classes feeling the brunt of whatever industrialization has to wield and a middle class caught in a cyber web. Many East Asian countries had a middle class primed to enter into cyber use and, as that class expanded, so has access to the many uses of the internet, not only in the workplace, but in the home. Despite varying degrees of government restrictions, these countries have been able to make extensive, communicative use of blogs, discussion forums and internet networking to wage huge protests and rallies. South Korean teens were able to organize one of the largest anti-government demonstrations in this century. Yet reputable social scientists and observers of democratic trends noted that misinformation sped across the internet faster than rumor in a small village, firing up students who accepted it without question and mobilized their protests electronically. While presumably, web forums are a place to debate both the pros and cons of an issue that did not take place in this instance. Anyone who wanted to enter the web discussion forums to critique the issues was not welcome and rudely dismissed. Whatever tools for communication the internet generates can be used for noble or life-saving causes, but they work just as well for mindless ones. The instant and frenzied gratification for the young people involved brings to mind the hysteria of shamanism with its reliance on fetishes and emotional release. Ideologies seeped in irrationality are aided and abetted by technology.

From the nations which use the internet heavily, we also learn of young people playing internet games for sixteen or seventeen hours a day. In Korea, desperate parents elect to send such youngsters to camps where they are forced to engage in physically demanding sports and activities and to take risks in the outdoors. As well, they are restrained from using the internet or watching TV for the duration of their stay. Boot camps for cyber addicted teens seem like a drastic measure. A million teens organizing themselves for protest based on misinformation and taking to city streets with fiery sticks is a nightmare. Is it we who have lost our way in modernity or has modernization failed us?

Every new technology ushers a new way of communicating and thinking, of responding and relating to each other and ourselves. This has always been so. While we all know of ways in which technology isolates individuals from society, intersubjectivity and action, we also know that technology brings people together, invites collaboration and creates new modes of collaborating as well as new language and concepts to do it with, and thus, it creates new norms for interacting and reflecting. We need to be sensitive to ways in which technological innovations can serve the humane values found in every society to continue thriving and advancing. But as societies little acquainted with the responsibilities of freedom in our past traditions and, being new to the competitive side of market globalization and modernization, our internal resources appear to be no match for the task. Whose task is it to bring subjectivity to citizens? How does a nation that has deliberately chosen modernity and modernization go about assisting the growth of subjectivity in its citizens? Marcuse wrote as witness of what not to do. Neither a materially satiated working class nor a self-absorbed middle class advance the lofty goals of modernity's vision.

Unfortunately, there is more to the endangerment of the modernity project than technology's potential to wed with consumerism and produce mindless, ineffectual citizens. Technology, as a tool of modernism, poses other dangers as well, but the culprit behind modernity's greatest endangerment may be modernity itself.

Any concept with the power to influence the structures and thrust of governance on so many levels is open to interpretation and criticism. In fact, its life expectancy, so to speak, depends on its potential to respond to criticism and new knowledge and to change course. As well, the concept must contend with other worldviews influencing governance. These views tend to take in and absorb or merge the concept's development into already established practices. I spoke of this phenomenon in relation to countries which came late to an acceptance of the modernization agenda and tend to fit modernity's development into their traditional structures of governance. The same tendency, of course, is true of modernity itself. Modernization has always had to contend with the lingering ghosts of colonialism and the constant rebirthing of nationalism. Now, modernization is endangered by ever reincarnated practices and ideologies of both colonialism and nationalism as well as with its proponents' failure to absorb new knowledge and information about the effects of modernization on the environment and what that means.

Modernization was first promoted as a way to freedom for all and, most importantly, a way of gaining control over nature, both in terms of controlling the harm nature could inflict and in transforming nature to serve human needs and desires. While this view is still prevalent, it began losing ground rapidly in the latter decades of the twentieth century when it became apparent that the accelerated advances in science and technology, while proliferating development and trade on a global level, were critically harming the environment. The damages provided insights into their human and ecological costs. Moreover, these new insights allowed many to see for the first time the inequities in social justice that modernization imposes, and has always imposed, in every society.

Just at this juncture, characterized by an awareness of the dangers inherent in modernization and neo-liberalism's rise, many countries decided to join the modernization project. They carried into their venture, hopes for freedom from want and the good life, but as I mentioned, they had no mature civil society and no institutionalized structures to voice dissent or seek alterations when modernization methods created more poverty, not less. Moreover, there were no models of success in terms of sustaining a good life for all to be found in the modernity of well-established developed nations. Indeed, just at the time many Asian nations were opting for development at long last, many Western nations began to deliberately dismantle the safeguards of regulating vital industries and services and were cutting funding for long established institutions which had guaranteed basic rights to food, shelter and education for their citizens.

Many critics believe that the problems of modernity and neo-liberal economic globalization are inherent in the concepts themselves. For example they believe that capitalism and modernity, of necessity, must cause ecological harm and injustice and harm to groups of people or markets will suffer and modernity cannot advance. Some even argue that history will work through all the injustice and harm and, that new resources, perhaps in outer space, will be found to replace those destroyed and that surviving members of one destroyed group will be the leaders of a similar cycle. Still, other argue that the ends do not justify the means, and, moreover, that ecological modernization is a possibility, and sometimes, even now, a reality. They further maintain that embracing ecological moderation policies will encourage standards based on justice for both people and their environment. This last belief, assuming that it is not too late, can come about only if we can envision modernity in a different way than we do now. My contention is that the revised vision is already here, that its roots can be found in the earliest rationalizations of subjectivity.

MODERNITY AS SUBJECTIVITY

Though it would not be apparent to an intelligent visitor from another planet today, the fundamental distinguishing feature of modernity is the awareness of the subject of his/her own existence as actor. Some Western intellectual historians assert that this self-awakening became manifest in the political form of the French Revolution of 1789 on one hand and in the form of German Idealism on the other. This historical perspective suggests that the process of individuation occurring in Korean society and elsewhere in this region requires a deeper reflection than is the case now on the ongoing changes in mentality being brought about by the rapid rationalization of social structure taking place.

In our attempt to link philosophy to reality, we will look now at some anthropological accounts which Kant and Hegel construed from their observations of the political and social conditions of their time. One of the political implications of Kant's transcendental theory of knowledge is the problem of subjectivity that is characteristic of creative spontaneity. Those who achieve subjectivity become the self-determining, free individuals that Kant presumes to be essential to his political philosophy. Subjectivity is also taken as the unique mark of human dignity (*Menschenwuerde*) in his moral philosophy.

Reading Kant, it is difficult to believe that he lived his whole life in the same city and never ventured more than a few miles outside of it. Yet, without aid of any of the modern means of communication we know today, he knew much about the world outside of his city, his country and Europe. He ranted against slavery and against wars and the oppressive means used to open up markets in far away lands. He never wavered in his premise that all men were subjects. The federation of states that he conceived included those lands that were considered by others to be inhabited by savages. Kant commented that, in his view, the practices of the Europeans were far more barbaric than those of the "savages.' Article III in the conditions of a Perpetual Peace is titled "The Rights of men as Citizens of the world in a cosmo-political system, shall be restricted to conditions of universal Hospitality."[6] He strongly believed that all nations want to trade but only under hospitable conditions. Under the conditions of an agreed upon practice of universal Hospitality, Anglo-European countries would be unable to treat foreign and strange lands as if they belonged to nobody whatsoever and available for them to conquer and plunder.

Yet, this same Kant, who insisted on hospitality among nations, well understood the conflicted, oppositional nature of all human beings. He is justly famous for his exploration of the "unsocial sociability" of human nature (ungesellige Geselligkeit)[7] Disciplining one's unsociability in order to get along in society was the mark of a civilized person. Human beings, as individuals, came to this discipline because they realized that they needed to live in society, that it was essential to survival. Nations would come to the notion of keeping a Perpetual Peace for the same reason. When Kant spoke of the abuses European traders inflicted upon countries weaker and less developed than their own, he might well have been predicting the problems of today, though he surely thought there would be a Cosmo-political constitution by now. What we have instead however are calls from civil society, from various non-governmental organizations for global governance to achieve social and environmental justice through a global-political constitution or laws because modernization, as it is practiced today, has created unparalleled inequality among citizens within a single nation and among nations. Kant did talk about the ruination of nature through war, colonization and coercive marketing methods, but there is no evidence that he thought modernity as he perceived might endanger the resources of the world. However, just as Kant believed that human beings would reconcile their oppositional natures in order to maintain a peaceful society, so I think his message would be the same regarding re-visioning modernity so that it can not only be sustained, but be worthy of being sustained. And he would have no difficulty associating that re-visioning with social and environmental justice.

For Hegel, subjectivity actualizes itself in labor. In work we relate to objects of nature and to our fellow-human beings. In labor too, one individual may subsume others through intersubjectivity, but in the end, those enslaved attain subjectivity when they realize the worth of their labor and rebel. Ideally, labor binds subjects together through its sociality and intersubjectivity. Labor is the objectification of human potentialities realized in the social act. Hegel is keen to point out that labor, which in essence is never solitary, allows human beings to receive the recognition from others that they inherently crave. This need for recognition is met in the division of labor within community. Labor is a universal element binding individual subjects in a community. Through the product of labor, individuals acquire mutual recognition as equals. As *homo laborans*, subjects are autonomous individuals bearing responsibility for others, and are thus collective as well.

Both Kant and Hegel were well aware of the consequences of a flourishing market economy, and their portrayal of subjectivity as awareness of one's ability to think and act independently, and to collaborate was certainly a response to the problems accruing to the modernization of German society at the dawn of the Great Industrial Revolution. Especially, the latter demanded the transcendence of a state in which individuals were objectified and treated as cogs in a market machine. He envisaged a society that fosters personal subjectivities and universal recognition of the free, thinking individual.[8] This thought is echoed in the Critical Theory of late capitalism with even stronger basis for doing so. First, there is even more evidence to suggest that subjectivity exists in all lifeworlds, and that the hall mark of subjectivity, free will, prevails even in the most authoritarian and oppressive of them. States may or may not transcend their oppressive operations and subjectivity may be stifled, but it exists and never ceases to find expression on some level.

HERMENEUTICS FOR A TRANSCULTURAL ETHICS

We exist in the world relating to other fellow-beings. The modes of social relationships vary within lifeworlds. After laboring together, early peoples began to relax together, family and neighbors came together to share food at the evening table. Communal relaxation at the end of long days soothed the pains of the body and lifted the spirits. Shared food and drink invited them to chant and dance life's burdens into oblivion, and the hardships of work receded as make-believe set in. Thus, in our earliest history of communal living did fantasy and play emerge. The concept of play is a universal conception, existing in every culture. The capacity to imagine and so to conjure up alternative realities is uniquely human. Through such play did metaphysics delineate the distinction between reality and appearance.

In imagination we are infinitely free to do what we will, but in real life we are confined to our bodies within given situations. Yet in playing with others, we glean the true meaning of what it is to be free. In imagination, human beings learn the genuine meaning of freedom of thought and expression, affirming our individual subjectivity against the actual world. In childhood human beings learn to revel in fairy tales, ruling the fairylands into which no outsiders are allowed. And out of imagination springs the power of creation, by virtue of which humans transform nature into something entirely new and, by this ingenuity, distinguish themselves from nature.

Through these distinctly human traits, Hegel's *homo laborans* becomes Weber's *Kulturmensch*. This is the authentic mode of human existence. Labor proclaims how free humans are by way of changing imaginary worlds into the actual world. True enough, the transformation more times than not brings new obstacles, but today, the very act of imagining change is being pitilessly endangered by our techno-scientific age. We cannot turn back the clock and summarily have philosophy reinstate human subjectivity to its original metaphysical position, but we can ask philosophy to ground subjectivity in all aspects of our lifeworlds and so restore its power to transform and influence those lifeworlds, and above all, to develop an ethics to promote and protect universal subjectivity.

At the turn of the twentieth century Husserl's transcendental phenomenology of subjectivity made its illustrious way as part of philosophical endeavors to secure human subjectivity from the threat of its reification, and the Existentialism of Heidegger and Sartre followed suit along with the Critical Theory of Horkheimer, Adorno, Marcuse and Habermas. Each of these philosophers tackled the problem of vanishing susbjectivity by approaching it from different perspectives and resources. The crisis of a vanishing subjectivity has never quite gone away, no matter what the perspective. At the dawn of the new millennium, industrializing societies of East Asia, having entered the cyber-world as well, are confronted with similar anthropological crises and philosophers are called upon to reinstate subjectivity in this precarious contemporary moment when cyber dreams and consumerism choke not only the subjects' propensity to oppositional reasoning and action, but also their creativity and will.

Sujectivity developes in modes other than labor and play. Human beings relate to other humans in the modes of social relationship such as love, hate, domination and death.[9] The notion of love has informed all cultures in human history. Love alone is capable of bringing together separate individuals and groups into communal solidarity. In love one learns the meaning of oneness with others and becomes imbued with a sense of wholeness. Hatred finds its infinite ways to divide; it often leads to violent strife, which separates victors and the defeated. This in turn creates notions of superior and inferior among fellow beings that justify political-social orders of domination and subjugation. Human history has witnessed numerous cases of this kind and continues to do so.

Awareness of one's mortality defines what it is to be human. The dread that I shall no longer exist *hic et nunc* reveals to me and to every individual the true meaning of being and non-being. Facing the immanent nullification of my own being, I come to see the dark abyss of nothingness, and struggle to regain my potentiality to prolong my existence. The inevitability of our own demise holds us captive in thought and imagination. Death illuminates the disparity between transience and eternity. Perhaps, philosophy derives its inner driving force from one's awareness of mortality, from our "being-toward-death" (*Zum Tode sein*),[10] while our moral consciousness attains its strength from the gnawing anxiety about what will become of us after death. Yet, we yearn for eternal life and envision it as a place where will be no more hate, quarrels, wars and destruction, a place where we can live together in perpetual peace and fulfill our potentials without hindrance.

In the evolution of human history oppositional categories are always paired and intertwined: unity and division, peace and conflict, and creation and destruction exist together in tension. The mediation involved in this complex of commonly acknowledged meanings imbued with oppositional tensions which humans acquire from childhood on through the modes of social relationships of love and hate, work and play, and living and dying takes place daily in our lifeworlds. These meanings, constantly nuanced through mediation, in turn constitute the basis of our intersubjective understanding by virtue of which we relate to our environments and fellow human beings in thought, feeling and action. Practical reasoning in every society grows through the mediations of primary and secondary social relationships and matures in articulation at those societal levels so that conciliation of divisions and hostilities can come to be addressed collectively. Mediating the oppositional elements of societal life, or as Kant would have said, our "unsocial sociability" takes place at every level. Historical contexts change, the scope of the concepts available to social mediation widens in each generation, but the tensions of oppositions and the ever emerging variations of their reconciliation can still be viewed as viable contributions to a theoretical foundation for establishing communities, even for establishing a global community of peace and harmony wherein each of us may realize all of our potentialities as freely as we can.

Democratic concepts such as "individual," "equality before the law," "social justice" and "human rights" are not given to us a priori. They belong to the legacy built by those philosophers and thinkers who reflected on humanity's relentless struggle for self-liberation from bondages in the past. These concepts have been able to reach so many through centuries of complicated and varied processes of dissemination and now have come to embrace nearly all of humanity. The complex of meanings, acquired through our social relationships of love, hate, work and play, and life and death, catalyses the connections, which are transcultureal. Today, most lifeworlds brim with potential schemata by which to render practices insuring human dignity and social justice for all human beings. Two more concepts, discussed briefly in this essay, have entered our general vocabulary, "environmental justice" and "sustainable modernity", sometimes associated with "sustainable development" but going beyond even that in its scope. We owe our understanding of the depth and importance of these concepts to the ever growing urging from civil society around the world to reinstate the essential vision of modernity, with its emphasis on equality. It is civil society, after all, from philosophers and critics to mobilized non-governmental organizations dedicated to the original notions of modernity that have pointed out to various national governments that subjectivity, equality, social justice and observance of human rights have gone missing in today's global economics. It is civil society that urges governments to pay attention to what scientists are telling us about our environment. It is civil society that informs the most vulnerable in our societies of the dangers the current neo-liberal ideology and managerial economics poses to them and their environment as well as to the environments of the world. And it is civil society that has called attention to the limits of modernization. What shall we do with our understandings?

Subjectivity demands agency or it is nothing at all. Conversely, action is ineffectual if knowledge and reflection do not inform it. This understanding urges me to advocate for education in critical thinking, problem solving and awareness of world threatening issues. I note that many universities throughout the world have courses, even majors in environmental studies and social justice. Such education should be a priority of modernizing countries, It should not wait until students reach university years, it can begin much sooner. There are fine programs featuring what early childhood educators refer to as a community of philosophical inquiry (CPI) for kindergarteners which explore several types of reasoning, including moral reasoning. Continuing education should certainly offer community courses in environmental studies for adults of all ages.

There are many other ways of educating citizens to subjectivity and action. I have mentioned above some of those I know about in Korea and elsewhere. It seems to me that those nations which have chosen modernization have the best chance of exploring it with their citizens of all ages. Hope exists in keeping the transculturated concepts of freedom, subjectivity and equality alive and growing through education, discussion and debate locally and globally.

NOTES

1. United Nations, *Alliance of Civilizations*, p. 5. Report of the High-Level Group. 13 November 2006 (New York: The United Nations, 2007).

2. In-Suk Cha, "Globalization, Cultural Identity and the Development of the Self," *Philosophy Facing World Problems*, the proceedings of the Twenty-First World Congress of Philosophy, Vol. 13 (Ankara: Philosophical Society of Turkey, 2007).

3. Herbert Marcuse, *One-Dimensional Man* (London: Routledge & Kegan Paul, 1964).

4. Don Ihde, "Philosophy of Technology, 1975–1995," *Journal of the Society for Philosophy and Technology* 1, nos. 1–2 (Fall 1995).

5. Tim Jordan, *Cyberpower* (London: Routledge & Kegan Paul, 1999), pp. 4–5

6. I. Kant, *Kant's Principles of Politics, including his essays on Perpetual Peace, A contribution to Political* Science, 1784, trans. W. Hastie (Edinburgh: Clark, 1891).

7. Kant, *Ideen zu einer allgemeinen Geschichte in weltbuergerlicher Absicht*, 1784 (*Idea for a Universal History from a Cosmopolitan Point of View*, 1784), IV. Und V. Saetze.

8. G. W. F. Hegel, *Dokumente zu Hegels Entwicklung*, ed. Johannes Hoffmeister (Stuttgart: Frommann, 1936), pp. 219–220. Cited in Schlomo Avineri, *Hegel's Theory of the Modern State* (London: Cambridge University Press, 1972), p. 11.

9. Eugen Fink, *Grundphaenomene des menschlichen Daseins* (Freiburg: Alber, 1979).

10. Martin Heidegger, *Sein und Zeit* (Tuebingen: Niemeyer, 1927).

SELECTED PAPERS FROM
THE XXII WORLD CONGRESS OF PHILOSOPHY

Rethinking Philosophy for the Resurrection of the Object of Knowledge

IOANNA KUÇURADI
MALTEPE UNIVERSITY, ISTANBUL

Abstract: The author of the paper starts by calling our attention to problems that make it necessary to rethink philosophy and puts her finger on one common factor at the origin of these problems. This is what she calls "the loss of the object of knowledge" in epistemology.

After she shows how the object of knowledge is lost in two prevailing epistemologies of the twentieth century—in pragmatism and logical empiricism—and the consequences of this loss for our lives, she gives examples of rethinking certain philosophical questions. These are the questions of what knowledge is and problems of norms related to the lack of distinction between epistemological kinds of norms. This rethinking also implies the necessity of rethinking philosophical education.

Why rethinking philosophy? Rethinking presupposes awareness of a problem, i.e., a discrepancy which leads to inquiry and often to new knowledge.

What are the problems which make necessary to rethink philosophy? A variety of theoretical and practical problems can be mentioned. In a paper I wrote in the year 1990, related to "modernity" and "postmodernity," I formulated this need as follows:

> we need perhaps neither to defend nor to reject modernity in whatever sense, neither to defend nor to reject modernization, also in whatever sense; we need new philosophical knowledge: an epistemology beyond the positivistic one—one which distinguishes not between science and metaphysics, but between knowledge and the other products of the human mind—; an ontology which has overcome the "great reduction" of Being into one of its species—an ontology beyond the dualism of the physical and the metaphysical—; an anthropology which does not deal with images or conceptions of the human being, but with its specificities which include also its possibilities; and an ethics which is neither normative nor meta-ethics, but which goes beyond these approaches and objectifies the ethical human phenomenon.[1]

Special Supplement, *Journal of Philosophical Research* pp. 375–387
DOI: 10.5840/jpr201237Supplement55

In order that philosophical knowledge has a humanizing impact on life, e.g., in order to deal with global problems without losing sight of their ethical aspects, we have to rethink the prevailing approaches in all these fields of philosophy.

Here I shall confine myself to present to you the result of my rethinking—during the past twenty-five years—of certain epistemological issues, which I had to rethink while dealing with ethical and human rights problems. At the root of all these issues, we see problems related to what I call "the loss of the object of knowledge."

A number of such epistemological issues is related to the right diagnosis and explanation of situations. They are the problems we face in *naming* or *labelling* a social or political situation and those faced in the attempts to explain it. Different theoretical or practical starting points—: different assumptions or approaches, e.g., different economic, social a political theories—lead, no wonder, to different "diagnoses," i.e., different labellings of the same situation, as well as to different explanation of, i.e., to ascribing different causes to, an objectively same situation.

The world community is now sufficiently aware of this impasse. Still, I am afraid, it is not sufficiently aware of the epistemological problems behind this impasse. For example, they call those different labellings and explanations of the same situations "looking from different viewpoints" and promote it, assuming that thus dogmatism can be avoided.

It is strange enough that, though perhaps the most cultivated philosophical discipline in the twentieth century appears to be epistemology, the epistemological tools that the prevailing views secure, help us too little in facing the difficulties we come across with respect to the diagnosis and explanation of the situations we have to confront.

THE LOSS OF THE OBJECT AND ITS CONSEQUENCES

Let us take here a bird's eye view to the prevailing approaches in epistemology in the twentieth century and their role related to the loss of the object.

In the twentieth century, pragmatism and logical empiricism with its various ramifications, seem to have played crucial yet different roles in this loss of the object of knowledge.

It is noteworthy that both these "schools" of philosophy have developed their respective touchstones for knowledge from their world-views, which they proposed in order to answer pressing psychological needs of their age. It is also noteworthy that both of them call themselves 'method' in the sense of 'approach,' or 'world-view,' and when they speak, they both look at the spectator—and *not* at the producer—of knowledge.

In the face of the turmoil created at the end of the nineteenth century by the development of the sciences and by their "truths" which were in disagreement with those of religion, pragmatism, by cutting the Gordian knot, was believed to have opened a way out for those who were at a loss: "The pragmatic method is primarily a method of settling metaphysical disputes that otherwise might be interminable"[2] says James. "Whenever a dispute is serious, we ought to be able to show some practical differences that must follow from one side or the other being right."[3] As we see here, this is the attitude of the spectator of discrepant statements on the same topic. To enable the spectator to show these practical differences, pragmatism formulates its criterion: "True ideas are those that we can assimilate, validate, corroborate and verify . . . Truth *happens* to an idea. It *becomes* true, is *made* true by events. If the consequences we have in mind follow, that means that our ideas agree with reality."[4] Here we also observe that 'idea' is meant to be any product of the human mind.

The main concern of logical empiricism is also to find a way to *become sure* of avoiding error—something which, of course, it never achieves, since it has to consider all propositions as 'hypotheses,' in the end. It develops its criterion of knowledge—verifiability, and later falsifiability—from its world-view, as we find it expressed in the manifesto (as I call it) of the Vienna Circle, i.e., in the text presented in 1929 to Moritz Schlick.[5] There we read: "The scientific world-conception is characterized not so much by theses of its own, but rather by its basic attitude, its points of view and direction of research." It is characterized "essentially by *two features*. First it is *empiricist and positivist*: there is knowledge only from experience, which rests on what is immediately given. . . . *Second*, the scientific world-conception is marked by application of . . . *logical analysis* . . . If such an analysis were carried through for all concepts, they would thus be ordered into a reductive system, . . . the 'constitutive theory' within the framework of which logical analysis would be applied by the scientific world-conception." This is what logical empiricism planned to achieve.

Still in the sciences, both in natural and so-called social sciences, not one but many frameworks, many 'models' were developed. To construct 'models' has constituted the main preoccupation in the sciences; and the term 'model'—concerning which a great confusion still prevails—appears to be one, if not the most, fashionable term in the Philosophy of Science.

Yet, the following fact which Hannah Arendt, in the sixties, pointed to, still escapes attention:

> The trouble is that almost every axiom seems to lend itself to consistent deductions and this to such an extent that it is as though men were in a position to prove almost any hypothesis they might choose to adopt, not only in the field of purely mental constructions like the over-all interpretations of history which are all equally supported by facts, but in the natural sciences as well. . . . The totalitarian systems tend to demonstrate that action can be based on any hypothesis and that in the course of consistently guided action, the particular hypothesis will become true, will become actual, factual reality. . . . In other words, the axiom from which the deduction is started . . . does not have to tally at all with the facts as given in the objective world at the moment the action starts; the process of action, if it is consistent, will proceed to create a world in which the assumption becomes axiomatic and self-evident. . . . Within the natural sciences things are not essentially different, but they appear more convincing because they are so far removed

> from the competence of the layman and his healthy, stubborn common sense, which refuses to see what it cannot understand . . .[6]

says Hanna Arendt. And what she says seems to be true not only for totalitarian systems, but for any social and political system.

Also her observations concerning 'contemporary science' seem to the point. The hallmark of this science appears to be what I call 'the loss of the object' we observe prevailing in most of the sciences. 'Science' is considered—by prevailing Philosophy of Science—to be a system of hypotheses or theories—these two terms being used as synonyms. For example, according to Popper, science is "a system of hypotheses, a system of unjustifiable anticipations: i.e., a system of anticipations by which we operate so long as they are corroborated, and which we may call neither 'true' nor merely 'more or less sure' or 'probable.'"[7] Thus "the activity of the scientific researcher consists of establishing propositions or systems of propositions, and of testing them systematically; what is established and tested in experience by observation and experiments are hypotheses, systems of theories."[8] "'Theory' is the net we throw in order to capture the 'world'—in order to rationalize, explain and master it."[9] 'To capture the world' means in Popperian terminology 'to make empirically testable prognoses.'

Is this conception of science, as worded by Popper, not in full agreement with Hanna Arendt's observations—still, critical observations—concerning 'contemporary sciences'?

Thus 'objectivity,' being once the ideal of the sciences, has given room to 'intersubjective validity,' which has constituted the ideal in 'science.' Application of the assumed intersujectively valid hypotheses or theories—or models, or approaches—to individual cases, which in turn 'proves' or 'corroborates' their validity, has become 'the method of science.' This latter observation applies not only to logical empiricism but to the dialectical approach as well.

Nevertheless, 'theories' or models on the same issue, go on increasing in number, and all of them seem justifiable at first glance. Still this form of much praised pluralism leaves people at a loss, and makes the spectators of knowledge look like novices in philosophy.

I think we are still not sufficiently aware of the consequences created by the loss of the object of knowledge in various areas of human activity; and as a remote consequence, I would mention—well aware, of course, that I may shock many among you here—the fashionable demand to respect all cultures equally.

Thus, at the beginning of the twenty-first century, we find ourselves in a situation parallel to that of the beginning of the twentieth century: we have many 'truths,' but this time 'secular truths,' on the *same topics*: we have different models for the diagnosis, explanation, evaluation etc. of the *same things*.

To come to grips with this situation—instead of questioning prevailing epistemology—we made pluralism a motto of our time, considering it to be a remedy against dogmatism, still without inquiring where pluralism is epistemologically possible.

Postmodernism seems to be an attempt to justify this pluralism—to legalize the facts in the name of freedom, considered to be a remedy to "the dogmatism of the big narratives" of modernity. Yet, owing to postmodernism, dogmas also—including the various fundamentalisms—found free hand to spread themselves. It is really noteworthy that the theoreticians of the fundamentalists are fascinated by postmodernism. Postmodernism appears to be the most extreme appearance of the loss of the object of knowledge.

For an objective naming of a situation we need clear concepts which can be the product of a philosophical definition of human facts and of a philosophical conceptualization of ideas.

EPISTEMOLOGICAL PROBLEMS IN THE DIAGNOSIS AND EXPLANATION OF SITUATIONS

How is it possible to make a right diagnosis and explanation of a situation—which is indispensable for the right evaluation of a situation, which, in turn, is indispensable for finding solutions which do not lose sight of human rights and of the ethical components inherent in every human situation?

Put very briefly:[10] A situation is not there out, it does not stand before our eyes, like you and me. It becomes the special situation it is, only when it is put forth, i.e., when we name it. This is the main reason why one and the same situation is often presented as a few different ones.

To put forth a situation amounts to become aware of the relationship between various *simultaneous events* which are the outcome of the situation, or its symptoms; it amounts to discovering, among their other different causes, the *common cause* of certain independent events which happen at that moment. This makes it possible to diagnose and name the situation under consideration correctly—as Dr. Rieux in the *Plague* of Camus does—which not only has implications for finding the proper measures to be taken in order to change this situation, but also implications for the legal treatment of those involved in it.

On the other hand, to explain a situation means to show how the situation came about. This amounts becoming aware of the way a number of *other* (earlier) *simultaneous events* were entangled around a human group and of the role that each of these independent events has played in the creation of the existing situation. This makes it possible to find out what has to be done to change this situation, yet in any direction or toward any purpose we might have. Thus, naming and explaining correctly a situation, though indispensable, are not sufficient for finding humane solutions to overcome them. Ethical value knowledge and knowledge of human rights have to play here also their role.

Thus we see that in the case of the right diagnosis of an existing situation the object of knowledge is the *common cause* of independent events, which is only one of the *causes* of each of them and in the case of a right explanation the object of knowledge is the entanglement, around a given human group, of simultaneous independent events. If we lose sight of this object, different labellings, as well as ascription of different causes is well possible. This is what is often called pluralism.

As you can see from these examples, by the term 'object of knowledge' I mean what, at any given moment, we wish, for different reasons, to know and consequently we objectify. To make this concept clearer, here allow me to objectify 'knowledge' and try to answer the question "what is knowledge?."

KNOWLEDGE AND ITS OBJECT

To objectify 'knowledge' let me start from language, as Aristotle did: knowledge, whatever it be, is always 'the knowledge of *something*.' Still when we look at some languages, at least some European languages, the word 'knowledge' appears to denote both the *activity of knowing* something and the *outcome* of this activity, i.e., the assertions somebody makes about something, the propositions, statements or whatever you might call them.

Knowledge, as one human activity among others, appears to be the general name of various *interwoven* activities—such as perceiving, conceiving, understanding, thinking-reasoning with all its various kinds; verification, justification, evaluation etc. Compositions of such activities play their part in single *acts* of knowledge-acquiring, consequently such activities can be isolated only artificially for epistemological purposes. And I think that, without a hair-splitting analysis of all of them, and of the different kinds of some of them, in view of determining their special imput to the general activity of knowing, it is not possible to attain sound knowledge *of* knowledge.

Now, every act of knowing, be it simple or complex, is intentional, i.e., it is intended to know something special, which the knowing person *objectifies* for a special practical or theoretical reason. Thus, 'every knowledge is knowledge of something' would, in the case of an *act* of knowledge, mean that the knowing person is oriented towards, and puts himself in relation to, something ontically *independent* of this act of his. By this act, something that *is*—in one or another way, or, modality—becomes an object of knowledge. Thus the object of every knowledge—of every piece of knowledge—or, *the known*, is a connection that the knowing person discovers and establishes successfully or unsuccessfully. The knowing person establishes *the object* of his special knowledge, i.e., he isolates, according to his intention, and tries to fix something that is.

Thus, the object of knowledge—of every piece of knowledge—appears to be something that *is*: in other words, it is not product of the act (or acts) that grasps it, it is ontically independent from this act; still its objectification is something that, by this act, the knowing person *does*, sometimes successfully and other times unsuccessfully, as I said.

The objectified and established connections are ontologically different, and the fact that the objectified is a connection established by the knowing person, makes for us difficult to grasp what knowledge is, since it is our habit to take for the object of knowledge only *real things*. Thus, the object of knowledge—of every act of knowing—is not the so-called 'external world' or whatever you may call it, but anything *being*, and being as it is, independently from the act of knowing that objectified it. This is also the object of every piece of knowledge—of the assertion or the proposition put forth as the outcome of this act—, i.e., the connections this sentence asserts.

This 'object of knowledge' has also to be distinguished from the 'object of inquiry' (or research), which is usually a problem, a discrepancy, or an *aporia* in the Platonic sense and which an inquiry intends to eliminate.

Now, when we look at propositions—or whatever one pleases to call them—i.e., to full sentences, which assert something, keeping an eye on the question of the object of knowledge, i.e., on what they make known independently of themselves; we see that there is a bulk of propositions which have no subject, i.e., they are not put forth as a result of an objectification, but which either *create* their 'object'—like a kind of beliefs—, or are inferences expressing an opinion, an 'ought,' 'must' etc. Norms are the outcome of such inferences.

I think, we have to restrict our concept of knowledge only to propositions which possess such an object. I also think that today's epistemology has to resurrect the object of knowledge. To do this, a new ontology seems necessary; but I shall not dwell here on this point.

Without the resurrection of the object of knowledge, today's epistemology will not, probably, become able to secure the necessary tools, which today's world needs for right diagnosis, explanation, evaluation etc. and for becoming able to establish, in an epistemically justifiable way, the content of ideas and principles proposed for action, social as well as political.

If we possess the will to produce *knowledge* of ideas, of norms, etc. epistemically and ethically justifiable, as well as if we possess the will to scrutinize the existing ones for selection and use, we have to try to find what we shall look at.

NORMS AND THEIR KINDS

Another group of problems we are faced with in dealing with global problems, is related to the lack of knowledge concerning the epistemological specificities of norms. Lack of epistemological knowledge on norms, e.g., lack of distinction among kinds of norm—let alone between the concept of norm and the concept of value—makes possible, for example the claim made in certain non-western circles, especially when they are accused of violations of human rights, that human rights are product of European culture—they are "European values"—, consequently they are different from the "values" of their cultures, ergo: They should not be accused.

The existence of norms, of different and changing norms, is a (human) fact, related to a specificity of being human: the establishing of social relations, i.e., the creation of social roles, assumed by concrete individuals.

Norms are *deduced* undeliberately or deliberately, in order to create an order in a given group, i.e., in order to secure measures for the right and wrong, consequently in order to determine the conduct of individuals, as well as the way how social relations will be established among the individual members of a given group. Whoever assumes or finds himself in a given role, has to behave in accordance with the norms constituting that role.

Norms are usually worded as ought-should-must or may propositions. This means that propositions of norms are not propositions of knowledge, i.e., they have no object independent of those who put them forth. Consequently norms are neither true nor false.

This is the main epistemological specificity of norms and also the origin of the difficulties faced in evaluating a given norm: propositions of norms can not be verified or falsified; their evaluation presupposes a different epistemological treatment.

Compared with propositions of knowledge norms are thoughts, deduced from epistemologically very different premises and by different kinds of reasoning.

The axiological specificity of a norm depends on the epistemological specificity of its premises. Its justification or "foundation" is related to the possibility of *going back* to its origin—to the premises from which it is deduced—and of seeing their epistemic specificity, i.e., whether the premises from which a given norm is deduced are knowledge or other norms and what kind of knowledge or norms.

This epistemological evaluation, which every norm has to undergo, is something quite different from *the ways of validating* or enforcing a norm. The latter are social procedures—different social or political procedures—, aiming at establishing a broad *consensus* on a given norm. To find out how a moral norm was *made valid* presupposes sociological research, while to find out how a legal norm was enforced, one has to read the minutes of the sessions of the bodies, which the enforcement of such a norm depends on.

What we see in the present world, is a search for *consensus* on given norms, *without taking into consideration the epistemological-axiological specificity of the given norms*. This is why, even in the development of professional codes and international (human rights) instruments no attention is paid to the epistemological specificity of the included norms. This is also one of the main dangers of "democratic" decisions in our present world. It makes possible the enforcement, by consensus or by the majority of votes, of norms which are contradictory to human rights.

What I said concerning the epistemological-axiological specificity of norms is true for both moral and legal norms.

What we call 'morals' are systems of norms, which individuals in a given group (or in a given culture) have to follow in their relations with others, in action: of norms of behaviour or conduct, as well as of norms of evaluation. They are the "good"s and the "bad"s prevailing in a given group—a given "society" or "culture."

Now, if we take some distance and look at these moral norms, i.e., if we objectify them, we easily observe that a part of such norms prevailing in given groups or "cultures" is different, and that it is also changing with the time within the same groups, that even a way of behaviour, once prohibited, becomes promoted or vice versa; we also see that the same single action—of yours or mine—is qualified by prevailing different norms on the same issue, simultaneously, as good and bad. This fact, which postmodernism, by losing sight of the specificity of another kind of norms, attempted to justify theoretically, has led especially young people and mainly in the so-called "Western society," to the (theoretical) rejection of all and all kinds of norms.[11] At present the debates concerning certain issues in bioethics, are also directly related to the lack of distinction between kinds of norms.

Still besides these different and changing norms, we also observe that another part of norms does not show, to a great extent, such a difference or change—for example "for one, to keep one's word." People in each culture or group are expected to obey—to follow or use—both these kinds of moral norms.

In view of this fact, the first distinction we have to make, is between the norms of evaluation—the so-called value judgements—and the norms of behaviour or conduct, though they can be easily translated into each other, since the role they are expected to play is different.

Norms of moral evaluation—or general proposition on what is good or bad—are expected to determine our evaluations, i.e., to be used in order *to determine the value* of an evaluated object—be it an action, a person, a situation etc.—; while norms of moral conduct or "ought-should" propositions are expected *to determine our actions* in life. In other words, norms of evaluation are supposed to lead those who use them as criteria, to the *knowledge of value* of given actions of yours or mine—which is not the case—; while norms of behaviour—moral rules or principles—are expected to determine actions carried out in given situations—your actions, my actions etc. And the 'ought' or 'should' of these latter norms of conduct or behaviour, are deduced from premises of different epistemic specificity and by different ways of reasoning.

Here I shall confine myself to pointing only at two kinds of such norms: those deduced in different given historical conditions *from experience by induction* and those deduced by the comparison of different given (human or historical) conditions in the light of the knowledge of certain specificities of *the* human being—or of what is called human dignity. The first kind of norms may be justified—if wished—statistically, the second by a kind of reasoning similar to *reductio ad absurdum*.

At the origin of the first kind of norms (of behaviour) are given natural-social conditions, as well as the conceptions related to *the* human being of different cultures. They are norms of behaviour relative to the existing conditions, possessing a *practical* function, in view of establishing or safeguarding *any* order in these existing conditions at the moment they are deduced. So long as the conditions in which they are deduced prevail, if deduced with sagacity, they are functional. But when these conditions change, they lose their function and meaning, i.e., the "ought"s or "must"s they express, lose their ground. Many traditional-customary ways of behaviour transmitted from generation to generation in a given cultural group, belong to this kind of norms. Thus we see that though in time the conditions wherefrom these norms are deduced do not exist any more—which means that there is no more a justifiable reason of the "ought" they express—, people in this group try to keep them going. We even see attempts to revive obsolete norms.

Still, in time, new norms on the same issue are deduced from the changed conditions, mostly incompatible with the old ones. And right here we find the point where the so-called "crisis of values," to a great extent, arises from. It seems that those who insist on keeping valid such norms, are unaware of the source wherefrom the "ought" or "must" of these norms is deduced, i.e., that they are unaware of their epistemic specificity.

Norms of this kind—to which many proverbs or products of practical wisdom also belong—are deduced, by evaluating the *effects* this or that way of behaviour has had, i.e., the benefit or harm they *mostly* (or often) caused to those who happened to behave in this or that manner. This kind of norms tell us, in fact, so much: when someone behaves in this or that way, *the probability of safeguarding his or her benefit or interests*, and sometimes those of the others, increases. In other words: when, in a given case, one is unable to make a right evaluation, but possesses the will to protect what is considered to be in such a case his or her benefit or interest—or that of the group he belongs—, it is more *probable* to protect it, if he behaves in the way the relevant norm (rule, etc.) demands. This does not, of course, exclude the possibility that, in a given case, following this norm one causes harm to his or her benefit or interest and to those of the others. The different norms which distinguish one culture from another are mostly norms of this kind. This is also the kind of norms which those who advocate equal respect to all cultures invite us to respect and which those who promote cultural identities wish to revive, without evaluating them, i.e., without taking into consideration the implications they bear, in the existing conditions, for the human beings who are born by chance by a mother and/or father brought up in a given cultural group.

As to the other kinds of norms (or "ought" propositions), originating in the knowledge in the value of the human being: they are deduced from this knowledge, directly or indirectly, in the face of the human or historical conditions doing harm to this value (e.g., "thou shall not kill," "no racial discrimination shall be made").

I would say that the reasoning which leads to the deduction of such a norm (or principle) is made—schematically—as follows: if the value or the specificity of the human being is such and such, or, since the human species possesses such and such potentialities, no one belonging to this species—you, me—should do anything that harms this value, i.e., which abolishes the *possibility* of the actualization of such potentialities. Such norms are often worded in the passive, i.e., they demand that no one belonging to the human species should undergo any treatment which abolishes the possibility of the actualization of such potentialities (for example: "no one shall be subjected to torture," etc.).

A typical example of this kind of norms is what we call human or basic rights. Human rights express—in fact, intend to express—ethical demands concerning how each and every individual belonging to the human species should be treated by and should treat other individuals in general (whoever they might be and whatever their special situation might be), if human dignity is to be protected in practice.

If we make such distinctions between kinds of norms—e.g., between universal norms, like human rights which bring demands for the treatment of every human being, and cultural norms which aim at creating or protecting social order (of any kind)—we see, for example, that to restrict, or put limitation to, a clearly conceived human right by law in order to protect . . . public morals (as expressed in art. 18 and art. 19 of the U.N. *International Covenant for Civil and Political Rights* and many other human rights instruments), it amounts to consider more important a cultural norm than a universal norm.

Philosophical/epistemological knowledge of norms secures us a tool in the evaluation of norms. It helps us, among other things, to distinguish among universal, general and cultural (culture specific) norms, and thus not to mix up their different functions in life. This, in turn, can help us develop codes and human rights instruments—or to revise the existing ones—, so that they can better serve the purpose for which they are developed. Can you imagine the implications will bear for the European Court of Human Rights, if shown—and, of course, approved by the necessary international formal procedures—, that a right in the *European Convention of Human Rights* is not a human/basic right?

RETHINKING PHILOSOPHICAL EDUCATION

As you see, awareness of the object of knowledge has implications not only for dealing with problems in the various disciplines of philosophy, but also for our life. This is why, in an age in which "anything goes," it would be useful to rethink, in connection with the object of knowledge, the teaching of philosophy and philosophical education in general. A number of Platonic dialogues can show us how it is possible to objectify what one wishes to know.

In these dialogues Socrates, when his interlocutor fails to answer his question concerning what something is (what virtue is, what knowledge is etc.), often asks him what he is looking at when he speaks (ποί ἀποβλέπεις), i.e., he asks his interlocutor what he is looking at when he answers his question. In other words he tries to show him that he was unable to grasp the object of the knowledge in question and that he does not answers his question, but a different one.

Socrates gives in the *Meno* one very clear example of how this objectification can be made—the example of σχῆμα, the shape. He starts with making a distinction between *a* shape and *the* shape—a crucial distinction indeed—and then asks Meno: "What is that what you call shape, which encompasess both the round and the straight, and according to which you don't say that the round is more shape than the straight?" or "what is that whose name is shape?"[12] What Socrates is asking Meno to find, is the *eidos*, the idea of the shape. Then Meno, following the same way, could perhaps answer, on his own account, the question of what virtue is. In other words: Socrates tries to help Meno to find *what* he will look at, to find *the object of knowledge* to which their inquiry aims at, and looking at this object to answer the question of what virtue is. This object is what is identical in all those things we call virtues—in courage, in justice, in temperance, etc. Meno does not manage to make this objectification. Aristotle will make it.

This Socratic method of inquiry into the *noeta*, the products of the human mind, is not any kind of reasoning—it is not induction, as many people assume[13]—but a special kind of objectification—objectification of the whatness, of what something is, of a kind of objects of knowledge. It is an attempt to find out not *any* common characteristic, but only what is essentially the same in all those individual things and which makes possible to call all of them by the same name.

It is also different from phenomenological reduction which aims at acquiring the same kind of knowledge and which is more similar to the Cartesian abstraction.

At present, as all of you know, so-called interactive education is promoted all over the world. Still, most of the teachers are not sufficiently trained in using the Socratic method of education, which is the best example of an education which assists the trainee to put questions and answer them himself or herself, by looking of the object of the knowledge. Thus he/she could be trained in so-called "critical thinking" which has to be understood as the capacity of going back to the object of given claims, and not as simply confronting or juxtaposing different views on a given issue.

In an age in which "anything goes" in the name of freedom and pluralism, in which we see new world problems created by the solutions introduced earlier in order to tackle other world problems, we need philosophy as an area of knowledge (*not* as a world view). For this, it is necessary that in any attempt to reflect and produce knowledge we don't lose sight of our object of knowledge. This is also a point that has to be seriously taken into consideration in philosophical education.

To row against the stream, when human dignity necessitates it, is a par excellence philosophical task.

I wish to close with Ingeborg Bachmann's words: Im Widerspiel des Möglichen mit dem Unmöglichen erweitern wir unsere Möglichkeiten (In the conflict between the possible and the impossible we enlarge our own possibilities).

NOTES

1. "Modernity as a Concept and as a Project of 'Modernity', Modernization and Beyond," in *Cultures in Conflict or in Dialogue*, ed. Mourad Wahba, 3rd Afro-Asian Philosophical Conference, Cairo 31 October–3 November 1990 (Afro-Asian Philosophy Association, 1991), pp. 93–94.

2. William James, "What Pragmatism Means," *The Moral Philosophy of William James*, ed. John K. Roth (New York: T. Y. Crowell, 1969), p. 276.

3. Ibid.

4. William James, "Pragmatism's Conception of Truth," in Roth, *The Moral Philosophy of William James*, p. 295.

5. "The Scientific Conception of the World: The Vienna Circle (Wissenschaftliche Weltauffassung: Der Wiener Kreis)," in *Empiricism and Sociology*, ed. Otto Neutrath, chap. 9, *Vienna Circle Collection*, vol. 1 (Dordrecht: D. Reidel Publishing Company, 1973), pp. 305–307.

6. Hannah Arendt, "The Concept of History: Ancient and Modern," in *Between Past and Future* (New York: Penguin Books, 1978), pp. 87–88.

7. Karl R. Popper, *Logik der Forschung* (Tübingen: J. C. B. Mohr/Paul Siebeck, 1971), p. 258.

8. Ibid., p. 3.

9. Ibid., p. 31.

10. For details see Ioanna Kuçuradi, *Etik*, fifth edition (Ankara: Türkiye Felsefe Kurumu, 2006), pp. 82–99.

11. Jeanne Hersch, "'Cultural Development': A Tentative Answer," *Philosophy and Cultural Development*, ed. Ioanna Kuçuradi and Evandro Agazzi, A Joint Publication of the International Federation of Philosophical Societies and the Philosophical Society of Turkey, 1993, pp. 31–32

12. *Meno*, 74 d–a.

13. See "Induktion," *Philosophisches Wörterbuch*, begründet von Heinrich Schmidt, Achzente Auflage, neu bearbeitet von Prof. Dr. Georgi Schischkoff (Stuttgart: Albert Kröner Verlag, 1969), p. 278.

SELECTED PAPERS FROM
THE XXII WORLD CONGRESS OF PHILOSOPHY

A Spiritual Turn in Philosophy: Rethinking the Global Significance of Confucian Humanism

TU WEIMING
HARVARD UNIVERSITY

Abstract: An exposition of the core Confucian text, the *Analects*, is a rich resource for thinking philosophically about aesthetics, ethics, and religion. Indeed, the *Analects* is an inspiration for doing philosophy as a dialogical, rather than a dialectic, dialogue and an edifying conversation. The four integrated dimensions of Confucian humanism as embodied in Confucius's "anthropocosmic" philosophy encompass the sacredness of earth, body, family, community, and the world. Specifically, the philosophy envisions that the full realization of the way of learning to be human consists of (1) the integration of the body and mind, (2) the fruitful interaction between the individual and society, (3) the sustainable and harmonious relationship between humanity and nature, and (4) the mutual responsiveness between the human hear-mind and the Way of Heaven. Furthermore, it transcends the concepts of rationality in the Enlightenment mentality and provides a philosophy of life rooted in the sensitivity, sympathy, and compassion inherent in human nature. Confucius's "anthropocosmic" philosophy is one of the most profound spiritual legacies in rethinking the human in the twenty-first century.

Contemporary philosophy, as an academic discipline, has been shaped by two significant turns in its methodological orientations: epistemological and linguistic. With a view toward the future, it is likely that a new turn, which I deliberately choose to characterize as the "spiritual," is in the offing. There are clear signs of this development. An obvious one is the return of philosophy to its original source of inspiration, namely "the love of wisdom." The relevance of Aristotelian ethics, the Stoic discipline, and the other forms of self-knowledge in the Greek heritage to the current modes of philosophizing are obvious.

Special Supplement, *Journal of Philosophical Research* pp. 389–401
DOI: 10.5840/jpr201237Supplement56

In a broader context, virtually all Axial civilizations—Hindu, Buddhist, Daoist, Confucian, and Judaic (and by implication, Christian and Islamic)—have become fields of inquiry for professional philosophers. This does not mean that philosophers have chosen to be "religious." The central concerns of philosophical analysis, such as epistemology, logic, philosophy of the mind, linguistic philosophy, and ontology remain dominant in philosophy departments all over the world. By and large, philosophy teachers self-consciously distance themselves from their colleagues in religious studies by insisting that free, disinterested, rational, and systematic exploration is significantly different from faith-centered or commitment-motivated studies.

The re-presentations of the thoughts of paradigmatic personalities, notably Buddha, Confucius, Laozi, Mencius, Xunzi, Zhuangzi, Shankara, Maimonides, and Ibn Arabi, in philosophical studies show the authentic possibility of a new mode of thinking as exemplified by the works of some of the most brilliant living philosophers. Confucian humanism like Buddhism and Daoism, is both philosophical and spiritual. It is a source of inspiration in our joint venture to rethink Asian philosophy as an integral part of current global reflections on the meaning of being human in the twenty-first century.

Historically, none of the major Axial-age civilizations in Asia—Hinduism, Buddhism, Confucianism, or Daoism—made a clear distinction between philosophy and religion. Virtually all philosophical contemplation is embedded in spiritual insight and cultivation. Indeed, without spiritual discipline, sophisticated intellectual reflection is impoverished. The confluence of disinterested analysis and experiential understanding, is a defining characteristic of the Axial modes of thinking. Actually, as philosophically seasoned historians, such as the French academician, Pierre Hadot, have convincingly demonstrated, for some Greek thinkers philosophy is a way of life exemplified by spiritual exercises. This is also the approach of Harvard professor Hilary Putman to Maimonides, Rosenweig, Buber, and Levinas in his lecture course on the "Four Jewish Thinkers." It seems obvious that philosophers in close collaboration or friendly competition with colleagues in other disciplines, such as religion, can produce a highly productive way of thinking in the twenty-first century. Needless to say, this is also a wholesome practice of returning to the core and source of the philosophical enterprise: self-knowledge.

Confucian humanism, unlike the secular humanism characteristic of the European Enlightenment, is a comprehensive and integrated vision of the human condition.

Traditionally, ideal Confucians assumed a variety of roles throughout their lives. As scholar-officials, they shouldered political responsibilities and performed educational functions in society. Like Indian gurus, they were teachers; like Buddhist monks, they were ethical exemplars; like Jewish rabbis, they were learned scholars; like Greek thinkers, they were wise men; like Christian priests, they were spiritual leaders; and like Islamic mullahs, they were community leaders. However, in the final analysis, their commitment to the improvement of the human condition, rather than to a reality outside or beyond this world compelled them to take on social responsibilities in their calling. Yet, their intellectual horizons and spiritual concerns were broader and deeper than academic disciplines such as ethics, political philosophy, or social philosophy.

Confucian humanism seeks to integrate four dimensions of human experience: self, community, nature, and Heaven. It is not a form of secular humanism, but a humanism that entails both naturalist and spiritual dimensions. As a holistic humanistic way of life it proposes that the agenda of human flourishing involves (1) sustained integration of the body and mind, (2) fruitful interaction between the self and the community, (3) harmonious relations between the human species and nature, and (4) mutual responsiveness between human hearts and minds and the Way of Heaven. A person so conceived is an observer, appreciator, participant, and co-creator of the evolutionary, indeed the cosmic, process. Human consciousness must be expanded from the self, family, community, nation, world, earth and ultimately, to the "great transformation" of the cosmos.

I would like to present a focused investigation of the *Analects*, the most celebrated and influential core text in the so-called Confucian cultural area—China, Korea, Japan, and Vietnam. My purpose is not to give a Sinological reading of this classic but to present my "personal" reflection on it. It is an attempt to think philosophically from Confucian roots. By the way, when I say "personal," I do not mean private or idiosyncratic. This is intended to be an "embodied" knowing that, hopefully, will be transparent and publicly accountable for comment and criticism. In other words, it is my desire to offer a "local knowledge" that hopefully is also globally significant.

The *Analects* is, I believe, the distillation of what must have been a series of rich, varied, spontaneous, timely, dynamic, memorable, and thought-provoking interchanges between Confucius and his disciples over the stretch of several decades. It may have taken more than two generations for the most intimate and knowledgeable followers of Confucius to compile the "book." It seems that they did not intend it to be a finished product. Rather, they may have deliberately chosen to make it open and receptive to new contributions, but it is obvious that they were cautious and judicious in their choice of each entry. The reason for this strategy is not difficult to imagine. Assuming that the purpose of the compilation was to remember of their Master, the paradigmatic personality whom they missed, adored, and respected, there were several ways to complete such a task. They could have chronicled the Master's most important activities, jointly authored an appreciative biography, or systematically recorded his core ideas. Instead, they opted for a highly personal style, recording authentically how he talked, acted, thought, and, most vividly, responded to specific questions. It works brilliantly.

As a classic, the *Analects* is open-ended. It lends itself to new additions as well as to divergent glosses, different commentaries, and novel interpretations. Its text, by nature, is receptive to an even-expanding network of contributors. It seems to be a vast public space with ample room to accommodate a variety of insights attributable to the Master.

Like the *New Testament* and the Socratic dialogues, the *Analects* is a source of inspiration for those who cherish the experience of directly seeing and hearing the Master's teaching. As several scholars have pointed out, Chapter X offers a subtle and nuanced depiction of Confucius's manner of dressing, walking, approaching superiors, meeting strangers, and receiving friends. Indeed, his facial expressions, his body language, and above all his ritual performances are vividly portrayed. This contextualized daily routine reveals his appropriateness in specific situations. In the eyes of his students, he evoked an aesthetic sense of elegance. He comes alive in lived concreteness rather than in abstract universalism. Even with the lapse of more than twenty-five centuries, an attuned ear can still hear his inner voice and sense his presence. Confucius's vibrant personality, indeed his humanness, is vividly revealed.

As digested conversations and condensed discourses, a dialogical mode pervades the *Analects*. This has profound implications for intercivilizational dialogue today.

The Golden rule in Confucian ethics is "Do not do to others what you would not want others to do to you." This statement is intentionally presented in the negative to emphasize the virtue of reciprocity. The assumption is that what is best for me may not be best for my conversation partner. Edifying conversation begins with sympathetic resonance. However, this passive statement must be guided by the principle of humanity: "In order to establish myself, I help other to establish themselves; in order to enlarge myself, I help others to enlarge themselves."

Therefore, tolerance of difference is a prerequisite for any fruitful dialogue. Yet merely being tolerant is too passive to go beyond self-indulgent egoism. We need to be acutely aware of the presence of the other before we can actually begin communicating. Awareness of the presence of the other as a potential conversation partner compels us to accept our co-existence, with an ever-expanding network of human relationships as an undeniable fact. This leads to a recognition that the other's role (belief, attitude, and behavior) is relevant and significant to us. In other words, there is an intersection where the two of us are likely to meet to resolve divisive tensions or to explore a joint venture. As the two sides have built enough trust to see each other face-to-face with reciprocal respect, a meeting of the hearts and minds becomes possible. Only then can a productive dialogue begin. Through dialogue, we can appreciate the value of learning from the other in a spirit of mutual reference. We may even celebrate the difference between us as the reason for expanding both of our horizons.

Dialogue, so conceived, is neither a tactic of persuasion nor a strategy of conversion, but rather it is a way of generating mutual understanding through sharing common values and creating a new meaning of life together. As we approach civilizational dialogues, we need to suspend our desires to sell our ideas, to persuade others to accept our beliefs, to seek approval of our opinions, or to evaluate our course of action in order to gain agreement with what we cherish as true, or to justify our deeply held convictions. Rather, the purpose is to learn what we do not know, to open ourselves up to multiple perspectives, to reflect on our own assumptions, to share insights, to discover tacit agreements, to explore best practices for human flourishing, and, above all, to cultivate the art of listening.

The art of listening, essential for personal knowledge, is cultivated as a precondition for elegance in verbal expression. The Confucian style of teaching, contrasted with the Socratic method, underscores experiential understanding and silent appreciation.

Learning, which features prominently in the *Analects*, involves practice as well as cognition. It is a spiritual exercise. One learns not only with the heart-and-mind but also with the body. Learning so conceived entails transforming the body as well as enlightening the mind. As the practice of the "six arts" (ritual, music, archery, charioteering, calligraphy, and arithmetic) clearly indicates, both physical and mental disciplines are required and learning and thinking ought to complement one another.

Implicit in this style of education is the existence of a fiduciary community, a community of trust. The fellowship of the like-minded that Confucius formed with his disciples was a voluntary association dedicated to improving the human condition through education. Modern historians interpret the traditional description of Confucius as the "First Teacher" in terms of his social role, namely, he was the first scholar to establish private schools in China. The students who gathered around Confucius, like Jesus' disciples, were not children but adults who were truth seekers, passionately engaged in the quest for the meaning of life. They were attracted to him by his great vision and profound sense of mission. His radiant and yet unassuming personality must have been a source of inspiration for them: "To store up knowledge in silence, to remain forever hungry for learning, to teach others without tiring—all this comes to me naturally."

Confucius may not have had a set curriculum, but the *Analects* offers sufficient evidence to support the view that his educational purpose was no less than learning to be human. The primary aim of education is character-building. What does this mean? Neo-Confucian thinkers interpreted this to mean "learning for the sake of the self" (quoting Confucius directly), "learning of the body and the heart-and mind," "learning of the heart-and-mind and human nature," "learning of the sage," "learning of the profound person," and "learning of human nature and destiny."

Self, body, heart-and-mind, human nature, sage, profound person, and destiny suggest that learning to be human covers the whole spectrum of our lifeworld. The assertion that Confucius is exclusively concerned about life and human affairs without being deeply immersed in a discourse on death and the spirit is untenable.

Surely he focuses his attention on life rather than death and in serving the human rather than serving the spirits. The implication is obvious: he considers understanding life is a precondition for understanding death, and serving the living to be a precondition for serving the spirits. But this implies that a full understanding of life necessitates an appreciation of death and serving the live man well requires the ability to serve the spirits well.

Undeniably there is a transcendent dimension in the Confucian form of life. Confucius also claims that only Heaven knows him. He strongly believes that his mission of cultural transmission is not only a human endeavor but also a fulfillment of the Mandate of Heaven. He is in awe of Heaven and he seems to have a tacit understanding of Heaven's creativity in the cosmic process.

Then what is Heaven? A general observation based on the teachings of his most prominent follower, Mencius, is in order. The uniqueness of being human is our inner ability to learn to become worthy partners of the cosmic process. This is predicated on the assumptive reason that we are empowered to apprehend Heaven through our self-knowledge.

As Mencius avows, if we can realize the full measure of our heart-and-mind, we will know our nature; if we know our nature, we will know Heaven. Surely existentially we cannot fully realize our heart-and-mind, thus, in practical terms, it is unlikely that we will ever know our nature in itself and, by implication, it is unlikely that we will ever know Heaven in its entirety. But in theory, and to a certain extent in practice, we can be attuned to the Way of Heaven; specifically, through our persistent moral endeavor we can realize a sympathetic resonance with Heaven.

Understandably, the highest manifestation of self-realization is the "unity of Heaven and humanity." This is the reason underlying the idea of "immanent transcendence" in Confucian humanism.

Confucius lived during a period of political disorder and social disintegration. The elaborate ritual tradition, refined by the Duke of Zhou, one of the most influential statesmen in pre-Confucian times, had become dysfunctional. Internecine warfare flared up between rival states. Several hermits tempted Confucius to withdraw from the world in order to enjoy a peaceful and tranquil life in communion with nature. The Master, though respectful of such an existential preference, was determined to pursue his own course of action: "I cannot associate with birds and beasts. Am I not a member of this human race? Who, then, is there for me to associate with? If the world were following the Way, I would not have to reform it" [18:6]. It is not surprising that among the historical religions (Judaism, Buddhism, Jainism, Daoism, Christianity, and Islam) Confucianism is unique in refusing to see a difference between the sacred and the secular and in regarding the secular as sacred. Confucius did not posit a spiritual sanctuary (church, temple, synagogue, monastery, or ashram) as a sacred place for contemplation, meditation, prayer, and worship. Nor did he envisage a holy land or the other shore as ultimately real and radically different from our lifeworld here and now. By committing himself to transforming the human condition from within, he was inevitably intertwined with the political affairs of his time. However, in regarding the secular as the sacred, he envisions that the ultimate meaning of life is realizable and indeed ought to be realized in ordinary human existence. He maintains that in thinking about the world, we should always take as the point of departure our existence as concrete living persons here and now. Thus, reflection on things at hand is the basis for ultimate self-realization. In this view, the political process begins at home. It is inseparable from one's way of living. What happens in the privacy of one's home is socially, anthropologically, and even cosmically significant. Implicit in this style of Confucian praxis is the creation of a discourse community through self-understanding and mutual learning. The group solidarity was not imposed by the Master according to a preconceived pedagogical model. Nor was it forged by a firm resolve to perform a clearly defined political and ethical function. Rather, the disciples gathered around Confucius were encouraged to develop their own potential as knowledgeable, cultured, ethical, and tasteful contributions to the public good. This constructive mode enabled them to practice their own paths of self-cultivation through reciprocal respect and mutual appreciation. Confucius urged them not to become utensils defined in terms of their functional utility but all-round profound persons capable of political action at different levels under all circumstances.

This is relevant to the contemporary situation. In a comparative civilizational perspective, this seemingly unique Confucian spiritual orientation—regarding the secular as sacred, or, more appropriately, rejecting the separation between the defiled earth and the sublime Heaven—has been embraced by most, if not all, major spiritual traditions in our age. Virtually all Axial-Age civilizations have undergone substantial transformations so that they can respond meaningfully to the crises of the modern world. No mainstream ethical or religious belief can afford to ignore environmental degradation, abject poverty, social disintegration, violence, crime, drugs, or terrorism as worldly affairs below the purview of their God-centered spirituality. Without a doubt, a defining characteristic of religion is its avowed compassion and love for humanity; thus, all forms of suffering, from brutal torture to routine boredom, are worries of spiritual leaders. However, since the "ultimate concern" is often directed otherwise, salvation is seldom to be found in the world here and now. Those who have identified themselves with the things that are God's rather than the things that are Caesar's would not consider politics as a calling, let alone accept the bureaucracy as the proper domain for spiritual commitment. However, nowadays spiritual and religious leaders are duty-bound to be politically concerned, socially engaged, and culturally sensitive.

The human condition today dictates that spiritual and religious leaders become proficient in two languages: one specific to their faith communities and one for global citizenship. Similarly, experts and professionals should also feel obligated to become bilingual. They must be able to address themselves to two overlapping linguistic communities. One is the expert language relevant to their profession and the other is the language of the public intellectual. Unless they are capable of rising above their own interest groups, they cannot properly situate their expertise or professionalism in an increasingly complex and interconnected global village.

What kind of society, or more appropriately community, did Confucius actually create to realize his vision of transforming our world from within? Since Confucius regarded himself as the guardian of the Way of human survival and flourishing, he appealed to the sages and worthies, who were the architects of the cumulative tradition, rather than a transcendent reality alone beyond human comprehension or a natural evolution without human participation. Although Confucius was never entrusted with a territory to put his idea of model government into practice, the social reality that he actually constructed turned out to be profoundly meaningful. The fellowship, as the result of his collaborative effort with his disciples, was open, flexible, communicative, interactive, inclusive, and mutually beneficial. He engaged his students not as a philosopher who methodically led them to see the essence of things step by step. There is nothing in the *Analects* that resembles the elaborate reasoning in the Socratic dialogue. Indeed, Confucius distrusted mere verbal persuasiveness, he despised glibness, and he resented clever expressions. Although he highly valued eloquence in diplomacy, lucidity in thought, and articulateness in literature, he preferred tacit understanding to effective argumentation. The former reminded him of the trickery in legal disputes, even litigiousness. In civil cases, he favored negotiation, mediation, or out-of-court settlements, rather than formalistic, arbitrary, or coercive mechanisms of control.

The ideal society that Confucius envisioned and the discourse community he created through exemplary teaching was a voluntary association. The primary purpose of such an association was to help facilitate the self-realization of each of its members. A polity based on such a social vision involves a reflectivity of both the political and intellectual elite and an effective procedure by which humane government is set into motion.

Confucius's determination to transform politics through moral strength, cultural values, social cohesiveness, and historical consciousness is often misunderstood as his naïve enthusiasm for the primacy of the political order. Rather, it is predicated on the perception that the ultimate purpose of politics is human flourishing. Surely, politics is intertwined with power, influence, and authority, but the purpose of politics is ethics through education. The maintenance of security and the sustenance of livelihood are not ends in themselves but rather they are conditions for human flourishing. The Confucian instruction that "from the ruler to the commoner all should regard self-cultivation as the root" is supposed to provide the basis for a fiduciary community, rather than to inculcate a mechanism of social control. To use Emile Durkheim's terminology, Confucius, through mutual understanding and corporate self-consciousness, brought about an organic solidarity. Among Confucius's disciples there were literati, farmers, artisans, soldiers, merchants, and practitioners of a variety of other occupations. The division of labor enriched the Confucian fellowship through its diversity of backgrounds and plurality of life-orientations.

Again, an issue of contemporary relevance looms large. How can the Confucian perception of a fiduciary community and social solidarity account for political legitimacy and democratic participation? Indeed, how can the Confucian style of governance accommodate human rights? Max Weber's critique of universal brotherhood as a premodern ideal incompatible with modern society, defined in terms of secularization, professionalization, and rationalization is also pertinent here. More seriously, if the Confucian self is perceived of as an inclusive individuality fixed in birth, rank, and status, it is definitely incapable of responding to the highly differentiated social roles that a modern person habitually assumes to play in a normal life in a post-industrial, if not postmodern, society. Certainly the idea of the self as a specific non-destructive and non-changeable identity is outmoded. But these charges against the Confucian tradition are one-sided. In a deeper sense, the real issue at stake is not only how to judge whether Confucian humanism can respond to modernist critiques, but also to explore the possibility of critiquing these modernist presuppositions from Confucian insights into rethinking the human. In the twenty-first century, a broad humanist vision embodying both Heaven (the ultimate source of meaning of life) and earth (nature) is necessary. Human interconnectedness and mutual dependence have forged and wired all members of the human species into one economic and scientific world. In this new reality or virtual reality the need for universal ethics to nurture the awareness of co-existence is obvious. Governance so conceived cannot work without a strong sense of responsibility of the elite. The idea of rights is based on individuality. It is imperative that, in addition to dignity, independence, autonomy, and freedom of the individual, a sense of responsibility, especially of the elite, be required. Since the quest for personal integration and authenticity has emerged as a crucial concern of the elite, can a functional equivalent of rights, especially economic and social rights, of the marginalized and underprivileged be derived from the responsibility of the elite? A society governed by responsible leaders committed to the well-being of the people is definitely more humane than a society dictated by the freedom, rationality, and self-interest of the elite. To respect the human rights of all people does not automatically lead to a polity that cares for their security, livelihood, and self-development.

Confucians believe that liberty without justice, rationality without sympathy, legality without civility, rights without responsibility, and individual dignity without social solidarity cannot bring about an enduring world order nurtured by a richly textured culture of peace. All five core values in the Confucian tradition—humanity, rightness, civility, wisdom, and trust—are not merely local values but rather universal values rooted in East Asian theory and practice.

Let us return to the *Analects*. Confucius's charisma lay in his magnetic power to draw a divergent group of energetic men to share his vision and mission to transform the world from within by tapping the mental and physical resources of each one of them through the art of self-cultivation.

It may not be farfetched to suggest that what Confucius created with his disciples was more than a community of the like-minded. It was a cultural movement that engendered a learning civilization based on a philosophy of self-cultivation. Confucian self-cultivation, far more complex than the personal quest for inner spirituality, is multi-dimensional. It involves not only the body and mind but also the total environment of one's existence. Confucius's own depiction of his spiritual journey is a case in point:

> At fifteen, I set my heart upon learning. At thirty, I took my stand. At forty, I had no delusions. At fifty, I knew the Mandate of Heaven. At sixty, my

> ear was attuned. At seventy, I could follow the desires of my heart without transgressing any rule. [2:4]

This pithy autobiographic note has inspired numerous interpretations. Obviously, Confucius lived up to his self-understanding that he was primarily a learner: "In a hamlet of ten houses, you will certainly find people as loyal and faithful as I, but you will not find one man who loves learning as much as I do."

Throughout his life Confucius persistently tried to improve himself. He fully acknowledged that sagehood or moral perfection were beyond his reach, and he learned without flagging and taught without growing weary. Indeed, he sought every opportunity to learn: "Put me in the company of any two people at random—they will invariably have something to teach me. I can take their qualities as a model and their defects as a warning." He frankly admitted that he had to acquire the cumulative wisdom of the past to make himself wise: "I was not born of knowledge, but, being fond of antiquity, I am quick to seek it."

Furthermore, he was deeply concerned that he might lapse in his self-cultivation: "Failure to cultivate moral power, failure to explore what I have learned, incapacity to stand by what I know to be right, incapacity to reform what is not good—these are my worries." In short, he was the sort of learner "who, in his enthusiasm, forgets to eat, in his joy forgets to worry, and who ignores the approach of old age."

Underlying Confucian education is the firm conviction that human beings are multifaceted. The reductionist mode of thinking is not only simplistic but also misleading. We are not merely rational animals, tool-users, or linguistic beings because at the same time, and under all circumstances, we are aesthetic, social, ethical, and spiritual. We can fully realize ourselves only if we care for our body, heart, mind, soul, and spirit. As we move from the center of our existence to meet ever-expanding and increasingly complex relationships, we embody home, community, nation, world, earth, and the cosmos in our sensitivity and consciousness. This is why true humanity is relational and dialogical as well as psychological and spiritual. Education must take as its point of departure the concrete, living person here and now, a person embedded in primordial ties, especially the affective bonds within the family.

By implication, in a modernist perspective, those ties, such as race, language, gender, status, age, and faith, are also relevant. In a way, each of us is fated to be that unique person, situated in a particular time and space, who has never existed before and will never appear again. Indeed, we are as different as our faces. Yet, Confucians also believe that the commonality and communicability of our heart-and-mind is such that our natures, in essence, are the same and that we can share our sights, sounds, emotions, wills, senses, tastes, and experience. This confluence of difference and similarity enables us to become what we ought to be not by severing the primordial ties that have made it possible for us to be concrete and living persons. Rather, we transform them into vehicles for self-realization. That is the reason why, as learners, our lives are enriched by encountering a variety of humans who are individually unique and who communally share a great deal of information, knowledge, and wisdom. Furthermore, our feelings, desires, motivations, and aspirations are personal but not necessarily private. We often reveal our intensely personal concerns to relatives, friends, colleagues, associates, and even strangers. Their sympathetic understanding of our inner worlds is profoundly meaningful to us.

Any attempt to reduce the variety of living experience to merely the physical, mental, or spiritual is counter-productive. Human beings are by nature psychological, economical, social, political, historical, aesthetic, linguistic, cultural, and metaphysical animals. The full realization of the human potential is never one-sided. Confucius believed that an enabling environment for human flourishing is "harmony without uniformity." A respect for difference is vitally important for the development of a wholesome community.

When Confucius was asked about the virtue of repaying maliciousness with kindness, he retorted: how will you repay kindness? Then he suggested, repay kindness with kindness and repay maliciousness with justice. The Confucian ethic implicit in this line of thinking is an ethic of situational appropriateness, political engagement, and social responsibility and care. It covers the whole range of our lived world. I would like to draw a few implications from the humanistic vision in the *Analects*. These are not evident in the text. Rather they are my interpretations and elaborations of the Confucian project.

My intention is to make these observations in the Confucian spirit but they may also be judged to be a misreading. I would like to show that, as a source of inspiration, the fruitful ambiguities in the *Analects* offer rich food for thought.

1. The idea of the "continuity of being." In this view the human is connected with all modalities of being: minerals, plants, and animals. If we probe deeply to find some linkages, the human is part of a continuum. But the uniqueness of being human is qualitatively different from all other modalities of being. The defining characteristics of the human are not reducible to any of the properties that have become constitutive parts of the human condition. For example, Xunzi observed:

> Fire and water possess energy but are without life. Grass and trees have life but no consciousness and feeling. Birds and beasts have consciousness and feeling but no sense of rightness. The human possesses energy, life, consciousness, and feeling, and in addition, a sense of rightness.

This idea of the human is predicated on two principles: interconnectedness and uniqueness. In short, the distinctiveness of the human is based not on separation but connection. The reason for this is that although an emergent property is not reducible to its constitutive parts, genetically and structurally it is always intertwined with all the elements that have contributed to the particular form of its existence.

2. Creationism or evolutionism may make a profoundly significant difference in understanding the origins of human nature, but for the Confucians, it is the structure of the human here and now rather than the genetic reasons that have made it, so that is the focus of attention. The uniqueness of the human, whether created or evolved, is intimately connected with Heaven, Earth, and the myriad things. In other words,

the human body is a microcosm of the cosmos. Its well-being is intimately united with the macrocosmic ecology.

3. The primary concern of human flourishing is to discover and recover the rich resources for self-knowledge, especially those that seem not to have been derived from social conditioning. We should try to understand and appreciate the depth and breadth of the innate capacities possessed by all humans. Admittedly, this is Mencius's rather than Xunzi's position, but it is noteworthy that even for Xunzi, although virtues will have to be internalized, a vitally important, indeed the most significant, inherent quality of the human mind is intelligence.

4. The innate capacity of the human to develop a moral sense or a learned capacity to internalize virtues is part of a much more elaborate and complicated picture. It is unlikely that reductionist definitions, such as the human being as a rational animal, tool-user, or endowed with linguistic ability, will capture the full measure of the way of being human. Human beings are by nature aesthetic, social, political, historical, and cosmological beings. They become fully human by bringing to fruition all dimensions that constitute concrete and living persons here and now.

5. Although ethics deals with the relationship between individuality and sociality, morality, as Confucians understand it, must be conceived in cosmological as well as anthropological terms. The full manifestation of humanity must transcend anthropocentrism. The tripartite division of aesthetics, ethics, and religion under the influence of Kierkegaard must be perceived in a new configuration. To use the same vocabulary to illustrate this point: feelings, such as commiseration, sympathy, or compassion, are the basis of morality. Aesthetics is not opposed to ethics. Ethics is not only rule-governed. It is also a manifestation of harmonized emotions. Religion does not require "a leap of faith." It is the result of the necessity to expand the ethical realm. If ethics does not raise the question of ultimate concern, it falls short of its full expression.

6. The "anthropocosmic" idea is predicated on a holistic and integrated humanism, substantially different from secular humanism. Morality, the way to learn to be human, must be rooted in nature and extended to Heaven.

7. Heaven features prominently in this discourse. Morality as an innate quality is inconceivable without constant reference to Heaven. Heaven is creativity in itself, but the advent of the human has made a difference. The human as a co-creator imitates but also participates in Heaven's cosmic transformation.

8. Heaven cannot be conceived merely in naturalistic terms. As the Heavenly Way is encoded in human nature, what the human does affects Heaven as well. Morality conceived of as a defining characteristic of learning to be human must be extended beyond individuality and sociality to embody a larger universe.

This "anthropocosmic" vision presupposes a unity between anthropological and cosmological perceptions of the human condition. In the language of the *Book of Change*, the cosmos is never a static structure but rather a dynamic process. In its constant unfolding, it always generates new realities by creatively transforming the existing order.

Learning to be human in the cosmic sense is learning to emulate Heaven's creativity, which is open, dynamic, transformative, and unceasing. Whether we came into being by the mysterious design of a transcendent reality or by a persistent evolutionary process, we find an intimate niche in the cosmos as our ultimate source and meaning of life.

This sense of wholeness and connectedness is captured by the opening lines of the so-called *Western Inscription* by Zhang Zai, an eleventh-century Confucian thinker:

> Heaven is my father and Earth is my mother, and even such a small being as I finds an intimate place in their midst. Therefore, that which fills the universe I regard as my body and that which directs the universe I regard as my nature. All people are my brothers and sisters, and all things are my companions.

Finally, a short concluding remark: Economic globalization is characterized by instrumental rationality, science, technology (especially information and communications technologies), professionalism, materialism, liberalization, technocratic management, legitimization of desires, and individual choice. The "economic man" is a rational animal conscious of his self-interest, motivated to increase his wealth, power, and influence by maximizing his profit in a relatively free market adjudicated by law. He embodies a host of modernistic values, such as freedom, rationality, rights consciousness, work ethic, knowledge, technical competence, cognitive intelligence, legality, and motivation. Yet other essential values requisite for social solidarity are either relegated to the background or are totally ignored, notably justice, sympathy, responsibility, civility, and ethical intelligence.

In a world characterized by materialistic and egocentric tendencies, the thirst for spiritual gratification often takes the form of fundamentalist extremism and exclusive particularism. Confucian humanism, as expressed in the *Analects*, is a balanced and open approach to the purpose of life. It offers a spiritual exercise essential for self-knowledge and it is a primordial wisdom that deserves our understanding and appreciation. Thank you for listening!

SELECTED PAPERS FROM
THE XXII WORLD CONGRESS OF PHILOSOPHY

Time and Self

MARK C. TAYLOR
COLUMBIA UNIVERSITY

ABSTRACT: Kierkegaard's critique of Hegel and Hegelianism anticipates major twentieth-century philosophical movements ranging from structuralism, existentialism, and phenomenology, to post-structuralism and postmodernism. This paper analyzes Kierkegaard's interpretation of the relationship between subjectivity and temporality in pivotal passages in *The Sickness Unto Death* and *The Concept of Anxiety*. Heidegger's account of the interplay between presentation (*Darstellung*) and representation (*Vorstellung*) imagination points to Kant's theory of the imagination and suggests the way in which the Kierkegaardian subject is constituted by an irreducible alterity that is never present but is always already past. The infinite qualitative difference of the divine is reflected in the inescapable interiority of the subject. Kierkegaard's abyssal other returns in Barth's wholly other God, Heidegger's aletheia, Derrida's différance, and Lacan's real. For each of these writers, subjectivity is haunted by another it can neither exclude nor appropriate. This interior exteriority is the condition of the possibility of both desire and hope.

2008 is the fortieth anniversary of that fateful year 1968, which a popular American book labels "the year that rocked the world." It did, indeed, rock the world in ways that are still being felt. The war in Viet Nam was raging and many American cities were burning as a result of race riots and I was a senior at Wesleyan University in the spring of '68. Looking back, it is hard to understand how anyone could have kept his or her mind on academic work: January, the Tet offensive; February, revocation of draft deferments; March, Prague spring; April, the assassination of Martin Luther King; May, universities across the world shut down; June, the assassination of Bobby Kennedy. The turmoil continued throughout the summer and reached a climax in August at the Democratic National Convention in Chicago. Three months later Richard Nixon was elected president.

Special Supplement, *Journal of Philosophical Research* pp. 403–418
DOI: 10.5840/jpr201237Supplement57

Far from these world historical events, other things were happening that went virtually unnoticed at the time. In 1968, two of Hegel's most influential interpreters died—Alexander Kojève and Jean Hyppolite. Just one year earlier Jacques Derrida burst on the scene with the publication of three major books—*Of Grammatology*, *Writing and Difference*, and *Speech and Phenomena*. Many of the ideas in these books had been worked out and first presented in Hyppolite's seminars. Kojève conducted a series of seminars in Paris in the 1930s, which were attended by figures who would shape intellectual life during the last half of the twentieth century and would exercise considerable influence on world politics: Merleau-Ponty, Georges Bataille, Jacques Lacan, André Breton, Raymond Aron and others. These lectures were published in 1947 under the title *Introduction à la lecture de la lecture de Hegel* and an abbreviated English version of the work, edited by Alan Bloom, appeared in 1969. Bloom went on to shape a generation of students who eventually became leaders in the neo-conservative movement whose ideology is in large measure responsible for the global crisis we now face. His most important students were Paul Wolfowitz, Richard Pearl and William Kristol. It is also instructive to recall that Kojève's notion of the end of history was appropriated by Francis Fukuyama for quite un-Hegelian purposes, i.e., the declaration of the triumph of global capitalism. Hyppolite's influence is not so obvious but it has been lasting. His monumental work, *Genesis and Structure of the Phenomenology of Spirit*, also published in 1947, remains, in my judgment the best work on Hegel's masterpiece. Hyppolite's seminars were as influential for Derrida, Foucault and Deleuze as Kojève's had been for a previous generation.

For me, 2008 is not only the anniversary of my graduation from college and marriage, but also the fortieth anniversary of my introduction to Kierkegaard. In the fall of 1967, I took a seminar from Stephen Crites entitled "The Dialectic of Self-Alienation and Reconciliation in Hegel, Feuerbach and Marx," and in the spring of 1968, I took the follow-up seminar—"Kierkegaard's Dialectic of Existence." As I have suggested, it was not always easy to keep one's mind on academic work during that tumultuous spring. Much to my surprise, however, the more Hegel and Kierkegaard I read, the more I found that their work helped me to understand what was happening around me. The conflict between Hegel's systematic philosophy and Kierkegaard's existential individualism prefigured and illuminated the tension between the system and the individual in the counterculture. It was Hegel, I discovered, who had first articulated the dialectic of self-alienation that people marching in the streets that had never heard his name invoked, and it was Kierkegaard, who had developed an account of the authenticity of individual experience for which so many young people seemed to be searching. What began in those classes forty years ago has become a life-long preoccupation. Along the way, Niels Jørgen Cappelorn and Peter Kemp, who were kind enough to invite me to deliver this endowed Kierkegaard lecture, have always been there to offer help when I have needed it. For that and much more, I would like to say publicly, "Thank you." Looking back on this long trajectory,

I might adapt Derrida's comment on Hegel: we will never be finished with the reading or rereading of Kierkegaard, and, in a certain way, I do nothing other than attempt to explain myself on this point. I am going to reconsider two pivotal texts on time and the self with which I have been wrestling for forty years. As I have read and reread Kierkegaard, I have become more and more impressed by his prescience. He anticipated many of the most important issues at stake in debates about postmodernism in ways that are uncanny. Today I would like to consider the implications of his work for post-Heideggerian philosophy, giving special attention to Derrida's writings.

I am going to concentrate my analysis on two of Kierkegaard's seminal texts with which I have been wrestling for four decades. Before citing those texts, however, a word about Derrida's seminal writings. It is possible, I believe, to read the history of twentieth-century philosophy and theology as an ongoing debate between Hegel and Kierkegaard. While Hegel's influence on Marxism and Kierkegaard's influence on existentialism are well-known, less often recognized is their respective influence on structuralism and post-structuralism. For a variety of reasons, structuralism in France was read as latter-day Hegelianism and Hegelianism as proto-structuralism. Kierkegaard, by contrast, was rarely cited in the arguments swirling around structuralism and post-structuralism. The reason for this is the role his thinking played in Sartre's existential humanism. With the emphasis on the decentering of the subject, the disappearance of the author and an insistent anti-humanism, structuralists and post-structuralists were not inclined to turn to Kierkegaard for insights. For those with eyes to see, however, Kierkegaard's ghost haunts many of the most influential post-structuralist texts. When I started reading Derrida's works in the late 1970s, it was obvious to me that his critique of structuralism repeated Kierkegaard's critique of Hegelianism. Though he did not acknowledge the importance of Kierkegaard for many years, by the end of his life, Derrida had become, in effect, a Kierkegaardian.

Today I would like to argue that in his subtle analysis of time and the self, Kierkegaard develops what can best be described as deconstruction *avant la lettre*. To support this claim, it will be necessary to return to Kant by way of Heidegger, or, more precisely Heidegger's reading of Kant in his book, *Kant and the Problem of Metaphysics*. I am now prepared to cite the two pivotal texts from Kierkegaard that I previously mentioned. The first is from *The Sickness Unto Death* and the second from *The Concept of Dread.*

> A human being is spirit. But what is spirit? Spirit is the self. But what is the self? The self is a relation that relates itself to itself or is the relation's relating itself to itself in the relation; the self is not the relation but is the relation's relating itself to itself. A human being is a synthesis of the infinite and the finite, of the temporal and the eternal, of freedom and necessity, in short, a synthesis. A synthesis is a relation between two. Considered in this way, a human being is not yet a self . . . .
>
> Such a relation that relates itself to itself, a self, must either have established itself or have been established by another.

> If the relation that relates itself to itself has been established by another, then the relation is indeed the third, but this relation, the third, is yet again a relation that relates itself to that which established the entire relation.
>
> The human self is such a derived, established relation, a relation that relates itself to itself and in relating itself to itself relates itself to another.[1]

> This now lies between 'was' and 'will become,' and naturally 'the one' cannot, in passing from the past to the future, bypass this 'now.' It comes to a halt in the now, does not become older but is older. In the most recent philosophy, abstraction culminates in pure being, but pure being is the most abstract expression for eternity, and against as 'nothing' it is precisely the moment. Here again the importance of the moment becomes apparent, because only with this category is it possible to give eternity its proper significance, for eternity and the moment become the extreme opposites, whereas dialectical sorcery, on the other hand, makes eternity and the moment signify the same thing. It is only with Christianity that sensuousness, temporality and the moment can be properly understood, because only with Christianity does eternity become essential.[2]

And now the detour—though it is not precisely a detour because, as we shall see, the question of the detour is precisely what is at stake—the detour from Heidegger to Kant as well as others in order to arrive back at these texts without having come full circle.

In 1784, Kant published a brief but influential essay entitled "What is Enlightenment?" in which he stresses the interrelation of reason and freedom.

> Enlightenment is man's release from his self-incurred tutelage. Tutelage is man's inability to make use of his understanding without direction from another. Self-incurred is this tutelage when its cause lies not in lack of reason but in lack of resolution and courage to use it without direction from another. *Sapere aude*! "Have courage to use your own reason!" That is the motto of enlightenment.[3]

While heteronomy involves determination by another, e.g., God, sovereign, parent or teacher, autonomy is the self-determination or self-legislation through which the subject gives itself the universal law of reason. Far from spontaneous or arbitrary, free actions are, from this point of view, both rational and normative. Though reason is deployed theoretically and practically, Kant insists on the primacy of practical reason. Reason and will are inseparable: reason is essentially an *activity*, and if activity is free activity it must be reasonable. In the Second Critique, Kant underscores the primacy of practical reason by arguing that freedom is "the keystone of the whole architecture of the system." Freedom, however, proves to be a complex keystone because it implies an irreducible ambiguity. The more closely one examines Kant's argument, the clearer it becomes that freedom involves not only autonomy but also what can best be described *an-archy*. In this context, the term *an-archy* does not mean the absence of form, which issues in disorder, confusion or chaos. Rather, *an-archy* suggests the absence (*an*, without) of any beginning (*arkhe*) and, by extension, the lack of an originary foundation. In other words, that which is anarchic is groundless. While Kant does not always seem to recognize the far-reaching implications of his argument, his critical philosophy demonstrates that autonomy presupposes *an-archy*, which is the non-foundational foundation or the groundless ground of the law that the self-legislating subject gives to itself. Autonomy and *an-archy* intersect in the activity of the imagination through which the interplay of word and deed deepens the contradictions of subjectivity. To understand the importance of these two aspects of freedom, it is necessary to consider why autonomy is impossible apart from *an-archy*.

The notion of autonomy is the structural principle around which all three critiques are organized. The theoretical and practical deployments of reason are isomorphic—in both cases a universal principle of reason is brought to bear on particular sense data. While theoretical reason organizes the sensible manifold of intuition through a priori forms of intuition and categories of understanding, practical reason controls idiosyncratic sensible inclinations through universal moral principles. Kant's three critiques are directed at the triple threat of skepticism, determinism and atheism. His critical philosophy prepares the way for the defense of religion in terms of moral activity rather than theoretical speculation. Every aspect of his argument is organized around a series of binary oppositions, which he both articulates and attempts to reconcile.

Autonomy/Heteronomy

Freedom/Determinism

Reason/Sensibility

A priori/A posteriori

Universality/Particularity

Objectivity/Subjectivity

Obligation/Inclination

Form/Matter

Kant's immediate successors were divided between those who thought he had not gone far enough and those who thought he had gone too far in formulating a comprehensive philosophical system that could mediate these oppositions. The former argued that his reconciliation of opposites remained incomplete and the latter insisted that his effort to synthesize opposites was misguided because it obscured the irreducible contradictions and inescapable aporiae inherent in thought and life. The unresolved tensions in Kant's work set the terms of debate in the nineteenth century and continue to influence critical reflection and practice down to the present day.

It has frequently been observed that Kant's "Copernican revolution" is the theoretical equivalent of the political revolution in France. Rarely noted but no less important is the fact that one of Kant's most significant philosophical innovations was his translation of ontology into epistemology. To understand the implications of this development, it is necessary to trace the religio-philosophical genealogy of Kant's epistemology all the way back to Plato and early Christian apologists. In Plato's myth of origin, the world is created by a Demiurge who brings together unchanging forms with the undifferentiated flux of matter. Within this framework the activity of creation is a process of *formation* through which order is brought to chaos. Early Christian apologists, eager to demonstrate that their religion did not involve unsophisticated superstition, which was politically subversive, reinterpreted fundamental theological principles in terms of Platonic philosophy. Instead of an intermediate being situated between eternity and time like the Demiurge, the Christian God, they argued, is the eternal creator of the world. For these apologists, Platonic forms become the mind of God or the Logos, which is understood as the eternal Son of the divine Father. Inasmuch as the Father always creates through the Son, the world is an expression of the divine Logos and is, therefore, logical, reasonable, or, in a more recent idiom, Logocentric. Human reason is the reflection of the Logos through which people can comprehend the world God has created. In Kant's account of theoretical reason, Platonic forms and the divine Logos become the forms of intuition and categories of understanding, and the undifferentiated flux of matter becomes the sensible manifold of intuition. Just as Platonic forms and the divine Logos are universal and unchanging, so the forms of intuition and categories of understanding are a priori rather than aposterior and are therefore universal. Alternatively, Kant's epistemology can be expressed in terms of contemporary information theory: the mind is programmed to process data. Knowledge results from the synthesis of the universal forms of intuition and categories of understanding and the particular data of sense experience. This information processing brings order to chaos by unifying the multiplicity of data we are constantly experiencing. The agency through which this synthesis occurs is the imagination—*die Einbildungskraft*. "Now, since every appearance contains a manifold," Kant argues, "and since different perceptions therefore occur in the mind separately and singly, a combination of them, such as they cannot have in sense itself, is demanded. There must therefore exist in us an active faculty for the synthesis of this manifold. To this faculty I give the title, imagination. Its action, when immediately directed to perceptions, I entitled apprehension. Since imagination has to bring the manifold of intuition into the form of an image, it must previously have taken the impressions up into its activity, that is, have apprehended them."[4] Since the imagination articulates objects, it is the necessary condition of the possibility of knowledge and as such is *transcendental*. To fulfill this function, the imagination must operate at the edge or on the border *between* understanding and sensation. Kant writes: "Obviously there must be some third thing, which is homogeneous on the one hand with the category, and on the other hand with the appearance, and which thus makes the application of the former to the latter possible. This mediating representation must be pure, that is, void of all empirical content, and yet at the same time, while it must be in one respect *intellectual*, it must in another be *sensible*. Such a representation is the *transcendental schema*."[5] Kant describes the operation of the imagination as the "schematization of the categories." In a manner reminiscent of the transcendent Demiurge who brings form to chaos and the transcendent God who creates through His Logos, the imagination deploys transcendental schemata to organize experience and thereby create the world in which we dwell.[6]

Kant realized that his interpretation of reason in both its theoretical and practical deployments deepens the contradictions of subjectivity by inwardizing the conflict between the various binary opposites he articulates. With the movement from heteronomy to autonomy, universality, which had been externally imposed, is inwardly legislated. In the Third Critique, devoted to aesthetic judgment, Kant attempts to mediate these oppositions through the notion of inner teleology. In contrast to every form of utility and instrumentality in which means and ends are externally related, inner teleology involves what Kant describes as "purposiveness without purpose" in which means and ends are reciprocally related in such a way that each becomes itself in and through the other and neither can be itself apart from the other. Kant illustrates this idea by describing the interplay of whole and part in the work of art.

> The parts of the thing combine of themselves into the unity of a whole by being reciprocally cause and effect of their form. For this is the only way in which it is possible that the idea of the whole may conversely, or reciprocally, determine, in its turn the form and combination of all the parts, not as cause—for that would make it an art product—but as the epistemological basis upon which the systematic unity of the form and combination of all the manifold contained in the given matter become cognizable for the person estimating it.[7]

Though not immediately obvious, this formulation of inner teleology marks a tipping point in cultural and social history whose ramifications are still emerging. In hindsight it is clear that the nineteenth century began with the 1790 publication of the *Critique of Judgment*. The distinction between external and internal teleology is the philosophical articulation of the transition from a mechanical to an organic schema for interpreting the world. What Kant discovered is the *principle of constitutive relationality in which identity is differential rather than oppositional*. The immediate implications of this insight were worked out by romantic artists and idealistic philosophers during the closing decade of the eighteenth century and early years of the nineteenth century. But the significance of Kant's insight is much farther reaching. The structure he identifies is the condition of the possibility of much modern as well as postmodern art, literature and philosophy. It also clears the space in which Kierkegaard's imagination roams.

The Third Critique extends the principle of autonomy from theoretical and practical reason to the work of art understood as both the process of production and the product produced. In contrast to art produced for the market, which is utilitarian and as such has an extrinsic purpose, fine art is not produced for any external end but is created for its own sake. Never referring to anything other than itself, high art is art about art, and is, therefore, self-referential and thus self-reflexive. But while seeming to be completely autonomous, the structures of self-referentiality and self-reflexivity are considerably more complicated than they initially appear. They presuppose something they cannot assimilate. The interruption of the self-referential circuit of reflexivity exposes aporiae that are the condition of creativity. The pivot upon which this analysis turns is the interplay of the imagination and representation in the production of self-consciousness.

For the young writers, artists and philosophers gathered in Jena in the years immediately after the publication of the Third Critique, Kant's critical philosophy opened the possibility of completing what began in France by shifting the revolutionary struggle from politics to philosophy and poetry. In a world without adequate social, political and economic institutions and ravaged by the early stages of industrialization, writers and critics sought to overcome personal alienation and social fragmentation by cultivating new forms of unification and integration. Kant glimpsed the possibility of a unity that nourished rather than repressed differences in his account of the reciprocity of inner teleology but he was unable to carry his argument through to its necessary conclusion. Given the limitation of knowledge established in the First Critique, he was forced to restrict his notion of beauty to a regulative idea that might or might not describe the way things really are in the actual world. Since the work of art figures reconciliation as nothing more than an unrealizable idea, it actually deepens the oppositions and fragmentation it is designed to overcome. To accomplish what both the French and the Kantian revolutions leave undone, romantics and idealists argue, it is necessary to realize the Idea by transforming the world into a work of art. As apocalypse by revolution gave way to apocalypse by imagination and cognition, consciousness turned inward and became self-conscious. By pushing itself to its limit, however, autonomous self-consciousness becomes an-archic. That is to say, the subject discovers that it has emerged from a groundless ground that it can never fathom. This fissure creates the opening for the postmodern critique of modernism, which Kierkegaard anticipates in his account of the self and time. Contrary to expectation, the transition from autonomy to an-archy, which is the condition of the possibility of postmodernism, passes through Hegel's speculative system.

Kant's successors realized that the inner teleological or self-referential structure he identified discloses the self-reflexive structure of self-consciousness. In self-consciousness, the subject turns back on itself by becoming an object to itself. Self-as-subject and self-as-object are reciprocally related in such a way that each becomes itself through the other and neither can be itself apart from the other. The structure of self-relation constitutive of self-conscious subjectivity presupposes the activity of self-representation.

Though it is not immediately obvious, at the precise point where self-consciousness seems to be complete, it approaches its constitutive limit. Dieter Henrich identified

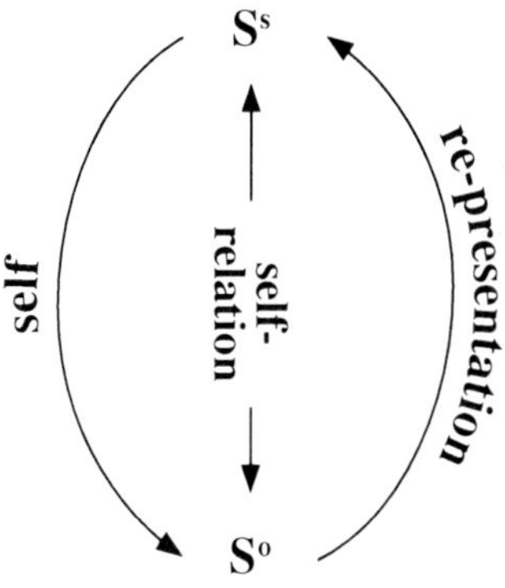

Self-Consciousness

the crucial issue question in commenting on Fichte's reading of Kant: "We might cast this question another way: Will ontological discourse always make use of the premise that something can be said about the mind that is not of the mind, and that the mind can say something that is of the mind about what is not of the mind, so that the two discourses can never be derived from one another—or even form a third discourse, thereby precluding any fully intelligible linear formulation?"[8] Henrich implies that the impossibility of explaining self-consciousness through linear models does not necessarily mean that the self-reflexivity of self-consciousness is circular. To the contrary, when consciousness turns back on itself, it discovers a lacuna without which it is impossible but with which it is incomplete.

This is the crucial point: the self presupposes self-consciousness, which, in turn presupposes self-representation. The self, in other words, becomes itself in and through a process in which it appears to present itself to itself. But how is this possible? If self-as-subject and self-as-object are codependent, neither can be the originary cause of the other. Then where does that which is represented to the self come from and through what agency does it emerge? The activity of self-representation, it seems, presupposes a more primordial presentation, which must originate elsewhere and emerge through some agency other than the self itself. Here thinking approaches the limit it both requires and cannot cross. "Thinking," as Jean-Luc Nancy explains in another context, "is always thinking on the limit. The limit of comprehending defines thinking. Thus thinking is always thinking about the incomprehensible—about this incomprehensible that 'belongs' to every comprehending, as its own limit."[9] This limit is the edge of chaos where order simultaneously dissolves and emerges. To understand what occurs along this border, it is necessary to consider the dynamics of representation in more detail.

The question of representation—*Vorstellung*—runs through all three critiques. In the First Critique, Kant argues: "A concept [*Begriff*] formed from notions [*Notio*] and transcending the possibility of experience is an idea [*Idee*] or concept of reason."[10] In the exercise of practical reason, Ideas that lie beyond experience and hence remain regulative are actualized as they become practically effective in moral activity. But postulates can no more be experienced than ideas and, therefore, yield no knowledge even though they are rational. An Idea or a postulate, Rodolphe Gasché explains, "is a representation by a concept of the concepts that serve to represent representation with consciousness."

> Representation here translates the German *Vorstellung*, a term Kant uses to designate the operation by which the different faculties that constitute the mind bring their respective objects before themselves. Yet when Kant claims that in spite of the impossibility of intuitively representing (and thus knowing) the ideas, they nonetheless play a decisive role in the realm of cognition, or that in the moral realm they acquire an at least partial concretization, he broaches the question of the becoming present of the highest, but intuitively unpresentable representation that is the idea. This is the problem of the *presentation*, or *Darstellung* of the idea, and it is rigorously distinct from that of representation. The issue is no longer how to depict, articulate, or illustrate something already present yet resisting adequate discursive or figural expression, but of how something acquires presence—reality, actuality, effectiveness—in the first place. The question of *Darstellung* centers on the coming into presence, or occurring, of the ideas.[11]

Coming into presence (*Darstellung*) is the condition of the possibility of representation (*Vorstellung*). But how does such presencing or presentation occur?

In his analysis of Hegel's concept of experience, Heidegger suggests a possible answer to this question when commenting on Hegel's claim that "science, in making its appearance, *is* an appearance itself."

> The appearance is the authentic presence itself: the *parousia* of the Absolute. In keeping with its absoluteness, the Absolute is with us of its own accord. In its will to be with us, the Absolute is being present. In itself, thus bringing itself forward, the Absolute is for itself. For the sake of the will of the *parousia* alone, the presentation of knowledge as phenomenon is necessary. The presentation is bound to remain turned toward the will of the Absolute. The presentation is itself a *willing* [emphasis added], that is, not just a wishing and striving but the action itself, if it pulls itself together within its nature.[12]

This remarkable insight complicates Hegelianism in a way that opens it up *as if* from within. Far from a closed system, which, as a stable structure, would be the embodiment of the Logos, the Hegelian Absolute here appears to be an infinitely restless will that wills itself in willing everything that emerges in nature and history and wills everything that exists in willing itself. Heidegger explains the implications of this reading of Hegel when he interprets the inconceivability of freedom in Kant's philosophy in a way that points toward his own account of the groundless ground of Being: "The only thing that we comprehend is its incomprehensibility. Freedom's incomprehensibility consists in the fact that it resists comprehension since it is freedom that transposes us into the realization of Being, not in the mere representation of it."[13]

The interplay of *Darstellung*—presentation—and *Vorstellung*—representation—occurs through the activity of *Einbildungskraft*—imagination. The etymology of *Einbildungskraft* is important for Kant's argument as well as its elaboration by his followers. *Bild* means picture, image, likeness or representation, and *Bildung* means formation, forming, generation and by extension culture as well as education. The verb *bilden* means to form, fashion, shape, mould, or construct. Finally, *Ein* means one. *Einbildungskraft*, then, is the activity of formation or construction by which something is fashioned into a unified image or representation. While Kant clearly and consistently distinguishes the theoretical and practical uses of reason, I have noted that he insists on the "primacy of practical reason." Cognition presupposes volition but willing does not necessarily presuppose thinking. The imbrication of thinking and willing lies at the heart of the imagination. In his analysis of aesthetic judgment in the Third Critique, Kant offers a definition of the imagination that proved decisive for many later writers, artists, philosophers and theologians: "If, now, imagination must in the judgment of taste be regarded in its freedom, then, to begin with, it is not taken as reproductive as in subjection to the laws of association, but as productive in exerting an activity of its own (as originator of arbitrary forms of possible intuitions)."[14] The imagination, then, involves two interrelated activities, which Kant describes as productive and reproductive. In its productive modality, the imagination figures forms that the reproductive imagination combines and recombines to create the schemata that organize the noisy data of experience into comprehensible patterns.

The imagination, in other words, both creates schemata that organize experience and disrupts and dislocates stabilizing structures. The figures that the productive imagination forms are *arbitrary* insofar as they are not determined by other figures but are *freely* formed and thus original. Freedom, in other words, is the condition of the possibility of the imagination and, therefore, of knowledge as well. Fichte was the first to recognize implications of this interpretation of the imagination that Kant himself did not fully realize. In *The Science of Knowledge*, he argues:

> Our doctrine here is therefore that all reality—*for us* being understood, as it cannot be otherwise understood in a system of transcendental philosophy—is brought forth solely by the imagination . . . Yet if it is now proved, as the present system claims to prove it, that this act of imagination forms the basis for the possibility of our consciousness, our life, our existence for ourselves, that is, our existence as selves, then it cannot be eliminated unless we are to abstract from the self; which is a contradiction, since it is impossible that what does the abstracting should abstract from itself.[15]

The argument once again turns on the relation between *Darstellung* and *Vorstellung*. Both theoretical and practical reason are impossible apart from representations. Representation, in turn, is impossible apart from antecedently given data. The question, then, becomes: How does *Darstellung* occur? How do representations *emerge*? Who or what gives that which is represented? According to Fichte, presentation is an act that "occurs with absolute spontaneity" and, therefore, *Darstellung* is "grounded" in freedom. Such freedom is not the freedom *of* subjectivity but the freedom *from* subjectivity through which both subjectivity and objectivity are posited or given.

While autonomy is self-grounded, *an-archy* is groundless. It "is not the diffraction of a principle, nor the multiple effect of a cause, but is the *an-archy*—the origin removed from every logic of origin, from every archaeology."[16] Heidegger describes the *an-archy* of freedom glimpsed in the presentational activity of the imagination as an abyss. In *Kant and the Problem of Metaphysics*, he explains: "In the radicalism of his questions, Kant brought the 'possibility' of metaphysics to the abyss. He saw the unknown. He had to shrink back. It was not just that the transcendental power of the imagination frightened him, but rather that in between [the two editions of the First Critique] pure reason as reason drew him increasingly under its spell."[17] This abyss or *Abgrund* from which all determination emerges is the groundless ground that is indistinguishable from nothing. Such an unfathomable ground is the nothing, the no-thing on which every foundation founders. Hegel explains the relationship between nothingness and freedom: "In its highest form of explication nothingness would be freedom. But this highest form is negativity insofar as it inwardly deepens itself to its highest intensity; and in this way it is itself affirmation—indeed absolute affirmation."[18] Negativity is affirmative insofar as it is the condition of creative emergence of everything that exists. Just as God creates freely *ex nihilo*, so the productive imagination creates freely out of nothing.

The self becomes itself in and through an other it can never fathom, which is nonetheless lodged within subjectivity as an inescapable interiority. The noncoincidence of the self with itself issues in its infinite restlessness. Heidegger brings the argument full circle by *not* closing the loop of self-reflexivity: "This original, essential constitution of humankind, 'rooted' in the transcendental power of the imagination, is the 'unknown' into which Kant must have looked if he spoke of the 'root unknown to us,' for the unknown is not that of which we simply know nothing. Rather, it is what pushes against us as something disquieting in what is known."[19] The analysis of the transcendental power of the imagination "reveals" the concealment at the heart of subjectivity. Contrary to the promises of Descartes, the inward turn of consciousness discloses the irreducible obscurity rather than the transparency of the self.

This obscurity harbors the *radical* temporality of subjectivity. The time of the subject is radical because it involves an uncanny past that is not a modality of the present. The past of *Darstellung* is not a past present but is a past that was never present because it is always already past. This absence of time is the nothingness that haunts subjectivity. This past that was never present eternally returns as the future that never arrives to disrupt the present that never is. In this way, the orignary absence of the past is the condition of the inescapable openness of the future. Since the past is never accessible, the present is never present and the future is never closed, subjectivity is infinitely restless.

With this understanding of the interplay of the imagination, temporality and subjectivity, it is necessary to return to the question of self-consciousness. Self-consciousness, I have argued, is self-reflexive and as such necessarily entails self-representation. Our investigation of the imagination now makes it possible to answer the question that we encountered at the limit of self-consciousness: Where does that which the self-conscious subject represents to itself come from? Since subject and object are codependent, the subject cannot give itself the object without which self-consciousness remains impossible. The presence of the object of self-representation must be given through the process of presentation or presencing, which cannot be effected by the self posited by it. As the condition of the possibility of presence, presencing is never present as such—nor is it absent. *The present, understood both temporally and spatially, is always a gift or present pre-sent by (the) nothing that is (not) present.* This no-thing gives by withholding, shows by hiding, approaches by withdrawing. Since that which is never present cannot be re-presented, representation includes as a condition of its possibility "something"—something that *is* (impossibly) nothing—that remains irreducibly unrepresentable.

If self-consciousness requires self-representation and representation is inevitably implicated with the unrepresentable, then the possibility of self-consciousness depends upon something it can never comprehend. The incomprehensible or unrepresentable is not simply outside or the opposite of consciousness and self-consciousness. To the contrary, as the condition of the possibility of (self-)representation, the unrepresentable is "inside" as an "outside" that cannot be assimilated. In the depths of interiority lies hidden the activity of an other that can never be known. This interior exteriority further complicates the structure of self-relation inherent in self-consciousness.

With these insights in mind we can finally return to the passages from *The Sickness Unto Death* and *The Concept of Anxiety*. The definition of the self that Kierkegaard presents in *The Sickness Unto Death* is, in effect, a parody of Hegel's account of spirit devised to subvert the reflexivity of the Hegelian subject as if from within. "The self is a relation that relates itself to itself or is the relation's relating itself to itself in the relation; the self is not the relation but is the relation's relating itself to itself." Kierkegaard, or more precisely, Vigilius Haufniensis, proceeds to describe this relational activity as effecting a synthesis between the finite and the infinite, the temporal and the eternal and freedom and necessity. At first glance, it appears as if Hegel could have written these words but closer examination suggests that Kierkegaard is turning Hegel's argument against itself. His argument suggests that the previous diagrammatic representation of the structure of self-representation must be revised.

In Kierkegaard's terms Self-as-Subject (S^s) and Self-as-Object (S^o) are joined in a relation that is their "negative unity." Insofar as each becomes itself in and through the other and neither can be itself apart from the other, S^s *is* not S^o and S^o *is* not S^s. But now Kierkegaard adds a qualification that opens a chasm between him and Hegel and anticipates Derrida's deconstruction of speculative metaphysics. The concluding sentence completes the argument: "the human self is such a derived, established relation, a relation that relates itself to itself and in relating itself to

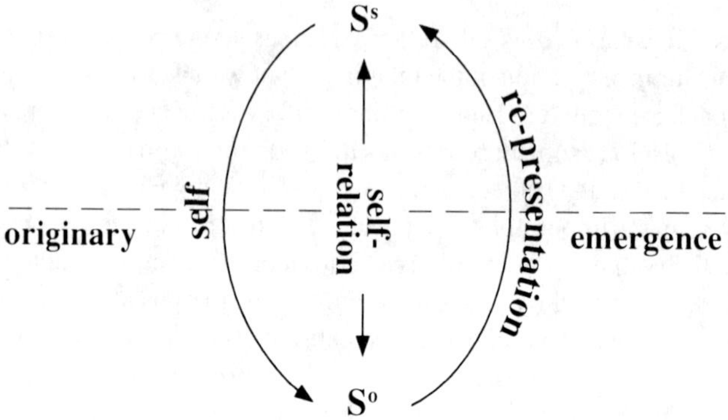

Self-Conscious Subjectivity

itself relates itself to another." Accordingly, the relation to altarity is constitutive of subjectivity; the self, in other words, cannot be itself without relating to an other. But who or what is this other and how is a relation to radical altarity possible without negating the very difference it attempts to affirm?

There are at least three possible answers to this question. First, the other to whom the subject relates might be other human subjects. From this point of view, self and other are bound in a constitutive relation of intersubjectivity. While Kierkegaard does not deny that being is always being-with, he does not regard intersubjectivity as constitutive of the self as such. The second possibility is that the other in relation to which the self becomes itself is God. Kierkegaard surely does believe that human beings are created by God. But how is God to be conceived? In one of his best-known formulations, Kierkegaard describes God as "infinitely and qualitatively different." But what does this mean? The phrase "infinitely and qualitatively different" is, like Karl Barth's term "wholly other," nothing more than a name for what cannot be named.

There is a third way to read altarity that is neither human nor divine. That which is infinitely and qualitatively different might be the condition of the possibility of all differences. Such a difference might be an immanent transcendence that allows the emergence of the subject's identity through the relation to an irreducible exteriority that is nonetheless *within* the self. To glimpse this elusive other, it is necessary to return to our discussion of the imagination in the constitution of the self-reflexive subject. As we have seen, the interplay of *Darstellung* and *Vorstellung* in the structure of self-reflexivity implies an antecedent exteriority that is constitutive of subjectivity. Insofar as the self relates itself to itself through the activity of self-representation, it presupposes an originary givenness that cannot be a function of the self itself. This givenness is what I have identified as the presentation or presencing of the present without whose representation is impossible. Presencing as such is never present but is always already past. Such past is not a past present but is a radical past that has never been present. Paradoxically, time and eternity meet in this radical past.

With this insight, it is possible to reconsider the question of time that Kierkegaard addresses *The Concept of Anxiety*. Criticizing what he regards as the atemporality of Hegel's logic, Kierkegaard writes, "Transition belongs in the sphere of freedom, for transition is a *state* and it is actual. Plato fully recognized the difficulty of placing transition in the realm of the purely metaphysical, and for that reason the category of *the moment* cost him so much effort." In the footnote from which I have already quoted, Kierkegaard proceeds to argue:

> The moment appears to be this strange entity [that which has no place], . . . that lies between motion and rest without occupying any time, and into this and out from this that which is in motion changes into rest, and that which is at rest changes into motion. Thus the moment becomes the category of transition, for Plato shows in the same way that the moment is related to the transition of the one to the many, of the many to the one, of likeness to unlikeness, etc., and that it is the moment in which there is neither one nor many, neither a being determined nor a being combined.[20]

The moment that makes presence possible is never itself present nor is it absent; rather, the moment is always withdrawing or slipping away. Forever in transition, the moment's place is no place—neither here nor there, neither one nor many, motion nor rest. As *always* already past, the moment is eternal. In the moment, eternity is neither present nor presence but is a radical past that was never present but eternally returns as the future that never arrives to disrupt the present that never is. For human subjectivity, being *is* time. Life is suspended between an unrecoverable past that we endlessly mourn and an open future that we face with a dread that harbors both despair and hope.

If Hegelianism is proto-structuralism and structuralism is latter-day Hegelianism, then Kierkegaard's deconstruction of Hegelian *Geist* anticipates Derridean deconstruction. Kierkgaard's "infinite, qualitative difference" prefigures Derrida's *différance* as the matrix within which difference and oppositions emerge. Heidegger reinterprets Kierkegaard's account of the relation between Christendom and philosophy to form his narrative of the western ontotheological tradition. Derrida, in turn, appropriates Heidegger's argument to present his own version of the western tradition in terms of logocentrism, which is characterized by the metaphysics of presence. If, as Hegel insists, the structure of spirit is dialectical opposition, then to oppose Hegel is to confirm Hegelianism and all it represents. As Kierkegaard warned us long ago, "to do the opposite is also a form of imitation." The challenge for the critic is to turn philosophy on itself in a way that exposes the non-dialectical other without which philosophy and the historico-cultural tradition of the West are impossible. This challenge is unending. As we take up this task ever again, Kierkegaard's deconstruction of western subjectivity could not be more timely. By rereading and rereading his writings, we can discern the opening of the imagination in which it is possible to translate the eternal return of the same into the eternal return of difference. It is not too much to say that our future depends on this opening as much as this opening depends on the future.

NOTES

1. Søren Kierkegaard, *The Sickness Unto Death*, trans. Howard and Edna Hong (Princeton, NY: Princeton University Press, 1980), pp. 13–14.

2. Søren Kierkegaard, *The Concept of Anxiety*, trans. Reidar Thomte (Princeton, NJ: Princeton University Press, 1980), p. 84 n.

3. Kant, "What is Enlightenment?," In *On History*, trans. Lewis White Beck (New York: Bobbs-Merrill, 1963), p. 3.

4. Immanuel Kant, *Critique of Pure Reason*, trans. Norman Kemp Smith (New York: St. Martin's Press, 1965), p. 144.

5. Ibid., p. 181.

6. I will consider further implications of Kant's account of the imagination below.

7. Immanuel Kant, *Critique of Judgment*, trans. James Meredith (New York: Oxford University Press, 1973), part 2, p. 21.

8. Dieter Henrich, *Between Kant and Hegel* (Cambridge, MA: Harvard University Press, 2003), p. 287.

9. Jean-Luc Nancy, *The Experience of Freedom*, trans. Bridget McDonald (Stanford: Stanford University Press, 1993), p. 54.

10. Kant, *Critique of Pure Reason*, p. 314.

11. Rodolphe Gasché, "Ideality in Fragmentation," Foreword to Friedrich Schlegel, *Philosophical Fragments*, trans. Peter Firchow (Minneapolis: University of Minnesota Press, 1991), pp. xix–xx.

12. Martin Heidegger, *Hegel's Concept of Experience*, trans. Kenley Dove (New York: Harper and Row, 1970), pp. 48–49.

13. Martin Heidegger, *Schelling's Treatise on the Essence of Human Freedom*, trans. Joan Stambaugh (Athens, OH: Ohio University Press), p. 162.

14. Kant, *Critique of Judgment*, p. 86.

15. J. G. Fichte, *The Science of Knowledge*, trans. A. E. Kroeger (Philadelphia: J. B. Lippincott, 1868).

16. Nancy, *The Experience of Freedom*, p. 13.

17. Martin Heidegger, *Kant and the Problem of Metaphysics*, trans. Richard Taft (Bloomington: Indiana University Press, 1997), p. 118.

18. G. W. F. Hegel, *The Logic of Hegel*, trans. William Wallace (New York: Oxford University Press, 1968), p. 162.

19. Heidegger, *Kant and the Problem of Metaphysics*, p. 112.

20. Kierkegaard, *Concept of Anxiety*, pp. 83–83.

SELECTED PAPERS FROM THE XXII WORLD CONGRESS OF PHILOSOPHY

Rethinking Philosophy as Power of the Word

Opening address to the XXII Congress of Philosophy

PETER KEMP
PRESIDENT OF THE CONGRESS;
EMERITUS PROFESSOR, UNIVERSITY OF AARHUS

Abstract: If 'power' means cultural and political influence, philosophy has become a global world power. Philosophical argumentation and reflection constitute a non-economical, non-technological, and non-military power by the word that is capable of challenging the other powers, exposing lies and illusions, and proposing a better world as dwelling for humanity.

Often the power of the philosophical word has been ignored, when philosophy was seen as pure description, pure reference, an innocent mirror, that forgets itself and make us present to things. However, if philosophy has the power of the word, not all kinds of philosophizing are necessarily good for humanity. It can be very seducing for a group, and give food for mass suggestion making that appeals to the worst part of ourselves. We have learnt to understand how philosophy in itself may not only enlighten and liberate, but also seduce and manipulate. Today, philosophy has lost its innocence; we cannot philosophize without reflection on our linguistic practice. But we philosophers are not only called to understand ourselves. We must also contribute to developing an understanding of the power of the word more generally. And as citizens of the world, we must recognize that humiliation of others might be the most brutal violence we can practice without directly killing.

Why are we philosophers coming together in a world congress for a whole week? What can we offer the world by our papers, symposia, lectures and discussions? Is all that nothing but sheer words, words, and more words? How can these words be important for the world today?

Special Supplement, *Journal of Philosophical Research* pp. 419–426
DOI: 10.5840/jpr201237Supplement58

Other researchers and scholars have special research fields; they represent special disciplines, special orders of research and education. But we philosophers have no special discipline. We can have discussions with researchers from all fields, and not only with researchers but also with technicians, with artists, with moralists, and so forth. We can enter their fields, but our activities do not belong to any of them. We are everywhere and nowhere. Our strength is not that we have to do with a particular area of research and thinking and that we can produce results by working in these particular fields, but it is our capacity to speak rationally about everything, to consider the role of everything in the whole. More than any other researcher and any other theorist we have only the language, only the speech, only the word. By using the philosophical concepts and discourse we have learnt remembering the thoughts of philosophers before us, we try to speak philosophically in our way, according to the conditions of our time; we try to rethink philosophy today, when we describe, analyse, argue, criticise, teach, propose, and so on. And if we discover a danger for humanity, for the world or for the individual or for a vulnerable group, we may feel it is our duty to propose a way of preventing the evil or the catastrophe, and we may warn humanity against hidden destructive forces or carelessness that might be disastrous, etc.

But whatever we, do the only power we have is the power of the word, the power of language, of speech as teachers, educators, lecturers, reviewers, opinion makers. A great philosopher in the twentieth century said: "The word is my kingdom—*la parole est mon royaume*—and I am not ashamed of it."

Sometimes political leaders and heads of institutions try to make us ashamed about it; they cannot see why they should support and give room for philosophy, since philosophy does not have a technical goal, and since it does not simply contribute to increasing the production of material goods or strengthening our technical capacity. Sometimes philosophers are even moved or excluded from universities and higher education because they are considered as useless if not dangerous for the established order. But nevertheless there are today many signs of the vivacity of philosophy, and philosophical thinking still plays an enormous role in the world.

The attendance to this congress shows it. The strong life of philosophical societies all over the world shows it. The creation of new centres for philosophy and of new philosophical societies shows it. The enthusiastic participation in the annual International philosophical Olympiads where high school pupils from many countries compete on writing the best philosophical essay shows it. And last, but not least: the continuing high level of publication of philosophical works in all important languages shows it. All over the world philosophers take the floor inside and outside scientific institutions, and they are well received in most places. Thus, if 'power' means cultural and political influence, philosophy has become a global world power. Truly, on our planet where wars and conflicts increase, the power of philosophy manifests itself by defending the freedom of thought, the freedom of expression of great values, the freedom of criticism of injustices, and freedom of dialogue crossing all cultural and national frontiers—in short, philosophy appears everywhere as the power of maintaining the will to peace. And maybe the world would be a worse place for human life without philosophy.

It follows that power does not necessarily equal domination over others, but can be liberating, give space for new possibilities, open new horizons, unveil hidden forces and chances.

One often forgets that the economical, technological, and military powers do not possess the monopoly on power in the world. Philosophical argumentation and reflection constitute a non-economical, non-technological and non-military power by the word that is capable of challenging the other powers, exposing lies and illusions, and proposing a better world as dwelling for humanity.

Often the power of the philosophical word has been ignored, when philosophy was seen as pure description, pure reference, an innocent mirror, that forgets itself and makes us present to things. This idea of philosophy as a mirror of nature has therefore been criticized both from a hermeneutical point of view and from a pragmatic point of view: Hans-Georg Gadamer showed in *Thruth and Method* (1960) that there is no description without interpretation of the historical situation in which we describe some thing and Richard Rorty declared in *Philosophy and the Mirror of Nature* (1979), that philosophy must focus on action that changes the world.

But already in 1955 the Oxford philosopher J. L. Austin gave lectures on speech acts. They were published in 1962 in the booklet *How To Do Things with Words*. He showed that a proposition that presents a meaning is an act, he called it a *locutionary* act, and he claimed that the *locutionary* act cannot be completely separated from what he calls an *illocutionary* act having a certain *force* in saying something. In other words, the total situation in which the utterance is issued, what Austin calls the total speech act, is always both *locutionary* and *illocutionary*. Already by selecting something we want to say and omitting other things we do not consider to be important, we have a certain influence on those who read or hear what we write or say. Thus, the word has always been a force in the world.

That means that philosophizing is never totally neutral. We philosophers have a responsibility to know how we do things with words.

However, if philosophy has the power of the word, all kinds of philosophizing are not necessarily good for humanity. In the twentieth century we have learnt how destructive and disastrous nationalistic, fascist, and other totalitarian thinking can be for humanity. It can be very seducing for a group, and give food for mass suggestion making appeals to the worst part of ourselves. And this part of ourselves is not only formed by our egoistic drives but it is also constituted by what Tomonobu Imamichi has called the "nosistic" drives, an egoism in plural (from latin: nos, we), a group-egoism that divides humanity in positions and considers as potential enemies everybody else or every foreigner belonging to another group, another nation, or another culture.

But the *illocutionary* element of language is not sufficient for an understanding of how our speech can be both good and evil. In the speech situation we not only find that the word has an influence by carrying a meaning from one person to another, by giving information about something to someone or by asking a question, making an appeal to someone, giving an order or offering an excuse. A speech act can also intend to form the other, for instance in order to dominate, to subjugate, to humiliate. Therefore there is a third aspect of speech acts, that the perspicacious J. L. Austin has mentioned but not developed very much, and that we have to give more attention to. This is the *perlocutionary* act that he defines as "the achieving of certain effects by saying something."

Today this *perlocutionary* act might be the most important kind of speech act we philosophers have to examine. But in all the philosophy of language we have developed in the twentieth century I do not find enough analysis of how language can achieve certain effects, and touch the other by saying something to the other.

It is true that since the linguistic turn in philosophy to which J. L. Austin contributed to in the 1950s many philosophers have been occupied by trying to understand language. There were, for instance, the analyses of ordinary language by Ludwig Wittgenstein and others, the phenomenology of language by Martin Heidegger, Maurice Merleau-Ponty and others, the hermeneutical reflections on interpretation of speech and text by Hans-Georg Gadamer and others, the reflection on poetic symbols, metaphors and narratives by Paul Ricœur and others, the theory of communicative action by Jürgen Habermas and his school, and many other forms of philosophy of language, whether in analytic or synthetic philosophy, whether inside or outside European culture.

Thanks to this linguistic turn, to this attention paid to language, we have learnt to understand how philosophy in itself may not only enlighten and liberate, but also seduce and manipulate. To promote enlightenment and liberation and to avoid seduction and manipulation have been the aims of philosophy since Plato prescribed reasonable talk, i.e., talk that we can agree on in a dialogue where every interlocutor is honest to himself and honest to others. Certainly, to Plato and later in particular to Søren Kierkegaard, both irony and what Jacques Derrida has called philosophizing in the margin may be reasonable. But seduction and manipulation—even when called philosophy—that tend to reduce people to blind instruments of an ideology or a flock with a leader who thinks for them, can never bring them to reason.

However, the reason for having philosophers is that they are the guardians of reason. Therefore it can only be counterproductive if philosophy is practised as an anaesthetic or, what is provocative but not better: hate-talk, speech of hatred. Indeed, the good philosopher is involved in his or her cause, speaks with enthusiasm about what he or she believes, and is sober-minded even in the hardest criticism. But hate-talk that uses insult and defamation against others, whether they are other philosophers or they are non-philosophers, for instance politicians, reduces the arguments to violence and makes philosophy to an egoistic or nosistic warfare.

Today, philosophy has lost its innocence; we cannot philosophize without reflection on our linguistic practice. Therefore more understanding of the *perlocutionary* act is needed in order to make us more conscious about how in every communication, from the most intimate to the most political sphere, we can both encourage and hurt, can both stimulate and repress others.

Not only because philosophers have the very visible power of the word are they therefore challenged by society to account for what they are doing by educating in philosophy and speaking in the public space, but also because they cannot explain their own activity without a reflection about the power of the word in general. And thereby they must recognize that this power is enormous. They cannot explain the illocutionary and the *perlocutionary* role of philosophy today without taking into account what we are doing to each other by speaking and writing as ordinary people and not only as philosophers in a world that we, perhaps more than ever, shape by our words.

I consider this account as one of the most urgent tasks for philosophers today who want to rethink philosophy and who want to apply their capacities in analysis and criticism of the most urgent problem we have in our time: How do we avoid by our words "the clash of civilizations," that Samuel P. Huntington has seen as the greatest threat to humanity in our century.

It follows that we philosophers are not only called to understand ourselves, the power of our philosophical word. We must also contribute to develop an understanding of the power of the word more generally. As members of the kingdom of the word we are responsible for teaching and explaining what words can do among people, not only in a single country but also among all people in the world belonging to different nations, different cultures, different languages, traditions, and religions.

Let me take an example from my own country, the effects achieved by the publication in September 2005 in the Danish Newspaper *Jyllandsposten* of some cartoons of the prophet Mohammed presenting him as a terrorist, for instance by a bomb in his turban. These cartoons were attended by some words of the editor saying that they should teach the Muslims to endure "disdain, insult and ridicule." The reaction in the Muslim world to this aggressive offence was heated and sometimes very violent; Danish flags were being burnt in many places and even some Danish diplomatic residences were burnt down.

At that time most other Danish Newspapers refused to publish the cartoons, but the Danish Prime-Minister Anders Fogh Rasmussen did not present a clear opposition to the publication in *Jyllandsposten* but declared that in Denmark there is freedom of speech and that the government could not and should not intervene in decisions that the newspaper was responsible for. When he was asked to apologize for the publication of the cartoons, he understood this as a demand to take the responsibility for something that the government had not done, and he refused to make any excuse. Few people in Denmark thought that it was a legal question and that the cartoons should have been forbidden by law, but many saw it as a moral question. But in the beginning the Prime Minister did not see it either as a legal question, nor as a moral question. However, when this year a Dutch filmmaker, Geert Wilders, constructed a short movie called FITNA on the internet that was extremely aggressive against Muslims, and then came to Denmark thinking that he would have the support of our Prime Minister, the latter took the sharpest distance to the movie. Such a moral distance could also have been taken to the Danish Newspaper. Why did he not do that?

The cartoons were defended in Denmark in the name of the right to freedom of speech. And more recently the Danish intelligence service told the press that three young people—a Dane and two foreigners—might have planned to murder the cartoonist (for security reasons proofs were not published). Then no Danish newspaper considered these three people as presumably simple criminals, but nearly the whole Danish press were seized by a kind of war logic and published the offensive cartoons in order to defend Denmark—the "country of freedom of speech"—against all its enemies. The result did not wait long; it was a bloody suicide attack on the Danish Embassy in Pakistan.

But I would ask: Was this unhappy story not the consequence of bad philosophy?

The idea of freedom of speech appears in the first Amendment to the Constitution of the United States of America from 1791 that declares that "Congress shall make no law . . . abridging the freedom of speech or of the press." This was proclaimed in order to protect the possibility of criticism of those in power. One and a half centuries later, the freedom of speech was conceived as a human right in article 19 of the Universal Declaration of Human Rights from 1948: "Every one has the right to freedom of opinion and expression."

However, in the wake of the French Revolution, thanks to the free speeches of courageous citizens, the Declaration of the Rights of Man and of Citizen from 1789 did not proclaim a right to free speech without limits. The reason given was that there is no freedom without responsibility; this corresponds to its definition of freedom in article 4 that says that freedom consists of the right to do everything that does not harm any other, and that the limits to this right must be determined by law.

Truly an absolute freedom of speech and expression is problematic. This is already true in the case of the claim of freedom of religion that historically precedes the claim of freedom of speech. Religious freedom has been claimed as a freedom of faith, and this has been claimed as a human right, but not without limits; because freedom to practice a religion that includes violence in order to force people to a confession has never been generally accepted as a human right. In other words freedom of religion is a right as long as it does not prevent everybody else from having the same freedom.

But also freedom of speech and expression is problematic if it is claimed without limits; it may be practised as violence if it is a *perlocutionary* act that hurts and humiliates others in order to dominate, repress, or oppress them.

There is a much more fundamental human right than the right of freedom of speech, and this is the right of freedom of thought. This freedom of thought was claimed by Voltaire in his *Philosophical Dictionary* from 1764 and many other European philosophers in the age of Enlightenment. The right to this freedom can be considered as absolute, if by thought is meant an inner conviction or a faith that does not include violence against others. Thus, there is an absolute freedom of conviction, but not an absolute freedom of expression of any thought.

The cult of public freedom of expression in a country such as Denmark is peculiar in comparison to what is normally admitted in Danish family life. Everybody knows that in a family or amongst friends you may think what you like about your wife or your partner, about your parents and your children, and about your closest friends. But if you want a good life together with them, you must always take care of the way you tell them your thoughts. Then you do not use the word as a weapon against them. Why should this use of freedom be otherwise in the great family we call humanity?

As members of this humanity, as citizen of the world, we must recognize that humiliation of others might be the most brutal violence we can practice without directly killing. Economic exploitation of a big part of the world population by a smaller, richer part is a big problem, but not the greatest problem; the greatest problem is the problem that consists in the lack of mutual recognition between peoples from different cultures, different language, different history, different race, and different religion. For instance, it would cost us Europeans and Americans nothing in money or capital to give this recognition. Nevertheless it seems to be much more difficult for us to practice than any renunciation of material goods. It demands a humility we do not possess.

The opposition between recognition and humiliation is indeed very instructive. To recognize the other is not only to accept the sheer existence of the other, but to refrain from violence against this person. Humiliation on the other hand is an attitude that is intended to give the other a feeling of inferiority, to injure the self-esteem of the other and the self-respect of a cultural community. When one's self-esteem is wounded it is the very relationship to the other human being that is hurt, because it cannot unfold itself without the other. Humiliation destroys our "living together" not only in personal relationships but also in the social life.

Humility is the opposite of pride and arrogance: it is to consider oneself as equal with every other human being. By contrast, humiliation of the other is not a virtue, it is a vice—being the attempt to dominate the other by forcing him or her to be humble. But enforced humility can never be true humility for that must come generously from the proper character of the individual and not from the outside or out of fear of the other. Humility is humbleness before the community to which we belong. In this sense, it is not a feeling of inferiority, but a feeling of belonging. And it consists in the conviction that none of us have our identity without what we receive from others. In fact, a human identity in a modern world is a synthesis of identities. As Amartya Sen says: "In normal lives, we see ourselves as members of a variety of groups—we belong to all of them."

Today we have several big problems we must resolve together. Therefore we must be cosmopolitan and this is no more a romantic dream but a very concrete task. Let me only mention three concrete problems: The problem of global warming and environment in general, the problem of intercultural co-existence, and the problem of financial globalisation. No peaceful solutions to these connected problems can be carried out if we do not learn to behave peacefully by language, i.e., to use language as a peace instrument and not as weapon. We live with the problems in a technological conjuncture, but we cannot master this conjuncture if we cannot master our language. Thus, we must rethink philosophy according to an eco-ethics, an ethics of our world as *oikos*, as dwelling for our good life together.

Therefore we need philosophy; we need the power of the word. This need is the deepest drive we have. A young Chinese man wrote to me when he had given up on finding money for attending our congress: I cannot come to the World Congress of Philosophy, but "philosophy will go on in my heart!"

He belongs to the kingdom of the word. He has the conviction that has brought us all together here in Seoul. He is with us in our burning wish: Long live philosophy!